THIRD EDITION

CHILDREN'S LITERATURE

An Issues Approach

MASHA KABAKOW RUDMAN

University of Massachusetts at Amherst

Longman *Publishers USA*

CHILDREN'S LITERATURE, Third Edition

Longman, 10 Bank Street, White Plains, N.Y. 10606

Associated companies:
Longman Group Ltd., London
Longman Cheshire Pty., Melbourne
Longman Paul Pty., Auckland
Copp Clark Longman Ltd., Toronto

Senior acquisitions editor: Laura McKenna
Production editor: Linda Moser/The Bookmakers
Cover design: Silvers Design
Cover illustration: Richard J. Murdock
Production supervisor: Richard Bretan

To Reva: daughter, friend, and colleague whose intellect, energy, humor, passion, and commitment make a difference in this world

Library of Congress Cataloging-in-Publication Data
Rudman, Masha Kabakow.
    Children's literature / Masha Rudman.—3rd ed.
       p.   cm.
    Includes bibliographical references (p.) and indexes.
    ISBN 0-8013-0537-3
    1. Children's literature—History and criticism. 2. Children's
literature—Bibliography. I. Title.
PN1009.A1R8 1995
028.1'62—dc20

94-6627
CIP

2 3 4 5 6 7 8 9 10-MA-98979695

Contents

CHAPTER 7 **DEATH**   141

PART III   SOCIETY   **175**

CHAPTER 8 **GENDER ROLES**   177

CHAPTER 9 **HERITAGE**   219

Foreword

Not too long ago, a friend told me, "I love your book *Greyling* and have read it over and over." As I tried to preen and look modest at once, she added, "I changed the ending, of course."

What my friend was doing was not just changing the ending but joining a long line of censors who down through the ages have marked stories for children with their own brand. Francis James Childs, the collector of the Child ballads, called such people the "blind beggar, the nursery maid, and the clerk."

Certainly I can understand the desire to tamper with the tale for morality's sake. But I wish my friend had not told me about her change. After all, the story had not been written in a vacuum, moral or otherwise.

All art is moral, a striving for the light. But unlike earlier moralities—which are consistent in their demands on men and women, and hence on artists—the moralities of today shift and change by decades, rather than centuries. Communications are swift today, the speed of light. And minorities that could previously be ignored are eloquent in their demand for redress, for justice. They are heard and reheard, and they cannot be denied.

Artists are aware, are made aware, of injustices. As individuals in an individual age, they create from an idiosyncratic sense of what is right. This is not to say that writers and other artists should try to be moralists and create propaganda. Propaganda is bad art. As Isaac Bashevis Singer reminds us, "In art, a truth that is boring is not true."

But the best writers write from the heart. Harlan Ellison, the science fiction writer, said, "I write what I am. There is no way to create literature."

If all art is moral, then all art becomes morality. What I write out of my own needs and ideas and ideals becomes a statement. That statement can be accepted or rejected by the reader. If the reader is an adult, the acceptance or rejection is probably a fairly conscious choice.

The child does not read that way. A child reads with the heart. If I write for children, I must be aware that children will accept what I write with their hearts. My morality becomes their morality. Heart to heart, body to body, blood to blood, a kind of literary eucharist.

Changing the ending can change the morality of a tale, but it changes the author's intent as well. That is not consistent with the idea of literature.

However, there are times when the morality of a book, even a fine literary work, is inconsistent with that of the teacher, the librarian, the parent. The answer then is not to force a change of endings or bring about the more extreme version of that—burn books. As a teaching device, changing the ending, characters, sex, and so on can be most productive. But arbitrarily changing the ending, without letting the child know that such a thing is happening is direct censorship that changes the author's intent, whether the intent was overt or covert.

Dr. Rudman offers many ways in which an educator can help to structure the reading and aid young readers in sorting out conflicting or inconsistent moralities. She does not necessarily throw out the book because its morality is outdated or its characters mouth inhumane statements. Rather, she suggests methods of dealing with these problems within the classroom or home. She does not necessarily recommend a book even though it is correct in its preaching, if preaching is all the book does. She is concerned with human relationships, with understandings, with morality. But she is concerned with literature, too. In a field that is all too often crowded with didactic moralists, Dr. Rudman is literature's champion.

As a writer, I thank Dr. Rudman for that concern. However, I must also point out that what she is offering is the second step in a two-step process. The first step, of course, lies with the authors and illustrators who create the materials with which children dream. We are the myth-makers.

We must write from the heart. Write from the heart, and you write your own truth. And if we have changed and grown inside, the truth we write will change and grow, too.

Then the children will be touched. Touch and pass it on. It is the only way.

Jane Yolen

Preface

HOW TO USE THIS BOOK

This book is designed for use as a text, a reference, and a guide to the study and selection of children's books. It focuses on the way issues of a social and developmental nature are treated in children's literature and how books may be used as bibliotherapy (to help children address personal and social problems).

Each chapter contains expanded and updated information and

1. An introduction to and exploration of a personal or social issue.
2. A list of criteria that most experts agree constitute a constructive and nonstereotypic approach to the issue. (The criteria have been greatly expanded from the second edition.)
3. A section discussing particular books relating to the topic as exemplars of how that issue is handled in children's literature.
4. Suggestions ("Try This") for activities teachers or other concerned adults can use to personalize and extend the reading of the chapter.
5. Activities for children as adjuncts and extensions of their reading.
6. An annotated reference list relating the topic to children and books and, where possible, a list of organizations providing supplemental materials on the issue at hand.
7. A selected list of recommended children's books pertaining to the topic. The age levels attached to the books are those suggested by the publishers in most cases, but readers are cautioned to use their own judgment on the appropriateness of any book to their intended audiences. No book of quality is too simple for any age level. There are,

however, books that are too complex or advanced for young children's developmental levels. The annotations reflect the criteria listed in the chapter. Cross-references to annotated references in other chapters are in brackets.

The Family section from the previous edition has been divided into separate chapters for greater ease of use. Abuse has now been separated from the Special Needs chapter, since it is more a social issue in its own right than a condition of an individual. The chapter on Abuse includes the issues of substance abuse and treats eating disorders as a form of substance abuse. The Special Needs chapter now includes a section on AIDS, reflecting the unfortunate increase of that disease. The second edition chapter War is now War and Peace and includes conflict resolution in order to reflect the way the world has been changing and the importance educators and other informed adults place on children's learning to make peace in their daily lives.

The chapter on Methodology has been eliminated because there are now many excellent sources for integrating literature into a reading program. In its stead are two new appendixes: Appendix A includes references for methodological help in using children's books in the classroom, as well as references conveying a theoretical foundation of the reading process. This appendix also contains titles providing activities for stimulating interest in reading and supplying practical guidelines for the classroom. Appendix C, the other new appendix, consists of a list of activities to use with children in order to extend their reading experiences. Appendix D has been modified to include awards pertinent to an issues approach, rather than an extensive listing of all book awards. Appendixes B and E (a list of books to use as resources for children's literature and a listing of publishers' addresses) remain essentially the same as in the second edition, but they have been updated.

As with the second edition, the annotated books constitute a comprehensive, but not all-inclusive, recommended list. Books are selected from publishers' catalogs, published annotated bibliographies, and various review journals such as *The School Library Journal, The Bulletin* of the Center for Children's Books, the *Bulletin* of the Council on Interracial Books for Children, *The Horn Book Magazine, Booklist, Booklinks,* specialized compendia of issues-related books (listed with the references at the end of each chapter), and recommendations from colleagues and students.

Prices are not included in the listings; they change too rapidly for accurate representation. Readers may contact publishers directly if local bookstores cannot supply the information.

Space limitations prevented the inclusion of author and title listings arranged by subtopic. Such listings are available for the following chapters: Abuse, Special Needs, Heritage, and War and Peace. They may be obtained from the author for the cost of duplicating and mailing at 224 Furcolo Hall, UMASS, Amherst, MA 01003.

More poetry and folklore are included in this edition than in the last one. Readers are invited to send recommendations for new entries to be included in future revisions of this text. I am an advocate of books and reading. If any titles have been omitted that are appropriate and of high quality, I invite your sending them for my consideration. I welcome comments and suggestions for improvement.

Some of the books in the lists are out of print. They are included here because of their value to the reader. They remain available in libraries, and it is possible that the public will demand their reprinting. Readers would be advised to contact publishers of books that are no longer in the bookstores. Perhaps some of the fine books that have unaccountably been discontinued will gain new life through these efforts.

ACKNOWLEDGMENTS

In an effort of this magnitude, spanning many years and thousands of books, a small army of people has been involved. The idea for the text arose from the format of my seminar on isues in children's literature. My students—most of them classroom teachers and librarians—wanted references for a thematic approach to children's books. They also wanted recommendations of books to help children with their emotional and social needs. On their instigation I wrote the first edition. The response to the book, the subsequent second edition, and the increasing acceptance of an issues approach has sustained me and motivated me to prepare this third edition.

First and foremost, my thanks to Jodi Levine without whom this edition would never have been completed. I appreciate her meticulous research, informed judgment, remarkable memory for titles and plots, and tireless hours of labor.

Similarly, to Su Flickinger I owe countless thanks for her careful and intelligent reading, commenting, and management of the text. Su is largely responsible for the final format. Her critiques and thought-provoking questions resulted in a far more balanced approach to a number of the issues.

I am grateful to other stellar students and helpers, including Rudi Dornemann for his expertise in computers, research skills, continuous searching for new titles, sense of humor, and, above all, keen intellect and ability to critique and question. Anna Pearce also provided astute recommendations for editing the text.

Vicki Blackgoat Sorci, Jerry Jaccard, and Deborah Harrison contributed insightful critiques of books involving Native Peoples' cultures, especially Dine, Southwest, Yupik, Athapaskan, and Inuit.

Robin Barnes tirelessly entered bibliographic data; devoted endless hours of research; and gave calm, quiet advice and perspective on African-American material.

Susan Rosenberg selected and advised on Holocaust literature sensitively and astutely.

I also thank Gloria Goldstine for her helpful research; Barbara Love for her responsiveness and openness each time I asked for advice and opinions about African-American perspective; Dee McWilliams for her support, research, organizational abilities, and time; Lee Liu for sharing her knowledge of Chinese heritage; Chieko Yamazaki for her expertise and thoroughness in critiquing books dealing with Japanese culture; Mike Mitchell for his computer assistance; Kimberley Russell for her entering of information and her helpful summaries; and Joanna Farewell for her expert typing, research assistance, and diligence in working with the subject index.

Research for this text also involved the efforts of a number of students, friends, and professionals in the field. People kept finding new articles and sources they thought I might be interested in reading; and their conversation and suggestions about children's literature in general and issues in particular were stimulating and constructive. Particularly helpful in this respect were Sondra Radosh and the entire staff of the Jones Library in Amherst, the reference staff of the University of Massachusetts Library, Pat Drake McGiffin and Sue Woodfork of the Amherst Public School libraries, and all the students in my children's literature seminars who supplied annotated lists of books. Sonia Nieto and Rudine Sims always serve as models and friends and are generous in their help. Publishers, too, were helpful in providing catalogs and review copies.

I would also like to thank the reviewers of this edition for their valuable insights and thoughtful suggestions. These reviewers include the following individuals:Helen Abadiano, Central Connecticut State University; Joyce Bergin, Armstrong State College; Stanley Bochtler, Buena Vista College; Gale Breedlove, University of South Carolina; Brenda Dales, Miami University; Daniel Hade, Pennsylvania State University; Sylvia Hutchinson, University of Georgia; Sandra Imdieke, Northern Michigan University; Marjorie Jones, St. Martin's College; Nicholas Karolides, University of Wisconsin, River Falls; Janice Kristo, University of Maine; Sandra Lott, University of Montevallo; Miriam Marecek, Boston University; Sue Mohrman, Texas A&I University; Diane Monson, University of Minnesota; JoAnn Muller, University of Northern Colorado; Ruth Sabol, West Chester University of Pennsylvania; Silver Stanfill, University of Alaska; Meritt Stark, Henderson State University; Charles Temple, Hobart and William Smith Colleges; Terrell Young, Washington State University; and Jack Zevin, Queens College.

To all these, and to those whom I have not named but who always have been supportive and ready to help, I acknowledge my debt and tender my thanks.

I must add my appreciation too, to my husband for his unflagging support and encouragement.

Introduction

Educators have within their power the means to inculcate values; develop skills; influence attitudes; and affect the physical, social, emotional, intellectual, and moral development of today's youth and tomorrow's adults.

Schooling should ensure the appropriate acquisition of competence in such basic areas as reading, writing, and computation; but skills taught in isolation or placed in meaningless contexts serve no function. Knowing how to read is useless unless one reads. Recognizing this principle, contemporary educators must provide many opportunities to support children's joy of reading by making available as many interesting, well-written books as they possibly can. Reading aloud; engaging in projects related to reading; having a silent reading time when everyone, including the teacher, reads for pleasure; and inviting authors to the classroom are but a few of the activities that create a climate favorable for reading.

Society needs to develop responsible decision makers; the process should begin as soon as a child begins to reason. Decision-making skills pertain not only to important long-range matters but also to everyday situations. When given the opportunity, even preschool children are able to select what clothing they will wear, what activities they will engage in and decide which friends they will play with. Adults often ask their children to decide on what specific gifts they will request for birthdays and special occasions. Young children frequently negotiate with one another over what games to play, what the rules will be, and when to begin and end the games. Though the extent of their choices may be limited, they should be encouraged to practice their skills and to evaluate the success of their decisions. Nonthreatening conversations about the outcomes of their choices can help children approach critical thinking, viewing, and reading with open minds and the expectation that their opinions are valuable.

The structure of the conventional classroom has changed and continues to change. Means are being sought to enable children to maintain and improve their decisionmaking and evaluative skills. Students are being encouraged to explore their environment and to extract from it whatever is meaningful to them. Reading, one of the most important areas of instruction in the schools, has emerged as a critical tool in developing the skills of independent and responsible critical thinking and behavior.

In the past, reading programs concentrated on the mechanical aspects of skills. Although concerned publishers and educators attempted to address comprehension and critical reading, the important part of reading instruction was confined to simple decoding, or word calling. Now, especially with the embracing of the "whole-language" movement with its emphasis on literature-based instruction and emergent literacy, teachers ask fewer "one-right-answer" questions, require children to think more deeply about what they read, and encourage children to select books they will enjoy reading.

The field of children's literature has kept pace with the direction of education as a whole. Teachers and librarians are able to approach the study of children's literature in a variety of ways. Probably the most widespread is the genre approach, which examines the different literary categories of children's books (e.g., folk tales, poetry, fiction, biography). There are many excellent sources and texts guiding students in this approach, which has the advantage of providing the adult with an overview of the field. The genre approach also attempts to assist readers in developing literary criteria for selecting and appreciating books. Some scholars advocate an exclusively literary approach, looking at the style, characters, plot, and structure of each book and analyzing it according to aesthetic criteria.

In keeping with contemporary aims of education, directions in publishing for children, and social needs, this author recommends an additional approach to the study of children's literature. A critical examination of the books in the light of how they treat contemporary social problems and conditions is a valuable adjunct to a literary perspective. Books are important influences on readers' minds. They can help in the construction of suitable bases for attitudes and behaviors. A critical, or issues, approach should therefore be included in the repertoire of courses and texts available to adult learners.

To assess the effectiveness in literature of issues of social and personal concern, the reader is required first to examine his or her own knowledge, attitudes, and prejudices. Psychologists and sociologists (cited in each individual chapter) have provided excellent advice for handling various problems constructively with children. Family relations, divorce, adoption, sibling rivalry, abuse, death, sexuality, old age, war and peace, special needs, gender roles, and different heritages are all potentially volatile and wrenching matters. Books afford the opportunity to explore and confront these issues with children by creating a protected vicarious situation.

The use of books to help children grapple with their personal problems and become aware of social concerns has become accepted as an important part of teaching. Librarians and counselors, as well as parents, search for books that mirror a problem they want to help a child resolve. The ancient library at Thebes bore the inscription: "Healing place of the soul." In using books to help children address emotional and social concerns, educators do not assume the role of psychologists or physicians but recognize that children today walk into the classroom grappling with many problems. Teachers, who next to parents spend the most time with young people, need the competence to handle children's questions and concerns, and books can help.

Adults who conduct this guidance through books (this practice is sometimes called "bibliotherapy") know that to be successful, the practice must not be specifically prescriptive or forced. When a book is assigned as medicine, the chances of its being accepted are slim. Rather, if informal strategies are used, such as amassing many books on a given theme, then the likelihood of success is enhanced. Book exhibits on a given theme; regular reading aloud by the teacher, other adults, or students; a list of recommended titles posted in an accessible area; and regular conferences between the teacher and child are some of the ingredients contributing to constructing a setting in which children will be attracted to reading about and then discussing their concerns.

Literature should be well written and appropriate to the child's developmental level. Teachers and librarians must continuously update their knowledge of what is available in children's books; thousands of titles are published each year. Adults must always be sensitive to the children's reactions. Ideally, the child reader should be able to identify with the character and action in the book. Then catharsis can take place, ultimately followed by insight. With insight, constructive behavior and attitudes can be reinforced and nurtured.

Especially in today's world, adults who work with children must understand and be knowledgeable about children's concerns. They should search for a variety of books to use as resources to help children deal responsibly with the issues. Those books that attempt to teach lessons should be analyzed for their accuracy, effectiveness, and intent. But readers should be aware that books that are not obviously didactic are the most potent. The aesthetic quality of a book is one of the most important factors affecting its impact.

This text examines literature for children from kindergarten through junior high school. Books for older children have consistently contained issues that relate to life's problems, but until quite recently, books for young children attempted to shield their audience from dissension and dilemmas of social import. That situation has drastically changed over the past two decades. There is almost no topic that is unmentionable in a child's book. Young children are encouraged to read and think about all the issues included in this text, and more.

Good works of literature contain many issues and provide good stories or well-designed factual presentations. Thus, the death of Charlotte in *Charlotte's Web* helps readers to understand and handle the concept of death, but the book is much more than a discussion and examination of this topic. Charlotte is a masterly literary creation. Her grappling with the ferocity of life as a spider, her friendship with Wilbur, and her cleverness and perspective on life enrich the experience of reading the book. To say merely that the book is about death would be to seriously mislead and do damage to appreciation of the book as a whole.

Sometimes books teach negative lessons without their authors' recognition of the fact. Even well-intentioned authors project their prejudices and values into their writing. They are limited by their own experiences and the resources to which they have access; no one person can know all the facts about anything. It is the intent of this text to encourage readers to ask questions about everything they read. Furthermore, this author hopes that after using this text readers will acknowledge that every work of children's literature has implications that bear examining. A critical perspective does not mean that when serious questions or negative messages are uncovered a reader should dislike the entire book or that it should be banned. It reflects an active effort on the part of a reader to deal with work that is demeaning, damaging, or stereotypic.

Criticizing a book is not the same as censoring it. No lover of books condones censorship. School boards and self-appointed watchdogs who demand the withdrawal of books from shelves threaten the process of education, as well as the freedom of speech. But critical analysis is necessary to maintain an atmosphere of lively interaction. Proponents of certain viewpoints have the right and obligation to speak out; readers have the right and obligation to accept or reject the arguments. Advocacy groups of all sorts are fervent in their comments about what they consider to be damaging in books. People may approve of and agree with some and vigorously oppose the views of others, but to silence any of them would constitute censorship. They should not ban or burn books; but they may urge, exhort, and publish articles of criticism. If their views spark controversy, so much the better for the health of the children's book industry. Children should be taught to become critics, too. This fits into an approach to problem solving that is rapidly gaining interest across the country. Many schools are incorporating curricula teaching problem-solving strategies.

Although book-talks and conversations with children about the plots, characters, and themes of books are not at all controversial, some communities have raised questions about the feasibility of discussing books containing sensitive issues. Self-appointed censors, as well as official decision makers about curriculum and materials of instruction, sometimes object to classroom discussions about politically volatile social or personal issues and take exception to specific books they think are potentially harmful to children.

Sometimes it is helpful if teachers invite parents into the classroom ahead of time to see the books they will be discussing. Parents may be given the option of choosing what their child will read from among a variety of titles or even that of having their child excluded from the classroom when a disapproved topic is being discussed. Most often, if a book is offered as an option rather than assigned reading, the situation is less likely to invite dissension. All education is political, and teachers and librarians must make their own decisions about how to handle potentially explosive topics and books. Ideally, each child will select his or her own reading material, and conversations and group discussions will follow in context and without undue fanfare.

An issues approach to children's literature includes an examination of problem situations in stories. It also fosters the development of those skills defined as critical reading, comprehension, and critical thinking. Many works of fiction are excellent vehicles for teaching history. It is therefore important for adults working with children to become ever more knowledgeable about the scope and materials of children's literature. This book is designed to serve that educational function.

This edition is divided into three major parts: Family, Life Cycle, and Society. Part One, Family, includes chapters on Siblings, Adoption and Foster Care, Divorce, and Family Constellations. Sex and Sexuality, Aging, and Death constitute Part Two, Life Cycle. Part Three, Society, contains chapters on issues of Gender Roles, Heritage, Special Needs, Abuse, and War and Peace.

PREVIEW

Chapter One: Siblings

The family is the first social structure. It provides a model for other relationships. This chapter explores sibling interaction, one of the foundations for children's future social behavior. Books in which characters are siblings present a variety of different models of interaction. Parents' behaviors in these books range from destructive and irresponsible to supportive and nurturing. An appreciation of different heritages can be found in these books as well. Sibling relationships also contain implications for gender role expectations and behaviors. Placing value on cooperative behavior is communicated in a number of the books.

Chapter Two: Adoption and Foster Care

The feelings of adopted children have been more acknowledged in recent years, particularly with the advent of legislation granting people the right to find out about their birth parents. Foster children, too, figure in a number of children's books, helping the reader to empathize with their issues. Some books mirror up-to-date aspects of adoption, such as interracial and international adoptions and the rights of birth parents, as well as adoptive parents, to permanent custody of children.

Chapter Three: Divorce

Books on divorce attempt to help young readers recognize that they are not alone and that their problems do have solutions. The amount of fiction and nonfiction about this issue increases steadily. Most books respect the child's perception and communicate that attitude. Some books, centering exclusively on the child, ignore the adults' reactions; others help young readers to understand the causes of their parents' dissension.

Chapter Four: Family Constellations

An evolving definition of family, as well as the appearance in children's literature of different lifestyles and configurations of families, forms the content of this chapter. Children need books that reflect their own family patterns and those of their friends. They also benefit from seeing family situations in books that differ from those they encounter in their daily interactions.

Chapter Five: Sexuality

Sex education arouses much controversy among educators and other members of any community. Although most professionals agree that sex education is necessary, the content, manner of presentation, materials, timing, quantity, and setting are all matters for argument. Consequently, many different presentations exist in books. Topics include reproduction, birth, puberty, homosexuality, abortion, and the relationship between sexual activity and love. Although it is more difficult for children to locate and acquire these books than to obtain those in any other category, children often manage to share what they do find with each other. Peer education and miseducation on this topic are greater than on any other. Adults must decide if and how they wish to intervene. Books can help.

Chapter Six: Aging

The median age in the United States is increasing. Like members of other special populations, elders are subject to stereotyping and misunderstanding. They appear in many children's books, sometimes as three-dimensional characters, sometimes as cardboard devices, most often in their unifunctional roles as grandparents. Criteria for appropriate presentation and a description of books containing a variety of elders are included here.

Chapter Seven: Death

Death has received much attention in literature for children. Different religious views, family reactions, problems, and methods of coping are presented in a great variety in books, some of which are extremely well written while others will not last long in readers' memories. Stereotypes are presented and surmounted. Painful situations are experienced. Important questions are brought to the readers' attention. This chapter, in common with the others, suggests activities for both adults and children in order to increase their understanding of the issues presented. It also discusses developmental stages of knowing about death and reacting to the death of loved ones.

Chapter Eight: Gender Roles

The role of the female is one that the public has been discussing actively. Male roles also need to be examined and perhaps redefined. The new feminist scholarship has greatly influenced the consideration of what it means to be male or female in this society. Different points of view are emerging. Language usage is one of the political and sociological aspects of this issue. Many annotations and references accompany the text in this and the other chapters. Readers are encouraged to seek out these resources to aid in formulating their own positions. The activities in this chapter are aimed at self-evaluation.

Chapter Nine: Heritage

More and more excellent books can be found that include characters in significant roles representing different heritages. People from any group other than the Christian white middle class once were missing from consideration or even actively distorted in most children's books. Children from many different cultures can now read about themselves and each other. Critical reaction to books dealing with various heritages is by no means uniform; opinions range from appreciation of good intentions on the part of the author to rejection of any book that is not written by a member of the group discussed in the book. This chapter presents and discusses some criteria for the reader's consideration. Its intent is to provide a context for detecting and overcoming stereotypes and developing an appreciation for the nation's rich and varied cultures.

The chapter contains a brief history of the peopling of America from prerecorded time to the present. Literature for children is represented and analyzed in many genres, including folklore, poetry, nonfiction, and fiction. Exemplary books are discussed. Different perspectives are shared, and suggestions are offered for further study.

Chapter Ten: Abuse

Physical, sexual, and emotional abuse; family violence; and incest are some of the topics that appear in contemporary children's literature. These topics reflect a new awareness of the prevalence of abusive conditions in American society today. This chapter includes discussions of the issues, as well as descriptions of the ways children's books incorporate what is known about the issue. Included are discussions of drug and alcohol abuse and an indication of how they are handled in the literature for children. Eating disorders also are considered an addiction; in this case food is the abused substance.

Chapter Eleven: Special Needs

This chapter deals with children's literature containing characters who have special needs. The category includes not only people who are mentally or physically disabled but also those with emotional problems. Gifted individuals are also included. A substantive portion of this chapter contains discussions of serious illnesses such as AIDS, cancer, and other life-threatening or debilitating diseases.

Chapter Twelve: War and Peace

As with each of the other issues, war and the attempt to create and maintain peace contain complexities beyond a simple discussion of right or wrong. Each war, whether it is global or confined to a small group of people, has individual characteristics differentiating it from others; but there are also universal factors to be considered. Books about war range from allegories and satires to realistic personal accounts. The burgeoning peace movement has entered literature appropriate to the developmental levels of very young children. Conflict resolution, noncompetitive games, a look at bullies, and at the negotiations friends use are all a part of this complex issue.

Children's books should be sought that convey the complex aspects of war. Occasionally books can be found that help the reader become aware of the ambiguous morality and the ambivalent outcomes surrounding this topic. Criteria for analysis of the books are suggested.

This text helps readers build a solid basis for forming opinions and developing attitudes. The more informed people are, the more constructive their behavior can be. Too often, people act out of ignorance. Education can serve as a key to positive action. In this author's opinion, it is the hope of the world.

part 1

Family

The family is a child's first social structure. It provides a model for other relationships. The first four chapters of this book deal with interrelationships in traditional families, as well as those that reflect the evolving definition of what constitutes a family. Chapter 1 examines books that provide a variety of perspectives on what it means to be or to have a sibling. Although few books handle the issues surrounding the position of the only child, they are also included in this chapter.

Adoption and foster care are covered in Chapter 2. Although these are not the most common situations, they are nevertheless becoming more important, especially because of the increase in international and intercultural adoptions. Legislation regulating both foster care and adoption has also received attention in the past few years. The issues surrounding these topics can also be classified as societal, but they are included in this part because they are first and foremost, family concerns.

The same is true of divorce, the subject of Chapter 3. Although the divorce rate seems to have stabilized in recent years, attitudes toward divorce are changing radically. Divorce is no longer a rare phenomenon. Children are more likely now to know at least a few people whose families have experienced divorce. Coping with the situation and its many ramifications, such as blended families and multiple siblings, has become much more important than examining the rights and wrongs of the decision to divorce.

The family constellations examined in Chapter 4 include single-parent families, extended families, and uniquely constituted units, as well as families that are bound into a larger community. It deals with families which have made a variety of adjustments in an attempt to effect a harmonious and mutually beneficial life together.

chapter 1

Siblings

Sibling relationships play an important part in how individuals feel about themselves and how they relate to other people. Sibling interaction often serves as a model for people in associating friends, new acquaintances, mates, and their own children and in relating to society in general.

Siblings who grow up together learn each other's characteristics in a way that no other people do, with little room for pretense. They have the opportunity to construct their own social order, and the advantage of built-in companionship. They may develop bonds that last throughout their lives and, when conditions are right, forge relationships of mutual support, pride, and love. Siblings also practice many skills of social interaction. They must develop strategies for living together that will be acceptable most of the time. Besides having to share their parents' time, attention, and love, siblings are forced to share physical space and possessions.

Siblings can test out behaviors with the relative security of knowing that their brothers or sisters probably will not have the option of leaving them forever, as is the case with friends. They can usually rely on getting honest reactions to their behaviors. Parents influence siblings' interactions in the ways that they deal with their children. Favoritism, a laissez-faire attitude, expectations (high or low), undue interference in children's relationships, or lack of proper supervision can all affect children's behavior, self-images, and perceptions of how society functions.

Another influential factor in the conduct between and among siblings is birth order. It is rare in literature that birth order does not play an important role. The only child is frequently depicted as a lonely, spoiled, self-centered individual who is unable to get along with peers, too adult-oriented, and in general, maladjusted. The eldest takes charge and cares too much about achievement. The middle child is often portrayed as squeezed, resentful, quick-tempered, overly sensitive, and rebellious. The youngest is usually seen as pampered, demanding, and favored but often feels like an outsider and yearns for acceptance. There are also positive aspects of each position: The only child and the eldest are often very successful in later life and assume positions of leadership. The middle child learns how to compromise and to make friends; he or she becomes a "people person." The youngest is everyone's darling and develops a strong positive sense of self.

Too often, the literature affirms stereotypes rather than recognizes that most people are not bound by impositions and expectations of birth order. The experiences of birth order may influence patterns of behavior, attitudes toward self, and strategies for coping; but, as Dr. Lucille K. Forer says, "Birth order is only one of many environmental factors important in developing and maintaining life roles."

Try This
What position do you occupy in birth order in your family? How has this position affected your relationship with your sibling(s)? How did it affect your relationship with your parents when you were growing up? Which of the books in the Bibliography at the end of this chapter most closely approximates your situation? Find someone who occupies the same birth order position as you. Share the book with that person to see how your perceptions and experiences match.

Other factors besides birth order affect a family's interactions. The number of years between children; the sex of the children; the economic, social, and emotional circumstances of the family during the time the children are being reared; the state of each person's health; the physical environment; the influence of peers and schooling—all these factors contribute to how members of a family perceive themselves and one another. Children's books offer a wide range of family settings for readers to experience vicariously. Some of the books can be very helpful in assuring children that, contrary to their fears, they and their family are normal.

Authors have represented families realistically as having internal struggles and problems, rivalries, and unpleasant relationships. In addition, they have begun to present useful models for parents and siblings to emulate in normal stress situations.

SUGGESTED CRITERIA

It is wise to seek out those stories that contain realistic solutions to problems. If real issues are presented, their effect is lessened if they come to a happy but unlikely resolution. A pat solution is also less valuable than one that indicates more thought and time should be given to the problem; it is far better to suggest that one answer will not suffice than to provide a simple solution. For example, the situation created by having a new baby in the house is usually resolved in life only for short periods of time. It needs constant reexamination and additional strategies as both the new arrival and the elder sibling(s) develop. Books that indicate this expectation are useful.

Parental behavior is an important element of stories concerned with sibling interaction. Models should be presented wherever possible in which parents behave humanely, responsibly, and plausibly. Although no parents are saints and some are cruel, their behavior should arise from the plot, with some rationale indicated. An explanation for characters' behavior always contributes to the quality of a story.

Parental and sibling roles should reflect a realistic pattern, but expectations need not be rigid or stereotypic. No matter what the behavior, it should be in the context of the story rather than imposed on it. Readers can judge for themselves whether any of the siblings is being either unjustly favored or victimized. Sometimes the author purposely describes such a predicament, leading young readers to examine their own reactions to the injustice; but it is helpful to find some books in which parents' concerned, equitable, and appropriate behavior can serve as a model.

The illustrations should attempt to demonstrate the universality of sibling interactions; a range of ethnic groups, economic circumstances, geographic locations, and family styles should be represented in a collection of books. If the setting is a city, there should be a representation of the multicultural nature of urban life. In any case, stereotypes, both visual and literary, should be avoided.

Ideally, all the characters—certainly each of the siblings—should be developed as three-dimensional individuals. Who are they? What makes them behave the way they do? What is their perspective? Do they function simply as foils for the protagonist, or are they people in their own right? If the author has not provided this information, readers should be invited to flesh out the other characters for themselves, to add depth to the story.

Sibling conflict should not be judged as abnormal. Books can help to provide the context for healthy reactions and interactions on the part of readers. Guilt should not be imposed, particularly since arguments and hostility between siblings are such an expected part of normal development.

Books are most effective when they have literary merit. The best lessons are those taught unobtrusively. Too obvious a message damages a story.

DISCUSSION OF CHILDREN'S BOOKS

The New Baby

The elder sibling, particularly when that child has been an only child up to the arrival of the new baby, is the subject of sympathetic concern in many books. These books are generally directed to three-to-six-year-old children, perhaps because these children react most keenly to new babies. Some books dealing directly with this topic are factual. They are designed to be read aloud in order to give information that will help the child to understand the process of adjusting to a new sibling. Fred Rogers's *The New Baby* is one such book. It is illustrated with photographs that show not only new babies but also their brothers and sisters in pleasant activities. The book attempts to involve elder siblings in an understanding of the baby's development so that they will not resent the baby's behavior. Some of the explanations will probably alleviate anxiety and anger and help the elder child feel more comfortable as a result of the additional knowledge.

The newly reissued *Everett Anderson's Nine Month Long*, by Lucille Clifton, demonstrates to older children that they are loved. The message that every family member is important is also communicated strongly in Sara Bonnett Stein's *That*

New Baby—one book in the "Open Family" series. As with the other books in this series, there are separate texts for parents and children. The advice to parents is both practical and psychologically sound. It helps families to recognize that jealousy and feelings of being displaced are normal and can be dealt with in a loving, accepting way. The photographs, both in black and white and in color, show an African-American family, adding to the universality of the message. The family contains two older siblings, a boy and a girl, and a grandmother who is a permanent member of the family. Books of this sort help to prepare parents for coping with the problem of sibling rivalry in a realistic, direct fashion. Teachers, counselors, and librarians may want to read such books so that they can recommend procedures to parents and children who are trying to deal with the arrival of a new baby.

The New Baby at Your House, by Joanna Cole, helps families prepare older siblings for the birth of a new baby. An advantage of this book is that it provides an invitation for children to participate in the process of welcoming a new baby, rather than to look on or merely "help." The book contains sections for parents as well as children. A number of the books on this topic emphasize the role the elder sibling can play in helping with the new baby. In Mary-Joan Gerson's *Omoteji's Baby Brother,* Omoteji, a Nigerian boy, feels left out and useless until he decides on the perfect contribution he can make to the festivities of his new brother's naming ceremony. Marc Brown's protagonist in *Arthur's Baby,* the eldest of three children, deals well with both his younger sister and the new baby. He demonstrates his knowledge of infants when he burps the baby and thereby stops her crying. A factor to be noted in this book is that Arthur is entirely aware that there will continue to be ups and downs in his relationship with his siblings; there is no once-and-for-all-time cure.

Some books deal with the topic of the sibling relationship as the main thrust of the story, while others only incidentally include the interaction between siblings within the context of the plot. Whether the intent is to look at this issue as a problem or a model, the young reader, assisted by the helpful adult, can find an array of books. Children who read these books or have them read to them can be asked to give suggestions about how they can help at home with their baby sisters or brothers. They can also dictate stories to their teachers or to older students or adults in the classroom or library. In these stories they can name themselves as the protagonists who have just experienced having a baby sibling come home to them. They can describe what they do to help with the new baby and illustrate their stories either with their own drawings or with photographs of themselves and their families. Their stories can be placed on the classroom or library shelves.

The best antidote to the poison of sibling rivalry is a feeling of self-worth, along with the knowledge that the family still loves and needs the person who is jealous. Kathryn Lasky's *A Baby for Max* affirms Max's place in the family, as well as his parents' assumption that Max is an important contributor to the baby's welfare. Little Rabbit's parents in Fran Manushkin's *Little Rabbit's Baby Brother* go to great lengths to reassure Little Rabbit that her baby brother conveys on her the important status of "big sister." The parents also encourage Little Rabbit to hold and comfort the new baby. Dorothy Corey's *Will There Be a Lap for Me?* is one of a number of books that deal with the mother's lap as a special place for children.

Patricia MacLachlan's *Arthur, for the Very First Time* describes a boy's gradual development from being very self-involved to appreciating and cherishing new life and others' feelings and ideas. Caring adults and a feisty, sensitive female friend help him in this evolution. Although not primarily about the acceptance of a new sibling, this book will help any reader, especially one who has been an only child, adjust to the coming of an infant.

Sometimes, no matter how well intentioned the parents are, children still feel unwanted. In both Russell Hoban's *A Baby Sister for Frances* and Ezra Jack Keats's *Peter's Chair,* the elder siblings run away from home. Neither runs very far, though, and both feel much better when they realize their parents want them back.

Try This
Rewrite any of the "new baby" books from the point of view of the new baby. Have children do the same thing. If they cannot write, have them retell the stories orally.

Sibling Rivalry

Authors often exhibit sympathy for the elder child but also consider the younger one. In *If It Weren't for Benjamin,* by Barbara Shook Hazen, the older brother gets to lick the icing spoon, uses scissors with points, and stays up late. The parents help the younger child to see that it isn't necessary to be identical to his sibling and that he is valued for who he is. He independently comes to recognize that he would miss Benjamin's telling him jokes, fixing his toys, and playing with him; but he also admits that there are times when he hates his brother.

Several books elaborate on this theme. In Crescent Dragonwagon's *I Hate My Brother Harry,* the little girl is permitted to express her ambivalent feelings toward her older brother. At the end of the book, she retains both the love and the hate. A little boy, in Judith Viorst's *I'll Fix Anthony,* dreams of the day he will be six years old and big enough to get back at his older brother who treats him badly. This sort of presentation reassures a child who has not achieved a purely loving relationship with a sibling that it is a condition shared by others.

A number of books reflect the problem of rivalry between siblings once the siblings have progressed beyond babyhood. One is Pat Brisson's *Your Best Friend, Kate,* in which Kate and her younger brother engage in a number of spats. Being forced to endure each other's company on a family car trip taxes their ability to get along. Their arguments are not ugly or threatening, though, and their underlying affection for each other is realistic and strong.

A more serious rivalry, one with unhappy consequences, is portrayed in Clyde Robert Bulla's *The Christmas Coat.* Hans and Otto's mother draws a chalk line down the middle of the boys' room to keep them from hurting each other. One day, they cross the line, disobediently open a box containing a beautiful coat, and tear the coat in half when they quarrel over who will try it on first. When they discover that the coat is to be a Christmas surprise for their next door neighbor, they work in concert to have it repaired. Each boy acknowledges blame and helps to make amends. This story could serve as the basis for children to discuss how to end destructive behavior and how to design some long-lasting solutions to the problems evidenced by Hans and Otto.

In a less destructive relationship, two mouse brothers in *Dear Brother,* by Vladimir Vagin and Frank Asch, are stimulated to cooperative behavior by the discovery of a batch of letters exchanged by two of their great-great uncles. The young brothers are so moved by the letters that they begin to develop a perspective on the importance of close sibling relationships.

Another book portraying sibling rivalry is Doris Orgel's *Bartholomew, We Love You.* While the reader's sympathy is expected to lie with the younger sister, the presentation is balanced enough so that the elder does not emerge as the victimizer. The happy ending is not that the younger one wins out but that they learn to share and cooperate with each other. This book is useful in its depiction of the parents, who in addition to both being working people, are impartial, understanding, and capable.

Twins

Twins are often considered to be two halves of the same child. A number of books usefully present twins experiencing the rivalry of ordinary brothers and sisters. Beverly Cleary's *Mitch and Amy* and Alice Bach's *The Smartest Bear and His Brother Oliver* are two that demonstrate this approach. The bear twins have understanding, responsive parents; but Mitch and Amy's parents unwittingly foster competition between the twins. Children can be encouraged to discuss what they might do as mothers and fathers to remedy the unfairness of the fictional parents. Katherine Paterson's *Jacob Have I Loved* revolves around Louise, who hates her favored twin sister. Only maturity and a sense of accomplishment in saving the life of a newborn baby help Louise to overcome her negative feelings.

Most books at least imply that siblings will grow out of their bickering and rivalry. For some readers, this may seem an unlikely development. They will be delighted with *Being a Twin/Having a Twin,* a factual photo essay on the experience of being a twin. Maxine B. Rosenberg and George Ancona show twins engaging in many activities. Their book contains photos and follows four sets of twins, up close and personal. The text points out that each child should be treated as an individual.

Aliki helps very young children to see that acknowledging differences between twins is very important in *Jack and Jake,* a charming picture book in which the twins' older sister is the only one who takes the time to know the twins well enough to discern their important differences even if they appear to be identical.

In Sylvia Fair's *The Bedspread,* twin sisters in their eighties or nineties spend all their time together at opposite ends of a very long bed. Although they do not agree on much, they do concur that their white bedspread is boring and begin to decorate it. Even though both sisters are ostensibly stitching the same items (the front door; the steps; their cat; the windows, walls, roof, and chimneys) their personalities and their individual recollections make the two ends of the spread very different. This time, instead of arguing over who is right, the sisters begin to see each other's point of view and even to enjoy it. Never patronizing, the author manages to convey the rivalry and the love and to communicate a valuing of differences, as well as an understanding that it is never too late to learn.

Cooperation and Love

Perhaps less realistic for some children, but certainly reflective of some experiences, are the books that describe helpful and loving relationships among siblings. If these books are not held up to readers as perfect examples to be emulated, they can serve to confirm positive feelings and perhaps provide alternatives to quarrelsome behavior. *I'm Telling: Kids Talk about Brothers and Sisters,* edited by Eric Arnold and Jeffrey Coeb, is a compilation of preteens' comments about their siblings. Readers gain the understanding that it is acceptable for siblings to bicker with one another and even to harbor resentment but that it is also normal for them to have times where they love and enjoy each other.

In John Steptoe's *My Special Best Words,* Bweela, although she is only three years old, lovingly and competently relates to her younger brother. They do have some verbal quarrels, but the reader recognizes this as part of the fun; the relationship remains strongly positive. June Jordan contributes a strong, coping family in *New Life, New Room.* The children are realistic, lively, and inventive, while both parents are tender to each other and to the children. The brother and sister in Patricia MacLachlan's *Seven Kisses in a Row* provide another excellent model for readers to appreciate. All the characters accept one another's idiosyncracies, have vivid personalities, and are amusing as well as captivating.

The oldest sister in Kady MacDonald Denton's *Janet's Horses* is clever in her games of make-believe with her younger siblings, and it is not a sacrifice for her to play with them. They all enjoy themselves enormously. In *Eat up Gemma,* by Sarah Hayes, Gemma's older brother doesn't suffer from jealousy; he helps the family solve the problem of the baby's not wanting to eat. The family here is African American, a welcome addition to the collection of multicultural literature depicting universal themes. Similarly, *Con Mi Hermano/With My Brother,* by Eileen Roe, describes two brothers spending quality time with each other. They are affectionate and respectful of each other. The book is written in both English and Spanish, and the characters have Latino features.

Two Athapaskan siblings' survival depends on their cooperating with each other, as well as their intelligence and fortitude, in *Toughboy and Sister* by Kirpatrick Hill. Although the children are young (ages seven and eleven) and the hardships they face seem insurmountable, their story is believable and inspiring.

Facing Responsibility

Siblings are often called upon to take care of one another to varying degrees, depending on the extremes of the situation. In Lucille Clifton's *Don't You Remember?,* the four-year-old girl is tended by her elder brother. He must postpone going back to school so that both parents can work and his sister can be adequately supervised. The statement is made that he will resume his schooling. The arrangement does not seem to be a hardship for him.

Dicey, in Cynthia Voigt's *Homecoming* and in the Newbery Award–winning *Dicey's Song,* and Mary Call, in the Cleavers' *Where the Lilies Bloom,* take over the management of their families. Mary Call's parents are both dead; Dicey's mother has abandoned them. Both girls hide the fact that they have no adult protection; they are occasionally resented by their siblings for their imperious attitudes; and they are superhuman in their ability to respond to emergencies and maintain the family. These stories end happily with adults stepping in and taking charge. In contrast, Karana, in *Island of the Blue Dolphins,* by Scott O'Dell, never receives the benefit of someone to take care of her when she and her brother are marooned on an island. She is in this predicament because of her sense of responsibility for her brother. Despite her efforts, he dies, and she must manage her own survival alone.

A functioning, accepting, mutually respectful family comes to life in Johanna Hurwitz's *Russell and Elisa.* Although seven-year-old Russell and his three-and-a-half-year-old sister Elisa exhibit normal rivalry, their parents are unfailingly understanding and consistent in their responses of love and support. They do not permit the children to run roughshod over each other, but they do allow them some leeway in their behavior. They listen and encourage the children to solve their own problems. None of the characters is demeaned, even when exhibiting behavior that might invite teasing. For example, when Russell goes for his first "sleep-over date" and experiences pangs of separation, his actions are not ridiculed but are given loving, and firm treatment. His parents permit him to choose whether to go through with the sleep-over. They set limits that are realistic and firm, and they are never punitive.

An additional strength of this story is that the children are treated even-handedly. They are both charming in their own ways, and each commits some acts that warrant reprimand. They are real children in their feelings and behavior. The parents are somewhat idealized, but not beyond the bounds of believability. This gentle book can serve as a model for children and adults, and the episodes are fun to read.

Fairy Tales and Folk Tales

Folk tales (including legends, myths, and fairy tales) deal with archetypes and symbols. Their emotional content carries much more weight than specific details of character and plot. Bruno Bettelheim points out that "the child carried away by sibling rivalry feels, 'That's me; that's how they mistreat me, or would want to; that's how little they think of me.' And there are moments—often long periods of time—when for inner reasons a child feels this way even when his position among his siblings may seem to give him no cause for it" (1977, p. 237).

In the conventional pattern of fairy tales, there are three siblings, and the youngest is something of a simpleton but kind-hearted and pure in thought. During the course of the story, the siblings usually must complete some challenge. Traditionally, the two older siblings fail because they are selfish; the youngest succeeds and wins a great reward. Bettelheim claims that "When in a fairy story a child is the third one, the hearer easily identifies with him [sic] because within the most basic family constellations the child is the third down, [from both parents] irrespective of whether he is the oldest, middle, or youngest among his siblings" (Bettelheim, 1977, p. 106). Contrary to what Bettelheim says, however, many adults, as well as children, reflect in conversation that when they encounter a number of stories confirming the stereotypic pattern children *do* associate literally with their own birth-order placement and strongly identify with the child who is in the same birth order as the reader.

One of the dangers here is a tendency to accept and internalize stereotypes. The common patterns in fairy and folk tales indicate that sibling rivalry is a phenomenon of a deep and lasting nature. Also in these tales, simple-mindedness is often equated with kindness while cleverness is looked at askance. What is more, designating the youngest member of the family as the "best" can cause problems with readers who unconsciously begin to believe these notions. Teachers or parents can introduce the idea of switching the characters around, so that the eldest is the sweet-tempered one, or the middle child wins out. This activity retains the emotional truth of the rivalry and the self-perception of being misunderstood and mistreated, but it eliminates the birth-order stereotype.

Characteristics can be changed, too, so that all siblings are of equal strength, beauty, and intelligence but the one who wins is both clever and kind. John Steptoe did just that in *Mufaro's Beautiful Daughters.* One of the special features of this stunning book is that both siblings are beautiful. Although one sister is selfish and narrow minded and the other is caring and open, their external features are equally lovely. This helps to dispel the stereotype that external beauty indicates goodness and does no damage whatsoever to the story. As a matter of fact, it enhances the quality of the folktale because readers can judge the characters by their actions rather than their appearance. An added advantage to this book is that it is derived from an African tale, and the beauty is exemplary of non-Caucasian standards.

In the same vein, the original Cinderella, *Yeh-Shen: A Cinderella Story from China,* by Ai-Ling Louie, which predates European versions by hundreds of years, adds dimension to any library collection. Ed Young's illustrations leave no doubt as to Yeh-Shen's beauty, even though she is not the "classic" European blonde with blue eyes.

It is always useful to have a variety of books available so that stereotypes will not become cemented into children's thinking. Such traditional tales as *The Three Little Pigs* or *The Three Billy Goats Gruff* help young readers to see that even when there are three siblings it is not necessary for the eldest to be nasty, the youngest to be simple and kind, or for there to be vicious rivalry among them. In some versions of *The Twelve Dancing Princesses,* it is the eldest princess who marries their rescuer; in some it is the youngest. Children might want to discuss what difference this makes. In many stories, the siblings cooperate and love each other dearly, as in the traditional European versions of *Hansel and Gretel, The Seven Swan Brothers, Snow White and Rose Red;* in several Latin American tales, such as *The Bad Wishers* and *The Hero Twins;* and in the Chinese tale, *The Seven Chinese Brothers,* retold by Margaret Mahy. A lively discussion might start with the question of what would happen to the story if these helpful siblings engaged in rivalry.

Try This
Search for fairy tales or folk tales that contain siblings as characters. Construct a chart showing how often the youngest, the middle child, or the oldest is the hero. List positive and negative characteristics according to the birth order of the siblings. Discuss the configuration the chart reveals.

Folk and fairy tales come to us from oral traditions passed down over generations by storytellers in every culture. It has always been the prerogative of the teller to embellish or adapt a tale according to the needs and conditions of the moment. Only when the tales are frozen in print does a particular version becomes inflexible. Even in print, each reteller builds on previous versions and fashions a new tale according to his or her pleasure and purpose. When children see the differences, productive discussions can arise around issues of stereotyping, patterns of behavior, and societal expectations.

Many books contain examples of different sibling relationships. In order to be guided into constructing a healthy mode of behavior, children need to see that they are normal, that they are valued, and that there are many acceptable ways of relating to one another. Adults and children will find many examples of the ways sisters and brothers are presented in a variety of books that provide models, test situations, and questions to explore. The greater the number and variety at readers' immediate disposal, the more beneficial the impact. Sibling rivalry will not be eliminated, but readers may learn to handle it with more comfort.

REFERENCES

Siblings

Bank, S. P., and Kahn, M. D. *The Sibling Bond.* Basic Books, 1982. The authors, clinical psychologists, offer a theory of the way siblings attach to each other and engage in lifelong relationships.

Bettelheim, B. *The Uses of Enchantment: The Meaning and Importance of Fairy Tales.* Vintage Books, 1977. The noted child psychiatrist proposes that fairy tales are enriching and satisfying literature for both adults and children and that they offer the possibility of learning about human beings' deepest problems and emotions. They help children cope with turmoil, make meaning of predicaments, and discern what moral behavior is. The book contains analyses of a number of popular fairy tales and discusses such issues as the child's need for magic, sibling relations, Oedipal conflicts and resolutions, fear of fantasy, and the use of fantasy to help in a child's development.

Dunn, J., and Kendrick, C. *Siblings: Love, Envy, and Understanding.* Harvard University Press, 1982. The authors studied responses of firstborn children to newborn siblings. They discovered that when children were included in the care of the new baby a warm and close relationship was more likely to develop.

Faber, A., and Mazlish, E. *Siblings without Rivalry.* Illus. by K. A. Coe. Norton, 1987. Sensible, realistic advice on how to handle sibling rivalry. One of the authors' points is that insisting on good feelings and refusing to acknowledge bad feelings can lead to a worsening of those bad feelings. Conversely, permitting children to express their negative feelings can, with guidance, often lead to good feelings and behaviors. The authors discuss if and how to intervene in children's conflicts.

Forer, L. K. *The Birth Order Factor: How Your Personality Is Influenced by Your Place in Your Family.* David MacKay, 1976. The author, a clinical psychologist, explores the opinions concerning birth-order influences on personality and discusses how people may change their patterns.

Hoopes, M. M., and Harper, J. M. *Birth Order Roles and Sibling Patterns in Individual and Family Therapy.* Aspen, 1987. A discussion of the characteristics of children based on birth order, the rules and boundaries families set, and the alliances that are formed within the family system.

Konig, K. *Brothers and Sisters: The Order of Birth in the Family* (4th ed.). Rudolf Steiner, 1984. The author believes in the influence of birth order on people and their behavior. He says there are only three types: the first-, the second-, and the third-born child. In larger families, the order repeats. He provides characteristics for each type.

Lamb, M. E., and Sutton-Smith, B., eds. *Sibling Relationships: Their Nature and Significance across the Lifespan.* Erlbaum, 1982. Discusses siblings as agents of socialization, effects of newborns on older siblings, patterns of sibling interaction in children from the very young through adulthood, sibling interdependence, birth order, and only children.

Reit, S. V. *Sibling Rivalry.* Ballantine, 1985. Suggestions to help families cope with sibling conflicts, reassuring readers that the process is a part of natural growth. Includes discussions of birth order, competition, a new baby, twins, and handling special occasions constructively.

Rudman, M. K.; Gagne, K. D.; and Bernstein, J. E. *Books to Help Children Cope with Separation and Loss* (4th ed.). Bowker, 1994. This reference work contains 49 titles and annotations on siblings, in addition to two chapters on bibliotherapy and psychological background on separation and loss.

Toman, W. *Family Constellations.* Springer, 1976. Analyzes different sibling positions and defines characteristics of siblings according to birth order and sex. Fun, but more like astrology than science.

BIBLIOGRAPHY

Adler, C. S. *The Lump in the Middle.* Clarion, 1989. (Ages 9-12.) Kelsey is a middle child whose mother is overly critical and always blames her when anything goes wrong. Her older sister is "perfect," and her younger sister is "cute" and takes advantage of that fact to tattle and cause trouble for Kelsey. Kelsey finally discovers that it's OK for each of the siblings to differ and comes to a better understanding of her mother, who begins to see that she has been somewhat unfair to Kelsey.

Adoff, A. *Hard to Be Six.* Illus. by C. Hanna. Morrow, 1991. (Ages 4-6.) [See Family Constellations]

Adorjan, C. *I Can! Can You?* Illus. by M. Nerlove. Whitman, 1990. (Ages 3-5.) A noncompetitive look at the differences in ability of two sisters. Although the younger acknowledges that the elder can accomplish certain tasks, such as reading and shoe tying, the younger one can tell a story and put her toys away. The story is told in rhyme and maintains a cheerful, developmental perspective that reflects a healthy self image and relationship.

Aliki. *Jack and Jake.* Illus. by the author. Greenwillow, 1986. (Ages 3-6.) In a rollicking story that is as much about individual differences of all people as it is about telling twins apart, it is the older sister who perceives the differences and understands the twins. She serves as their champion, admonishing everyone to pay more attention to each twin's personality rather than focusing merely on physical traits.

Andry, A. C., and Kratka, S. C. *Hi, New Baby.* Illus. by T. di Grazia. Simon & Schuster, 1970. (Ages 2-6.) Addressing elder siblings, this well-illustrated book provides facts about new babies. It also points out situations that these siblings will have to cope with. The authors suggest activities that children can do to help themselves, their baby siblings, and the family climate in general.

Anholt, C. *Aren't You Lucky!* Illus. by the author. Little, Brown, 1990. (Ages 4-8.) A young girl tells of her adjustment to a new baby brother from the long wait through the pregnancy, and learning to accept someone else competing for attention. At first everyone tells her she's fortunate. As the baby grows older, people begin to tell her how lucky the baby is to have her for a sister. Charmingly written and illustrated.

Arnold, E. H., and Loeb, J., eds. *I'm Telling: Kids Talk about Brothers and Sisters.* Illus. by G. B. Karas. Little, Brown, 1987. (Ages 8–13.) One of the best aspects of this book is its clear message that arguing with and resenting siblings is normal, just as loving and enjoying each other is. Told in children's own words, the situations and observations are truthful, funny, and helpful.

Asch, F., and Vagin, V. *Dear Brother.* Illus. by the authors. Scholastic, 1992. (Ages 6–10.) Two mouse brothers find a collection of old letters that their great-great-granduncles sent to each other over a span of years. Reading about these long-ago brothers' feelings for each other causes the younger mice to appreciate their own relationship.

Bach, A. *The Smartest Bear and His Brother Oliver.* Illus. by S. Kellogg. Harper, 1975. (Ages 5–8.) Ronald wants to be different from his twin, Oliver. In order to demonstrate that they recognize their differences, the boys' parents wisely give each a different gift. Although the story's characters are bears, human siblings can identify with the situation.

Banish, R. *I Want to Tell You about My Baby.* Illus. by the author. Wingbow, 1982. (Ages 5–8.) Narrated by a young boy, the story in photographs and text tells about the mother's pregnancy, the birth of a new baby boy, and the older brother's activities and feelings after the baby comes home. The child's emotions are accepted and handled in a loving way.

Bauer, M. D. *A Question of Trust.* Scholastic, 1994. (Ages 11 and up.) Brad and Charlie are brothers who seem to fight with each other constantly. Their mother has left them, and they live with their father. Each of the boys react to their mother's leaving in a different way; their personalities appear to be opposite, but there are no easy judgments to be made here.

Bertrand, C. *Mr. and Mrs. Smith Have Only One Child, but What a Child!* Illus. by the author. Lothrop, Lee & Shepard, 1992. (Ages 5–8.) Cementing the image of the only child as the most favored, wonderful, and self-confident child in the world, the author-illustrator celebrates the energetic, imaginative Ursula, an only child who is her parents' darling. This translation from the French adds humor to the meager store of books representing only-children.

Bider, D. *A Drop of Honey.* Illus. by A. Kojoyian. Simon & Schuster, 1989. (Ages 6–9.) "A small quarrel may lead to big trouble" is the warning Anayida receives from her mother after she argues with her brothers. It is only after a dream about spilling a drop of honey triggers many unpleasant events that Anayida understands her mother's words. The illustrations sensitively capture the Armenian people, their dress, and their customs.

Blume, J. *Tales of a Fourth Grade Nothing.* Illus. by R. Doty. Dutton, 1972. (Ages 9–12.) Children find this book very amusing. Peter's younger brother, Fudge, is a monster. The child is spoiled, inconsiderate, and undisciplined. Not only is Fudge permitted to run rampant, but the parents are made to look foolish, though pleasant. Both parents try to control Fudge's behavior too often through trickery, and sometimes win out. In the sequel, *Superfudge,* (1980), Fudge and Peter now have new sibling Tootsie to contend with.

Bode, J. *Truce: Ending the Sibling War.* Watts, 1991. (Ages 12 and up.) The author interviewed many teenagers across the country and found that 25 percent had dangerous relationships with their siblings. This book reports on the lives and problems of several of these teenagers, generally discusses the problems, and suggests ways of resolving them. The author recommends strategies to help young people cope with their problems. These include developing different daily routines, changing one's diet, and working out. She also advises readers how to "rework the family script."

Bogart, J. E. *Daniel's Dog.* Illus. by J. Wilson. Scholastic, 1990. (Ages 5-8.) Daniel copes with his feelings of being left out by the arrival of a baby sister by playing with a "ghost dog," his special imaginary friend. Daniel's mother supports him lovingly. Daniel is an affectionate and bright child who plays well with his new sibling and is a good friend to his peers. The family is African American; the friend is Asian American.

Bonsall, C. *The Day I Had to Play with My Sister.* Harper, 1972. (Ages 3-7.) The narrator tries to teach his little sister to play hide-and-go-seek, but she cannot or will not follow the rules. The book takes no sides but helps readers to understand the elder brother's point of view.

Brennan, J. *Born Two-gether.* Illus. by L. Brennan. J & L, 1984. (Ages 5-8.) A photo-essay on how it feels to be a twin. Unfortunately there are no examples shown of any twins who are not Caucasian.

Brisson, P. *Your Best Friend, Kate.* Illus. by R. Brown. Bradbury, 1989. (Ages 7-9.) During her family's extended automobile tour of eleven states, Kate and her brother Brian fight. Although the arguments distress the children's parents, Kate shows that she cares about her brother by leaving him an encouraging note when he stays behind to visit an aunt while Kate and her parents return home. The book models the inevitability of sibling clashes and the underlying love that permeates the relationship.

Brown, M. *Arthur's Baby.* Illus. by the author. Little, Brown, 1987. (Ages 5-8.) Arthur saves the day when he demonstrates his knowledge of burping babies to keep them happy. The two older siblings deal with the arrival of the new baby and show no signs of jealousy or resentment. The parents prepare their children well for the new arrival, but Arthur's friends warn him of dire times ahead. The story is amusingly told and illustrated, and there are no unrealistic resolutions to problems.

Browne, A. *Changes.* Illus. by the author. Knopf, 1990. (Ages 5-8.) After Joseph's father cryptically tells him that things are going to change, Joseph notices strange happenings: the teakettle takes on ears, paws, and a tail; and menacing creatures such as alligators, snakes, and gorillas appear indoors. When Joseph's father and mother return home with a newborn sister, Joseph seems to be comforted that this was the forewarned change. The anxiety that pervades the story is the result of the fear of change that occurs with a new sibling. This book reaches children at a much deeper feeling level than cognitive analysis can convey.

Buckley, H. E. *"Take Care of Things," Edward Said.* Illus. by K. Coville. Lothrop, Lee & Shepard, 1991. (Ages 4-7.) When his older brother Edward leaves on the bus for his first day of school, Tom worries that he will be lonely. Edward tells Tom to "take care of things," and Tom does his best to live up to this request. His babysitter assures him that he has done exactly what needs to be done and that Edward will be proud. Edward confirms this when Tom greets him at the bus. A lovely model of a special sibling bond with the added bonus that Tom appears from the illustrations to be of Asian heritage.

Bulla, C. R. *The Christmas Coat.* Illus. by S. Wickstrom. Knopf, 1989. (Ages 7-10.) Hans and Otto drive their mother to distraction with constant fighting. One day, they destroy a beautiful coat they have disobediently unwrapped from its fancy package. When they discover that the coat was to be a Christmas surprise for the young boy next door they are finally ashamed of themselves and work in concert to have the coat repaired. A catharsis occurs as each boy is finally able to shoulder some blame and help make amends. The story ends with hope that they will understand how their fighting is selfish and hurtful, especially to their loving mother. Although the story is somewhat exaggerated, the elements of the plot are not far-fetched.

Bulla, C. R. *Keep Running, Allen.* Illus. by S. Ichikawa. Crowell, 1978. (Ages 5-8.) Allen races to keep pace with his older brothers and sister. One can easily empathize with his frustration as he never quite catches up. He finally attains peace when he gives up trying and stops to rest in a soft grassy field, only to find his siblings joining him.

Byars, B. *Go and Hush the Baby.* Illus. by E. A. McCully. Viking, 1971. (Ages 3-8.) The elder brother is called upon to entertain the crying baby while their mother finishes several tasks. The boy does this with imagination and good will. At last the baby falls asleep, and the brother is free to go out and play.

Cameron, A. *The Stories Julian Tells.* Illus. by A. Strugnell. Knopf, 1981. (Ages 7-10.) This first in a series introduces the reader to a loving, African-American family. The father provides a model as a caring, consistent, firm parent who finds the time and energy to intervene wisely in his sons' disputes. Bright and imaginative, Julian manages, with his parents' help, to extricate himself from thorny situations. Julian and his brother have some altercations, but for the most part they are good company for each other.

Carlson, N. *Harriet and Walt.* Illus. by the author. Carolrhoda, 1982. (Ages 4-6.) Harriet resents having to take her younger brother Walt with her when she goes out to play in the snow. Harriet calls Walt a dummy several times, but when her friend George loudly agrees with her, Harriet gets angry with him, sympathizes with the toddler, and takes him away to play. The pictures and language are charming, and the humorous plot makes sense. Harriet has not had a permanent change of heart toward her brother, she is maintaining her exclusive prerogative to call him names.

Carlson, N. *Poor Carl.* Illus. by the author. Penguin, 1989. (Ages 4-6.) Baby Carl's big brother can think of many disadvantages to Carl's position. He can also list several instances in which Carl is to be envied. On balance, Carl is most fortunate to have a big brother like the narrator. This story expresses well the ambivalence experienced by older siblings upon the arrival of a new baby. It is constructively designed and provides some good models.

Carlson, N. S. *The Half Sisters.* Illus. by T. di Grazia. Harper, 1970. (Ages 8-12.) Luvvy's father has three daughters by his first wife, and three from his current marriage. Luvvy is the oldest of the second set. She longs to be accepted by her older sisters and is impatient with the demands for attention made on her by her younger sister Maudie. When Maudie dies, Luvvy is distraught. The author portrays well the position of the middle child and the anguish over losing a sibling.

Caseley, J. *Silly Baby.* Illus. by the author. Greenwillow, 1988. (Ages 5-7.) Every time Lindsay hears about the new baby she says, "Silly baby." Lindsay is not tolerant of the baby's behavior until she sees in her own baby album some evidence of similar behavior.

Caseley, J. *Starring Dorothy Kane.* Greenwillow, 1992. (Ages 7-9.) This chapter book for younger readers is written from the perspective of Dorothy, the middle child in a loving and supportive family. They overcome obstacles by turning them into adventures with positive results. Dorothy is a little too good to be true, but she and her family provide a pleasant and comforting alternative to nasty bickering.

Cleary, B. *Mitch and Amy.* Illus. by G. Porter. Morrow, 1967. (Ages 8 and up.) Fraternal twins Mitch and Amy are always squabbling. Their parents unwittingly foster competition between them. Still they enjoy being twins and manage to handle their arguments good-naturedly.

Cleary, B. *Ramona the Brave.* Illus. by A. Tiegreen. Morrow, 1975. (Ages 8-12.) Ramona, six years old, is trying to be brave despite the fact that she thinks her parents love her elder sister more than they love her. Her parents eventually comfort her and persuade her that she is loved. Her sister also helps. A loving family. An excellent book, as are all the books in the *Ramona* series.

Cleaver, V., and Cleaver, B. *Me Too.* Lippincott, 1973. (Ages 9-12.) Lydia assumes responsibility for the teaching and care of her retarded twin sister, Lornie. She must cope with their father's departure, their mother's despair, and the neighbors' disapproval. Finally, she accepts the impossibility of her task. This is a realistic look at how much responsibility a sibling can take.

Cleaver, V., and Cleaver, B. *Where the Lilies Bloom.* Illus. by J. Spanfeller. Lippincott, 1969. (Ages 9 and up.) Mary Call's relationships with her siblings range from protective to hostile. She takes over responsibility for all of them (including her elder sister) when her father dies. The story is believable, and the reader understands and appreciates each of the siblings.

Clifton, L. *Don't You Remember?* Illus. by E. Ness. Dutton, 1973. (Ages 3-7.) Desire Mary Tate, four years old and very lively, considers herself to have the best memory in her family. One of her three older brothers has taken a year off from school to care for her. Her parents both work, and her ambition is to grow up and work at the plant, "just like Daddy." This African-American family equitably shares all their labor.

Clifton, L. *Everett Anderson's Nine Month Long.* Illus. by A. Grifalconi. Holt, Rinehart, & Winston, 1978 (reprinted 1989). (Ages 3-6.) Everett's mother tries to prepare him for a new baby brother or sister, reinforcing that there is sufficient love to go around, but Everett fears he'll miss the special time alone with his mother. In a conversation with his step-father, Mr. Perry, Everett learns to see that he is a special part of the growing family. The fact that the family is African American adds positively to readers' sense of the universality of the need to prepare young children for the arrival of a sibling.

Cole, J. *The New Baby at Your House.* Illus. by H. Hammid. Morrow, 1985. (Ages 3-6.) The focus of this useful book is to help families prepare older siblings for the birth of a new baby. In separate sections for adults and children, the author provides ideas for specific activities and behaviors that will ease the difficulties. A special advantage to this book is that it genuinely invites children to participate in welcoming a new baby rather than remaining onlookers or mere "helpers."

Cole, J., and Edmondson, M. *Twins: The Story of Multiple Births.* Illus. by S. Raciti. Morrow, 1972. (Ages 10-13.) The logistics of multiple births are explained and illustrated. In this easily understood scientific explanation, fraternal and identical twins are identified. The effects of fertility drugs on multiple births are explained. Simple terms and good illustrations abound.

Colman, H. *The Secret Life of Harold the Bird Watcher.* Crowell, 1978. (Ages 8-11.) Harold prefers nature to athletics. In his fantasies, he imagines himself a hero. He finally acquires a friend who also likes to make believe. A sympathetic portrayal of an only child of working parents.

Conta, M. M., and Reardon, M. *Feelings between Brothers and Sisters.* Illus. by J. M. Rosenthal. Raintree, 1974. (Ages 6-10.) Color photographs illustrate the questions asked by siblings about important issues such as helping one another, fighting, jealousy, teasing from older siblings, sharing, competition, and loneliness. The last picture displays middle-aged brothers who still argue yet continue to work and be friendly with one another. The variety of questions within the book could be used as a means to promote discussion.

Corcoran, B. *A Trick of Light.* Illus. by L. Dabcovich. Atheneum, 1973. (Ages 9-12.) Casandra and Paige are fraternal twins. They are growing up, and Paige wants to have friends of his own. Casandra is hurt, bitter, and jealous, wanting Paige to herself as her best friend. Casandra learns to live with the idea of independence from her twin.

Corey, D. *Will There Be a Lap for Me?* Illus. by N. Poydar. Whitman, 1992. (Ages 4–7.) Kyle's mother is pregnant. Her lap, Kyle's special place, keeps getting smaller and smaller. After the baby is born, it takes awhile, but Kyle's mother finally invites him onto her lap again. The illustrations show an affectionate African-American family; Kyle is by no means neglected during the time his mother's lap is unavailable. Everyone, including his mother, offers substitutes; but it is clear that her lap is special.

Cummings, P. *Jimmy Lee Did It.* Illus. by the author. Lothrop, Lee & Shepard, 1985. (Ages 5–7.) Angel believes her brother Artie when he says a character named Jimmy Lee performs the mischief that goes on in the house. She tries her best to capture Jimmy Lee, but he is elusive and only appears when Artie is around. As with all of Pat Cummings' work, the family pictured here is African American.

Dale, P. *Bet You Can't.* Illus. by the author. Lippincott, 1987. (Ages 3–6.) A brother and sister engage in some bantering about whether each of them can carry a basketload of toys and whether they can clean up the mess of their spilled toys. The expressive illustrations of two very attractive children of African-American heritage carry the story even more than the simple, direct captions floating comic-book style in balloons from the characters' mouths. The story is an excellent model of how siblings can cooperate while engaging in some mild rivalry.

Daly, N. *Look at Me.* Illus. by the author. Viking, 1986. (Ages 3–5.) Josh's antics are so beguiling to his big sister and her friend that they join with him in his play. A good strategy for younger children to try when they're feeling excluded.

Denton, K. M. *Janet's Horses.* Illus. by the author. Clarion, 1990. (Ages 3–6.) A fine model of how older children can have a good time with their younger siblings. Janet's imagination and the younger children's willingness to go along with it convey a sense of joy. The situation is realistic and the relationship is not far-fetched.

Dickinson, M. *Alex and the Baby.* Illus. by C. Firmin. Deutsch, 1982. (Ages 5–8.) Alex resents an infant visitor but eventually enjoys playing with her. Alex's mother is relieved when the baby leaves and expresses her appreciation for Alex.

Dragonwagon, C. *I Hate My Brother Harry.* Illus. by D. Gackenbach. Harper, 1983. (Ages 5–8.) Sometimes a young girl hates her older brother, and sometimes she loves him. Their parents are helpful to both children. The engaging text demonstrates the caring, as well as the rivalry, between the two siblings.

Edelman, E. *I Love My Baby Sister (Most of the Time).* Illus. by W. Watson. Lothrop, Lee & Shepard, 1984. (Ages 2–5.) The older sister in this story is usually tolerant of the often negative behaviors of her new baby sister. The children's parents nurture the two siblings equally and provide a solid base and model for a loving relationship. Both children's behavior is believable, and there is no gross exaggeration for the purpose of humor. The book avoids cliché; there is no sudden change of heart or reversal of behavior. The illustrations are amusing, showing a realistically disorganized but comfortable household.

Edwards, D. *My Naughty Little Sister Storybook.* Illus. by S. Hughes. Clarion, 1990. (Ages 5–8.) The English flavor of this set of stories is as important to the stories as are the plots. At no time does the older sister's recounting of the adventures of her "naughty little sister" degenerate into condescension. The younger sibling's inquisitive and open-hearted behavior is both endearing and humorous. Although the story is narrated by the older sister, the younger child's point of view is clearly conveyed, permitting young readers to empathize with both characters.

Ehrlich, A. *The Random House Book of Fairy Tales.* Illus. by D. Goode. Random House, 1985. (Ages 7-10.) [See Gender Roles]

Epstein, B., and Davis, D. *Two Sisters and Some Hornets.* Illus. by R. Wells. Holiday House, 1972. (Ages 5-8.) Sibling spats continue through old age. This humorous story tells of a childhood incident recalled by two elderly sisters about what happened when they had an encounter with hornets. They react in old age in much the same way as they did as little children: The older sister is smug and superior and the younger sister is petulant.

Fair, S. *The Bedspread.* Illus. by the author. Morrow, 1982. (Ages 5-8.) Two elderly twins have never stopped engaging in sibling rivalry. The two sisters conduct their business from opposite ends of the same very long bed. One day they agree that their plain white bedspread is boring, and they decorate it. The resulting artwork is based on the same topic, their house; but each sister's side of the spread is vastly different from the other's. The sisters begin to appreciate each other's point of view when they share the impressions and memories of their childhood. The story conveys appreciation for individual differences and an understanding that even at an advanced age siblings may not necessarily live in total harmony with each other.

Galbraith, K. O. *Roommates and Rachel.* Illus. by M. Graham. McElderry, 1991. (Ages 4-6.) This is one of the few books that discusses the arrival of a new baby into a family where there is more than one older sibling. Mimi and Beth, the two older sisters, continue their normal argumentative interactions, and they both resent the new baby. They hit upon the bright idea of having their mother bring baby Rachel to their classrooms for a special sharing time. By the end of the story, the girls are realistically comforting their new baby sister and not resenting her quite so much.

Gauch, P. L. *Dance, Tanya.* Illus. by S. Ichikawa. Philomel, 1989. (Ages 5-8.) Although Tanya is too young to take ballet lessons with her older sister Elise, she loves to dance and takes every opportunity to do so. The happy ending shows Tanya proudly going off to lessons when she has finally become old enough. The illustrations demonstrate the loving acceptance and encouragement that the family (including grandparents, an aunt, and an uncle) gives to each child. There is no rivalry here, but there is admiration, mutual love, and enormous warmth.

Gerson, M. *Omoteji's Baby Brother.* Illus. by E. Moon. Walck, 1974. (Ages 4-8.) Omoteji, who lives in Nigeria, is a member of the Yoruba people. He feels left out when a new baby is born because there seems to be no way he can help. Finally, he composes a song for his new brother and presents it as his gift at the naming ceremony.

Glenn, M. "Maria Preosi." In *Class Dismissed: High School Poems.* Illus. by M. Bernstein. Clarion, 1982. (Ages 10 and up.) Maria seethes because she is always compared to her sister Tracy. She bottles up her anger and allows it to eat away at her. Readers might be asked to suggest scenarios for Maria so that she can express her feelings without a destructive outcome.

Gray, G. *Send Wendell.* Illus. by S. Shimin. McGraw-Hill, 1974. (Ages 3-9.) Wendell, who has six siblings, is the one always expected to run errands, but he does not have anything important of his own to do. After his Uncle Robert's visit, Wendell does have things of his own to do, especially including writing letters to Uncle Robert.

Greenfield, E. "Reggie." In *Honey, I Love.* Illus. by D. and L. Dillon. Crowell, 1978. (Ages 6 and up.) Reggie's younger sister is unhappy because he is more absorbed in playing basketball than in paying attention to her. The tone of the poem is regretful but accepting and brings up the issue of the separate interests of family members.

Greenfield, E. *She Come Bringing Me That Little Baby Girl.* Illus. by J. Steptoe. Lippincott, 1974. (Ages 5–8.) Kevin is jealous of the attention the new baby gets. When his mother permits him to hold his new sister and to show her off to his friends, Kevin begins to feel happy again and to plan for what he and his sister will eventually do together. The rivalry is handled lovingly on the part of the parents. Steptoe's illustrations are beautiful.

Greenfield, E. *Sister.* Illus. by M. Barnett. Crowell, 1974. (Ages 10 and up.) Doretha is afraid she'll be just like her troubled older sister Alberta. They look alike, and sometimes Doretha feels as resentful and rebellious as her sister. Doretha is helped to be herself by a school run by and for African Americans. A well-written, interesting book.

Greenfield, E. *Talk about a Family.* Illus. by J. Calvin. Lippincott, 1978. (Ages 10 and up.) Genny, who idolizes her older brother, is unrealistically hopeful that when he returns from the army he will be able to fix their parents' problems. The siblings rely heavily on each other for emotional support; and although the parents decide to separate, the family will not be destroyed.

Greenwald, S. *Alvin Webster's Surefire Plan for Success (and How It Failed).* Illus. by the author. Little, Brown, 1987. (Ages 9–12.) Alvin is anxious about the upcoming birth of his baby brother. His parents are overly solicitous and very intellectual. When Alvin is given a guinea pig to care for, he experiences firsthand a process similar to parenting. He finally understands what it means to accept and love a creature regardless of looks or talents.

Grimm, J., and Grimm, W. *The Golden Goose.* Illus. by D. Duntze. North-South, 1988. (Ages 7–10.) Because of his generous and open nature and through the help of a magical old man, Simpleton wins the hand of the princess. As with many other tales of this nature, Simpleton's two older brothers, favored by their parents, are selfish and mean.

Grimm, J., and Grimm, W. *Hansel and Gretel.* Illus. by M. Felix. Creative Education, 1983. (Ages 7–10.) This beautifully designed and dramatically illustrated tale of two siblings who survive because of their mutual love and protection is told in the traditional story. The witch, even with her red eyes and bone-filled hair, conveys a sense of deadly beauty. The story invites much discussion about what the father could have done and why the stepmother was so cruel. Children can also talk about the relationship of the siblings with each other.

Grimm, J., and Grimm, W. *The Queen Bee.* Illus. by P. Dumas. Creative Education, 1984. (Ages 7–12.) This edition keeps faithfully to the traditional version: Three brothers, the youngest of whom is kind and thoughtful, set out on a journey and encounter an enchanted castle. To set the castle free from its enchantment, the brothers attempt to accomplish three tasks. Only the youngest brother, with the help of creatures he has befriended, is successful. He marries the youngest princess, and his two older brothers marry the other two princesses. The illustrations in this book are unusual: The characters are depicted as beautiful children dressed in modern clothing. The youngest brother is of African origin while the other children appear Nordic. Readers can make their own illustrations for this and other Grimm tales, adding details they feel are important.

Grimm, J., and Grimm, W. *Snow White and Rose Red.* Illus. by R. Topor. Creative Education, 1984. (Ages 7–10.) The two sisters in this story are unfailingly loving and kind to each other and to their mother. They exemplify filial virtue. They befriend a bear and try to help a cantankerous and ungrateful dwarf. In the end, the bear becomes a prince after killing his mortal enemy, the dwarf. He marries Snow White and his brother marries Rose Red. There are few changes to this tale in any of its retellings. The differences are in the illustrations, which children might find interesting to compare.

Grimm, J., and Grimm, W. *The Three Feathers.* Illus. by E. Schmid. Creative Education, 1984. (Ages 8–10.) Three brothers, the youngest of whom is viewed as a simpleton, three feathers for indicating where the brothers should journey, and three tasks, plus one extra to prove who was most fit to rule the kingdom, form the structure of the plot. In this version, the older brothers consistently underestimate Dummling's abilities and don't try to compete with him. Children might enjoy comparing these siblings with other fairytale threesomes.

Guthrie, D. *Not for Babies.* Illus. by K. K. Arnsteen. Simon & Schuster, 1993. (Ages 5–8.) One summer day, Andrew, the oldest of four children, becomes fed up with all the noise and chaos in his house. He decides to sleep in the yard, something that is "not for babies." In the morning when he comes in for breakfast, he is happy that he got away, but he has discovered that he missed his family. Children might wish to discuss ways they have found to secure some privacy in a full house.

Hallinan, P. K. *We're Very Good Friends, My Brother and I.* Illus. by the author. Ideals, 1990. (Ages 4–6.) The two brothers in this cheerful rhyming book enjoy each other and prefer togetherness to solitude. A bit idyllic, but examples of shared activities are realistic and appropriate.

Halloran, P. *Oh Brother! Oh, Sister!* Illus. by K. E. Shoemaker. Milliken, 1989. (Ages 4–6.) Although this book is part of a basal reading series, it stands on its own as literature. The brief and simple (but not simplistic) poems with illustrations that depict children of all heritages and conditions of ability address many aspects of sibling interactions without judgment or didacticism. New siblings, father–son relations, rivalry, birth order, and teasing are but a few of the issues uncovered here. The book is sensitive and endearing.

Harper, A. *It's Not Fair.* Illus. by S. Hellard. Putnam, 1986. (Ages 3–5.) The story first describes what the new baby's privileges are (much to the jealous annoyance of the elder). The second half of the book is devoted to pointing out many things the elder is permitted that the baby is not.

Havill, J. *Jamaica Tag-Along.* Illus. by A. S. O'Brien. Houghton Mifflin, 1989. (Ages 5–8.) When Jamaica permits a little boy to play with her as she builds a sand castle, her big brother joins them. The story is a gentle model of empathic behavior and provides a strategy for younger siblings to entice older siblings into a good relationship. As always, O'Brien's illustrations depict attractive children in a multiracial setting. See also *Jamaica and Brianna* (1993) [War]

Hayes, S. *Eat up, Gemma.* Illus. by J. Ormerod. Lothrop, Lee & Shepard, 1988. (Ages 4–6.) The illustrations show a tightly knit African-American family engaging in many activities, all the while worried about the baby's lack of interest in eating any food. Gemma's older brother uses his powers of observation, ingenuity, and genuine concern for his baby sister to concoct a meal that is enticing to her. In *Happy Christmas, Gemma* (1986), there is no rivalry; but there certainly is the sense of how the brother and baby sister differ in their responses and abilities.

Hazen, B. S. *If It Weren't for Benjamin.* Illus. by L. Hartman. Human Sciences, 1979. (Ages 5–8.) Told through the perspective of the younger brother, this book provides an excellent model of how a loving family helps with the problem of sibling rivalry.

Hazen, B. S. *Why Couldn't I Be an Only Kid like You, Wigger.* Illus. by L. Grant. Atheneum, 1975. (Ages 5–8.) Two boys, one from a large family and one an only child, want to exchange places. Each thinks the other has a better life, but they end up appreciating their own lives. A good book for discussion dealing with family size and numbers of siblings.

Hellard, S. *Billy Goats Gruff.* Illus. by the author. Putnam, 1986. (Ages 5-8.) The Norwegian tale is retold entertainingly and reassuringly in this book. No one, not even the troll, gets hurt; and ultimately the troll reforms and permits all travelers to cross his bridge. The three goat brothers cooperatively design the plan for crossing the bridge. The "lift the flap" design of the book adds enjoyment.

Hendrickson, K. *Getting Along Together: Baby and I Can Play.* Illus. by M. Megale. Parenting Press, 1985. (Ages 3-5.) Activities for interacting positively with a new baby. It also assures older siblings that their negative feelings are normal and that they can report these feelings to their parents without fear of being labeled evil. The follow-up book, *Fun with Toddlers,* carries similar messages for siblings of toddlers.

Hill, K. *Toughboy and Sister.* McElderry, 1990. (Ages 9-12.) Eleven-year-old Toughboy and his younger sister survive at an isolated campsite near the Yukon River. Their mother died the past autumn; their father brought them to the camp to spend the summer and then died upon his return from an alcoholic binge. Details of how the pair subsist and the underlying information about modern, changing Athapaskan life enrich the story. The children's feelings toward each other and their mutual contributions to coping with their situation are convincing.

Hills, E. S. *Evan's Corner.* Holt, Rinehart, & Winston, 1967. (Ages 4-8.) Evan, his three elder sisters, and his younger brother Adam live with their parents in a very small apartment. Evan fixes up a place of his own, but he is not totally satisfied until he recognizes Adam's needs too.

Hoban, R. *A Baby Sister for Frances.* Illus. by L. Hoban. Harper, 1964. (Ages 4-8.) Frances's new baby sister, Gloria, has disrupted the family's schedule so Frances runs away (to under the dining room table). When her parents talk about how they miss her, it is really a child's dream come true to hear how sorry people are that she is gone. All the *Frances* books are worthy additions to any library.

Hoberman, M. A. *Fathers, Mothers, Sisters, Brothers: A Collection of Family Poems.* Illus. by M. Hafner. Joy Street, 1991. (Ages 5-10.) [See Family Constellations]

Hogan, P. Z. *Sometimes I Get So Mad.* Raintree, 1980. (Ages 5-10.) Karen, the older sister, realizes at the end of the book that her younger sister can be fun. The text also explores relationships between friends and deals with the ways a child can express angry feelings. It shows that conflicts do not have to ruin relationships, their resolution can make relationships stronger.

Hooker, R. *Sara Loves Her Big Brother.* Illus. by M. Apple. Whitman, 1987. (Ages 3-5.) Sara's big brother is a model of tolerance. Although Sara clearly adores him, her behavior is often annoying and disruptive. The brother is not a martyr, and Sara is not a monster. Even when Sara invades her brother's room, she is never destructive or malicious. Parents do not appear here to intervene between the siblings. Apparently the two children can work things out by themselves.

Howard, E. F. *The Train to Lulu's.* Illus. by R. Casilla. Bradbury, 1988. (Ages 5-8.) The watercolor paintings capture the events, as well as the feelings of the characters, in this reminiscence of the first time Beppy and her sister Babs have ridden alone on a train. They are going from Boston to Baltimore to spend the summer with their Aunt Lulu. The simple text details the specifics of the ride and conveys to the reader the warm relationship between the sisters and the secure, loving involvement of the entire family.

Hurwitz, J. *Russell and Elisa*. Illus. by L. Hoban. William Morrow, 1989. (Ages 4–7.) Three-and-a-half-year-old Elisa and her seven-year-old brother Russell experience normal rivalry and enact believable and constructive solutions. Their parents are involved in their lives, firm without punishing, and loving without overindulging. Children will find models here and reflections of their own feelings. Gender roles are equitable and natural: both parents perform household tasks, and nurture the children.

Hutchins, P. *You'll Soon Grow into Them, Titch*. Illus. by the author. Mulberry, 1983. (Ages 3–6.) Titch's parents buy new him clothes when all his hand-me-downs from his older sister and brother are still too large for him. Titch has heard, "You'll soon grow into them" too often. But when his baby brother is born, Titch donates his too-small clothes to the baby and assures him, "You'll soon grow into them." The story is a gentle reminder that all children need to be acknowledged as worthy individuals.

Jarrel, M. *The Knee-Baby*. Illus. by S. Shimin. Farrar, Straus & Giroux, 1973. (Ages 5–8.) The little boy wants very much to be held on someone's lap, hugged, and cuddled. His mother spends much time with the new baby. Finally, his mother gives him a turn on her lap and he is satisfied.

Johnson, A. *Do like Kyla*. Illus. by J. E. Ransome. Orchard, 1990. (Ages 4–7.) Told from the perspective of the younger sister as she imitates older sister Kyla's actions and words. Kyla good naturedly permits the younger child to tag along. The young child is thrilled when she initiates, and big sister Kyla imitates, her good-night window tapping to see if birds are asleep.

Jones, A. *So, Nothing Is Forever*. Houghton Mifflin, 1974. (Ages 12 and up.) Three children from an interracial marriage, fifteen-year-old Talene, thirteen-year-old Joey, and two-year-old Adam, refuse to be separated and put into different foster homes when their parents are killed in a car crash. They decide to stay with their disapproving maternal grandmother even though they are unsure of her welcome. Their eventual acceptance is satisfying. The sibling bond is very strong here.

Jordan, J. *New Life, New Room*. Illus. by R. Cruz. Crowell, 1975. (Ages 6–9.) A new baby is expected; and ten-year-old Rudy, nine-year-old Tyrone, and six-year-old Linda, because their apartment has only two bedrooms, must decide how to live together in one room. With their parents' help they decide what to keep and what to throw away. The sensitive portrayal reflects every family member's feelings. This is a joyous, loving, and constructive book.

Keats, E. J. *Peter's Chair*. Illus. by the author. Harper, 1967. (Ages 5–8.) Peter has a new baby sister. His parents are giving all his old furniture to the baby. He feels excluded and "runs away" with his chair to just outside their house. When he realizes that he has outgrown his chair, hears his parents' supportive words, and smells dinner, he returns to the family and resolves to tolerate his sister.

Kimmel, E. A. *Nanny Goat and the Seven Little Kids*. Illus. by J. Stevens. Holiday House, 1990. (Ages 5–8.) A wicked wolf tricks the seven goat siblings into letting him into their house, and they and their mother are gobbled up. The mother resourcefully snips a hole in the wolf's skin so that they can all escape (after loading the wolf's stomach with heavy stones, so that he drowns.) The story demonstrates that even in folk tales siblings can be noncompetitive and happy together. One caveat: The wolf is depicted with an eye patch, perpetuating the old stereotype of disabilities equated with wickedness. Otherwise, the illustrations and writing combine to make an entertaining story. Ed Young's *Lon Po-Po* (Philomel, 1989) is another version of this tale.

Klein, N.. *Naomi in the Middle*. Illus. by L. Grant. Dial, 1974. (Ages 7–10.) Naomi, age seven, the narrator, and her elder sister Bobo, age nine, have a typical sibling relationship. When they hear of their mother's pregnancy, Naomi contemplates the problems of being the middle child and Bobo is gloomy. The story shows how a loving family handles sibling relationship problems.

Lacoe, A. *Just Not the Same.* Houghton Mifflin, 1992. (Ages 5-8.) [See War and Peace]

Lasky, K., in the words of M. B. Knight. *A Baby for Max.* Illus. by C. G. Knight. Aladdin, 1987. (Ages 3-7.) Max is involved with his new sibling's arrival well before the baby is born. He accompanies his mother to her doctor, visits the hospital beforehand, and helps his father make a changing table. Max is resentful of all the attention the baby gets and wishes at times that the baby would disappear. But all in all, Max looks forward to an equitable relationship with his sibling. The photographs and text combine to make an engrossing, informative, and supportive story.

L'Engle, M. *A Ring of Endless Light.* Farrar, Straus, Giroux, 1980. (Ages 11 and up.) [See Death]

Little, J. *Home from Far.* Illus. by J. Lazare. Little, Brown, 1965. (Ages 9-12.) [See Death]

Livingston, M. C. *Poems for Brothers, Poems for Sisters.* Illus. by J. Zallinger. Holiday House, 1991. (Ages 8-12.) Memories, perceptions, arguments, and friendships are all part of this varied collection of poems about siblings.

Louie, A. L.. *Yeh Shen: A Cinderella Story from China.* Illus. by E. Young. Putnam, 1988. (Ages 8 and up.) [See Gender Roles]

Lowry, L. *All about Sam.* Dell, 1988. (Ages 8-10.) Told from the perspective of the younger child, this engaging story presents Sam, Anastasia Krupnik's younger brother, as a charming and mischievous child whose natural curiosity and literal interpretation of language often get him into trouble. Everyone, including Anastasia, loves Sam. A sequel is *Attaboy Sam!* (1992). [See Family]

Lowry, L.. *A Summer to Die.* Illus. by J. Oliver. Houghton Mifflin, 1977. (Ages 10 and up.) [See Death]

Lyon, G. E. *Borrowed Children.* Orchard, 1988. (Ages 10-13.) Mandy is responsible for caring for her siblings, including two older brothers. When her mother becomes very ill after giving birth, Mandy must leave school and care for the baby, her mother, and the entire household full time. A visit to her grandparents helps her see her family in perspective and understand the important roles siblings play in each others' lives.

MacLachlan, P. *Arthur, for the Very First Time.* Illus. by L. Bloom. Harper, 1980. (Ages 9-12.) [See War and Peace]

MacLachlan, P. *Seven Kisses in a Row.* Illus. by M. P. Marrella. Harper, 1983. (Ages 7-10.) An affectionate and humorous story about Emma, an outspoken and engaging seven year old, her brother Zach, who understands and loves her, and the five days they spend with their aunt and uncle while their parents are at an "eyeball convention." All the characters learn to adjust to and accept each other's differences.

MacLachlan, P. *Unclaimed Treasures.* Harper, 1984. (Ages 9-12.) In a beautifully told story flavored with mystery and romance, twins Willa and Nicholas interact with other colorful characters, survive the birth of a new sibling, and reinforce and support each other's feelings.

Magorian, M. *Who's Going to Take Care of Me?* Illus. by J. Graham Hale. Harper, 1990. (Ages 4-6.) Karin has been her brother Eric's protector and guide when they attended daycare together. Now that Karin is going to kindergarten, Eric is worried about who will take care of him. He feels small and vulnerable until he realizes that he is an "old timer" at daycare now and can be a helper to a new child there. A lovely picture book from the author of the acclaimed *Good Night, Mr. Tom.*

Mahy, M. *The Seven Chinese Brothers.* Illus. by J. and M. Tseng. Scholastic, 1990. (Ages 7-10.) This is a respectful version of the Chinese folktale. The illustrations of the brothers are richly detailed and realistic. The brothers' feats are presented as re-markable talents rather than freakish attributes, and the brothers' concern for each other and their wish to help oppressed people override any other motive for exercis-ing their talents.

Malecki, M. *Mom and Dad and I Are Having a Baby!* Illus. by the author. Pennypress, 1982. (Ages 5-10.) The child narrator describes the entire procedure of home birth with all family members in attendance.

Manushkin, F. (created by L. Bate). *Little Rabbit's Baby Brother.* Illus. by D. de Groat. Crown, 1986. (Ages 5-8.) Without succumbing to the cliché happy ending of the magi-cal turnaround of the elder sibling, the author provides children with strategies for dealing with negative feelings about new siblings. In this story, the older sibling recognizes that she can retain her sense of self while being a big sister. The parents not only acknowledge the competence and value of their firstborn but also attend to the new baby. The author wisely controls Little Rabbit's "running away" from home by having her stay just outside the house while the parents loudly and clearly communi-cate that they want her back home with them. She adopts some rituals to make her relationship with her baby sibling more manageable, and she is wonderfully supported by her parents (although there are also times when they express their annoyance at her behavior.)

Markham, M. M. *The April Fool's Day Mystery.* Illus. by P. Estrada. Houghton Mifflin, 1991. (Ages 7-10.) [See Gender Roles]

Mattmuler, F. *We Want a Little Sister.* Lerner, 1972. (Ages 4-8.) This book is different from most others that focus on a new baby because there are already three children in the family. All the children are allowed to visit their mother and baby sister in the hospital. The family atmosphere is positive, and the comments and activities of the family in-clude all the children.

Mayer, M. *The Twelve Dancing Princesses.* Illus. by K.Y. Craft. Morrow, 1989. (Ages 7-10.) A young farm-lad discovers the secret of how the bewitched princesses wear out their shoes. Unlike the hero in other versions, however, he does not reveal the secret to the king. He and the youngest princess have fallen in love. Finally, the princess chooses to break the spell. The illustrations are luminous and filled with elegant detail. Children can discuss the differences in detail and related implications between this and other versions.

McCully, E. A. *New Baby.* Illus. by the author. Harper, 1988. (Ages 3-6.) This story about a young mouse child who feels displaced by the newest baby contains no words, so that readers can invent their own text. An older sibling helps the little one feel useful, and harmony is restored.

McKenzie, E. K. *Stargone John.* Illus. by W. Low. Holt, 1990. (Ages 8-10.) For a time, John's only ally is his older sister Liza. John talks infrequently, hates school, suffers from a punitive and incompetent teacher, and remains illiterate until he befriends Miss Mants, a retired teacher, now elderly and blind. By the end of the story, John has demonstrated that he is as capable of learning as any child, especially when his teacher is responsive and kind.

McPhail, D. *Sisters.* Illus. by the author. HBJ, 1984. (Ages 3-6.) A tender commentary on two sisters who differ in age, interests, and attributes; enjoy certain activities; argue over some possessions; and love each other very much. The line drawings show two equally attractive, lively girls in a realistic setting.

Minarik, E. H. *No Fighting, No Biting.* Illus. by M. Sendak. Harper, 1958. (Ages 6-10.) Cousin Joan is reading when Willy and Rosa disturb her with their fighting. She quiets the pair by telling a story about two alligator siblings whose fighting leads to danger. Willy and Rosa continue to bicker, then subside to silent reading. The story portrays a realistic situation where an older child is bothered by younger children.

Moncure, J. B. *My Baby Brother Needs a Friend.* Illus. by F. Hook. Children's Press, 1979. (Ages 4-6.) Illustrated with colorful and realistic drawings, this book shows specific ways siblings can interact with a new baby. It also anticipates activities they will share when the baby is older.

Mulligan, K. *Kid Brother.* Lothrop, Lee & Shepard, 1982. (Ages 12 and up.) Brad's older brother Tom is perfect. Brad has difficulty not being Tom's shadow. After a visit with an eccentric older aunt in Albuquerque, Brad finally discovers who he is and what he wants to do apart from his brother.

Murrow, L. K. *The Ghost of Lost Island.* Holiday, 1991. (Ages 8-12.) The story begins with Gabriel strongly resenting his older sister Ginny's bossiness, but their mutual adventure ultimately brings them together. The story is believable and interesting, and the Maine coast setting is a perfect backdrop to the family interaction and mystery.

Naylor, P. R. *All Because I'm Older.* Illus. by L. Morrill. Atheneum, 1981. (Ages 5-8.) John must keep his two younger siblings out of mischief during a trip to the supermarket because he is the oldest. Eldest children will appreciate John's solution to his dilemma.

Ness, E. *Do You Have the Time, Lydia?* Dutton, 1971. (Ages 5-8.) Lydia and her brother live with their father on a tropical island. Lydia is a well-intentioned elder sister, but she is busy with so many activities that she bitterly disappoints her younger brother who craves her company. She makes up by determining to change her ways.

O'Dell, S. *Island of the Blue Dolphins.* Houghton Mifflin, 1960. (Ages 10 and up.) [See Gender Roles]

Oneal, Z. *Maude and Walter.* Illus. by M. Chambliss. Lippincott, 1985. (Ages 4-7.) Maude is not the underdog in this book, although she is Walter's younger sister. She persuades him to play with her by offering him needed materials, such as her ribbons for the tail of his kite, and by the force of her logic, such as reminding him of his promises to her. Although Maude wins in her encounters with Walter, he is not demeaned. He emerges as a pleasant, caring, reasonable person who doesn't mind being helped by his clever little sister and responds amiably to her negotiations.

Oppenheim, J. *Wake up, Baby!* Illus. by L. Sweat. Bantam, 1990. (Ages 4-6.) The protagonist is an imaginative little girl who tries to contain her impatience at having to wait for an outing until her baby sibling awakens. She imagines all sorts of creative ways of waking the baby, none of which works. Finally she falls asleep, and her mother and the baby have to awaken her. An atmosphere of mutual love and support is communicated despite the simple language of the predictable text.

Orgel, D. *Bartholomew, We Love You.* Illus. by P. G. Porter. Knopf, 1973. (Ages 8-12.) Kim is Emily's younger sister. She thinks that Emily is prettier, smarter, more talented, and more favored. In the end, the two sisters learn to share somewhat more happily. The mother works in a laboratory; the father is a machinery designer. They are understanding, competent people. The book is realistic and useful.

Ormerod, J. *101 Things to Do with a Baby.* Illus. by the author. Puffin, 1984. (Ages 5-8.) In this merry romp of a book, the message is amusingly conveyed that all siblings are valued and that constructive activities are more appealing than destructive ones.

Pankow, V. *No Bigger Than My Teddy Bear.* Illus. by R. Pate. Abingdon, 1987. (Ages 4-8.) Dustin tells what it is like to have a premature sibling. Pictures show the care given the premature infant in the hospital. Dustin learns how to treat his new sibling by practicing on his teddy bear. This provides a helpful strategy for young readers.

Patent, D. H. *Babies!* Illus. with photos. Holiday House, 1988. (Ages 6–10.) Beautiful photographs demonstrate the stages of a child's development from birth to two years of age. The diversity of children photographed enhances the text.

Paterson, K. *Flip-Flop Girl.* Lodestar, 1994. (Ages 9–12.) [See Death]

Paterson, K. *Jacob I Have Loved.* Crowell, 1980. (Ages 10 and up.) Sarah Louise, the older and stronger twin, always feels outdone by her frailer, prettier, talented sister. Eventually, Louise becomes a nurse-midwife, delivers twins, and exorcises all her old hates and fears concerning her sister.

Pfeffer, S. B. *Twin Surprises.* Illus. by A. Carter. Holt, 1991. (Ages 7–9.) An easy-to-read story about Crista and Betsy, twin sisters who each wants to give the other a surprise birthday party. Although the story is somewhat predictable, it does acknowledge the difficulty making birthdays and other occasions special for each twin. These twins appear well adjusted and able to maintain their individuality. Crista and Betsy's relationship suffers some strain in the sequel, *Twin Troubles* (1992).

Roe, E. Translated into Spanish by J. Mintzer. *Con Mi Hermano/With My Brother.* Illus. by R. Casilla. Bradbury, 1991. (Ages 4–6.) A younger child spends quality time with his elder brother. The text is written in both Spanish and English. The older sibling is a model of patience and nurturing. He genuinely enjoys his younger brother, and the two are affectionate and respectful with each other. The characters all have Latino features; and although there is no attempt here to depict Latino culture, it is useful to have a book that depicts a universal positive theme where the characters are not the usual white, blond, and blue-eyed family.

Rogasky, B. *The Water of Life.* Illus. by T. S. Hyman. Holiday House, 1986. (Ages 9–12.) The classic pattern of three brothers, the youngest a hero, is illuminated by the brilliance of Trina Schart Hyman's illustrations. It's unfortunate that the rivalry among the brothers is unresolved when the older brothers retreat into exile. The princess in the story is a worthy mate for the kind and open-hearted youngest brother.

Rogers, F. *The New Baby.* Illus. by J. Judkins. Putnam, 1985. (Ages 3–8.) As with all his books, Mr. Rogers understands children's feelings and helps deal with them constructively. He validates children's angry and jealous reactions to new siblings and allays their fears of rejection.

Root, P. *Moon Tiger.* Illus. by E. Young. Holt, 1985. (Ages 5–8.) A little girl journeys in her dreams with her toy tiger. Although she has been angry at her younger brother, her magical journey erases sufficient jealousy and frustrations so that she shares the experience with her brother. The illustrations demonstrate the magic and power needed to enable the older sister to overcome her angry feelings.

Rosenberg, M. B. *Being a Twin/Having a Twin.* Illus. by G. Ancona. Lothrop, Lee & Shepard, 1985. (Ages 5–10.) The book offers close-up looks at four pairs of twins, identical and fraternal. Ancona's photographs beautifully capture the spirit and feelings of twinhood. Although only one birth in every 89 produces twins, the photos and text clearly indicate that they belong to all sorts of families of many backgrounds and heritages.

Rosenberg, M. B. *Brothers and Sisters.* Illus. by G. Ancona. Clarion, 1991. (Ages 6–10.) Each of three chapters is told from the perspective of a sibling in a different birth position: eldest, youngest, and middle. The text discusses pros and cons but focuses on the positive. The color photographs demonstrate the active and often joyful interactions.

Rowland, P. T. *Our New Baby.* Illus. by N. Backes. Pleasant, 1990. (Ages 3–5.) There are three versions of this pretty, interactive book: Caucasian, African American, and Asian

American. The text is identical, while the features of the baby's face differ. In each, the baby is tended by the young reader's lifting a flap, pulling or pushing a tab, or zipping a zipper, thus inviting an older sibling to interact with the new arrival.

Sachs, M. *The Bears' House.* Illus. by L. Glanzman. Doubleday, 1971. (Ages 9-12.) Fran Ellen, her brother, and two sisters try to manage their household after their father has deserted them and their mother has suffered a nervous collapse. The relationship among the siblings is generally protective and loving. The book is more complex and painfully involved than most stories about sibling survival.

Samson, J. *Watching the New Baby.* Illus. by G. Gladstone. Atheneum, 1974. (Ages 8-11.) This book, which describes the newborn baby in terms of physical development and relationship to the world, is useful for siblings who ask many "why" questions about new babies. The photographs show many happy relationships between newborns and elder siblings.

Samuels, B. *Faye and Dolores.* Illus. by the author. Bradbury, 1985. (Ages 4-8.) Although Faye and her younger sister Dolores sometimes argue, they are usually kind and loving to each other and manage to play together in a satisfying way.

Scott, A. H. *On Mother's Lap.* Illus. by G. Coalson. McGraw-Hill, 1972. (Ages 5-8.) Michael and his family are Inuit. The story is simply told: Mother makes room on her lap for everyone, making Michael very happy. The book acknowledges rivalry and models the mother's gentle, nonreproaching manner of dealing with it.

Scott, A. H.. *Sam.* Illus. by S. Shimin. McGraw-Hill, 1967. (Ages 4-8.) Sam is very much the baby of the family. His two elder siblings are not unkind, but they do not want him touching their things. Sam's mother realizes that he needs to do something special by himself. The rest of the family applauds when Sam is permitted to bake a raspberry tart.

Sendak, M. *Outside over There.* Illus. by the author. Harper, 1981. (Ages 5 and up.) Ida, the protagonist, searches for her infant sibling who has been kidnapped by goblins (who turn out to look just like the baby). Ida's father is away on a voyage, and Ida's mother is in the arbor. Of course, Ida is successful. The book is a visual delight; and like many of Sendak's other works, it has a dreamlike and symbolic quality. It is also controversial; some readers believe it is more for adults than for children.

Sharmat, M. *Goodnight, Andrew, Goodnight, Craig.* Illus. by M. Chalmers. Harper, 1969. (Ages 3-8.) Two brothers, put to bed by their father, finally fall asleep after the elder brother promises the younger one he will play with him in the morning. A loving family relationship all around.

Sharmat, M. W. *I'm Terrific.* Illus. by K. Chorao. Holiday House, 1977. (Ages 5-8.) Jason Everett bear is an only child who enjoys his mother's total attention and approval. Eventually Jason must decide to stop being a "mother's bear" and start being his own person.

Shyer, M. F. *Here I Am, an Only Child.* Illus. by D. Carrick. Scribners, 1985. (Ages 3-6.) An only child lists numerous negative factors that attend his status. He also acknowledges that many advantages come from his position. The presentation is, all in all, balanced; and the child finishes the story satisfied that he is an only child.

Smith, A. W. *Sister in the Shadow.* Atheneum, 1986. (Ages 11 and up.) An excellent book about the effects of birth-order expectations. Sharon is confused and jealous when her younger sister becomes more popular than she. Sharon gains perspective during her summer job as a mother's helper when she learns how the death of a child has affected her employers' family.

Steel, D. *Max Runs Away.* Illus. by J. Rogers. Delacorte, 1990. (Ages 4–7.) Five-year-old Max feels neglected and angry because his parents spend much of their time and energy on his lively two-year-old twin sister and brother, who damage his room and his favorite teddy bear. Max runs away, but after about ten minutes he realizes that this is dangerous and returns to school. His teacher comforts him, reminds him of the dangers of running away, and calls his father, who has already repaired all the damage done by the twins. Max's parents help him to see how vital the family is to them all. The book primarily teaches a lesson; but the story is a good one, and all the characters are appealing.

Stein, S. B. *That New Baby.* Illus. by D. Frank. Walker, 1974. (Ages 3–8.) This is one in the series of "Open Family Books for Parents and Children Together." It contains a text for parents that points out that most elder children are jealous of younger ones to some extent. Through beautiful photographs (of an African-American family) and an excellent text, the message comes through that every family member is valued. The advice to parents is practical, direct, and psychologically sound.

Steptoe, J. *Baby Says.* Illus. by the author. Lothrop, Lee & Shepard, 1988. (Ages 3–6.) Big brother is patient, loving, and helpful with his baby sibling although there are many occasions for "uh-oh's." The overriding effect is one of affection and good humor in this African-American family.

Steptoe, J. *Mufaro's Beautiful Daughters: An African Tale.* Illus. by the author. Lothrop, Lee & Shepard, 1987. (Ages 7–11.) This gloriously illustrated retelling of a Southern African folktale has a "Cinderella" theme minus stepsisters or stepmother. Here, two sisters are very beautiful, but one, Manyara, is competitive, selfish, and underhanded, while the other, Nyasha, is cooperative, generous, and honest. They are loved equally by their father. In the end, when Nyasha marries the king, there is no indication that Manyara has changed or that Nyasha has become more astute about her sister's character. Children might want to write some sequels to the story to further explore the siblings' relationship.

Steptoe, J. *My Special Best Words.* Illus. by the author. Viking, 1974. (Ages 5–8.) [See Sex and Sexuality]

Steptoe, J. *Stevie.* Illus. by the author. Harper, 1969. (Ages 7–10.) Robert experiences the pangs of sibling rivalry over Stevie, a young boy who stays at Robert's house. But Robert misses Stevie when he leaves.

Stevenson, S. *Do I Have to Take Violet?* Illus. by the author. Dell, 1987. (Ages 4–8.) Elly resents having to play with her younger sister, Violet, and makes her feelings known. Once she accepts that they must play together, however, they have a wonderful time and find creative, imaginative ways to play with one another. It must be pointed out, however, that certain aspects of the girls' play (alone on the rocks near the ocean) are dangerous and inappropriate without adult supervision.

Thomas, I. *Walk Home Tired, Billy Jenkins.* Illus. by T. di Grazia. Harper, 1974. (Ages 5–8.) It is time to go home from the playground, and Billy Jenkins is very tired. His sister Nina lovingly and imaginatively makes the trip home a series of magical rides for the two of them. Illustrations of the people, the city, and the African-American siblings are beautiful.

Tyler, L. W. *My Brother Oscar Thinks He Knows It All.* Illus. by S. Davis. Puffin, 1989. (Ages 4–8.) A young girl tells of her troubles with her older brother, Oscar. Oscar already knows how to ride a bike and skateboard, insists on playing teacher when they play school, and won't let her play with his friends. He is very proud of his younger sister, however, when she is the star of the school's sports day. Despite their competition, both children seem proud of who they are.

Van Leeuwen, J. *Amanda Pig and Her Big Brother Oliver.* Illus. by A. Schweninger. Dial, 1982. (Ages 5-8.) Also all others in this series. Amanda adores her older brother and wants to do everything he does. Their father is nurturing, and Oliver is amazingly understanding. Eventually, Amanda heeds her mother's advice and becomes involved in a block-building project by herself.

Viorst, J. "Some Things Don't Make Any Sense at All." In *If I Were in Charge of the World and Other Worries.* Atheneum, 1982. (Ages 5-10.) The young child in the poem wants to know why his mom just had another baby, especially since she's told him that he's terrific. Wonderfully humorous, this hits the mark of sibling jealousy.

Viorst, J. *I'll Fix Anthony.* Illus. by A. Lobel. Harper, 1969. (Ages 5-8.) Anthony is thoroughly nasty and mean to his younger sibling. The younger boy, dreaming of the day when he will become six years old, imagines revenge. Excellent for demonstrating the younger child's perspective.

Voigt, C. *Homecoming.* Atheneum, 1981. (Ages 10 and up.) [See Family Constellations]

Voigt, C. *Sons from Afar.* Atheneum, 1987. (Ages 12 and up.) James and Sammy search for their long lost father to discover more about themselves. Although they never find him, they do learn about themselves and their relationship as brothers. This is one of the books in the Tillerman family saga.

Wade, B. *Little Monster.* Illus. by K. Kew. Lothrop, Lee & Shepard, 1992. (Ages 4-7.) Mandy grows tired of hearing her mother tell everyone how perfect she is. She envies her little brother's mischievous exploits. For a full day, Mandy becomes a monster and thoroughly enjoys infuriating her parents. At the end of that day, this close-knit African-American family are all able to laugh about it; and her parents assure Mandy that they love her no matter what.

Walter, M. P. *My Mama Needs Me.* Illus. by P. Cummings. Lothrop, Lee & Shepard, 1983. (Ages 3-7.) Jason's attempts to help his mother with his new baby sister get mixed reactions of appreciation and dismissal. At last his mother understands his anxiety and reassures him that he is always needed and loved. This story is told through the eyes of a young African-American child.

Watson, J. W., et al. *Sometimes I'm Jealous.* Illus. by I. Trivas. Crown, 1986. (Ages 3-7.) The story tells about a child's feelings of loss as well as gains when a new baby usurps his status as youngest of the family. The child acknowledges that he likes his mom and dad to pay attention solely to him. The short text for parents at the beginning gives good advice, notably that the new baby is not a toy for the older sibling.

Watts, B. *Snow White and Rose Red.* Illus. by the author. North-South, 1988. (Ages 6-10.) Two sisters are very loving and cooperative in this story. They befriend a bear and help him defeat his enemies. He eventually turns into a handsome prince. Snow White marries him, and Rose Red marries his brother. Each sister has a distinctive personality, but they never compete or argue. They are obedient, kind, and loving. The illustrations communicate a sense of innocence.

Williams, B. *Jeremy Isn't Hungry.* Illus. by M. Alexander. Dutton, 1978. (Ages 4-7.) Jeremy and Davey's mother is busy. She asks Davey to feed little Jeremy, but Jeremy decides to play with the food instead of eat it. Davey discovers that taking care of his little brother isn't easy and begins to appreciate his mother's task.

Williams, D. *Walking to the Creek.* Illus. by T. B. Allen. Knopf, 1990. (Ages 7-10.) Twin brothers take a long walk to the creek on their grandfather's land. In addition to making observations about the world of nature they continuously encounter, the boys demonstrate how different they are from each other and how well they get along. The dreamlike illustrations and language filled with imagery deepen the readers' understanding of the natural world and the characters of the boys.

Woodruff, E. *Tubtime.* Illus. by S. Stevenson. Holiday House, 1990. (Ages 4-7.) Three active sisters, from about three to six years of age, enjoy a bath together after romping in the mud. They delightedly blow bubbles containing gigantic fantastical creatures while their mother is on the phone. When Father enters the bathroom, he is invited to blow his own big bubble. Readers are left guessing what will be contained within it. The girls' relationship is free of rivalry in their shared adventures.

Wright, B. R. *I Like Being Alone.* Raintree, 1981. (Ages 7-10.) With the support of her Aunt and her parents, Brenda constructs a tree house so she can get away from her siblings and have some time alone. She values her privacy but does not reject her numerous siblings.

Young, R. *The New Baby.* Illus. by the author. Viking, 1987. (Ages 3-5.) Some good modeling here by the parents as they take turns with "alone-time" with each child, involve the older child in helping with the baby, and provide affection and attention equitably. A pleasant story in which a young boy adapts nicely to the new baby.

Zolotow, C. *Big Sister and Little Sister.* Illus. by M. Alexander. Harper, 1976. (Ages 5-8.) No one likes always to be the one who must be "taken care of." By showing that sometimes big sisters need help too, perhaps both big and little sisters can see a way to a happier relationship.

Zolotow, C. *Timothy Too!* Illus. by R. Robbins. Houghton Mifflin, 1986. (Ages 4-7.) A young boy wants to play with his older brother, to the point of being a pest. When the younger child finally finds his own playmate, the older brother finds that he misses the younger sibling's attention. A book with which both younger and older siblings can identify.

chapter **2**

Adoption and Foster Care

When children live in a household for extended periods of time, they should become part of the family structure. Adopted children are legally entitled to all the rights of biological family members. They are permanent additions to the family. Foster children, however, can lead a tenuous existence. At any moment, for any of a variety of reasons, they may be moved out of their current homes. On the other hand, many foster children know the identities of their birth parents and siblings. They often know why they were removed from their original homes, and they may realistically expect at some point to be returned to biological parents. This chapter discusses books dealing with issues of both foster and adopted children and provides criteria for judging the efficacy of these books.

Until recent years, adopted children rarely had much information about their birth parents, if any. Ordinarily, birth records are sealed when an adoption is completed. Kansas and Alaska are the only two states with open-records laws that automatically permit access to birth records. Other states require varying procedures; and the burden falls on the petitioner requesting to see adoption records. Ostensibly intended to protect the child from the stigma of illegitimacy, the practice of maintaining closed records also aims to shield birth parents from later recriminations by the child. This practice also may reassure adoptive parents by "guaranteeing" the permanence of a child's new identity.

Recently, however, advocates for adopted children have agitated for a loosening of the regulations, especially for children who have reached the age of eighteen. Advocates argue that adoptees need to learn about their biological heritage and medical history. Although they may not want to meet their birth parents, they may want to find out why they were given up for adoption, or they may want to learn about other members of their family of origin. Some psychologists believe that finding out about their birth parents helps adopted children feel more secure.

This need to know about their origins sometimes results in extensive legal searches, culminating in frustration, partly because records are not always up to date. Advocacy agencies (see the list at the end of this chapter) have been formed to help adoptees in their quest. In the best situations, adoptees have the support of their adoptive parents in the search. Birth parents are often relieved to be located and eager to learn about their relinquished child. This discovery can also be traumatic. One point of view contends that although painful, ultimately it is better for all concerned to have up-to-date knowledge. Another perspective is that the pain is too great and biological parents have the right to privacy. There is general agreement that adopted children belong with their nurturing parents.

Try This

Write a story using any or all of the following scenarios:

> Imagine that you are adopted. You are happy with your parents, but you want to find out about your birthparents. What will you do?
>
> Imagine that you relinquished your child for adoption. Why did you make this decision? What would you do if your child contacted you after eighteen years?
>
> Imagine that you are an adoptive parent. Your child wants to locate his or her birth parents. How do you feel and what do you do?

Self-image is a problem for foster children and adopted children. The foster child in one story points out that when a child thinks his own mother doesn't have any use for him, he can't have much use for himself. A child has difficulty understanding that parents sometimes love their children so much that they are willing to relinquish them to the care of others to guarantee their welfare. Children tend to see only the rejection, not the protection. They often feel unworthy of love and respect, despite verbal and demonstrated reassurances on the part of their adoptive parents. Books can help these children and their peers look at situations that impel parents to relinquish their children to the care of others.

Most adoptions are arranged by agencies, placements that are carefully controlled and monitored. Foster care is usually less meticulously overseen. After a trial period, adoptive families have the reasonable expectation that they can settle into a permanent relationship. When a foster child remains "unadoptable," there is always the chance that his or her current placement may be terminated abruptly.

SUGGESTED CRITERIA

Language is an important factor in books about adoption. The term *birth* mother or father is preferable to *real* mother or father. The message should convey that the people who nurture, love, and accept a child are truly the parents of that child.

The "happy" ending for adopted children should not be that their birthparents claim them. This may be an expected and appropriate outcome to stories about foster care, but adoptions should be presented as permanent arrangements achieved after serious thought by both sets of parents. Recent court cases notwithstanding, stories about truncated adoptions should indicate that this rupture is not the usual pattern.

The pitiful orphan so frequently encountered in Victorian novels can be a stereotypic cardboard figure. While circumstances may be painful and perhaps tragic, readers should be led to empathize with characters, not pity them. Adopted and foster children should have qualities that make them distinct and memorable characters aside from their condition. Similarly, adoptive parents should be depicted as real people, not as saints or devils. Plots must be believable.

When possible, the life of the family should be like that of any other family, except for special emotional considerations attendant upon adoption and foster care. Oversimplification of family interactions should be avoided. Foster care should not automatically be linked to abusiveness.

If traumas, catastrophes, and tragedies occur, they should take place in the context of the plot, not as automatic consequences of adoption.

DISCUSSION OF CHILDREN'S BOOKS

Foster Care

Probably the finest example of a well-written, moving, multidimensional book on this topic is *The Great Gilly Hopkins* by Katherine Paterson. Gilly is a bright, manipulative, angry eleven year old who has been shifted from one foster home to another. Sometimes her behavior is the cause of her removal from a foster home. Gilly has been wounded by foster parents who she thought loved her. Now she says, "I can't go soft—not while I'm nobody's real kid—not while I'm just something to play musical chairs with." She maintains a dream that her mother loves her and wants to take care of her. In reality, Gilly's birth mother has no intention of ever reclaiming her.

Another foster child figures in this book. In contrast to Gilly, William Ernest is shy, fearful, and unable to express himself. He and Gilly become part of the household managed by Mame Trotter who, despite a lack of education, emerges as a woman with limitless good sense, patience, and love. Mame is a remarkable human being. She accepts people and life as they are. She is generous and sensitive. Unfortunately, Gilly learns to appreciate her qualities too late for Trotter and Gilly to make their relationship permanent.

Gilly learns some hard lessons in this story. The outcome of the book is not a fairy tale happy ending, but the reader knows that all the characters will endure. Every person encountered in this book is interesting and three dimensional. Miss Harris, the teacher who recognizes Gilly's intelligence and anger, helps Gilly see school in a different light and turn away from her past disastrous encounters. Mr. Randolph, Trotter's neighbor, contributes some lessons in perseverance and love of literature. The story is fast moving and consistently engrossing. Foster children, as well as their peers, will gain insight from this excellent book.

In Betsy Byar's *The Pinballs,* children in the care of Mr. and Mrs. Mason (understanding and loving foster parents) have many emotional problems; but they come to achieve a sense of family with one another. The author describes each child's background so that readers can understand their behavior. One of the boys has been deserted by his mother and injured by his alcoholic father; one was raised by two very old women; the girl, Carlie, has been abused by her stepfather (the third in a series) and becomes cynical and suspicious of everyone.

Patricia MacLachlan's *Mama One, Mama Two* sensitively and delicately addresses issues of foster care. Intended for a young audience, the story describes the relationship between Maudie, whose mother is emotionally ill and cannot take care of her, and Katherine, Maudie's foster mother. Katherine is all that a foster parent should be: affectionate, patient, responsive, dependable, and steadfast, but willing to relinquish the child to her birth mother when "Mama One" is ready to resume responsibility. Maudie's anxieties and needs are acknowledged, as are the positive factors in her life. In *Baby,* the same author more deeply explores the feelings of the foster family. Sophie is a toddler whose mother leaves her with Larkin and her family. They all love Sophie so much that the thought that her mother might reclaim her is a constant cause of anguish. Sophie enriches their lives, and engages them all. When the inevitable happens and Sophie's mother returns, both the reader and the family accept and understand the appropriateness of the return but mourn the loss of the child.

Occasionally, foster children become eligible for adoption. In Gail Radley's *The Golden Days,* Corey is afraid that his foster mother will reject him because she is expecting a birth child. These fears prove groundless, and he learns that the love and nurturing capacities of his adoptive parents are boundless. Instead of having to leave, he is assured of a permanent home. It turns out that Corey's foster mother was an orphan who wished in vain for an adoptive parent to take her away from the institution where she lived. Later she determined to help a child because she herself had never been helped.

The same conditions pertain in *When the Road Ends,* by Jean Thesman, in which Mary Jack, Adam, and Jane are foster children who know harsh and abusive circumstances. They finally find a home with a woman who needs them as much as they need her. It would be a good idea to invite children to look into the rules governing foster care in their particular town or state and discuss the possibilities for permanent placement of foster children. In general, the foster care system aims to return children to their biological families whenever possible; and in order to be realistic, books need to reflect this intent.

Adoption

Not many books are available that meet all the criteria for well-constructed and helpful literature on this topic. Some factual books give good advice, but others either oversimplify issues or present information in a dry style. Some books have been written by adoptees with strong points of view to convey. This can lend authenticity to a book, but some authors are so intent on persuading their readers that they lose perspective and become strident.

Books like Linda Walvoord Girard's *Adoption Is for Always* are designed to inform younger children about the facts and feelings of adoption. For older children, *Adoption and Foster Care,* by Kathlyn Gay, helps readers understand the range of responses to this issue. This book uses actual narratives by various adoptees. Similarly, Jill Krementz's *How It Feels to Be Adopted* contains interviews with nineteen adopted children, ages eight to sixteen, telling their individual stories. The author's photographs underline the book's authenticity. Roslyn Banish and Jennifer Jordan-Wong's *A Forever Family* is in the format of a photograph album of eight-year-old Jennifer. Jennifer leads the reader through the events leading up to her adoption and her new "forever family." Jennifer's new family is large, extended, biracial, and loving. Her experiences in foster homes, and now in her permanent home, have been positive.

High quality fiction about adoption is even less plentiful. Miska Miles's *Aaron's Door* provides the reader with a model of a concerned father who literally breaks down the barrier separating Aaron from the family that will provide him with a permanent loving home. *Abby,* by Jeannette Caines, directly and openly deals with adoption and how to handle it in a happy family.

Contemporary complications such as court cases of children not wanting to be "harassed" by their birth parents and of adoptions being contested and overturned because the birth mother and father have changed their minds have found their way into the literature. Eve Bunting's *Sharing Susan,* based loosely on an actual case, tells about Susan, who was switched at the hospital with another newborn. When the error is discovered twelve years later, one child has died; and Susan and her parents are afraid that she will be forced to return to her birth parents. In this story, a kind of mutual custody arrangement is the result of an out-of-court solution to the problem. The ending in no way pretends that the answers are easy or that anyone is truly happy with the outcome.

International and interracial adoptions have increased in number over the past few years, as have books describing these situations. Brent and Melissa Ashabranner's *Into a Strange Land* is about young refugees, mostly Vietnamese and Cambodian, who live with foster families in the United States. Linda Walvoord Girard's *We Adopted You, Benjamin Koo* tells from a child's perspective how Koo Hyun Soo came from Korea to be adopted and become Benjamin Koo Andrews, an American citizen. It also tells how his sister Susan was adopted from Brazil. The narrative deals honestly with issues of intercultural adoption and the joys and concerns of ordinary adoption. The parents try hard to maintain a sense of the children's cultures of origin while encouraging them to enjoy their adoptive culture. Joanna Halpert Kraus tells a similar story of her own family's experiences in *Tall Boy's Journey.* Susi Gregg Fowler leads the reader through a few of the complexities of international adoptions in *When Joel Comes Home* and ends on a celebratory note.

Although no children's books have focused on controversial issues about interracial and international adoptions, it is wise to consider the different points of view about the benefits and disadvantages of raising children in a culture or society different from that of their biological origins. Such organizations as the National Association for the Advancement of Colored People (NAACP) and the National Association of Black Social Workers advise against interracial adoptions, arguing that children in such families have problems determining what their identity is and where they belong. Issues of rearing a child in a different religion from that of his or her birth parents can be examined as well. Thus far, the research is inconclusive on this matter.

Certainly, adoption and foster care are important dimensions of many children's lives. It is to be hoped that children's book authors will respond to the need for appropriate literary fare dealing with these issues.

REFERENCES

Adoption and Foster Care

Achtenberg, R. "Not in the Best Interest," *Utne Reader* 45 (Nov./Dec. 1991): 57. Briefly discusses the legal status of lesbian and gay couples who want to adopt or manage to adopt. Affirms the importance of a will assigning guardianship to the remaining nonbiological parent.

Bolles, E. B. *The Penguin Adoption Handbook: A Guide to Creating Your New Family.* Penguin, 1984. A guide to permanent adoption, as well as temporary fostering, this reference supplies strategies for traditional and untraditional adoptions and discusses adoption laws state by state. It cautions about "legal quagmires."

Bunin, S. "Up with Adoption." *Parents* 65 (Jan. 1990): 78–80. The author shares her point of view as an adoptive mother, discussing how the unthinking questions or responses of others reinforce negative stereotypes of adopted children.

Caplan, L. *Open Adoption.* Farrar, Straus & Giroux, 1990. A case study of an open adoption, including problems between the adoptive parents and the birth mother. The book contains an excellent history of adoption procedures in the U.S. and the development of the open adoption movement.

Child Welfare 72 (May/June 1993). This entire issue is on adoption. It contains articles on open adoption, transracial adoption, and adoption statistics in the United States.

Eastman, K. S. "Foster Families: A Comprehensive Bibliography." *Child Welfare* 64 (Nov./Dec. 1985): 565–585. An extensive reference list of articles and books related to foster children and families.

Flango, V. E. "Agency and Private Adoptions, by State." *Child Welfare* 69 (May/June 1990): 263–275. Lists and analyzes data on numbers of adoptions across the United States in 1987. Provides sources for this information.

Gilman, L. *The Adoption Resource Book.* Harper, 1984. The author, an adoptive parent, provides numerous possible scenarios for adoption. She discusses agencies, international adoption, and independent searches; furnishes many addresses of resources; and discusses how to prepare for and raise an adopted child.

Lifton, B. J. *Lost and Found: The Adoption Experience.* Harper, 1988. The author is a strong advocate for open-adoption and open-record laws. In her interviews with adoptees, birth parents, and adoptive parents, she brings to light feelings attendant upon the search by the adopted child for his or her birth parents. She avers that even when the results are negative the search was worthwhile.

Meyer, C. H. "A Feminist Perspective on Foster Family Care: A Redefinition of the Categories." *Child Welfare* 64 (May/June 1985): 249–258. The author invites a reconceptualization of foster care, raising foster-parenting to a professional level and taking into consideration what is known about the benefits of children retaining their primary families.

Moisa, R. "Indians Resist Non-Indian Adoption." *Utne Reader* 45 (Nov./Dec. 1991): 58. The author outlines the history of adoption of Indian children by non-Indian parents and raises questions about this practice.

Pardeck, J. T., and Pardeck, J. A. "Helping Children Adjust to Adoption through the Bibliotherapeutic Approach." *Early Childhood Development and Care* 44 (Mar. 1989): 31–37. This article describes some problems adopted children face and recommends books to help such children handle these situations.

Powers, D. "Of Time, Place, and Person: *The Great Gilly Hopkins* and Problems of Story for Adopted Children." *Children's Literature in Education* 15 (Winter 1984): 211–219. The author uses the story of *The Great Gilly Hopkins* by Katherine Paterson to look at various concerns and problems foster children face.

Rudman, M. K.; Gagne, K. D.; and Bernstein, J. E. *Books to Help Children Cope with Separation and Loss (4th ed.).* Bowker, 1994. This reference work contains about fifty titles and annotations on adoption and foster care.

Scanzoni, L. D. "Should White Parents Adopt Black Children?" *Utne Reader* 45 (Nov./Dec. 1991): 59–60. The author briefly outlines some of the issues surrounding interracial and transracial adoption and reports the position of the National Association of Black Social Workers denouncing this practice as "racial and cultural genocide." She concludes that despite the difficulties there is value in these adoptions "when they are undertaken properly."

Sharp, P. "Foster Care in Books for Children." *School Library Journal* 30 (Feb. 1984): 28–31. This article discusses treatment of the theme of foster care and provides an annotated list of more than 40 books for children.

Sherman, L. L. "In the Homes of Strangers: The World War II Evacuation of British Children in Children's Literature." *School Library Journal* 35 (April 1989): 42–43. Discusses 14 children's books that deal in some way with the temporary fostering of British children to escape the blitz of London in World War II. Some of these children were away from their homes for as much as five years, while for others it was a more temporary situation. The books are varied in style, content, and quality.

Tremitiere, N. A. "I Should Have Had Black Parents." *Utne Reader* 45 (Nov./Dec. 1991): 60. A short essay written by a black woman who was adopted by white parents. She concludes that though she and her parents love each other dearly her path would have been easier had she been reared by black parents.

RESOURCES

Adoptee-Birthparent Support Network. P.O. Box 23674, L'Enfant Plaza Station, Washington, DC 20026. Provides search assistance to adoptees and birthparents who want to locate biological relatives.

Adoptees in Search. P.O. Box 41016, Bethesda, MD 20814. Works to increase public awareness of present adoption practices and laws, especially as they affect adopted adults.

Adoption and Family Reunion Center. P.O. Box 1860, Cape Coral, FL 33910. [(800) 477-SEEK.] Seeks to make adoption a more humane institution through education with emphasis on the need for openness and understanding. Works to allow adoptees access to their birth records.

Adoptive Families of America. 3333 Hwy. 100 N, Minneapolis, MN 55422. Acts as an umbrella organization for adoptive parent support groups.

Adoptive Parents' Committee, Inc. 210 Fifth Ave., New York, NY 10010. One of the oldest parent groups in existence.

Child Welfare League of America. 440 First St. N.W., Ste 310, Washington, D.C. 20001. Publishes materials on adoption and standards for placement and care.

Committee for Single Adoptive Parents. P.O. Box 15084, Chevy Chase, MD 20825. Provides members with information and assistance and informs public and private agencies of legislation and research applying to single-person adoption. Publishes *The Handbook for Single Adoptive Parents.*

Concerned United Birth-Parents. 2000 Walker St., Des Moines, IA 50317. [(800) 822-2777.] Seeks to open birth records to adoptees and their birth parents and develop alternatives to the current adoption system.

Family Service Association of America. 44 E. 23 St., New York, NY 10010. Provides counseling before and after adoption.

International Concerns Committee for Children. 911 Cypress Dr., Boulder, CO 80303. Helps those interested in adoption of children from foreign countries.

International Soundex Reunion Registry. P.O. Box 2312, Carson City, NV 89702. A central reunion agency for biological relatives and adults 18 years old or older who were adopted, orphaned, or separated from their parents by war or divorce or were foundlings, foster children, or wards of the state. The service seeks reunions with next of kin by birth and knowledge of personal heritage for medical, genetic, and personal reasons. There is no charge for the service.

Latin America Parents Association. P.O. Box 339, Brooklyn, NY 11234. Helps people seeking to adopt children from Latin America and assists those who have already adopted.

Liberal Education for Adoptive Families. 23247 Lofton Ct. N., Scandia, MN 55073. Seeks legislative and agency policy reform. Also provides postadoption client counseling, training, and technical assistance for public and private agencies; public education seminars; and media presentations.

National Adoption Assistance Center. 444 Lincoln Blvd., No. 107, Venice, CA 90291. Assists birth parents in finding the best possible homes for their children and helps adoptive parents find adoptable children.

National Adoption Center. 1218 Chestnut St. Philadelphia, PA 19107. [(800) TO-ADOPT.] Provides information on adoption, including intercountry adoption, children with special needs and state and federal adoption laws.

National Adoption Information Clearinghouse. 11426 Rockville Pike, Suite 410, Rockville, MD 20852. Distributes information on many types of adoption and foster care. Publishes fact sheets and directories of adoption agencies.

National Coalition to End Racism in America's Child Care System. 22075 Koths, Taylor, MI 48180. Attempts to assure that all children requiring placement, whether through foster care or through adoption, are placed in the earliest available home most qualified to meet their needs.

National Committee for Adoption. 1930 17th St. N.W., Washington, DC 20009. Works to protect the institution of adoption and ensure the confidentiality of all involved in the adoption process.

North American Council on Adoptable Children. 1821 Univ. Ave. Suite N-498, St. Paul, MN 55104. Provides direct assistance to local and state advocacy efforts and acts as a clearinghouse for adoption information.

Operation Identity. 13101 Blackstone Rd., N.E., Albuquerque, NM 87111. Supplies information to searching adults on search procedures and advises on available research sources.

Organized Adoption Search Information Service. P.O. Box 53-0761, Miami Shores, FL 33153.
Maintains confidential search files and a cross-match birth registry. Offers special search
help for those unable to pursue their own search.

Orphan Voyage. 2141 Rd. 2300, Cedaredge, CO 81413. Helps build relationships between
adult adoptees and their birth families.

Reunite, Inc. P.O. Box 694, Reynoldsburg, OH 43068. Educates the public on the need
for adoption reform, encourages legislative changes, and assists in adoptee, adoptive
parent and birth-parent searches.

Right to Know. P.O. Box 1409, Grand Prairie, TX 75051. Receives and stores information
volunteered by adopted children, adoptive parents, and natural parents.

BIBLIOGRAPHY

Adler, C.S. *The Cat That Was Left Behind.* Ticknor & Fields, 1981. (Ages 11 and up.)
Thirteen-year-old Chad has recently become a foster child to the Sorenic family. Because
of Chad's past experiences in foster homes, he has little trust for this new foster family.
The Sorenics, especially his stepsister Polly, work very hard at building Chad's trust
within the family. By the story's end, Chad has accepted the family, who are making
plans to adopt him.

Ames, M. *Without Hats, Who Can Tell the Good Guys?* Dutton, 1976. (Ages 10–12.) Eleven-
year-old Anthony Lang, Jr., has been sent to live with the Diamonds, "until his father
can come back for him." He is not happy with this family at first. Eventually he learns
to care about Hildy, his sister; Mr. and Mrs. Diamond; and even senile Mrs. Puckett.
When his dream of someday living with his father is shattered, Tony's love for his foster
family supports him through that difficult period of his life. A realistic insight into the
life of a foster child.

Ashabranner, B. and Ashabranner, M. *Into a Strange Land.* Putnam, 1987. (Ages 11 and
up.) The dramatic stories of young refugees, mostly Vietnamese and Cambodian, who
escaped incredible hardship and threat and came to havens in America. The authors
explain how foster families are selected and adjustments made so that the young people
can have stable environments and access to educational programs.

Awiakta, M. *Rising Fawn and the Fire Mystery.* Illus. by B. Bringle. St. Luke's, 1983. (Ages
10 and up.) The family of Rising Fawn, a Choctaw child, has been killed by marauding
whites; and she has been adopted by a well-meaning Christian white couple ignorant
of her culture and background. Told through the child's perspective, customs and beliefs
of native and white people are compared. The Cherokee author is a fine poet. This story
can spark discussion of the benefits and detriments of interracial adoptions.

Banish, R. and Jordan-Wong, J. *A Forever Family.* Illus. by R. Banish. Harper, 1992. (Ages
5–8.) Eight-year-old Jennifer leads the reader through photos that reflect her life. Through
this vehicle, Jennifer talks about herself and the events leading up to her adoption and
her new "forever family" which is large, extended, biracial, and loving. Her experiences
in foster homes, and now in her permanent home, have been positive.

Bawden, N. *The Finding.* Lothrop, Lee & Shepard, 1985. (Ages 9–12.) Alex is found as a
newborn in the arms of a statue of a sphinx. He runs away, is held hostage, and is
finally found again by his adoptive family in the arms of the same statue. The ending is

believable because of the author's mastery of her craft. Issues of adoption, including jealousy of the adopted child's siblings, are handled well.

Blue, R. *A Quiet Place*. Illus. by T. Feelings. Watts, 1969. (Ages 9–12.) Nine-year-old Matthew, a foster child, spends his spare time in his "quiet place" at the library. He has been to a variety of foster homes, and only his current one has been like a real home. When the library is slated to be closed for two years, Matt feels threatened again with loss, despair, and fear of being abandoned by his foster parents. Only through their loving reassurance does he overcome his fear.

Bunin, C., and Bunin, S. *Is That Your Sister?* Illus. with photos. Pantheon, 1976. (Ages 6–12.) A six-year-old child explains adoption. She is of a different race from her parents and has become an "expert on explanations." A warm, true story with photographs of the family.

Bunting, E. *Sharing Susan*. Harper, 1991. (Ages 9–12.) This story is based on an actual case that earned newspaper headlines over a long period of time. Susan Moretti and her parents are notified that Susan is really the biological child of Mr. and Mrs. Stobbel. She and another infant, Marlene, were switched in the hospital at birth. The story sympathetically details everyone's feelings and reactions. Unlike the historical case, this one is resolved in an out-of-court settlement by Susan's returning to her birth parents and visiting the parents she has known for twelve years during holidays and over the summers. The arrangement is somewhat easily arrived at, but the anguish of all parties is palpably portrayed.

Byars, B. *The Pinballs*. Harper, 1977. (Ages 9–12.) Three foster children, or "pinballs" as Carlie labels them, are sent to stay with the Masons. Each has a problem that must be confronted, discussed, and accepted. Carlie, the ringleader, helps both Thomas J. and Harvey and matures into a sincere, loving sister. A well-written and sensitively handled story.

Caines, J. *Abby*. Illus. by S. Kellogg. Harper, 1973. (Ages 5–8.) Abby is an adopted child loved by her parents and her older brother Kevin, although he upsets her sometimes. The illustrations of this loving African-American family add to the impact of the book.

Cassedy, S. *Lucie Babbidge's House*. Crowell, 1989. (Ages 9–12.) Lucie is oppressed by her fellow residents in an orphanage. She is shy, unkempt, friendless, and unable to stand up for herself. After a series of adventures and near tragedies, Lucie finds that she can finally speak out for her rights. In this story, a fantasy world is a key to freedom rather than a symptom of mental illness.

Cohen, S. *Coping with Being Adopted*. Rosen, 1988. (Ages 10–12.) A practical book that tells through both interviews with adopted children and some healthy doses of good advice by the author how to handle problems such as prejudicial negative comments and behavior by outsiders about interracial adoptions. The author evenhandedly discusses searching for birth parents and urges adopted children to get to know themselves well before attempting to find their biological parents.

Duprau, J. *Adoption: The Facts, Feelings, and Issues of a Doubled Heritage*. Messner, 1981. (Ages 12 and up.) This book explores changes in adoption laws and policies over the years, describes the present-day adoption process and examines the conflicts and feelings of the child, adoptive parents, and birth mothers. Detailed, objective, sensitive, readable, and extensive.

Eige, L. *Cady*. Illus. by Janet Wentworth. Harper, 1987. (Ages 9–12.) Formerly shuttled from house to house by unloving, punitive family members, twelve-year-old Cady now lives with a silent, mysterious woman whose physical features are like his own. Cady eventually learns that she is his paternal aunt and that the father he thought was dead is living close by. Although Cady's father has never recovered from his wife's death, he and Cady together weather the death of a loved pet fox; and Cady begins to feel that he belongs. The author employs spare, dramatic description and dialogue to convey the characters' feelings rather than trying to label them. Some discussion could arise over why secrecy was necessary before Cady could eventually become part of the family.

Fowler, S. G. *When Joel Comes Home.* Illus. by J. Fowler. Greenwillow, 1993. (Ages 5-8.) A young girl waits with great anticipation for her parents' friends' newly adopted baby Joel to arrive. She makes elaborate plans for greeting them at the airport and looks forward to holding the new baby. When the day arrives, things don't go quite as planned but so many friends turn out to greet the new family that it is like a party.

Freudberg, J., and Geiss, T. *Susan and Gordon Adopt a Baby.* Illus. by J. Mathieu. Random House/Chldrn's Telev. Wkshp, 1986. (Ages 3-6.) Susan and Gordon of Sesame Street become baby Miles's adoptive parents. The book emphasizes that now they will be Miles's parents forever and that when someone new enters the family there is plenty of love to go around. Although didactic in intent, it is written in simple (not simplistic) language and helps children not only deal with the issues of new siblings but also understand the adoptive process.

Garfield, L. *Fair's Fair.* Illus. by S. D. Schindler. Doubleday, 1983. (Ages 7-10.) In a satisfying blend of fantasy and Victorian flavor and with lavish illustrations, this story tells of two orphans who find a permanent home with a rich benefactor because of their bravery and generosity. Not a real-life situation but one in which the characters' feelings and behavior are believable.

Gay, K. *Adoption and Foster Care.* Enslow, 1990. (Ages 11 and up.) The author uses interviews and anecdotes to convey the situations of adoptive families and children. The book describes several placement procedures and airs the many debates engendered by this emotional process. Children whose races are different from those of their potential parents, children with special needs, children born overseas, and foster parents who wish to adopt are all part of an ongoing set of controversies. The author's tone is reasoned and empathic.

Girard, L. W. *Adoption Is for Always.* Illus. by J. Friedman. Whitman, 1986. (Ages 5-7.) Although Celia has known she was adopted since she was young, she has just begun to ask questions. Her adoptive parents answer her openly and explain details of the adoption procedure, but Celia still becomes upset and does not like it that she is adopted. The language is current and sensitive ("birthmother" and "birthparent" for example). Celia is neither pitiful nor idealized. Such issues as why birth parents gave the child up for adoption, anxiety over whether the adoption can be overturned, and strategies for coping are handled well in this book.

Girard, L. W. *We Adopted You, Benjamin Koo.* Illus. by Linda Shute. Whitman, 1989. (Ages 6-10.) In accurate, respectful language (including "birthmother" and "first mother") nine-year-old Koo Hyun Soo tells the story of how he was adopted from Korea and became Benjamin Koo Andrews, an American citizen. He also includes the story of how his sister Susan was adopted from Brazil. The narrative deals honestly with the issues of intercultural adoption and with the joys and concerns of ordinary adoption.

Greenberg, J. E., and Carey, H. H. *Adopted.* Illus. by B. Kirk. Watts, 1987. (Ages 5-8.) Reassuring and clarifying language characterizes this book for young children. The adoptive parents and grandparents are careful to express positive and loving feelings toward the children and to credit their birth parents with goodness and constructive intentions. The photos add considerably to the value of the book.

Hoberman, M. A. *Fathers, Mothers, Sisters, Brothers: A Collection of Family Poems.* Illus. by M. Hafner. Joy Street, 1991. (Ages 7-10.) [See Family Constellations]

Holland, I. *Alan and the Animal Kingdom.* Dell, 1977. (Ages 9-12.) Alan has been shipped from one relative to another since his parents died. His love for animals seems greater than his love for or belief in people. Alan eventually learns to put his trust in his "new" family.

Hunt, I. *Up a Road Slowly.* Follett, 1966. (Ages 9-12.) Seven-year-old Julie and her nine-year-old brother Chris are sent to live with their Aunt Cordelia when their mother dies. Their father can't cope with the situation. The story describes their growth and acceptance of their situation. Excellent characterization with realistic interaction and dialogue earned this book the Newbery Medal.

Kraus, J. H. *Tall Boy's Journey.* Illus. by K. Ritz. Carolrhoda, 1992. [See Heritage]

Krementz, J. *How It Feels to Be Adopted.* Illus. by the author. Knopf, 1991. (Ages 10 and up.) Nineteen children, ages eight to sixteen, tell in their own words what it feels like to be adopted. Both concerns and benefits are discussed; and although each person tells a different story, the net effect is one of self-acceptance and security in the midst of a loving family. The author's photographs underline the book's authenticity.

Lapsley, S. *I Am Adopted.* Bradbury, 1974. (Ages 5-8.) A simple picture book about two adopted children, Charles and Sophie, narrated from a child's point of view. Charles describes their everyday activities; and the family's love, warmth, and caring shine through.

Lindsay, J. W. *Open Adoption: A Caring Option.* Morning Glory, 1987. (Ages 12 and up.) A helpful book about the adoption process. Much of the content came out of the author's experiences as a teacher in a Teen Mother program. Open and closed adoption, how agencies function, the rights of each individual, emotional reactions and confidentiality are discussed through vignettes and profiles of people and agencies.

Lindsay, J. W. *Pregnant Too Soon: Adoption Is an Option.* Illus. by P. Morford. Morning Glory, 1988. (Ages 12 and up.) This helpful book focuses on the plight of the teenage unwed mother and offers many details about how to apply the option of adoption rather than abortion or "forced" marriage. It answers many questions and personalizes information.

Livingston, C. *Why Was I Adopted?* Illus. by A. Robins. Lyle Stuart, 1978. (Ages 4-10.) A thorough and humorous presentation of the whys and hows of adoption. The "special-ness" of being adopted is kept in perspective. It includes common questions with down-to-earth answers.

MacLachlan, P. *Arthur, for the Very First Time.* Illus. by L. Bloom. Harper, 1980. (Ages 9-12.) [See Gender Roles]

MacLachlan, P. *Baby.* Delacorte, 1993. (Ages 11 and up.) [See Death]

MacLachlan, P. *Mama One, Mama Two.* Illus. by R. Bornstein. Harper, 1982. (Ages 5-11.) Maudie is living with a foster family until her birth mother is well enough to care for her. Mama Two often tells Maudie the story of how she became a foster child. The story and illustrations show warmth and understanding. Maudie is tenderly accepted as part of her new family and is given love and reassurance. Mama Two will relinquish Maudie to Mama One's care when the time comes, but she will remain available.

Malotki, E. *The Mouse Couple.* Illus. by M. Lacapa. Northland, 1988. (Ages 7-10.) [See Heritage]

Martin, A. M. *Yours Turly, Shirley.* Holiday House, 1988. (Ages 9-12.) [See Special Needs]

Miles, M. *Aaron's Door.* Little, Brown, 1977. (Ages 9-11.) Aaron, a newly adopted boy, trusts no one. He is afraid of loneliness and rejection and closes himself off by hiding behind his bedroom door. When Aaron's door is finally broken down, his wall against the world crumbles, and he begins to trust.

Mills, C. *Boardwalk with Hotel.* Bantam, 1985. (Ages 9-12.) Jessica is shocked when her baby sitter comments that her parents adopted her only because they thought they couldn't give birth to children of their own. She begins to question her parents' love and fears that she is not as valued as her younger siblings, her parents' birth children. Ultimately she comes to understand that she is a beloved member of the family. The story is written in a humorous and honest fashion. Unfortunately the grandmother is a stereotypic character.

Montgomery, L.M. *Akin to Anne: Tales of Other Orphans.* Bantam, reprinted in 1990. (Ages 10 and up.) The author knows from personal experience what it means to be orphaned and to live with people who provide adequate physical care but inadequate emotional care. These 19 short stories contain a range of characters and themes, with the theme of the orphan constant. Delightfully written, each story has a satisfying ending.

Montgomery, L.M. *Anne of Green Gables.* Bantam, reprinted 1984 (copyright 1908). (Ages 10 and up.) Anne Shirley is the protagonist and quintessential orphan in the classic multivolume series set in Prince Edward Island, Canada. Anne is spunky, dramatic, bright, and desperately searching for a loving and secure home. The charm of the writing, the strong portrayal of the setting, the depth of the characters, and the quality of the emotional tone combine to make these stories inviting for contemporary readers.

Myers, W. D. *Me, Mop, and the Moondance Kid.* Illus. by R. Pate. Yearling, 1988. (Ages 9-12.) A multiethnic group of boys and girls, some living in a Catholic institution for orphans, are friends and players on the same Little League team. Although two brothers, Moondance and T.J., get adopted, the children remain close friends. The happy ending is satisfying and not beyond believability. The characters are all-around children involved in more than their quest for adoption.

Myers, W. D. *Won't Know till I Get There.* Viking, 1982. (Ages 11 and up.) Earl Goins has gone from one foster home to another. Although his mother refuses to have him, she refuses to permit him to be permanently adopted. He finally arrives at the comfortable home of the Perrys, where he causes many problems but also finds understanding.

Nickman, S. *The Adoption Experience: Stories and Commentaries.* Messner, 1985. (Ages 11 and up.) This book, written by a psychiatrist, includes commentaries after each vignette as springboards for discussion. Many aspects of adoption are included in the stories, journal entries, and commentaries, such as blended families, finding one's birth family, special needs, and interracial and international adoptions. The author avoids stereotypes and provides good models of self-help and self-reflection.

Nixon, J. L. *A Family Apart; Caught in the Act; A Place to Belong;* and *In The Face of Danger.* Bantam, 1989. (Ages 10 and up.) These four titles constitute the *Orphan Train Quartet.* The author was inspired to write this series by the actual orphan trains that transported more than 100,000 children from New York City slums to new homes in the west and midwest. The Children's Aid Society sponsored the well-intentioned place-ment program from 1854 to 1929, followed by other groups. The characters in the stories are fictional, but they represent some experiences foster children endured as a result of this program.

Okimoto, J. D. *Molly by Any Other Name.* Scholastic, 1990. (Ages 12 and up.) When Molly is seventeen years old, she seeks out both her birth mother and a clearer explanation of her origin. Although she is of Asian descent, she doesn't know to which Asian group she belongs. It is difficult to believe that Molly would have no clue as to her heritage, especially since her adoptive parents have always been direct with her about her adoption. Despite this flaw, the book explores a dilemma that many adoptive families encounter. Molly's parents suffer anxiety when she wants to find her birth mother. The book clearly presents the procedures Molly uses to locate her birth mother and helps readers to understand each person's perspective. The ending leaves Molly with her adoptive family, happier for being informed, and with hopes for good relationships in the future.

Paterson, K. *The Great Gilly Hopkins.* Crowell, 1978. (Ages 9 and up.) Gilly seems to enjoy making people dislike her. In reality, she craves love and security. Gilly dreams of being reunited with her birth mother. She is placed with Trotter, a wise and loving foster mother, and William Ernest, the painfully insecure little boy who is also Trotter's foster child. All the characters are vivid individuals. This masterly writing helps readers better understand foster care problems.

Pellegrini, N. *Families Are Different.* Illus. by the author. Holiday House, 1991. (Ages 4-7.) Nico and her sister are of Korean heritage. Their adoptive parents are American Caucasians. The intent of the story is to communicate that differences are fine if the family is loving. The language and illustrations are simple, and the story works well.

Piepgras, R. *My Name Is Mike Trunsky.* Illus. by P. R. Haag. Child's World, 1979. (Ages 7-10.) Although Mike has a good relationship with his foster family, he really wants to see and be with his mother. The dialogues between Mike and his friends and Mike and his foster family give a clear depiction of foster care. There is possibility of a permanent reunion between Mike and his mother at some time in the future.

Radley, G. *The Golden Days.* Macmillan, 1991. (Ages 10-12.) Corey, a foster child, has been placed in a succession of homes. In his present home, Corey fears that since his foster parents are expecting a baby they will send him back to the orphanage. He has become close to Carlotta, an elderly woman who hates being confined to a nursing home. The two run away together and struggle to survive, but Corey and Carlotta both realize that they cannot manage on their own. The happy ending is satisfying because it is plausible and because the characters have endeared themselves to the reader. Corey and Carlotta both learn what it means to be part of a family.

Rosenberg, M. B. *Being Adopted.* Illus. by G. Ancona. Lothrop, Lee & Shepard, 1984. (Ages 7-10.) Interviews and black-and-white photos tell the stories of three children who have been adopted into families with heritages different from their own. The book discusses issues of adoption common to most adoptive families and those pertaining to multiracial and intercultural families. The author's personal involvement (she is an adoptive parent) contributes to the book's authenticity and balance.

Rosenberg, M. *Growing up Adopted.* Bradbury, 1989. (Ages 10 and up.) A well-documented account of how adopted children view their situations. Each interview presents many details of the adoption, as well as the feelings and perspectives of all concerned parties. The author stresses that adoption is permanent and that adoption is more open and less shrouded in secrecy than it once was.

Sachs, M. *A December Tale.* Doubleday, 1976. (Ages 9-11.) [See Abuse]

Sobol, H. L. *We Don't Look like Our Mom and Dad.* Illus. by P. Agre. Coward McCann, 1984. (Ages 6-9.) Eric and Joshua Levin are brothers by adoption. Each was born in Korea and adopted as a baby. Their Caucasian parents try to maintain the boys' sense of heritage by cooking Korean food and reading books about Korean culture. They retell the story of each boy's adoption and try hard to address issues of prejudice. The photos clearly depict a family that is close knit, active, and secure in mutual love. The Levins provide a model of addressing the joys and concerns sparked by interracial and international adoptions.

Stein, S. B. *The Adopted One.* Illus. by E. Stone. Walker, 1979. (Ages 3–8.) One of the *Open Family* series. Four-year-old Joshua, who is adopted, questions his mommy about his birth mother. The accompanying text for adults explains why children ask certain questions, and the story and illustrations model helpful ways of responding to these questions.

Thesman, J. *When the Road Ends.* Illus. by R. Wisnewski. Houghton Mifflin, 1992. (Ages 10–up.) Mary Jack, the narrator, is twelve years old and strong and competent beyond her years. She takes care of another foster child, Jane, who has been horribly abused. Mary Jack helps maintain the delicate balance of stability at the home of their foster parents. The three foster children (the third is Adam, a fourteen-year-old boy who is angry and often on the edge of violence) endure the sullen, neurotic Mrs. Percy and the well-meaning but weak Father Matt Percy (an Episcopal priest). Although the story never crosses the line into sentimentality, the situation is sometimes heart rending. The plight of foster children and the blundering of well-intentioned but ineffectual adults are underlying threads in the well-paced and well-drawn plot. Although the ending is happy, it is not far fetched. The author carefully lays the foundation for resolution of the characters' problems.

Turner, A. *Through Moon and Stars and Night Skies.* Illus. by J. G. Hale. Harper, 1990. (Ages 5–8.) A child retells for himself and his mother the familiar tale of his arrival in the United States from an Asian country (probably Korea). He recalls his plane flight and his arrival. He especially remembers the feelings of safety that followed his fears. The child's perspective adds an important component to young readers' understanding of international adoption.

chapter 3

Divorce

Since 1988, after two decades of considerable change, the proportion of marriages ending in divorce has remained fairly steady at 9.7 percent (*World Almanac,* 1992). In essence, this means that almost one out of every two marriages ends in divorce. In the past two decades, divorce has become, except for people who consider it unacceptable for religious reasons, an acceptable option when a marriage has failed. Duration is not the only criterion by which to judge that a marriage is happy. People may choose to stay together for reasons that are less than constructive. Wives once endured all kinds of hardships within marriage because they feared that life would be more difficult if they were divorced. Husbands stayed with women they no longer cared for because it was economically unfeasible to pay for divorce and its aftermath. Men were responsible for total support of their families. Marriages also continued "for the sake of the children." These pressures still exist, but gradually people are recognizing that they must work together to keep marriages going well and that if their efforts fail they must work together to separate successfully.

Separation and divorce are now less costly to arrange. What was once an ugly, painful, and drawn-out procedure has in many states been simplified and made easier. Today the process is less arduous when both partners decide to dissolve their contract; though divorce is never easy, and agreeing to a final settlement can still be a painful process that takes years to complete. Many states have instituted "no-fault" divorce laws acknowledging that when there has been an irreparable breakdown of the marriage no one is at fault.

Although our social structure is in transition, the preponderant values continue to include the traditional expectations of lasting marriage. Ending a marriage by any means except the death of one spouse is still considered by many to constitute failure, partly because of a sense that commitments have been broken and partly because of the implicit expectation that people who work hard enough can overcome all obstacles. Just as adults agonize over what they could have done to save a marriage, the children blame themselves. They imagine that if they had done their jobs as "good children" their parents would still be together. These children may worry whether their parents will continue to love and care for them and fret about being deserted by the remaining parent and about never seeing the absent parent. They often worry about being supplanted in their parents' affections, and they question their own self-worth.

If divorce is an unusual occurrence in the community, a child's peers sometimes avoid him or her as though divorce were contagious. Peers may have difficulty knowing what to say to help a child who no longer lives with both parents. In communities where divorce is less rare, children who have experienced the same situation can be very helpful to one another by sharing feelings and offering support. A sensitive adult can arrange for this to take place.

A large percentage of all divorcing couples have children under eighteen. Agencies specializing in family help, as well as organizations such as Parents without Partners, give advice and support. Books can be used as tools by parents, teachers, librarians, and children on a regular "come to me whenever you need me" basis.

SUGGESTED CRITERIA

The literary quality of any written work, including those dealing with divorce, can enhance or lessen its effectiveness. Fiction should offer more than the issue of divorce to carry readers' interest. Books intended to convey information must do so with accuracy in a noncondescending, jargon-free fashion. The topic of divorce must be kept up to date because statistics and state laws change rapidly. On the other hand, children's psychological response to divorce has changed little. If a book communicates children's feelings and suggests some effective ways to deal with them, no matter what the date of publication, it can be useful.

Books should present the topic realistically. One pitfall to avoid is the "happy" ending in which parents are reunited as a result of their child's behavior or intervention. Although estranged couples sometimes get back together, this outcome does not usually occur as a result of their children but because they themselves rethink or change their own relationship. This resolution does not help readers trying to cope with divorce. Many children unrealistically believe that they have power to save their parents' marriages, taking on a burden that serves them badly.

Generally, books should also refrain from establishing blame. A divorce is almost always a complicated situation with no simple cause. Blame-fixing can be destructive because it maintains anger and mitigates against a mediated solution.

Plots should make it clear that one argument between parents, no matter how heated, is not sufficient reason for a divorce unless physical violence is involved. This can reassure children who are afraid that if their mother and father disagree it automatically means their marriage will end.

Good books demonstrate clear channels of communication and responses to children's questions. Sudden surprises when the fictional children thought their parents were doing fine or cases where a parent suddenly returns or unaccountably changes behavior are detrimental to a child's understanding of the situation.

The most helpful books about divorce acknowledge the full range of children's feelings, such as hopes, fears, anger, guilt, sadness, and love. They are models for supportive peer and adult behavior, providing options for everyone. Although they may not end happily, they do demonstrate that life can go on constructively. Books on this topic can be used with children experiencing the problem with their peers (so that empathy can be stimulated) and with parents, who often need to learn how to manage their responses.

The audience determines how a book will be used. If a child's parents have just divorced, the book may be used as therapy, comfort, and perhaps a source of information and suggestions for behavior. If the audience is a group of children who have never come into contact with divorce and are now responding inappropriately to a peer involved in a divorce, a book can stimulate empathic and supportive behavior. Sometimes a book for children is a useful tool for reaching a parent, helping him or her understand and deal with a child more constructively. In the process of reading to a child, a parent may also derive comfort, support, and ideas.

Try This

Select three books from the Bibliography at the end of this chapter. (1) What factors would make you recommend the book? (2) Which readers would most appreciate this book? (3) What problems are left unresolved by these books? Discuss your reactions with someone who has done the same activity.

Books containing even the briefest mention of divorce usually communicate both the author's attitude and the prevailing societal point of view quite clearly. Religion, upbringing, and ethical standards contribute to children's attitudes toward people involved in divorce. Accurate information contributes to a healthy perspective. Helping adults must face their opinions and prejudices knowledgeably before they attempt to work with children who are coping with the problem at first hand. Assumptions about behavior of these children; attitudes toward the preservation of marriage and causes of divorce; understanding of how to get up-to-date information about divorce rate, regulations, and support organizations are all factors that contribute to the ways an adult can be helpful.

DISCUSSION OF CHILDREN'S BOOKS

Breaking Up

Books describing divorce usually offer hope for the eventual happiness and stability of the children whose parents have separated or divorced. The pattern of these books includes the child's bewilderment and unhappiness over the separation, the difficult period of adjustment when arrangements are first being negotiated, the problem of living with one parent while visiting the other periodically, and the settling down to a satisfactory everyday existence with the single parent. The books do not pretend that the children's hoped-for happy ending—

the reconciliation of father and mother—will ever occur. They do recognize the fears and guilt feelings of children, and they present realistic situations.

Beth Goff's *Where Is Daddy?* follows this pattern, exploring the trauma for a very young child who experiences not only the disappearance of her father from the household but also the partial loss of her mother who, for the first time, must leave the house to work. In this book, Janeydear, her mother, and her dog go to live with her maternal grandmother. The child is terrified that if she exhibits any anger or bad temper her mother will behave like her father and not return. She considers herself the culprit in the divorce. If she had behaved well, her father would not have left. Her well-meaning but harassed grandmother unwittingly contributes to this feeling. The child becomes fearful, quiet, and withdrawn.

Finally, the adults recognize how Janeydear feels and try to make her more comfortable. The mother takes Janeydear to her place of business. Now Janeydear can picture her mother at work instead of worrying about where she is. Her grandmother accompanies them, becoming a partner in the process. The grandmother begins to play with Janeydear and relaxes some of her rules about permitting the dog in the house. And Janeydear's father visits her and answers her questions. The characters are somewhat oversimplified but not stereotyped. They have enough individuality that the story can stand on its own without being used exclusively as a lesson. Commenting at the end of the book, psychiatrist Dr. John F. McDermott describes both the usual reactions of a young child to divorce and some of the difficulties that adults face. He recommends this story as a bridge to help restore perspective to children and parents. Young children may appreciate the opportunity to role-play this story and others like it.

Another book conveying a similar message for older children is Peggy Mann's *My Dad Lives in a Downtown Hotel.* When Joey's father leaves him and his mother and moves into a hotel, Joey is convinced that his father does not love him. He imagines that if he reforms, his father will be willing to come back home. He goes to visit his father armed with a list of promises that he will keep in order to be a better person. Joey's mother also wants the father to come back home. The father seems callous about their feelings and rejects any contact with Joey's mother even though she invites it. He avoids mentioning her in conversation with Joey. He inconsiderately drops in on Joey and his mother to collect some of his belongings.

The book specifically describes the child's feelings. Apparently the father has never been a companion for the boy. Now that he and the mother are divorcing, he pays more attention to his son. The divorce brings all kinds of improvements in the behavior of both parents toward him. Joey also discovers that many children at school are in the same situation, and they decide to form a social club. It promises to serve as a support for them.

The book presents a realistic portrayal of separation. The mother is not dependent, clinging, or nagging. Although obviously the injured party, she is not a martyr. She continues to work and to care about her appearance, and she tries to devise special ways of attending to Joey's needs. She is an excellent model despite keeping alive a hope that her husband will return. The husband, although inconsiderate, is not really a villain. Children could devise a "What if . . . ?" exercise, telling how Joey might respond if his father did not visit regularly or if he remarried. When Joey's first attempt to bring his parents back together fails, he accepts the permanence of their separation.

Most books concentrate on children's feelings. Some should help children acknowledge their parents' feelings, too. Books like those just described are useful for children enduring the painful beginnings of life after divorce. They help make them aware that other people have gone through the same experience and had the same ugly and confused feelings. They present a positive way of relating to both parents and of coping with the problems.

One negative aspect of many books for older readers is the assumption that the mother is at fault. The mother is blamed for the breakup of the marriage, and the father is almost always pleasant, understanding, and admirable. Except for the mother's attitude, there is no indication of any real cause for the divorce. Readers may find it an interesting exercise, in cases like this, to attempt to reconstruct the couple's courtship and marriage to understand how they came to marry in the first place.

Aftermath of the Divorce

Books describing people's lives after divorce are much more varied than those dealing mainly with the period during and immediately after the breakup. In general, many problems are clearly confronted, but the prospect of a blissful solution is less assured.

In Beverly Cleary's *Dear Mr. Henshaw* ten-year-old Leigh's correspondence with his favorite author, Mr. Henshaw, prompts him to set his feelings into writing. Although he wishes his father were more attentive and understanding, he is coping well with the situation. *Strider,* the sequel, further demonstrates Leigh's ability to handle his parents' breakup and his father's behavior.

Sometimes a child's nightmare comes true in these books. The parents do not want anything to do with their children. They can even abuse them both physically and psychologically. These books may be useful in stimulating peer empathy or encouraging discussion about the negative feelings of a child who believes, accurately or not, that he or she is being victimized. If a child becomes upset by these books, an adult can provide supportive guidance and offer books presenting different aspects or resolutions.

In *Chloris and the Creeps,* by Kin Platt, a child responds destructively to her parents' new lives. Chloris and her younger sister Jenny live with their mother. Their father remarries after the divorce and commits suicide when his second marriage breaks up. Jenny appears to have adjusted to the situation, but Chloris has constructed a fantasy about her father. Aided and goaded by her paternal grandmother, she resents and blames her mother for what realistically was her father's failing. She glorifies and romanticizes this weak, self-centered, self-destructive man who in reality was impatient with his daughters, unfaithful to his wife, and inconsiderate of everyone. The mother finally marries a loving man who is solicitous of the children. Jenny is very happy, but Chloris still cannot accept the situation, although she is tremendously supported by her new stepfather. Her performance of a series of outlandish acts indicates that she is still enmeshed in her fantasy world. Finally, she is jolted into reality when she discovers that her beloved father left money to her younger sister but not to her.

I, Trissy, by Norma Fox Mazer, ends with the hope that Trissy will respond to positive efforts on her behalf by her father, mother, and stepfather. Trissy's behavior, like Chloris's, is damaging and self-centered. Nonetheless, the adults' concern for her is apparent throughout the story, and the reader can see that she will accept their help and eventually recognize her own individuality, valued apart from what her mother and father do with their personal lives.

Children who resent any independent life their parents want to lead may find comfort and a source of perspective in these books which describe divorce in terms of children's negative and inappropriate behavior. An appropriate class exercise is to write a "Dear Abby" letter from the character and devise the answer from "Dear Abby."

Managing

Although most divorce settlements award custody of children to one parent, shared or joint custody is another possibility, one with both advocates and critics. Joint custody does not necessarily imply that children must stay for a specified amount of time with either parent. Nor does it require the actual physical presence of a parent. In this situation, both parents share responsibility for making decisions about their children. Although the couple is no longer married, when this custody arrangement operates optimally, they still function together as parents. Families have structured many workable arrangements. Children may live in one parent's house for a specified amount of time (two or three days a week, one or two weeks, several months, and even alternate years). Some couples have the children stay in one home while the parents shift from one dwelling to another. When the children do the "commuting," some parents arrange to have identical furniture, clothing, and toys in their houses so that the children will feel comfortable. Parents often make sure that their residences are in the same school district so that the transition from house to house is feasible.

Even if custody is not shared or joint, many families are careful to assure the children that they have two parents although the primary care is the responsibility of one. Parents want their children to be members of two-parent families in the emotional and nurturing sense, even if the parents do not live together. Both an adjunct parent (any adult who functions in a parenting role) and the new partner of either parent also contribute to the nurturing process. The phrase "single-parent family" has replaced the outmoded "broken family" because of the recognition that any loving entity is a "whole" family. Now a new term is needed broad enough to indicate that, although the parents are divorced, they continue to be involved in concerned and loving relationships with their children.

Nevertheless it would be foolish to pretend that there are no problems particular to the everyday management of living after a divorce settlement has been reached. At present, it remains more likely that one parent will have primary care of the children. If this task falls to the mother, the difficulties of taking on a full-time job outside the home and providing adequate care for the child are considerable. Several books recognize this fact and explore solutions. *Mushy Eggs,* by Florence Adams, describes the relationship between two young boys and their babysitter. There is no problem until the sitter wants to retire and return to her native Italy. Then the boys are hurt and angry that she is leaving them.

A gentle, somewhat uneventful book, *Mushy Eggs* contains some important unobtrusive messages. The mother is an excellent carpenter and uses her skills to build bookcases, closets, and a boat for the boys to play in. The boys maintain a close relationship with their father, who continues to visit them on Sundays and to whose apartment they sometimes go to play. The boys have responsibilities for the maintenance of their house. They are unhappy when their beloved sitter leaves, but their mother wisely manages to take a week's vacation to help alleviate their sadness. Soon she finds a new sitter who appears to be warm and responsible. Although the boys do not love her immediately, they accept her and become optimistic about the future.

Books of this sort are helpful not only to children who think that divorce means the end of the world for them but also to parents who need good role models to emulate. The mother in this book is a comfortable, independent, and caring person who is managing the situation well. Her daytime job is to work with computers. She finds helpers to care for the children from breakfast through dinnertime.

In Crescent Dragonwagon's *Always, Always,* custody is amicably shared by a young girl's parents, even though their lifestyles are totally different. The daughter adjusts well from one parent to another, although she is subject at times to moments of anxiety. Although the parents cannot live with each other, they both love their daughter very much. Louis Baum's *One More Time* is another custody story, told in picture book form, that indicates that life can be pleasant when a child must share time between two parents. In this story, Simon and his father spend a perfect Sunday in each other's company. It is only at the end of the book, when Simon's father bids him "goodbye," that the reader understands that Simon's dad doesn't live with him. Simon endures anxiety at the separation, but he knows he will see his father again soon. Books such as these help reassure children that parents, though often separated from them, can be trustworthy.

Advice can come in many forms. Whether imbedded in a story or didactically administered through nonfiction, it can be directed at children or aimed specifically at parents. One nonfiction work, *The Boys and Girls Book about Divorce* by Richard A. Gardner, is written for children and is recommended by Parents without Partners. The book, a comprehensive discussion of divorce, contains an introduction for parents, guiding their behavior and describing their children's feelings.

The book is directly and practically written. Dr. Gardner, a psychiatrist, reassures children who feel unworthy and suspect that their parents do not love them. If their suspicions are true, he says, they should not waste time and energy looking for love where it does not exist but should search in appropriate places where it can be found. He gives advice on how to get along with divorced parents and with stepparents. Although his advice places the responsibility for healthy adjustment on the children's shoulders, adults involved in this kind of situation can benefit from it. A similar book with varying differences in the actual advice is Eda LeShan's *What's Going to Happen to Me?*. The author reassures children that their parents will always love them, whereas Gardner tries to persuade children that they are lovable even if, as sometimes happens, their parents do not love them.

Dinosaurs Divorce, by Laurene K. Brown and Marc Brown is a straight-talking book that uses a comic strip style and humor to convey important and serious messages. It reassures children that they are not to blame when their parents divorce. For those children whose parents are not divorced or divorcing, the book is helpful in fostering understanding of children who are going through this trauma. Its implicit advice to parents is also useful.

Several books now deal with new relationships and adjustments that children must make when divorced parents acquire other partners and when they may also need to interact with stepsiblings. In Doris Orgel's *Midnight Soup and a Witch's Hat,* Becky is jealous and resentful of her stepsister Hope, but she finally understands that Hope's fears are even more intense, and being a reasonable young woman, manages to make the relationship work. In *My Mother Got Married (and Other Disasters),* by Barbara Park, Charlie hates that his mother remarried. He feels left out and unloved. In *Dear Dad, Love Laurie,* by Susan Beth Pfeffer, Laurie cannot tolerate her mother's dating. For a further exploration on this aspect of the aftermath of divorce, see Chapter 4, "Family Constellations," which reviews blended families and other forms of family constructs resulting from divorce and other circumstances.

Many sociologists and psychologists are making predictions about the future of marriage. Almost everyone agrees that attitudes and arrangements are changing. Few people agree on what the outcomes will be. Meanwhile, the phenomenon of divorce remains a difficult issue. The appropriate and sensitive use of books to help deal with resultant problems can ease pressure, helping not only the individuals most directly involved but also interested and concerned outsiders.

REFERENCES

Divorce

Bienenfeld, F. *Helping Your Child Succeed after Divorce.* Illus. by children of divorcing parents. Hunter House, 1987. Focuses on the benefits of joint custody. Stresses the importance of two parents cooperatively parenting the children. Good list of resources.

Bonkowski, S. E.; Bequette, S. Q.; and Boomhower, S. J. "A Group Design to Help Children Adjust to Parental Divorce." *Social Casework* 65 (March 1984): 131-37. Helpful for teachers, counselors, and other professionals who might want a model for conducting discussion sessions with children who need to develop coping strategies.

Bonkowski, S. E.; Bequette, S. Q.; and Boomhower, S. J. "What You Don't Know Can Hurt You: Unexpressed Fears and Feelings of Children from Divorcing Families." *Journal of Divorce* 9 (Fall 1985): 33-45. Useful analysis of letters of children participating in a divorce adjustment group.

Cantrell, R. G. "Adjustment to Divorce: Three Components to Assist Children." *Elementary School Guidance and Counseling* 20 (Feb. 1986): 163-73. Primarily for educators to assist them in developing techniques for working with children in need of counseling.

Defrain, J.; Fricke, J.; and Emlen, J. *On Our Own: A Single Parent's Survival Guide.* Heath, 1987. More than 1000 divorced single parents participated in this study of single parenthood brought about by divorce. The book discusses the issues of custody, adjustment by the various members of the family, money matters, relationships, and parenting skills.

Emery, R. E. *Marriage, Divorce and Children's Adjustment.* Developmental Clinical Psychology and Psychiatry Series, vol. 14. Sage, 1988. Reviews studies relating to children's adjustment. Includes clinical perspective and academic and behavioral effects of divorce on children.

Fineman, M. *The Illusion of Equality: The Rhetoric and Reality of Divorce Reform.* University of Chicago Press, 1991. Discusses legislation on divorce and what effect this legislation has, particularly on women and children.

Freeman, E. B. "When Children Face Divorce: Issues and Implications of Research." *Childhood Education* 62 (Nov./Dec. 1985): 130–36. Helpful for teachers and other educators dealing with children experiencing divorce. Suggestions for strengthening teacher–student relationships and a resource list are included.

Furstenberg, F. F. *Divided Families: What Happens to Children When Parents Part.* Harvard University Press, 1991. Focuses on economic consequences of divorce, particularly on children.

Garanzini, M. J. "Recognizing and Responding to the Child of Divorce." *Momentum* 15 (May 1984): 8–12. Helpful suggestions for teachers who want to ease adjustment for students experiencing divorce in the family.

Hetherington, E. M., and Arasteh, J. D., eds. *The Impact of Divorce, Single Parenting, and Stepparenting on Children.* Erlbaum, 1988. Sixteen papers presented at the 1985 National Institute of Child Health and Human Development conference tackle issues related to the effect of divorce on children, including stepparenting, self-esteem, and parental conflict.

Kalter, N., and Plunkett, J. W. "Children's Perceptions of the Causes and Consequences of Divorce." *Journal of the American Academy of Child Psychiatry* 23 (May 1984): 326–334. Interviews with children who discuss their ideas and perceptions concerning divorce, its causes, and its aftermath.

Lebowitz, M. L., ed. *The Children's Divorce Center Reading Guide: A Guide to Help You Choose and Use Divorce-Related Books.* Children's Divorce Center, 1986. A list of 300 books with brief annotations for use with children, adolescents, parents, educators, and other professionals.

Mitchell, A. K. *Children in the Middle: Living through Divorce.* Tavistock, 1985. Describes perceptions of issues such as separation, parental conflict, and emotional difficulties of children and their parents.

Nofsinger, M. M. *Children and Adjustment to Divorce: An Annotated Bibliography.* Garland, 1990. An extensive annotated bibliography of articles for social workers, health professionals, educators, and parents, involved with children who have been affected by divorce.

Pardeck, J. A., and Pardeck, J. T. "Bibliotherapy Using a Neo-Freudian Approach of Children of Divorced Parents." *School Counselor* 32 (March 1985): 313–318. Identifies bibliotherapy as a useful approach in working with children who may have emotional or behavioral problems as a result of divorce in the family. Describes appropriate techniques and resources.

Randolph, M. K., and Gredler, G. R. "Children of Divorce." *Techniques* 1 (Oct. 1984): 466–479. Suggests school as a valuable haven for children undergoing divorce-related problems. Recommends bibliotherapy as an important technique in helping these children. An annotated booklist is included.

Rudman, M. K.; Gagne, K. D.; and Bernstein, J. E. *Books to Help Children Cope with Separation and Loss,* 4th ed. Bowker, 1994. This reference work includes more than 35 titles and annotations on the topic of divorce.

Wolchik, S. A., and Wolchik, P., eds. *Children of Divorce: Empirical Perspectives on Adjustment.* Gardner, 1988. A thorough discussion of divorce and its ramifications for children and families by nationally recognized scholars. Includes parental, social, and environmental pressures. Identifies helping relationships and strategies for treatment.

RESOURCES

Journal of Divorce and Remarriage. Binghamton, New York: Haworth Press. All issues are filled with articles pertinent to this topic.

Parents without Partners, Inc. 8807 Colesville Rd., Silver Springs, MD 20910. National organization with more than 300 local chapters that provides support for single parents.

BIBLIOGRAPHY

Adams, F. *Mushy Eggs.* Illus. by Marilyn Hirsch. Putnam 1973. (Ages 3–8.) David and Sam live in New York with their mother, a computer operator, and their wonderful baby-sitter, Fanny, while their father lives in New Jersey. When the boys learn that Fanny is going away, they become very sad. In this story of a family after a divorce, the mother functions well, and the children are cooperative and understanding.

Adler, C.S. *The Silver Coach.* Coward, McCann & Geoghegan, 1979. (Ages 9–12). Chris and her younger sister Jackie spend the summer with their paternal grandmother. Their parents are divorced, and this summer marks their acceptance of the situation.

Anderson, P. S. *A Pretty Good Team.* Children's Press, 1979. (Ages 6–8.) Jeff senses something is wrong between his parents. Then the mother, preoccupied with her own problems, blurts out to Jeff that she and his father are going to get a divorce. The discussion section at the end of the book is very useful.

Avi. *Sometimes I Think I Hear My Name.* Pantheon, 1982. (Ages 11 and up.) Conrad's aunt and uncle try to protect him from finding out that he lives with them because his divorced parents really do not want him. When both his parents demonstrate that they are incapable of giving him love and security, he finally accepts himself and his situation. Part of the plot involves Conrad's relationship with a lonely, angry and rejected young girl whose upper-class parents are emotionally abusive.

Bailey, M. *The Facts about Single-Parent Families.* Crestwood, 1989. (Ages 8–10.) [See Family Constellations]

Banks, A. *When Your Parents Get a Divorce: A Kid's Journal.* Illus. by C. Bobak. Puffin, 1990. (Ages 7–10.) A useful workbook for helping children vent their feelings and understand that they are not alone in their emotions. Questions and activities include such items as comparing the mother's home with the father's, listing people they can talk to, and determining what makes them happy. The message to parents at the end of the journal succinctly summarizes good, practical advice. Unfortunately, the cartoonlike illustrations picture predominately white, middle-class children in limited family constellations. This can be partially offset by having readers draw their own illustrations.

Bauer, M. D. *Face to Face.* Clarion, 1991. (Ages 11 and up.) [See Family Constellations]

Baum, L. *One More Time.* Illus. by P. Bouma. Morrow, 1986. (Ages 5–8.) Simon and his father experience a wonderful day together. At the end of the story, the father deposits Simon at home and leaves to return to his own separate place. Only then is it clear that Simon's father spends Sundays with him as part of a custody arrangement.

Berger, T. *How Does It Feel When Your Parents Get Divorced?* Illus. by M. Shapiro. Messner, 1977. (Ages 8-12.) Sensitive photographs help illustrate a child's feelings about divorce. Although not in story form, the book is easy to read and excellent for children eight years old and up as it states and explores real feelings.

Blue, R. *A Month of Sundays.* Illus. by T. Lewin. Watts, 1972. (Ages 8-10.) When Jeff's parents divorce, he moves to New York with his mother. With the help of Matthew and his adopted mother, Jeff begins to enjoy city life and gets used to his new situation. A useful book for children who feel that divorce and a change of lifestyle signal the end of the world.

Blume, J. *It's Not the End of the World.* Bradbury, 1972. (Ages 10-12.) Karen and her sister and brother try to get their parents back together and worry about whether their parents love them. A friend whose parents are also divorced introduces Gardner's book, *The Boys and Girls Book about Divorce,* to Karen.

Boegehold, B. *Daddy Doesn't Live Here Anymore: A Book about Divorce.* Illus. by D. Borgo. Western, 1985. (Ages 4-7.) A note to parents advises how to help children weather a divorce. Casey goes through the stages of denial, bargaining, anger, guilt, and grief. She acts out her feelings by playing with dolls. The ending leaves some unfinished business, and that is all to the good.

Boyd, L. *Sam is My Half Brother.* Illus. by the author. Viking, 1990. (Ages 3-6.) [See Family Constellations]

Brown, L. K., and Brown, M. *Dinosaurs Divorce.* Illus. by the authors. Little, Brown, 1986. (Ages 5-10.) Important information and attitudes are conveyed in this deceptively light-hearted look at divorce. The characters are dinosaurs, and the format is like a comic book. Such messages as "You are not to blame" and "Look for ways to show anger that don't hurt yourself or others" are made accessible to a wide age range with diverse problems.

Cain, B., and Bemedek, E. *What Would You Do? A Child's Book about Divorce.* Saturday Evening Post, 1976. (Ages 6-8.) This book deals with questions a child may have about divorce and with concomitant problems such as moving, entering a new school, and making new friends.

Caines, J. *Daddy.* Illus. by R. Himler. Harper, 1977. (Ages 6-8.) A sensitive book about an African-American child whose father comes to get her each Saturday. The anxiety of the transition is described, as are the pleasures of the time spent with Daddy and his new mate, Paula.

Christianson, C. B. *My Mother's House, My Father's House.* Illus. by I. Trivas. Atheneum, 1989. (Ages 5-8.) Joint custody is explored in this story, where the child shuttles back and forth from one parent to the other every three or four days. The situation is understandably difficult for the child, and she wistfully dreams of a time when she can stay in her own place all the time and enjoy visits from her parents.

Cleary, B. *Dear Mr. Henshaw.* Illus. by P. O. Zelinsky. Morrow, 1983. (Ages 8-11.) Ten-year-old Leigh Botts writes regularly to his favorite author, Mr. Henshaw. He takes the author's advice and begins a diary. Through his writing, we understand Leigh's feelings about his parents' divorce, his difficulties at school, and his wishes and dreams. All this is told humorously and sensitively in this compelling book. In the sequel, *Strider* (1991), Leigh continues to write in his diary and to let the reader in on his development as a person and his reaction to his parents' divorce. A dog named Strider, abandoned by his owner, helps Leigh in his recovery from feelings of abandonment by his father.

Clifton, L. *Everett Anderson's Year.* Illus. by A. Grifalconi. Holt, 1974. (Ages 4-8.) Reinforces the loving world that Everett lives in. His mother manages well, even though the father has left them. Everett, who misses but still loves his father, is also coping well.

Dragonwagon, C. *Always, Always.* Illus. by A. Zeldich. Macmillan, 1984. (Ages 6-9.) A young girl spends summers in Colorado roughing it with her father and the rest of the year in New York with her sophisticated mother. Despite the differences in their lifestyles and values, both parents love their daughter. She recognizes this and adjusts well to their divorce and to their expectations of her.

Fleming, A. *Welcome to Grossville.* Scribner, 1985. (Ages 9-11.) Michael and Jenny's lives are changed by the sudden news that their parents are divorcing and that they must move to a new town, a smaller house, and diminished financial comfort. The move is difficult for Michael until he makes friends and starts coping with the fact of the divorce. Along with Michael and his sister, readers can build a repertoire of coping strategies.

Fox, P. *The Moonlight Man.* Bradbury, 1986. (Ages 12 and up.) [See Abuse]

Gardner, R. A. *The Boys and Girls Book about Divorce.* Illus. by A. Lowenheim. Science House, 1970. (Ages 12 and up.) Written by a child psychiatrist, this book discusses a child's feelings about divorce. It provides many practical suggestions for adjustment to the new situation. The author confronts all the problems realistically. His advice is reasonable and helpful.

Girard, L. W. *At Daddy's on Saturdays.* Illus. by J. Friedman. Whitman, 1987. (Ages 4-6.) This book provides a fine model for children and parents in dealing with divorce. The parents are clear in their communication with Katie. They promise that they will always tell her the truth and will always love her, although they no longer love each other. They relieve her of any feelings of guilt and arrange for her to see her father regularly. They do not expect her to be free of hurt, but they do the best they can.

Glass, S. M. *A Divorce Dictionary: A Book for You and Your Children.* Little, Brown, 1980. (Ages 10 and up.) This text defines and explains vocabulary associated with divorce and shows how each term applies in actual circumstances through anecdotes and case histories.

Glenn, M. "Jason Talmadge." In *Class Dismissed: High School Poems.* Illus. by M. Bernstein. Clarion, 1982. (Ages 11 and up.) Jason feels unwanted by both his birth father and his stepfather. He thinks bitterly that his parents want to exclude him from their lives.

Glenn, M. "Richie Miller." In *Class Dismissed: High School Poems.* Illus. by M. Bernstein. Clarion, 1982. (Ages 11 and up.) The bickering in Richie's house is constant. His parents threaten each other with divorce but never follow through. The home atmosphere is tense and ugly.

Goff, B. *Where Is Daddy? The Story of a Divorce.* Illus. by S. Perl. Beacon, 1969. (Ages 4-7.) A little girl who cannot understand her parents' divorce blames herself and fears that her mother will not come back whenever she goes off to work. Gradually her mother and grandmother help her to accept the new situation and stop blaming herself. Parents will also find this book informative and useful.

Greenfield, E. *Talk about a Family.* Illus. by J. Calvin. Lippincott, 1978. (Ages 10 and up.) [See Siblings]

Hazen, B. S. *Two Homes to Live In: A Child's-Eye View of Divorce.* Illus. by P. Luks. Human Sciences, 1978. (Ages 4-8.) Niki comes to accept that although her parents have divorced no one has divorced her. She also discovers that many children's parents are divorced and it is acceptable to have pajamas in two places.

Helmering, D. W. *I Have Two Families.* Illus. by H. Palmer. Abingdon, 1981. (Ages 5-8.) Patty and Michael experience normal anxieties when their parents divorce. They live with their father but regularly visit their mother and her new partner. Both parents love and care about them. Their adjustment seems complete.

Hurwitz, J. *DeDe Takes Charge*. Illus. by D. de Groat. Morrow, 1984. (Ages 8-10.) DeDe loves both her parents dearly and tries to prevent their divorce, but it is not the catastrophe DeDe feared. Both parents are portrayed with flaws, but both care about their daughter. The mother fares well after the divorce.

Ives, S. B.; Fassler, D.; and Lash, M. *The Divorce Workbook*. Waterfront, 1985. (Ages 5-8.) Filled with good, practical ideas for children to vent their feelings and adopt some coping strategies. Helpful information about the legalities of divorce is also included.

Jayanti, A. *Silas and the Mad-Sad People*. Illus. by E. Beier. New Seed, 1981. (Ages 5-8.) Silas hates that his mother and father fight all the time. He is confused and angry. Both parents care deeply about Silas and explain carefully to him what is going to happen because his father is moving out of their house. Finally, Silas understands better about grownups and their problems and accepts reassurance that his parents will continue to love him despite their permanent separation. The book is didactic, but it serves as a good model for parents to talk to their children.

Kindred, W. *Lucky Wilma*. Illus. by the author. Dial, 1973. (Ages 4-8.) Wilma and her father Charlie spend every Saturday together. They visit museums and parks and play lovingly and happily together. At the end of each Saturday, Wilma's father returns to his own house and Wilma goes home to her mother. The book demonstrates that children need not be miserable because of parents' divorcing.

Krementz, J. *How It Feels When Parents Divorce*. Knopf, 1984. (Ages 8 and up.) As with her other books of interviews, the author has captured young people's feelings with depth and detail. Nineteen children of varying backgrounds express their views and experiences. Many problems are aired, pain is uncovered, and issues are explored.

LeShan, E. *What's Going to Happen to Me?* Four Winds, 1978. (All ages.) A guide for children whose parents separate or divorce. It addresses divorce honestly, looks at feelings of all kinds, and makes suggestions for coping, along with a "further reading" section. LeShan acknowledges that divorce is a painful and frightening experience for children. She underlines the importance of being aware of children's feelings.

Lexau, J. *Emily and the Klunky Baby and the Next-Door Dog*. Illus. by M. Alexander. Dial, 1972. (Ages 5-8.) A young girl resents her little brother and becomes upset that her divorced mother cannot pay more attention to her, so she attempts to run away to her father's house. Her mother expects too much from her, and the pressure is more than the child can tolerate. When the mother recognizes the problem, she sets aside her own work to attend to her children.

Livingston, M. C. *There Was a Place and Other Poems*. McElderry, 1988. (Ages 8-12.) A number of poems in this short but effective collection allude to divorce. In one, a child remembers a time when both parents were together and happily smiling and wonders what happened to change their lives. Another underscores the importance of not calling any family "broken"; as long as the people consider themselves a family unit, they are intact. Other poems deal with custody, missing the absent parent, and blended families. The author is a talented poet with a fine sense of children's feelings.

Mann, P. *My Dad Lives in a Downtown Hotel*. Illus. by R. Cuffari. Doubleday, 1973. (Ages 8-12.) Joey blames himself for his parents' divorce, but after spending time with his father, talking with his mother, and finding a friend who also has no father living at home, Joey accepts the situation more calmly.

Mazer, N. F. *I, Trissy*. Delacorte, 1971. (Ages 9-12.) Trissy blames her mother for her parents' divorce. Eventually, she begins to be able to see both herself and her parents in a realistic light. She behaves in a very self-centered manner throughout the entire book. She, not her parents, is the cause of problems in the aftermath of the divorce. Her parents' understanding provides a base for her to build a more mature and responsible way of behaving.

Miner, J. C. *Split Decision: Facing Divorce.* Illus. by Vista III Design. Fearon, 1982. (Ages 10 and up.) Ann tries desperately to reunite her divorcing parents. When she fails, she demands joint custody in the hope that she will help them resolve their differences. She does not succeed, but the parents manage to become civil to each other and take Ann's feelings into consideration. The situation is didactically but realistically described.

Moore, E. *Something to Count On.* Dutton, 1980. (Ages 9–12.) Lorraine and Jason's parents separate. The children blame themselves. Lorraine, a bright, talented, but disruptive fifth grader narrates this story about separation, family life, friendship, and the difference a good teacher can make. Most of all, the book helps readers understand the feelings and responses of a seemingly unmanageable child.

Morris, J. K. *The Crazies and Sam.* Penguin, 1983. (Ages 10–12.) Sam is a casualty of divorce. His father, with whom he lives, is overly structured and distracted, and his mother places a higher priority on her job than on Sam's feelings and needs. Sam engages in some self-destructive behavior by attaching himself to an emotionally disturbed woman. As a result, he is held in her apartment against his will. When Sam finally escapes and returns to his father (who promises to pay more attention to him), he recognizes that he must accept both his parents as they are and try to manage his own life in a more balanced fashion. This book helps to expose the painful truth that there is not always a happy resolution after a divorce and that children bear a great portion of the responsibility for their own successful adjustment.

Newfield, M. *A Book for Jodan.* Illus. by D. de Groat. Atheneum, 1975. (Ages 6–10.) Jodan is heartsick at her parents' divorce though they both reassure her that they love her. She and her mother move to California; her father remains in Massachusetts. At the end of a holiday visit, her father gives her a special book that he has made. It recalls their happy times together and serves as a secure reminder of her father's love.

Nickman, S. L. *When Mom and Dad Divorce.* Illus. by D. de Groat. Messner, 1986. (Ages 10 and up.) Through the vehicle of seven stories on various aspects and stages of divorce, the psychiatrist-author suggests coping strategies and advises children of their rights. His tone is sympathetic and practical.

Norris, G. *Lillian.* Atheneum, 1968. (Ages 8–12.) Lillian's parents divorce, and she is afraid her mother will stop loving her now that she is so busy with her job. With her mother's help, Lillian grows more self-reliant and self-confident and less fearful. Readers will find their own anxieties mirrored in this book.

Okimoto, J. D. *My Mother Is Not Married to My Father.* Putnam, 1980. (Ages 7–10.) Cynthia and her younger sister make an excellent adjustment to their parents' divorce and their mother's subsequent dating.

Orgel, D. *Midnight Soup and a Witch's Hat.* Illus. by C. Newsom. Viking, 1987. (Ages 7–10.) The divorces and blended families in Becky's life are all very civilized. However, Becky resents the surprise she gets when she flies to a long-anticipated visit with her dad and finds his new mate's daughter, Hope, there to detract from the attention Becky wants exclusively from her dad. The adults in the story all try to be understanding and reasonable. Their efforts pay off.

Paris, L. *Mom Is Single.* Illus. by M. Christianson. Children's Press, 1980. (Ages 8–12.) A child describes the changes in his life since his parents' divorce. He shows some of his feelings of anger, fear, and resentment. The photographs emphasize that this is a realistic situation. The book ends on an accepting note.

Park, B. *Don't Make Me Smile.* Knopf, 1981. (Ages 9-12.) Charles is devastated when his parents decide to divorce. He compares divorce to helplessly watching a car smash your bicycle. "It's all smashed to pieces, and it will never be the same. It's too late. That's divorce." A psychiatrist helps Charlie say what's on his mind without yelling. His perceptions are humorously stated and hit the mark.

Park, B. *My Mother Got Married (And Other Disasters).* Knopf, 1989. (Ages 8-10.) [See Family Constellations]

Paulsen, G. *Hatchet.* Bradbury, 1987. (Ages 12 and up.) Brian is upset because he has seen his mother embracing a man before she and his father were separated, and he obsesses over that as the cause for his parents' divorce. On his way to visit his father, he is stranded in the Canadian wilderness by a plane crash and must survive on his wits and ingenuity. In the end, he returns to his mother and learns to cope with his father's somewhat neglectful ways. The story is a dramatic adventure, not only of physical survival but also of understanding the frailties of one's parents. Although some of the language is graphic, it is appropriate to the context of this well-crafted novel.

Peck, R. *Father Figure.* Viking, 1978. (Ages 11 and up.) [See Death]

Pfeffer, S. B. *Dear Dad, Love Laurie.* Scholastic, 1989. (Ages 8-11.) Although Laurie has fairly well recovered from her parents' divorce, she is upset that her mother is dating. She is also angry and jealous because her friend has been accepted into a program for gifted and talented children and she has not. The book consists of Laurie's letters to her dad, who has moved to Missouri. Laurie's mother and father maintain a friendly and mutually respectful relationship. No blaming is even hinted at in this book, which reflects many children's feelings and anxieties. The story provides a model of how successful a divorce can be. The humor, screamingly funny at times, enhances the plot; and the characters emerge as real and sympathetic. Unfortunately, the author does not pay as much attention to the needs of reporting accurately about gifted students or programs for the gifted.

Pfeffer, S. B. *Make Believe.* Holt, 1993. (Ages 9-12). Jill and Carrie have been best friends all their lives, as have their parents. When Jill's father announces that he wants a divorce and moves in with the young woman he now loves, the friendships are seriously threatened. It is difficult for Carrie to understand her friend's behavior, and it is impossible for Carrie's mother to understand her husband's seeming openness to maintaining his friendship with Jill's dad. The book reveals how friends can help when a child's world is disrupted by divorce. It also reflects the many perspectives and positions of people involved in a divorce.

Platt, K. *Chloris and the Creeps.* Chilton, 1973. (Ages 12 and up.) Chloris cannot accept her parents' divorce, her father's subsequent suicide, or her mother's dating and eventual remarriage. She is hateful and destructive to her mother and stepfather. Through therapy and patience, Chloris's mother, sister, and stepfather nurture her to a point where she may be able to change her attitude and behavior.

Pomerantz, B. *Who Will Lead Kiddush?* Illus. by D. Ruff. Union of American Hebrew Congregations, 1985. (Ages 5-8.) The story revolves around a Jewish couple who divorce but retain their involvement with Jewish ritual. The father phones his daughter every evening and visits her several times a week. He shares Sabbath with her every other week, and gives her a kiddush cup so that she will think of him every time she makes the blessing over wine. The religious observance strengthens this family even in its new configuration.

Pursell, M. S. *A Look at Divorce.* Illus. by M. S. Forrai. Lerner, 1977. (Ages 6–10.) Photos and text combine to present a matter-of-fact look at divorce, addressing changes in parents' feelings and family patterns. Reassuring comments for young readers predict eventual better family relationships.

Richard, A., and Willis, I. *How to Get It Together When Your Parents Are Coming Apart.* Willard, 1988. (Ages 11 and up.) Interviews with young people make up most of the book. Separate sections address various issues such as marital problems, the divorce process, and adjustment after the divorce. Various sources for help are listed.

Rofes, E., ed. *The Kids' Book of Divorce.* Lewis, 1981. (Ages 8 and up.) Twenty students, ages 11 to 14, of Cambridge's Fayerweather Street School discuss various aspects of divorce, including custody arrangements, and how they were first told about their parents' divorce. This book's impact lies in the faithful reproduction of children's words as they respond to divorce and describe how they feel.

Ruby, L. *Pig-out Inn.* Houghton Mifflin, 1987. (Ages 10 and up.) Dovi Chandler's mother has taken over a truck stop in a small town in Kansas. Tag, a nine-year-old boy, is left there, apparently abandoned by his father. Tag's parents are involved in a custody battle. His father has kidnapped the boy and is now trying to evade the police. In the end, joint custody is awarded, and Tag has the best of all possible worlds. Although the story is written in a light style, some of the issues are heavy. Everyone's perspective is presented fairly, and no harsh judgments are made.

Savitz, H. M. *Swimmer.* Apple, 1986. (Ages 7–10.) Skipper's whole life changes when his father moves out of their house, which now must become a boarding house so that Skipper and his mother can survive economically. When his father moves to New York and each parent argues for custody, Skipper is torn. He finally decides to stay with his mother.

Schuchman, J. *Two Places to Sleep.* Illus. by J. LaMarche. Carolrhoda, 1979. (Ages 5–10.) A seven-year-old boy lives with his father after his parents are divorced, and has trouble accepting the situation, although he visits his mother on weekends. He is just beginning to adjust to his new lifestyle and needs reassurance that he is still loved. This book might be especially helpful for a child living with a single male parent.

Severance, J. *When Megan Went Away.* Illus. by T. Schook. Lollipop Power, 1979. (Ages 7–12.) Shannon and her mother are unhappy because Megan, her mother's lover, has left. The feelings a child experiences when one of the nurturing adults in the house has left are well stated. The difference here is that it involves a lesbian relationship.

Sinberh, J. *Divorce Is a Grown-Up Problem.* Illus. by N. Gray, Avon, 1978. (Ages 3–8.) This book is written to help young children better understand their reactions to the divorce of their parents. Feelings such as fear, anger, sadness, alienation, and confusion are acknowledged. The book ends on the reassuring note that both parents still love the child. The author includes a brief preface for parents and some helpful advice for coping with the situation.

Sitea, L. "Zachary's Divorce," in *Free to Be You and Me,* ed. by C. Hart. McGraw-Hill, 1974. (Ages 5–8.) The aftermath of divorce is described through the eyes of Zachary, a young boy. He feels as if *he* has been divorced. His mother is supportive, understanding, and coping. Zachary feels very much out of control and dominated by the grown-up world, but time will pass and he will begin to feel better. A very useful little story.

Slepian, J. *Getting on with It.* Four Winds, 1985. (Ages 11 and up.) Berry stays with her grandmother while her parents are arranging for a divorce. She has difficulty understanding the situation because her parents have never fought. She becomes more aware of life's complexities and unlearns many stereotypes during the course of the summer. Some of the other issues in the book are old age, the Holocaust, and sexuality.

Smith, D. B. *The First Hard Times*. Viking, 1983. (Ages 10 and up.) Ancil resents her new stepfather and her family's acceptance of him. Her friend Lloyd helps her to cope.

Smith, R. K. *The Squeaky Wheel*. Delacorte, 1990. (Ages 10-12.) Mark is a likable boy who makes friends easily and gets along well in school. His parents' divorce has shattered his once-idyllic life, but at the end of the book it looks as if Mark will be happy again. Most of the occurrences are believable, except for the mother's gesture of inviting the father to join them for Thanksgiving just to please Mark. Otherwise, the author takes into consideration the difficulties everyone must endure as a result of the decision to divorce. The characters and the intricacies of the plot are workable, and the coping strategies are reasonable and helpful.

Sobol, H. L. *My Other-Mother, My Other-Father*. Illus. by P. Agre. Macmillan, 1979. (Ages 10 and up.) Andrea tells how she feels about being a stepchild and about the advantages and disadvantages of having two sets of parents. Her relationships seem to work out fine, making this a very positive book. The photographs show good interaction among all parties involved.

Spilke, F. S. *The Family That Changed: A Child's Book about Divorce*. Illus. by T. O'Sullivan. Crown, 1979. (Ages 5-8.) The book helps parents to inform their preschoolers about divorce. Very much an introduction to impending divorce, the book anticipates anxieties and fears.

Stanek, M. *I Won't Go without a Father*. Illus. by E. Mill. Whitman, 1972. (Ages 6-9.) Steve is angry and jealous of anyone who has a father. However, with the support of his uncle and grandfather he learns to become less defensive and more accepting of his family situation.

Stevenson, L. C. *Happily After All*. Houghton Mifflin, 1990. (Ages 8-12.) When Rebecca's adored father dies, she is stunned to learn that she must now live with her mother Rachel who, Rebecca has been told, deserted her when she was a baby. Gradually, the truth emerges: Her father kidnapped her, lied, and used his influence as a prominent attorney to deny custody to Rachel. Rebecca must adjust not only to her father's death but also to an entirely new lifestyle with her mother. The author provides detailed and insightful portraits of each of the characters, even the minor ones. The issues of bereavement, sudden change, and adjustment to different people and circumstances are well drawn. The subplot of a foster child who is exploited and abused by his father adds dimension to the story. Although all is settled rather neatly in the end, the resolution is believable.

Stinson, K. *Mom and Dad Don't Live Together Any More*. Illus. by N. L. Reynolds. Annick, 1984. (Ages 4-6.) Aimed at young children, this story conveys the feelings of anxiety spurred by the fact of parental divorce. The book deals with vacations, custody, parents' new relationships, and what will happen when the children grow up. It also reassures children that their fears can be addressed and that they can be safe and happy.

Stolz, M. *Leap before You Look*. Harper, 1975. (Ages 12 and up.) Jimmie adores her father and resents his remarriage. Living with her mother, brother, and grandmother and aided by her friend Chris, who is bothered by several divorces in her family, Jimmie gradually adjusts to the situation and becomes reconciled with her father.

Surowiecki, S. L. *Joshua's Day*. Illus. by P. R. Vevitrall. Lollipop Power, 1972. (Ages 3-6.) Joshua, who lives with his mother, goes to a day-care center while she works. She is coping well without a husband, and Joshua seems fine.

Vigna, J. *Grandma without Me.* Illus. by the author. Whitman, 1984. (Ages 4-8.) Although a young boy is attached to his paternal grandmother, he is somewhat cut off from her when his parents divorce. They correspond with each other and try in many ways to make the best of this bad situation, but it is difficult. The book demonstrates the importance of thinking about the impact of divorce on the extended family.

Vigna, J. *Mommy and Me by Ourselves Again.* Illus. by the author. Whitman, 1987. (Ages 5-8.) Amy's parents are divorced and her father never comes to see her. Now her mother's boyfriend, Gary, has left. Amy and her mother both miss Gary, and Amy fears more desertions in her young life. Her mother tries to explain how difficult it is to establish a successful relationship, but she is still hopeful.

Voigt, C. *A Solitary Blue.* Atheneum, 1983. (Ages 12 and up.) Jeff's mother Melody has deserted him and his father, ostensibly to help unfortunate people in the world. In reality, Melody is beautiful and charming but dishonest and superficial. When the divorce is finalized and Melody sues for custody, Jeff elects to stay with his father. The story tells of the process both Jeff and his father engage in, with the help of friends, to develop a loving relationship. Although Jeff has been neglected by both parents, after he and his father are emotionally united, Jeff is able to become independent and strong.

White, A. S. *Divorce.* Illus. by G. Giles. Watts, 1979. (Ages 8 and up.) A frank book on the mechanics and terminology of divorce. The text deals with feelings, the law, and the courts.

chapter 4

Family Constellations

In early colonial times, the American family was the major manufacturer of food, clothing, and household goods. Furthermore, the family home was workplace, hospital, and school. No other source of social stability was as strong as the family. The structure of the seventeenth-century family of European origin was generally patriarchal, with the father as the acknowledged authority and head of the household.

The multifaceted nature of the population affected the structure of the family. As Steven Mintz and Susan Kellogg report, the Native American peoples were composed of more than two hundred distinct groups, "each with its own political structures, language, economy, and patterns of family and kinship." African-American families were controlled by the laws governing slavery in the colonies.

In the seventeenth century, many harsh restrictions were imposed on free blacks, as well as slaves; and in colonies like Virginia, regulations prohibited them from entering into contracts of marriage. Nevertheless, slaves established strong family and extended kinship systems. Families told stories and passed music, crafts, and medical knowledge on to their children. The inhumane practice among plantation owners of separating and selling family members resulted in a communal sense of family, where every black adult was responsible for nurturing the children. Older black men were called "Uncle"; women were called "Aunt"; and the young people were all brothers and sisters. Despite deliberate attempts to destroy slaves' sense of family, they managed to engage in the rituals of courtship, the rites of marriage, and the rearing of children.

The eighteenth and nineteenth centuries brought about changes in the family as grown children moved away from their family farm and therefore ceased to be dependent on their parents for economic survival. This led to a decrease in parental control over the marriages of their children and a change in the concept of marriage as a property settlement or economic arrangement between the parents of the couple.

As the economic situation of the country changed, so too did the social and educational climate. The Industrial Revolution influenced the way people lived, furnished their homes, and earned their livings. With the growth of cities, a variety of specialized public institutions such as almshouses, free public schools, and artisans' workshops began taking on some of the responsibilities heretofore reserved to the family.

The nineteenth century saw the rise of a new white middle class, and with it a sense of the family as a haven for parents and children, with the father as breadwinner and the mother as caretaker and decision maker for the children's upbringing. Childhood and dependency were prolonged. Intimacy and affection among family members were encouraged as part of this new family entity. Immigrant groups came in larger numbers and joined the working class, often as family groups all working at the same mill or factory. This century was also the setting for a different idea of the rights of women. More women were employed, permitted property rights, and granted a greater degree of freedom than they had had before. Divorce laws became more flexible.

Family constellations have been changing rapidly since the beginning of the twentieth century. Class differences, ethnic influences, economic circumstances, the "sexual revolution," a dramatic rise in single-parent families, a movement from the concept of the parent-as-authority to a more flexible and permissive role, the influence of media such as film and television, and the opening of more and more options for lifestyle have all influenced the design and function of the family.

Today a definition of family can range from two parents, one male and one female, living together with one or more children (the nuclear family) to any number of people of any age or sex who choose to live together and nurture one another. The extended family can range from biological kin to a network of concerned and loving people. The literature for children reflects this evolution. In the past decade, books have depicted a number of family constellations in addition to the nuclear. Single-parent families with either mothers or fathers as heads of the household, extended families, communes, single parent mothers who were never married, blended families with multiples of stepparents and step-siblings, same-sex parents, and families where children are living with relatives other than their parents appear with some degree of frequency.

SUGGESTED CRITERIA

Libraries containing books that reflect a variety of lifestyles and family configurations best serve their clients. Even when a community contains a preponderance of conventional families, children should be able to read about the wider world. Nontraditional families should be depicted respectfully, not as though they are oddities to be deprecated. Authors should refrain from passing judgment on any particular family constellation; if there is conduct to be censured, it should occur in the context of the story rather than as a blanket condemnation of a particular lifestyle. Nontraditional families should not always be used as vehicles for presenting problems. Different choices of lifestyle should be appreciated. Marriage should not always constitute the happy ending to a single parent's dilemmas.

Characters should be three-dimensional; no person should be totally evil or good. Stereotypes should be avoided (such as the "typical" harried single mother or inept father.) All family members, including grandparents, should be people in their own right who exhibit behavior consistent with their individual personalities in the context of the story.

Large families are not necessarily noisy or poor; small families are not always lonely or affluent. A balance should be represented through the literature.

Blended families are shaped in many ways and have multiple interactions. A library collection should represent this variety.

Wherever possible, the positive and negative aspects of family life should be balanced. Members of different ethnic groups should be shown in a variety of family settings and patterns, as should inhabitants of urban or rural areas and people of varying ages and different economic standings.

Stepparents should have virtues as well as flaws; they should not automatically be classified as wicked or beneficent.

Happy endings where all conflict is resolved forever are neither realistic outcomes nor good literature. The process of working out conflicts should be included whenever solutions are effected. Change should take time and not occur without cause. Emotions should be expressed, honored, and dealt with.

Try This

Find one picture book, one novel, and one fairy or folk tale dealing with families. Prepare a critique of each according to the above criteria. Discuss what comments you would make to young readers if the book falls short in any areas or if it adheres to all the criteria.

DISCUSSION OF CHILDREN'S BOOKS

Single-Parent Families

Nonfiction depicting the normalcy and the pleasant aspects of single-parent families can be excellent adjuncts to stories about fictitious families. Marilyn Bailey's *The Facts about Single-Parent Families,* and Sara Gilbert's *How to Live with a Single Parent* contain advice and information that can enlighten children living with a single parent, as well as peers who may be experiencing other configurations.

Brendan's Best-Timed Birthday, by Deborah Gould, presents young readers with a picture of a wonderfully competent single father. Lee Bennett Hopkins's *Mama* is also competent; but because of the family's serious economic difficulties, she often resorts to shoplifting to provide her sons with what she thinks they should have. Cynthia Rylant offers adolescent readers a special relationship between Anne, a single mother, and her son Chip in *A Kindness.* Their relationship is threatened when Anne becomes pregnant, decides to bear the child, and refuses to disclose anything about the father of her unborn child. Readers' empathy flows to both the boy and his mother, and the story ends without cliché resolutions but with Chip's awareness that he is not responsible for his mother's life. This complex situation offers readers many perspectives on sensitive issues.

Several books include well-functioning single-parent families where the parent is in fact a grandfather. Mary Stolz's *Storm in the Night* and *Go Fish* describe a loving and mutually supportive relationship between a child and his grandfather. Pat Cummings's illustrations portraying the characters as African Americans adds to the universality of the situation. *Stone Fox,* by John Reynolds Gardiner, contributes another instance where a grandfather and grandson constitute the family.

Blended Families

Some stories show the difficulties of living with new stepparents and stepsiblings. The title of Barbara Park's *My Mother Got Married (and Other Disasters)* signals the emotional tone of the book. In this story, Charlie eventually feels somewhat more positive but fears that his mother no longer cares about him. His feelings will strike a chord with many readers. In *The Not-So-Wicked Stepmother,* by Lizi Boyd, Hessie is worried that she will be disloyal to her birth mother, with whom she lives most of the time, if she succumbs to liking her stepmother. Conflicting loyalties are often an issue in this sort of situation. For her book, *Talking about Stepfamilies,* Maxine B. Rosenberg interviewed a number of stepchildren from children through adults to discover their feelings about blended families. Their responses were mixed, but they agreed that their situation caused them to think seriously at an early age about how families were constituted.

Extended Families

Families with several branches that consist of grandparents, as well as cousins, aunts, and uncles, abound in the literature. Virginia Hamilton makes clear the importance of family ties in *Cousins,* offering readers the opportunity to know several members of an African-American family in Ohio. Carmen Lomas Garza, mostly through her paintings, shares her memories of her Mexican-American family in *Family Pictures; Cuadros de Familia.* Elizabeth Fitzgerald Howard's stories, set in Baltimore about fifty years ago (including *Aunt Flossie's Hats (and Crab Cakes Later),* are flavored with the tang of the extended family.

In *Tallahassee Higgins* by Mary Downing Hahn, the title character would be in sad shape if her aunt and uncle did not agree to take her in after her mother decides to go off with the latest of her lovers. In Patricia MacLachlan's *Arthur for the Very First Time,* Arthur learns much about himself at the rural home of his great aunt and uncle. The six-year-old child in Arnold Adoff's *Hard to Be Six* is fortunate indeed to have an extended family willing to listen to him and sympathize with his concerns. In *The Wednesday Surprise,* by Eve Bunting, a young child is able to teach her grandmother to read without impinging on the grandmother's dignity or sense of competence, proving that support can be a two-way street.

Extended families come in all colors and shapes in the literature. They offer not only a model of how a supportive community works but also a chance for children to try out their intergenerational communication skills and to develop an appreciation of points of view other than their own.

Folk and Fairy Tales

No specific folk or fairy tales are included in this chapter's bibliography because these tales contain family situations symbolically designed to represent archetypes or symbols. Stepparents are usually wicked; parents are disposed of in order to permit the child to become the adventuring hero; siblings represent wickedness versus good, and the youngest child generally illustrates the forces of virtue. If parents survive, they are all giving and loving; there are rarely grandparents, cousins, aunts, or uncles. Children might be invited to invent families for any of the fairy or folk characters they encounter. They might then weave stories around these characters so as to involve the families.

Loving, helpful, communicative families exist in stories alongside nasty, abusive, closed-mouthed relatives. When reading stories that focus on family relations, adults do well to invite children to talk about their own families and compare them to those in the books. Children should not be urged to reveal family secrets but to see how the book-families measure up to reality and how, if possible, they can serve as models or barometers for real behavior.

REFERENCES

Family Constellations

Achtenberg, R. *Preserving and Protecting the Families of Lesbians and Gay Men.* National Center for Lesbian Rights, 1990. Provides clear information, both legal and social, on issues regarding gay and lesbian families. The topics discussed are child custody and visitation, including adoption and foster care, and the rights of gay and lesbian partners regarding benefits, legally recognized marriage, and access to the partner in case of illness or death.

Atkinson, J. "The Portrayal of Parents in Young Adult Fiction: Authors Have Their Say." *Journal of Youth Services in Libraries* 1 (Spring 1988): 310-320. Several authors of fiction for young adults comment on their treatment of adolescents as part of a larger family. The writer of the article decries critics who insist on their own standards for evaluating these works and defends focusing on adolescent needs, concerns, and tasks.

Bracken, J., and Wigutoff, S., with Baker, I. *Books for Today's Young Readers: An Annotated Bibliography of Recommended Fiction for Ages 10-14.* Feminist Press, 1981. [See Chapter 1]

Bunkers, S. "We're not the Cleavers: Images of Nontraditional Families in Children's Literature." *The Lion and the Unicorn* 16 (June 1992): 115-133. After making the case for children's books reflecting the diversity of families in contemporary America, the author discusses more than 60 books on divorced families, single-parent families, extended families, adoption and foster care, and lesbian or gay parents.

Burner, J. "All in the Family: Parents in Teen Fiction." *School Library Journal* 35 (Nov. 1989): 42-43. Reviews several young adult novels in which adolescents grapple with their sense of family ties.

Ciborowski, P. J. *Survival Skills for Single Parents!* Focus on Parenthood Series. Stratmar Educational Systems, 1988. Presents helpful information regarding many daily living skills relating to single parenting. Includes ideas on dating, dealing with visitation, and custody issues.

Coleman, M.; Marshall, S. A.; and Ganong, L. "Beyond Cinderella: Relevant Reading for Young Adolescents about Stepfamilies." *Adolescence* 21 (Fall 1986): 553–560. Discusses the presence of stepchildren in today's classrooms and recommends the use of books to overcome stereotypes, invite empathy on the part of peers, and provide information to children who are experiencing the situation. Brief discussion of several books, more than 60 recommended books listed, as well as seven adult references.

Council on Interracial Books for Children. *Bulletin* (Special Issue on Parenting) 9 (1978). Contains several articles on child-rearing books and single parenting. Provides criteria, lists of resources, and book critiques.

Davidson, C. *Staying Home Instead: How to Quit the Working-Mom Rat Race and Survive Financially.* Heath, 1986. The author advocates that mothers stay at home rather than opting for careers outside the home. She refutes the idea that to work outside the home constitutes liberation, discusses the problems of career mothers and offers alternatives to nine-to-five jobs.

Dorn, L. *Peace in the Family: A Workbook of Ideas and Actions.* Pantheon, 1983. Addresses parental support groups, explores the role of the family as "the first and most influential educational arena," and provides activities for handling conflict.

Ehrensaft, D. *Parenting Together.* Free Press, 1987. The author wants to reach an audience of parents who *choose* to parent together, not those who feel forced to do so. She calls this the "mothering duet." She presents both the pitfalls and the advantages of dual parenting.

Gongla, P. A., and Thompson, E. H. Jr. "Single-Parent Families." In *Handbook of Marriage and the Family,* edited by M. B. Sussman and S. K. Steinmetz. Plenum, 1987. Presents thorough profile of single-parent families in terms of demographics, functioning, economics, social relationships, and effects of divorce on parents and children.

Greif, G. L. "Children and Housework in the Single Father Family." *Family Relations* 34 (July 1985): 353–57. Recommends that fathers encourage household help from sons as well as daughters. Discusses ways in which older children can participate in sharing responsibilities.

Greif, G. L. *Single Fathers.* Lexington, 1988. Presents fathers' perspectives on child rearing, household management, balancing careers. Compares responses of single fathers with those of single mothers.

Horner, C. T. *The Single-Parent Family in Children's Books: An Annotated Bibliography.* Scarecrow, 1988. Includes an annotated list of 622 children's books published between 1965 and 1986 pertaining to single-parent families.

Lodato, F. J. *Parenting Alone.* Sunday, 1986. Presents a psychological perspective on issues concerning single parents. Includes ways to deal with being left alone, sharing values with children, explaining sexual mores.

Miller, K. S. "Family Composition and Its Effect On the Behavior of Children." Doctoral dissertation, Emory University, 1989. Looks at various family compositions and their effects on how children behave. The author found that family composition did have some impact on the behavior problems some children exhibited.

Mintz, S., and Kellogg, S. *Domestic Revolutions: A Social History of American Family Life.* Free Press, 1988. Deals with changing definitions of family and with the evolution of the American family from the fundamental social unit to a loosely configured, diverse institution consisting of almost any grouping of two or more people domiciled together.

Packard, V. *Our Endangered Children: Growing Up in a Changing World.* Little, Brown, 1983. Probes the causes and conditions that lead to putting children at risk in today's society. Some concerns explored are single-parent families, inadequacy of caretakers, "latch-key" children, lack of interaction with a variety of adults, children's feeling of being a burden, unsafe neighborhoods, unpredictable eating arrangements, overuse of television as entertainment, and unskilled or self-absorbed parents, all leading to children's isolation, loneliness, and peril. The author makes recommendations and describes programs that counterbalance the risks.

Pardek, J. T., and Pardek, J. A. "Helping Children Cope with the Changing Family through Bibliotherapy." Paper presented at the Annual Meeting of Social Workers, New Orleans, La., Jan. 31–Feb. 3, 1985. Discusses the background and use of bibliotherapy as a way of helping children deal with issues that arise because of changes in the family. Includes a list of appropriate children's books.

Platt, P. *Survival Skills for a Weekend Father.* Orcas, 1987. Practical compendium of information for single fathers on child rearing, including school visits, holidays, and household management.

Schlesinger, B. *The One-Parent Family in the 1980s: Perspectives and Annotated Bibliography, 1978–1985.* 5th ed. University of Toronto Press, 1985. Extensive bibliography which includes Canadian and U.S. materials.

Schwarcz, J. H., and Schwarcz, C. "Love and Anxiety in the Supportive Family." In *The Picture Book Comes of Age: Looking at Childhood through the Art of Illustration,* American Library Association, 1991. A substantive discussion of how picture books reflect family relations. Many examples of picture books and their themes are provided.

Stewig, J. W. "Fathers: A Presence in Picture Books?" *Journal of Youth Services in Libraries* 1 (Summer 1988): 391–395. The words and content of 100 picture books selected at random (excluding alphabet, concept, and information books) were analyzed for their representation of men and their roles. Fathers appeared in fewer than half the books. There was a paucity of professional jobs or roles depicted, and only one grandfather was shown in a professional role. Fathers were shown performing personal tasks such as playing with children, giving advice, eating, and general caretaking; but few of these roles appeared often. The author recommends that more attention be paid in picture books to the roles of men, so that children may receive a sense of fathers' occupations and activities.

Swerdlow, A.; Bridenthal, R.; Kelly, J.; and Vine, P. *Household and Kin: Families in Flux.* Feminist Press, 1981. A reasoned and informative look at the contemporary family in flux, from a historical, anthropological, sociological, and psychological perspective. The authors explore the changing concepts of what a family is and how it may evolve in the future.

Wayman, A. *Successful Single Parenting: A Practical Guide.* Simon & Schuster, 1987. Practical suggestions for single parents in checklist format. Discussion includes money, dating, management, children's attitudes, and behavior.

Zwack, J. M. "The Stereotypic Family in Children's Literature." *The Reading Teacher* 26 (Jan. 1973): 389–391. The author is concerned about the lack of alternatives to the nuclear family as presented in children's books.

RESOURCES

Center for the Family in Transition. 5725 Paradise Dr., Corte Madera, CA 94925. Studies families in separation, divorce, and remarriage.

Child Welfare League of America. 440 First St. N.W., Suite 310, Washington, D.C. 20001. Publishes materials on standards for child welfare practice.

Family Research Council of America. 515 Second St. N.E., Washington, DC 20002. Includes professionals working in counseling, academia, or research concerning family issues. Provides family expertise to government agencies, members of Congress, the media, and the public. Publishes a newsletter.

Gay and Lesbian Parents Coalition International. Box 50360, Washington, DC 20004. Provides information on gay parenting and supports the passage of legislation to eliminate discrimination. Publishes a newsletter and a directory of support groups.

National Center for Lesbian Rights. 1663 Mission St., Suite 550, San Francisco, CA 94103. A legal resource center and national public-interest law firm working in the areas of adoption rights, domestic partner benefits, and child custody. Provides a multicultural network of lawyers, activists, and supporters; legal services; and advocacy on a national level, as well as publications and information on lesbian and gay family rights in the United States and Latin America. (Spanish telephone advice and newsletter available.)

National Council on Family Relations. 1910 W. County Rd. B, Suite 147, St. Paul, MN 55113. Members include organized groups, agencies, and family-life professionals. Disseminates information and research on families. Offers a national on-line bibliographic database. Publishes two journals, a newsletter, and a directory of members.

Parents without Partners. 8807 Colesville Rd., Silver Spring, MD 20910. [See Divorce]

Single Dad's Lifestyle. P.O. Box 4842, Scottsdale, AZ 85258. Publishes a magazine for single-parent fathers who have custody, wish to gain custody, or seek more meaningful visitation experiences. Also publishes an annual list of fathers' rights groups.

Sisterhood of Black Single Mothers. 1360 Fulton St., Suite 423, Brooklyn, NY 11216. Seeks to develop positive self-images in single mothers and acts as a referral service to assist members in seeking aid from institutions. Attempts to strengthen the black family through information, health care, and education. Publishes a newsletter.

Stepfamily Association of America. 602 East Joppa Rd., Baltimore, MD 21204. Serves as a national self-help and referral organization for stepparents. Provides educational materials and children's services. Publishes a quarterly magazine. Membership includes single parents.

BIBLIOGRAPHY

Because so many books for young readers include and involve family interactions, the following list is of necessity incomplete. The books listed here represent the best of selected aspects of the family and are meant as exemplars to which readers can add.

Adler, C.S. *In Our House Scott Is My Brother.* Macmillan, 1980. (Ages 11 and up.) Scott is Jodi's stepbrother. His mother Donna recently married Jodi's father. The marriage is a disaster, as is Scott's behavior. Donna's alcoholism and emotional immaturity finally cause the marriage to break up, and Scott must leave the only secure family he has known in his life. A sad ending, but one that points up the importance of family and of mature behavior on the part of adults.

Adoff, A. *Black Is Brown Is Tan.* Illus. by E. A. McCully. Harper, 1972. (Ages 3–8.) Positive feelings of warmth, energy, and togetherness are conveyed in this story of an interracial family who convey good feelings about themselves.

Adoff, A. *Hard to Be Six.* Illus. by C. Hanna. Morrow, 1991. (Ages 4–6.) Narrated in verse by the six-year-old boy in this loving and close-knit biracial family, the story tells of his frustrations at not being able to do all the things his capable ten-year-old sister can do. His sister is understanding about his feelings, and every member of his family tries to assure him of his worth. Finally, his grandmother helps him the most by reminding him of his deceased grandfather who believed in "taking time slow, making life count, and passing love on." The illustrations are realistically drawn closeups of each family member that create a pictorial album.

Albert, B. *Where Does the Trail Lead?*. Illus. by B. Pinkney. Simon & Schuster, 1991. (Ages 6-9.) A poetic exploration of a perfect day in the life of a child. The plot follows the boy in his explorations of an island off the coast of New England and ends with a family picnic. The scratchboard illustrations form an ideal accompaniment to the text. The child and his family are African American.

Auch, M. J. *Glass Slippers Give You Blisters.* Holiday House, 1989. (Ages 9-12.) Kelly's mother is still smarting from her own mother's unconventional behavior, and she does not want Kelly to be treated the same way. The conflict between generations is realistic.

Bailey, M. *The Facts about Single-Parent Families.* Crestwood, 1989. (Ages 8-10.) Comforting, practical information about the circumstances, problems, and "the bright side" of living in a single-parent household or family. Although most of the book refers to divorce, other reasons for the creation of single-parent families are also discussed. The photographs make it clear that this arrangement is not restricted to any particular ethnic group.

Bang, M. *Ten, Nine, Eight.* Illus. by the author. Greenwillow, 1983. (Ages 4-6.) Not only is this a clever counting book, (backward from ten to one) but the lively text also provides the reader with an affectionate father-daughter relationship and a model of an African-American family in a universal setting.

Banks, A. *Alone at Home: A Kid's Guide to Being in Charge.* Illus. by C. Bobak. Penguin, 1989. (Ages 7-10.) A manual for children who, through choice or necessity, must spend significant blocks of time alone at home. Advice for parents is also provided. Such topics as safety, communication, siblings, and beneficial activities are discussed.

Bates, B. *Bugs in Your Ears.* Holiday House, 1977. (Ages 10-12.) Carrie finds her life completely changed when her mother marries a man with three children. The adjustment of the blended family is depicted humorously and realistically. Carrie accepts her new family gradually as she lets go of her fantasized memory of her alcoholic birth father.

Bauer, C. F. *My Mom Travels a Lot.* Illus. by N. W. Parker. Warne, 1981. (Ages 4-6.) The positives and negatives of having a mom whose work takes her away from home much of the time. Children might be invited to continue the format of "The good thing about it is. . . . The bad thing about it is. . . ." to reflect on their own family situations.

Bauer, M. D. *Face to Face.* Clarion, 1991. (Ages 11 and up.) Although Dave, his stepfather, is a good man who loves him, Michael craves the company, attention, and love of his birth father who deserted him. When his father invites Michael to spend time with him, Michael discovers that he is not the man he longed for all his growing-up years. Finally, Michael is happy to be Dave's son.

Beck, M. *The Wedding of Brown Bear and White Bear.* Illus. by M. H. Henry. Little, Brown, 1989. (Ages 4-6.) In this subtle example of a biracial marriage, the plot is simple, the pictures are pleasant. Two bears are attracted to each other, engage in a courtship, and marry. Their friends joyfully celebrate with them.

Bode, J. *Truce: Ending the Sibling War.* Watts, 1991. (Ages 12 and up.) [See Siblings]

Boyd, L. *The Not-So-Wicked Stepmother.* Illus. by the author. Viking, 1987. (Ages 4-7.) Hessie has been influenced by the fairy tale depictions of stepmothers. She is taken aback when Molly, her father's new wife, is pretty, kind, and more than willing to spend time with her. The summer is an idyllic one for Hessie. All the adults in her family care about her happiness. One wonders why she can spend time with her dad only in the summer and why she had no acquaintance with Molly before the marriage. In the sequel, *Sam is My Half Brother (1990),* Hessie's father and Molly inform her as soon as baby Sam is born and again invite her to visit for the summer. The parents in this blended family behave with just the right degree of structure, responsiveness, and genuine communication. Hessie's readiness to accept Sam is followed in short order by her unhappiness at no longer being an only child. Her quick and positive turnaround is somewhat difficult to believe, but the book shows how blended families can function well.

Bradman, T., and Browne, E. *Wait and See.* Illus. by E. Browne. Oxford, 1987. (Ages 5–8.) When Jo and her mom (members of a biracial family) go shopping in their multicultural neighborhood, Dad stays home and cooks lunch. They run into a few obstacles, including the dog's eating the lunch Dad prepared, but all is resolved. The story and pictures reflect the warmth and joy of a multicultural community.

Brenner, B. *A Year in the Life of Rosie Bernard.* Harper, 1971. (Ages 8–12.) [See Gender Roles]

Bunting, E. *A Perfect Father's Day.* Illus. by S. Meddaugh. Clarion, 1991. (Ages 3–5.) Four-year-old Susie takes her father on a Father's Day outing designed to do all her father's favorite things. From the child's perspective, father and daughter are in perfect harmony with each other, with the father good-naturedly enduring all the activities Susie thinks are his favorites (including eating fast-food and buying balloons). The reader is convinced that this really was a perfect day for everyone.

Bunting, E. *The Wednesday Surprise.* Illus. by D. Carrick. Clarion, 1989. (Ages 5–9.) [See Aging]

Burt, M. S., and Burt, R. B. *What's Special about Our Stepfamily? A Participation Book for Children.* Illus. by R. Parisi. Doubleday, 1983. (Ages 5–8.) The book is most appropriate for readers in the midst of divorce in their family, but others who hope to be of help can also benefit from its interactive nature. After each paragraph or so, there are questions for young readers to answer. Such issues as residence, stepfamilies, communicating, finances, and visitations are discussed in some detail.

Butterworth, W. *LeRoy and the Old Man.* Four Winds, 1980. (Ages 12 and up.) [See Aging]

Byars, B. *The Not-Just-Anybody Family.* Illus. by J. Rogers. Delacorte, 1986. (Ages 9–12.) [See Death]

Cameron, A. *The Stories Julian Tells.* Illus. by A. Strugnell. Knopf, 1981. (Ages 7–10.) See also *More Stories Julian Tells* (1986), *Julian, Secret Agent* (1988), and *Julian, Dream Doctor* (1990) This series introduces readers to a loving, joyful African-American family consisting of Julian, his younger brother Huey, and their parents. The father provides a model as a caring, consistent, firm parent who finds the time and energy to intervene wisely in his sons' disputes. Bright and imaginative, Julian manages, with his parents' help, to extricate himself from thorny situations. Julian and his brother have some altercations, but for the most part they are good company for each other.

Charlip, R., and Moore, L. *Hooray for Me!* Illus. by V. B. Williams. Parents Magazine, 1975. (Ages 5–8.) Many kinds of families, including blended and extended, are illustrated here.

Cleaver, V. *Sweetly Sings the Donkey.* Lippincott, 1985. (Ages 10 and up.) Because Judson, her father, is a dreamer and her mother, Martha, is a self-centered, dependent person, fourteen-year-old Lily takes responsibility for her two brothers and for managing the home and family. Martha deserts the family, and Judson becomes ill; but Lily remains strong and determined to maintain the family.

Clifford, E. *The Summer of the Dancing Horse.* Illus. by M. B. Owens. Houghton Mifflin, 1991. (Ages 9–12.) Bessie and Sam Cobb and their mother are struggling because their father is ill with tuberculosis. Mrs. Cobb is a strong, practical woman who sustains the family by selling her baked goods to the local store. The story involves an abused child, an almost magical horse that has been taught to dance by a young man who was killed in the war, and the people of the town where the Cobbs live.

Collins, J. *My Father.* Illus. by J. Dyer. Little, Brown, 1989. (Ages 5 and up.) This illustrated song, with words and music by noted performer Judy Collins, conveys the sense of a family whose dreams are an important part of their togetherness. The essence of the story is the relationship of a father with his three daughters and the lasting effect of his love.

Cooper, M. *I Got a Family.* Illus. by D. Gottlieb. Holt, 1993. (Ages 4–8.) In rhyming verse, a young girl celebrates the many members of her extended family and the different ways they show their love.

Crews, D. *Bigmama's.* Illus. by the author. Greenwillow, 1991. (Ages 5–8.) The author fondly recounts a childhood memory of the train ride with his mother, sisters, and brother (Daddy will follow later) to his grandmother Bigmama's for the annual family reunion. The children love Bigmama's farm, full of animals and complete with a hand pump for water. The illustrations convey the children's pleasure.

Delton, J. *My Mother Lost Her Job Today.* Illus. by I. Trivas. Whitman, 1980. (Ages 5–8.) [See Gender Roles]

Dutton, R. *An Arab Family.* Illus. by J. B. Free. Lerner, 1985. (Ages 7–10.) All the titles in this series (which include families from China, Egypt, France, India, Israel, Jamaica, Nigeria, Pakistan, Sri Lanka, West Germany, Aboriginal Australia, Brazil, Chile, Ireland, Morocco, Singapore, and Zulu South Africa) are informative in text and photo and reveal a close personal look at family life. The focus on economics and geography represents people's day-to-day lives.

Eichler, M. *Martin's Father.* Illus. by B. Maginnis. Lollipop Power, 1971. (Ages 3–7.) Martin and his father live together. The story describes the commonplace daily activities the two engage in together. A gentle, matter-of-fact presentation.

Ellis, S. *A Family Project,* 2nd ed. McElderry, 1988. (Ages 9–12.) Family dynamics play an important part in the entire story, but the main focus is on the birth of a new baby eleven years after the last baby arrived. Jessica, her older brothers, and her entire family, as well as her friends, are enthusiastic about the birth. Jessica in particular has a strong affinity with the baby and is devastated when the baby dies and her mother experiences an emotional breakdown. The family rallies around to cope with the tragic loss and the traumas associated with it.

Elwin, R., and Paulse, M. *Asha's Mums.* Illus. by D. Lee. Women's Press, 1990. (Ages 5–8.) [See Sex and Sexuality]

Fassler, D.; Lash, M.; and Ives, S. B. *Changing Families: A Guide for Kids and Grown-Ups.* Waterfront, 1988. (Ages 8 and up.) An activity book inviting children and parents to explore jointly their feelings about being a family. Some information is given; but for the most part, the pages are almost blank so that with the help of adults young readers can personalize the stories and messages. This book can serve as a model for other issues.

Feelings, M. *Zamani Goes to Market.* Illus. by T. Feelings. Seabury, 1970. (Ages 6–9.) The book, inspired by the Feelings's visit with a West Kenyan family, tells how Zamani at last becomes old enough to accompany his father and brothers to market. A sense of the setting and people is communicated, as are the universal emotions of love and family caring.

Flourney, V. *The Best Time of Day.* Illus. by G. Ford. Random House, 1979. (Ages 5-8.) Cleaning his room, playing with his friends, making his own lunch, and shopping for groceries with mom, William is on the go from morning to night, but he always has time for his favorite part of the day when his daddy comes home from work. Although published some years ago, the story of a competent child in an African-American family remains timely and provides a good model.

Friedrich, L. *Teen Guide to Married Life.* Watts, 1990. (Ages 12 and up.) Illustrated with photos of people of all ethnic backgrounds, including interracial couples, the book discusses choosing the right partner, planning a family, solving problems, and such nitty-gritty items as managing money and sharing household responsibilities. The tone is conversational; the advice is straightforward and noncondescending.

Galloway, P. *Jennifer Has Two Daddies.* Illus. by A. Auel. Women's Educational Press, 1985. (Ages 5-8.) Jennifer's parents are divorced, and her mother has remarried. Now Jennifer has two men who function as fathers for her, although she understands that there is a difference between her birth father and her stepfather. When Jennifer becomes terribly anxious about her father's business trip and afraid he will not return, her step-father and mother help her to resolve her fears and permit her to make a long-distance phone call that gives her father the opportunity to lovingly reassure her that he will indeed return to her. A somewhat idealized picture, but certainly a model to aspire to.

Gardiner, J. R. *Stone Fox.* Illus. by M. Sewall. Harper, 1980. (Ages 10-12.) This single-parent family is headed by a grandfather who has lost his will to live because his farm is about to be forfeited for nonpayment of taxes. His grandson Willie and their sled-dog take over the responsibilities of the farm. When Willie enters a race to win the tax money, he faces unbeatable competition from Stone Fox, a Native American. In the end, thanks to Stone Fox, Willie and his dog win the race, but the dog dies.

Garza, C. L. (as told to H. Rohmer). *Family Pictures/Cuadros de Familia.* Illus. by the author. Children's Press, 1990. (Ages 5-8.) The author grew up in Kingsville, Texas, a town near the Mexican border. This collection of paintings and accompanying anecdotes presents a striking and intense view of the community's way of life. The text appears in both English and Spanish.

Gauch, P. L. *Christina Katerina and the Time She Quit the Family.* Illus. by E. Primavera. Putnam, 1987. (Ages 7-9.) Christina Katerina rebels against routine and anything that hints of someone else's authority. Her mother enters into an elaborate scheme in which Christina has the run of part of the house and can do what she wishes in the confines of her own space. After she does this for several days, she and her family reach a compromise that welcomes her back into the family without loss of face.

Gay, K. *Changing Families: Meeting Today's Challenges.* Enslow, 1988. (Ages 12 and up.) In what could also be an accessible reference work for adults, the author lays out the scope and breadth of the issues surrounding today's family structures. She points out that 43.4 percent of all American families are headed by single parents. She discusses interracial families, older families, single-parent families, and working families and looks at religious communities and communes.

Gay, K. *The Rainbow Effect: Interracial Families.* Illus. by the author. Watts, 1987. (Ages 12 and up.) A personal yet comprehensive look at multiracial families. Drawing on interviews with many families, the author discusses issues such as interaction within the families; dealing with prejudices, and discrimination; acceptance within the community; and the experiences of biracial children. Includes photographs of the families.

Geras, A. *Golden Windows and Other Stories of Jerusalem.* Willa Perlman, 1993. (Ages 9–12.) The five short stories in this book evoke a strong sense of family life in Jerusalem in the first half of the twentieth century. War, Jewish heritage, short supplies of food, family arguments, responsibilities for the care of younger siblings, and respect for elders are some of the factors in each of these extremely well written stories.

Getzhoff, A., and McClenahan, C. *Stepkids: A Survival Guide for Teenagers in Step Families.* Walker, 1984. (Ages 11 and up.) Many topics are included that young people may think are their unique problems, including what is normal and what is not, what to call your stepparent, what to do about feelings of sexual attraction to a stepparent, and how to give yourself permission not to love a stepparent. Much of the advice is basic ("Remind yourself periodically that your parents are responsible for their decision to divorce, not you"), but it is good advice, nevertheless. This book can serve as an introduction to more complex interactions.

Gilbert, S. *How to Live with a Single Parent.* Lothrop, Lee & Shepard, 1982. (Ages 10 and up.) One of the valuable aspects of this book is its inclusion of a wide variety of real situations and people. The author reinforces feelings and assures readers that they are not unique. Gilbert speaks directly to young people experiencing a single-parent family. Her advice is sensible and sympathetic.

Glassman, B. *Everything You Need to Know about Stepfamilies,* 2nd ed. Rosen, 1991. (Ages 8–10.) In simple and succinct language, the author defines terms relating to changing families and provides information about the causes and consequences of the changes. He also dispenses advice about how to handle such problems as stepparents' wanting to replace rather than complement a child's absent parents or the issue of names and whether or not they should be changed.

Goffstein, M.B. *Family Scrapbook.* Illus. by the author. Farrar Straus & Giroux, 1978. (Ages 8–11.) Seven tales of a Jewish family and their everyday adventures are sensitively, amusingly, and lovingly told.

Gould, D. *Brendan's Best-Timed Birthday.* Illus. by J. Rogers. Bradbury, 1988. (Ages 5–8.) After his father gives him a stopwatch for his birthday, Brendan times everything: How long it takes his father and him to frost the cake, lick the bowl, blow up balloons, complete a treasure hunt, and on and on throughout the entire party. Brendan's father is the only adult in evidence, and he has baked the cake and supervises the party. This is a model of a competent and nurturing father.

Green, C. J. *The War at Home.* McElderry, 1989. (Ages 10–12.) Family ties are all-important in this story set in Oakridge, Tennessee, during World War II. Mattie is the protagonist, but all the family members figure strongly in the plot, especially Otis, Mattie's cousin, who is abandoned by his parents and eventually adopted by Mattie's family. Grandparents, a younger sibling, and cousins are intertwined with the backdrop of the war and the mysterious and menacing atmosphere of the father's workplace. It is never explicitly stated that the father is involved in making the atomic bomb, but to informed readers that knowledge places an additional layer of complexity on the story.

Greenfield, E. *Honey, I Love.* Illus. by L. and D. Dillon. Crowell, 1978. (Ages 6 and up.) [See Heritage]

Greenfield, E. *Talk about a Family.* Lippincott, 1978. (Ages 10 and up.) [See Siblings]

Grode, P. *Sophie's Name.* Illus. by S. O. Haas. Kar-Ben, 1990. (Ages 4–7.) When Sophie Davida Finkle-Cohen informs her parents that she wants to change her name, they express no opposition. As the story unfolds, different family members tell stories of her family heritage, incidentally bringing out how she has received her names. Sophie decides that she is proud of her name and will keep it. The point is made without belaboring that one's heritage is something to treasure.

Hahn, M. D. *Tallahassee Higgins*. Clarion, 1987. (Ages 10 and up.) Tallahassee loves Liz, her mother, even though Liz periodically deserts her in favor of any in a string of male friends. She even enjoys their free-wheeling though poverty-laden lifestyle. She anguishes over her mother's decision to send her to her conventional Uncle Dan and Aunt Thelma. Although Thelma is irritable and disapproving, Dan is kind and supportive. Tallahassee finds a grandmother but always pines for her mother. Ultimately, Tallahassee must learn how to adjust to a family life without her mother.

Hamilton, V. *Cousins*. Philomel, 1990. (Ages 10–12.) Cammy is part of a large family, as well as a close-knit African-American community, in rural Ohio. Some vivid portraits are painted here of the various cousins. The 97-year-old grandmother, who, although living in a nursing home, is still an important element in the family's lives, and particularly Cammy, whose responses to her grandmother, mother, brother, and her troubled cousin Patty Ann form the substance of the story. Cammy's problems at school, her raging jealousy of Patty Ann, and her anguish over her grandmother's condition set the stage for her reaction to Patty Ann's death by drowning. The reappearance in her life of her father and the support of the rest of the family, particularly her grandmother, help Cammy to refocus her emotions and to look forward to continuing her life.

Hamilton, V. *M.C. Higgins, the Great*. Macmillan, 1974. (Ages 12 and up.) An interesting and complex story of an African-American family living in the mountains of Ohio. M.C. is the unusual hero of the story. The plot involves family love and pride and the process of growing up.

Harvey, B. *Immigrant Girl, Becky of Eldridge Street*. Illus. by D. K. Ray. Holiday House, 1987. (Ages 7–10.) The protagonists are a Jewish family of nine people sharing a three-room flat in a tenement in New York's Lower East Side in the early part of the twentieth century. The noise, people's lack of patience with a language other than English, the forced departure from some time-honored customs, and the struggle against poverty are juxtaposed against the genuine love of family members for one another while striving to become a part of their new community and holding on to basic customs and beliefs.

Hautzig, E. *A Gift for Mama*. Illus. by D. Diamond. Puffin, 1987. (Ages 8–10.) Set in Poland, the story revolves around Sara and her family. One Mothers' Day, Sara determines to flout family tradition and buy a gift rather than make one, just as the grownups do. At first her mother is disappointed; but when family members and friends show her the wonderful sewing Sara did for them to earn the money for her gift, Mama is touched and appreciates Sara's gift after all. Each of the family members is a support to Sara, and it is clear that family unity is strong.

Hickman, M. W. *When Andy's Father Went to Prison*. Illus. by L. Raymond. Whitman, 1990. (Ages 8–10.) Andy and his mother have relocated in order to be closer to his father, who is in prison. Andy deals with his conflicting emotions of family loyalty and fear that his classmates will ostracize him if they find out about his father. He finds an understanding teacher and good friends. When the story ends, his father is about to be paroled. It's unfortunate that Andy's younger sister is hardly mentioned. One wishes that her point of view had been considered as well.

Hoberman, M. A. *Fathers, Mothers, Sisters, Brothers: A Collection of Family Poems*. Illus. by M. Hafner. Joy Street, 1991. (Ages 5 and up.) Family constellations, interactions, joys, and hardships are all included in this exuberant celebration of family.

Hopkins, L. B. *Mama,* 2nd ed. Illus. by S. Marchesi. Simon & Schuster, 1992. (Ages 10 and up.) [See also *Mama and Her Boys,* new ed. 1993] The young narrator and his brother live with their mother; their father has left them. Mama is a hard-working, generous woman who changes jobs frequently and always manages to bring something home from work without paying for it. Mama's overflowing love for her children sustains the family despite her shoplifting habit.

Hort, L. *How Many Stars in the Sky?.* Illus. by J. E. Ransome. Tambourine, 1991. (Ages 5-8.) One night, while a mother is away on business, neither her son nor his father can sleep. They take their dog on a drive into the country, trying to count the stars. As a special treat, they sleep out under the stars and return at sunrise, looking forward to telling the mother about their adventure and, perhaps, to counting the stars with her one night in the future. The combination of text and paintings radiates affection between the child and his father. The warmth of the night sky serves as a metaphor for the love in this family. This is an example of a universal story exemplified through the portrait of an African-American family.

Howard, E. F. *Aunt Flossie's Hats (and Crab Cakes Later).* Illus. by J. Ransome. Clarion, 1991. (Ages 6-9.) A wonderful affirmation of the power of story and the importance of family. Aunt Flossie owns many hats, each of which, like the patches on a quilt, calls up reminders of what happened when Aunt Flossie was wearing it. The flavor of Baltimore in bygone days, the appreciation of the relationship between the two young girls and their great-aunt, and the togetherness of the family—coupled with sensitively drawn illustrations rich in detail—make this a book to use with many children in many different situations.

Howard, E. F. *The Train to Lulu's.* Illus. by R. Casilla. Bradbury, 1988. (Ages 5-8.) [See Siblings]

Isadora, R. *At the Crossroads.* Illus. by the author. Greenwillow, 1991. (Ages 4-8.) A group of black South African children eagerly awaits the return of their fathers, who have spent ten months working in the mines. They form a band and play music while they wait. Finally, the truck arrives with their fathers. Although apartheid is not specifically mentioned, the harsh reality of life for blacks in South Africa is evident from the illustrations: The families live in tin shacks and get clean water from a communal pump, the children bathe in washtubs and have makeshift toys, and families are separated from one another for most of the year. Nevertheless, a spirit of respect, love, and community is conveyed.

Isadora, R. *Over the Green Hills.* Illus. by the author. Greenwillow, 1992. (Ages 4-8.) Zolani, his mother, and his baby sister, who live in a coastal village in South Africa, set out on foot to visit Zolani's grandmother, who lives over the hills. They bring with them a lovely assortment of gifts. Friends along the way give them things too, including the first book Zolani has ever owned. The grandmother is a competent woman who lives alone. Zolani's mother cares for him and his sister while his father, a fisherman, is away at sea. The people are hard working and live simple lives. Their sense of love, joy, and pride in their community is strong.

Jenness, A. *Families: A Celebration of Diversity, Commitment, and Love.* Illus. by the author. Houghton Mifflin, 1990. (Ages 8 and up.) Black-and-white photos accompany the words of seventeen children talking about their diverse families. (The book began as an interactive photographic exhibit in the Boston Children's Museum.) Each of the children pictured here lives in a different family constellation. Represented are single parents, gay and lesbian parents, several cultures, and families with adopted and foster children, as well as biological children, only children, families with many children, and blended families.

Jenness, A., and Rivers, A. *In Two Worlds: A Yup'ik Eskimo Family.* Illus. by A. Jenness. Houghton Mifflin, 1989. (Ages 9-12.) Filled with the family members' own narrative, the book portrays a contemporary Yup'ik family coping with changing times while honoring tradition. Jenness's respect and affection for the family clearly emerge. The details of daily living, interactions among family members, worries, and joys are all communicated.

Johnson, D. *What Will Mommy Do When I'm at School?.* Illus. by the author. Macmillan, 1990. (Ages 5-8.) A little girl, about to start school for the first time, worries that her mother will be lonely since they have never been apart for very long. When her mother tells her that she will be beginning an adventure of her own, a new job, the little girl is relieved. Mother and daughter look forward to telling one another about their new experiences at the end of each day. The theme of this loving, gently reassuring book is universal. The family shown in the illustrations is African American.

Joosse, B. M. *Jam Day.* Illus. by E. A. McCully. Harper, 1987. (Ages 5-8.) Ben lives with his divorced mother. He envies families with lots of people, noise, and activity. When he and his mother visit his grandparent and the rest of his extended family to make jam for a day, Ben realizes that his family extends beyond the boundaries of his house.

Joosse, B. M. *Mama, Do You Love Me?.* Illus. by B. Lavallee. Chronicle, 1991. (Ages 4-7.) An imaginative child challenges her mother's unconditional love. Although the love is always there, the mother makes it clear that the child's behavior has consequences. The glossary explains the origins and locations of some of the items and animals mentioned in the story. The setting, as conveyed by the text and stylized illustrations, is pan-Alaskan rather than a specific village or group. Children may want to write personal versions of this story using their own specialized vocabularies.

Juneau, B. F. *Sad but O.K.: My Daddy Died Today.* Blue Dolphin, 1988. (Ages 9-12.) [See Death]

Kyte, K. *In Charge: A Complete Handbook for Kids with Working Parents.* Knopf, 1983. (Ages 10 and up.) Sensible ideas and advice for young people whose parents work outside the house.

Lash, M.; Loughridge, S. I.; and Fassler, D. *My Kind of Family: A Book for Kids in Single-Parent Homes.* Waterfront, 1990. (Ages 6-11.) An excellent workbook for children who live with a single parent, no matter what the reason. The problems, special circumstances, hopes, feelings and wishes of children in these families are presented in a format that invites children to contribute their own responses and ideas. A good communication guide for adults.

Lindsay, J. W. *Do I Have a Daddy?: A Story about a Single Parent Child.* Illus. by C. Boeller. Morning Glory, 1991. (Ages 4-7.) Including a special section of advice for single parents, the book provides one model of how to respond to a child's questions when he or she wants to know about an absent parent.

Livingston, M. C. *Poems for Fathers.* Illus. by R. Castilla. Holiday House, 1989. A variety of poems by a variety of authors about a variety of fathers. The author's *Poems for Mothers* (1988) and *Poems for Grandmothers* (1990) are companion volumes.

Livingston, M. C. *There Was a Place and Other Poems.* McElderry, 1988. (Ages 8-12.) [See Divorce]

Lowry, L. *Attaboy, Sam!* Illus. by D. deGroat. Houghton Mifflin, 1992. (Ages 7-10.) One of a series of lighthearted books about a very well educated middle class family who love each other and accept each other's foibles and actions. In this one, each family member tries to construct a gift for Mrs. Krupnik's thirty-eighth birthday. Each of the gifts is a disaster, but Sam saves the day.

Lowry, L. *The Giver.* Houghton Mifflin, 1993. (Ages 10-12.) This Newbery Award winner tells of a utopian community where everything is so "blanded out" there are no intensity of feeling, no conflict, and no decision making on the part of individuals. As a matter of fact, there are no colors in this Utopia, no animals, no climatic extremes, and no lasting pain. At the age of twelve, children are given their life assignments, which are selected for them by a group of elders after careful observation and deliberation. Jonas, the protagonist, is selected to be the receiver of memory from an elder who is the Giver. After he has received some memories and becomes able to see color, feel emotions, and suffer physical and mental pain, Jonas and the Giver decide to challenge the community to change its passive lifestyle. Jonas leaves the community with a baby who has been targeted for euthanasia because he whimpers at night and sets out into a new world. The reader is not certain what will happen to the community or, for that matter, to any of the characters in the story. Questions of decision making, the role of family, and the pros and cons of utopian living are raised by this provocative book.

Lowry, L. *Rabble Starkey.* Houghton Mifflin, 1987. (Ages 10 and up.) Rabble (short for Parable) and her mother Sweet Hosanna live in an apartment above the Bigelows' garage. Sweet-Ho is a caretaker for the family, especially for baby Gunther and Rabble's friend Veronica. Mrs. Bigelow has suffered an emotional breakdown. Despite all the hardships, the book focuses on how well the family system works and how family structure and support sustain each of the characters. When Rabble and Sweet-Ho must move on, the goodbyes are tearful but not tragic; the two families are intact.

MacLachlan, P. *Arthur, for the Very First Time.* Illus. by L. Bloom. Harper, 1980. (Ages 9-12.) [See Gender Roles]

MacLachlan, P. *Journey.* Delacorte, 1991. (Ages 10 and up.) Journey's grandparents are his real family, but it takes him a long time to recognize it. His parents have deserted both him and his sister; and for too long, Journey yearns for his mother's return. He is aided in his healing and comprehension by his grandfather's photographs, which help him to focus on what is real and acknowledge what is imagined. As with all her work, the author challenges the reader's depth of perception and at the same time opens new pathways to understanding.

MacLachlan, P. *Sarah, Plain and Tall.* Harper, 1985. (Ages 8 and up.) Families can be constituted in many ways. In this story, Sarah, a mail-order bride, arrives to be mother to Anna and Caleb and wife to the widowed Jacob, their papa. Although the perspective is Anna's, each family member's feelings emerge: Sarah's longing for the sea and her love for the children and for Jacob; Caleb's desire for a home where song and laughter are easy companions; Jacob's intense grief at his wife's death, his love for his children, and his admiration and respect for Sarah; and Anna's mixed emotions at being supplanted in her task of mothering and her yearning for her own mother, combined with her love for Sarah, undergird the simple plot. Sarah is not a savior, but she acts as a catalyst as the family members resolve their feelings of loss. *Skylark* (1993) continues the story and takes the family through the hardship of drought.

Mark, J. *Trouble Half-way.* Illus. by D. Parkins. Atheneum, 1985. (Ages 10-12.) The story, set in England, details the development of a close, strong relationship between Amy and her new stepfather.

Martin, A. M. *Bummer Summer.* Holiday House, 1983. (Ages 9-12.) Kammy finds it difficult to adjust to her new stepsiblings and to Kate, her new stepmother. Her father is understanding but firm about the necessity for Kammy to get along with the newly constituted family. He and Kate decide to send Kammy to summer camp so she can get away from her bothersome stepsiblings "until things settle down." They stipulate that

Kammy can decide to come home after two weeks. The summer camp experience predictably works out for the best, and the reader has some assurance that the new family will be fine.

Maury, I., translated by A. Munoz. *My Mother and I Are Growing Strong (Mi Mama y Yo Nos Hacemos Fuertes).* Illus. by S. Speidel. New Seed, 1978. (Ages 5–8.) Emelita and her mother work hard at the jobs that were her father's before he was imprisoned. Emelita feels a responsibility for raising her father's spirits when she visits him. The entire family is strong, despite their difficult circumstances.

Maury, I. *My Mother the Mail Carrier (Mi Mama, la Cartera).* Illus. by L. McCrady. Feminist Press, 1976. (Ages 7–12.) Written in Spanish and English, the story shows how a single parent is an effective mother, mail carrier, and person all at the same time. The son, Lupito, loves his mother very much and is proud of her.

Mazer, N. F. *C, My Name Is Cal.* Scholastic, 1990. (Ages 10 and up.) Cal's father abandoned him and his mother when Cal was five, and his mother now works as a housekeeper and caregiver. Suddenly, Cal's father reappears. The book ends with Cal and his father struggling to establish some kind of a relationship, a possible but difficult and awkward task. The difficulties between Cal's parents are well handled. The father is not forgiven for running out on his family, but he is portrayed as a sad, immature person who never learned to handle responsibility or stay in one place. Cal is torn between loyalty to his mother and anger mixed with curiosity about his long-absent father. There are no ecstatic reunions; Reestablishing ties is a slow process. The book leaves hope for a positive future.

McDonnell, C. *Count Me In.* Viking, 1986. (Ages 12 and up.) Kate's parents are divorced. Her mom has remarried, and her dad is about to do so. Although she likes her stepfather, Kate has mixed feelings about her mother's expecting a baby. Finally, she recognizes that she must develop her own relationships with friends in order to feel that she belongs.

McPhail, D. *Ed and Me.* Illus. by the author. HBJ, 1990. (Ages 6–8.) The young girl who narrates the story is comfortable living with her father, who seems to be a loving and nurturing parent. He appreciates the qualities of the old truck they call Ed, and he treats the truck with a respect and caring. The activities in the story always include the father as well as the girl.

Merrill, S. *Washday.* Seabury, 1978. (Ages 5–7.) [See Gender Roles]

Modesitt, J. *Mama, If You Had a Wish.* Illus. by R. Spowart. Simon & Schuster, 1993. (Ages 4–6.) In this gentle book, Mama Rabbit reassures Little Bunny, patiently answering each of his questions, that she loves him as he is and wants him to be himself. A lovely model of a mother-child relationship.

Montgomery, L.M. *Akin to Anne: Tales of Other Orphans.* Bantam, 1988. (Ages 11 and up.) [See Adoption and Foster Care]

Morris, A. *Loving.* Illus. by K. Heyman. Lothrop, Lee & Shepard, 1990. (Ages 5 and up.) Stunning-color photographs depict families of various compositions, backgrounds, settings, and heritages actively engaging in loving activities with children.

Myers, W. D. *The Mouse Rap.* Harper, 1990. (Ages 10–12.) Mouse has adjusted to the fact that he and his mother are a family entity, and now that his father wants to return, Mouse feels ambivalent. In addition to capturing the voices of the young people in this Harlem neighborhood, Myers also reveals the complexity of the parents' relationship. The plot gets complicated with a story of hidden loot and a dance contest that somehow turns into a career for one of the young men, but it is light and pleasant.

Newman, L. *Heather Has Two Mommies.* Illus. by D. Souza. Alyson, 1991. (Ages 4-6.) When Heather, a child of lesbian parents, begins her first day of preschool, she is saddened to hear other children talking about their daddies. Her understanding teacher uses this as an opportunity to discuss diversity in families. The children all draw pictures of their families, showing a variety of constellations including single, divorced, and same-sex parents, adopted children, and family members with disabilities. Heather begins to understand that it is not the composition of her family that is important but that she is loved. The relationship between Heather's mommies is shown as supportive and loving. Heather knows the specifics of her birth, including which mother carried her and that an artificial insemination occurred. Some readers may feel that the subject of artificial insemination is too mature for this book's target audience, but the text is gentle and reassuring.

Nixon, J. L. *Maggie, Too.* HBJ, 1985. (Ages 9-12.) First of a series (*Maggie Makes Three* and *Maggie Forevermore* follow this one). Maggie's relationship with her widowed father is a bumpy one, especially when Maggie is exiled to her grandmother's house so that her father can marry a much younger woman. Maggie finds a large extended family, full of affection and unexpected excitement.

Nolan, M. S. *My Daddy Don't Go to Work.* Illus. by Jim LaMarche. Carolrhoda, 1978. (Ages 5-8.) The father in this story stays home and does the cooking and cleaning because he cannot find a job. His wife goes to work. He is anxious and thinks of looking for employment somewhere else. The entire family agrees that it is important for them to stay together, so the father continues to stay at home. The family is African American.

O'Neal, Z. *A Formal Feeling.* Viking, 1982. (Ages 12 and up.) [See Death]

Oppenheimer, J. L. *Gardine vs. Hanover.* Crowell, 1982. (Ages 12 and up.) The focal point of this book is the relationship between stepsiblings and the effect on each child of joining two families.

Park, B. *My Mother Got Married (and Other Disasters).* Knopf, 1989. (Ages 8-10.) Some of the problems in this sometimes funny, earnestly presented story are resolved; but most of them realistically remain in some state of transition. The story is told from the perspective of Charlie Hickle, who finds it difficult to accept that his mother has remarried. He resents his stepfather and two stepsiblings, and he believes that his mother does not care about his feelings. The book is engagingly written. It would be a worthwhile activity to retell the story from each character's perspective.

Paterson, K. *Come Sing, Jimmy Jo.* Dutton, 1985. (Ages 10 and up.) Jimmy Jo is part of a family of singers who are much in the public eye. The intricate plot contains many characters and circumstances; for example, Jimmy Jo's biological father and grandparents are not the people he thought they were. He finally recognizes that his family is the group of people who love and nurture him, and he symbolically expresses this by joining them in singing "Will the Circle Be Unbroken?"

Patrick, D. L. *The Car Washing Street.* Illus. by J. Ward. Tambourine, 1993. (Ages 5-8.) Matthew's street is a special place every Saturday morning. People pour out of their houses onto Matthew's street with cleaning supplies and use hoses and hydrants to wash their cars. Matthew's family does not own a car, but they like to join in the festive occasion and enjoy the community activity. The neighbors are like a small community— a family unto themselves—and the mood is joyous. All the characters are Hispanic or African American.

Pellegrini, N. *Families Are Different.* Illus. by the author. Holiday House, 1991. (Ages 4-7.) [See Adoption and Foster Care]

Pinkney, G. J. *Back Home.* Illus. by J. Pinkney. Dial, 1992. (Ages 6–9.) Ernestine Avery Powell journeys alone by train for a brief visit with her kinfolk in the place where she was born. The importance of maintaining a family connection comes through strongly, even though cousin Jack is derisive of Ernestine's fancy dress and city ways and hurts her feelings. Ernestine perseveres, and she and Jack become friends. Jerry Pinkney's water-colors lovingly portray the people and the setting.

Porte, B. A. *Harry's Mom.* Illus. by Y. Abolafia. Greenwillow, 1985. (Ages 5–8.) Harry lives with his dad, but his extended family loves and supports him emotionally. They remind Harry that his mother died in an accident while driving her race car and that she was brave, smart, and affectionate. Harry misses her, and so does the rest of the family, but the strength of the family prevails here, not the grief.

Porte, B. A. *I Only Made up the Roses.* Greenwillow, 1987. (Ages 10–12.) Narrated in the first person by Cydra, the story tells about her family and how she fits into it. Her step-father is African American. Her birth father is a shadowy figure who never keeps his promises and, indeed, never appears in the story. A picture of a strong, loving, proud, supportive family extending over generations and across color barriers emerges here. The telling of family stories is an important element.

Porte, B. A. *Taxicab Tales.* Illus. by Y. Abolafia. Greenwillow, 1992. (Ages 5–9.) Abigail and Sam Rabinowitz's father regales the family with stories each night when he returns from his job as a taxicab driver. Their mother, an artist and former cab driver, illustrates his sometimes exaggerated tales. Abigail, also a storyteller, retells some of her favorites here. The family presents a lovely model of cooperation and support, and the often-humorous tales are cleverly illustrated.

Qualey, M. *Everybody's Daughter.* Houghton Mifflin, 1991. (Ages 12 and up.) Beamer, 16, spent the first ten years of her life on a commune in Minnesota. The group has since disbanded, but most of the former members still live nearby and meet regularly in her parents' bait shop below their house. Beamer feels somewhat suffocated by the continuing presence of these people in her life and begins to rebel against it. She becomes aware of the impact of her upbringing on the way she interacts with the world. Armed with this new self-knowledge, she makes peace with the many people who love her. This book paints a portrait of a unique family situation that is neverthe-less loving and supportive and of a young woman coping with coming into adulthood and finding independence, not only from her parents but from a whole network of close, loving friends.

Rosenberg, M. B. *Living in Two Worlds.* Illus. by G. Ancona. Lothrop, Lee & Shepard, 1986. (Ages 10 and up.) Black-and-white photos illumine the text with images of children and their parents representing a number of different racial backgrounds. The explanations of race and the descriptions of each of the family members in these interracial families focus only on the positive aspects of being biracial.

Rosenberg, M. B. *Talking about Stepfamilies.* Bradbury, 1990. (Ages 9–12.) The author inter-viewed many stepchildren (from age 8½ to age 41) in order to find out how they felt about being part of a stepfamily. She found, in general, that children of blended families view their families as different from the norm, even though this arrangement is much more common now than it ever was before. The people interviewed also agreed that they were more flexible because of the need to conform to different sets of rules and adapt to a variety of personalities. Further, they began at an early age to think about marriage, relationships, and the importance of family.

Roy, J. *Soul Daddy.* Gulliver, 1990. (Ages 11 and up.) Hannah and Rosie are twins. Their father Joe left to pursue his musical career before they were born. (In fact, he didn't know their mother was pregnant.) Now, he has reentered their lives. Joe is of African heritage; the girls have been raised in an all-white neighborhood by their white mother. The plot is complicated and many issues are raised, including what it means to be black women in a racist society.

Rylant, C. *A Kindness.* Orchard Books, 1988. (Ages 12 and up.) Chip and his mother Anne enjoy a mutually respectful and loving relationship. Anne has never married. When Chip is fifteen years old, Anne becomes pregnant and refuses to discuss who the father is. The birth of baby Dusky heals Chip's hurt. Issues of fatherhood and motherhood and of the role of love in sexual relations are raised.

Rylant, C. *The Relatives Came.* Illus. by S. Gammell. Bradbury, 1985. (Ages 4-7.) A rollicking, crowded, noisy family visit in which at times the relatives seem like an invading horde but are always welcome. The illustrations aptly reflect the closeness of the family and the special quality of the Appalachian setting.

Samuels, V. *Carry Go Bring Come.* Illus. by J. Northway. Four Winds, 1989. (Ages 4-7.) On Marcia's wedding day, the entire household is preoccupied with the preparations. Leon is awakened so that he can help too, but he gets so worn out from all his carrying and running that he is exhausted. The family shown experiencing this universal theme is African American.

Schaffer, P. *How Babies and Families Are Made (There Is More Than One Way).* Illus. by S. Corbett. Tabor Sarah, 1988. (Ages 5-8.) [See Sex and Sexuality]

Sharmat, M. *Sometimes Mama and Papa Fight.* Illus. by K. Chorao. Harper, 1980. (Ages 4-8.) Kevin and his sister become upset when their parents argue loudly. They learn, however, that dissension can be part of family life without necessarily leading to divorce.

Shasha, M. *Night of the Moonjellies.* Illus. by the author. Simon & Schuster, 1992. (Ages 5-8.) Mark helps his grandmother and other family members at their seaside refreshment stand. At the end of a long, busy, and noisy day, Mark's grandmother takes him out to sea on a fishing boat where they deposit a glowing creature they call a moonjelly into the ocean along with thousands of other glowing creatures. The textured pastel illustrations glow with the warmth of the family's cooperative enterprise and from the reflections of the sand, sea, sun, moon, and ocean.

Shelby, A. *We Keep a Store.* Illus. by J. Ward. Orchard, 1990. (Ages 5-8.) A young African-American girl tells about the joys of keeping a family store. Located on their property, it is not just a place to shop, but a community meeting place as well. In the winter, friends and neighbors gather around the stove to tell stories and share news. In the summer, they take their chairs out on the porch. For the young narrator the store provides community and helps the family to stay close.

Simon, N. *All Kinds of Families.* Illus. by J. Lasker. Whitman, 1976. (Ages 5-8.) The title reflects the aim of the book, to show that many patterns of family life are of value. Sadness and joy are depicted, as well as the role of the family as a support system.

Simon, N. *Wedding Days.* Illus. by C. Kieffer. Whitman, 1988. (Ages 4-7.) An exploration of the ritual of marriage, including brides and grooms of all ages, religions, and backgrounds. Simple but accurate language details wedding customs.

Smalls-Hector, I. *Jonathan and His Mommy.* Illus. by M. Hays. Little, Brown, 1992. (Ages 4-7.) Jonathan likes to go walking and talking with his mother. They have a loving relationship. The mother is not embarrassed to join in her son's play and fantasies. The characters are African American, and the setting is urban, but the theme is universal.

Smith, D. B. *Return to Bitter Creek.* Viking, 1986. (Ages 9-12.) Lacey's mother Campbell has adopted a lifestyle different from her Appalachian family's. Lacey's grandmother is unaccepting and judgmental until David, Campbell's lover, is killed in an automobile accident. Then the grandmother sees how deep the relationship was and what a good person David was. To make amends, she creates a quilt that clearly includes David, Campbell, and Lacey, weaving them permanently into the family. Extended family, cousins, and a sense of community add to the family structure presented here, in contrast to the lifestyle that Campbell had chosen.

Snyder, Z. K. *Libby on Wednesday.* Delacorte, 1990. (Ages 10 and up.) Libby, a seventh grader, lacks social skills and has few friends outside of her eccentric extended family (her mother is absent but maintains contact) who share the decaying mansion her grandfather built. Gender role stereotyping is carefully avoided. The issue of the extended family constellation is handled deftly. No member of the family is a stereotype, and each is an individual who functions distinctly from his or her family role. At first, Libby is embarrassed because of the eccentricities of her living situation; but once she sees that her friends are truly interested in her family and do not consider her situation "strange," she lightens up.

Sobol, H. L. *My Other-Mother, My Other-Father.* Illus. by P. Agre. Macmillan, 1979. (Ages 10 and up.) Andrea tells how she feels about being a stepchild and about the advantages and disadvantages of two sets of parents. Her relationships seem to work out fine, making this a positive book. The photographs show good interaction among all parties involved.

Soto, G. *The Skirt.* Illus. by E. Velasquez. Delacorte, 1992. (Ages 9-12.) Miata Ramirez leaves her dancing skirt, which was her mother's when she was a girl in Mexico, on the school bus. Miata and her best friend Ana manage to retrieve it. On the day of the folkloric dance recital, Miata's mother gives her a new skirt; but Miata decides to wear both skirts, one over the other. The Mexican-American community is a supportive one in which neighbors and cultural traditions are respected. Miata's father, a welder, is proud of his skills and his family. Spanish words, although not translated, are understandable in context.

Steptoe, J. *Daddy Is a Monster Sometimes...* Illus. by the author. Harper, 1980. (Ages 5-8.) Bweela [See *My Special Best Words* in Family] talks about her relationship and her brother's with their father, especially when he gets angry with them. Despite these times, the love in the family is real and comes across nicely.

Stock, C. *Sophie's Knapsack.* Illus. by the author. Lothrop, 1988 (Ages 4-7.) Sophie and her parents leave the city on a camping trip. The warmth of their feelings for each other shines through both in the illustrations and in the details of the setting and the ordinary events of the trip.

Stock, C. *Thanksgiving Treat.* Illus. by the author. Bradbury, 1990. (Ages 4-7.) A large family gathering demonstrates that each member is needed and valued. The little boy feels left out of his family's Thanksgiving preparations until his grandfather finds a wonderful way for him to contribute to the feast.

Stolz, M. *Go Fish.* Illus. by P. Cummings. Harper, 1991. (Ages 7-10.) The grandfather-grandson duo from *Storm in the Night* demonstrate an intact family with only one parent, this time a grandfather. The relationship between the two is respectful and playful.

Stolz, M. *Leap before You Look.* Harper, 1975. (Ages 12 and up.) Jimmie adores her father and resents his remarriage. Living with her mother, brother, and grandmother and aided by her friend Chris, Jimmie gradually adjusts and reconciles with her father.

Stolz, M. *Storm in the Night.* Illus. by P. Cummings. Harper, 1988. (Ages 5-8.) The story is set in the midst of a storm that has caused all electrical power to go out. Although his grandson cannot admit to a fear of storms, the grandfather recounts a story about the days when he was young and terrified of a storm, thus helping pass the time and comfort the child. The poetic language complements the deep, rich illustrations of this African-American family.

Surowiecki, S. L. *Joshua's Day*. Illus. by the author. Lollipop Power, 1972. (Ages 4–6.) Joshua, who lives with his mother, goes to a day-care center while she works. She is coping well without a husband, and Joshua seems fine.

Swentzell, R. *Children of Clay: A Family of Pueblo Potters*. Illus. by B. Steen. Lerner, 1992. (Ages 7–10.) The entire family is involved in collecting clay and shaping it into pots and figures, which they then decorate and bake. The traditional and spiritual aspects of this family enterprise are aptly and respectfully conveyed. Photographs display the beauty of the finished pieces.

Taylor, M. D. *The Gold Cadillac*. Dial, 1987. (Ages 9–12.) A trip south that begins as a prideful family journey encounters disaster in the form of bigotry, but the family remains strong and surmounts the ugliness. See also *Song of the Trees* (1975), *Roll of Thunder, Hear My Cry* (1976), *Let the Circle Be Unbroken* (1981), *The Friendship* (1987), *Mississippi Bridge* (1990), and *Road to Memphis* (1990).

Taylor, S. *All-of-a-Kind Family Downtown*, new ed. Illus. by B. Krush and J. Krush. Follett, 1988. (Ages 8–12.) Fourth in the series containing *All-of-a-Kind Family, More-All-of-a-Kind Family, All-of-a-Kind Family Uptown*, and *Ella of All-of-a-Kind Family*, which describe a Jewish family with five sisters and one brother growing up in New York in the early twentieth century. The sisters do everything together and always think of one another's feelings. The family is pious, just, loving, and cooperative. Although the children occasionally do naughty things, they always confess and set it right. The books convey a flavor of the era.

Thomas, M., ed. *Free to Be . . . a Family*. Bantam, 1987. (Ages 5 and up.) Stories, poems, and songs about families of all sizes, colors, and styles.

Uchida, Y. *The Happiest Ending*. McElderry, 1985. (Ages 9–12.) The third in a series about Japanese-American families in California during the Depression years. This time Rinko tries to intervene in an arranged marriage because she wants the bride to be romantically involved with the groom. Family unity, the extended family of the community, and pride of heritage are important ingredients here.

Voigt, C. *Dicey's Song*. Atheneum, 1982. (Ages 9 and up.) Dicey has protected and tended her younger siblings throughout a difficult year. Their mother has been hospitalized for mental illness; and they are now living with their maternal grandmother, a strong and eccentric woman. The relationship between Dicey and her grandmother constitutes the major portion of this sensitive and intricate book. This is the sequel to *Homecoming* (1981), in which Dicey and her siblings are abandoned by their mother and must make their way without parental help. Dicey's strength carries them through.

Walter, M. P. *Mariah Keeps Cool*. Bradbury, 1990. (Ages 7–11.) Mariah's half-sister Denise comes to stay, and Mariah and her sister Lynn must help Denise to adjust to a new way of behaving. The family's rules make sense, and Lynn responds well to the loving structure. *Mariah Loves Rock* (1988) first introduced this lively character. The family is African American.

Whelan, G. *Bringing the Farmhouse Home*. Illus. by J. Rowland. Simon & Schuster, 1992. (Ages 5–10.) Five branches of the family convene at the farmhouse to divide the heirlooms left by the grandmother. They compose five piles of treasures roughly equal in sentimental and monetary value and draw lots. Then they trade with each other for individual items they want. The family is remarkably amiable about the whole enter-prise. The grandmother has been dead for a while, and the grieving is over. Now the business of living and remembering is begun. The family interaction makes it clear that the memories are precious, and they agree to share the possessions even after they have made their claims. The large family is close knit and will remain so.

Willhoite, M. *Daddy's Roommate*. Illus. by the author. Alyson, 1990. (Ages 4-8.) [See Sex and Sexuality]

Williams, V. B. *A Chair for My Mother*. Illus. by the author. Greenwillow, 1982. (Ages 5-8.) An example of how a loving, cooperative family functions. This family consists of a grandmother, mother, and daughter. The mother works hard in a restaurant and comes home tired. The family saves coins from tips and odd jobs and finally amasses enough to purchase a really comfortable chair for the mother. The same family is depicted in *Something Special for Me* (1983), in which the coins are spent on a gift for Rosa, the daughter. A third book in the trilogy is *Music, Music for Everyone* (1984), in which the grandmother is ill, and Rosa and her friends form a band so that they can not only earn money but also lighten the grandmother's feelings.

Williams, V. B. *"More More More," Said the Baby*. Illus. by the author. Greenwillow, 1990. (Ages 2-5.) Three families of different heritages and configurations demonstrate the rapture of playing with, kissing, and hugging their babies.

Worth, R. *The American Family*. Illus. by R. Sefcik. Watts, 1984. (Ages 12 and up.) An overview of the American family, where it has been, where it is now, and where it seems to be going. The twentieth century is covered in most depth, the sexual revolution and women's movement being important aspects of family change. Photos show families of varied races. There is a helpful chapter on divorce, enumerating common causes and investigating how it feels for children at various ages. Worth also lets young readers in on what divorce feels like for the parents. An entire chapter is devoted to the single-parent family.

Wyman, A. *Red Sky at Morning*. Holiday House, 1991. (Ages 10-12.) Set in Indiana in the early years of the twentieth century, the story details the hardships many families endured, including a devastating diphtheria epidemic. Through strength of will and an amazingly optimistic outlook, Callie overcomes the death of her mother, her father's desertion, her sister's forced servitude, and her grandfather's illness. The author makes it plausible that in the end the entire family, including the wayward father, is reunited and can look forward to an easier life.

Zolotow, C. *This Quiet Lady*. Illus. by A. Lobel. Greenwillow, 1992. (Ages 4 and up.) A sense of family continuity is shown through the photographs of her mother's life dis-played by the young protagonist.

part 2

Life Cycle

Being born, aging, and dying are biological experiences that (except for those who die before they are aged) constitute our life cycle. In all cultural, economic, social, or political conditions, values and attitudes surrounding these topics vary radically from one group to another and, indeed, from one individual to another. Opinions about instruction concerning reproduction and sexuality, aging, and dying range from the view that it is entirely the responsibility of those at home to the belief that it is the mandate of the educational system. Some people favor sex education but discourage information about sexuality. Some support teaching about death and dying while others prefer to leave discussion of these matters to the clergy. Many people consider aging to be a topic unworthy of any consideration or discussion and avoid even thinking about its implications.

In the three chapters that make up Part 2, each of these life situations is examined as it is included in numerous works of children's literature. As with all the other themes included in this book, as many perspectives are presented as possible, with criteria for selection gleaned from both experts and experienced practitioners.

chapter 5

Sexuality

Mary S. Calderone, for many years the director of the Sex Information and Education Council (SIECUS), advises that the presence of sexuality in all human beings should be affirmed as a developing and continuing force from birth to death. Almost everyone agrees that there should be some instruction on this topic for young children; but when it comes to specifically determining who, what, where, when, and how it is to be given, opinions vary widely. Most parents want to have a say in the manner of the instruction. Some parents object to any mention of the topic at school, while others wish that the schools would handle the issue totally.

Sex education has not yet become a comfortable topic in either schools or libraries. Because of the controversial nature of the information, libraries often either maintain shelves of books to be read "by permission only" or simply do not purchase the controversial literature.

At present, children receive sex instruction in a variety of ways. They sometimes learn about the process in a totally satisfactory manner from parents who are knowledgeable and comfortable in their beliefs and attitudes. They are sometimes helped in their search for information by sympathetic and informed teachers, counselors, or friends. They can also acquire needed details from objective librarians who know what the resources are and how to handle them. Nevertheless, most of the time children receive answers, both accurate and inaccurate, from their peers. They also seem to be adept at acquiring pornographic material aimed at titillation rather than education. Much of their informal education comes from movies and television and from the fiction they read, which do not consciously try to instruct in matters sexual but succeed in imparting many implicit lessons.

Most educators agree that this healthy and positive attitude toward sex is necessary to any program of sex education. How then, can an interested, supportive adult convey facts, attitudes, and values to inquisitive young people? What information is necessary? Where can materials be found? What steps can be taken to help young people feel comfortable about the topic and informed enough to behave responsibly? What constitutes responsible behavior, especially in an era when AIDS and other sexually transmitted diseases are of such concern? What values remain valid?

Before an attempt is made to answer these questions, it would be useful for adults to examine their own attitudes and values.

Try This

Answer these questions as honestly as you can.

Of the following, what was the primary source of most of your information about sex: Your parents? Teachers? Books? Peers? Experience? Other?

How much time elapsed between your learning about puberty and its onset?

How well prepared did you consider yourself to handle the new situations and physical conditions imposed by puberty?

How did you feel about your body when you were a teenager?

How do you feel about your body now?

What is your opinion about premarital or extramarital sex for yourself? For an eventual (or current) spouse? For your children (if you have any or expect to have any)? For other people?

How linked do you think sex and love should be? For men? For women?

How "special" do you consider sexual intercourse to be in a relationship between two people?

What is your opinion of homosexuality?

What is your definition of pornography?

What, if any, are your personal rules about sex?

What are your opinions about masturbation?

What taboos, if any, do you hold for yourself?

How do you react to "dirty" jokes? To X-rated films?

How generalized or universal would you like your attitudes to be?

How do you feel about people who disagree with you?

Who do you feel should be responsible for educating children about sex?

When do you believe sex education should begin?

In an attempt to teach children about sex, attitudes come strongly into play, but feelings are usually colored by knowledge and experience. Sometimes students know more about sex than their teachers and have engaged significantly in sexual activities.

Where should direct information about sexuality and sexual practices begin, and where should it end? Some people believe that instruction ends with marriage. Some believe it should stop when a person has experienced intercourse. ("After all," they reason, "What more would anyone need to know?")

Any material aiming to instruct about sex should stress the broad range of sexual behavior, feelings, choices, and responses in human relationships, not only those aspects of behavior labeled sex acts. Thus, sexuality rather than sex should be emphasized. Current research in physiological responses, family relations, education, and psychology should be taken into consideration in any program of instruction as should the implications of the ways in which people can act on their feelings. Societal concerns and people's responsibility for their own behavior are a legitimate part of this topic. An overemphasis on physiology and too much duplication of known facts should be avoided. This kind of education should be perceived as a developmental program based on acknowledged human sexual conditions and needs from birth to old age.

The content of sex education is important. For adolescents in particular, whose formal sex instruction is too often linked with units on drugs, crime, and other abuses, instruction on sex should be integrated into the regular curriculum. For all children, this integration is important. Books that present sexuality in the light of normal and positive human interaction generally are regarded as the most positive influences.

Even after it is accepted that sexuality and learning about sex are appropriate to all ages, the specific question of direct, formal instruction remains. How can the questions of a child who cannot yet read be handled? How much information is appropriate for a nine year old? How can positive values and behaviors be presented in a manner acceptable to a twelve year old? How can adults ensure that the information is up to date? How can it be affirmed that values and personal behavior are constructive?

Try This

Do this with a group of classmates or colleagues. Without signing your name, write three questions about sex or sexuality, each on a three-by-five card. Your questions may pertain to physiological facts about your own body or that of someone of the opposite sex, or they may be about sensations, processes, or myths. They may reflect a desire to clarify or to be initially informed.

Place all questions in a box. Draw the questions out one at a time. Who in the group has some answers? What sources can you find, in addition to peers, that can provide answers? Answer or attempt to answer every question in this box. How comfortable is the group with this procedure?

The presentation of information about sex varies according to the developmental level of the student. Infants and young children receive most of their ideas by experiencing the way people interact in front of them and with them. Children accustomed to seeing their parents in affectionate embraces will probably feel different about their own sexuality from children whose families are undemonstrative. Children receive many messages from the way adults respond to their games of "doctor." Adult reactions to children's masturbation also teach lessons. The pattern of adults' answers to children's questions in general guides children toward the specific questions about sex they can risk. Adult conversations overheard by children also form a powerful part of the informal educational system. Comments about the behavior of married couples, reactions to films and television, and responses to the way other adults dress and behave are components of sex instruction.

Most educators, counselors, and psychologists, as well as religious advisers, agree that it is important for adults to help children feel comfortable with their sexuality, curiosity, and behavior. A guilty or furtive feeling arising from sexual activity is not helpful. Experts also advise adults to take into consideration a child's physical, intellectual, and emotional development in determining the extent of the information to be given in response to specific questions.

You may have heard about young John who asked his mother, "Mommy, where did I come from?" Mother then launched into an elaborate and detailed description from the progress of the egg to possible positions for intercourse. After a long lecture, to which the child listened attentively, the mother asked John what else he wanted to know. "Well," he said, "Timothy comes from Baltimore, and I still don't know where I come from." On the other hand, when children do ask us pointed and specific questions, we should try not to evade them or give incomplete answers. When they ask how the sperm and egg got together, they really do want to know about intercourse.

Reproduction education is not all there is to sex education. The facts of reproduction are, of course, an important element; but not all sexual activity includes intercourse, and human beings engage in many forms of sexual activity for reasons other than the desire to have children.

Children want to know about the opposite sex, their own bodies and how they are constructed, and why. They want to be reassured that they are normal, and they need to grow to accept themselves, their bodies, and their functions with ease and self-liking. Many adults should reexamine their own feelings about sex and refrain from imposing negative feelings on their children.

Of primary importance in any good program of education is the interaction between learners and teachers. Good sex education programs benefit from discussions among peer groups and adult leaders—parents, counselors, teachers, and other interested adults. Multiaged sessions among students are not recommended because of the readiness of some children to acquire greater detail than others and because it is generally acknowledged that younger children are usually satisfied with briefer answers.

William A. Block, a doctor specializing in sex education, identifies three developmental levels of sexuality: the dormant stage, the awakened period, and the active stage. He assigns age levels to these stages; but as with any developmental concept, ages vary according to the group and the individual. He suggests that the first stage lasts until about age nine, the second until age fourteen, and the third to age nineteen. He does not mention adults because he is primarily interested in providing a public school program of sex education. Block advises adults to take the stage of the child into consideration whenever questions need answering. He asserts that in the dormant stage, children are inquisitive but not intensely concerned about sex. The greatest preoccupation occurs during the awareness period, when sexual curiosity and exploration are high. He believes that this is perhaps the most critical time for education (Block, 1972).

Most adults draw upon books and other materials to help them in their explanations. Many children actively seek out books and other references to help guide their quest for information. There are many books now available that have, as their primary intent, the sexual instruction of young children. An equally large number of books instruct without, perhaps, intending to do so. The first category of books is usually in the realm of nonfiction; the second lies within fiction and fantasy. Not all nonfiction is necessarily successful in teaching the lessons it purports to communicate. Values and attitudes lie close to the surface, influencing the factual information. Adults and children should be alert to hidden messages and respond to them knowledgeably.

In recent years, many books have been directed toward a very young audience of preschool and primary school children. Authors and publishers have recognized that children become interested in matters sexual before their teenage years. Some books are consciously written to enable the parent to serve as an interpreter to the young child. They represent a wide range of attitudes, values, and information and can be used as valuable tools for education.

Many books have been written specifically for sex education. Most are nonfiction and heavily didactic. The illustrations vary, including carefully objective approaches and clinical diagrams unattached to human bodies; sweet, romanticized paintings of affectionate parents and amiable babies; and explicit cartoons or photos depicting sex play and intercourse. The words are equally as varied, with dry, detailed scientific explanations; sentimental descriptions with euphemisms substituted for anatomical labels; and slyly humorous observations phrased in vernacular terminology.

One aim of this chapter is to acquaint concerned adults with the variety, intent, styles, and general usefulness of the books; it is hoped that adults may thus acquire the resources to help young readers select and benefit from quality literature. Since books go into and out of print frequently, it would be wise to check the collection in local and school libraries.

SUGGESTED CRITERIA

Whether or not the intent is didactic, both fiction and nonfiction communicating information about sexuality should take into consideration the reader's developmental level. An appropriate amount of information should be transmitted.

What is included should be accurate, stated with carefully selected terminology. Some books consciously use vernacular terms because their intent is to eliminate some of the mystery and high-handedness that some adults communicate or to demonstrate that their authors are on the young readers' level. Some authors, perhaps out of fear that clinical terms will confuse a child, use euphemistic language (like "a special opening" instead of "vagina"). This itself can be confusing. Accurate dictionary terms are preferred to either the vernacular or the euphemistic.

In all books, the approach should maintain human dignity. Distortions in the guise of humor should be avoided. A balanced presentation, neither heavy and dour nor frothy and caricatured, is preferable.

Values should be communicated clearly with the author's acknowledgment of the intent. Books should indicate that there are many attitudes and values about sex and should not impart feelings of guilt to readers who disagree with the message of the book. No book can be acceptable to all people; no book should attempt to make all readers conform to its point of view.

Indicating consequences of various behaviors is much more effective than moralizing.

Care should also be taken to avoid perpetuating myths or falsehoods (like the fiction that a person will go blind if he or she masturbates).

Books should likewise acknowledge and value sexuality in all human beings; sexual activity should not be relegated solely to young adults.

Sex should be part of enjoyable, healthy living rather than a problem; but when problems are presented, they should be realistic. The solutions should be feasible rather than contrived or romanticized. The "happy ending" should not always be marriage.

Sex education should be more than reproduction education. When the intent is to communicate only the facts of birth, there should at least be an indication to the reader that there is more to be learned.

Care should be taken to include a discussion of the roles and functions of both sexes; for example, the father's role should not be left out of the birth process.

In books giving sexual information, both sexes should be invited to learn; boys are inquisitive about girls, and girls about boys. In books addressed to either sex, facts about both sexes should appear.

Gay, lesbian, or bisexual characters should be portrayed as fairly as hetero-sexual characters are. They should not be exclusively victims or persecutors, nor should they be ridiculed or feared because of their sexual orientation. (The term *orientation* is generally favored over *preference,* although this may be a matter of dispute, even among the gay, lesbian, and bisexual population, some of whom aver that they have opted for their way of life. Current research seems to indicate that sexuality is genetically linked, but there are no conclusive studies as yet.)

The cause of characters' sexual orientations should not be attributed to difficult family situations. Love between two people of the same sex should be treated in the same respectful and straightforward manner as love between two people of opposite sexes.

Characters should not be punished because they are gay, but societal pressures should be reported with accuracy.

A happy ending should not be that a gay, lesbian, or bisexual character "reforms" or falls in love with a person of the opposite sex.

Although homosexual exploration should be treated as part of heterosexual development, the expectation should not necessarily be that all young people will "outgrow this stage" in order to be accepted.

Sensitive authors communicate a tolerance of those who disagree with them and do not try to impose guilty feelings on them.

Too much information conveyed through words or pictures can be threatening to young children. When the emphasis is on mature bodies and advanced sex play, the implications can make the intended young audience overly anxious.

Stereotypes about the interest, arousability, capability, and behavior of males and females should be overturned.

Expectations that marriage is the aim of every woman and that all couples will want to have children should be handled as opinion rather than fact.

Care should be taken to provide different perspectives; far too many books present their view of morality as the only proper way.

Illustrations should take into account the injunction against stereotypes; multiethnic characters of different ages, classes, conditions of ability, and sexual orientation should people these books.

Prurient or demeaning humor should be avoided. Books should not stoop to ridicule. Books with titillating intent are in danger of imparting negative and uncomfortable lessons rather than constructive ones.

The aim of sex education materials and literature about sexuality should be to make each reader comfortable, responsible, and informed about his or her sexuality and about sexual activities in general.

DISCUSSION OF CHILDREN'S BOOKS

Books for Young Children

Most books on this topic for young children describe the birth process. They rarely take into consideration other aspects of sexuality in a child's life. John Steptoe's *My Special Best Words* is one of the exceptions. In this book, three-year-old Bweela lives with her one-year-old brother and their father. Bweela tries to toilet-train her brother, and the two children romp together in the bathroom. The illustrations help convey their sense of joy and comfort with their bodies, themselves, and each other. As usual, Steptoe is educational while simultaenously disturbing the complacency of some of the reading public.

Andry and Schepp's *How Babies Are Made* is designed for very young children. Although flowers and animals are discussed in addition to human beings, this information does not become confusing. The context is always in terms of what a child wants to know. The illustrations are pleasant, attractive paper sculptures, neither caricaturing or demeaning. Clear and nonjudgmental, the text uses simple, accurate language.

Did the Sun Shine before You Were Born?, by Sol and Judith Gordon, deliberately and successfully avoids sexist implications. The illustrations picture children engaged in different activities that are not stereotypically gender-linked. Love and affection are illustrated. Options for different lifestyles are presented as normal and viable, with choices presented in many forms. Different heritages are pictured. The entire book presents a balanced, positive, healthy view of life and sex.

Sometimes, otherwise excellent books miss the opportunity to educate readers about a balanced sex-role perspective. Some of them contribute accurate and useful details but imply that the main role of the father in the birth process is to stand and wait. Perhaps readers should write to publishers suggesting that these books be revised in light of contemporary needs. Parents would do well to guide their children so that questions are encouraged and answers are provided.

The Birth of Sunset's Kittens, by Clara Stevens, is useful in prompting questions. Although it is designated for seven-to-ten year olds, it can easily be absorbed and enjoyed by younger children, especially if interested adults are present to provide direction. The explicit photographs help to satisfy curiosity. The vocabulary is informative. Uterus, amnion, placenta, and umbilical cord are described; but the term *vagina* is inexplicably avoided. Nevertheless, the book is informative enough to be useful with a wide variety of children.

Books for Older Children

Nonfiction.   Many books for children eight years old and older recognize that they will be interested in details and description of the sex act, as well as the birth process. Most of these books also take into consideration the questions of approaching puberty. The presentations vary widely in the factual books. Depending on the intent and viewpoint of the authors, the tone of these books ranges from the objective, almost clinical, to the intensely personal.

Wardell Pomeroy's books, *Boys and Sex* and *Girls and Sex,* are direct and frank. He addresses readers twelve years of age and older, treating topics that concern them now, not years later. He speaks about masturbation, sex play, homosexuality, petting, dating, and intercourse. He expresses his opinions, but labels them as such and indicates his rationale.

Eric Johnson's book *Love and Sex in Plain Language* is exactly what the title promises. Dealing with personal and social values and with the pleasure of sex, as well as some of the problems, it stresses personal responsibility on the part of each individual. The book is aimed at readers as young as ten years of age. It speaks frankly but in a calm and reassuring tone.

Fiction.   Works of fiction, particularly if they are well crafted, can convey lessons more effectively than many books calculated to teach. The lessons may sometimes be unintentional on the part of the authors, but impressionable readers learn them nevertheless. In recent years, fiction has included such previously taboo topics as premarital sex, sex play, and homosexuality.

Both *I'll Get There. It Better Be Worth the Trip,* by John Donovan, and *The Man without a Face,* by Isabelle Holland, deal briefly with relationships between individuals of the same sex. In each case, the hero is a young teenager who fears he has gay tendencies. In each case, an older male reassures the hero that love for another male is normal and does not need to develop into a sexual relationship. Most books of fiction and nonfiction maintain the attitude that homosexuality is to be avoided at almost all costs and that gays and lesbians are "sick" people. The two books mentioned above handle the situation in a fairly reasonable manner, but the societal fear comes through. Helping to provide a rational counterbalance, Clayton Bess's *Big Man and the Burn-out* introduces Mr. Goodban, a compassionate and competent teacher and a model gay man valued as a member of the community.

Also dealing with this topic, but in a much more comprehensive and direct manner, is Nancy Garden's *Annie on My Mind.* The story is powerful in its character portrayal and intensity. In this novel, Liza and Annie are lovers. The development of their relationship is the topic of the story. Also figuring in the plot are two female teachers—lifelong lovers who are fired by the school committee for their sexual orientation. The issue is dealt with sensitively, providing a reasoned view of homosexuality. The story is a beautifully written love story, free from didacticism or fluff.

Love stories reflecting sexual alliances between men and women include Cynthia Rylant's compilation of stories titled *A Couple of Kooks and Other Stories about Love.* Characters of varied ages, economic conditions, and social classes are described in the throes of their relationships. The author's prose is as evocative as poetry. Both *Ludell* and *Ludell and Willie,* by Brenda Wilkinson, provide a model of a mutually respectful and affectionate friendship that ripens into love. It is to be hoped that increasing numbers of books will portray friendships and courtships, both heterosexual and homosexual.

Menstruation is a frequent topic in novels written for readers ten years of age and up. Some books deal with the emotional issues and problems created by peers who are entering adolescence. In Judy Blume's *Are You There, God? It's Me, Margaret,* several of the girls feel as though they are in a competition to see who will begin to menstruate first. So much pressure is placed on these girls to grow up that one of them lies about having her period in order to be one-up on her friends. Self-image hangs desperately on size of breasts and condition of puberty. Readers should probably be guided through this book by sympathetic adults. Perhaps a box like the one recommended in Try This on page 101, into which young people could place their questions, would help. Several small group sessions might be organized to answer the questions. It would be useful for the teacher to read the questions in advance and come prepared with some sources for answers.

Judy Blume presents the problems of boys and their entry into puberty in *Then Again, Maybe I Won't.* Tony has nocturnal emissions. He uses binoculars to watch a female neighbor in the nude. Since the information may not be sufficient for inquisitive readers, the question box may help, but it is more likely that some informal discussions at which young people can compare their experiences and feelings would be productive.

Norma Klein presents unconventional attitudes in many of her books. In *Mom, the Wolf Man and Me,* Brett's mother has never been married, and Brett does not want her to be. Brett's image of marriage is negative. She is afraid that she and her mother will become stereotypes if her mother marries. She indicates that she is comfortable with sexual information; she learned much of it at school. She and her mother have a frank, open relationship in which her mother answers all her questions honestly.

Honor Arundel also discusses controversial sexual behavior in her novels, but she also presents the consequences and describes the motivations and situations leading up to the problems that arise. In *The Longest Weekend,* Eileen is an unwed mother. Her mother is understanding to the point of loving the infant and taking over its care. The author attempts to remain nonjudgmental, but in the end Eileen marries Joel, the father of the child. A number of issues here provide opportunities for fruitful discussion. The students can discuss what they would have done in Joel's or Eileen's place. They can ask what their parents would have done under the circumstances the book describes.

Any discussion of sex is more valuable if parents and children can talk together. Although situations can be arranged where peers have discussions under the guidance or direction of a knowledgeable adult, in the long run parents and children should understand and respect one another's points of view and come to terms with their value systems. Books can help. They can be vehicles for understanding and exploration, but they cannot take the place of close, supportive family interaction. Librarians, teachers, parents, and counselors can accumulate materials that present different approaches and convey an assortment of attitudes as resources on which to base their discussions. No matter what emerges as the selected set of values, it will inevitably be more constructive if it has been influenced by accurate information and an increased awareness and appreciation of human sexuality.

REFERENCES

Sexuality

Anderson, D. E. "Gay Information: Out of the Closet," *School Library Journal* 38 (June 1992): 62. A plea to provide accessible information and materials, including fiction, for young people who are gay, lesbian, or bisexual. The author suggests several titles worthy of inclusion in a library collection.

Bess, C. "In Protest," *Voice of Youth Advocates* 10 (Feb. 1988): 274-275. The author of *Big Man and the Burnout* describes a speech he gave supporting the inclusion of positive homosexual characters, particularly teachers, in books for children.

Block, W. A. *What Your Child Really Wants to Know about Sex and Why.* Prentice-Hall, 1972. A straightforward presentation, stressing the importance of recognizing children's sexuality. Divides children's development of sexuality into three stages: the dormant period, age five to nine; the awakened period, age ten to fourteen; and the active period, age fifteen to nineteen. Recommends patterns of answers to questions about sex depending on the stage of the child. Also suggests some useful activities for the classroom.

Brewer, J. S. "A Guide to Sex Education Books: Dick Active, Jane Passive." *Bulletin of the Council on Interracial Books for Children* 6 (1975) Nos. 3 and 4. An excellent analysis of the general attitude that books convey about sex. Brewer criticizes the stereotype of a passive role for females. She points out the negative attitude toward homosexuality and comments that bisexuality is rarely discussed. In this review of fifteen sex education books, Brewer's comments are incisive and informative.

Brick, P. "Fostering Positive Sexuality." *Educational Leadership* 49 (Sept. 1991): 51-52. One of a series of articles in this issue focusing on sexuality education. The author indicates that every teacher is a sexuality educator in informal ways, as well as with formal instruction. She recommends using children's literature as a catalyst for discussion.

Council on Interracial Books for Children. *Bulletin* 14 (1983) Nos. 3 and 4. The entire double issue deals with how homosexuality is and should be handled in materials for an audience of children.

Frank, J. "Sexuality in Books for Children." In *Issues in Children's Book Selection,* Bowker, 1973. Asks what is the appropriate age level for fiction treating sex explicitly. Lists criteria for acceptable books as integrity of purpose, authenticity, moral and social validity, and resolutions offered. Praises several books and suggests that parents, teachers, and librarians recommend acceptable books to young readers.

Grannis, C. B. "Publishers Can Play a Key Role in Sex Education." *Publishers Weekly* 203 (March 12, 1973): 30-331. A report of a conference combining religious leaders, SIECUS, and publishers' representatives to set guidelines for publishing information about sex. Consensus was that sexuality should be stressed rather than sex. Sexuality includes "love, intimacy, fidelity, family life" and the way people regard themselves physically.

Haffner, D. W., and De Mauro, D. *Winning the Battle.* Sex Information and Education Council, 1991. Guidelines on how to establish a sex education program that enlists the cooperation of the community.

Hanckel, F., and Cunningham, J. "Can Young Gays Find Happiness in YA Books?" *The Wilson Library Bulletin* 50 (March 1976): 528-534. The authors offer comments on several novels that depict gay characters and point out the perils of stereotyping and of punishing characters because of their sexual orientation. They provide guidelines for evaluation drawn up by the ALA/Social Responsibilities Round Table's Task Force on Gay Liberation.

Hilu, V., ed. *Sex Education and the Schools.* Harper, 1957. Despite the age of this book, it is timely and useful now. The contributors, Mary Calderone, Alan Guttmacher, Millicent McIntosh, and Richard Unsworth, engage in conversation with one another, offering their recommendations for healthy conveying of information and attitudes about sex.

Jenkins, C. "Heartthrobs & Heartbreaks: A Guide to Young Adult Books with Gay Themes." *Out/Look* (Fall 1988): 82-92. Informative criteria are offered for providing a basis of discussion about novels containing gay characters. In addition, the author summarizes and critiques a number of books with gay themes published between 1969 and 1988.

Jenkins, C.A., and Morris, J. L. "Recommended Books on Gay/Lesbian Themes." *Bulletin of the Council on Interracial Books for Children* 14 (Nos. 3 and 4, 1983): 16-19. More than twenty-five books, mostly for readers over twelve years of age, are described and recommended.

Mercer, J. B. "Innocence Is a Cop-out." *Wilson Library Bulletin* 46 (Oct. 1971): 144-146. Pleads for recognition that children are reading and understanding books at a young age, even when topics such as sex and drugs are included.

Sears, J. T. "Helping Students Understand and Accept Sexual Diversity." *Educational Leadership* 49 (Sept. 1991): 54-56. The author has written extensively on the topic of sexuality education and issues for gay and lesbian youth. Excellent reference list.

Selverstone, R. "Sexuality Education Can Strengthen Democracy." *Educational Leadership* 49 (Sept. 1991): 58-60. Describes a classroom format using popular songs to encourage classroom discussion among adolescents about issues of sexual values and behavior.

Ward, J. V., and Taylor, J. M. "Sexual Education in a Multicultural Society." *Educational Leadership* 49 (Sept. 1991): 62-64. Points out that most sex education is based on developmental theories and studies of white, middle-class males. The authors provide useful guidelines for making sex education available and pertinent to young people of all backgrounds.

Whitlock, K., and Dilapi, E. M. "Friendly Fire: Homophobia in Sex Education Literature." *Bulletin of the Council on Interracial Books for Children* 14 (Nos. 3 and 4, 1983): 20-23. Provides guidelines for evaluating sex education materials for treatment of homosexuality.

Williams, R. F. "Gay and Lesbian Teenagers: A Reading Ladder for Students, Media Specialists and Parents." *The ALAN Review* 20 (Spring 1993): 12-17. Pointing out the likelihood that teachers will have gay and lesbian students in their classrooms, the author urges teachers and librarians to make relevant literature available to their students. He offers some simple suggestions and an annotated bibliography.

Wolkstein, D. "Old and New Sexual Messages in Fairy Tales." *Wilson Library Bulletin* 46 (Oct. 1971): 163–166. Interprets a number of fairy tales as means of exploring sexuality and responding to sexual needs. Recommends that new tales show sexuality and sensuality as important factors of life.

RESOURCES

Alyson Publications, Inc., 40 Plympton St., Boston, MA 02118 (617) 542-5679. Publishes titles with gay, lesbian, and bisexual themes.

American Association of Sex Educators, Counselors, and Therapists, 435 N. Michigan Ave., Suite 1717, Chicago, IL 60611.

Center for Family Life Education, Planned Parenthood of Greater Northern New Jersey, 575 Main Street, Hackensack, NJ 07601. Publishes and distributes materials for teaching safe sex to teens and young adults. Materials include publications for education of very young children as well.

National Federation of Parents and Friends of Gays. 8020 Eastern Ave, N.W., Washington, DC 20012. Assists children, parents, and spouses of gays. Provides support groups and provides information through educational materials and speakers.

Sex Information and Education Council, 130 West 42nd St., Suite 2500, New York, NY 10036. Clearinghouse for information and materials on sexuality education. Provides assistance to schools for comprehensive sexuality education.

BIBLIOGRAPHY

Andry, A. C., and Schepp, S. *How Babies are Made.* Illus. by B. Hampton. Little, Brown 1984. (Ages 3–10.) This book starts with flowers and animals and then discusses human reproduction. The pictures, a combination of cartoon and collage, are not at all demeaning. The text contains accurate information, gently and objectively conveyed. A widely useful book.

Arundel, H. *The Longest Weekend.* Thomas Nelson, 1969. (Ages 12 and up.) Eileen, a young unwed mother, struggles with her parents' wishes and her own feelings and desires. The author is not judgmental, but the happy ending is that Eileen and Joel (the father of the child) marry. Interesting complications and realistic dialogue make this a good book for discussion.

Bess, C. *Big Man and the Burn-Out.* Houghton Mifflin, 1985. (Ages 12 and up.) Abandoned by his mother when he was very young, Jess is an angry, frustrated young man without friends. He is very close to Sid, his step-grandfather, but he and his grandmother seem unable to get along. Mr. Goodban, Jess's favorite teacher, is an openly gay man living with his long-time partner. While he does not discuss his lifestyle, he does not hide it either; and the community accepts him. There is a scene in which Jess and his friend Meechum are chastised by Jess's grandmother for engaging in sexual exploration. Sid states that this behavior is natural and that if this is an indication of who Jess is, they must accept it because they don't want to drive Jess away.

Blume, J. *Are You There, God? It's Me, Margaret.* Bradbury, 1970. (Ages 10 and up.) Margaret and her friends are preoccupied with their physical maturation. They talk constantly about breasts, menstruation, and boys. The story hits home with many pre-adolescent girls.

Blume, J. *Then Again, Maybe I Won't.* Bradbury, 1973. (Ages 10 and up.) Tony is an adolescent learning how to deal responsibly with his new sexual feelings. Blume is explicit about young people's fears and curiosity. In this book, she presents the phenomena of nocturnal emissions and uncontrollable erections and manages to do so in a humorous context.

Bode, J. *Different Worlds: Interracial and Cross Cultural Dating.* Watts, 1989. (Ages 12 and up.) An initial discussion of bigotry and its roots frankly discloses the problems teenagers have when their parents do not understand their dating members of other races or religions. Interviews with parents, teens, social workers, and therapists provide hope for a more open multicultural community in the future.

Boston Children's Hospital, with Masland, R. P., Jr. *What Teenagers Want to Know about Sex: Questions and Answers.* Little, Brown, 1988. (Ages 10-13.) Structured in brief question-and-answer segments, the book attempts to be factual and nonjudgmental. The author uses the term *sexual preference* rather than *sexual orientation,* and this should invite some discussion. No extensive explanations, implications, or examinations of emotional fallout are given; but the facts are available, and the message is clearly communicated that it's OK to ask questions.

Brenner, B. *Bodies.* Illus. by George Ancona. Dutton, 1973. (Ages 8-10.) A happy combination of didacticism and fun. Sexuality is viewed as normal. Photographs depict children clothed and unclothed without embarrassment or condescension.

Calderone, M. S., and Johnson, E. W. *The Family Book about Sexuality.* Illus. by V. Cohen. Harper, 1981. (Ages 11 and up.) Lengthy, exhaustive treatment of the factual, emotional, and attitudinal aspects of sex and sexuality. Appropriate for adolescents of both sexes. Emphasis on normalcy of curiosity and feelings, along with responsibility for one's actions. Nonjudgmental; matter-of-fact, explicitly illustrated. Very carefully prepared.

Cole, J. *Asking about Sex and Growing Up: A Question-and-Answer Book for Boys and Girls.* Illus. by A. Tiegreen. Morrow, 1988. (Ages 8-12.) Basic and specific information not usually offered in books for this age level, such as sexual arousal, masturbation, birth control, and safe sex. The primary message is that it is important to be inquisitive and to find answers to any and all questions.

Cole, J. *How You Were Born.* Illus. by H. Hammid et al. Morrow, 1984. (Ages 5-8.) Beginning with guidelines to parents for using the book, the author addresses the child reader. Details and photographs of the development of the fetus and the concurrent development of the pregnant woman's body are included. The photos depict people from various cultures and show fathers as well as mothers actively involved with the infants. Although there is no mention of intercourse, the book represents the process of reproduction and birth factually and clearly.

Cole, J. *My Puppy Is Born.* Illus. by M. Miller. Morrow, 1991. (Ages 5-8.) A revised and expanded version of the 1973 edition, with color photographs showing the birth of a puppy and all its attendant consequences and activities.

Dragonwagon, C. *Wind Rose.* Illus. by R. Himler. Harper, 1976. (Ages 5-9.) A poetic, joyful celebration of the fruits of a loving relationship between a man and a woman. The mother explains to Wind Rose all the details of her conception and birth that are suitable for her level of understanding.

Elwin, R., and Paulse, M. *Asha's Mums.* Illus. by D. Lee. Women's, 1990. (Ages 5-8.) Asha has two mothers, and this never presents a problem until her teacher insists that she have a form filled out correctly, with just one mother's name. It is never explicitly stated, but it becomes evident that Asha's parents are both women who share her mothering.

Asha is much more concerned about possibly missing a class trip than she is about her nontraditional family structure. Particularly because of the general lack of books addressing this situation, this is a useful addition to a collection about different lifestyles and sexual orientations.

Faison, E. *Becoming.* Illus. by C. Ercin. E. Patterson, 1981. (Ages 3–6.) Illustrated with children from different heritages, the text contains a clear and accurate representation of the conception and birth of a child. The birth is attended by the father and by a woman who could be either a doctor or a midwife. The birth may be taking place at home or in a hospital. Love and sex are connected. A very positive book.

Garden, N. *Annie on My Mind.* Farrar, Straus & Giroux, 1982. (Ages 12 and up.) Liza and Annie are lovers. They have moved into this relationship gradually, and it is solid. The story includes two female teachers, lovers for many years, who are fired because Liza and Annie use their house as a rendezvous. The book dispels many stereotypes about lesbians and offers a sensitive portrayal of the characters and the choices they make. A powerful work.

Girard, L. W. *You Were Born on Your Very First Birthday.* Illus. by C. Kieffer. Whitman, 1983. (Ages 5–8.) A father and mother love each other and show affection and joy in the birth of their child. The book contains a description of gestation from embryo to birth.

Gitchel, S., and Foster, L. *Let's Talk about . . . S-E-X (Spanish version: Hablemos Acerca del . . . s-e-x-o).* Planned Parenthood of Central California, 1982. (Ages 9–12.) The format is straightforward, and the information is clearly stated. The authors respect their audience. The book provides some "fill-in-the-blanks" activity sheets for children and parents to complete together. All in all, a positive guide.

Gordon, S. *Girls Are Girls and Boys Are Boys.* Illus. by F. C. Smith. Prometheus, 1991. (Ages 5–8.) This excellent book reflects the author's awareness of a multiethnic audience. It focuses on an acknowledgment of the needs and emotions of both girls and boys. The language is clear, communicating information and constructive values directly.

Gordon, S., and Gordon, J. *Did the Sun Shine before You Were Born?* Illus. by V. Cohen. Third Press–Joseph Okpaku, 1974. (Ages 5–8.) The book is characterized by realistic illustrations and clear, accurate terminology. Much incidental learning is included: a boy with a doll, a female doctor, loving sexual relations (rather than clinical), multiethnic representation, the option not to get married or have children, the depiction of different kinds of families (including one-parent families), and sexual organs shown without exaggeration, distortion, or romanticizing. A balanced view.

Hanckel, F., and Cunningham, J. *A Way of Love, A Way of Life: A Young Person's Introduction to What It Means to Be Gay.* Photos by A. Olson. Illus. by L. Stein. Lothrop, Lee & Shepard, 1979. (Ages 12 and up.) This book, written for the sophisticated reader with a basic knowledge of physical and emotional sexuality, attempts to present the view that gender identity and erotic preference are established very early in life and should be accepted as they are. Portraits are included of representative gays living fulfilled, productive lives. The authors see the primary audience as young people who are gay or uncertain of their sexual orientation; it is informative for others as well. This forthright look at sexual preferences defines terms (slang as well as formal usage), explains male and female physical and sexual development and various kinds of sexual relationships. The authors include extensive references and an index.

Hayes, D. *No Effect.* Godine, 1994. (Ages 11 and up.) In a breezy and accessible style, the author deals with such deep issues as coping with effects of a father's death, the challenges of being a single parent, and the "raging hormones" of the adolescent. Tyler, the hero, is a likable young man whose tribulations form the plot. He mourns his father, admires and respects his mother, and falls madly in love with one of his teachers. Fortunately, he has plenty of support from the adults around him and from his friends. The author provides some models for how not to deal with adolescents, as well as some good examples of how to interact with and help them.

Heron, A. *How Would You Feel If Your Dad Was Gay?*. Illus. by K. Kovick. Alyson, 1991. (Ages 7–10.) This is clearly not literature, and most of the story line is tract; but it is a needed book. The authors present the dilemmas experienced by some children whose parents are gay. They provide several perspectives on how to address the issue, focusing particularly on some people's need for secrecy and others' need for disclosure. The realistic illustrations include African Americans as well as Caucasians.

Holland, I. *The Man without a Face*. Lippincott, 1972. (Ages 12 and up.) Charles is emotionally drained by his mother's multiple divorces and his eldest sister's cruelty to him. When he becomes attached to his tutor, he fears that he is sexually attracted to him, only to learn later that the tutor is homosexual. Charles ultimately comes to recognize his own feelings as admiration and gratitude. The tutor loves the boy in return and neither abuses nor misinterprets the boy's love for him. Unfortunately, the tutor's death neatly removes him as a potential problem.

Johnson, E. W. *Love and Sex and Growing Up,* new ed. Illus. by V. Cohen. Bantam, 1990. (Ages 9–12.) In precise terminology, refraining from slang, the author aims to correct misinformation and negative values. He includes a glossary and a brief factual self-quiz at the end of the book. The information given is appropriate for this age level.

Johnson, E. W. *Love and Sex in Plain Language,* revised ed. Harper, 1985. (Ages 10 and up.) A discussion of personal and social values surrounding love, sex, birth, and sex-related concerns. Talks plainly of erections, pleasurable sex relations, and the fact that humans engage in sexual activities for reasons other than reproduction. Stresses personal responsibility. An informative, balanced presentation.

Johnson, E. W. *People, Love, Sex, and Families: Answers to Questions That Preteens Ask.* Illus. by D. Wool. Walker, 1985 (Ages 9–12.) Based on questions from one thousand fourth, fifth, and sixth graders from different communities across the country, this book addresses informational rather than methodological issues. It also includes advice based on a clear value system reflecting respect for individuals.

Kerr, M.E. *Night Kites.* Harper, 1986. (Ages 12 and up.) Erick Rudd's eighteenth year is traumatic: He becomes emotionally and sexually involved with his best friend's girl, and his beloved and revered older brother Pete reveals not only that he is gay but also that he has AIDS. The story centers on Erick and his conflicting emotional relationships with his friends, lovers, and family. The other characters, who are not as thoroughly developed as Erick, often serve as foils for his feelings and actions; but the story works well to present the real dilemmas some teenagers encounter when the values and expectations they have grown up with are suddenly overturned.

Kitzinger, S. *Being Born.* Illus. by L. Nilsson. Putnam, 1986. (Ages 9–12.) Direct and clear language describe intercourse, fetal development, and birth. Equally direct and graphic photos illustrate the text. They include pictures of actual childbirth, suckling babies, and fetuses. The text not only presents information but also conveys a sense of emotion and ties sexual intercourse to love.

Klein, N. *It's Not What You Expect.* Pantheon, 1973. (Ages 12 and up.) Sex is handled casually in this book. Abortion, the logical solution to unplanned pregnancy, is accepted without trauma by the characters; further, it is not punished. Premarital sexual intercourse is the expected mode. All the characters are comfortable in their heterosexual relationships. When the father has a summer affair, he is welcomed home without recrimination. The mother was more experienced sexually before marriage than the father. This book can generate much discussion.

Klein, N. *Mom, the Wolf Man, and Me.* Pantheon, 1972. (Ages 10 and up.) More an indication of alternative lifestyles than information about sex, the story tells of Brett and her mother, who until now has never been married. Brett does not mind that her mother's male friend sleeps over, but she does object to her mother's plan to get married. Brett's mother has always been frank with her, and Brett has received sex education at school and is informed about many matters, including contraception.

Koertge, R. *The Arizona Kid.* Little, Brown, 1988. (Ages 13 and up.) Sixteen-year-old Billy goes to Arizona to spend the summer with his uncle, who is gay. During the summer, Billy falls in love, engages in intercourse, and comes to know his uncle and better understand the latter's lifestyle. Billy's uncle has to deal both with friends dying and with his own fears and change in lifestyle. He provides support and guidance for Billy in his new relationship and insists that Billy practice safe sex. Billy is exposed to some of the discrimination his uncle has to contend with, although the whole family is understanding and accepting.

Kolodny, N. J.; Kolodny, R. C.; and Bratter, T. E. *Smart Choices.* Little, Brown, 1986. (Ages 11-15.) Advice about many problems teenagers face, including how to talk to parents about controversial issues. The authors offer good examples, clarifying and demystifying a wide range of topics, including homosexuality.

Landau, E. *Different Drummer: Homosexuality in America.* Messner, 1986. (Ages 11 and up.) The reassuring and informative chapter titled "A Fact Sheet" sets the record straight about homosexuality and society's attitudes toward homosexual practices. The remainder of the book includes interviews with a number of homosexuals, both male and female, and gives advice about how to deal with parents, with the AIDS crisis, and with the repressive laws in certain states. As always, the author is well informed and clear in her presentation.

Levoy, M. *Three Friends.* Harper, 1984. (Ages 12 and up.) Joshua is terribly self-conscious about what he believes to be his underdeveloped body. Karen's parents are divorced, and she is bitterly angry at her father for deserting her and her mother for another woman. Her friend Lori, an artist, is uncomfortable with her bisexuality. When Lori attempts suicide, Joshua and Karen help her confront her feelings. The characters are well drawn, and their conflicts and anxieties reflect many adolescents' dilemmas.

MacLachlan, P. *Unclaimed Treasures.* Harper, 1984. (Ages 10-12.) [See Siblings]

Madaras, L., with Saavedra, D. *The What's Happening to My Body? Book for Boys.* Illus. by J. Aher. Newmarket, 1988. (Ages 9 and up.) Also *The What's Happening to My Body? Book for Girls.* Newmarket, 1983. A thorough, specific, unembarrassed, direct, accurate, and informative guide to puberty and sexuality. The author provides answers to often-asked questions and to some questions that many boys and girls may be too shy to ask.

Marzollo, J. *Getting Your Period: A Book about Menstruation.* Illus. by K. Williams. Dial, 1989. (Ages 11-15.) Physiological and emotional aspects of menstruation are presented openly, specifically, and thoroughly in this helpful book. Premenstrual syndrome (PMS), issues of privacy and body image, and even such mundane considerations as the use of sanitary products are included. There is also good advice on nutrition. The illustrations represent internal and external organs of both males and females. The overall tone is one of respectful appreciation of the human body and its functions.

McGuire, P. *It Won't Happen to Me: Teenagers Talk about Pregnancy.* Delacorte, 1983. (Ages 12 and up.) Interviews with fifteen young women, each of whom talks candidly about her sexual activity and pregnancy. The narrative includes the fathers and their involvement (or lack of it), the various options the young women have selected, and a discussion of venereal disease. The author does a remarkable job of letting the young women speak for themselves.

Miller, D. A., Ph.D, and Waigandt, A., Ph.D. *Coping with Your Sexual Orientation.* Rosen, 1990. (Ages 11 and up.) The most helpful chapter in this well-balanced book is the first one, which dispels many myths about homosexuality. In the other chapters, the authors present vignettes that end with questions about how the reader would respond. Some of these are not helpful because they may leave the reader at a loss. Nevertheless, for readers who take the opportunity to talk to knowledgeable adults, the vignettes may serve as starting points. The appendixes include a good list of resources and additional books to read.

Murrow, L. K. *Twelve Days in August.* Holiday House, 1993. (Ages 13 and up.) Todd O'Connor is confronted with a dilemma when his soccer team falls apart because of the viciously homophobic behavior of Randy, its star player. Because Randy is jealous of the playing ability of a newcomer to the team named Alex, he spreads the rumor that Alex is gay. The author never discloses whether Alex is gay, but that is not the issue. The problem is resolved when the characters recognize that teamwork is important and that respect for individuals is critical to the success of the team. An interesting component of the story is the introduction of Todd's uncle, an admirable gay character. The story may motivate good discussion about the responsibility of people to respond to scapegoating on the part of their group members. It may also spark questions and dialogue about targeting people who may or may not be gay.

Naylor, P. R. *Reluctantly Alice.* Atheneum, 1991. (Ages 8–11.) One of a series of books about Alice, now in seventh grade and preoccupied with the perplexities of sexuality and love. Her brother and father have adoring women vying for their affection (Alice's mother died some years earlier.) Boy-girl relations and physical development play a part in this humorous story that will probably touch chords, especially for preteen girls.

Newman, L. *Heather Has Two Mommies.* Illus. by D. Souza. Alyson, 1991. (Ages 4-6.) [See Family Constellations]

Ottens, A. J. *Coping with Romantic Breakup.* Rosen, 1987. (Ages 12 and up.) A practical book of advice, helping adolescents to separate constructive responses from self-destructive reactions after the painful breakup of a romantic attachment. The author recommends positive strategies and maintains a respectful and empathic tone.

Pomeroy, W. B. *Girls and Sex,* 3rd ed. Also *Boys and Sex,* 3rd ed. Dell, 1991. (Ages 10 and up.) In these companion books the author carries on a conversation with his readers about sex and sexuality, addressing each of the sexes and their concerns. While he is always careful to respect the reader's dignity, at the same time, he is very direct. Myths are explained; facts are presented; and, above all, readers are reassured of their "normalcy."

Reading, J.P. *Bouquets for Brimbal.* Harper, 1980. (Ages 12 and up.) Macy and Annie are best friends. Although Macy does not know it, Annie is a lesbian. Both girls become involved in sexual relationships when they work at a summer stock theater. At first, Macy cannot tolerate her friend's involvement with a woman, but in the end the two young women develop a stronger, more mature friendship.

Rench, J. E. *Understanding Sexual Identity: A Book for Gay Teens and Their Friends.* Lerner, 1990. (Ages 11 and up.) The intended audience is assured that they are "OK" and that their feelings of anxiety about homophobia and violence are appropriate and can be handled. The author asserts that sexual identity can neither be changed nor caused by anyone. Sensitive issues such as AIDS are discussed. Although the tone is subjective, the information is presented factually and is accompanied by ample advice.

Rylant, C. *A Couple of Kooks and Other Stories about Love.* Orchard, 1990. (Ages 12 and up.) The author employs an array of voices, both male and female. As in all her work, Rylant's sense of place and character illuminates the stories. Love is the topic in its infinite variety and unlimited affiliations. Old men and women, mentally disabled people, and young men and women are the subjects of these stories, all experiencing love and encountering their sexuality. It is important for young readers to see the connection between sex and love; all too often the link is merely biological.

Rylant, C. *A Kindness.* Orchard, 1988. (Ages 12 and up.) [See Family Constellations]

Schaffer, P. *How Babies and Families Are Made (There Is More Than One Way).* Illus. by S. Corbett. Tabor Sarah, 1988. (Ages 5–8.) Describing many specifics about the physiology and emotions of intercourse and reproduction, the book conveys a value system without passing judgment on behavior. It also proposes an expanding definition of family and includes people with different conditions of ability and background.

Scoppettone, S. *Happy Endings Are All Alike.* Harper, 1979. (Ages 12 and up.) Jaret and Peggy love each other. They must decide how they will resolve the societal pressures placed on them because of their lesbian relationship. Male chauvinism and rape are part of the drama.

Scoppettone, S. *Trying Hard to Hear You.* Harper, 1981. (Ages 12 and up.) Jeff and Phil become involved in a homosexual relationship. The story spans the events of a summer and the revelation of this relationship to their peers. The subject and events are handled realistically, and the conclusion does not change the boys' sexual orientation or make any value judgments.

Severance, J. *When Megan Went Away.* Illus. by T. Schook. Lollipop Power, 1979. (Ages 7–12.) [See Divorce]

Shannon, G. *Unlived Affections.* Harper, 1989. (Ages 12 and up.) Willie Ramsey's father never knew that he existed, and his mother died when he was still too young to know her. His grandmother, a taciturn, bitter woman who raised him, has just died, and Willie is preparing to sell the contents of her house and go to college. In going through the things in the house, Willie discovers that his father was gay. He also learns that his parents loved each other deeply and that his father was a man to be proud of. In finding out about his family, Willie also finds the courage and the ability to think about making a commitment to the young woman he loves. The story is skillfully told through a combination of the letters Willie's father wrote to Willie's mother and a narrative that opens Willie's thoughts to the reader. The father's perspective as he becomes more and more certain of his sexual orientation is well portrayed, as is Willie's evolving understanding.

Simon, N. *Don't Worry, You're Normal: A Teenager's Guide to Self-Health.* Harper, 1986. (Ages 11 and up.) Direct, clearly conveyed information; accurate terminology; and avoidance of condescension are features of this helpful book, which deals with the details of sexual development, sexuality, sexual behavior, and other issues of concern to adolescents.

Slepian, J. *Getting on with It.* Four Winds, 1985. (Ages 11 and up.) [See Divorce]

Stefoff, R. *Adolescence.* Chelsea House, 1990. (Ages 11 and up.) One of the Life Cycle series of books that is part of *The Encyclopedia of Health,* this volume presents a literate and thoughtful investigation of the definition, history, and factors involved in becoming an adolescent in today's United States. Physical, emotional, and societal factors are explored.

Steptoe, J. *My Special Best Words.* Viking, 1974. (Ages 5-8.) Bweela, three years old, lives with her one-year-old brother Javaka and her father. Javaka is not yet toilet trained, so Bweela teaches him. The book is full of "special" words, including the family's personal bathroom language. The illustrations are explicit: Javaka has a penis. A frank, educational, and endearing book.

Valentine, J. *The Day They Put a Tax on Rainbows and other Stories.* Illus. by L. Schmidt. Alyson, 1992. (Ages 5-8.) Fantasies with children as heroes and with gay or lesbian parents in some of the families. Issues of gender stereotyping, greed, and responsibility are handled well. Both heterosexual and homosexual love are respectfully presented as normal. The stories are fun and deserve a place on the shelves alongside more traditional fairytales.

Voigt, C. *Come a Stranger.* Macmillan, 1986. (Ages 12 and up.) Mina has a discouraging experience at dance camp, partly because puberty has caused her body to change and partly because she is African American. Back home, Mina falls in love with Tamer Shipp, a minister who offers her abiding friendship. In the end, she finds a new love interest in Dexter, a young man closer to her age and interests. Friendship, as well as sexuality, figures strongly in this story.

Wilkinson, B. *Ludell and Willie.* Harper, 1977. (Ages 11 and up.) [See Heritage]

Willhoite, M. *Daddy's Roommate.* Illus. by the author. Alyson, 1990. (Ages 4-8.) A young boy describes spending weekends with his father and Frank, his father's live-in boyfriend. He is a happy, well-adjusted child who understands and accepts his father's new relationship. The story is a bit saccharine but otherwise well done. It avoids stereotypes and provides reassurance.

Winthrop, E. *A Little Demonstration of Affection.* Harper, 1975. (Ages 12 and up.) Jenny fears that she has incestuous feelings toward her brother Charles. Her family never shows affection outwardly. Jenny is so moved by her brother's hugging her that she believes she is abnormal. Eventually her father helps her handle her feelings.

Yolen, J. *The Gift of Sarah Barker.* Viking, 1981. (Ages 11 and up.) Two young Shaker teenagers fall in love. The characters are well drawn, as is the dilemma that faces Abel and Sarah: how to reconcile their feelings of love for each other with the edicts of their religious community which, among other things, strictly enforces separation of the sexes. Sexuality and love are treated with honesty and respect.

Zindel, P. *My Darling, My Hamburger.* Harper, 1969. (Ages 12 and up.) A novel dealing with abortion, premarital sex, and interpersonal relationships.

chapter 6

Aging

American society is no longer dominated by the young. People may still worship at the altar of perpetual youth, but the nation's median age is rising steadily. The substantial part of the population over 65 years old cannot be ignored. According to the National Institutes of Health, by the year 2040 the population over age 65 in the United States may constitute over one-fourth of the U.S. population.

Different cultures have responded to the phenomenon of aging in a variety of ways. Some, particularly in Asia, venerate their elders. They respect the experience and knowledge that accrue with age, and they assign to elders almost magical qualities of wisdom and ability. At the opposite end of the spectrum are some groups, especially nomadic communities, who expect their aged members to disappear gracefully once they become burdensome and can no longer fend for themselves. Between these two extremes lies a great range of attitude and behavior toward elders, some prescribed and ritualized, some purely idiosyncratic.

Stereotypes about elders often inhibit the rest of the population from treating them humanely and rationally. On the one hand, lip service is paid to respecting elders' wisdom and experience. On the other hand, old people are often forced into retirement homes or segregated into communities restricted only to "senior citizens." Society sometimes behaves as if old people do not exist or wishes that they did not. Several generations of family rarely live in the same house now, so that children have fewer opportunities to interact with elders every day.

Fortunately, the elder population is not waiting for others to rescue it. Through such organizations as the Gray Panthers and the American Association of Retired Persons and through activities such as elder hostels they have been taking charge of their own advocacy and have helped educate the rest of the population about their abilities and needs. Problems have been imposed upon them not through their own failings but as a function of unresponsive social and governmental services. Pressure to withdraw from the work force, insufficient social security benefits, hoodlums who prey upon them, inadequate and expensive medical care, and a society that tends to ostracize the elderly all present barriers difficult to overcome.

Try This

Answer these questions, and be prepared to discuss your responses.

1. Where should elders live? (With their families? daughters? sons? siblings?)
2. What should the regulations be about retirement age? (Should there be a mandatory retirement age?)
3. Complete this statement: "Elders are . . ." (e.g., kind, crotchety, forgetful, wise, gentle, weak, strong, foolish, uninterested in sexual activity, prudish, expendable, vital to society, etc.)

A society that excludes its elders deprives itself of first-hand encounters with the wealth of past experience these people afford, not only of world and local history but also of cultural and family roots. Children need the multigenerational perspective elders can provide. They also need models for treating people with dignity and respect no matter what their age. Books can aid in the development of a mutually rewarding interaction with elders. There are many descriptions of the aged in children's books, and many of them are accurate and constructive.

SUGGESTED CRITERIA

Although old age is the last developmental stage of life, aging and death should not automatically be linked with each other. The emphasis should be on life and its interactions and activities. Death is a separate matter and should be confronted as such. It would be helpful to accumulate a variety of books, some of them describing old characters who recover from their illnesses rather than die as a result of them. It is nevertheless reasonable to expect elders to think and talk about death, and to acknowledge some sort of preparation for dealing with it.

It should also be recognized that there is a world of difference between some 65 year olds and some 80 year olds. Even though everyone can point to specific elders (like Grandma Moses, George Burns, or Bob Hope) who were more active than some 40 year olds at advanced ages, it must be acknowledged that most 85 year olds are less vigorous than most 70 year olds. Thus, though old age is developmental, there are stages within aging itself.

Although it may be realistic to describe elders with any of a variety of physical conditions such as arthritis, it is unfortunate if they are seen only as victims of physical infirmity.

When senility (infantile behavior, total loss of memory of recent events, or loss of contact with reality) is included as part of a plot, it should be factually accurate and not presented so as to devalue the afflicted elder. Children need to know about this problem, but the library should be balanced with books that describe capable, intellectually competent elders as well. Senility is less prevalent in the aged population than is commonly imagined, and the myth that all elders become senile should be counteracted. All characters, no matter what their intellectual capacity, should be treated with dignity.

Another myth that needs to be dispelled is that elders function primarily in relation to their families. Some people never marry and continue to be active participants in society; some live far from their families or choose to spend relatively small amounts of time with their relatives. Books should reflect the variety of possible relationships. Elders should appear in roles additional to and other than those of grandparents. Children should recognize that there is as great a variety among elderly people as there is among the rest of the population. Children should be helped to see that they may find many opportunities to interact with elders who are not in their immediate families and who have identities separate from their family ties.

Elders have as many varied personalities and responses as young people. Individuality does not disappear with age. It should not be assumed that people over 65 have lost their distinctive character traits.

The sexuality of elders should also be acknowledged. They are not necessarily without sex partners by choice, and their faculties can remain active as long as they live. They should be shown as individuals capable of establishing new relationships and of engaging in continuing marriages to long-time partners.

Children should not always be rescuers of elders, and elderly people should not always be victims. The image of the helpless, dependent old person should not dominate the literature. It is demeaning and condescending to present the child-hero as the more intelligent, assertive, perceptive character. Two-way friendships between children and elders should be depicted realistically, with each partner contributing to these relationships. On the other hand, elders should not be required to be heroes in order to be accepted and respected.

All characters should be treated with dignity. The qualities of elders should not be ridiculed or made to seem quaint because of the association with old age.

Elders should not be required to function as seers, saints, or sages. Their exclusive reason for existence should not be to serve others.

Elders are entitled to the same foibles and flaws as the rest of the population. Just as young people are not always beautiful, elders are not always physically unattractive. Elders should not automatically be crotchety, forgetful, wicked, or feeble. Many retain an energy level that equals and even surpasses a young person's.

Characters over 65 should, when feasible, be pictured as active people engaged in vital projects. The stereotype of the passive, sedentary senior citizen should not be the dominant image. However, this does not mean that the problems specific to aging—such as medical issues, fixed income, forced retirement, and others imposed by societal insensitivity—should be ignored. In books where an old age, nursing, or retirement home figures in the plot, it should not be represented as the expected place of residence for all elders. In reality, only about 5 percent of the aged population (up to age 70) lives in such institutions. Most live in their own homes or share housing with one another or with their families. When placement of an old person in such a residence is deemed necessary, it should be described realistically and in appropriate perspective; the decision should be reached after mutual consultation with all concerned. If this is not the case, the reader should be made aware that the situation is not a model one.

Since elders belong to a range of cultures, classes, and communities, their diversity should be depicted in the books that make up the classroom or library collection. Children must learn to refrain from pigeonholing the elderly population in any way. Books should focus on elders primarily as people, then, perhaps, as old people.

DISCUSSION OF CHILDREN'S BOOKS

A number of recently published books for children eight years of age or younger describe the loving affinity between young children and grandparents or other elders. Such titles as *Just Like Max* and *Song and Dance Man,* by Karen Ackerman, show a grandfather and a great-uncle with work-identities that are important to them and to the children. Another remarkable great-uncle figures in Diane DiSalvo's, *Uncle Willie and the Soup Kitchen,* in which the elder teaches by example that doing for other people has no age restrictions. Sally Wittman has also created a lively, vital elder in the person of *The Wonderful Mrs. Trumbly.* She is attractive, newly married, still active in teaching and engaged in her own interests, as well as capable of befriending a young student. A whole group of elders who are distinct individuals are pictured in wonderful illustrations by Julie Vivas and described in delightful text by Mem Fox in *Wilfrid Gordon McDonald Partridge.* The story describes the affection of young W.G.M. Partridge for the elderly residents of the nursing home next door and shows that his feelings are reciprocated by all the elders. Their idiosyncrasies are acknowledged without nastiness, and it is understandable that the young boy would want to be with them.

Eve Bunting's *Summer Wheels* contains an elder who becomes an important influence on many of the children in his neighborhood, not only because he supplies them with bicycles to ride but also because he provides them with a model of respectful behavior that arms them for societal living. The same author also contributes a touching story in *The Wednesday Surprise,* in which a young girl and her grandmother engage in a mutually satisfying project. The bibliography at the end of this chapter is filled with many such close and caring intergenerational collaborations.

For older children, Eth Clifford's *The Remembering Box* demonstrates that young people are capable of becoming involved with older people's stories and memories. In this story, Joshua genuinely enjoys his grandmother's reflections on her youth. Similarly, in *The Gift,* by Helen Coutant, Anna learns to value the way her friend, old Nana Marie, sees the world. In *Mrs. Abercorn and the Bunce Boys,* by Lisa Fosburgh, Otis and Will engage in a mutually satisfying and supportive friendship with a lusty, hardy old woman. Janni Howker offers some unforgettable and unique older characters in *Badger on the Barge and Other Stories.* In each of the stories a young person and an elder interact in some way so as to affect both their lives. A grandmother who refuses to be relegated to the rocking chair even when she is at the point of death adorns Richard Peck's

Those Summer Girls I Never Met, changing forever the way her two grand-children think about elders.

Try This
Make a list of all the characteristics of elders in all of the books the class has read. What's missing? What patterns emerge? Discuss gender, heritage, and class differences and similarities.

Some books deal with what to do when an elder can no longer care for him or herself. Barbara Dugan's *Loop the Loop* is a bittersweet story about a friend-ship between Mrs. Simpson, a very old woman who gets around in a wheelchair, and Anne, a girl about seven years old. Because Mrs. Simpson is not permitted to take her cat to the nursing home that will become her permanent residence, Anne decides to care for it and brings her own beloved doll to Mrs. Simpson so that she will have something to cuddle and talk to. Children might benefit from a discussion of what restrictions are necessary and which might be harmful, especially in the light of recent research demonstrating the healing effects of pets.

Another story of old age that presents a somewhat positive resolution of the problem of infirmity is Rose Blue's *Grandma Didn't Wave Back*. Debbie's grand-mother has been living with the family for more than five years. Debbie and her friends have always enjoyed Grandma's cooking and her company. But now the grandmother lapses into and out of senility, even beginning to do things that are potentially harmful to herself. The solution is her placement in a very painstak-ingly selected care center overlooking the ocean. At first Debbie is resentful of her parents for "sending her grandmother away," but the elder reassures her grand-daughter that she will be comfortable there and looks forward to occasional visits from her family. She tells Debbie to visit when she can but not to think of her all the time because Debbie's life is still ahead of her.

The family in this book does not have to worry about the cost of the facil-ity. They care about the feelings of everyone involved and can select the most appropriate arrangement. The story provides one model for making pivotal decisions while lovingly and respectfully involving an elder who is coping with a serious disability.

Both these books can be used to stimulate comparisons and discussions of what constitutes a good institution. A class visit to a local nursing home could be used to follow up this sort of discussion or even to introduce the topic. Often a holiday provides the impetus for a visit from children. If a child in the class has a grandparent in a nearby home or housing development for elders, the class can adopt that grandparent. The more comfortable children begin to feel about elders and the more contact they have with them, the more prepared they will be to deal with the issues surrounding old age when they arise.

Another useful practice is to invite elders who belong to a golden age club or who attend a local elders' group to come to the classroom to read stories to the children, help them with projects, or even just sit and be available for affec-tion. This practice permits children who live far away from their grandparents to experience some of the attention elders often enjoy giving children. It also provides a service to the elderly community by valuing them for what they can do and demonstrating that there is a special place and function for them.

One of these projects (visiting a "retirement ranch") is described in *Just like a Real Family,* by Kristi Holl. June, one of the sixth graders involved in the activity, is assigned to a cranky, laconic old man named Franklin Cooper. After a period of time, June, her mother, and Mr. Cooper become very closely involved with each other.

A Figure of Speech, by Norma Fox Mazer, deals with old age in a painful but forthright manner. The grandfather is full of aches and pains. He is forgetful, his apartment is messy, and he slobbers over his food. Most of the members of his family treat him with disrespect. He has an apartment in the basement of his daughter's house, and this arrangement is all right until one day his college-age grandson comes home newly married, requiring a place for himself and his wife. Eventually the old man is moved out. The family is worried about lack of privacy, added responsibilities, and economic burdens—a not uncommon situation in today's world. Only Jenny understands, respects, and responds warmly to the old man.

The old man and Jenny run away from home when they discover that the family is about to put him into an institution that regards elders as worthless and helpless. This sort of institution is, perhaps, not the rule, but the description is believable. The grandfather tries to dissuade Jenny from running away with him, but she insists on going. He carefully prepares for the venture, aware of the potential difficulties.

Mazer includes some excellent dialogue concerning the words people use to describe old age and death. The grandfather tolerates no euphemisms about his age or his eventual death. He leaves notes taped to the refrigerator indicating his displeasure at such phrases. He announces that he has no intention of "passing away"—he will die. *A Figure of Speech* does not mince words; it raises questions about old age, suicide, and death that have no easy answers. The issues of morality and responsibility are important for both adults and children. Children may benefit from telling the story from the perspective of each of the characters, including the parents.

Dealing with a strong and complex woman and raising questions about the positives and negatives of aging is Norma Farber's *How Does It Feel to Be Old?*. Older readers can benefit from the insights and wry humor of this beautifully crafted poetic reflection. The powerful illustrations can spark much discussion as well.

Sometimes elders may appear to be helpless when in reality they are not. Martha Whitmore Hickman portrays such a person in *When James Allen Whitaker's Grandfather Came to Stay.* At first it seems that the grandfather will be residing permanently with his daughter and her family. But as time goes on, even though he tries to make the best of it, he misses his home and independence. He finally decides that he must return to Massachusetts. But instead of "toughing it out" without any special preparations, he wisely arranges to have renters so he will not be alone and invites his family to spend summers with him so their interaction can continue. His decision is based on his own needs, and he is caring and firm about it; but he also considers his family's feelings.

In books, as in life, there are no easy answers and no absolutes. Each elder is different from every other. Each situation is also different. In one case, a nursing home is an excellent solution to a difficult situation; in another instance, it could be the worst option. The purpose of accumulating a variety of books is to find several alternative solutions for a given situation. Children should question, argue, design several possible approaches for handling a dilemma, and seek out more books and articles confirming or contradicting their ideas.

REFERENCES

Aging

Alfonso, S. R. "Modules for Teaching about Young People's Literature. Module 2: How Do the Elderly Fare in Children's Books?" *Journal of Reading* 30 (Dec. 1986): 201-203. One of a series of modules "designed to give preservice and inservice teachers a look at various issues across several genres" of children's literature. This one is focused on stereotyping of the elderly.

Ansello, E. F. "How Older People Are Stereotyped." *Bulletin of the Council on Interracial Books for Children* 7 (6, 1976): 4-10. Discusses how picture books treat aged characters, provides a format for critiquing books, and generally decries the negative image conveyed. This article is in two parts in an issue that is devoted entirely to the topic of aging.

Fillmer, H. T., and Meadows, R. "The Portrayal of Older Characters in Five Sets of Basal Readers." *Elementary School Journal* 86 (May 1986): 651-662. The authors found 553 references to older characters in five reading series. Most were white, male, healthy, and financially comfortable. Although there were few negative stereotypes, elders were represented unrealistically.

Horner, C. T. *The Aging Adult in Children's Books and Nonprint Media.* Scarecrow, 1982. The volume includes a comprehensive annotated bibliography of more than 300 children's books, with an informative and reasoned introduction exploring the many facets of the depiction of elders in literature.

Kazemek, F. E., and Rigg, P. "There's More to an Old Person Than Appears." *Journal of Youth Services in Libraries* 1 (Summer 1988): 396-406. The authors present the thesis that "reading good literature about old people is important for American youngsters." They describe and analyze the value of 40 children's books representing cultural diversity. They point out that literature, among its other virtues, helps young people to see the world through other eyes, gain access to different models of living, and appreciate old people in their infinite variety.

Luszcz, M. A. "Characterizing Adolescents, Middle-Aged, and Elderly Adults: Putting the Elderly into Perspective." *International Journal of Aging and Human Development* 22 (2, 1985-86): 105-121. The authors determined that attitudes of groups assorted according to age reflect stereotypes when broad categorical decisions are required, but the stereotypes break down if individual or known people are characterized.

Mitchell, J.; Wilson, K.; Revicki, D.; and Parker, L. "Children's Perceptions of Aging: A Multidimensional Approach to Differences by Age, Sex, and Race." *The Gerontologist* 25 (2, 1985): 182-187. The researchers piloted a methodology for measuring children's perceptions and found that attitudes or perceptions should be viewed as a multidimensional concept and that children should not be encouraged to polarize their responses. They also found that children did not consistently view elders in either a negative or a positive light but had varying opinions of each individual.

Rutherford, W. M. *An Exploratory Study of Ageism in Children's Literature.* Doctoral dissertation, University of the Pacific, Stockton, Calif., 1981. Eighty books for children were analyzed for stereotyping. The test instrument and coding procedure are useful for similar future studies.

Schwarcz, J. H., and Schwarcz, C. "Grandparents and Grandchildren." In *The Picture Book Comes of Age: Looking at Childhood through the Art of Illustration,* pp. 47-61. American Library Association, 1991. Analyzes 12 children's books containing grandparents as important characters. Discusses the variety of elders' roles and personalities and observes that not enough books reflect the reality of some negative characteristics of elders. Concludes that the presence of grandparents enriches children's lives.

Valeri-Gold, M. "Bridging the Generations: Helping Students Understand the Elderly (K-7). Choosing and Using Children's Books." *Livewire* 2 (Dec. 1985): 10-13. Recommends a number of children's books and suggests criteria for selecting books for children.

Watson, J. "A Positive Image of the Elderly in Literature for Children." *Reading Teacher* 34 (April 1981): 792-798. Provides an extensive list of books, prefaced by a useful discussion, that can be used with young readers to help them acquire a positive attitude toward old people.

RESOURCES

American Association of Retired Persons (AARP). 1909 K. St., NW, Washington, DC 20049. Provides a variety of benefits for people 50 years of age and older, including advocacy, a newsletter, discounts on various goods and services, and information on aging.

ELDER LINE. 1-800-AGE-INFO. Directs callers from Massachusetts or New Hampshire to agencies across the country that can best help them find good home care for their elderly family members. An arm of Massachusetts Home Care Agencies.

Grandparents Rights Organization. Suite 600, 555 S. Woodward Ave., Birmingham, MI 48009. Deals with visitation and custody rights issues of grandparents.

Gray Panthers. 311 S. Juniper St., Suite 601, Philadelphia, PA 19104. An advocacy organization providing information and support for elder issues.

National Council on the Aging. 600 Maryland Ave., SW, Washington, DC 20024. A national nonprofit membership organization advocating a more equitable society for elders. Conducts research and produces publications.

The Too Faraway Grandparents' Newsletter. P.O. Box 71, Del Mar, CA 92014. Offers tips on how to sustain relationships with grandchildren over a distance.

BIBLIOGRAPHY

Ackerman, K. *Just Like Max.* Illus. by G. Schmidt. Knopf, 1990. (Ages 6-9.) Aaron lives in a house with his parents, his sister, his aunt, his grandparents, and his Great-uncle Max. He treasures the times he spends watching Max create the clothing he sews for "the fancy people." After Max has a stroke, Aaron tries to cheer him up by demonstrating what he has learned about sewing, much to Max's delight. When Aaron grows up, he becomes a writer and emulates his great-uncle's work habits and the pleasure he took in them by becoming a model for the younger generation. It is unfortunate that Aaron's mother and aunt do not seem to value Max and his stories, but Aaron more than makes up for it.

Ackerman, K. *Song and Dance Man.* Illus. by S. Gammell. Knopf, 1988. (Ages 5-8.) The children's grandfather continues to practice his song and dance acts after his retirement. His grandchildren enjoy dressing in costumes and watching him perform. They appreciate him for his talents and his identity as a separate person, and they adore him as their grandfather. The book won the 1989 Caldecott medal.

Addy, S. H. *A Visit with Great-Grandma.* Illus. by L. Halverson. Whitman, 1989. (Ages 5-8.) The story celebrates heritage and the relationship of a young girl to her Czechoslovakian great-grandmother. Even though neither can speak the other's language, the two communicate through traditional food, looking at pictures, and, above all, love.

Aliki. *The Two of Them.* Illus. by the author. Greenwillow, 1979. (Ages 4-10.) The young girl is deeply loved and cared for by her grandfather. She cares for him when he is sick and fondly remembers him after his death.

Ancona, G. *Growing Older.* Illus. by the author. Dutton, 1978. (Ages 10 and up.) An excellent book of biographies, drawing on different heritages and illustrating the beauty and energy of the lives of people who have now grown old.

Anderson, L. *Stina's Visit.* Illus. by L. Anderson. Greenwillow, 1989. (Ages 5-8.) In this affectionate story of friendship, Stina and her grandfather surprise grandfather's friend Stretchit on his birthday. Stretchit tells them several very tall tales and then gives Stina a memento of one of his tales (a washtub) to take home. The contrasts and similarities between the two old men enrich the story. This is a sequel to *Stina* (1988), in which the grandfather displays tenderness and companionship as he and his granddaughter weather a storm together.

Baker, J. *Millicent.* Illus. by the author. Andre Deutsch, 1980. (Ages 5-12.) Remarkable vivid illustrations accompany a text that leads the reader into the mind of a wonderful old woman who comes to the park every day to feed the pigeons.

Ballard, R. *Granny and Me.* Illus. by the author. Greenwillow, 1992. (Ages 3-6.) Annie and her grandmother engage in many wonderful activities—reading stories, going to the beach, driving around, baking, and especially looking at photos of the family. Annie learns about herself and her family through this close relationship.

Baylor, B. *The Other Way to Listen.* Scribner, 1978. (Ages 5-8.) A young boy learns from his friend, an old man, how to take the time to listen to what few people can hear—seed pods bursting open and all the other wonders of nature.

Blue, R. *Grandma Didn't Wave Back.* Illus. by T. Lewin. Watts, 1972. (Ages 7-10.) It is difficult for Debbie, who loves her dearly, to understand why her grandmother must go to live in a nursing home. In the end, all agree that it is the best course of action.

Borack, B. *Grandpa.* Illus. by B. Shecter. Trumpet, 1967. (Ages 5-7.) Illustrated with simple lines and soft colors, the correspondingly warm, simple story explores a mutually respectful and rich relationship between a young girl and her grandfather. The grandfather models behavior other adults would do well to emulate: He stops tickling the child when she says she has had enough, answers her letters in writing, sits quietly by her side without needing to speak, and responds to her needs for humor and comfort.

Bornstein, R. L. *A Beautiful Seashell.* Illus. by the author. Harper, 1990. (Ages 5-8.) A great-grandmother gives her great granddaughter a sense of the past and a precious gift for the future. The child and the old woman rock together in a chair, and the child learns about the great-grandmother's feelings, as well as her family's background.

Brenner, B. *A Year in the Life of Rosie Bernard.* Harper, 1971. (Ages 8-12.) Rosie's mother has died; and despite his promise to keep Rosie with him, her father must bow to economic pressures and take an acting job that keeps him on the road. He therefore brings Rosie to her maternal grandparents' house in Brooklyn. Rosie, a spunky, bright, sensitive, and engaging girl, spends a year with this family and grows to love and appreciate them. The grandparents particularly emerge as strong.

Bunting, E. *Summer Wheels.* Illus. by T. B. Allen. HBJ, 1992. (Ages 7–10.) The Bicycle Man is an elder who spends his time working with children in an inner city neighborhood in Los Angeles. He permits them to borrow bicycles on a sign-out basis and interacts with them as a friend and counselor. Lawrence, one of the boys who appreciates and benefits from the Bicycle Man, learns how to understand other people's issues without condemning them. In addition to the genuinely touching story, a realistic model of an interracial friendship is presented.

Bunting, E. *The Wednesday Surprise.* Illus. by D. Carrick. Clarion, 1989. (Ages 5–9.) Anna and her grandmother prepare a surprise timed especially for Anna's father's birthday. The story builds a sense of suspense. The surprise turns out to be that Anna has taught her grandmother to read. The love and respect of Anna and her grandmother for each other shine through the story. The grandmother is depicted as a strong woman who decided on her own how to overcome the illiteracy she perceived to be a handicap.

Burningham, J. *Granpa.* Illus. by the author. Crown, 1984. (Ages 4–6.) Most of the book reveals a loving and active relationship between a little girl and her aged grandfather. In addition to reading to her; telling her stories; and taking her fishing, sledding, and to the park, the grandfather respects her questions and concerns. After the grandfather sickens and dies, we see the saddened little girl taking her baby sibling for a walk. It looks as though the child's relationship with her grandfather will serve as a model for interaction with her sibling. The crayon-and-ink drawings project an expressive and childlike quality, conveying the characters' emotions as well as the fullness of their relationship.

Butterworth, W.E. *LeRoy and the Old Man.* Four Winds, 1980. (Ages 12 and up.) LeRoy goes to stay with his grandfather, whom he is meeting for the first time in his life. LeRoy's father has deserted him and his mother. The grandfather is unforgiving of his son, but he takes in his grandson and teaches him his value system. The old man is capable, strong, and well respected by his community. LeRoy and his mother will eventually make a permanent home here. The family is African American.

Caines, J. *Window Wishing.* Illus. by K. Brooks. Harper, 1980. (Ages 5–8.) Grandma Meg is not old, but she is a grandmother; and it is important for children to encounter a variety of women who are grandmothers. Grandma Meg leads a very active life. When the two children visit her, she takes them fishing and "window wishing" (her name for looking in the windows of shops and wishing for what they can one day have). Unconventional in many ways, Grandma Meg provides her grandchildren with memories they will cherish. The characters are African American.

Cameron, A. *The Most Beautiful Place in the World.* Illus. by T. B. Allen. Knopf, 1988. (Ages 8–10.) Juan lives in his grandmother's house in Guatemala. Even though he is only seven years old, he works as a shoeshine boy. Together the boy and his grandmother define the most beautiful place in the world as one where "you can hold your head up . . . and be proud of who you are . . . and where you love someone a whole lot and you know that person loves you."

Carlstrom, N. W. *Blow Me a Kiss Miss Lilly.* Illus. by A. Schwartz. Harper, 1990. (Ages 8–10.) Miss Lilly, an elderly woman, is young Sara's best friend. The two spend much time together telling stories, gardening, and canning jam. One day, Miss Lilly goes to the hospital, where she later dies. Sara's family adopts Miss Lilly's cat, which helps Sara with her grief. The next spring, Sara visits Miss Lilly's garden and feels as if Miss Lilly is blowing her a kiss. Miss Lilly is a bit of a stereotype—she wears her grey hair in a bun, lives in a little white cottage, cans jam, and drinks tea. A stereotypic expectation is confirmed when the elderly protagonist dies at the end. It is strange that neither character seems to have any other friends. However, the relationship between the two protagonists occupies the center of attention, and it is a model intergenerational friendship. The story has substance, and the characters are strong.

Carlstrom, N. W. *Grandpappy.* Illus. by L. Molk. Little, Brown, 1990. (Ages 6-9.) The ordinary events of a day for Nate and his grandfather impart all kinds of learning to the boy and demonstrate what a model the old man is. His love of life, respect for all people, generosity, strength, thoughtfulness, intelligence, caring, and wisdom are reflected in each of his actions and in his conversations with his grandson.

Caseley, J. *Dear Annie.* Illus. by the author. Greenwillow, 1991. (Ages 5-8.) Annie and her grandfather maintain a correspondence from the time she is born. At first Annie's mother does the actual writing, but in good time Annie takes over. The postcards and the thoughts expressed on them are wonderful models for young readers.

Caseley, J. *When Grandpa Came to Stay.* Illus. by the author. Greenwillow, 1986. (Ages 5-8.) Benny handles with aplomb Grandpa's coming to stay after Grandma dies and adjusts well to helping Grandpa recuperate from a stroke. Then one day, when Grandpa cries, Benny goes into a tizzy, after which he is ashamed of himself. Grandpa understands Benny's behavior and explains that he too has behaved badly in his time. The two then visit Grandma'a grave and renew their mutually satisfying relationship.

Clamenson, S. *Where Is Grandma Potamus?* Illus. by S. Gantner. Grosset & Dunlap, 1983. (Ages 4-7.) Grandma Potamus takes Stanley and Bebe to Playland although she is very sleepy because she was out dancing very late the night before. After an adventure at the amusement park, Grandma Potamus goes dancing late into the next night with a pilot she meets at the park. A good model of an active older woman.

Clifford, E. *The Remembering Box.* Illus. by D. Diamond. Houghton Mifflin, 1985. (Ages 7-10.) Joshua and his grandmother enjoy a very close relationship based on respect and unconditional love. Part of their interaction involves going through a box of the grandmother's treasures, each of which calls forth stories and emotional memories. When Joshua is ten years old, his grandmother gives him a remembering box of his own, tells him more stories about her growing up, and dies serenely. Joshua is left with a powerful sense of enduring love, a foundation of memory, and an appreciation of his heritage.

Coats, L. J. *Mr. Jordan in the Park.* Illus. by the author. Macmillan, 1989. (Ages 5-8.) Beautifully illustrated, this book helps young readers to see that elders were once babies, children, young people, and young adults. Mr. Jordan is very much an individual and is not now identified solely by his role as a grandfather. An excellent book for raising awareness and understanding of older people.

Coutant, H. *The Gift.* Illus. by V. Mai. Knopf, 1983. (Ages 7-10.) Nana Marie, an old woman, and Anna, a shy young girl, befriend each other and continue their friendship after Nana Marie loses her sight. Anna's gift to her friend is a detailed accounting of each day as Nana Marie has taught her to see and experience it.

Davis, M. S. *Something Magic.* Illus. by M. O. Young. Simon & Schuster, 1991. (Ages 3-6.) A grandmother is shown as an active woman: She canoes, tends a farm, bakes, and digs for clams. She is also attuned to her granddaughter's feelings: She recalls the grandfather with love and empathizes with the pain of the loss of the child's kitten. The illustrations successfully convey the magical connection between the young child and the older woman. The story helps young readers to appreciate the continuity with the older generations.

Delton, J. *My Uncle Nikos.* Illus. by M. Simont. Crowell, 1983. (Ages 5-8.) In both its illustrations and gentle text, this book shows a warm relationship between a young girl and her uncle, a productive, accepting, happy, older Greek man.

De Paola, T. *Now One Foot, Now Other Foot.* Illus. by the author. Putnam, 1981. (Ages 5-8.) When his grandfather suffers a stroke, Bobby helps him to walk again, just as his grandfather once helped him.

Dexter, A. *Grandma.* Illus. by the author. Harper, 1992. (Ages 4-8.) A young girl has trouble keeping up with her energetic grandmother as they share a wonderful day at the beach. Grandma is seen chasing her granddaughter with crabs, playing arcade games, racing up hills, and operating a chain saw, in addition to baking cookies and cleaning the house. The clever, lighthearted text and bright, bold illustrations combine to create a picture of an older woman who defies stereotypes.

DiSalvo-Ryan, D. *Uncle Willie and the Soup Kitchen.* Illus. by the author. Morrow, 1991. (Ages 7-10.) Uncle Willie is a model for older people who continue to be productive and community minded. He is no self-pitying, crotchety elder. He takes his young nephew with him to work in the soup kitchen where he regularly volunteers. The two share a loving and respectful relationship.

Dorros, A. *Abuela.* Illus. by E. Kleven. Dutton, 1991. (Ages 5-8.) Rosalba, a young girl of Latino heritage, spends time with her loving *abuela* (grandmother). She imagines that she and her grandmother fly above New York City, visiting different places along the way. Many Spanish phrases are worked into the reading. A glossary lists all these words. The colorful mixed-media collages augment the text.

Dugan, B. *Loop the Loop.* Illus. by J. Stevenson. Greenwillow, 1992. (Ages 5-8.) Mrs. Simpson, a very old woman, and Anne, a young girl, spend their summer together enjoying such activities as feeding the ducks in the pond, playing cards and Scrabble, and playing with Mrs. Simpson's cat and Anne's favorite doll. Mrs. Simpson also demonstrates her remarkable prowess as a yo-yo player. The story is told from Anne's point of view, and the reader feels her anguish when Mrs. Simpson is hospitalized with a broken hip and seems more out of touch with reality than usual. Later, Anne visits her in the nursing home where she will stay for the foreseeable future. Anne smuggles Mrs. Simpson's cat in for a visit (no cats are permitted in the home) and leaves her beloved doll with Mrs. Simpson. The portrait of the vigorous old woman is engaging. The ending raises many questions about how to handle some of the problems attendant upon extreme old age and physical disabilities.

Eige, L. *The Kidnapping of Mister Huey.* Harper, 1983. (Ages 9-12.) Willy, age 14, and Mister Huey, an old man, become friends. To protect Mister Huey from being sent to a run-down, unappealing old age home, Willy and Mister Huey run away. They find an abandoned town where they camp out for two weeks. When they are inevitably discovered, Willy prevails on his parents to help Mister Huey keep his house. All works out for the best as each of the characters emerges stronger and more hopeful. Running away has helped Willy to mature and given Mister Huey confidence in his ability to maintain his independence. It is not a good idea to offer running away as a solution to a family problem, but in this case it turns into a positive action.

Epstein, B., and Davis, D. *Two Sisters and Some Hornets.* Illus. by R. Wells. Holiday House, 1972. (Ages 5-8.) [See Siblings]

Fair, S. *The Bedspread.* Illus. by the author. Morrow, 1982. (Ages 5-8.) [See Siblings]

Farber, N. *How Does It Feel to Be Old?* Illus. by T. S. Hyman. Dutton, 1979. (Ages 7-12.) A sensitive, joyous and often humorously poetic book. The grandmother speaks frankly about her feelings. Never maudlin or self-pitying, she asserts independence and the "right to be me" as themes throughout the poem.

Flournoy, V. *The Patchwork Quilt.* Illus. by J. Pinkney. Dial, 1985. (Ages 5–8.) Tonya's grandma uses scraps from the entire family to start her "masterpiece," a quilt that becomes a family project when the grandmother becomes too ill to work on it. The grandmother recovers and resumes work on the quilt (counteracting the stereotype that when old people get ill they do not get well). The grandmother's dialect enhances the flavor of the story. This African-American family is tightly knit and mutually nurturing.

Fosburgh, L. *Mrs. Abercorn and the Bunce Boys.* Illus. by J. Downing. Four Winds, 1986. (Ages 10–12.) The friendship between Mrs. Abercorn and the brothers Otis and Will helps sustain all of them. The boys' mother works hard as a waitress and has little time for them. Her boyfriend Bink drinks a lot of beer. Mrs. Abercorn is estranged from her son and grandson. She is a fast-driving, intelligent, talented woman whose age does not prevent her from living life to the fullest. The end of summer signals the boys' departure, but the friendship will continue.

Fox, M. *Wilfrid Gordon McDonald Partridge.* Illus. by J. Vivas. Kane Miller, 1985. (Ages 5–9.) One of the charms of this endearing book is that it is effortless and natural for Wilfrid to enjoy the company of the elderly people who live in the old people's home next door. His helpful approach to assisting Miss Nancy Alison Delacourt Cooper find her memories can spark many creative responses on the part of young readers.

Gauch, P. *Grandpa and Me.* Illus. by S. Shimin. Coward, McCann & Geoghegan, 1972. (Ages 5–8.) A grandfather and his grandson spend a wonderful summer together.

Geras, A. *Apricots at Midnight and Other Stories from a Patchwork Quilt.* Illus. by D. Caldwell. Atheneum, 1982. (Ages 8–12.) Aunt Pinny is a storyteller. She is also an old woman who has lived a rich and passionate life because of her understanding of others' needs, her imagination, and her zest for living.

Goffstein, M.B. *Fish for Supper.* Illus. by the author. Dial, 1976. (Ages 3–8.) An active grandmother gets up early and likes to fish. The language and line drawings are simple and appealing.

Goldman, S. *Grandma Is Somebody Special.* Illus. by the author. Whitman, 1976. (Ages 4–7.) Grandma goes to school, works, and lives in the city. Her stories about her life and relationships indicate that she is not afraid to show emotions such as anger but that she harbors no grudges. She is an attractive, lively old woman.

Gray, L. M. *Miss Tizzy.* Illus. by J. Rowland. Simon & Schuster, 1993. (Ages 6–9.) Miss Tizzy entertains, interacts with, and feeds the neighborhood children. She is remarkably active and inventive, and she inspires the children to perform acts of kindness to people in the community. When she becomes ill, the children feed and entertain her. This elder, an African-American woman (whose age and heritage are identified only by the illustrations) provides an excellent model for multicultural and intergenerational harmony.

Greenfield, E. *Grandmama's Joy.* Illus. by C. Byard. William Collins, 1980. (Ages 6–8.) Rhondy has lived with her grandmother since she was a baby. Grandmama calls Rhondy her "Joy" and always says everything will be all right as long as she has her joy. When Grandma finds out they must move, not even Rhondy can make her happy until she reminds Grandmama that they still have each other.

Greenfield, E. *Grandpa's Face.* Illus. by F. Cooper. Philomel, 1988. (Ages 5–8.) Tamika's grandfather leads a vigorous and independent life. He is an actor in summer theater. One day he inadvertently frightens Tamika with an angry, hard, cold face that makes Tamika think he does not love her any more. When she expresses her fears, her grandfather reassures her that this was not his real face and that he loves her dearly. Not only is this a vital portrait of a vigorous old man, but also it is an intimate and thoughtful portrayal of a loving African-American family.

Griffith, H. V. *Georgia Music*. Illus. by J. Stevenson. Greenwillow, 1990. (Ages 5-8.) The girl and her grandfather enjoy each other's company when she visits him for the summer at his cabin in Georgia. They garden, fish, lie on the grass, and listen to the grandfather play "Georgia Music" on his harmonica. The next summer, the old man goes back with them to Baltimore because he is tired and depressed. But the grandfather languishes in his new home until his granddaughter tries to play his music. Then it seems that the old man has a chance to recover. The mood created by the author and illustrator underlines the affection and respect of the grandfather and granddaughter for each other. The grandfather's difficulty in adjusting to his move to a new home is understandable and sympathetically handled.

Griffith, H. V. *Grandaddy's Place*. Illus. by J. Stevenson. Mulberry, 1987. (Ages 4-6.) When Janetta is about 3 or 4, her mother takes her on a train to meet her grandfather, who lives on a small farm in Georgia. The mother seems oblivious of her daughter's fears of hornets, a mean cat, and a very scary, very big mule. The grandfather, on the other hand, is very understanding. He helps his granddaughter appreciate him and his world by telling her stories, teaching her to fish, and introducing her to the animals. By the end of her visit, she has given names to all the previously scary animals. The illustrations and text show a loving affinity between a shy little girl and her attentive grandfather. In *Grandaddy and Janetta* (1993), the story continues as Janetta makes a train trip to visit her grandfather all by herself.

Hamm, D. J. *Grandma Drives a Motor Bed*. Illus. by C. Robinson. Whitman, 1987. (Ages 6-8.) [See Special Needs]

Hartling, P. Translated from the German by E. D. Crawford. *Old John*. Lothrop, Lee & Shepard, 1981. (Ages 10 and up.) Every character in this story has passion, flaws, and a strong personality. The process of inviting an old person into the family's home is well modeled: John's feelings are honored, he selects all the possessions he wants to take with him, the family design their home with him in mind, and all family members, even the children, are consulted about their wishes. Old John is sometimes cantankerous. He is also tender and funny. He becomes involved in a relationship with a woman, so his sexuality is acknowledged. Altogether a fine book.

Henkes, K. *Grandpa & Bo*. Illus. by the author. Greenwillow, 1986. (Ages 4-7.) Bo and his grandfather share an idyllic and busy summer, even taking time to celebrate Christmas because Grandpa is with Bo only every other Christmas. They also share the same wish on a shooting star. The soft grey pencil drawings on a cream-colored background further reinforce the low-key but strong connection between these two.

Hest, A. *The Crack-of-Dawn Walkers*. Illus. by A. Schwartz. Penguin, 1988. (Ages 4-6.) Sadie and her grandfather have established a ritual where they visit their favorite shops, talk about the old country, eat delicious food, and engage in long and intimate conversations. On alternate Sundays, Sadie's younger brother Ben receives this privilege. Sadie is jealous. She is comforted, but not entirely mollified, by her grandfather's loving and truthful response to her feelings. The grandfather is an interesting man with an identity beyond that of being a grandfather.

Hewett, J. *Rosalie*. Illus by D. Carrick. Lothrop, Lee & Shepard, 1987. (Ages 5-8.) Every member of the family loves and appreciates Rosalie, a dog who in human terms would be almost 100 years old. Contrary to stereotypic patterns, Rosalie remains alive at the end of the book, a model of aging and the nurturing that can occur in a family setting.

Hickman, M. W. *When James Allen Whitaker's Grandfather Came to Stay.* Illus. by R. Hester. Abingdon, 1985. (Ages 4–9.) After James Allen's grandmother dies, his grand-father comes from Massachusetts to North Carolina to stay with James Allen's family. He is an astute old man who keeps busy and remains genuinely helpful. He deflects patronizing or overly solicitous behavior. The grandfather is an excellent model of an elder who is not senile or infirm but is temporarily displaced because of the loss of his lifelong partner. It is clear that his decision to leave his daughter's house to be on his own again is reasoned and workable and that his life will continue to be fulfilling and active.

Hines, A. G. *Grandma Gets Grumpy.* Illus. by the author. Clarion, 1988. (Ages 6–10.) Grandma is usually patient and tolerant of messes in her house when her granddaughter comes to visit. Her patience is tried to the limit one night when she babysits for all five of her grandchildren at once; and she finally gets grumpy. The grandchildren learn that Grandma still loves them even though she sets limits on their behavior in her home.

Hines, G. *A Ride in the Crummy.* Illus. by A. G. Hines. Greenwillow, 1991. (Ages 5–8.) A grandfather sharing a train ride with his grandson takes the opportunity to recount the story of a favorite train ride with his family in an old steam engine long ago.

Hoff, S. *Barkley.* Illus. by the author. Harper, 1975. (Ages 4–8.) Barkley, an old circus dog, finds a way to be useful and valued even though he is old. The problems of old age are recognized, and a happy solution is proposed in this "Early I Can Read" book.

Houston, J. *Akavak.* Illus. by the author. HBJ, 1990. (Ages 10 and up.) Akavak and his grandfather make a perilous journey so that the old man can return to his brother and his former home before he dies. Although Akavak survives the extreme hardships of the journey, the grandfather does not. Nevertheless, the grandfather is in no sense portrayed as a victim, nor is he romanticized. He is strong of spirit and competent to the end. One wishes that the author had made it clearer that this is not an Inuit legend but a story told by a respectful outsider using Inuit sources.

Howker, J. *Badger on the Barge and Other Stories.* Greenwillow, 1984. (Ages 11 and up.) Five tales of intergenerational encounters, some of them friendships. The stories are sometimes poignant, sometimes funny. The young people are invariably affected by the words and behavior of the elders.

Hurd, E. T. *I Dance in My Red Pajamas.* Illus. by E. Arnold McCully. Harper, 1982. (Ages 4–8.) Jenny's grandparents are active people, and the three of them have a wonderful time when Jenny comes to visit. Although the grandparents have somewhat gender-spe-cific roles, Jenny participates with both of them, carrying wood and building a house for the cat with Grandpa and cooking with Grandma. They enjoy a messy meal of blue-berry pie and then dance together. A positive relationship is shown between a child and an older couple who are still very much in love.

Irwin, H. *The Lilith Summer.* Feminist Press, 1979. (Ages 10 and up.) Twelve-year-old Ellen and seventy-year-old Lilith don't like each other very much; but each has been tricked into thinking she is "sitting" for the other. They discover the ruse, continue to collect their sitter's pay, and begin to enjoy each other's company. Ellen learns much about the depth and breadth of a number of old people. Lilith has a companion with whom to read, write poetry, go on outings, and watch birds.

Irwin, H. *What about Grandma?* Atheneum, 1982. (Ages 12 and up.) Eighty-year-old Wyn is a grandmother. She is also a mother, dear friend, and attractive woman. She is so full of life and energy that the reader is as shocked as the characters to learn that Wyn has a terminal illness and will die soon. She and her family and friends prepare together for her death; and in so doing, they become wiser.

Isadora, R. *Jesse and Abe.* Illus. by the author. Greenwillow, 1981. (Ages 4-8.) Jesse enjoys visiting his grandfather, Abe, at work backstage at a Broadway theater. Jesse learns how much his grandfather is valued one night when Abe is late for work.

Johnson, A. *When I Am Old with You.* Illus. by D. Soman. Orchard, 1990. (Ages 5-8.) In a rapturous daydream, a young boy imagines being old alongside his beloved grandfather, with both of them enjoying periods of action as well as intervals of quiet and rest. Each of their activities is one in which they already engage or could easily engage, so this is an exercise in the art of the possible. The partnership of this author and illustrator is felicitous, with the right amount of feeling and cultural character in both the words and the pictures.

Kesselman, W. *Emma.* Illus. by B. Cooney. Doubleday, 1980. (Ages 5-8.) Based on the life of artist Emma Stern, who was old, lonely, and unappreciated by her family. When she started to paint, she became contented and appreciated. The story deals with the need to be valued and shows that old people can learn new skills and become creative.

Ketner, M. G. *Ganzy Remembers.* Illus. by B. Sparks. Atheneum, 1991. (Ages 5-8.) As a young girl and her grandmother spend the day in the nursing home where Ganzy, the great-grandmother lives, the sights and sounds of the day remind Ganzy of stories from her youth—some real and some embellished—which she shares with her daughter and great-granddaughter. This humorous story with its watercolor illustrations shows that the very old were not always that way and that the stories of their lives can be fascinating to the young people who love them.

Kimmelman, L. *Me and Nana.* Illus. by R. Burton. Harper, 1990. (Ages 4-8.) Natalie anticipates a day with her Nana, who enjoys building with blocks, ice skating, baseball games, and crazy-colored nail polish. The two always have a wonderful time together (even though Natalie's mother feels guilty for leaving her daughter for the day). The illustrations are bright and cheerful, and the grandmother is attractive and active. The book avoids gender-stereotyped activities.

Klein, L. *Old, Older, Oldest.* Illus. by L. Kessler. Hastings House, 1983. (Ages 7-10.) A humorous, factual examination of lifespans and behavior. The book palpably makes the point that aging is a relative process, especially where human beings are concerned.

Knox-Wagner, E. *My Grandpa Retired Today.* Illus. by C. Robinson. Whitman, 1982. (Ages 5-9.) The young boy and his grandfather clearly share a loving relationship. When the grandfather retires, the boy helps him to overcome his depression.

Landau, E. *Growing Old in America.* Illus. with photos. Julian Messner, 1985. (Ages 11 and up.) A comprehensive, positive compendium of interesting information about the elderly population in the United States. The challenges encountered because of retirement are recounted; and a day at a busy senior center is described, as well as the factors involved in living in an adult community. Different chapters explore medical, financial, and legal facets of aging. Also included is a view of elders in other countries. The focus here is the process of aging as a developmental part of life.

Langone, J. *Growing Older: What Young People Should Know about Aging.* Little, Brown, 1991. (Ages 11 and up.) Fascinating statistics ("During Julius Caesar's reign, the average life span of a Roman was twenty-five years." "By 2050 there will be more than a million people living in the United States who are over one hundred years of age.") and some direct quotes from young people about their perceptions of elders and the aging process begin this informative and well-written book. The author dispels some myths, affirming that elders are capable of learning new things, being active in their professions or avocations, engaging in vigorous exercise such as weight-lifting, and participating in and enjoying sexual activity. Langone urges young people to plan for their aging, both by taking care of themselves physically and developing healthful habits and by mentally deciding on what kind of elder they envision becoming.

Lasky, K. *I Have Four Names for My Grandfather.* Illus. by C. G. Knight. Little, Brown, 1976. (Ages 6–9.) Photographs beautifully illustrate this loving book about a young boy and his special relationship with his grandfather.

Lasky, K. *My Island Grandma.* Illus. by E. McCully. Frederick Warne, 1979. (Ages 5–8.) Explores a close relationship between a strong, dynamic, creative grandma and her young granddaughter. The setting is a Maine island in summer.

Leiner, K. *Between Old Friends.* Illus. by M. H. Arthur. Watts, 1987. (Ages 6 and up.) Four children describe friendships with an older person or adult couple. The people vary in background and heritage; the book counteracts stereotypes about middle-aged and old people and about their relationships with young people. Much more than surface information is provided. These elders are active, independent, interesting, and diverse. Their interactions with the children are based on mutual respect. The book provides models for cross-generational friendship. The photographs reinforce the text.

LeShan, E. *Grandparents: A Special Kind of Love.* Illus. by T. Taggart. Macmillan, 1984. (Ages 8–13.) LeShan explores and celebrates the special bond between grandchildren and grandparents. She explains the differences between grandparenting and parenting and emphasizes the importance of family history in relationships. She also presents situations such as extended families and estrangements. She gives excellent advice on how to handle difficulties, even such serious situations as the death of a grandparent.

Levin, B. *The Trouble with Gramary.* Greenwillow, 1988. (Ages 10 and up.) Merkka's yard is filled with truck bodies, old school buses, and scrap metal. The town has been putting pressure on her family to clean up their "mess" because they fear it will scare tourists away. Gramary (Grandma Mary) gets revenge on the town naysayers when her artistic talents are discovered by out-of-town collectors who buy her welded sculptures. In the end, she dies of a stroke; but she has won the respect (if not the friendship) of her critics. The elders in this story, especially Gramary, are strong-willed, independent, unique individuals who stick to what they believe.

Levoy, M. C. *A Shadow like a Leopard.* Harper, 1981. (Ages 11 and up.) In order to prove his worth to a street gang, fourteen-year-old Ramon Santiago robs an old man, Arnold Glasser, at knifepoint. Glasser is an artist; Ramon is a poet. The two form a surprising alliance and help each other find a way out of their problems. Both are intelligent, talented, and unwilling to conform to what others want to force them to be.

Lindbergh, R. *Grandfather's Lovesong.* Illus. by R. Isadora. Viking, 1993. (Ages 3 and up.) In poetic verse illustrated with watercolor landscapes showing the changing seasons, a young boy and his grandfather celebrate the many ways they love each other.

Livingston, M. C. *Poems for Grandmothers.* Illus. by P. Cullen-Clark. Holiday House, 1990. (Ages 5–8.) This collection of poems celebrating grandmothers features older women who are political activists and working women, as well as homemakers. Grandmothers are shown as a diverse group of loving people.

Lloyd, D. *Grandma and the Pirate.* Illus. by G. Tomblin. Crown, 1985. (Ages 5–8.) Robert spends an idyllic day at the beach with his grandmother. She participates actively in his games and is an enthusiastic partner in his fantasies. She is a model of a capable person who is in her late middle years. The reader may be somewhat distracted because the boy and his grandmother seem more suitably dressed for a cool day in the park while everyone else in the pictures is wearing bathing suits. Nevertheless, the illustrations reinforce that this is not a woman who is glamorous or svelte, but a person aglow with health and love for her grandson and for life.

MacLachlan, P. *Journey.* Delacorte, 1991. (Ages 8-14.) [See Family Constellations]

MacLachlan, P. *Through Grandpa's Eyes.* Illus. by D. Ray. Harper, 1979. (Ages 6-9.) [See Special Needs]

Mathis, S. B. *The Hundred Penny Box.* Illus. by L. and D. Dillon. Viking, 1975. (Ages 6-9.) Michael loves his Aunt Dew. He understands her feelings. She is one hundred years old but still communicates and remembers. Michael is protective of Aunt Dew's feelings and distressed by his mother's seeming lack of understanding.

Mazer, N. F. *A Figure of Speech.* Delacorte, 1973. (Ages 12 and up.) Unable to deal with her grandfather's old age and senility, Jenny's parents want to put him in a home. Jenny objects, as does her grandfather, who would rather die. This is a powerful but upsetting story. Its realism leaves the reader shocked.

McKenzie, E. K. *Stargone John.* Illus. by W. Low. Holt, 1990. (Ages 8-10.) [See Siblings]

Melton, D., compiler. *Images of Greatness—A Celebration of Life,* 2nd ed. Illus. by the author. Landmark, 1987. (Ages 10 and up.) An excellent and inspiring compilation of quotes from well-known people who lived to old age. Included are Eleanor Roosevelt, Albert Einstein, Victor Hugo, Seneca, S.I. Hayakawa, Eubie Blake, and many others.

Moore, E. *Grandma's House.* Illus. by E. Primavera. Lothrop, Lee & Shepard, 1985. (Ages 5-8.) Kim spends the summer at her grandmother's country home. The summer "begins with strawberries and ends with plums," and they share the fruit with the many animals that live near Grandma's house. Grandma is independent and lives alone. The relationship between grandmother and granddaughter is gentle and loving. In the sequel, *Grandma's Promise* (1988), Kim and her grandmother share a winter adventure in the country when the electricity goes out. They feed birds, watch deer, stack wood, go ice skating, and sleep by the wood stove.

Murrow, L. K. *Dancing on the Table.* Illus. by R. Himler. Holiday House, 1990. (Ages 8-12.) Jenny, who has enjoyed a close connection with her grandmother, resents the fact that Nana is now getting married. Her wish comes true when the wedding is sabotaged, and she must deal with her guilt over the consequences. In addition to creating an engaging set of characters and evoking a vivid sense of the setting of Brights Island, the author has provided young readers with a lively, idiosyncratic, spunky older woman. It is not at all difficult to believe that Nana is sexually active and attractive. Charlie Streeter, her new husband who adores her, is a strong and caring man in his own right. This is an excellent story to blast stereotypes of the aging process.

Nomura, T. *Grandpa's Town.* Illus. by the author. Kane/Miller, 1989. (Ages 5-8.) Yuuta and his mother go to visit his Grandpa Gen, who lives in a small town in Japan. His wife died a year ago, and they are worried that he is lonely and want him to live with them. Grandpa brings Yuuta to the public bath with him; and on the way, Yuuta meets many of Grandpa's friends. He realizes what a strong community his grandfather has. Gen is a fine model of an independent, self-sufficient older person. His family and friends love him, and his grandson respects his autonomy. The text is in Japanese and English, and the stylized illustrations convey a sense of life in Gen's village.

Oppenheim, S. L. *Waiting for Noah.* Illus. by L. Hoban. Harper, 1990. (Ages 5-8.) Noah loves to hear his Nana tell stories, especially the story about the day she spent waiting for him to be born, dreaming of all the wonderful things she would do with her grandchild. Nana is an active woman who bicycles, wears jeans, and prunes trees. The gentle text and tender illustrations show that Nana and her grandson adore one another.

Orr, K. *My Grandpa and the Sea.* Illus. by the author. Carolrhoda, 1990. (Ages 5-8.) Lila and her family live on St. Lucia, where her grandfather still fishes in the traditional way from a dugout canoe, never taking more than his fair share. When younger fishermen with large commercial boats put him out of business, he becomes depressed. The grandmother, an independent and resourceful woman, helps the family by opening a bakery. The grandfather tries to adapt to a life on land, but he is not happy. He finally comes up with the idea of farming sea moss, which is becoming scarce. Through trial and error, he becomes successful, sustaining himself while staying on the sea which he loves. This beautifully illustrated book shows an active older man, respected in the community, who is able to adapt to new situations and maintain his independence. It also shows some of the life and culture of St. Lucia and the implications of modern technology for the traditional island lifestyle.

Palmer, K. S. *A Gracious Plenty.* Illus. by the author. Simon & Schuster, 1991. (Ages 5-8.) Great Aunt May lives alone, but she is never lonely. Her house is filled with friends, relatives, and wonderful objects. She is a loved and loving woman who shares a special relationship with her nephew's children.

Pearson, S. *Happy Birthday, Grampie.* Illus. by R. Himler. Dial, 1987. (Ages 5-8.) In anticipation of a visit to her grandfather on his eighty-ninth birthday, Martha buys him a gift and makes him a special textured and raised-lettering birthday card he can read despite his blindness. Although at one time he knew English, he now speaks only his native Swedish. He is able to read the card, however, and is so moved that he says "I love you, too" in English to Martha. This is a beautifully written and sensitive story. Despite the language barrier, Martha and Grampie are able to communicate. The family drives two hours to visit him each week. One of the nurses in his nursing home speaks Swedish, so he is not cut off from society. Martha is trying to learn Swedish too so she can speak directly to her grandfather. The illustrations nicely complement the text.

Peck, R. *Those Summer Girls I Never Met.* Delacorte, 1988. (Ages 12 and up.) Drew and his sister Stephanie have been coerced into taking a cruise with their grandmother, Connie, whom they hardly know. She was once a musical star, and she has been hired to entertain on the cruise because most of the passengers are elderly people who remember her with nostalgia. Stephanie is at a stage of wanting to avoid all members of her family; Drew looked forward to a summer chasing girls. In addition to being surprised by how interesting their grandmother is, the teenagers begin to appreciate how much stamina older people have. The two siblings establish a mutually loving and respectful relationship as a result of getting to know their remarkable grandmother. Peck's style of humor mixed with tenderness is effective.

Peters, L. W. *Good Morning, River!* Illus. by D. K. Ray. Little, Brown, 1990. (Ages 7-10.) Katherine, a six year old, and her friend Carl, an old man, live near the river. Together they explore the river through its seasonal changes. When the river is frozen, Carl's booming voice creates echoes, which he says are the river answering him. Katherine's voice is not strong enough to cause an echo. When Carl gets sick one autumn, he loses his booming voice. Katherine has grown enough by then to take over their morning ritual of talking to the river and having it answer. The intergenerational friendship is a good model. Carl and Katherine enjoy exploring their world together, and Carl teaches his young friend a great deal. It is unfortunate that, as occurs in many other books about such friendships, Carl suffers a debilitating illness that spurs Katherine to develop her own abilities. Fortunately, Carl is able to return to his home and live independently, though weakened. The watercolor illustrations nicely complement the text.

Pitts, P. *Racing the Sun.* Avon, 1988. (Ages 10-12.) While this story does not contain specific cultural information, it does dramatically and movingly convey the dilemma of being true to one's heritage while becoming part of a larger American society. The grandfather in this story teaches his grandson the value of challenging oneself physically and spiritually.

Pochocki, E. *The Mushroom Man.* Illus. by B. Moser. Green Tiger, 1993. (Ages 7-10.) An old man who lives alone is a figure of derision and abuse on the part of the children and adults of his community. He tends a mushroom farm, where he is almost content with his life, except that he craves a friend. After a failure with a cat as a pet and friend, he develops a satisfying friendship with a remarkable mole, who keeps house and cooks for him and offers excellent companionship. The book is a mixture of fantasy and reality. The combination of text and illustrations works well.

Pochocki, E. *Wildflower Tea.* Illus. by R. Essley. Green Tiger, 1993. (Ages 7-10.) An old man who lives alone is not a figure of pity. He takes good care of himself; has an excellent knowledge of nature; and enjoys collecting berries, flowers, and other ingredients with which to brew his special tea when the chill of November arrives. Children may discuss what constitutes happiness for them, and what their conception of loneliness is.

Polacco, P. *Mrs. Katz and Tush.* Illus. by the author. Bantam, 1992. (Ages 5-8.) [See Heritage]

Pople, M. *The Other Side of the Family.* Holt, 1986. (Ages 10 and up.) During World War II, Kate is sent from London to Australia where her grandparents live to be safe from German bombers. Her stay with her paternal grandmother is not at all what she has been led to expect. Her grandmother is deaf but refuses to admit her deafness to anyone. She manages without hearing aids by reading people's lips. Her son, Kate's father, who is ashamed to admit the poverty of his family, has, in effect, deserted his mother. Other plot elements include the ostracization of a local Italian family because of a misunderstanding about why the father has remained in Italy during the war. The story deals with the results of miscommunication.

Provost, G. *David and Max.* Jewish Publication Society, 1988. (Ages 10-14.) [See War and Peace]

Robinson, J. *The Secret Life of T.K. Dearing.* Illus. by C. Robinson. Seabury, 1973. (Ages 8-11.) T.K.'s grandfather feels useless at home. He wants to play with T.K. and his friends in this story about an independent old man and a basically understanding family.

Rogers, P. *From Me to You.* Illus. by J. Johnson. Orchard, 1987. (Ages 5-8.) Lace trims the grandmother's christening gown and later is applied to the grandmother's wedding gown. She uses it to trim her daughter's bassinet, and at last a bit of it is handed down to her granddaughter as a decorative kerchief. Using the lace as the artifact of continuation, the grandmother tells her granddaughter how she grew up. Rhyme is used to make the narrative sound like a song. A paragraph at the end of the book sums up the life of the real grandmother, born in 1906.

Ruby, L. *This Old Man.* Houghton Mifflin, 1984. (Ages 12 and up.) Greta has been placed in a group home for young women whose home situations are intolerable. She befriends most of the young women in the home, as well as a fifteen-year-old Chinese-American boy whom she accompanies daily when he takes dinner to his aged grandfather in the hospital. Greta's therapist helps her to see that she views the old man in many complicated ways, including imbuing him with power that she would like to attain. The old man is revered by his family; and although they are poor, he is well cared for. No character in this well-crafted book is stereotypic. The only thoroughly irredeemable character is a young thug from China who exhibits no concern for his family or his heritage.

Schertle, A. *William and Grandpa.* Illus. by L. Dabcovich. Lothrop, Lee & Shepard, 1989. (Ages 6-8.) William travels by bus to visit his grandfather. Together, they sing songs, swing on swings, cook dinner, and climb to the roof to watch the stars. Grandpa tells William stories about the days when he was young and talks about Grandma, who is now dead. Grandpa is shown as a loving, nurturing, active, and independent man. William sees parts of his grandparents in himself.

Schwartz, D. M. *Supergrandpa.* Illus. by B. Dodson. Lothrop, Lee & Shepard, 1991. (Ages 5–8.) Although Gustaf Hakansson was 66 years old, he felt and acted young and was in wonderful shape. He rode his bicycle everywhere. When he saw an advertisement for the Tour of Sweden, a 1,000-mile bike race, he decided to enter. His family was not supportive, and the judges denied him entry because of his age. He decided to race anyway; and after riding an additional 600 miles to the entry point, he actually finished first. Because he was not an official participant, he was denied his prize. However, his inspiring ride won recognition from the whole country, even the king. He went down in history as Supergrandpa. This book, based on a historical figure who became a folk hero in Sweden, shows what can be accomplished by determination and ability.

Scott, A. H. *Grandmother's Chair.* Illus. by M. Kelleher Aubrey. Clarion, 1990. (Ages 5–8.) A photograph album and a child's chair handed down from the grandmother help readers see the continuity between the generations. Now the child will inherit the chair and will preserve it for her own future child. The grandmother is pictured as a woman just beyond middle age in excellent shape.

Sechan, E. *The String Bean.* Illus. with photos. Doubleday, 1982. (Ages 7–12.) Based on a film, the story tells of an old woman whose life is drab until she discovers a flowerpot and plants a seed. Although her first attempt ends in disappointment, she will continue to plant seeds. Next time she will succeed.

Shulevitz, U. *Dawn.* Illus. by the author. Farrar, Straus & Giroux, 1974. (Ages 5–8.) A subtle but moving communication of the relationship between a young child and a grandfather. The illustrations beautifully convey the message.

Skolsky, M. *Carnival and Kopeck.* Illus. by K. A. Weinhaus. Harper, 1979. (Ages 7–10.) Hannah helps her grandmother learn to read and write in English, and Hannah's grandmother plays with her, tells her stories, and cooks delicious food. Because both of them have strong personalities, they sometimes clash; when that happens, they are unhappy until the problem is resolved.

Skorpen, L. M. *Grace.* Harper, 1984. (Ages 9–12.) Sara teams up with her new friend Amy to torment Grace, an old woman who lives alone next door. Not until Sara is forced to apologize to Grace does she realize how lonely and afraid the old woman is. Sara becomes her friend and visits regularly throughout the summer. Grace is terrified of dying in an institution; she wants to die in her own bed at home. At the end of the summer, she has her wish. After Grace's death, Sara reconnects with her old friends. She has come of age. The story is written in a style that is spare and intense.

Skorpen, L. M. *Old Arthur.* Illus. by W. Tripp. Harper, 1972. (Ages 3–8.) Arthur is too old to be a good farm dog anymore, so he runs away from the farmer who wants to kill him. Although he spends time in a dog pound, he finally ends up as a valued pet for a little boy. A beautiful story about the positive attibutes of old age.

Slepian, J. *Getting on with It.* Four Winds, 1985. (Ages 11 and up.) [See Divorce]

Smith, R. K. *The War with Grandpa.* Illus. by R. Lauter. Delacorte, 1984. (Ages 8–10.) Peter's grandfather, grieving over the death of his wife, comes to live with Peter and his parents. Without consultation, Peter's room is taken over by his grandfather, and Peter is moved to the guest room. Peter is furious over the arrangements and decides to declare war on his grandfather until he regains his old room. At first Peter's grandfather is sedentary and spiritless. Once Peter has played a few tricks on him, he perks up and engages in as many pranks as Peter. He seems to gather strength from the battle of wits. Eventually, Peter and his grandfather figure out a solution they both can live with. The importance of communication is stressed. Children may be invited to discuss the potential dangers of the tricks and to debate whether or not the characters' mischievous and self-centered behavior avoids being demeaning or dehumanizing.

Sobol, H. L. *Grandpa: A Young Man Grown Old.* Illus. by P. Agre. Coward, McCann & Geoghegan, 1980. (Ages 10 and up.) The life of Morris Kaye, a Jewish immigrant—a modest, dignified, "young man grown old"—described in words and actual family photographs from two vantage points: Morris's, as he looks back on seventy-eight years, and that of his seventeen-year-old granddaughter Karen, who loves and respects him for what he has accomplished and for the part he has played in her own growing up.

Stock, C. *Thanksgiving Treat.* Illus. by the author. Bradbury, 1990. (Ages 4–7.) [See Family Constellations]

Stolz, M. *Storm in the Night.* Illus. by P. Cummings. Harper, 1988. (Ages 5–8.) [See Family Constellations]

Strangis, J. *Grandfather's Rock.* Illus. by R. Gamper. Houghton Mifflin, 1993. (Ages 6–9.) In an Italian variation of a universal folktale, the story tells of a beloved grandfather whose family makes the difficult decision to have him live in a home for the aged because they are in difficult economic circumstances. The children devise a clever way of conveying the message that they want the grandfather to remain with them. They make the father think about his own future when he becomes old. What is more important, they decide to help with the chores of the farm and to work together so that there will be enough food for all. The father and children value the grandfather's stories, and the father is grateful for the care his father gave him when he was young. It is regrettable that the mother does not participate actively in the resolution of the problem.

Stren, P. *There's a Rainbow in My Closet.* Illus. by the author. Harper, 1979. (Ages 8–10.) Emma's grandmother is ideal: She understands Emma's art, plays funny and imaginative games with her, reads stories, permits her to do outlandish (but not unsafe) things like eat ketchup sandwiches, sometimes stays up all night talking, and always takes her side. The book is not a fantasy, but it is certainly every child's dream come true.

Tate, J. *Gramp.* Harper, 1979. (Ages 9–12.) Simon understands that his grandfather needs to feel useful and keep busy in order to preserve his health and vitality. Through extraordinary perseverance, Simon helps accomplish this.

Voigt, C. *Dicey's Song.* Atheneum, 1982. (Ages 10 and up.) [See Family Constellations]

Ward, S. G. *What Goes Around Comes Around.* Illus. by the author. Doubleday, 1991. (Ages 5 and up.) Isabel's grandmother is an amiable, eccentric woman who wears high-top sneakers, tap dances, and keeps a parrot that swears. She sews for a living and makes and gives away soup for fun. One day Isabel spends the day making the rounds with Grandma Rose, taking soup to friends and needy strangers. Whenever Grandma Rose gives away some of her soup, the person receiving it offers something in return. During her day with Grandma, Isabel sees the joy Rose brings to others by sharing her gift. She decides to accompany her grandmother regularly and to give away her paintings. This well-written, joyful story presents an older woman who defies stereotypes and demonstrates the rewards of sharing.

Wittman, S. *The Wonderful Mrs. Trumbly.* Illus. by M. Apple. Harper, 1982. (Ages 5–9.) Mrs. Trumbly is a vibrant, elderly, energetic teacher, portrayed in the illustrations as a senior citizen. Not only does she lead a productive professional life, she enjoys a romantic relationship with Mr. Klein, the music teacher. The story presents a well-rounded picture of two older people with enjoyable, active lives.

Worth, R. *You'll Be Old Someday, Too.* Illus. with photos. Watts, 1986. (Ages 11 and up.) The author presents a realistic picture of the condition of elders in American society and asks readers to think about "What kind of old age will I have?" Information on such areas as the economic and physical aspects of aging, health care, and death-related issues is offered. The author describes coordinated efforts between young and old and options for elders such as life-care communities. In-depth attention is paid to the family. Also included are profiles of inspiring older people.

Wright, B. R. *Getting Rid of Marjorie.* Holiday House, 1981. (Ages 9–12.) Emily is devastated when she learns about her grandfather's sudden marriage to a stranger named Marjorie. Emily schemes to get rid of Marjorie so that she and her grandfather can regain their special close relationship. Never bordering on the sentimental, this story helps destroy some stereotypes about old people and their needs.

Yep, L. *Child of the Owl.* Harper, 1977. (Ages 11 and up.) Casey moves in with his grandmother who lives in Chinatown and learns to cope with the generation gap.

Zalben, J. B. *The Fortuneteller in 5B.* Holt, 1991. (Ages 10–12.) Madame Van Dam, an elderly fortune teller, moves into the apartment upstairs from Alexandra and her mother, who are still mourning the death of Alex's father. After an initial period spent fearing the old woman, Alexandra gets to know her and hears about her experiences as a child in a concentration camp. In addition to the intergenerational friendship, the blasting of stereotypes about elders, and the universality of grieving, the story informs the reader about the treatment of gypsies at the time of the Holocaust.

Zolotow, J. *I Know a Lady.* Illus. by J. Stevenson. Greenwillow, 1984. (Ages 5–8.) An old woman who lives alone is generous to neighbors and their pets. Only by implication is there any reciprocal contact, but the pictures show the children interacting with the woman, and the child-narrator declares her love for the old woman. Discussion could ensue on how children could show their appreciation for the old woman's kindnesses.

chapter 7

Death

Until recently, books dealing realistically with death were categorized almost as pornography. Enamored of youth and trying to remain young forever, Americans like to pretend that death does not exist. Dying people have been shunned as though dying itself were a contagious disease. This society values beauty, comfort, boundless productivity, and control over life, preferring not to confront death, which is associated with pain and fear of the unknown. For some people, death appears to be a punishment and an ever-present threat. Even to those for whom death is a valid end to earthly life or a transcendental episode in the balance of the universe, there are negative aspects.

We miss our loved ones, our great ones, our kind ones. But more and more we have come to realize that, even if we do not talk about it, death will not go away. Courses concentrating on questions, concerns, and issues associated with death and dying are being offered on campuses across the country. Parents and teachers find themselves increasingly called upon to answer children's questions, prompted not only by the children's actual experiences but also by their encounters with these concepts in books.

Before deciding to work with children on the facts, attitudes, and problems surrounding the themes of death and dying, an adult must decide how he or she feels about these topics. Helping others to cope with or understand a situation is difficult unless we know our own feelings. Once we know what our attitudes are, we can more easily go beyond them and accept the ideas of others in an ongoing growth process. Having a strong opinion today does not mean that we will have the same idea tomorrow, especially if we receive and assimilate more information that either confirms or changes our attitudes.

Try This
Design a questionnaire to discover your attitudes toward dying and death. After you have answered its questions, try to think of others you

can ask. Compare your questionnaire with a friend's. Are there questions that appear on both lists? If so, do your friend's answers differ from yours? Are there questions either of you cannot or will not answer? Talk about your differences and similarities. Now consider how you would handle these questions with children.

Some sample questions might be these:

How do I feel about dying (fearful? resigned? unconcerned? panicked?)

What are my beliefs about an afterlife?

Which comes closest to my perception of death? (random? fated? under our control? necessary for the balance of nature?)

Who should teach children about death? (family? ministers? school? a combination?)

If I were dying, what would I want people to tell me? (that I would recover? that I had ____ months to live?)

Given that I must, how do I prefer to die? (quickly or suddenly? slowly, with time to plan?)

What sort of funeral do I want? (elaborate? private? none?)

How do I want my body disposed of? (cremation? donated to hospital? buried?)

What is my definition of death?

At what stage of development does an unborn child become a living person?

Who should decide that death has occurred? (family? physician?)

What conditions should be set for defining death? (brain-dead? coma?)

When is it right to kill? (never? war? self-defense?)

When, if ever, is suicide an appropriate act? (never? terminal illness?)

How much should children be protected from the facts of death?

How extensively should children be included in the rituals of mourning?

After you have begun to explore your own feelings, start to exchange ideas with children. Sometimes they will ask you questions you cannot answer, just as you have asked yourself very difficult questions. Often they want confirmation that others feel as they do and can accept those feelings, even when they are unpleasant. On occasion the conversation will reveal misconceptions ("My grandma died yesterday, but she'll come back in time for my birthday if I'm good.") Accept all statements without contradiction, waiting to comment until you have a fairly coherent idea of how the child perceives death. Then you can decide whether to use this information to build curriculum, reassure the child, correct erroneous information, or refer the matter to another professional for further handling. Several excellent sources of advice on how to talk to children about death can be found in libraries and bookstores (see the Reference Section at the end of this chapter.)

DEVELOPMENTAL STAGES

It is useful for adults to be aware of the stages through which children progress in their perception of death and of the usual responses to the death of a loved one. It is believed that even infants are attempting to cope with and understand the concept of loss when they play such games as peek-a-boo and drop-the-object. According to psychologists, this indicates babies' attempts to control their world. They are reassured whenever the "lost" object or person reappears.

Until children are about five years old, they cannot conceive of death as permanent. They imagine that dead people are still alive and can perhaps be found somewhere else. Because children are so self-centered at this stage, they think of everything and everyone in the light of their own desires and experiences. When they reach the age of five or six, they still consider the world through their own needs; but they have begun to acknowledge the weight of their experiences. At this stage, until they are about nine years old, they personify death and believe they can control it through magic, trickery, or just the force of their wishes.

By the time they get to be nine years old, they are usually able to acknowledge that death is permanent, universal, and inevitable. In short, they have reached the stage most adults achieve. It has been found that children who have had the opportunity to talk about and deal with the idea of death seem to be able to handle the idea of loss and death in a more stable and constructive manner than children who have been "shielded" from exposure to the issue.

Adults and children react to death in an almost universal fashion, all the while thinking that each is the only one ever to feel this way. The first response is usually denial. "You're joking!" "I don't believe it!" "Tell me it isn't so." Bargaining sometimes enters into the equation here: "If I do my homework every day this week, please make my dog come back to life." As with most areas where stages are involved, people rarely leave one before they enter the next. Thus, even years after someone has died, we may think we see him or her walking down the street; or we may think to ourselves, "I must tell Mother about this," even when Mother has been dead for a long time.

Another stage is anger: at God, at the person who has died, at the world, and finally at oneself. The self-anger can turn into guilt. "If I had been better or behaved differently, she wouldn't have died." Sometimes the guilt becomes self-castigation: "Why am I alive when he is dead? He was a much better person than I." Understandably, the sense of guilt leads to grief and depression, usually the last stage before achieving acceptance. The length of the stages varies from person to person and situation to situation. Some people never arrive at the acceptance stage. The stages are flexible in sequence and duration, but knowing about them helps people to anticipate how they will feel and provides an understanding of what is "normal."

SOME QUESTIONS TO EXPLORE

How can we help children accept their feelings about the death of people they love? What do we want children to know about death? How much realism can they tolerate? How much detail should we present about the act of dying? Do we want them to believe that it is painless? How much should we dwell on pain? How can we handle issues of abortion, suicide, euthanasia, the controversies surrounding the definition of death, customs of mourning, funerals, the hereafter, and all the religious teachings concerning death? How protected should children be from the fact that we do not usually know in advance when we will die, and that the oldest people do not always die first? This list is by no means exhaustive. Add your own questions.

Try This
Read some of the factual books about death, along with the articles annotated at the end of this chapter and any others that you find listed in *Library Literature* or *The Education Index* concerning death and children's books. List some of the answers these sources provide to the above questions. Note those that are most congruent with your philosophy. Plan arguments for those with which you disagree.

SUGGESTED CRITERIA

When the topic of death is included in a book for children, the author should incorporate a developmental point of view, responding to the stages children pass through in their internalized knowledge about death. Younger children cannot comprehend too many abstract concepts; older children need factual, realistic circumstances as well. Books that reflect folkloric notions, like the personification of death, may be confusing for younger children not yet developmentally aware of their own magical thinking. Useful for the younger child are the simple, realistic stories of individual encounters with death. Older children are more able to understand the allegorical or mythic implications of a story and therefore to appreciate its intent.

Books about death should reflect a regard for the experiences of the reader. Even picture books and stories can acknowledge that most of the ideas, feelings, and questions expressed by very young children evolve from their personal experiences. While it is not uncommon for a young child to have experienced the death of a pet, a grandparent, or another elderly family member, a child sometimes must face the untimely death of a parent, sibling, young relative, or friend.

Children's feelings should be acknowledged and respected. Children should be supported in learning that their emotions are valid, even when these feelings are perceived as negative.

The stages of denial, fear, anger, guilt, grief, and acceptance should be presented as normal. Also recognized should be children's understandable desire to get on with their lives and not spend inordinate amounts of time with grieving adults. Books are more helpful when they acknowledge and describe the mourning process rather than pretend that death is easily handled, not really a loss, or something to be borne stoically.

Wherever possible, books should model appropriate ways for those who are bereaved to receive emotional support from a caring community. Gathering together for mutual assistance, sharing in the commemoration of the life and accomplishments of the dead person, exchanging personal verbal expressions of support, and valuing memories and the artifacts of memory, such as photographs, are helpful expressions of constructive mourning that can increase the positive impact of a book.

The language describing death should refrain from euphemisms. People and animals die. Death should not be equated with sleep, a vacation, or a trip.

Books that demonstrate children's active participation in the rites of mourning are very helpful. Much discussion should accompany the reading of books where children are left without any explanations, are "guarded" from information about the death of a loved one, or are "protected" from taking part in family activities.

Books should make it clear that dead people or pets cannot be replaced. If a new pet is offered to a child, it should not be expected to take the place of the one that died but should be a new experience in itself. The dead pet is part of the child's history, to be remembered not dismissed. Similarly, there should never be a hint that a person who has died is expendable or interchangeable with someone else.

Death must be presented as permanent, especially to younger children who would be confused by allegorical or abstract stories of ghosts, afterlife, devils, or bargaining with death. Authors need to make clear that when people die they do not come back to life.

A collection of books is required to emphasize that not only old people die and that there are many possible causes for death. Children should be helped to understand that death cannot usually be anticipated and that death is not always fair.

The beliefs and practices of different cultures should be presented in a respectful manner, without implying that they are quaint or abnormal.

DISCUSSION OF CHILDREN'S BOOKS

Books for children deal with suicide and with the deaths, both sudden and expected, of very young people, parents, grandparents, and pets. They describe feelings of rage, sorrow, loneliness, helplessness, and resignation. They include looks at upper-class, lower-class, and middle-class families as they handle death. Books contain Native American rituals and customs, Jewish and Christian procedures and beliefs, and glimpses into countries other than the United States. One can read about the responses of adults and children, males and females, and people of various races. There are books aimed at the very young, at intermediate ages, and at older children. They reflect a wide range of information and attitudes about death. Children, perhaps with the help of a knowledgeable adult, can utilize those books most nearly corresponding to their developmental levels and needs.

Reading these books invites many activities. Children can locate contradictory ideas and set up a debate. One controversy might revolve around funerals and the purpose they serve. Evidence supporting different positions can be located in the literature. Children may enjoy writing stories stemming from their reading, adopting the same position as the one expressed in the book or an opposing one. It is always an excellent practice to accumulate a class or personal library containing books that collectively present a balance of the many different aspects and facts about death. Be certain that the library includes picture books, folk tales, modern fiction, nonfiction, poetry, literary fantasy, and realistic fiction so as to reach the widest audience and present the greatest diversity. Death may be the major theme, or it may be included as an adjunct to the rest of the story.

Books for Young Children (to Age 7)

Funerals.   The death most frequently encountered by a young child is probably that of an animal. Authors use this experience to help children cope with and learn about some of the rituals, practices, and beliefs surrounding death. Following the experts' advice about including children in the ceremonial aspects of death, several authors have written stories in which children conduct a funeral for a dead animal. In 1958 Margaret Wise Brown's book *The Dead Bird* appeared. The first book of its kind for young audiences, it describes the physiological manifestations of death as well as the burial service the children accord the dead bird. The story is somewhat impersonal; the bird is not a pet but simply a dead bird found in the path. But the illustrations by Remy Charlip convey the emotions of the children in a way the simple text does not attempt. The language is at the level of the early grades in school, or even preschool, but describes clearly what is happening. It also communicates that an important part of the process of mourning is being glad to be alive. As the children conduct a funeral, they sing to the bird. They cry because it is dead, but they are glad that they can participate in this ceremony. Their tears are as much a response to the beauty of their own singing and fragrance of the flowers as they are mourning for the death of the bird.

The Tenth Good Thing about Barney, by Judith Viorst, is another book in which an animal dies and receives a funeral. When the child's cat Barney dies, he loses his appetite and refuses to do anything but go to bed and cry. The empathic mother suggests a funeral service, which the child's parents and his friend Annie attend. The mother tells the child to think of ten good things about Barney to recite at the funeral. He can think of only nine. The mourning period is portrayed realistically, with the funeral helping to relieve the acuteness of the loss but some of the hurt remaining until the boy realizes that the tenth good thing is that Barney has become a part of nature.

A surprisingly large number of books include funerals, stressing their usefulness in helping children cope with emotions. For the family in Virginia Lee's *The Magic Moth,* the funeral helps to focus their grief over the death of a young child. A minister also helps the family in this book, which concentrates on how siblings react to a sister's death. Smith's *A Taste of Blackberries* also describes the death and funeral of a child and the reactions of his closest friend.

For seven to ten year olds, Jane Resh Thomas's book *Saying Good-bye to Grandmother* plumbs the extent to which each component of a funeral contributes to coping with death. In *Grandfather's Laika,* by Mats Wahl, a boy and his grandfather are comforted by the ritual of visiting their dog's grave. Some stories recount practices, such as the covering of mirrors in Jewish homes, as in Joan Fassler's *My Grandpa Died Today.* Ann Turner's *Houses for the Dead* describes the customs of many cultures, both ancient and contemporary. Children can benefit from learning about the universality of ritual.

Reacting to Death. In Sandol Warburg's *Growing Time,* as in Judith Viorst's *The Tenth Good Thing about Barney,* the cyclical nature of the universe and the concept that death is necessary for the sustenance of new life are presented so that young children can understand and accept them.

The younger sister in *When Violet Died* decides to give one kitten in each generation the same name as its mother, ensuring that she will always have a cat with that name. She is excited by her invention, knowing all the while that nothing lasts forever but telling herself that she has almost granted her cat eternal life. For some readers this will be a technique for softening a loss.

It is very useful for children to recognize as early as possible that books are not gospel just because they are in print. They must accept the challenge of disagreeing with an author whose ideas conflict with theirs. Adults should encourage this kind of critical thinking, teaching children to evaluate authors' suggestions, investigate "facts," and use their own experience and judgment. If a child accepts the author's idea, that is fine. If a child refutes this idea, the child should be invited to consider the issue further and contribute his or her own point of view. Children may want to write to the author or publisher with a list of questions or comments. They are almost certain to receive a response.

In life as in books, well-meaning friends or family sometimes try to replace a dead loved one. For example, when a child's pet dies, the parents may buy another animal immediately, hoping to assuage the child's grief and perhaps attempting to demonstrate that though death is final life goes on. Sometimes this is an attempt to pretend, "Your dog didn't really die; you still have a dog." In *The Old Dog,* by Sarah Abbott, the boy accepts the new puppy, but not as a substitute. He regrets that the old dog is not there to welcome the new one; and although he intends to nurture the puppy, the old dog is still in his thoughts.

In *A Taste of Blackberries,* the child offers himself as a substitute to his best friend's mother, and she is comforted and touched by the offer. At the moment of bereavement, the gesture provides a measure of solace even though both of them know that no substitution is possible.

Most books for young children stress tolerance of the reactions of children when someone or something they love dies. Anger, withdrawal, refusal to eat, tears, confusion—all are acceptable behavior in the stories. *Growing Time* beautifully demonstrates how adults can be supportive of a young child when death has occurred. Each adult adds another perspective and another piece of information to help the boy cope with the death of his dog. The boy is permitted resentful feelings and grief. He is finally ready to accept the finality of death and the responsibility of caring for another dog.

In *A Taste of Blackberries,* the boy at first denies his friend's death; he cannot face it. Gradually, with the help of supportive adults, he begins to believe and then to accept the idea. This death is difficult because it is sudden and violent and occurs while the child's friends are present. The child, Jamie, dies of bee stings. The idea of being unable to prevent an accident is difficult even for an adult to handle.

The boy, Ben, in *The Old Dog,* reacts in a typical young child's fashion. He misses all the functions that the dog performed for him, as well as its company and all the happiness it gave him. For many young children, it is the permanence of death that is incomprehensible; and their immediate reactions do not necessarily reflect their true feelings. The boy in *My Grandpa Died Today* is permitted to play and behave in his normally cheerful fashion after his grandfather dies, even though his parents are in mourning at home. The grandfather in this book dies painlessly in his rocking chair after forewarning his grandson, saying he is not afraid to die and that he knows the grandson is not afraid to live. The child is encouraged not to feel guilty about wanting to play. He knows that his grandfather's spirit is with him. Although the book is didactic, it successfully communicates feelings and conveys the intent to protect and support the child in his responses to his beloved grandfather's death.

A parent's grief gets in the way of appropriate mourning in *Nadia the Willful* by Sue Alexander. In this beautifully told story, Nadia's brother Hamed has died, and their father has proclaimed that no one must speak his dead son's name. Wiser than her father, Nadia realizes that remembering and talking about her brother eases her grief. She finally manages to persuade her father of this and helps him to accept Hamed's death.

In Charlotte Zolotow's *My Grandson Lew,* a young boy misses his dead grandfather and calls for him in the middle of the night. Lew and his mother share their loving memories and comfort each other through their conversation. This tender portrait can serve as a model to people who are afraid to talk about deceased loved ones with their children.

Another book that accomplishes the same modeling is *Time for Uncle Joe,* by Nancy Jewell. In this gentle recollection, a little girl mourns for her beloved uncle but keeps his memory alive. She recalls his jokes, the details of his appearance, and the activities they shared. She also feels comforted by the fact that she has retained some of his possessions and is able to touch and look at them. In so doing, she has him with her in spirit even though she knows he is never coming back. The book is a loving tribute to the dead man while it affirms the love and sensitivity of the child.

Books for Older Children

Death is not an easy topic about which to write or talk. Many adults have yet to resolve questions and anxieties surrounding this issue. Death in the abstract is difficult enough; but real, immediate death can be so traumatic that it defies the ability to cope with feelings and thoughts. Religion, upbringing, personal experiences, and the opinions and help of those we respect have a great deal to do with our own attitudes and methods of handling the situation. Many books directly concerning this topic are helpful in different ways. Some of them are more suitable for the much older child because of the specificity and the magnitude of the issue involved.

In some books, the characters do not respond heroically or admirably to death. One of the characters in *Meet the Austins,* by Madeleine L'Engle, is a girl who behaves unpleasantly after the death of her father. She capitalizes on the fact that she is an orphan, using her circumstance as an excuse to throw temper tantrums, disregard the feelings of others, and make people miserable when they are near her. The Austins, who have invited her to live with them, teach her to relate to other people in a less selfish and obnoxious fashion. The parents are absolutely perfect: wise, understanding and knowledgeable, always responding sympathetically and appropriately, never professing to know why loved ones must die or what plan governs life and death. The responses of the children to the death of their close family friend and to the intrusion of the orphan are presented well.

Jess, the protagonist in Katherine Paterson's *Bridge to Terabithia,* is stunned by the death of his dearest friend Leslie. The two of them have an imaginary kingdom they visit regularly. Jess feels guilty, and his feelings of guilt are compounded by the fact that on the day Leslie died he was away on a pleasure trip with his art teacher. After Jess passes through the stages of mourning, he emerges from the experience much more attuned to other people's feelings.

In Jean Little's *Home From Far,* Jenny has difficulty recovering from the traumatic death of her twin brother Michael, in a car accident. Her parents become foster parents to a little girl and her older brother. The foster son's name, coincidentally, is Michael. Jenny resents him bitterly, suspecting that her parents are trying to replace her dead brother. She is also angry with her mother for disposing of all her twin's possessions. At last Jenny and her mother talk about their feelings and realize that the mother has simply been trying to spare Jenny pain. The mother uncovers all their mementos of Michael so that she and Jenny can both begin to remember him with love and joy. Jenny can also begin to participate in a positive relationship with the living Michael.

In Candy Dawson Boyd's *Breadsticks and Blessing Places,* Toni's grief over the death of her best friend Susan is realistically presented. Her problems and their solutions are believable. Transitions are gradual, and Toni learns that her grief will not magically disappear but that she can learn to live with it. The book presents strong families within a supportive African-American community with dreams and aspirations. The children, all of African-American heritage, come from varied socioeconomic classes and family situations. One wonders why, although Toni's grief is a disruptive factor in school and she has difficulty functioning for many weeks, no one suggests counseling. Nevertheless, this is a well-crafted story of a strong community of people holding one another together in difficult times.

In Virginia Hamilton's *Cousins,* Cammy is jealous of her pretty, smart, rich cousin, Patty Ann, even though it is clear that Patty Ann suffers from an eating disorder and is highly nervous. When Patty Ann drowns while rescuing Elodie, a far less popular cousin, Cammy's grief and guilt overwhelm her. She denies having seen Patty Ann die and experiences recurrent nightmares in which Patty Ann comes to haunt her. The situation is exacerbated when the school teacher and Patty Ann's mother's insist on erecting a shrine of sorts to Patty Ann in the classroom. All the children are affected negatively by this unhealthy fixation on the dead child, but none more severely than Cammy. At last, with the support of her heretofore-absent father and of other loving and empathic family members, and with her grandmother's help in placing death in perspective with living, Cammy confronts her feelings and becomes ready to resume her life.

Attitudes toward death on the part of different cultures can also be found in books for young readers. *The Big Wave,* by Pearl S. Buck, describes how two Japanese villages face death caused by natural disasters. Buck's aim is to help young people learn not to fear death and to recognize that life is stronger than death.

Maia Wojciechowska tries to present the perspective of a bullfight aficionado in *Shadow of a Bull,* winner of a Newbery medal. She asserts that the bullfight is the Spaniard's way of defeating death. These books in some measure try to explain the wish to fight, kill, and die gloriously. A noble death defeats death, according to the message in these books. In another Newbery medal book, *The Cat Who Went to Heaven,* by Elizabeth Coatsworth, the author attempts to express a Buddhist point of view. The idea of dying in ecstasy is particularly Eastern but may be of interest to Western readers. Research into Buddhism and other non-Western cultures can profitably ensue from a reading of this book.

Some authors present a resigned, accepting response to death. Others acknowledge strong emotion even when that emotion is rage. Some people admire stoic silence. In several poems, Edna St. Vincent Millay advocates anger and resentment. In "Dirge without Music," she responds to the idea that the dead enrich the earth, making it possible for other things to grow: "I know, but I do not approve. And I am not resigned."

All these approaches provide the opportunity for demonstrating that, given the same information and similar circumstances, not everyone responds in the same way. This must be seen as valid and valuable.

Suicide

Grover, by Vera Cleaver and Bill Cleaver, concerns the suicide of a boy's mother. Knowing she has a terminal illness, she shoots herself because she cannot bear the thought of going through all the changes she knows will occur if she permits the illness to take its natural course. The authors do an excellent job of describing how adults try to shield children from the truth and in the process sometimes harm them more than they help. Grover initially displays little external reaction to his mother's death, but in his dealings with his friends he exhibits his grief and pain. He explodes into blind rage when a nasty, somewhat demented woman taunts him about his mother's suicide. He seems able, partly because of the support of his friends and partly because of an understanding housekeeper, to rebuild his own life. His father, however, cannot cope, grieves constantly, and resents the boy's normalcy. The situation is realistic and disturbing.

Suicide is the result of a long series of painful events in Norma Fox Mazer's *A Figure of Speech.* The eighty-three-year-old grandfather decides to kill himself rather than be sent to a home for the aged. Some of the people in this story are extremely insensitive to each other's feelings. They are especially cruel, without meaning to be, to the old man and his granddaughter Jenny. Her love for her grandfather almost saves him, but in the end it becomes apparent that they are both powerless to keep him from being sent to live in a place that would destroy his dignity and sense of self. This story and *Grover* may both help readers examine their feelings and raise some questions about the absolute right or wrong of the desperate act of suicide.

Other books, fiction and nonfiction, that discuss suicide try to point out that while it is important to be alert to signals suicidal people may send out, it is futile to feel responsible or guilty if the person succeeds in committing suicide. *Face at the Edge of the World* by Eve Bunting details the trauma Jed suffers when his friend, Charlie, commits suicide. As is not the case in a number of other novels of this type, Jed succeeds in uncovering the reasons for his friend's act. *Teenage Suicide,* by Sandra Gardner with Gary Rosenberg, M.D., and *Teen Suicide: A Book for Friends, Family, and Classmates,* by Janet Kolehmainen and Sandra Handwerk, are two works of nonfiction that contribute not only information and advice but also a list of available resources.

Factual Books

Herbert S. Zim and Sonia Bleeker have written *Life and Death* which briefly includes some life processes but concentrates on death. The authors describe the scientific process of maturation and dying. The book, which contains much anthropological and other scientific information, is directed at children nine years of age and older. It clarifies some misconceptions, such as equating death with sleep. It states, "With death, all of the life processes, such as growth, movement, awareness, and reactions, stop—finally and permanently" (p. 19). Details, including a description of a death certificate, health officers who verify and report a death, funeral arrangements and costs, different kinds of burial (historic and contemporary), and mourning customs are provided in a nonjudgmental, dispassionate style. The authors express their point of view in several instances, hoping that readers will accept death as part of life and in its larger context in terms of the rest of the world. Many readers may find this to be a valuable book for explaining death to children who have recently experienced the death of someone close to them. The book can also serve to prepare children for understanding death when they hear about it or ask about it. It can be a tool for generating questions.

Another book that speaks directly to children about the facts of death is *Death Is a Noun,* by John Langone. The author includes discussions of critical contemporary issues. He comments on suicide; euthanasia; the problem of when to declare a person legally dead; and questions of capital punishment, murder, and abortion. He also talks about personal dilemmas of how to face death, ideas about life after death, and the weighty implications whenever a decision about life and death is made.

Langone represents several viewpoints in each chapter. He includes an impressive amount of information, usually leaving it to the reader to decide on the answer. He contends: "About all one can do is affirm the right of all to speak, to listen to the opposing views, consider both society as a whole and the individual, and then make a decision based on one's own conscience" (p. 106). The author does not abdicate responsibility; he does interject his own ideas and his sense of morality. He wants people to make life as mutually beneficial and as productive as possible. He selects quotations and uses facts judiciously and persuasively. Young people need a fair degree of maturity to appreciate this book thoroughly. Younger children, depending on their precocity, may have more difficulty but may nevertheless be able to handle the content.

Joanne E. Bernstein's books on helping children to handle separation and loss are among the best sources for children and adults alike. One of her books for young readers, *Loss and How to Cope with It,* not only explains the stages of mourning, assuring children that they are normal to feel the way they do, but also adds reassuring advice about how to handle these feelings. Information—presented in a readable, anecdotal format—is directed not only to people who have experienced the death of a loved one but also to their friends and to those who might want to know how to react to mourners.

Immortality and the Supernatural

Most secular experts on talking about death to children advise that an adult should frankly state that he or she does not know whether there is an afterlife or a place called heaven. In works of nonfiction read in the public school classroom, discussion of heaven or hell might be interpreted as conflict of church and state. But there are a number of works of fiction, especially for the older reader, that involve ghosts, spirits, demons, supernatural events, and the notion of an afterlife. When children are mature enough to recognize the fantasy or imaginative design of the story, then they may reflect on what the author has presented without undue confusion or anxiety. Discretion on the part of the adult is needed so that all views are respected and none imposed.

In C.S. Adler's *Ghost Brother,* the author grapples with the issues of hoping against hope that a loved one is returning, the idea of ghosts, the dilemma of trying to take a dead loved one's place, the appropriateness of the grieving process, and the resolution of those inevitable rivalries and negative feelings siblings have for each other. She raises the issues and lets the reader judge how to resolve them.

In Bernal C. Payne Jr.'s *The Late, Great Dick Hart,* the main character not only encounters the ghost of his best friend, but he is also invited into heaven and given the option of choosing his date of death. The heaven he sees is not peopled with angels on snowy white clouds but is reminiscent of ordinary places on earth. Aside from the issues of immortality, this book raises questions of what life is all about, the definition of friendship, and the choices people make in life.

A different view of immortality is presented in a book that might be difficult for younger children to read to themselves but could be read to them. Certainly, children aged nine and up could handle the prose themselves. *Tuck Everlasting,* by Natalie Babbitt, is worth the effort for younger readers. The story tells of a family that has discovered and drunk from a spring containing the water of eternal life. Many questions are raised about the value of life and death, all in the context of an exciting and well-written adventure story. Each character displays a different perspective for the reader to explore and ponder.

Books in Which Death Is Incidental

Most books for young readers concentrate on elements other than death. Death nevertheless occurs in many books and figures importantly in their plots. It appears either as an incidental happening or as a plot strategy in all genres of literature including folk tales, classics, romantic novels, and poetry. Sometimes death is seen in a religious light. Sometimes it occurs almost as an author's afterthought. It often conforms to some literary expectation; for example, the parents of young protagonists are killed off so that the children can have heroic adventures.

In some classics the young heroes, male or female, are angels on earth while alive, carrying out their mission of tenderness and virtue, and are "gathered back to God" while they are still very young. The writing is usually sentimental, with the quaintness of a period piece. The attempt is made to teach children to admire and emulate this good and kind soul who was lent to us mortals for such a brief period. One logical conclusion a child could reach, however, would be quite the opposite from the one intended—to vow never to be that good in order not to die so young. The idea is not so far fetched as it first may seem; forced didacticism often backfires. Goodness can be presented in such a saccharine and exaggerated fashion as to discourage its practice.

Hans Christian Andersen's stories almost always display a strong moralistic tone. His characters often die as a reward for a good life. Andersen's characters go to a specific place after they die; there is no doubt about life after death. Religion plays a very important part in his tales and, of course, figures heavily in his messages about death. Children may be interested in studying Hans Christian Andersen's life in order to see how it affected his writing.

Teachers may find it difficult to deal with this approach if they are uneasy about either offending or supporting any given religious attitude about the hereafter. One way of handling the dilemma is to suggest that students make a study of the different religious approaches to death. Additional research can include a comparison of modern and ancient beliefs. Other extensions of this sort of study would lead to comparative mythology, an examination of fairy tales and folk tales from around the world, or an inquiry into anthropological aspects of societies and their customs surrounding death. It is always a fruitful educational experience to acquire information about beliefs and customs other than one's own since this knowledge makes us more inquisitive and less judgmental or narrow.

Death as punishment is often used in literature as a deterrent to wickedness. In literature, as in real life, this threat is usually ineffectual: The wicked continue to be evil and continue to be justly killed. Witches, dragons, ogres, and giants die. So too do most, if not all, of the hero's enemies. The death is often violent and described in gory detail.

Villains, unless they repent, must die. What sort of attitude does this rule create in us? How can we help our students move from the "eye for an eye" morality expressed so convincingly in our folklore? How much does this philosophy actually seep into our sense of social and political justice? For instance, why is it that in oldtime cowboy films we know that a character who has committed a certain kind of crime will die in the end? We not only anticipate this ending, we require it. Questioning this accepted pattern may lead us to discussions of capital punishment, justice, and the causes and nature of crime. The teacher can begin asking this kind of question in order to work with the level of moral and social development the students have acquired.

Although it is but one of the many components, death is a factor in the modern classic *Charlotte's Web,* by E.B. White. Wilbur is threatened with death during the first part of the book, and Charlotte dies near the end; but the book emphasizes the idea that life goes on. Although he no longer actively grieves, Wilbur never forgets Charlotte. Her children remain as her legacy, along with memories of her special characteristics and talents. Friendship, love, and tolerance of those with different lifestyles are strong themes in this beautifully written book. Death is handled so sensitively that it would probably provide a measure of comfort to readers trying to deal with the death of someone dear to them. It also can provide the basis of an interesting discussion about life cycles, as well as the function of death and its aftermath for the living.

There are hundreds more books containing mention of, concentration upon, and implications of death. Some of these can be useful in helping readers cope with their own fears and problems, while others can help readers in uncovering attitudes and thoughts of which they had been unaware. Some books may, if the reader is not careful, convey ideas that are detrimental. Alert adults will be able to more readily guide and respond to children by making available as much variety as the literature can provide.

REFERENCES

Death

Apseloff, M. F. "Death in Adolescent Literature: Suicide." *Children's Literature Association Quarterly* 16 (Winter 1991–92): 234–237. Analyzes two books for older readers in which suicide is a major theme and discusses their bibliotherapeutic value.

Berman, D. B. "The Facilitation of Mourning: A Preventive Mental Health Approach." Doctoral dissertation, University of Massachusetts, 1977. Presents a curriculum based on research and experience to help young children develop a concept of death and the ability to mourn. Helps teachers and other concerned adults to address children's question on the subject of death. Provides suggestions for activities and books to use with preschoolers.

Chaston, J. D. "The Other Deaths in *Bridge to Terabithia.*" *Children's Literature Association Quarterly* 16 (Winter 1991–92): 238–240. The author cautions against relying too heavily on bibliotherapy as a "cure" for a grieving child. He uses the example of *Bridge to Terabithia,* in which all the protagonist's reading on death does not help prepare him for the tragic death of his friend. He quotes Katherine Paterson, who says books should not be used to tell readers what to feel but may be useful in helping readers to "listen to the sounds of their own hearts."

Cunningham, B., and Hare, J. "Essential Elements of a Teacher In-Service Program on Child Bereavement." *Elementary School Guidance and Counseling* 23 (February 1989): 175–183. Offers practical suggestions for setting up in-service programs for teachers to help them teach about death and grieving. Lists several criteria, including promoting awareness of children's bereavement patterns and perceptions of death, examining one's own attitudes, role-playing, and awareness of community and curricular resources.

Danielson, K. E. "Death: Realism in Children's Books." Paper presented at the Plains Regional Conference of the International Reading Association (Nov. 7–9, 1985). Discusses children's developmental stages in understanding death and their role in children's literature. Reports the reactions of a sixth grade class exposed to a variety of books on this subject. An annotated bibliography is provided.

Davis, G. L. "A Content Analysis of Fifty-Seven Children's Books with Death Themes." *Child Study Journal* 16 (1986): 39-54. The author determined that most books portray the grieving process unrealistically and that a disproportionate number of the books focus on the death of young people, which is a relatively rare occurrence. He calls for books focusing more on the feelings of the dying individual. He also cites an improvement in quality and realistic representations since 1969.

Doherty, S. "Teaching Kids How to Grieve." *Newsweek,* Nov. 13, 1989, p. 73. The article reports on an experimental class in a public school in Los Angeles where children who have recently lost family members to violence can learn to express and deal with their grief.

Gibson, L. R., and Zaidman, Laura M. "Death in Children's Literature: Taboo or Not Taboo?" *Children's Literature Association Quarterly* 16 (Winter 1991-92): 232-233. In this introduction to an issue devoted to the subject of death in children's literature, the authors give a brief overview of the history of death in children's books then advocate the inclusion of this subject in books for young readers.

Goodwin, C., and Davidson, P. M. "A Child's Cognitive Perception of Death." *Day Care and Early Education* 19 (Winter 1991): 21-24. Discusses how increasing longevity and impersonal institutions such as funeral homes have made death distant for many children. Provides suggestions for educators and parents on how to answer children's questions and discuss the concept of death. Recommends activities designed to familiarize children with life's cycles.

Grollman, E. A., ed. *Explaining Death to Children.* Beacon, 1983. Chapters are contributed by experts on various aspects of death education. Several religions are represented. Psychologists explain children's perceptions and reactions to death. Advice is given on how to converse with children about this topic.

Grollman, E. A., ed. *Talking about Death: A Dialogue between Parent and Child,* 3rd ed. Beacon, 1991. A conversation including children's questions and the answers understanding parents would provide.

Hunt, C. "Dead Athletes and Other Martyrs." *Children's Literature Association Quarterly* 16 (Winter 1991-92): 241-245. The author identifies three categories of books which deal with death for adolescents. She discusses their appeal and critiques the flaws of each category. She warns against books in which a dead hero is idealized or an unwanted minor character is done away with, advocating instead books in which the protagonists work through their feelings.

Kelly, E. B. *Dealing with Death: A Strategy for Tragedy.* Phi Delta Kappa Educational Foundation, 1990. This informative booklet helps teachers deal with students experiencing a tragedy. It offers suggestions both for dealing with the whole class and for helping the grieving students when they return to school.

Kubler-Ross, E. *On Children and Death.* Macmillan, 1983. Many aspects of this difficult topic are dealt with in a comprehensive and analytic fashion. The author's spiritual outlook permeates the text. She provides many examples of situations that form the basis of her contentions about children and death.

Kubler-Ross, E. *On Death and Dying.* Macmillan, 1969. In what has become a classic the author explores the stages terminally ill people progress through upon learning of their impending death. The stages are denial, anger, bargaining, depression, acceptance, and hope.

McCornack, B. "Helping Young Children Deal with Death." Paper presented at the Conference of the National Association for the Education of Young Children, Washington, D.C., Nov. 14-18, 1990. Presents information from a workshop on helping preschool teachers discuss death with young children. Refers to 16 books appropriate to read with children.

Moore, D. W.; Moore, S. A.; and Readence, J. E. "Understanding Characters' Reactions to Death." *Journal of Reading* 26 (March 1983): 540-544. Presents an approach to help students respond to literature that contains death as a theme. Outlines the Kubler-Ross stages of response to death and invites students to analyze characters' reactions according to those stages.

Moore, T. E., and Reet, M. "Who Dies and Who Cries: Death and Bereavement in Children's Literature." *Journal of Communications* 37 (Autumn 1987): 52-64. Discusses how fictional accounts of the death of a significant person in a child's life reveal stereotypes of tearful girls and stoic boys, with little natural grief.

Oaks, J., and Bibeau, D. L. "Death Education: Educating Children for Living." *The Clearinghouse* 60 (May 1987): 420-422. Advocates the inclusion of death and dying in the curriculum of all children from kindergarten to twelfth grade, and offers guidelines and suggestions for doing so.

Papadatos, D., and Papadatos, C., eds. *Children and Death.* Hemisphere, 1991. Part of a series on death education, aging, and health care, this is a compilation of papers presented by acknowledged experts on the topic of death at the International Conference on Children and Death held in Athens in 1989. The 27 chapters range from a discussion of the developmental levels of knowing about death to parental adjustment to the loss of a child.

Pyles, M. S. *Death and Dying in Children's and Young People's Literature: A Survey and Bibliography.* McFarland, 1988. A series of book talks in which the author explores the treatment of death. Folklore about death, the deaths of friends and relatives, and one's own death are all examined.

Rudman, M. K.; Gagne, K. D.; and Bernstein, J. E. *Books to Help Children Cope with Separation and Loss,* 4th ed. Bowker, 1993. This reference work contains 80 titles and annotations on death in addition to two chapters on bibliotherapy and psychological background on separation and loss.

Sadler, D. "Grandpa Died Last Night: Children's Books about the Death of Grandparents." *Children's Literature Association Quarterly* 16 (Winter 1991-92): 246-250. Surveys 29 books for children centering around the death of a grandparent. The author identifies four stages: the relationship between child and grandparent, the grandparent's illness, the grandparent's death, and the child's mourning and recovery. He compares and contrasts the themes in the different books, pointing out highlights and suggesting helpful criteria. He stresses the special influence of these books in helping children to see the importance of perpetuating family values and traditions.

Schaefer, D., and Lyons, C. *How Do We Tell Children?: Helping Children Understand and Cope When Someone Dies.* Newmarket, 1986. Different scenarios, such as suicide, the death of a close family member, murder, and death by accident are handled deftly and compassionately. Funeral rituals are mentioned in the context of the emotional release they provide. Another positive aspect of this book is that the authors keep in mind children's developmental levels and advise parents and teachers accordingly. An excellent resource.

Schowalter, J. E.; Buschman, P.; Patterson, P. R.; Kutscher, A. H.; Tallmer, M.; and Stevenson, R. G., eds. *Children and Death: Perspectives from Birth through Adolescence.* Praeger, 1987. This volume integrates research from various disciplines and ranges in topics from a report on outstanding children's books about death, a manual for medical students on chronic illness and death in children, developmental aspects of children's concepts of death, and varying views on death education.

Stambrook, M., and Parker, K. C.H. "The Development of the Concept of Death in Child-hood: A Review of the Literature." *Merrill-Palmer Quarterly* 33 (April 1987): 133-155. A critical review of the literature studying how children's concepts of death evolve and change as they mature. Suggestions for further study.

RESOURCES

American Academy of Child and Adolescent Psychiatry. P.O. Box 96106, Washington, DC 20090-6106. Provides brief, informative "Fact Sheets" on topics such as "Children and Grief" and "Teen Suicide."

International Association for Widowed People. P.O. Box 3564, Springfield, IL 62708. Offers widowed people and their families a better understanding of death. Publishes newsletters, a magazine, and a membership directory. Maintains a library and speakers' bureau.

BIBLIOGRAPHY

Adler, C.S. *Carly's Buck.* Clarion, 1987. (Ages 10 and up.) Some difficult aspects of mourn-ing and coping with the death of a loved one are handled in depth in this story of a child who cannot let go of the regret and resentment she feels over her own and her father's treatment of her mother before the mother's death. Another painful loss and the sensitive intercession of a friend finally help Carly to overcome her guilt and rage.

Adler, C.S. *Daddy's Climbing Tree.* Clarion, 1993. (Ages 9-12.) Jessica refuses to believe that her adored, lively, nurturing father is dead. Even his funeral and the comments of visiting friends and family fail to persuade her of the truth of this awful and sudden loss. Only after making an odyssey to their previous home does Jessica acknowledge her father's death. Even though the reader meets the father only briefly, his personality and place in the family are firmly established. Each character's individual perspective is well handled here, and the reaction to death by accident is accurately and sensitively depicted.

Adler, C.S. *Ghost Brother.* Clarion, 1990. (Ages 9-12.) Wally's adored older brother Jon-o keeps appearing to him, even though Jon-o has been dead for more than a week. His ghost urges Wally to become more adventuresome and outgoing, in short, more like him. Wally's mother is consumed by her grief, having relied on Jon-o for emotional and practical support since the boys' father died eight years earlier. In a moving novel, the author demonstrates the power of the sibling attachment and the grappling with a deep loss.

Agee, J. *A Death in the Family.* Grosset & Dunlap, 1967. (Ages 12 and up.) A portrayal of the effects of a man's death on the rest of his family, with tremendous insights into the world and emotions of children.

Alcott, L. M. *Little Women.* Little, Brown, 1868. (Ages 8 and up.) [See Gender Roles]

Alexander, S. *Nadia the Willful.* Illus. by L. Bloom. Pantheon, 1983. (Ages 6-9.) Nadia, a feisty Bedouin girl, disobeys her father's command not to speak even the name of his dead son, Hamed. Realizing that remembering her brother eases her grief, Nadia ulti-mately helps her father to accept Hamed's death.

Allen, T., ed. *The Whispering Wind: Poetry by Young American Indians.* Doubleday, 1968. (Ages 10 and up.) [See Heritage]

Ancona, G. *Pablo Remembers: The Fiesta of the Day of the Dead.* Lothrop, Lee and Shepard, 1993. (Ages 7–10.) [See Heritage]

Anderson, L. C. *It's O.K. to Cry.* Children's Press, 1979. (Ages 5–8.) After the death of a favorite uncle, a nine year old tries to explain death to his five-year-old brother who cannot understand its finality. Included in the book is a discussion of death in terms that can easily be understood.

Arundel, H. *The Blanket Word.* Nashville: Nelson, 1973. (Ages 12 and up.) Jan begins to grow up after returning from school to observe her mother's painful death from cancer, the funeral, and the rest of her family's reaction to the whole situation.

Babbitt, N. *Tuck Everlasting.* Farrar, Straus & Giroux, 1975. (Ages 10 and up.) The Tuck family inadvertently achieves immortality after drinking from a magical spring. They are threatened by all sorts of enemies and problems because of their inability to die. The story is poetically written, and its depth invites readers to ponder the questions raised here long after the book is ended.

Bartoli, J. *Nonna.* Illus. by J. E. Drescher. Harvey House, 1975. (Ages 5–8.) When the grandmother dies, everyone in the family, including the father and mother, cries. The funeral is described, the extended family arrives, and everyone mourns together. The family then resumes life, remembering both grandparents lovingly.

Bauer, M. D. *On My Honor.* Clarion, 1986. (Ages 10 and up.) Guilt torments Joel because he feels complicity in the drowning of his friend Tony. Although he tried to dissuade Tony from endangering himself and he did everything he could to rescue his friend, Joel lies about the incident and pretends he was not involved. Joel's father responds with understanding once the truth is out; but Joel faces a challenge of self-confrontation.

Bernstein, J. E. *Loss and How to Cope with It.* Clarion, 1977. (Ages 10 and up.) An excellent resource for people of any age, though it is directed at children. It contains anecdotes of informative personal experiences affirming the necessity for the mourning process, reassuring people that their reactions are normal and helping them to handle their emotions. Resources for further reading are provided at the end.

Bernstein, J. E., and Gullow, S. V. *When People Die.* Illus. by R. Hauserr. Dutton, 1977. (Ages 6–10.) One woman's death, coming at the end of a productive life, is portrayed as an example of the aging process, mourning, and beliefs about an afterlife. The photographs help convey the messages.

Blume, J. *Tiger Eyes.* Bradbury, 1977. (Ages 11 and up.) Davey is fifteen years old. Her father has been killed by a thief, and the family is in dire economic straits. The book deals with issues of loss and security and the problem of coping with irrational tragedy.

Bolton, C. *Reunion in December.* Morrow, 1962. (Ages 12 and up.) A fifteen-year-old girl has a hard time adjusting to the sudden death of her father and the actions of the rest of her family after his death.

Boyd, Candy D. *Breadsticks and Blessing Places.* Macmillan, 1985. (Ages 9 and up.) Twelve-year-old Toni struggles to deal with the death of her best friend Susan and get on with her life. The swift removal of Susan's belongings from the classroom and the open-casket funeral make the death harder for Toni to tolerate. Finally, Mattie (her other best friend, whose father has died) helps Toni to create her own ritual for saying goodbye to Susan and accepting her loss.

Boyd, C. D. *Circle of Gold.* Scholastic, 1984. (Ages 9–12.) The death of the father in the Benson family causes a vacuum that takes massive efforts on everyone's part to fill. Much of the responsibility falls on eleven-year-old Mattie's shoulders. She finally communicates her fortitude and determination to her mother, and it looks likely that the family will become whole again.

Brooks, M. *Two Moons in August*. Little, Brown, 1991. (Ages 12 and up.) A year after her mother's death, sixteen-year-old Sidonie, her older sister Roberta, and their father are still disjointed. The father has buried himself in his work, often distancing himself from his daughters. Roberta has overburdened herself by attempting to fill the shoes of her mother. Sidonie has become very introverted, but finally tires of grieving alone and vows to bring the other survivors out of their shells. She arranges a long-needed reunion with her mother's sisters and acknowledges that long-term healing is a collaborative effort.

Brown, M. W. *The Dead Bird*. Illus. by R. Charlip. Young Scott, 1958. (Ages 3-8.) Some children find a dead bird, conduct a funeral, and visit the grave every day until they forget. One of the first books for young children on this topic.

Buck, P. S. *The Big Wave*. Illus. with prints by Hiroshige and Hakusai. John Day, 1948. (Ages 8-12.) When a Japanese boy's family dies in a tidal wave, his friend's family helps him to deal with death and fear through an affirmation of life.

Bulla, C. R. *The Christmas Coat*. Illus. by S. Wickstrom. Knopf, 1989. (Ages 7-10.) [See Siblings]

Bunting, E. *The Empty Window*. Illus. by J. Clifford. Warne, 1980. (Ages 7-10.) Joe, a young boy, is dying. He loves to look out his window at some wild parrots. When he receives one of the parrots as a gift, he sets it free in a symbolic acceptance of his own life and death. The response of his friends to his condition is well handled in this sensitive book.

Bunting, E. *Face at the Edge of the World*. Clarion, 1985. (Ages 12 and up.) Couched in the form of a mystery, the story deals with the unsettling issue of teen suicide. Jed, the protagonist, uses his powers of observation and his love for his friend Charlie to uncover the reasons for Charlie's suicide. Included are also such issues as drug abuse, media exploitation, bigotry, and adults' inappropriate responses.

Bunting, E. *The Happy Funeral*. Illus. by V. Mai. Harper, 1982. (Ages 7-10.) The book contains descriptions of Chinese-American funeral rituals and tells of a perspective on life that accepts death as a fitting end.

Bunting, E. *A Sudden Silence*. HBJ, 1988. (Ages 10 and up.) [See Abuse]

Burningham, J. *Granpa*. Illus. by the author. Crown, 1984. (Ages 4-6.) [See Aging]

Byars, B. *A Blossom Promise*. Illus. by J. Rogers. Dell, 1987. (Ages 9-12.) In this fourth volume of the "Blossom Family" series, (the others are *The Not-Just-Anybody Family, The Blossoms Meet the Vulture Lady,* and *The Blossoms and the Green Phantom*) besides continuing to mourn the father of the family, the characters have several brushes with death. Vern, the eldest brother, nearly drowns; both family dogs nearly die; and Pap, the grandfather, suffers a near-fatal heart attack. None of the characters dies, but the process of dealing with the possible tragedy is believably presented.

Byars, B. *Goodbye Chicken Little*. Harper, 1979. (Ages 9-12.) Jimmie feels guilty because he couldn't stop his uncle from taking a dare and drowning as a result of it. He is helped to overcome his guilt and his negative feelings about himself when his unconventional family celebrates Uncle Pete's life with a huge party rather than morosely mourning his death. An unusual story.

Carlson, N. S. *The Half Sisters*. Illus. by T. di Grazia. Harper, 1970. (Ages 8-12.) [See Siblings]

Carrick, C. *The Accident*. Illus. by D. Carrick. Seabury, 1976. (Ages 6-10.) After his dog Bodger is run over and killed, Christopher must deal with feelings of depression and guilt. Christopher blames himself as much as the truck driver for the accident because he called the dog across the road. The boy finally finds a way to deal with his feelings when he and his father look for the right stone to mark the dog's grave.

Caseley, J. *When Grandpa Came to Stay.* Illus. by the author. Greenwillow, 1986. (Ages 5-8.) [See Aging]

Clardy, A. F. *Dusty Was My Friend: Coming to Terms with Loss.* Illus. by E. Alexander. Human Sciences, 1984. (Ages 5-10) Although this book has didactic intent, it is nevertheless a well-crafted story. Benjamin, the narrator, evidences and discusses the stages of mourning when he learns about his friend Dusty's death. His message grants permission to young readers to acknowledge the validity of their feelings of grief.

Cleaver, V., and Cleaver, B. *Grover.* Illus. by F. Martin. Lippincott, 1970. (Ages 9-11.) Grover's mother, who knows she is dying of cancer, shoots herself. Grover understands and accepts his mother's action better than his father. He is able to cope with his grief with the help of his friends and a sympathetic housekeeper.

Cleaver, V., and Cleaver, B. *Where the Lilies Bloom.* Illus. by J. Spanfeller. Lippincott, 1969. (Ages 9 and up.) [See Gender Roles]

Clifford, E. *The Killer Swan.* Houghton Mifflin, 1980. (Ages 10 and up.) Lex's father has committed suicide, and Lex tries to understand why it happened. He blames himself and his mother, and he feels angry and confused. He finally realizes, through a symbolic encounter with a pair of swans, that he can never know the whole answer, but he must resume his own life.

Clifton, L. *Everett Anderson's Goodbye.* Illus. by A. Grifalconi. Holt, 1983. (Ages 5-8.) The sensitive black-and-white line drawings enhance the emotional impact of a child's mourning for his father. The stages of mourning are pictured and acted out by Everett Anderson, and responded to lovingly and supportively by his mother. Death is difficult for anyone to cope with, but this book poetically and clearly conveys the healing process over the passage of time.

Coatsworth, E. *The Cat Who Went to Heaven.* Illus. by L. Ward. Macmillan, 1990 (Originally published in 1958). (Ages 9-11.) An artist paints the legend of Buddha in which he is spurned by a cat and the cat does not go to heaven. The artist, however, takes pity on his cat and paints it into the picture. The cat then dies in ecstasy.

Cohen, M. *Jim's Dog Muffins.* Illus. by L. Hoban. Greenwillow, 1984. (Ages 5-8.) After Muffins is killed by a car, Jim has a hard time dealing with his grief. He becomes withdrawn and pushes away friends who try to comfort him. His teacher understands that he "needs time to feel sad," but this is difficult for his friends to understand. His friend Paul finally helps him to cry, laugh, and get on with his life. The book presents a reassuring message that life goes on and that it is OK to feel sad.

Cohn, J. *I Had a Friend Named Peter.* Illus. by G. Owens. Morrow, 1987. (Ages 5-8.) Using the fictionalized story of the accidental death of a young child, the book advises adults about handling the issue of death with children. The book also speaks to a child audience, inviting young readers to acknowledge their feelings and help peers when they need comforting. The importance of participation in ritual and the necessity for understanding and accepting children's feelings are highlighted.

Corso, G. "Italian Extravaganza." In *On City Streets,* edited by N. Larrick. Illus. by D. Sagarin. Lippincott, 1968. (Ages 7 and up.) The death of an infant and the elaborate trappings of the funeral impress the child narrator in this poem.

Coutant, H. *First Snow.* Illus. V. Mai. Knopf, 1974. (Ages 5-8.) Lien and her family have come from Vietnam to New England. It is winter, and Lien's grandmother is dying. Lien asks her grandmother to explain what dying means. She understands when her grandmother directs her to experience the snow. Recognizing the cyclical nature of life, she is content.

Deaver, J. R. *Say Goodnight, Gracie.* Harper, 1988. (Ages 12 and up.) When her closest friend Jimmy is killed by a drunken driver, Morgan is numbed by the loss and withdraws from the world. Finally, with professional help, Morgan confronts her denial, anger, fear, and guilt and decides to rejoin the living.

Dobrin, A. *Scat.* Four Winds, 1971. (Ages 5–8.) An eight-year-old boy says good-bye to his dead grandmother by playing his harmonica at the cemetery. This makes him feel better because, although his grandmother hated jazz, he knows that she would understand.

Dolan, E. F. *Matters of Life and Death.* Watts, 1982. (Ages 12 and up.) Controversial societal issues such as abortion, contraception, and euthanasia are presented here with broad, equitable, forthright, and intensive coverage. Examples from newspaper articles flavor the debate.

Donnelly, E. *So Long, Grandpa.* Trans. by A. Bell. Crown, 1981. (Ages 8–11.) When Mike's grandfather dies after a long and painful battle with cancer, he has prepared his grandson for his death, going through a kind of rehearsal by taking Michael to the funeral of an old friend. Each of the family members reacts in a different way.

Dragonwagon, C. *Will It Be Okay?* Illus. by B. Shecter. Harper, 1977. (Ages 3–7.) The little girl asks her mother to assuage her fears about all sorts of things and finally asks what will happen if her mother dies. Her mother assures her that her love will never die and that her memories of their time together will comfort her.

Dragonwagon, C. *Winter Holding Spring.* Illus. by R. Himler. Macmillan, 1990. (Ages 7–10.) After Sarah's mother dies, Sarah and her father spend time together walking, working in the garden, and helping each other to heal the hurt of the mother's death. Sarah's father is a loving and intelligent man. Sarah is a thoughtful and sensitive eleven year old. Together they realize that although they will always miss their loved one they hold her in their lives, and she is not lost to them.

Duncan, L. *Killing Mr. Griffin.* Little, Brown, 1978. (Ages 12 and up.) A chilling story of a group of high school students who inadvertently, but directly, cause the death of their English teacher. The major portion of the book explores the reactions to his death and builds a picture of each of the characters, including Mr. Griffin.

Ellis, S. *A Family Project.* McElderry, 1988. (Ages 9–12.) [See Family Constellations]

Enright, D.J. "Along the River." In *Don't Forget to Fly,* edited by P. Janeczko. Bradbury, 1981. (Ages 10 and up.) A comparison of two suicides found in the river from the perspective of the poet as a child and as a young man.

Erwin, J. "Death." In *Miracles: Poems by Children of the English-Speaking World,* edited by R. Lewis. Simon & Schuster, 1966. (Ages 8 and up.) Relating death to the "growing of people which cannot be stopped," the poet accepts the finality of death in this five-line poem.

Fairless, C. *Hambone.* Illus. by W. Edelson. Tundra, 1980. (Ages 5–8.) Hambone, Jeremy's pet pig, must be slaughtered. Jeremy's sister Stoner helps him deal with Hambone's death. They construct a memorial, a special pot where all the pig's favorite items are buried, and they plant what turn out to be prize-winning tomatoes.

Farley, C. *The Garden Is Doing Fine.* Illus. by L. Siveat. Atheneum, 1975. (Ages 10 and up.) Corrie's father is dying of cancer. She cannot accept the fact until just before his death. Then, at last, with the help of an elderly friend, she realizes that her father's life has been an important factor in her life and in others' lives. She understands that his spirit and memory will be retained and that he leaves a legacy of joy and love. Corrie's feelings of hope, superstition, despair, and anger mirror many readers' responses to death.

Fassler, J. *My Grandpa Died Today.* Illus. by S. Kranz. Behavioral Publications, 1971. (Ages 3–8.) A boy's grandfather dies, and he feels sad and empty until after the funeral, when his parents encourage him to go outside and play. At first he feels guilty about resuming his normal activities, but then he realizes that this is what his grandfather would have wanted for him. The grandfather has tried to prepare the boy for this circumstance. Jewish mourning customs, mentioned in this book, might provide a context for the discussion of other cultures' rituals.

Fenton, E. *The Morning of the Gods.* Delacorte, 1987. (Ages 12 and up.) After the death of her mother, when Carla travels to Greece, she comes in contact with her mother's background. Carla becomes involved in a political plot, returns to America, and finally to Greece again, where she has made an important spiritual connection with her mother and with herself. The author deftly handles the emotional tone and the importance of the setting to Carla's coming to terms with her grief.

Fleischman, P. *Rear-View Mirrors.* Zolotow, 1986. (Ages 12 and up.) Olivia's long-absent father arranges to see her because he knows his death is imminent. After he dies, Olivia undertakes a ritual marathon bicycle ride similar to one her father had accomplished. The successful completion of this ride helps her to feel that she can lay her father to rest and now become her own person.

Gardner, J. *In the Suicide Mountains.* Houghton Mifflin, 1977. (Ages 12 and up.) Three people who feel that society has short-changed them set out to commit suicide, but before they reach their destination, many things occur to make them change their minds. The tale, a reworking of traditional German and Russian folk tales, is intended to reach some of the many American adolescents who attempt suicide.

Gardner, S., with Rosenberg, G., M.D. *Teenage Suicide.* Messner, 1985. (Ages 12 and up.) A comprehensive look at suicide, including many details about possible causes and the signals people may emit if they are contemplating taking their own lives. Prevention programs are described, and resources for help are listed.

Gerstein, M.. *The Mountains of Tibet.* Harper, 1987. (Ages 7 and up.) Reincarnation and the philosophical notion of the choices we make in life are presented in a picture book that can be appreciated at many levels. The illustrations are framed and enclosed when they depict the real world; they take the form of mandalas when they refer to the world beyond. The story is about the options a newborn is offered at birth of where to live and what form to take. The child chooses exactly the life he led before, only this time he decides to be female. Not a story about death, but more about a non-Western concept of the cycle of life.

Giff, P. R. *The Gift of the Pirate Queen.* Illus. by J. Rutherford. Dell, 1982. (Ages 8–10.) [See Siblings.]

Gipson, F. *Old Yeller.* Harper, 1956. (Ages 12 and up.) As a part of the process of growing up, a boy learns to deal with his grief over his devoted dog's death.

Girion, B. *A Tangle of Roots.* Scribner's, 1979. (Ages 11 and up.) Beth's mother dies suddenly of a cerebral hemorrhage. The story details all Beth's reactions, the Jewish ritual of the funeral and mourning, and the way the family tries to readjust their lives afterward. Beth's relationships with her friends and her family change after her mother's death. All the responses are believable, and the pace of the book is appropriate to the topic. Beth's disbelief when she is told of her mother's death, her grief and reassessment of her own life, her fear of desertion, and her gradual recovery are well developed.

Gould, D. *Grandpa's Slide Show.* Illus. by C. Harness. Lothrop, Lee & Shepard, 1987. (Ages 6-8.) Grandpa was an amateur photographer and the master of ceremonies at family slide presentations. A short time after he dies, the immediate family gathers for a nostalgic show of slides from various family vacations and outings. This ceremony helps the family to vent their feelings and to focus on the good times they have shared and will continue to experience, always holding the grandfather in loving memory. The illustrations support the realistic, intimate tone of the text.

Graeber, C. *Mustard.* Illus. by D. Diamond. Macmillan, 1982. (Ages 6-9.) Alex does not want to accept the fact that his cat Mustard is not only old but seriously ill. Finally, when the cat is in extreme pain and medicine does not seem to help him, Alex's parents take the cat to the veterinarian so he can "die in peace." Alex sees Mustard's dead body, and the cat is buried. Alex's father weeps, and the family agrees that they are not yet ready for another cat. A well-constructed and informative book, as well as a moving story.

Grant, C. *Phoenix Rising.* Atheneum, 1989. (Ages 11 and up.) Jess's adored older sister Helen has died of cancer at age eighteen, and Jess is inconsolable. She has nightmares, feels physically ill, and finds it difficult to concentrate. A combination of a helpful friend's visits and reading her sister's diary finally helps her begin to come to terms with her sister's death. The story details Helen's feelings at having cancer and the extreme emotional response that Jess suffers. It also reveals how each family member unsuccessfully tries to deal with Helen's death. This is not a comforting book, but it is a strong and compelling portrait of a family in crisis.

Greenberg, J. E., and Carey, H. H. *Sunny: The Death of a Pet.* Illus. by B. Kirk. Watts, 1986. (Ages 5-8.) Many useful details are provided here: Ken's developmentally appropriate reactions to the death of his dog, the idea of storing the pet's things in a special place to help Ken remember, and the acceptance of a new pet, not as a replacement but as an individual in its own right. The book is a good model of coping for young pet owners.

Greene, C. C. *Beat the Turtle Drum.* Viking, 1976. (Ages 9-12.) A loving family suffers mightily because of Joss's accidental death. The shock, the pain of the bereavement, the palpable physical symptoms of grieving, and the handling of well-meaning condolences are portrayed with keen insight and deft language.

Gunther, J. *Death Be Not Proud.* Harper, 1949. (Ages 12 and up.) The true story of a young man's hopeless but courageous fight against a brain tumor, written by his father. A moving story for adolescents.

Hamilton, V. *Cousins.* Philomel, 1990. (Ages 10-12.) [See Family Constellations]

Harlan, E. *Watershed.* Viking, 1986. (Ages 12 and up.) The plot presents the dilemma of brothers raised in the same house but very different from each other. In this case, Noel is so vulnerable that he kills himself when he is caught and punished for an act of mischief. The rest of the family react in their own individual manners. The book contributes to the growing number of stories emphasizing the importance of listening and observing closely.

Hay, S. H. "For a Dead Kitten." In *Reflections upon a Gift of Watermelon Pickle,* edited by S. Dunning, E. Lueders, and H. Smith. Scholastic, 1966. (Ages 9 and up.) Wondering how the soft tiny body of a kitten could "hold so immense a thing as death," the poet speaks of putting away things that belonged to the cat. The reaction of bewilderment is a natural stage in mourning.

Hazen, B. S. *Why Did Grandpa Die? A Book about Death.* Illus. by P. Schories. Golden, 1985. (Ages 5-8.) Neither euphemisms nor avoidance are employed in this well written and clearly presented book for young readers. Molly's reactions to her grand-father's death are denial, fear, anger, and grief. She benefits from her understanding and loving family, participates in family rituals of remembrance, and acknowledges the healing effects of the passage of time. Storytelling is recommended as a means of honoring and transmitting a family's traditions and values.

Heegaard, M. E. *Coping with Death and Grief.* Lerner, 1990. (Ages 9-12.) The book describes such factors as funerals, cremation, different ways people die (e.g., suicide, accidents), and other details children are inquisitive about. The author helps readers understand that their negative feelings are normal and that there are a number of ways they can cope with their loss. The tone of the book is neither abstract nor condescend-ing. The information is provided gradually in small doses. Children are given permis-sion to remain children rather than having to suddenly become adults. They are assured that they cannot "fix" people's grief but that they can listen and respond.

Hermes, P. *You Shouldn't Have to Say Good-bye.* HBJ, 1982. (Ages 10 and up.)While Sarah's mother is dying of cancer, she prepares her daughter for her death in many loving and thoughtful ways. After she dies, Sarah is comforted by her mother's diary. Affirmation of life is the key theme.

Hesse, K. *Poppy's Chair.* Illus. by K. Life. Macmillan, 1993. (Ages 4-8.) Leah is constantly reminded of her grandfather's absence on her first visit to her grandmother's house since his death. She misses him sorely and has a difficult time adjusting to his death. At first, she will not even look at his picture. Her grandmother helps her to work through some of the pain and learn to remember him with love.

Hoopes, L. L. *Nana.* Illus. by A. Zeldich. Harper, 1981. (Ages 4-8.) The little girl's grand-mother has just died. Recalling her lessons on how to observe and be a part of nature, the little girl feels that she has found a way to keep her grandmother with her at all times.

Hunter, M. *A Sound of Chariots.* Harper, 1972. (Ages 12 and up.) When a young girl's father dies, she learns to cope and to rechannel her grief into creative energy.

Hyde, M. O. *Meeting Death.* Walker, 1989. (Ages 10 and up.) This book covers a wide variety of topics related to death. The information is presented in detail, perhaps too much for some young readers; but all the facts are well researched and interesting. Cultures other than mainstream American are mentioned, and critical issues are raised. The book is not comforting, but it is informative for readers who are inquisitive about the various aspects of death and dying.

Jewell, N. *Time for Uncle Joe.* Illus. by J. Sandin. Harper, 1981. (Ages 5-9.) An evocative, loving memorial to the child's uncle, the book takes the reader through Uncle Joe's activities and habits. The smells, sounds, and sights he enjoyed and his personal objects are all woven into the book so that by the end, the reader too mourns and lovingly remembers.

Jordan, M. *Losing Uncle Tim.* Illus. by J. Friedman. Whitman, 1989. (Ages 8-10.) [See Special Needs]

Jukes, M. *Blackberries in the Dark.* Illus. by T. B. Allen. Knopf, 1985. (Ages 8-11.) So many of Austin's memories are tied to the things he did with his grandfather that it is difficult for him to visit his grandmother's farm the year after his grandfather died. His grandmother makes certain that they continue their traditional family activities so that they lovingly remember the grandfather while enjoying each other in the here and now.

Jukes, M. *I'll See You in My Dreams.* Illus. by S. Schuett. Knopf, 1993. (Ages 6-10.) A young girl visits her beloved uncle in the hospital where he is dying. She is determined to say good-bye. She prepares for the experience by imagining herself as a skywriter piloting her plane across the sky and writing her good-bye in the sky, adding the words, "I love you," and "I'll see you in my dreams." Then she and her mother visit her uncle, not knowing if he knows she's there but knowing in her own heart that being there is important. The book is a tribute to the strong bonds a child can form with a beloved relative and to the power of performing the ritual of a last good-bye.

Juneau, B. F. *Sad but O.K. My Daddy Died Today.* Blue Dolphin, 1988. (Ages 9–12.) Told in the language of 9-year-old Kelly, the book details the dying and death of Kelly's 34-year-old father from a malignant brain tumor. His family do everything they can to make his last weeks comfortable. The book provides an excellent model of how to cope with the impending death of a close family member.

Justice, D. "Sonnet for My Father." In *Don't Forget to Fly,* collected by P. Janeczko. Bradbury, 1981. (Ages 10 and up.) Spoken by the poet to his dying father, this sonnet deals with the pain and understanding between the two men as death approaches. The poet recognizes the continuity of life and the finality of death.

Kaldhol, M. *Goodbye Rune.* Illus. by W. Oyen. Kane/Miller, 1987. (Ages 5–8.) Sara's friend Rune dies in an accidental drowning while he and Sara are playing together. Sara's parents answer her questions with clear and compassionate explanations. The poetic language and flowing paintings support the story. Children might wonder at Sara's apparent lack of guilty feelings about her possible role in Rune's death, and an interesting discussion might ensue.

Kantrowitz, M. *When Violet Died.* Illus. by E. A. McCully. Parents Magazine, 1973. (Ages 5–8.) After their bird dies, the children have a funeral, realizing that living creatures do not last forever.

Klagsbrun, F. *Too Young to Die: Youth and Suicide.* Houghton Mifflin, 1976. (Ages 12 and up.) By means of case histories, the author analyzes different forms and causes of suicide in adolescents. She assuages some fears, assures readers that it is not hereditary, and warns people of its symptoms. She also appends useful lists of resources.

Kolehmainen, J., and Handwerk, S. *Teen Suicide: A Book for Friends, Family, and Classmates.* Lerner, 1986. (Ages 10 and up.) Contains information about the prevalence of suicide among young people, warning signs, and organizations designed to help. Vignettes of people who attempted suicide, their friends, and people who succeeded in committing suicide illuminate the discussion. Myths are debunked.

Krementz, J. *How It Feels When a Parent Dies.* Knopf, 1991. (Ages 8 and up.) Intended as a support for children who have lost a parent or who know someone who has, this book contains the experiences of 18 children between the ages of 7 and 16 who have lost a parent. The stories, told in the children's own words, are honest and often moving.

Kubler-Ross, E. *Questions and Answers on Death and Dying.* Macmillan, 1974. (Ages 13 and up.) Series of questions concerning family feelings, staff (hospital) involvement, the dying patient, funerals, and the like. A good book to help with the discussion of death or preparation for the death of a friend or family member.

Kunz, R. B., and Swenson, J. H. *Feeling Down: The Way Back Up.* Illus. by M. McKee. Dillon, 1986. (Ages 9–12.) The book focuses on Stephanie, a teenager who has attempted suicide, and the effect of this attempt on her two brothers. A therapist intervenes and helps the entire family to respond appropriately.

Langone, J. *Dead End: A Book about Suicide.* Little, Brown, 1986. (Ages 12 and up.) The author is a competent researcher whose exploration of difficult and sensitive topics contributes a scholarly and rich source of information. In its detailed presentation, the book provides facts and investigates thorny societal issues such as the right to die, influence of media, role of peers, and advisability of discussing this volatile topic.

Langone, J. *Death Is a Noun: A View of the End of Life.* Little, Brown, 1973. (Ages 13 and up.) A hard-hitting survey of all forms of death: natural, euthanasia, abortion, capital punishment, murder, and suicide. How to face death, whether that of a loved one or one's own, is explicitly dealt with. A book only for the mature reader.

Lanton, S. *Daddy's Chair.* Illus. by S. O. Haas. Kar-Ben Copies, 1991. (Ages 5–8.) Michael's dad has died of cancer. Michael makes a sign, placing it on his father's chair so that no one else will sit on it. The family comes to "sit shiva," the Jewish custom of mourning for seven days and tells stories about Michael's dad. Finally, Michael decides he will sit in his father's chair whenever he wants to have special memories of his dad. The book respectfully describes Jewish customs of mourning. It is an honest, uncondescending, sensitive presentation.

Lasky, K. *Beyond the Divide.* Macmillan, 1983. (Ages 11 and up.) [See Gender Roles]

Lasky, K. *Home Free.* Four Winds, 1985. (Ages 11 and up.) The protagonist is fifteen-year-old Sam, and the plot revolves around his involvement with the people of the town to which he and his mother have returned after his father's death in an automobile accident. Several deaths are encountered and handled, and the reader is invited to join in the exploration of the interrelationship of life and death.

Lee, V. *The Magic Moth.* Illus. by R. Cuffari. Seabury, 1972. (Ages 8 and up.) Mark-o comes to accept his sister's long illness and death from a heart defect. After the funeral, he preserves her memory in the symbol of a moth that comes out of its cocoon when his sister dies.

L'Engle, M. *Meet the Austins.* Vanguard, 1960. (Ages 8–12.) A friend of the family is killed in a plane accident, and the orphan daughter comes to live with the Austins, making them realize the difficulties of dealing with the aftermath of death. The orphan is a spoiled brat, changing the conventional stereotype.

L'Engle, M. *A Ring of Endless Light.* Farrar, Straus & Giroux, 1980. (Ages 11 and up.) The fourth in the Austin family series, this book focuses on Vicky, whose family is staying on the island where her dying grandfather lives. Vicky and her brother John become close friends in this story. Vicky's rivalry with her sister and her loving and protective relationship with her younger brother Rob also figure in the plot. Vicky discovers that she has the gift of communicating with dolphins. The book is an investigation of love, life, and coming to terms with death.

LeShan, E. *Learning to Say Good-By.* Macmillan, 1976. (Ages 7 and up.) This book, by a noted educator and family counselor, is clearly, concisely, sensitively, and beautifully written. It answers a child's questions and discusses fears and fantasies regarding the death of a parent. An excellent resource for the family.

Little, J. *Home from Afar.* Illus. by J. Lazare. Little, Brown, 1965. (Ages 10 and up.) Jenny resents the two foster children her parents have taken into their home after her brother Michael is killed in a car accident. Jenny deals with her grief, her mother's inappropriate behavior, and her resentment.

Little, J. *Mama's Going to Buy You a Mockingbird.* Penguin, 1984. (Ages 11 and up.) Jeremy and his sister Sarah struggle to keep from being overwhelmed by the consequences of their father's illness and eventual death. Their parents find it difficult to communicate what is going on during the inexorable progress of the father's cancer. Although the funeral (which the children wisely decide to attend) is not a personalized one, the grieving process is well defined and presented with strong emotion but without sentimentality.

Littledale, F. *Ghosts and Spirits of Many Lands.* Illus. by S. Martin. Doubleday, 1970. (Ages 12 and up.) These tales from around the world examine different countries' beliefs about death and life after death.

Lowry, L. *A Summer to Die.* Illus. by J. Oliver. Houghton Mifflin, 1977. (Ages 8–12.) Thirteen-year-old Meg sees her beautiful, popular sister Molly enter the hospital at Christmas time and soon after die of cancer. Because Meg has been kept uninformed of her sister's condition, she is shocked by the death. She has always been jealous of her sister, and now she must come to terms with her feelings. Her friends help her to overcome her guilt and begin to accept herself.

MacLachlan, P. *Baby.* Delacorte, 1993. (Ages 11 and up.) The death of a newborn child wounds Larkin's family, particularly the mother, to the extent that they cannot address their grief. The arrival of Sophie, a toddler whose mother leaves her for the family to foster and love for a while, changes all their lives. They all love Sophie so much that the thought of her mother's reclaiming her is a constant cause of anguish to each family member. Sophie's mother returns, the family finally confronts the death of their birth child. They name him, remember him, and mourn him.

MacLachlan, P. *Cassie Binegar.* Harper, 1982. (Ages 8–11.) Cassie finds it difficult to recover from her grandfather's death, especially because the last time they were together they had an unresolved argument. She suspects that this disagreement might have contributed to his death. Her grandmother helps her to overcome most of her bad feelings. Each character in this thoughtful story adds to the readers' understanding of human interaction and reaction to loss.

MacLachlan, P. *Sarah, Plain and Tall.* Harper, 1985. (Ages 8–10.) [See Family Constellations]

Madenski, M. *Some of the Pieces.* Illus. by D. K. Ray. Little, Brown, 1991. (Ages 7–10.) A year after the death of his father, Dylan, his mother, and his baby sister share memories of their special times within the family. Dylan reflects on how some of the pain has subsided and how memories and pictures can now bring happiness rather than sorrow. After they strew the last of the father's ashes in the river, Dylan realizes that his father is now in the ocean, mountains, garden, and river and that the family holds the memories. The rituals the family has developed may serve as models for people to design their own comforting ceremonies.

Madison, A. *Suicide and Young People.* Clarion, 1978. (Ages 12 and up.) This investigation of the causes of suicide among young people is not alarmist but presents the seriousness of the situation. Sources of help for young readers who feel they are suicidal are listed.

Madler, T. *Why Did Grandma Die?* Raintree, 1980. (Ages 5–8.) When Heidi's grandmother dies, Heidi is angry and worried. She is sure that by wishing hard she can get her grandmother back. Heidi's supportive family finally persuades her that it is all right to grieve. They share her tears and help her deal with the finality of death. They also permit her to participate in the funeral proceedings.

Mann, P. *There Are Two Kinds of Terrible.* Doubleday, 1977. (Ages 11 and up.) The first kind of terrible is breaking your arm on the first day of summer. The other kind, for Robbie, is having your mother enter the hospital for tests, never to return. While trying to cope with his mother's death, Robbie realizes that his father feels it even more. He recovers by building a new relationship with his father.

Marsoli, L. A. *Things to Know about Death and Dying*. Silver, 1985. (Ages 9-12.) The information in this book is given with a strong dollop of comforting commentary, emphasizing that death is natural and that people's feelings are to be respected. The author reminds readers that everyone concerned needs comfort and acknowledgment of his or her feelings. She includes coverage of death in the media, as well as a look at some public rituals for commemorating the deaths of heroes or famous people, and recommends ways people can help one another in times of grief.

Martin, A. M. *Slam Book*. Holiday, 1987. (Ages 12 and up.) Because of his ailing heart, Liza's father knows he will die within six months. The story tells of the preparations on the part of the entire family to survive the father's death and brings us to the aftermath of the death. Despite the thorough preparation, the actuality brings much pain and difficulty. Each family member mourns in his or her own way, and each has his or her own individual difficulties.

Martin, A. M. *With You and without You*. Holiday, 1986. (Ages 12 and up.) The story confirms that no matter how carefully and extensively people try to prepare for the death of a loved one, the reality is that the massive loss surpasses the expectation. This story is especially valuable because each member of the family reacts to the father's death in a way appropriate to his or her developmental level. Through constant communication and mutual assistance, the family members make some hard decisions and go on with their lives.

McLean, S. *Pennies for the Piper*. Farrar, Straus & Giroux, 1981. (Ages 10 and up.) Ten-year-old Victoria and her mother have tried to plan adequately for what they know is inevitable: the mother's approaching death from heart disease. Victoria knows that she will be placed in the care of an aunt but has really not thought through what her mother's death will mean to her. Also in the story is a young boy whose mother has neglected, abused, and finally rejected him. The book provides readers with a remarkable view of the human spirit.

Mellonie, B. *Lifetimes*. Illus. by R. Ingpen. Bantam, 1983. (Ages 5 and up.) In simple and poetic language, this gentle and informative book helps readers to understand the lifetimes of all living creatures. The essence of the story is that all living things have a limited span on this earth and that beginnings and endings are occurring all the time.

Mendoza, G. *The Hunter I Might Have Been*. Astor Honor, 1968. (Ages 8-10.) A young boy shoots and buries a sparrow. He is so affected by the death that he never touches a gun again.

Miles, M. *Annie and the Old One*. Illus. by P. Parnell. Little, Brown, 1971. (Ages 6-8.) A Navajo girl futilely tries to prevent the predicted death of her grandmother. In the end, she accepts death as a necessary part of life.

Nicleodhas, S. *Gaelic Ghosts*. Holt, Rinehart & Winston, 1963. (Ages 9-11.) Tales about chilling, scary ghosts and friendly, helpful ghosts who return from the dead in Scotland.

Oneal, Z. *A Formal Feeling*. Viking, 1982. (Ages 12 and up.) Anne finds it difficult to come to terms with her mother's death, even more so because her father already has a second wife, and Anne resents the precipitousness of his remarriage. After much discussion with her brother and soul searching on her own, Anne remembers what a difficult time they had with her mother. She begins to put her mother's memory in perspective and finally becomes able to let go of her pain and resentment, reconcile with her father, and live her own life again.

Orgel, D. *The Mulberry Music*. Illus. by D. Payson. Harper, 1971. (Ages 9-12.) Libby is comforted by the music at the funeral as she remembers the death of her beloved grandmother. The story demonstrates how effectively children can participate in the immediate response to the death of a loved one. Also demonstrated is the harm of not informing children about what is happening.

Pank, R. *Under the Blackberries*. Illus. by the author. Scholastic, 1991. (Ages 5-8.) When Sonia's beloved cat Barnie is killed by a car, she moves through the stages of mourning his death. The ritual of a funeral is comforting to her, and she plants a rosebush on his grave. When the family gets a new kitten, Sonia loves it and allows it free run of the garden, except for Barnie's rosebush, which will remain his alone.

Paterson, K. *Bridge to Terabithia*. Illus. by D. Diamond. Crowell, 1977. (Ages 9-12.) A beautifully written story about the friendship of a boy, Jess, and a girl, Leslie. Leslie, who runs as swiftly as Jess, is bold and willing to take chances. Jess is sensitive and artistic. When Leslie dies suddenly, Jess goes through each of the stages of mourning, from denial to guilt, anger, and grief. In the end he decides to give others some of the "magic" Leslie taught him in their imaginative play, and he begins with his little sister.

Paterson, K. *Flip-Flop Girl*. Lodestar, 1994. (Ages 9-12.) Vinnie and her younger brother find their own ways of coping with the death of their father. For both, the death has been traumatic; and their responses are not always in their own best interests. Vinnie's friend Lupe open-heartedly helps her and her brother, even though she is grieving for her dead mother and bears the burden of grappling with the issue of whether her father was the murderer. As with all her books, the author has provided readers with all-too-human characters. Their flaws as well as their strengths make a story rich with dilemmas and emotion.

Paterson, K. *Park's Quest*. Dutton, 1988. (Ages 11 and up.) [See War and Peace]

Payne, B. C., Jr. *The Late, Great Dick Hart*. Houghton Mifflin, 1986. (Ages 10 and up.) Dick Hart comes back from the grave to invite his best friend Tom to join him in an idyllic afterlife where everyone stays the age he or she most prefers. Tom is tempted, but he realizes that he is already different from the way he was six months ago and wants to live to see what life will be like in subsequent years. His encounter with Dick's ghost helps Tom free himself from the grief that has hung over him since Dick's death. He is also ready to relinquish his idealized image of his friend.

Peavy, L. *Allison's Grandfather*. Illus. by R. Himler. Scribner, 1981. (Ages 6-8.) Erica is afraid to ask the many questions she has about her friend Allison's dying grandfather, preferring to remember him the way she knew him. This book demonstrates that even when children do not openly ask questions they still have concerns. Sometimes adults have to answer questions that go unasked.

Peck, R. *Father Figure*. Viking, 1978. (Ages 11 and up.) Byron and Jim's mother takes her life when she can no longer tolerate her cancerous condition. The boys and their mother have been staying with their well-to-do grandmother, who now finds that she cannot deal with both her grief and the boys' needs. She sends them to their estranged father for the summer. The story tells how seventeen-year-old Jim finally lets go of his rage at his father's desertion, his mother's death, and his grandmother's aloof and controlling behavior. He also finds it possible to stop serving as a hovering father figure to eight-year-old Byron. Through Jim's telling of the story, the reader understands each of the characters, even the grandmother. It helps that the author is such a master at injecting humor into even the most serious topics.

Peck, R. *Remembering the Good Times*. Delacorte, 1985. (Ages 12 and up.) Trav, a disturbed young man, was sent away by his parents for shoplifting. He returns to learn of the murder of a family friend and kills himself. He signals his intent by giving away his valued possessions. The suicide leaves his friends and family angry and confused. His friends Katey and Buck, the recipients of his gifts, are bereft at Trav's action. They help the reader to reflect more deeply on the implications of Trav's life and death.

Pevsner, S. *How Could You Do It, Diane?*. Clarion, 1989. (Ages 12 and up.) The story begins five days after the suicide of Bethany's older sister Diane. She has left no note explaining her decision. The family is shocked and devastated. Bethany is obsessed with finding an explanation for the suicide, but she finds no satisfactory answers. All family members are plagued with guilt. Finally, after entering therapy, they are able to stop blaming themselves and each other. The characters are well developed and the plot is realistic and engrossing.

Pomerantz, B. *Bubby, Me, and Memories.* Illus. by L. Lurie. Union of American Hebrew Congregations, 1983. (Ages 5-8.) A few days after her grandmother dies, the young narrator tells about her memories of her "bubby" (the Yiddish word for grandmother.) She also takes the reader through the Jewish customs of mourning and relates her feelings to the information her parents give her about the finality of death and the process of grieving. The author is an educator and applies her knowledge of child development to this well-told story.

Powell, E. S. *Geranium Morning.* Illus. by R. Graef. Carolrhoda, 1990. (Ages 5-8.) Timothy's dad has died in an automobile accident. Frannie's mother has died after a long illness. Both children help each other go beyond their guilt and grief. This simple narrative accomplishes its intent of helping children know they are not alone in their mourning and that "if-only's" do not bring back people who have died.

Rhodin, E. *The Good Greenwood.* Westminster, 1971. (Ages 12 and up.) Louis dies in an accident with a gun. Mike, his best friend, does not like what the townspeople do to destroy the memory of Louis and to make him into somebody he was not.

Richter, E. *Losing Someone You Love: When a Brother or Sister Dies.* Putnam, 1986. (Ages 10 and up.) Each narrator in this book has experienced the death of a sibling, some recent, some long ago. The narrators' raw emotions are expressed graphically. Despite this, their words are comforting because survivors of losses of great magnitude know they are not alone and that their feelings are important. The honesty of their responses is one of the strengths of this compelling presentation.

Rofes, E., E., and the Unit at Fayerweather Street School. *The Kids' Book about Death and Dying: By and for Kids.* Little, Brown, 1985. (Ages 10 and up.) As is indicated by the title, children compiled this book. They interviewed people of all ages and talked to professionals in hospitals, suicide prevention centers, hospices, funeral homes, and burial places. The book includes legal definitions of death, funeral and burial customs, causes of death, and especially, feelings about death. This is a comprehensive and readable work.

Rogers, F. *When a Pet Dies.* Illus. by J. Judkins. Putnam, 1988. (Ages 4-6.) Mr. Rogers discusses common feelings and reactions about the death of a pet and encourages families to talk about these feelings. He is aware of the developmental level of the child audience and presents his material with clarity, describing the process and stages of mourning and the rituals surrounding death. He avoids euphemisms and assures children that their feelings of anger, guilt, sadness, and acceptance are normal and that in time they will feel better. The photos illustrate the feelings of the children and the parents' comforting behavior.

Rylant, C. *Missing May.* Orchard, 1992. (Ages 11 and up.) Aunt May and Uncle Ob have made Summer feel that she is a beloved part of their family ever since she was six years old. When Aunt May dies, Summer and Uncle Ob find it difficult to survive the loss.

Uncle Ob retreats to his bed, goes on a spiritual odyssey, and ultimately decides to return to an active life. The author is good at creating characters with whom readers can empathize. The death is a difficult one, not only for the characters in the book to deal with but also for the readers.

Saint-Exupery, A. de. *The Little Prince*. HBJ, 1943. (Ages 8 and up.) A little prince from another planet comes down to earth to explore and, in the end, "returns to his planet" after being bitten by a poisonous snake. A mystical allegory about life and death.

Sanders, P. *Death and Dying*. Illus. with photos. Watts, 1991. (Ages 7-10.) The book explores such questions as these: What is death? What is dying? What is a funeral for? Is death the end of life? What do people feel when they know they will die? Why are people afraid of death? What happens after death? The language is simple, but the answers are presented in enough depth to be worthwhile. The photographs showing a diverse population add to the effectiveness of the book.

Schotter, R. *A Matter of Time*. Philomel, 1979. (Ages 11 and up.) Lisa Gilbert's mother is dying. The book provides a model for how a family can helpfully anticipate death and its attendant feelings afterward. While the grieving must occur, it is made more bearable when it has been worked through ahead of time.

Schwandt, S. *Holding Steady*. Holt, 1988. (Ages 12 and up.) In a complex story involving alcoholism, bullying, ecology, and coming of age, as well as coming to terms with the death of a parent, Brendan Turner struggles with his feelings of jealousy because he thinks his dead father favored his younger brother. After behaving in a foolhardy manner, he listens to his brother and accepts the fact of his father's love, thereby releasing himself from his guilt and anger.

Shreve, S. *Family Secrets*. Knopf, 1979. (Ages 9-12.) The death of a pet and suicide are but two of the issues included in the stories in this collection. Seen through ten-year-old Sammy's eyes, the events are described with sensitivity and humor. Sammy goes through the stages of mourning when his dog dies, and his parents wisely aid him in the process.

Simon, N. *The Saddest Time*. Illus. by J. Rogers. Whitman, 1986. (Ages 7-10.) The author is masterly in her understanding of developmental issues and the importance of acknowledging emotions. In the three stories presented here, the death of a young child, an old woman, and a man somewhat younger than middle age are dealt with honestly and sensitively. Fears, mixed emotions, and guilt are demonstrated as likely responses to death. Advice about how to handle grief is included in the body of each episode.

Simon, N. *We Remember Philip*. Illus. by R. Sanderson. Whitman, 1979. (Ages 7-12.) Mr. Hall's son Philip has died in a mountain-climbing accident. Philip's class helps Mr. Hall through his grief by asking him to bring slide pictures of Philip and deciding to do something special to show him they care. They plant a tree in the school yard and dedicate it to Philip's memory. Mr. Hall feels strengthened by this gesture of love.

Smith, D. B. *A Taste of Blackberries*. Illus. by C. Robinson. Crowell, 1973. (Ages 7-10.) Jamie dies of an allergic reaction to a bee sting, and his friend feels guilty and lonely. He cannot believe it happened until after the funeral, when he offers himself as a substitute son to Jamie's mother when and if she wants one.

Smith, J. *Coping with Suicide: A Resource Book for Teenagers and Young Adults*. Rosen, 1986. (Ages 12 and up.) In this two-part book, the first section tells the story of a teenager who committed suicide and then discusses theories about suicide and people who attempt it. The second half of the book is a manual on crisis intervention. Exercises and information about communicating with people in crisis, advising them on how to get further help, and surviving the suicide of a close friend or relative are included.

Stein, S. B. *About Dying.* Illus. by D. Frank. Walker, 1974. (Ages 4-10.) One of the "Open Family" series. A description is given of the death of a pet bird. The mother factually and supportively deals with the child's questions and needs. Then the grandfather dies, and again the child is helped by ritual, family support, and answers to questions. An excellent resource for adults and children, discussing reactions and stressing the need to keep pleasant memories alive.

Stevenson, L. C. *Happily after All.* Houghton Mifflin, 1990. (Ages 8-12.) [See Divorce]

Thesman, J. *The Last April Dancers.* Houghton Mifflin, 1987. (Ages 12 and up.) On the day Cat St. John is sixteen years old, her father commits suicide. This complex novel shows several ways of handling a shocking death, some of them less beneficial than others. Cat's grandmother, for example, never accepts the reality of her son's death and lingers in denial and anger. The book will appeal to adolescents grappling with their sexual feelings as well as their relationships with their parents. Although no issue is completely resolved, the reader is not left dissatisfied; the conclusions are realistic.

Thomas, J. R. *Saying Good-bye to Grandmother.* Illus. by M. Sewall. Clarion, 1988. (Ages 7-10.) The mother, father, and young girl travel from their home to the home of the grandparents in order to attend the funeral of the grandmother. From the breakfast the family eats on the way to the funeral to the exquisitely painful, bittersweet memories each of the family members contributes, including the step-by-step progression of the funeral, the author's careful specificity helps the reader to experience and understand the process of mourning.

Tolan, S. *Grandpa—and Me.* Scribner, 1978. (Ages 9-12.) Kerry's grandfather has become embarrassingly and dangerously senile. In a remarkably mature fashion, Kerry tries to protect him, but she cannot. In his last lucid act, the grandfather decides to commit suicide rather than lose total control. A thought-provoking book.

Turner, A. *Houses for the Dead.* David McKay, 1976. (Ages 10 and up.) Ten separate cultures from prehistoric to contemporary times are described in terms of how they mourn their dead. By means of personalized stories in each of the settings, the author presents the myths, rituals, and practices surrounding the death of a member of that culture. A fascinating and comforting book.

Turner, A. *A Hunter Comes Home.* Crown, 1980. (Ages 11 and up.) Several deaths occur in this story of a boy becoming a man. Jonas's father and brother die prematurely in a blizzard, and their death is bitterly mourned. His grandfather drowns while teaching Jonas how to become a fisherman, but his death comes at the end of a long, active life; and his life is celebrated at his death. The book tells of the decisions Jonas must make about his identity as an Inuit and as an individual.

Varley, S. *Badger's Parting Gifts.* Illus. by the author. Lothrop, Lea & Shepard, 1984. (Ages 7-10.) Badger tries to prepare his beloved friends for his death; but when he dies, they all grieve. In the spring they participate in a memorial that helps them to reflect on all the good and kind things Badger did for them, creating a legacy of warm feelings. A lovely model is created of affirming the value of a life well lived.

Vigna, J. *Saying Goodbye to Daddy.* Illus. by the author. Whitman, 1991. (Ages 6-10.) In this realistic and moving book, Clare deals with her feelings of guilt, anger, denial, and grief after her father's death in a car accident. She is helped and supported by her understanding mother and grandfather, who let her have her father's wallet, full of mementos, and the doll house he built before he died to comfort her when she feels especially sad.

Viorst, J. *The Tenth Good Thing about Barney.* Illus. by E. Blegvad. Atheneum, 1971. (Ages 5-9.) Barney, a boy's pet cat, dies. The boy's parents encourage him to have a funeral and to think of ten good things about the cat so that he will not feel so bad about its death. He finally recognizes that the death of the cat contributes to the cycle of life.

Wahl, M. *Grandfather's Laika.* Illus. by T. Nygren. Carolrhoda, 1990. (Ages 5–8.) Matthew and his grandfather spend a lot of time together playing with Laika, the golden retriever. Laika grows very old and sickens, and it is clear she is not going to get well. The grandfather, as gently as possible, explains to Matthew that he will take Laika to the vet where she will be given an injection and die. Matthew and his grandfather visit Laika's grave and mourn together. The book deals with euphemisms, the inevitability of death, and the importance of memories.

Warburg, S. S. *Growing Time.* Illus. by L. Weisgard. Houghton Mifflin, 1969. (Ages 5–8.) A little boy's beloved dog dies, and the boy's family helps him to understand and accept the pet's death. Each adult he questions adds to his store of knowledge and comfort.

White, E.B. *Charlotte's Web.* Illus. by G. Williams. Harper, 1952. (Ages 9 and up.) Charlotte the spider saves the life of her friend Wilbur the pig. When Charlotte finally dies, Wilbur treasures her memory and cares for her children, grandchildren, and great-grandchildren.

Wilhelm, H. *I'll Always Love You.* Crown, 1985. (Ages 4–7.) This story amply meets the criteria for dealing with death, especially for young children. A child's dog, Elfy, dies; and the child knows that Elfy will never return. He is encouraged to mourn together with his family. He refuses the offer of a new pet because he knows that he is not yet ready to accept one. He is comforted by the knowledge that every night he has ritually told his dog that he will always love him. He knows that his love will continue even after his dog's death. The illustrations successfully convey the book's emotional tone.

Wojciechowska, M. *Shadow of a Bull.* Illus. by A. Smith. Atheneum, 1964. (Ages 9–12.) Although death is feared in this book, "brave" death invites admiration. Manolo fears that he is a coward because he does not want to be a bullfighter. The plot's resolution creates a happy ending for Manolo, and maintains the concept of the "noble" death.

Wright, B. R. *The Cat Next Door.* Illus. by G. Owens. Holiday House, 1991. (Ages 6–8.) The young narrator dreads going to her grandparents' home this summer because it is the first one since her grandmother died. She remembers all the special times she and her grandmother shared. She remembers the cat next door, who especially favors the little girl and of whom the grandmother has said, "She'll love you forever." The grandmother has also told the child that memories make special events and feelings last forever. When the cat comes by this sad summer with two kittens trailing behind her, the little girl is relieved of her grief and acknowledges that she will carry her grandmother's memory with her forever. The story affirms the healing power of time and memory.

Yolen, J. *The Stone Silenus.* Philomel, 1984. (Ages 10 and up.) Because Melissa has constructed a romanticized version of her now-dead father, she cannot face the fact of his death. Some dramatic encounters with a psychotic young man finally jolt her into acknowledging that her father was not the idol she worshiped. The lesson here is that it is important to have a clear vision of the person who died in order to cope with the loss. The author's skill and poetic language make the story believable and free of melodrama.

Zindel, P. *The Pigman.* Harper, 1968. (Ages 12 and up.) The story of two teenagers who discover an unhappy, lonely old man who cannot accept his wife's death. They mistreat and exploit him and then regret it after he dies of a heart attack.

Zolotow, C. *My Grandson Lew.* Illus. by W. P. duBois. Harper, 1974. (Ages 3–8.) A little boy and his mother share loving memories of the boy's dead grandfather. The mother helps the child cope with this grief through these positive reflections.

part 3

Society

Although gender, heritage, and ability are factors present at birth, these factors have become issues because of the way society reacts to them. Abuse in all its forms, as well as global, local, and personal conditions of conflict are patent manifestations of society's failure to establish a healthful environment for each individual and group. The issues discussed in this part affect people's interactions; potential for economic, political, and social power; and views of the world. Each issue is laden with bias, but each has the potential to be handled in a more socially productive manner. Children's books reflect many ways to make the world a better place. Without being doctrinaire, they can provide an aesthetic context for thought and action.

chapter **8**

Gender Roles

What began more than 100 years ago as women's battle for the vote has broadened today into a quest for equal opportunity and respect for both men and women. People of all classes have become conscious of the feminist movement and the issues involved in it. Men, too, have added their voices and energy, recognizing that liberation from stereotypic and destructive roles is essential for everyone, not only for women.

Although media such as television, radio, motion pictures, magazines, newspapers, comic strips, adult books, and children's books continue to produce traditionally stereotyped programs, situations, and characters, they also reflect the growing awareness of the change in gender role definitions and behaviors. The trend is positive, signifying the concerns of an increasingly independent and enlightened public.

A study conducted by the Wellesley College Center for Research on Women, commissioned by the AAUW, was released in 1992. "How Schools Shortchange Girls" revealed that the American educational system inadequately meets girls' needs. The study traced girls' education from preschool through high school. It charged male and female teachers with neglecting girls in class in favor of boys, even encouraging boys to call out answers while discouraging girls by telling them to "raise their hands." Teachers also selected activities more suited to the learning styles and interests of boys. In addition, the study found that standardized tests evidenced bias toward boys. Citing problems with females' self-esteem and a resultant diminished academic performance, the study made specific recommendations for schools attempting to address these problems.

These findings are the more distressing because of the perception that women's rights have advanced greatly in recent years. National and state legislation acknowledges the importance of affirmative action and of guaranteeing a measure of gender equity in the workplace. The women's movement is represented by such leaders as Carol Gilligan, Mary Belenky, Jill Tarule, Betty Friedan, the National Organization for Women, the Feminist Majority, Faye Waddleton, Pat Schroeder, Gloria Steinem, Robin Morgan, Mary Daly, Maya Angelou, Alice Walker, Toni Morrison, and the Wellesley College Center for Research on Women, among many others. They have reported much research and affected the way many educators think and behave on issues of gender discrimination. New television programs with strong women as protagonists and men in nurturing roles and advertising agencies' heightened awareness of the requirement for more equitable gender presentations have helped educate the general public.

Nevertheless, a great gap still remains between the new attitudes and behaviors that demonstrate them. Men who take on what used to be considered women's tasks tend to be looked at askance. Men who are gentle, passive, self-effacing, religious, and emotional open themselves to criticism despite the fact that these are human characteristics. Though few people question the desire of women to climb to the level of esteem men enjoy, they fail to understand that a man would consent to give up his "superior" position. Traditional men's tasks, characteristics, and behaviors generally remain those valued. Certain men are apprehensive about their ability to remain independent and secure without the measuring rod of the "inferior" women beneath them. To some minds, there are also questions about the impact of equal job opportunities on the economy. Further, they fear that the future of the family as it is now constituted is jeopardized with so many mothers working and with the newfound independence and opportunities for women.

Once people become aware of their preconceptions and fears, they can begin to deal with today's realities. American society is in transition. It is important that everyone have a sense of the options available in order to choose consciously and productively.

People's roles are linked with their personality characteristics. Male traits are valued above female; male roles are the more favored. Housekeeping, child nurturing, nursing, serving as a flight attendant, and holding other jobs traditionally assigned to women are regarded as inferior to working at jobs conventionally reserved for men. A doctor is more valued than a nurse, a pilot more than a flight attendant, an athlete more than a cheerleader. Until recently, young girls did not aspire to positions of authority. Female lawyers, police, physicians, judges, and pilots are still considered the exception and, the "strange ones" in some areas.

An anecdote circulating among many women's groups concerns the attitudes of these females toward themselves: The riddle was told at a party of a man and his son who were involved in a tragic automobile accident. The father was killed, and the son was rushed to a hospital for emergency surgery. Just before performing the operation, the surgeon looked at the child and exclaimed, "My God, that's my son!" The questions is, how could that be? None of the people at the party could come up with the right answer. They guessed that the surgeon was mistaken, that it was a long-lost son, or that the dead man was the boy's stepfather. Although the people at the party were all physicians and surgeons, both male and female, not one of them guessed that the surgeon was the boy's mother. Similarly, when children in school are queried as to their occupational aspirations, most girls continue to select jobs conventionally open to females while most boys select those conventionally open to males, even when their parents are employed in unstereotypic positions.

Try This

Recognizing that each of us is at a different level from everyone else in our attitudes toward masculine and feminine characteristics and roles, complete the following chart to inform yourself more completely about your own position. Be honest with yourself; no one else need see this. The purpose of this self-test is to help you recognize and articulate your own attitudes so that you can examine the areas that are likely to influence you in your work with children. If you are uncomfortable with some of your responses, use this information to determine what your next step will be.

Attribute	Admirable in				Usually found in			
	Men	Women	Both	Neither	Men	Women	Both	Neither
Intelligence								
Leadership								
Compassion								
Physical Strength								
Preoccupation with Appearance								
Ambition								
Assertiveness								
Acquiescence								
Loquacity								
Religious Faith								
Flirtatiousness								
Obedience								
Tenacity								
Independence								
Good manners								
Strong emotions								
Self-control								
Quick temper								

Some occupations considered to be lower-status jobs remain largely reserved for men. Ditchdigging (at least in the United States), heavy janitorial work, professional gardening, street cleaning, garbage collecting, and even dishwashing are considered to lie in the male domain when they are performed for payment. Some of these jobs are slowly being opened to females, in approximately the same proportions and with the same public reaction of shock as jobs in the more highly prestigious areas. Female toll collectors, road workers, truck and bus drivers, and gasoline station attendants can be seen. At the same time, more male nursery-school teachers, telephone operators, flight attendants, and nurses are also in evidence. The number of males taking hitherto female assignments is not as great as the movement in the other direction, but it is discernible.

Try This

Draw up a list of occupations you believe are primarily the responsibility of men. Draw up a similar list of occupations for women. Rank them by prestige, salary level, and interest. Present the list without the gender designation to an elementary school class. Have the students mark which jobs they feel are available to them. Compare the gender of the students with your designated list, and discuss the results with the students.

Most advocates of women's rights say that women should feel comfortable if they decide not to join the paid labor force. A woman who chooses to remain a full-time housekeeper and mother should be supported in those roles. Information and encouragement about all available career and leisure-time options should be available to everyone. Similarly, males and females should feel free to behave as they choose without other people's constraints being forced upon them, as long as they are within legal and ethical boundaries. Society, however, has exerted such a strong influence on gender role behavior that it is sometimes difficult to say whether a certain role indicates a person's natural inclination or shows simply that the person has been socialized into thinking that it is.

In an article entitled "Guns and Dolls" (*Newsweek,* May 28, 1990) Laura Shapiro examines the difficulties of exploring this question. Citing the work of many researchers in biology, anthropology, sociology, and psychology, the author concludes that while some sex-stereotyped behavior may be genetically determined (hormones play a large part in this contention), early socialization and the messages people communicate, even to infants, are important in shaping children's behaviors and teaching them societal expectations for their gender roles. Jerome Kagan, in *The Nature of the Child,* finds that both boys and girls express empathy and concern for others. Carol Gilligan and Grant Wiggins argue that psychologists need to investigate behavior going beyond narrow definitions of stages and development to a focus on relationships and particular social and cultural contexts.

Books for children have reflected societal attitudes in limiting choices and maintaining discrimination. Most traditional books show females dressed in skirts or dresses, even when they are engaged in activities for which this sort of costume is inappropriate. Illustrations have conventionally placed females in passive observer roles, while males have been pictured as active. Studies have demonstrated that illustrations confirm the subordinate, less valued role of the female and stress the active, adventuresome, admirable role of the male. Too often a happy ending for a story occurs when a "tomboy" reforms and becomes a "proper" young lady. When a female is permitted to retain her active qualities, it is usually made clear to the reader that she is the notable exception and that all other girls in the story are "normal"; that is, interested in dolls and clothing, passive, obedient, graceful, and pretty according to northern European standards.

Publishers of children's reading texts sometimes consciously maintain this situation because they try to appeal to boys' interests. Their contention has been that since most of the children in need of remedial reading are boys, boys should have stories that will especially appeal to them. They have not been as concerned with girls because they have subscribed to the belief that girls will read anything while boys stay away from stories that have girls as main characters. This phenomenon has held true to a certain degree. Some boys have been taught to be embarrassed if they enjoy fairy tales and stories with emotional relationships. But although girls may read a greater variety of books, boys enjoy books that have active female characters. Charlotte and Fern in E. B. White's *Charlotte's Web*, Mary and Laura in the Laura Ingalls Wilder series, and Alice in Lewis Carroll's *Alice in Wonderland* attract boys and girls who enjoy reading well-constructed stories. All readers relate to heroes, male and female, who are well balanced in their action and inventiveness.

Publishers have now recognized that sexist bias harms everyone, male and female. Many publishers of children's texts issue guidelines to authors and artists to assist them in using nonsexist, nonracist language and images.

SUGGESTED CRITERIA

Wherever possible, characters should be individuals, consistent with their own personalities and the context of their situations. Males and females can be portrayed negatively if they appear as individuals rather than stereotypes and if the negative characteristics are not generalized to include all people of that character's gender.

Occupations should, within the context of literary consistency, be gender free. Women and men should be pictured doing similar tasks and with roughly the same distribution of responsibility and prestige. Male behavior should not be the standard for which to strive.

Achievements should be judged equally, not through a filter of gender role differences. Attributes such as mechanical competence should not be restricted by gender. A woman should not be complimented for throwing a ball well "for a girl." Nor should a man be praised for taking care of a house "as competently as a woman could." Work should not be stereotyped as *women's work* or as *a man-sized job.*

In at least some books, adults should be seen to function both as parents and in their breadwinning occupations. Fathers and mothers should be shown sharing responsibility for care of the house and children and for decisions about their lives.

Both cooperation and competition between males and females should be part of the action of some books. Competition should not be the sole mode of relating.

Clothing should be functional and differentiated. Males and females should be dressed in clothing consistent with their personalities and appropriate to their activities, economic situation, and historical setting, rather than wearing gender-stereotyped "uniforms."

Females need not always be weaker, shorter, or more delicate than males. A normal range of differences is preferable. Illustrations showing real people in real situations convey a message well. Imaginative and impressionistic illustrations can also be important in affirming or combating stereotypes. Males and females should be logical or emotional depending on the situation. Both males and females should be independent when appropriate and dependent upon each other when that is in context.

In biographies of men or women, the subjects should not appear too good to be true. Although sensationalism or "exposes" should be avoided, the heroes' flaws should not be deliberately concealed. People should be neither romanticized nor vilified. The facts about historical figures should be well researched. The author's bias should not impinge on the evidence.

The use of language plays an important part in communicating equal valuation of the sexes. Language has been used as an effective tool both for imprisonment in and release from gender role constraints. The universal pronoun until recently has been *he*. *Man* has stood for person, no pronouns in the singular form represent both males and females. Various alternatives to *he, his,* or *him* can be found by rewording to eliminate unnecessary pronouns, recasting into the plural, or replacing masculine pronouns with *one, she or he,* or alternating male and female pronouns.

In references to humanity at large, terms that exclude females (such as fireman rather than fire fighter) should be avoided. The word *man* does not represent the generic person or people. In cases where *man* must be used, special efforts should be made to ensure that pictures and other devices make explicit that the term includes females. Words such as *humanity, human beings, human race,* or *people* may be used for the plural. *Person, candidate, individual, adult, child,* or *worker* may be suitable terms for the singular generic person. For *man-made,* try *artificial, synthetic, manufactured, constructed,* or *of human origin.*

Sometimes language bias is subtle. Be on the lookout for male words always first in the order of presentation. Appreciate the authors who alternate the order, sometimes using *women and men, her or his, gentlemen and ladies,* and so on.

The language used to designate females and males should be equitable. In speaking of college *students,* a term that serves to describe both males and females, *co-eds* should not be used. Like a male shopper, a woman in a grocery store should be called a *customer, consumer,* or *shopper,* not a *housewife.* Note that *gentleman* and *lady, wife* and *husband,* and *mother* and *father* are role words. Women should be referred to by their roles only if their counterparts are also called by their role names. (Thus, *ladies* and *gentlemen,* not *ladies* and *men.*) Ms. is the female counterpart to Mr.

Women should not be referred to as *girls,* men should not be called *boys.* The suffixes *ess* and *ette* should be avoided. (Thus, *poet, author, Jew, usher.*) Generic terms such as *doctor, nurse, pioneer, farmer,* or *settler* should be assumed to include both men and women. Modified titles such as *woman doctor* or *male nurse* are unnecessary.

Books must exemplify literary quality. If a story is primarily a didactic device, it is likely to be neither lasting nor effective. A gripping plot, vivid characters, or moving descriptions make more of an impact than a string of gender-appropriate pronouns. Above all, both males and females should be treated with dignity and respect for their individual characteristics.

Try This

Examine an article in today's newspaper, any current magazine, or a children's book of your choice. Place a piece of masking tape over each word that does not meet one or more of the criteria for nonsexist language. For example, if *congressman* is used as the generic term instead of *senator* or *representative,* place a piece of tape over that word. Write an appropriate nonsexist word on the masking tape. Ask children to try this activity.

Teachers, counselors, parents, and librarians are accepting the responsibility for guiding young people to a better sense of the options a nonsexist society makes available to them. Children's literature can help. Although many books retain conventional patterns and attitudes, an increasing number are entertaining and enlightening and challenge the traditional constraints of gender role behavior, encouraging young readers to accept more contemporary and societally constructive ideas.

DISCUSSION OF CHILDREN'S BOOKS

Folk and Fairy Tales

It is reasonable to expect that since folk and fairy tales rely so strongly on patterns and traditions they reflect a heavily gender role stereotyped format. Most of them do. The hero is often strong, brave, active, highly extroverted, nonintellectual, and willing to take great physical risks. He usually initiates action and controls the situation. Conversely, the typical female protagonist is weak, demure, passive, in need of rescuing, never scholarly, and, above all, obedient. She is seldom in control of her own destiny. Her greatest reward is to become the bride of her prince-rescuer and serve him happily ever after. Sometimes females such as servants, witches, fairy godmothers, and wicked stepsisters, who are not constrained by the burden of being protagonists, can be powerful and intelligent— even ugly, strong, and disobedient.

Most western folk and fairy tales are derived from and mirror early nineteenth-century European values and ideas, the result of the transcription of these tales from the oral tradition by such folklorists as the Grimm brothers and Andrew Lang. Fortunately, other collections reflecting the oral tradition without being held hostage by this perspective are available to children. Rosemary Minard, for example, compiled *Womenfolk and Fairy Tales* because of her desire to provide children a literary diet well balanced with fantasy that offers an image of the female appropriate for contemporary times. She retells a variety of African, Irish, Scandinavian, Japanese, Chinese, and other stories. They contain such characters as women who perform daring and clever deeds, a mother who rescues her child from the fairies, and some females who trick the wicked wolf. The stories are stimulating; the females are admirable. Males are not denigrated.

Other excellent works include Ethel Johnston Phelps's *Tatterhood and Other Tales* and *The Maid of the North: Feminist Folk Tales from around the World.* Suzanne Barchers's *Wise Women: Folk and Fairy Tales from around the World* presents stories in which women of all ages and in many roles are depicted as heroes. The origins of the stories are respected, and the research is meticulous. In addition to these compilations, a number of individual tales can be found in which neither men nor women are demeaned and gender roles do not dictate the behavior of the characters.

An activity children might find engaging and illuminating is to compare different versions of the same tale, examining the language, characterization, stream of events, and author's perspective. "Cinderella" lends itself admirably to this investigation, especially with more than 1000 variations available. *Yeh Shen: A Cinderella Story from China,* by Ai-Ling Louie, with stunning illustrations by Ed Young, is a retelling of the first known Cinderella story. The details differ markedly from those of classic European versions. The common threads include the unhappy lifestyle of the lowly Cinderella, a nasty stepmother, the search by the prince, and the eventual marriage of Cinderella to the prince. Cinderella's character is adventurous and active, however, rather than passive and dull.

One Arthurian tale retold many times over the ages appears in Phelps's *The Maid of the North* as "Gawain and the Lady Ragnell." It differs from some of the other versions in the way the characters are treated, the language, and the philosophical basis for the telling. The king will die if he cannot solve a riddle posed by the villain: "What is it that a woman desires above all else?" In the Phelps version, the answer is "The power of sovereignty—the right to exercise her own will." In another retelling, the answer is given as "To have her own way." In the Phelps version, Lady Ragnell, who has been transformed into a hideous hag, knows the answer to the riddle; and in return for saving the king's life, she specifies that Sir Gawain must consent to marry her of his own free will. In another version, she tricks King Arthur into promising to give her one of his knights in marriage. (Ostensibly, any one will do.) The Phelps tale accords dignity and a sense of relationships to the characters that is absent in other renderings.

Richard A. Gardner has created several tales with a didactic intent. Dr. Gardner's *Fairy Tales for Today's Children* was written in a light fashion. "Hans and Greta" describes both children as equally intelligent and courageous. They return home after vanquishing the witch knowing that they cannot change their stepmother. However, they agree to use their own natural qualities to try to get along with her when she is in good moods and avoid her when she is in bad moods. "The Ugly Duck" does not turn into a swan but learns to cope with his different appearance. "Cinderelma" never meets a fairy godmother but goes to the ball because of her own initiative. After agreeing to marry the prince, she stays with him at his castle; and they mutually decide that they are not suited for each other. She eventually starts her own business and marries a man who shares her interests. The fantasy in Dr. Gardner's stories is not so rich as that in traditional fairy tales, and the lessons are explicit. They are taught humorously but their point is clear—counteracting the myths of romantic, unreflective love at first sight and happily-ever-after weddings.

Jane Yolen, an author who has written many contemporary fairy tales with a flavor of the traditional, makes no attempt to teach lessons. Her aim is to stretch the imagination and communicate a sense of universality. Her language is poetic, her plots complex. She usually manages within the context of the fairy tale to create characters who are active, intense, thoughtful, and complete, whether they are males or females.

Yolen's collections, *The Hundredth Dove* and *The Girl Who Cried Flowers and Other Tales,* contain women with special characteristics as central figures. Jennet, the hero of Yolen's adaptation of the ancient Scottish tale of *Tam Lin,* demonstrates her courage and tenacity along with her wild spirit. This version respects tradition and retains most of the symbols of the sixteenth-century ballad. These women are unique in their qualities, as are the women in Yolen's other stories. In *The Emperor and the Kite,* Djeow Seow uses ingenuity and courage to rescue her father, the emperor. In *The Girl Who Loved the Wind,* Danina manages to escape from the sheltered and safe world that her father has designed for her. In *The Magic Three of Solatia,* Sianna becomes the wise and just ruler of her country. She also demonstrates bravery, inventiveness, intelligence, compassion, and the ability to be a wonderful mother.

Any collection of fairy or folk tales has lessons to teach and morals to impart. Young readers should be helped to recognize what they may be absorbing. They should become aware of messages being communicated. One activity that students can use with any fairy tale is to note who initiates the action. Is it a male or a female? What would happen in any of these tales if the initiator's sex were changed? Another activity could be to list those qualities considered admirable in females and those considered admirable in males in specific stories and to discuss how this matches contemporary opinions. Another approach might be to reconstruct the setting of the tale to see what changes the readers would render in the society to make the tale more contemporary.

Classics

Classics are stories that have withstood the test of time and remain popular over many years. Most people also ascribe to classics a certain literary quality and a sense of universal appeal. This second characteristic is not true of all acknowledged classics. *Little Women,* for example, is generally considered to be a "girl's book." Some stories such as *Charlotte's Web* are thought of as modern classics because their popularity may endure for a long time. Most classics are products and reflections of their time that manage to supersede the temporal; they indicate a sense of timelessness, at least in the values that they impart to the reader.

Frances Hodgson Burnett's *The Secret Garden* contains a number of interesting characters. The hero is bold, assertive, capable of initiating her own behavior, and independent. One of the boys is at first weak, spoiled, and dependent. Another is kind, gentle, and wise beyond his years with a capacity for loving and nurturing that is admired by everyone else in the book.

Little Women, by Louisa May Alcott, also contains several unusual characters, Marmee and Jo in particular. Jo is one of literature's exemplars of the active young woman. Most of the values transmitted by this book concern people's relationships to each other as respected individuals. There is also much emphasis on the responsibility of each human being to care about every other person. Unfortunately the book's title and reputation classify it "for girls only." Perhaps in the future this will no longer be the case, and boys will be permitted to enjoy it without fear of embarrassment.

A classic may be used to compare modern times with those of the book's setting. Often a book will contain assertions that are no longer valid but were perhaps appropriate for the time. Students could select classics and comment on what, in their opinion, made each book a classic. Then they could produce some suggested changes to make these classics contemporary in social terms. Debates could be held on whether to amend the classics. Students could examine all the work of selected authors, such as Alcott or Burnett, for evidence of consistent attitudes toward males and females. Students could construct bulletin boards of the "best-balanced characters," being certain to leave space for opposing opinions, comments, and additions. The main purpose of all these activities is to give students the experience of comparing contemporary expectations with historical treatment of males and females in high-quality books.

Nonfiction

Factual books aimed at providing appropriate gender role models can sometimes send messages different from those their authors intended. For example, some books ostensibly telling the reading audience that males and females can aspire to the same careers in fact indicate that competition between the sexes is the expected norm. Much more beneficial are books such as Eve Merriam's *Mommies at Work* and *Daddies at Work*. Each of these books for young children begins with a description of nurturing and tender parental roles and behaviors. Each one also concludes that parents like best of all to come home to their children. And each book includes, without comparison to other people or allusion to gender, a long list of possible occupations for parents. Both books picture families of a variety of ethnic backgrounds.

Some of the most convincing and positive books encouraging readers to build an acceptance of new roles for both males and females are those that describe real people already doing real things that defy stereotypes. These books are particularly effective when they are illustrated with photographs. *My Mom Is a Runner,* by Mary Gallagher Reimold, is one such book. The mother in this family is a seriously committed runner, sometimes competing in marathons. The reader has no idea what else the mother does, but her running is valued by every member of her family. The color photographs provide a further basis for building new attitudes on the part of young readers.

A book for older readers, Trudy J. Hanmer's *Taking a Stand against Sexism and Sex Discrimination,* invites activism. The details alone are dramatic, including the projection that by the twenty-first century 99 percent of people on welfare will be women and dependent children unless something is done to turn the situation around. The author traces the history of sexism in the United States and advises readers on how to become involved in taking a stand against sexual harassment and gender discrimination. Finally, as inspiration, the author offers profiles of young people who have taken stands and won against sexism.

History and Biography

Histories of the women's movement include such titles as Dale Carlson's *Girls Are Equal Too,* Elaine Landau's *Women, Women, Feminism in America,* Janet Harris's *A Single Standard,* and Ruth Warren's *A Pictorial History of Women in America.* Of special interest is *American Women: Their Lives in Their Words* by Doreen Rappaport. Through the voices of the women themselves, some famous, some not well known, the book documents their roles in each period of American history. These histories are valuable, fascinating, and illuminating. Students' research would benefit from the use of these books in addition to standard historical texts and encyclopedias.

Famous women ought to be included as part of the regular social studies curriculum rather than a separate category. Significant authors, artists, and scientists deserve to be studied as representatives of their professions, regardless of their sex. Students can update their textbooks by doing research on women previously not included. Student-authored additions can be appended to the texts.

Biographies should become part of the accepted compilation of texts used in studying history, to help make it come alive. A visit to any library or bookstore produces evidence that biographies of males far outnumber those of females, out of proportion to their representation in history and society. However, it is heartening to see the increasing number of books about women who have made important contributions to the world. Recent biographies have been written of women who are activists, poets, performers, artists, authors, scientists, members of the military, and local, national, or international political leaders.

Readers must become alert to biographers' biases. Because of the difficulty in determining what the truth is and where the author romanticizes, distorts facts, or vilifies the subject, access to more than one book about any given individual is beneficial. For example, in reading about Sarah Emma Edmonds, who disguised herself as a man for several years during the Civil War and served as a soldier and as a spy, one can uncover many disputes about what really happened and what she really did. Reading one biography invites the assumption that the hero not only hated being a woman but also had no regard for any women. The reader might be puzzled by the lack of insight provided into Emma's character, thoughts, and motivations. Few details of her life in the army are provided. The reader is expected to be satisfied with vague explanations of separate pup tents and cursory physical examinations. *Behind Rebel Lines: The Incredible Story of Emma Edmonds, Civil War Spy,* by Seymour Reit, however, develops character and permits the reader to share her feelings. The character's emotions are no more than informed speculation on the part of the author; but the account of his research for the book is impressive. During the course of the book, Reit never lets the reader forget that the main character is a woman. Emma retains the qualities of an attractive young woman even when pretending to be a man. True, she wants to prove to her father that she can be as good as any boy; but the reader does not feel she is resentful of her womanhood. In one book, she seems to be a strange creature, out of place in this world, always wishing to be a man. In *Behind Rebel Lines* there are excellent reasons for her actions, and she is in control of her situation. She is a pitiful figure in one book, an admirable one in the other.

An interesting project for students would be to research this and other little-known characters to compose their own versions of the character's life. Reading differing books such as those described above could lead students to debate the authors' believability. Since most notable people have been subjects of several biographies, it would not be difficult to find such information. Another activity for a group of students could be to assemble as many different versions of a subject's life as they could find. Each group member would read one or more of the accounts, and all would compare notes. Criteria could be designated for judging the accuracy of a book. In cases of general agreement about the details of a person's life, they could decide which of the biographies was the most appealing, most useful, or best written.

Harriet Tubman is one woman about whom a number of books have been written, all of them in accord about the details of her remarkable life. The points of view are generally consistent—that Harriet was a brave, successful, and unusual woman. However, the methods of presentation vary from straightforward telling of the story to acquainting the reader with the horrors of slavery. Jacob Lawrence's *Harriet and the Promised Land* relies on the power of illustrations to convey the difficulty of Harriet's tasks and the strength needed to endure. Lawrence's book is controversial because some critics believe the illustrations are too harsh for children, perhaps even demeaning of black people although the artist is himself black. Readers should know about the controversy so that they can judge for themselves how they feel about the pictures. Students should be encouraged to recognize that they must read with a critical mind, whether the work is fact or fiction.

Other African-American women who helped the cause of their people and were courageous and strong are the subjects of biographies. Sojourner Truth, Juliette Derricotte, Maggie Mitchell Walker, Ida Wells Barnett, Septima Poinsette Clarke, Charlotte Forten, Shirley Chisholm, and others can be found on the biography shelves. Most of the authors are respectful of their topic and knowledgeable about their subjects.

Belva Lockwood, Amelia Earhart, Florence Nightingale, Eleanor Roosevelt, Grace Hopper, Emily Dickinson, Edna St. Vincent Millay, Chris Evert Lloyd, Maria Tallchief, Elizabeth Blackwell, Lucy Stone, and numerous others in many fields of endeavor can also be found in books. Most of these women defied social convention and family pressure to accomplish what they did. Most of them endured ridicule and abuse but persevered. *Nellie Bly, Reporter,* by Nina Brown Baker, describes the challenging and socially effective reporting done by this woman. The book also bemoans the fact that Nellie Bly is probably better remembered for her stunt of going around the world alone in fewer than 80 days than she is for her work in cleaning up insane asylums, prisons, and other abusive institutions. Bly had a life in which fame, prosperity, poverty, and adversity were all ingredients. Whatever she achieved was the result of her own initiative after struggling against opposition.

Margaret Sanger, Pioneer of Birth Control, by Lawrence Lader and Milton Meltzer, also describes a woman who had to overcome tremendous barriers. Sanger was a determined woman. She was roundly criticized for her controversial views about marriage and for her ideas of appropriate behavior for women; but her work far outlasted her notoriety and continues to have far-reaching consequences for the world. This biography, like many of the others, makes no pretense that its subject is uncontroversial or flawless. According to the text, personal contentment is not necessary for public good. People are described who dare to be different because of principle, not whim.

Linda Peavy and Ursula Smith wrote *Dreams into Deeds: Nine Women Who Dared,* a provocative book containing succinct but sensitive biographies of nine influential women. Young readers can interview men and women they know, who may even now be making significant contributions. A series of these interviews, written for publication, might be appropriate for the school newspaper or even for a text compiled by the students for use in their history classes.

Portrayal of Women and Girls

Many works of fiction have as their main characters girls who dare to be different. Sometimes, as with the young women in Scott O'Dell's *Island of the Blue Dolphins* and Jean Craighead George's *Julie of the Wolves,* this difference spells survival. In both books, the young women are alone in the wilderness and must cope with their environment in order to remain alive. In both cases, the heroes face their situations with courage and intelligence. Julie must also cope with problems of a personal and societal nature throughout the book. Her spiritual survival becomes an issue. For Karana, the challenge is physical. Readers may want to experiment with changing the gender of the characters to see if this affects the story.

But these young women are rarities. They are the striking examples set against the more conforming females. Many books make it clear that the strong-willed, intelligent, self-managing, disobedient female heroes are anomalies. How comfortable are young girls using these females as models? How admirable and believable do young males find them to be? Some female heroes are extremely lonely and unhappy young women, despite their bravado. Like Louise Fitzhugh's *Harriet the Spy,* they crave friends and want others to like and accept them. Their adventures and the ideas they act upon are humorous and clever. But what child would want to be in their situations? These supergirls do not lead enviable lives, although their exploits are fun to read about.

Shabanu, the title character in Suzanne Fisher Staples's *Shabanu, Daughter of the Wind,* takes her aunt as a model of a woman who rejects the traditional roles forced upon her as a member of a Muslim nomadic group. At one point, Shabanu tries to emulate her aunt; but she at last determines that her family is more important than her personal happiness. Here is an example of a woman who dares to be different but at last decides to submit, not in spirit but in deed, to the customs of her culture. The story raises many questions that young readers could debate productively.

A number of books provide readers with examples of delightful girls whose differences and deviations from the expected gender role norms may at times cause some problems but who, in the long run, maintain their characteristics and achieve their hopes. Rosie Bernard, to whom we are introduced by Barbara Brenner in *A Year in the Life of Rosie Bernard,* is bright, unconventional, passionate, and feisty. She experiences many negative emotions, she is sometimes foolhardy, and she is not always obedient or even sensible; but her exploits are unfailingly understandable, and readers find it easy to empathize with her. Christina Katerina, who appears in Patricia Lee Gauch's stories, *Christina Katerina and the Box* and *Christina Katerina and the Time She Quit the Family,* is an attractive, imaginative girl. She provides an energetic model of another nonstereotypic girl who is decidedly *not* suffering or ostracized.

With the exception of grandmothers (see bibliography to Chapter 6), women are rarely main characters in children's books, usually appearing incidentally as mothers, teachers, or adult foils for the plot. Miss Rumphius, the title character in the book by Barbara Cooney, is a glorious exception to this practice, as is the title character of *My Great Aunt Arizona,* by Gloria Houston. Both women are intelligent and adventurous, though Miss Rumphius travels the world whereas Arizona dreams of travel and imbues her young students with her visions of faraway places. Both women are respected for their legacies of inspiration and work for the public good. Miss Rumphius remains unmarried and childless. Although Great Aunt Arizona marries and becomes a mother, her influence is exerted as a teacher.

Some grandmothers worthy of mention are the active, alert, nurturing grandmothers in stories for young children such as *Something Magic,* by Maggie Davis, and *Grandma's House,* by Elaine Moore. In each of these (and in many others) the elder woman is shown as an individual who is a person in her own right. Similarly, the grandmother in Eve Bunting's *The Wednesday Surprise* is also a compelling character; as the recipient of her granddaughter's literacy lessons, she makes it clear that she has entered into this tutoring program creatively and with strength. The grandmother in Liza Ketchum Murrow's *Dancing on the Table* demonstrates her liveliness and love of life. Her impending marriage and relocation are the cause for a crisis for her granddaughter, who relies enormously on her grandmother's presence.

Mothers fare less well in children's books, although the mother in *A Wrinkle in Time,* by Madeleine L'Engle, is beautiful and brilliant. The fact that she is a scientist working in a laboratory is also useful in a contemporary book. Mothers working outside the home generally have to put up with much criticism in fiction; their children often seem to suffer from their lack of time and interest. M.E. Kerr's *Dinky Hocker Shoots Smack* and several other books contain children who resent their mother's involvement outside the house. These mothers are unable to handle the situation well. The daughters are interesting, active characters, and they communicate their feelings in sometimes dramatic ways, redeeming the books from sexist accusations. Children might benefit from discussing what they would do if their mothers behaved as these mothers do. The mothers in *The Terrible Thing That Happened at Our House,* by Marge Blaine, and *Mushy Eggs,* by Florence Adams, manage to maintain their jobs and a nurturing role with their children.

Contrary to reality, not many fictional mothers have paid jobs. The role of the mother in most children's books is still that of the housekeeper and cook. Differing from this is Vera B. Williams' series of books about a working class family of women, where the mother serves food in a diner. These books focus on the young girl as the protagonist, but the mother and grandmother also figure strongly in each of the stories. The series consists of *A Chair for My Mother, Something Special for Me,* and *Music, Music for Everyone.* They provide a picture of a collaborative, lively, and loving circle of women working hard, each in her own way.

A book that centers on the problem of a mother's losing her job is *My Mother Lost Her Job Today,* by Judy Delton. The mother and her little girl discuss the situation, comfort each other, and plan for the future. For children who live in homes where both parents work outside the house, Kathleen Kyte has written a book of advice called *In Charge: A Complete Handbook for Kids with Working Parents.*

Activities in which children are asked to describe the work their mothers and fathers do and then to try to find matching characters in books may reveal that parents' jobs are rarely described. The students may then write job descriptions for these parents. An activity related to books of fiction could have children describe the characteristics of "ideal" parents. They could then locate books that contain parents matching these descriptions and books that conflict with or differ from the descriptions. They then can be encouraged to rethink and expand their descriptions and add those qualities they consider beneficial. They can search for fictional working mothers who are members of different ethnic heritages and compare their treatments in the stories.

Students can list positive qualities for boys and girls, again matching characters in literature. They can compare their lists with one another's, and with the books and even categorize the descriptions according to age levels.

Portrayal of Men and Boys

The feminist movement contends that its quest is for a change in the status not only of women but also of men. Human liberation is the goal. Young readers, as well as concerned adults, can apply to males the same criteria suggested for females; males have also been victimized by stereotypic expectations. Readers may observe how young male characters are treated and expected to act. They may reflect on the literary role of the father and watch for the imposition of a competitive system in which males are required to win. When stories are free of these restrictions, they may be recommended to friends. Publishers and authors are receptive to letters from readers and take into consideration their comments and suggestions.

Patricia MacLachlan's books avoid stereotypes and tell wonderfully crafted, humorous, engaging stories. In *The Sick Day,* Emily's father stays home with her when she is sick (her mother is at work) and lovingly and tenderly responds to her needs. Other fathers, such as Ramona Quimby's father in the *Ramona* books by Beverly Cleary and Bweela and Javaka's father in *My Special Best Words* and *Daddy Is a Monster... Sometimes,* by John Steptoe, are models of nurturing adult males, not because they are perfect fathers but because they exhibit characteristics that counteract stereotypes.

In *June Mountain Secret,* by Nina Kidd, young Jen spends the day trout fishing with her father. She is not at all stereotypical. She plays with bugs and salamanders, climbs rocks, and is agile with a fishing rod. Her father helps her to learn the secrets of trout behavior, and she finally brings in her fish. The magic of catching it is enough; she releases it unharmed. Her father teaches her, serves as a companion, and presents a model of a loving, patient, nurturing male.

The grandfather and his friend Jake in Nette Hilton's *The Long Red Scarf* are rugged men. Grandpa wants a long red scarf like the one Jake wears. He asks Great Aunt Maude to make him one. She tells him she can prime pumps and move cattle but cannot knit. He asks cousin Isabel, but she's too busy building furniture and preparing a room for her new baby. Jake tells him that he made his own scarf and Grandpa can do the same thing. Grandpa grumbles and mutters, but after his next cold fishing trip, he agrees. When the book ends, he has not only knitted his own scarf, but he and Jake have knitted an outfit for the new baby, too—to keep her warm when they take her fishing. This picture book light-heartedly dispels sex-role stereotypes and shows an elder who, though initially resistant to being a man who knits, discovers that he likes his new skill enough to pursue it.

Although it is a good idea to show that men have important roles as fathers and grandfathers, it is also valuable to see men depicted unstereotypically in their everyday activities. *Magical Hands,* by Marjorie Barker is a rare book that has as its main characters four working-class, middle-aged men, close friends who share a work ethic and an appreciation of their friendship. They meet daily for lunch and engage in conversation that reveals one another's wishes for a special birth-day celebration. William, the cooper, secretly sets about fulfilling each of his friends' wishes. To his surprise, his birthday wish, too, is fulfilled by someone's "magical hands." The story conveys a sense of caring and nurturing on the part of males. It is also a touching story of mature friendship. The illustrations by Yoshi portray the men and their settings respectfully, realistically, and with depth.

Readers should note books that deviate from the artificial requirements that males must be interested only in sports, never cry, have only male friends, and always be strong and brave. Peter, the protagonist in *A Special Gift,* by Marcia L. Simon, loves to dance, but he is intimidated by his peers and reluctant to let them know of his talent. Finally, he comes to accept and value his special inter-ests. Dance is also an option for males in Rachel Isadora's two books, *Max* and *My Ballet Class.*

A work of nonfiction, *Oh Boy! Babies!,* by Alison Herzig and Jane Mali, describes, through dialogue and photographs, an elective course on child care. This course is offered to fifth and sixth graders in an all-male school. Real babies are brought into the classroom; and the boys learn to bathe, diaper, feed, and nurture the infants.

For older children, Jess, in *Bridge to Terabithia,* by Katherine Paterson, is sensitive and artistic. Furthermore, his best friend is female. Ramon, in *Shadow like a Leopard,* by Myron Levoy, rejects the macho facade his father and peers try to impose on him; and in *Alan and Naomi,* also by Levoy, Alan patiently and tenderly befriends Naomi in an attempt to help her regain her equilibrium after she has been traumatized by her father's brutal murder. Amir, the sensitive and almost magical young man in Joyce Hansen's *The Gift Giver,* brings his special peace-making gifts to a group of his peers in a way that changes their community. Gary Paulsen's young hero of *Hatchet* and *The River* survives his encounters with life-threatening crises as a strong, but not macho male.

Slowly but surely, books and the media are reflecting society's direction. Active critical reading and responding will help speed the process.

REFERENCES

Gender Roles

Bauer, M. D. "Sexism and the World of Children's Books." *The Horn Book* 69 (Sept.–Oct. 1993): 577–580. A plea to include in literature both genders' grappling with individua-tion and relationships without demanding male behavior as the standard to achieve.

Belenky, M. F.; Clinchy, B. M.; Goldberger, N. R.; and Tarule, J. M. *Women's Ways of Knowing.* Harper, 1986. Provides perspectives redefining, acknowledging, and articulating the value of women's thoughts and perceptions. This work, along with Carol Gilligan's *In a Different Voice* (Harvard University Press, 1982) has served as the basis for research and commentary on women's approaches to learning, thinking, interacting, and teaching.

Bracken, J., and Wigutoff, S., with Baker, I. *Books for Today's Young Readers: An Annotated Bibliography of Recommended Fiction for Ages 10-14.* Feminist Press, 1981. Gender, ethnicity, acculturation and racism, peer friendships, special needs, families in transition, foster care and adoption, and views of elders are some of the categories specified in the descriptions and analyses of books. Good discussion and format.

Broverman, I. K.; Broverman, D. M.; Clarkson, F. E.; Rosenkrantz, P. S.; and Vogel, S. R. "Sex-Role Stereotypes and Clinical Judgments of Mental Health." *Journal of Consulting and Clinical Psychology* 34 (Feb. 1970): 1-7. Revealing report of a study conducted with clinical psychologists, demonstrating that male characteristics are viewed as positive for adults and female characteristics are not. The study concludes that unstereotypic sex-role behavior is viewed as abnormal.

Clark, E. C. "Missing in Action: Confederate Females in Civil War Novels." *The Lion and the Unicorn* 15 (Dec. 1991): 15-26. A convincing indictment against the demeaning treatment of Southern women and girls during the Civil War era in fiction for young people.

Council on Interracial Books for Children. *Bulletin* (Special Issue on Romance Series for Young Readers) 12 (Nos. 4 and 5, 1981). Articles analyzing and criticizing the sexist implications of many romance novels popular with young readers. Listing of books on male–female friendships (such as *Bridge to Terabithia* and *Growin'*) as an antidote to the romances.

Council on Interracial Books for Children. "Ten Quick Ways to Analyze Books for Racism and Sexism." *Bulletin* 5 (No. 3, 1974): 1. Criteria to use when examining children's books. Incisive and useful.

Council on Interracial Books for Children. *Winning "Justice for All."* U.S. Department of Health, Education and Welfare, 1980. A social studies and language arts curriculum to help children overcome stereotypes, particularly those of gender role.

Epstein, C. F. "Ideal Images and Real Roles: The Perpetuation of Gender Inequality." *Dissent* 31 (Fall 1984): 441-447. Despite evidence that women and men are equally competent in most areas, many people still cling to preconceived notions about "women's strengths" versus "men's strengths." The author, however, points out that societal changes are forcing people to reexamine these notions in favor of a more egalitarian, less dichotomous system.

Gersoni-Stavn, D. "Feminist Criticism: An Overview." *School Library Journal* 20 (Jan. 1974): 22. A thoughtful article reviewing the negative stereotyping of girls in children's books. Encourages criticism that supports both males and females. Also pleads for maintenance of aesthetic standards. Gives excellent advice to readers and critics.

Gersoni-Stavn, D. *Sexism and Youth.* Xerox, 1974. A worthwhile resource book examining the socialization of females in society; omission of females from history; and stereotyping in picture books, television, and other media. Books for children are reviewed and examples given of imprinting gender typecasting on children.

Gilligan, C.; Ward, J. V.; and Taylor, J. M., eds. *Mapping the Moral Domain.* Harvard University Press, 1988. Scholarly chapters by prominent researchers in gender psychology and sociology contribute to a new understanding of moral behavior and the tension between the morality of caring and the morality of justice. Frameworks and definitions of child, adolescent, and adult development form much of the subject matter.

Honig, E. L. *Breaking the Angelic Image: Woman Power in Victorian Children's Fantasy.* Greenwood, 1988. Uncovers the existence of independent female characters and the beginnings of a feminist movement in late nineteenth-century stories for children. The author analyzes the roles of mothers, spinsters, girls, and magical women in Victorian literature for children.

John, E. G. "Searching for Great-Great-Grandmother: Powerful Women in George MacDonald's Fantasies." *The Lion and the Unicorn* 15 (Dec. 1991): 27-34. Although the focus here is on elders and their unstereotypic treatment in some of MacDonald's fantasies, the overall image is of women who genuinely like and care for each other.

Kazemek, F. E. "Literature and Moral Development from a Feminine Perspective." *Language Arts* 63 (March 1986): 264-272. Explores the relationships between children's literature and moral development and makes a case for including "female morality" as a perspective. Books exemplifying this viewpoint are described, along with suggestions for their use in the curriculum.

Kolbenschlag, M. *Kiss Sleeping Beauty Good-Bye.* Doubleday, 1979. Basing her comments on Sleeping Beauty, Goldilocks, Beauty, and the princesses who inhabit the fairy tales, the author examines their characteristics and interactions and relates them to today's society.

Kuznets, L. R. "Two Newbery Medal Winners and the Feminine Mystique: *Hitty, Her First Hundred Years* and *Miss Hickory*." *The Lion and the Unicorn* 15 (Dec. 1991): 1-14. Discusses the two Newbery Award winners as representative of society's attitude toward independent women, with *Hitty* more liberating than *Miss Hickory*. The author provides excellent analytic evidence for her view.

Lanes, S. "On Feminism and Children's Books." *School Library Journal* 20 (Jan. 1974): 23. Urges differentiation between art and propaganda. Criticizes books that display male or female characteristics rather than universal human behavior. Although Lanes agrees with the cause of feminism and welcomes healthy propaganda, she cautions against an unbalanced preoccupation with propagandistic literature in a total reading diet.

Langerman, D. "Books and Boys: Gender Preferences and Book Selection." *School Library Journal* 36 (March 1990): 132-136. Summarizes several studies and makes recommendations for stocking a library containing a wide range of books.

Lehnert, G. "The Training of the Shrew: The Socialization and Education of Young Women in Children's Literature." *Poetics Today* 13 (Spring 1992): 109-122. The history of how females have been portrayed in children's literature, often reflecting the norms of the society in which the book was written.

Lieberman, M. "Some Day My Prince Will Come: Female Acculturation through the Fairy Tale." *College English* 34 (Dec. 1972): 383-395. Analyzes the Lang versions of fairy tales and demonstrates their negative effects on women. Beauty and passivity are presented as the most important female qualities in these tales; marriage is a female's greatest reward. The author argues powerfully that fairy tales inculcate stereotypic sex-role behaviors.

Lurie, A. "Fairy Tale Liberation." *New York Review of Books* 15 (Dec. 1970): 42-44. The author argues that folk and fairy tales can help prepare children for women's liberation, since so many of the female characters are strong. She then suggests collections of tales.

Nilsen, A. P. "Women in Children's Literature." *College English* 32 (May 1971): 918-926. Critiques Caldecott Award winners from 1951 to 1970. Suggests several causes of unfairness toward females in children's books. Recommends that good books be written with interesting, strong females so that both boys and girls will want to read them.

Osmont, P. "Teacher Inquiry in the Classroom: Reading and Gender Set." *Language Arts* 64 (Nov. 1987): 758–761. Examines the reading preferences of early elementary-aged boys and girls and makes recommendations for the inclusion of books holding an appeal for boys, who often have an anxiety about or a dislike of reading.

Pickhardt, I. "Sexist Piglets." *Parents* (Dec. 1983): 32–37. Discusses studies showing that many children, beginning at age five, go through a prolonged stage in which they engage in gender-specific behavior and roles. It reassures parents that most children will grow out of this stage and provides suggestions for helping them to do so.

Prida, D., and Ribner, S. "Feminists Look at 100 Books: The Portrayal of Women in Children's Books on Puerto Rican Themes." *Bulletin of the Council on Interracial Books for Children* 4 (Spring 1972). Commentary, analysis, and annotated bibliography of children's books containing Spanish-speaking female characters. The same damaging stereotypes adhere to Puerto Rican female characters as to their Anglo counterparts, perhaps with greater intensity.

Rigg, P. "Those Spunky Gals: An Annotated Bibliography." *The Reading Teacher* 39 (Nov. 1985): 154–160. Provides a list of recommended books in several categories, including multicultural books, which feature strong, competent females.

Scott, K. P. "Effects of Non-Sexist Reading Materials on Children's Preferences, Sex-Role Attitudes, and Comprehension." Paper presented at the Annual Meeting of the National Reading Conference, St. Petersburg Beach, Fla., Nov. 30–Dec. 2, 1978. (ERIC Document Reproduction Service No. ED 169 496.) Summarizes research indicating that student interest in reading material may be enhanced by using more substantive stories about females; comprehension is increased and attitudes toward role behavior are more flexible. The plea is made for more research into the impact of materials with nontraditional male role models.

Shapiro, L. "Guns and Dolls." *Newsweek* (May 28, 1990), pp. 56–65. Explores the debate over the roles of society and biology in influencing gender-specific behavior in children.

Smith, N. J.; Greenlaw, M. J.; and Scott, C. J. "Making the Literate Environment Equitable." *The Reading Teacher* 40 (Jan. 1987): 399–407. Read-aloud preferences of 254 elementary school teachers showed an unintentional but strong bias towards books with male protagonists. The authors provide a list of sources for unstereotyped children's books.

Snee, B. "Sexism and Ten Techniques to Combat It through Children's Books," 1979. (ERIC Document Reproduction Service No. ED 188 168.) Summarizes the studies to date on sexism in children's books. Includes ideas for activities to use in classrooms to lessen sexism.

Stewig, J. W. "Fathers: A Presence in Picture Books?" *Journal of Youth Services in Libraries* 1 (Summer 1988): 391–395. In a randomly selected sample of 100 picture books, the researchers found that fathers appeared in only 40. Few professional activities for fathers or grandfathers were depicted. The authors conclude that children need more diverse images of fathers in order to obtain a clear image of what it means to be a father.

Tibbetts, S.-L. "Sex Differences in Children's Reading Preferences." *The Reading Teacher* 28 (Dec. 1974): 279–281. Examines the assumption that girls will read anything but boys will read only books pertaining to boys and their interests. Concludes that this bias is societally imposed, thus a societal change is needed.

Trousdale, A. "The True Bride: Perceptions of Beauty and Feminine Virtue in Folktales." *The New Advocate* 2 (Fall 1989): 239–248. In a cross-cultural look at the portrayal of and expectations for women in Cinderella-like stories, the author compares the role of physical beauty in the European tales to its role in tales from China, Africa, and America.

Tyack, D., and Hansot, E. *Learning Together: A History of Coeducation in American Schools.* Russell Sage, 1992. A thorough and well researched history defending coeducation and exploring the differences of opinions about gender abilities and characteristics. The authors discuss sexual discrimination as a major factor in consideration of schooling.

Unsworth, R. "Welcome Home, I Think: The Changing Role of Fathers in Recent Young Adult Fiction." *School Library Journal* 34 (May 1988): 48–49. Although the author is pleased with a recent trend of including fathers as major characters in young adult fiction he points out the predominance of abusive, neglectful, or otherwise troubled fathers who are portrayed.

Weitzman, L. J.; Eifler, D.; Hokada, E.; and Ross, C. "Sex Role Socialization in Picture Books for Pre-School Children." *American Journal of Sociology* 77 (May 1972): 1125–1150. The Caldecott Award winners in particular are examined in light of their influence on acceptance of sex-role stereotyping. Other award winners and popular books for children are also analyzed. Illuminating article, evidencing careful research.

Wellesley College Center for Research on Women. *The AAUW Report: How Schools Shortchange Girls.* AAUW Educational Foundation, 1992. Susan McGee Bailey is principal author of this widely read and quoted report. Many other scholars contributed. Gender bias is demonstrated in every aspect of schooling, such as testing, curriculum, vocational education, and after-school activities. Offers recommendations for changes in national policy.

Zipes, J. *Don't Bet on the Prince.* Gower, 1986. A collection of modern fairy tales with feminist themes or nontraditional female characters, some aimed at children and others at adults. Also included are essays analyzing the role of female characters in fairy tales.

RESOURCES

Equity Policy Center. 2000 P St., N.W., No. 508, Washington, DC 20036. Concerned with global women's issues and developments.

Feminist Press. City University of New York, 311 East 94 Street, New York, NY 10128. Publications include news, issues, and events in women's studies.

International Center for Research on Women. 1717 Massachusetts Ave., N.W., Suite 302, Washington, DC 20036. Designed to improve the productivity and incomes of women in developing countries worldwide.

Lollipop Power Books. P.O. Box 277, Carrboro, NC 27510. Publisher of nonsexist, multiracial books for children. Shows both boys and girls as "adventurous, independent, emotional, and expressive."

National Foundation for the Improvement of Education: Resource Center on Sex Roles in Education. 1201 16th St., N.W., Rm. 628, Washington, DC 20036. Seeks to improve the quality of education empowering teachers. Offers grants. Publishes *Blueprint for Success: Operation Rescue.*

National Organization for Women (branches in each state). Central Office: 1000 16th St., N.W., Ste.700, Washington, DC 20036. Works for legal, social, and economic equality through organization and advocacy.

New Seed Press. P.O. Box 9488, Berkeley, CA 94709. A collective committed to publishing nonsexist, nonracist stories for children that actively confront issues of sexism, racism, and classism.

NOW Legal Defense and Education Fund. 99 Hudson St., 12th Fl., New York, NY 10013. Sponsors and publishes studies on gender equity.

Organization for Equal Education of the Sexes. P.O. Box 438, Blue Hill, ME 04614. Biographies and data on women, teacher guidelines, and classroom posters.

Wellesley College Center for Research on Women. Wellesley, MA 02181. Research and studies on women including current issues of girls in American education, curriculum change, stress affecting men and women, child care, women in the sciences, and public policy concerning women.

Women's Action Alliance. 370 Lexington Ave., New York, NY 10017. Publishes *Equal Play,* a semiannual journal for educators, parents, and others on nonsexist child raising and education of young children.

BIBLIOGRAPHY

Aaseng, N. *Florence Griffith Joyner.* Lerner, 1989. (Ages 10-12.) The style of writing and the material included create an intimate look at the famous athlete. Joyner's accomplishments, as well as her feelings, are explored. This volume is part of a series called "The Achievers." Another in this series is *Zina Garrison: Ace,* by A.P. Porter (1991).

Adams, F. *Mushy Eggs.* Illus. by M. Hirsch. Putnam, 1973. (Ages 5-10.) [See Divorce]

Adler, C.S. *The Once in a While Hero.* Coward, McCann & Geoghegan, 1982. (Ages 9-12.) Patrick, who has five sisters, enjoys the company of girls as much as he does that of boys. When a bully keeps badgering him, he worries that he will be unable to handle it, but eventually all turns out well, and he acknowledges that he likes himself as he is. The conventional fight with the bully occurs, but with a twist that makes the reader agree with Pat that it is unnecessary to be a hero all the time.

Adler, D.A. *A Picture Book of Eleanor Roosevelt.* Illus. by R. Casilla. Holiday House, 1991. (Ages 5-8.) In simple, descriptive language, the author narrates the highlights of this remarkable woman's life. Although he admires her greatly, he does not idealize or romanticize her. He includes some of the problems she encountered and conveys an understanding of her contributions, apart from her position as the president's wife.

Adoff, A. *Flamboyan.* Illus. by K. Barbour. HBJ, 1988. (Ages 4-9.) Flamboyan is "a tall and strong young girl" who lives on a lush island and who dreams of flying. The story is an idyll of the young girl's flight over her island and a lovesong to the generic Caribbean locale.

Adoff, A. *I Am the Running Girl.* Illus. by R. Himler. Harper, 1979. (Ages 7-11.) A book-length poem about a young woman who loves to run. Other women are shown joyously celebrating their abilities.

Alcott, L. M. *Little Women.* Little, Brown, 1868. (Ages 10 and up.) Portraits of four sisters in a loving family (Meg, Jo, Beth, and Amy), each with an individual personality and a different vision of her future. Jo is one of the classical literary sources of the active female.

Alda, A. *Sonya's Mommy Works.* Illus. by the author. Messner, 1982. (Ages 5-8.) Sonya has responsibilities, develops self-confidence, and spends quality time with each parent. She also has an understanding grandmother. A realistic and specific picture of a family with two parents who work outside the home.

Alexander, L. *The Philadelphia Adventure.* Dutton, 1990. (Ages 12 and up.) The fifth in the series of stories about Vesper Holly, a strong, courageous young woman of the nineteenth century. Alexander's interlacing of fiction with historical events makes this a compelling adventure. Readers may want to revisit *The Wizard in the Tree,* in which Mallory, a young kitchen maid, heroically helps a wizard.

Alexander, S. H. *Sarah's Surprise.* Illus. by J. Kastner. Macmillan, 1990. (Ages 6–8.) Seven-year-old Sarah and her mother go on a somewhat hazardous expedition to gather mussels. Sarah's mother reassures her that she will take care of Sarah, that Sarah is strong, and that if she goes slowly and carefully, she will be fine. The tables are turned when Sarah's mother slips and hurts her ankle. Sarah uses all the comforting words her mother gave her and goes for help. The story values caring as well as strength.

Ancona, G. *And What Do You Do?* Illus. by the author. Dutton, 1976. (Ages 8–12.) Excellent photographs illustrating the careers of 21 people. The introduction states that despite the depicted gender of the person performing the work, each job can be done by either a man or a woman.

Andersen, H. C. *The Snow Queen.* Illus. by S. Eidrigevicius. Creative Education, 1984. (Ages 8–10.) Gerda, one of the classic strong heroes of fairy tales, employs her female intuition and concern for others to rescue Kay, a boy who has been her childhood companion. A number of females, each of them a unique individual, figure in the story.

Anderson, W. *Laura Ingalls Wilder, A Biography.* Harper, 1992 (Ages 9–12.) The biography supplies interesting facts about both the author of the "Little House" series and the series itself. Wilder was 60 years old when she began writing it. The biography makes the stories even more vivid and reinforces what a strong woman Laura Ingalls Wilder was.

Angel, J. *One-Way to Ansonia.* Bradbury, 1985. (Ages 11 and up.) Rose Olshansky is a dynamic, free-thinking hero. Her life is difficult: Her father is a ne'er-do-well who takes advantage of her loyalty; she attends night school and works seven days a week and most nights. Positive and negative elements of turn-of-the-century New York City for immigrants and women are graphically described.

Asbjornsen, P.C. *The Squire's Bride.* Illus. by M. Sewall. Atheneum, 1975. (Ages 7–10.) Retelling of an old Norwegian tale in which a young woman outwits the old squire who wants to force her to marry him.

Aylesworth, J. *Mr. McGill Goes to Town.* Illus. by T. Graham. Holt, 1989. (Ages 5–8.) A group of men want to get their tasks done, but they cannot finish all by themselves, so each, in this cumulative rhyming story, helps the others; and they all get to go to town for some recreation. A lovely model of cooperation, with the unusual inclusion of adult males in mutually helping roles.

Barchers, S. I., editor and reteller. *Wise Women: Folk and Fairy Tales from around the World.* Illus. by L. Mullineaux. Libraries Unlimited, 1990. (Ages 10 and up.) Sixty-one tales from all over the world, retold true to their origins, in which women are intelligent, bold, and resourceful heroes. The tales are grouped by the roles of the women: daughters, sisters, maidens, attendants, wives and mothers, and mature women. The collection is probably intended for adults, but it is readable enough for ages 10 and up.

Barker, M. *Magical Hands.* Illus. by Yoshi. Picture Book Studio, 1989. (Ages 7–10.) A beautiful and touching book, its main characters are four working-class, middle-aged men who are close friends and reflect a departure from the stereotype. The illustrations portray the men and their settings respectfully and realistically.

Bauer, C. F. *My Mom Travels a Lot.* Illus. by N. W. Parker. Puffin, 1988. (Ages 5–8.) A young child presents the good and bad aspects of his mother's frequent business trips. In balance, he suffers from her absence, but he is secure in the fact that she always returns home. His father seems to be an adequate, if not totally successful caretaker.

The topic is controversial, and this little book may help stir conversations about the phenomenon of a mother who must frequently leave her family.

Berry, C. *Mama Went Walking.* Illus. by M. C. Brusca. Holt, 1990. (Ages 4-6.) Sarah and her mother go on many imaginary adventures together in which Sarah manages to rescue or solve problems for her mother. But when Sarah is truly frightened, her mother is there to comfort her. A loving, creative relationship is depicted here.

Billings, C. W. *Grace Hopper: Navy Admiral and Computer Pioneer.* Illus. with photos. Enslow, 1989. (Ages 9-11.) Admiral Hopper has consistently challenged authority and found new and better ways to accomplish what needs to be done. She is the first woman to earn the rank of admiral in the U.S. Navy. The book focuses largely on her expertise in computers, but the details of her life and the energy of her spirit come through clearly.

Blaine, M. *The Terrible Thing That Happened at Our House.* Illus. by J. C. Wallner. Parents' Magazine, 1975. (Ages 5-10.) When a young girl's mother resumes her career, she feels as if her world has fallen apart. She is intolerant of the new lifestyle and resentful of her parents' new roles. She wants her old, comfortable life back again. After a confrontation, the family together decides on a course of action satisfactory to all. The solution is a good one.

Brenner, B. *A Year in the Life of Rosie Bernard.* Harper, 1971. (Ages 8-12.) [See Aging]

Briggs, C. S. *At the Controls: Women in Aviation.* Illus. with photos. Lerner, 1991. (Ages 8-12.) Filled with information, well presented, and concise, this book is not a diatribe against a sexist system, but it does point out discrimination against women in aviation. It also provides excellent models for young readers to admire and emulate.

Brooks, P. S. *Beyond the Myth: The Story of Joan of Arc.* Lippincott, 1990. (Ages 12 and up.) This work of nonfiction reads like a novel and contains a rich palette of characters. Joan emerges as an intelligent, devout, courageous, and human young woman.

Brown, D. P. *Belva Lockwood Wins Her Case.* Illus. by J. Watling. Whitman, 1987. (Ages 8-12.) Not only does this well-written and extensively researched biography describe the life of a courageous and determined woman, it also tells in lively detail of the historical battle women waged for their rights. In addition, the fight for equal rights for people of color and for American Indians emerges clearly in the text. Belva Lockwood was the first woman to run for president of the United States and the first to earn the title of doctor of law. The author weaves Ms. Lockwood's personal life into the events so that the reader comes to know her as a real person, not only as a hero.

Brusca, M. C. *On the Pampas.* Illus. by the author. Holt, 1991. (Ages 7-10.) Told from the perspective of a young girl from Buenos Aires who is visiting her grandparents and other family members on a ranch in the Pampas, the story and illustrations reveal the lifestyle of a working cattle ranch and the active participation of the girls in the work of the ranch.

Buckley, H. E. *Someday with Father.* Illus. by E. Eagle. Harper, 1985. (Ages 4-8.) A little girl, in bed with a broken leg, fantasizes about all of the things she will do with her father when her cast comes off: fishing, sailing, hiking, and skiing. Her father's promises help her keep her spirits up while she waits. Here is a picture of an active girl and a nurturing male.

Bunting, E. *A Perfect Father's Day.* Illus. by S. Meddaugh. Clarion, 1991. (Ages 4-8.) [See Family Constellations]

Bunting, E. *The Wednesday Surprise.* Illus. by D. Carrick. Clarion, 1989. (Ages 5-9.) [See Aging]

Burnett, F. H. *The Secret Garden.* Lippincott, 1911. (Ages 9–12.) A sensitive, assertive girl comes to live in a new place and discovers a secret garden, new friends, and how to care about others. Males and females in this classic are free of gender stereotypes.

Burt, O. *Black Women of Valor.* Illus. by P. Frame. Messner, 1974. (Ages 9–12.) Four black women who demonstrated their courage and ability: Juliette Derricotte, Maggie Mitchell Walker, Ida Wells Barnett, Septima Poinsetts Clark. The book also lists many other black women of valor.

Byars, B. *A Blossom Promise.* Illus. by J. Rogers. Dell, 1987. (Ages 9–12.) [See Death]

Byars, B. *The Midnight Fox.* Illus. by A. Grifalconi. Viking, 1968. (Ages 10 and up.) Tommy's parents leave on a long-planned trip to Europe. He does not like sports, hates camp, does not like animals, and would rather spend his time with his best friend or constructing models. He reluctantly agrees to spend the time while they are gone on a farm. When he gets there, he discovers a fox and frequently observes her. In the end, he is able to save the lives of the fox and her baby. The story is gentle and beautifully written. Tommy is not required to change in order to be happy. He remains his own self and is content.

Caines, J. *Just Us Women.* Illus. by P. Cummings. Harper, 1982. (Ages 5–8.) Aunt Martha and the young narrator of the story are about to embark on a wonderful trip where the two of them will do just exactly as they please. A joyful account of the relationship between a niece and her aunt and their sense of independence.

Caines, J. *Window Wishing.* Illus. by K. Brooks. Harper, 1980. (Ages 5–8.) [See Aging]

Carlstrom, N. W. *Wild Wild Sunflower Child Anna.* Illus. by J. Pinkney. Macmillan, 1991. (Ages 5–8.) Anna, an enthusiastic, energetic child spends a summer morning exploring the meadows and streams near her home. The text is poetic and descriptive. Anna, who is African American, engages in nongender-stereotyped activities such as catching frogs and looking under rocks for bugs. The theme is universal, and the illustrations are lovely.

Caseley, J. *The Cousins.* Greenwillow, 1990. (Ages 5–8.) Two cousins are as unlike as any two people can be, but each is valued and encouraged by her family, each has excellent self-esteem, and each enjoys being an individual. Moreover, the two cousins do not compete but enjoy each other's company.

Cleary, B. *Beezus and Ramona.* Illus. by L. Darling. Morrow, 1955. (Ages 7–10.). Others in the series by Beverly Cleary: *Ramona the Brave* (1975), *Ramona and Her Father* (1975), *Ramona and Her Family* (1977), *Ramona and Her Friends* (1980), *Ramona and Her Mother* (1980), *Ramona, Age Eight* (1981), *Ramona the Pest* (1982), *Cutting up with Ramona!* (1983), *Ramona, Forever* (1984), *The Ramona Quimby Diary* (1984), *The Beezus and Ramona Diary* (1986), *Ramona, Mouse* (1990), and *Ramona Quimby* (1990). All the stories portray a sparkling, bright, creative character in the person of Ramona. In some of the stories, where Ramona's father feels unfulfilled, the family supports his quest for a satisfying way of making a living.

Cleaver, V. *Sweetly Sings the Donkey.* Lippincott, 1985. (Ages 10 and up.) Lily is the fourteen-year-old protagonist and the anchor of her dysfunctional family. Her father is weak and unable to support them emotionally or economically. Her mother, who is self-centered and dependent, eventually runs away with another man. Lily cares for her two brothers and maintains the household. She is a survivor who knows how to make friends and become part of a nurturing community.

Cleaver, V., and Cleaver, B. *Where the Lilies Bloom.* Illus. by J. Spanfeller. Lippincott, 1969. (Ages 9 and up.) Mary Call, a fourteen-year-old Appalachian girl cares for her family after the sickness and death of their father, whom she and her siblings bury. In order to keep from being separated, they pretend their father is still alive. Her strength is impressive but is insufficient without the help of her siblings and some outsiders.

Clifton, L. *Don't You Remember?* Illus. by E. Ness. Dutton, 1973. (Ages 3–7.) [See Siblings]

Climo, S. *The Egyptian Cinderella.* Illus. by R. Heller. Crowell, 1989. (Ages 6–8.) In this ancient tale based on fact (a Greek slave, Rhodopis, married the Pharaoh Amasis in the twenty-sixth dynasty and became his queen), Rhodopis, a young Greek woman, has been sold as a slave in Egypt. She looks different from the Egyptian women because she has light, curly hair and fair skin. (Rhodopis means "rosy cheeked" in Greek.) The "Cinderella" elements include the fact that Rhodopis is forced to work as a servant, she has tiny feet, her slipper is lost (it is carried off by a falcon to the Pharaoh.), and she marries the prince (Pharaoh).

Cohen, N. *Jackie Joyner-Kersee.* Illus with photos. Little, Brown, 1992. (Ages 9–12.) One of a series of "Sports Illustrated for Kids" books, this journalistically styled biography of a great athlete reads easily and smoothly. The person emerges as well as the athlete.

Cole, N. *The Final Tide.* Macmillan, 1990. (Ages 10 and up.) Geneva is a strong willed and independent young woman, and her parents eventually accept the fact that she will follow her own path. She manages to convince her grandmother to move to town near some of the family where she can have new experiences and Geneva can continue her education. The characters are well developed, and the plot is interesting and realistic.

Cooney, B. *Miss Rumphius.* Illus. by the author. Viking, 1982. (Ages 5–9.) Alice Rumphius's artist grandfather impresses upon her that she must do something to make the world more beautiful. She lives an active and adventure-filled life. When she becomes old, she plants lupine seeds in many places and in so doing beautifies her world. As a very, very old woman, she passes her legacy on to her niece, who also promises to make the world more beautiful.

Cosner, S. *War Nurses.* Illus. with photos. Walker, 1988. (Ages 10–12.) The photographs alone would make this book worth stocking in the library. They depict the conditions female nurses endured as well as their activities during war times from the Civil War to the present. The book contains chapter titles such as ". . . Sight-seers, do-nothings, idlers, time-killers, fops, and butterflies . . ." (describing the attitudes of some men toward women's wanting to serve as nurses on the battlefield.) Sexism was a serious factor preventing much progress in women's participation in medical help for the armed services. The author presents the case for the women in low-key but authoritative and swift-moving prose.

Dana, B. *Young Joan.* Harper, 1991. (Ages 11 and up.) In contrast to some other biographies of the saint, this book focuses on Joan as a mystic. Its language is poetic and inspirational.

Davis, M. S. *Something Magic.* Illus. by M. O. Young. Simon & Schuster, 1991. (Ages 3–6.) [See Aging]

Delton, J. *My Mother Lost Her Job Today.* Illus. by I. Trivas. Whitman, 1980. (Ages 5–8.) A young girl is frightened because her mother comes home angry and hurt, having just lost her job. The two give each other loving support. They determine that everything will eventually be resolved and may even turn out better than before.

DePaola, T. *Oliver Button Is a Sissy.* Illus. by the author. HBJ, 1979. (Ages 4–7.) Oliver loves to walk in the woods, read, and draw—not activities many of the boys in his class engage in. His parents send him to dancing school "for the exercise." His peers tease him persistently. When Oliver takes part in a talent show and does not win, he is crushed; but his family and (surprisingly) his peers applaud, praise, and acknowledge him. It is important that Oliver doesn't have to win a prize to have his talents and interests recognized. It is helpful that children whose interests may not match their peers' can see that they too have value.

De Pauw, L. G. *Seafaring Women.* Houghton Mifflin, 1982. (Ages 10 and up.) Women have been pirates, warriors, traders, whalers, and sailors, as this interesting book reports. Here are accounts of females who went to sea.

Ehrlich, A. *The Random House Book of Fairy Tales.* Illus. by D. Goode. Random House, 1985. (Ages 7–10.) This dramatically illustrated collection includes such Grimm tales as "The Twelve Dancing Princesses" and "Hansel and Gretel." It also includes the Perrault variant of "Cinderella" and the de Beaumont tale "Beauty and the Beast." The tales are simply told, with most of the details that are usually included in the conventional versions. This is a good basic compilation of the European versions of these stories.

Eichler, M. *Martin's Father.* Lollipop Power, 1971. (Ages 5–8.) [See Family Constellations]

Ellis, A. L. *The Dragon of Middlethorpe.* Holt, 1991. (Ages 12 and up.) Kate is the hero of this tale, set in medieval times. She grapples with the taboos and assumptions that keep women in a subordinate role. Kate vanquishes a dragon. She also investigates the differences between the real and imagined, the true and false.

Epstein, V. S. *The ABC's of What a Girl Can Be.* Illus. by the author. VSE, 1980. (Ages 5–9.) An openly didactic but light rhyming alphabet book indicating that any occupation is open to females. The list, including union leader, TV quiz program MC, ophthalmologist, and rancher, adds interesting options to children's thinking.

Epstein, V. S. *History of Women Artists for Children.* VSE, 1987. (Ages 10 and up.) A beautiful and informative book describing some women artists and their work. Beginning with prehistory and including women artists from the sixteenth century through contemporary times, the text is interesting, and the reproductions are well produced.

Fitzhugh, L. *Harriet the Spy.* Harper, 1964. (Ages 9–12.) An amusing, brash portrayal of a sometimes stubborn eleven-year-old girl who wants to be a spy and writes down all her observations of family and community life in her secret notebook. Harriet is clever and inventive but not very sensitive to other people's feelings. None of the other children in the book is gender stereotyped.

Florian, D. *People Working.* Illus. by the author. Crowell, 1983. (Ages 3–6.) In a colorful and ebullient book, people of all ages and backgrounds are shown busily at work. Males and females work both together and at separate tasks, at home, under the ground, on land and water, in cities and in the country, and this book shows them all. Fun.

Fox, M. *Shoes from Grandpa.* Illus. by P. Mullins. Orchard, 1989. (Ages 3–6.) Jesse receives a variety of gifts of clothing from her loving, generous family. She appreciates their good intentions but asks for jeans, clearly because she needs clothing appropriate to her activities, such as skate-boarding. The pattern of the text is that of "The House That Jack Built"; and each family member is free of stereotypic trappings.

French, F. *Maid of the Wood.* Illus. by the author. Oxford University Press, 1985. (Ages 7–10.) To pass the time, four men construct and adorn a little wooden doll. When the doll is finished, one of the men endows her with life, and then argues with the other three over who shall keep her. The girl settles the issue by dancing away to explore the world on her own. The surprise ending acknowledges a female's sovereignty over herself, counteracting the message of women being men's property.

Gardner, R. A. *Dr. Gardner's Fairy Tales for Today's Children.* Illus. by A. Lowenheim. Prentice-Hall, 1974. (Ages 8 and up.) Four tales loosely adapted from classical fairy tales.

The characters behave in a rational, constructive fashion rather than adhering to traditional patterns. The stories are fun.

Gauch, P. L. *Bravo, Tanya.* Illus. by S. Ichikawa. Philomel, 1992. (Ages 4-8.) The dance teacher's counting gets in the way of Tanya's dancing in rhythm with the other children. At last, when she is acknowledged for the music inside her, she is able to override her teacher's counting and dance to her teacher's satisfaction. This is the second book about Tanya. The first, presenting Tanya's introduction to dance classes, is *Dance, Tanya* (1989).

Gauch, P. L. *Christina Katerina & the Box.* Illus. by D. Burn. Coward-McCann, 1971. (Ages 4-8.) Christina Katerina is an imaginative, creative child who transforms a refrigerator box into a series of wonderful playthings: a clubhouse, a race car, a castle, and a dance floor, all to the dismay of her mother. It is unfortunate that Christina Katerina's playmate has the nickname "Fats" and consistently ruins the game through his clumsiness, but the friendship between the two children has realistic ups and downs. Another story in this series is *Christina Katerina and the Time She Quit the Family,* Illus. by E. Primavera (Putnam, 1987). [See Family]

Gauch, P. L. *This Time, Tempe Wick?* Illus. by M. Tomes. Coward, McCann & Geoghegan, 1974. (Ages 7-10.) Temperance Wick, a bold, unselfish girl, defies rebellious American soldiers in order to protect her mother, house, and horse during the Revolutionary War.

George, J. C. *Julie of the Wolves.* Illus. by J. Schoenherr. Harper, 1972. (Ages 12 and up.) An Inuit girl runs away from an unhappy situation. Living in the frozen wilderness, she courageously makes friends with the wolves and learns their ways. She must face problems not only of individual survival but also of the changing ways of her people.

Geras, A. *Apricots at Midnight and Other Stories from a Patchwork Quilt.* Illus. by D. Caldwell. Atheneum, 1982. (Ages 9 and up.) Aunt Pinny is a storyteller. She has lived a rich and passionate life because of her understanding of others' needs, her imagination, and her zest for living. The stories are absorbing.

Geras, A. *Voyage.* Atheneum, 1983. (Ages 10 and up.) Mina takes charge of her brother and mother on their long journey to America and also manages to buoy up the spirits of most of the passengers in steerage. She is an exuberant, self-assured, artistic girl whose energy enlivens the voyage. Another passenger on the ship, Clara Zussmann, is an elderly version of Mina. Her provision of small luxuries in the midst of deprivation adds quality to the voyage that enriches all the passengers. Geras's prose is elegant and moving.

Goldreich, G., and Goldreich, E. *What Can She Be? A Lawyer.* Illus. by R. Ipcar. Lothrop, Lee & Shepard, 1973. (Ages 7-12.) Ellen Green is a lawyer, wife, and mother. She has a varied clientele and is shown to be an able attorney, as well as a competent, happy, well-adjusted woman. An excellent, well-conceived book, part of a series devoted to describing women in professions formerly considered to be for men only. The series contains descriptions of a musician, an architect, a veterinarian, a film producer, a farmer, a geologist, a newscaster, a police officer, and a computer scientist. Different heritages are represented. The women are portrayed as having outside lives, as well as being competent at their work.

Gould, A. *The First Lady of the Senate: A Life of Margaret Chase Smith.* Windswept House, 1990. (Ages 8-10.) A simply written, clearly admiring but balanced presentation of the life and work of an independent and courageous senator, Margaret Chase Smith.

Gould, D. *Brendan's Best-Timed Birthday.* Illus. by J. Rogers. Bradbury, 1988. (Ages 5-8.) [See Family Constellations]

Green, C. J. *The War at Home.* McElderry, 1989. (Ages 10-12.) [See Family Constellations]

Greene, B. *Philip Hall Likes Me, I Reckon, Maybe.* Illus. by C. Lilly. Dial, 1974. (Ages 9–12.) Beth Lambert is African American, eleven years old, and extraordinarily bright and competent. She is a lively, ambitious, successful young woman who wants to be a veterinarian; and the reader knows she will succeed. Some of the action in the book revolves around the issue of Beth's competition with her friend Philip. Their relationship is further explored in the sequel, *Get on out of Here, Philip Hall* (1981).

Greenfield, E. "Harriet Tubman." In *Honey I Love.* Illus. by D. and L. Dillon. Crowell, 1978. (Ages 6 and up.) Using vernacular language, the poet describes a child's perception of Harriet Tubman's courageous exploits. All the poems in this collection are personal, evocative, and well crafted.

Greeson, J. *An American Army of Two.* Illus. by P. R. Mulvihill. Carolrhoda, 1992. (Ages 8–10.) Tells of how Rebecca and Abigail Bates drove off the British army by playing "Yankee Doodle" and fooling the British into thinking that the American troops were nearby. The two young women actually lived in Scituate, Massachusetts, during the War of 1812; and the story may be true.

Hahn, M. D. *Tallahassee Higgins.* Clarion, 1987. (Ages 10 and up.) [See Family Constellations]

Hamilton, L. *Clara Barton.* Chelsea House, 1988. (Ages 9–12.) Part of a series, "American Women of Achievement," this biography deals with the political infighting and opposition Clara Barton had to endure. Barton was an activist for all people, especially the underserved. Others in this series include women whose biographies are not ordinarily accessible, including Marian Anderson, singer; Ethel Barrymore, actor; Agnes De Mille, choreographer; Emma Goldman, political revolutionary; Karen Horney, psychoanalyst; Mahalia Jackson, gospel singer; Jeanne Kirpatrick, diplomat; Emma Lazarus, poet; Julia Morgan, architect; Louise Nevelson, sculptor; Sandra Day O'Connor, Supreme Court justice; Mae West, entertainer; and Phyllis Wheatley, poet.

Hamilton, V. *Sweet Whispers, Brother Rush.* Philomel, 1981. (Ages 12 and up.) [See Special Needs]

Hanmer, T. J. *Taking a Stand Against Sexism and Sex Discrimination.* Watts, 1990. (Ages 10 and up.) This excellent work of nonfiction reads as compellingly as a novel. The author cites many dramatic facts, such as, "Of the brightest high school graduates who *do not* go on to college, 70 to 90 percent are females". Likewise, "Although 50 percent of the people now attending law school are women, very few women become partners in law firms. . . ." The book includes history, as well as contemporary events and issues. Black and white photos provide effective visual references.

Hansen, J. *The Gift-Giver.* Walker, 1980. (Ages 10 and up.) [See Heritage]

Hart, C. *Delilah.* Illus. by E. Frascino. Harper, 1973. (Ages 6–8.) Delilah is an active, happy girl who enjoys drums and playing basketball. She helps her father fix dinner on "his night" to cook. Acceptance of other-than-usual roles and interests for women and men are portrayed here. Delilah has good relationships with both parents. Told from the perspective of the child.

Herman, H. *The Forest Princess.* Illus. by C. P. Duinell. Over the Rainbow, 1974. (Ages 5–10.) A modern-day fairy tale in which a princess wakes a sleeping prince with a kiss and then enchants him with her independence and self-assurance.

Herzig, A., and Mali, J. *Oh Boy! Babies!* Illus. by K. Thomas. Little, Brown, 1980. (Ages 10 and up.) An all-male school offers an elective on baby care to fifth and sixth graders, with real babies. This is a delightful book full of photographs and quotations that show the boys learning to hold, bathe, diaper, feed, and love babies.

Hilton, N. *The Long Red Scarf.* Illus. by M. Power. Carolrhoda, 1990. (Ages 5–8.) Grandpa wants a long red scarf to keep him warm when he goes fishing, like the one his friend Jake wears. He asks a succession of women to make him one; but they decline because of all their other activities. Jake then teaches Grandpa how to knit, and the two men embark on some knitting projects. The illustrations are cheerful and complement the text nicely.

Hoehling, M. *Girl Soldier and Spy: Sarah Emma Edmundson.* Messner, 1959. (Ages 10 and up.) A well-written account of this unusual woman. The author always refers to her hero as a woman, and it is as a woman that Sarah accomplishes her adventures. Her qualities are womanly, even when she is pretending to be a man. The author values women and presents the story so that readers may do so as well.

Hoffman, M. *Amazing Grace.* Illus. by C. Binch. Dial, 1991. (Ages 6–9.) Grace is a talented child whose classmates try to deter her from trying out for the part of Peter Pan because she is African American and female. Her supportive mother and grandmother reinforce her positive self-image, and Grace wins the part, clearly the best-qualified for the role. The story and pictures convey a sense of power and pride.

Homan, D. *In Christina's Toolbox.* Illus. by M. Heine. Lollipop Power, 1981. (Ages 4–6.) Although safety measures are not followed when Christina is hammering and sawing, if these dangers are pointed out, this book amply demonstrates that girls and women can be skillful carpenters.

Hopkins, L. B. *Girls Can Too!* Illus. by E. McCully. Watts, 1972. (Ages 5–8.) A book of positive poems about the different things girls can do, think, and feel.

Hopkins, L. B. *I Loved Rose Ann.* Illus. by I. Fetz. Four Winds, 1976. (Ages 7–10.) Harry tells why he is so angry at Rose Ann, whom he used to love. The book's value lies not only in the humor of the story but especially in the second part of the book, which tells the same story, this time from Rose Ann's perspective. From Rose Ann's account we gain much information about stereotyping and its consequences, but not in a didactic or heavy-handed manner.

Hopkins, L. B. *Mama.* Illus. by S. Marchesi. Simon & Schuster, 1977. (Ages 10 and up.) [See Family Constellations]

Hotze, S. *Summer Endings.* Clarion, 1991. (Ages 12 and up.) The book chronicles the feelings and events of Christine's summer while the family awaits word about the father, who is trapped in Poland by World War II. Christine is an avid baseball fan who watches every game and collects baseball cards. Her sister works in a factory packing parachutes to help the war effort. The mother is strong and independent; and although she misses her husband terribly she is capable of supporting her children both financially and emotionally.

Houston, G. *My Great Aunt Arizona.* Illus. by S. C. Lamb. Harper, 1992. (Ages 4–8.) Great aunt Arizona was an imaginative, capable, and intelligent Appalachian woman who taught school for 53 years and inspired generations of students with her stories of the far-away places she visited only in her mind.

Howard, M. L. *The Ostrich Chase.* Illus. by B. Seuling. Holt, Rinehart & Winston, 1974. (Ages 10–12.) Khuana, a young woman of the Bushman tribe, violates tradition by learning to hunt and to build fires. Because of these skills, she is able to save her grandmother's life and conquer the desert. She nevertheless remains interested in "womanly things." She is an admirable character.

Hunt, I. *Up a Road Slowly.* Follett, 1966. (Ages 12 and up.) Julie goes to live with a strict aunt when her mother dies. Julie learns to admire her aunt enough to want to stay with her rather than returning to live with her remarried father.

Hurmence, B. *Tancy.* Clarion, 1984. (Ages 12 and up.) [See Heritage]

Hurwitz, J. *Russell and Elisa.* Illus. by L. Hoban. Morrow, 1989. (Ages 4–7.) [See Siblings]

Igus, T.; Ellis, V. F.; Patrick, D.; and Wesley, V. W. *Book of Black Heroes Volume II: Great Women in the Struggle.* Just Us, 1991. (Ages 10 and up.) More than 80 outstanding black women are pictured and described here. They are activists, educators, writers, performing and fine artists, athletes, entrepreneurs, lawyers, policy makers, scientists, and healers. The brief descriptions encourage the reader to learn more.

Isadora, R. *Max.* Illus. by the author. Macmillan, 1976. (Ages 5–8.) Max accompanies his sister to her dance class and recognizes the advantages of such a class. He joins in and enjoys it as much as he does his sports.

Isadora, R. *My Ballet Class.* Greenwillow, 1980. (Ages 6–8.) A very simple story of a girl attending her ballet class. The teacher is a man, and boys also attend the class. Rachel's father calls for her after class, carrying a younger child.

Isadora, R. *No, Agatha!* Illus. by the author. Greenwillow, 1980. (Ages 5–8.) Agatha accompanies her parents on a ship to England. The adults try to make her conform to what "nice" little girls do, but she is lively and irrepressible.

Iverson, G. *Margaret Bourke-White: News Photographer.* Illus. by M. Bourke-White. Creative Education, 1980. (Ages 8–11.) The photographs are more powerful than the text in this biography, but the account of this intrepid photographer's life is accurate and respectful.

Jacobs, W. J. *Mother, Aunt Susan, & Me: The First Fight for Women's Rights.* Coward, McCann & Geoghegan, 1979. (Ages 9–12.) In an interesting format, the reader is introduced to Sojourner Truth, Susan B. Anthony, and Elizabeth Cady Stanton, the mother of the teenaged narrator of the story.

James, B. *The Red Cloak.* Illus. by the author. Chronicle, 1989. (Ages 6–9.) In this "Tam Lin" retelling, Jan is a young girl who rescues her friend Tam from the elves. Except for the ages of the protagonists and their boisterous everyday play, the story line is the traditional one, and the magic works well in the context of the tale.

Kerr, M.E. *Dinky Hocker Shoots Smack.* Harper, 1972. (Ages 11 and up.) Dinky, an overweight girl who is emotionally distraught because her socially conscious mother neglects her in favor of various projects, acts out and publicly embarrasses her mother in order to gain attention. The mother is portrayed as an unfeeling do-gooder whose public image is more important than her daughter's needs. This book might stimulate debates about whether this outcome is a necessary by-product of a mother's service to the community.

Ketteman, H. *Not Yet, Yvette.* Illus. by I. Trivas. Whitman. (Ages 4–7.) Yvette and her father clean the house, bake, shop for a gift, buy flowers, and prepare a festive table in honor of the veterinarian-mother's birthday. Not ostentatious in its gender role equity, the points are made in the context of the story. The characters of the lively young girl and her competent father are well drawn. The family is African American.

Kidd, N. *June Mountain Secret.* Illus. by the author. Harper, 1991. (Ages 5–8.) Young Jen spends the day trout fishing, eating, rock climbing, and catching salamanders with her father. This is a satisfying story of a young girl bonding with her father. She dresses just like him—in hip waders, a fishing vest, and a safari hat. Her father is a loving, patient, nurturing teacher. The book also contains a strong ecological message, and its beautiful illustrations of the story line are peppered with labeled diagrams of river creatures, western forest wildlife, and fishing gear.

Kimmel, E. A. *The Four Gallant Sisters.* Illus. by T. Yuditskaya. Holt, 1992. (Ages 5–8.) In this adaptation of a Grimm folk tale, four orphaned sisters disguise themselves as men to go out into the world to learn trades and support themselves. After seven years, when they have all become masters of their respective crafts, they are enlisted into the king's service where they heroically rescue four princes from the clutches of a dragon. When their sex is revealed, they marry the princes. The princes they marry love them for their skills, valor, and companionship, not their beauty.

King-Smith, D. *Sophie's Snail.* Illus. by C. Minter-Kemp. Dell, 1991. (First published in England in 1988.) (Ages 5-8.) The British flavor adds to the charm of this chapter book that chronicles Sophie's daily adventures. Her interactions with her twin brothers, her great-great-great aunt, and her parents demonstrate her spunk. She is active, inquisitive, naughty, bright, and endearing. Even though the author insists on using the term "lady farmer" as Sophie's ambition, the message is one of respect for the child's individuality.

Kingman, L. *Georgina and the Dragon.* Illus. by L. Shortall. Houghton Mifflin, 1972. (Ages 7-10.) Georgina Gooch is determined to live up to her suffragist great-grandmother's tradition. She crusades for equal rights and manages to raise the level of consciousness of her whole neighborhood. She is fun—her energy and intelligence are outstanding.

Klein, N. *Girls Can Be Anything.* Illus. by R. Doty. Dutton, 1973. (Ages 5-8.) Marina's friend Adam tells her she has to be the nurse or stewardess when they play; but Marina's parents inform her that she can be anything, even a doctor, a pilot, or U.S. president. Marina reports this to Adam, and they change the way they play.

Klein, N. *Mom, the Wolf Man and Me.* Pantheon, 1972. (Ages 10 and up.) [See Family Constellations]

Krauss, R. *I'll Be You and You Be Me.* Illus. by M. Sendak. Bookstore, 1973. (Ages 8 and up.) Warm ideas in poetry about friendship between boys and girls.

Kudlinski, K. V. *Rachel Carson: Pioneer of Ecology.* Illus. by T. Lewin. Viking, 1988. (Ages 7-10.) One of a series called "Women of Our Time." The story of Carson's life is told in simple and personal language, so that readers have a sense of the person underneath the celebrity. Some of the other titles in the series include *Dorothea Lange: Life Through the Camera; Dolly Parton: Country Goin' to Town; Our Golda: The Story of Golda Meir; Mary McLeod Bethune: Voice of Black Hope;* and *Carol Burnett: The Sound of Laughter.*

Lader, L., and Meltzer, M. *Margaret Sanger, Pioneer of Birth Control.* Crowell, 1969. (Ages 12 and up.) A biography of Margaret Sanger, who fought to make birth control a right for all women, especially for poor women. She was strong enough to maintain her own individuality.

Landau, E. *Women, Women: Feminism in America.* Messner, 1970. (Ages 12 and up.) Presenting a case for equality of the sexes, the author describes many instances of discrimination as the basis for her argument. She also tells of countries, such as Israel and Sweden, where great advances in the cause of equality have been made. A well-written, persuasive book.

Larche, D. W. *Father Gander's Nursery Rhymes.* Illus. by C. Blattel and J. Blair. Advocacy, 1985. (Ages 5 and up.) To update the original rhymes so as to change messages perceived to be sexist or racist, the author has altered the Mother Goose rhymes to reflect that intent. The rhymes are still fun and lyrical, and the illustrations whimsically echo the messages of inclusiveness and equity. Not a substitute for, but rather an addition to, the original.

Larrick, N., and Merriam, E., eds. *Male and Female under 18.* Avon, 1973. (Ages 8 and up.) Comments and poems contributed by girls and boys, aged eight to eighteen, reflecting how they feel about their sex roles. The responses range from strong support of tradition to militant anger.

Lasker, J. *Mothers Can Do Anything.* Illus. by the author. Whitman, 1972. (Ages 3–8.) This book demonstrates the variety of jobs mothers can hold, including scientist, artist, and lion tamer. The illustrations are fun, and the message is important.

Lasky, K. *Beyond the Divide.* Macmillan, 1983. (Ages 11 and up.) Meribah Simon joins her father, Will, who has been excommunicated by their Amish community, in his journey westward. This is the story of Meribah's strength of character and personal courage and her anger at injustice. Meribah copes with many deaths, including her father's. She is adopted into the Yahi community after they save her life. This complex, rich story raises many moral and philosophical issues.

Lasky, K. *My Island Grandma.* Warne, 1979. (Ages 7–10.) [See Aging]

Lawrence, J. *Harriet and the Promised Land.* Simon & Schuster, 1968. (Ages 5–8.) In verse and colorful pictures, this book describes the courageous Harriet Tubman, who escaped from slavery and helped many others to escape as well. Her life was difficult and unconventional, and she persevered in her heroic actions despite grave danger.

L'Engle, M. *A Wrinkle in Time.* Farrar, Straus & Giroux, 1962. (Ages 12 and up.) [See Special Needs]

L'Engle, M. *The Young Unicorns.* Farrar, Straus, 1968. (Ages 12 and up.) A mystery set in New York with a blind musician, Emily, and a scientific whiz, Sue, as heroes. The other books in the Austin family series also contain strong and unstereotypic female characters. The males, too, are free of gender-role impositions.

Leiner, K. *Both My Parents Work.* Watts, 1986. (Ages 5–9.) Black and white photographs illustrate working families from a wonderful array of ethnic, social, and economic backgrounds. The criterion for "work" is that people get paid, so the person who stays home and works at maintaining the family is not included in this book, but such diverse occupations as housekeeper (for others), horse trainer, psychologist, farmer, reporter, procedure writer, police officer, and firefighter are among those listed and pictured here. The families cooperate, cope with problems, and remain proud of one another. A worthwhile and engaging book.

Levinson, I. *Peter Learns to Crochet.* Illus. by K. Sutherland. New Seed, 1973. (Ages 5–8.) Peter wants to learn to crochet, but he has trouble finding someone to teach him until he asks his teacher, Mr. Alvarado.

Levoy, M. *Alan and Naomi.* Harper, 1977. (Ages 10 and up.) [See War and Peace]

Levoy, M. *Shadow like a Leopard.* Harper, 1981. (Ages 11 and up.) To prove his worth to a street gang, fourteen-year-old Ramon Santiago robs an old man, Arnold Glasser, at knifepoint. Glasser is an artist; Ramon is a poet. The two characters form a surprising alliance and help each other find a way out of their problems.

Lewis, M. *Ernie and the Mile-Long Muffler.* Illus. by M. Apple. Coward, McCann & Geoghehan, 1982. (Ages 6–9.) When Ernie is at home with the chicken pox and bored, he learns to knit from his Uncle Simon, a sailor. Ernie decides to knit a mile-long muffler as a project. He doesn't quite make it, but along the way he learns about arithmetic, friendship, and perseverance. Uncle Simon is a great character and a wonderful model for male adults.

Little, J. *Hey World, Here I Am!.* Illus. by S. Truesdell. Harper, 1986. (Ages 8–12.) Told through the personality of Kate Bloomfield, these poems reflect a sensitive young woman's feelings and impressions of the world. Her friendship with Emily Blair, her feelings about being Jewish, her observations about teachers and school, all tell a personal story that becomes universal.

Lofts, N. *The Maude Reed Tale.* Illus. by A. and J. G. Johnstone. Thomas Nelson, 1972. (Ages 10 and up.) The setting is the Middle Ages. Maude, about twelve years old, has a twin brother who runs away from home to become a minstrel. Maude wants to be a wool merchant. The conflicts of personal and societal values, as well as the cleverness of the hero, make the book a vital one. The writing is of excellent quality.

Louie, A. L. *Yeh Shen: A Cinderella Story from China.* Illus. by E. Young. Putnam, 1988. (Ages 8 and up.) Found in a book from the T'ang dynasty (A.D. 618–907), this story predates the earliest European version of Cinderella by about 1000 years, leading scholars to believe that this was one of many folk and fairy tales adapted from Asian sources by European retellers. A magical fish and an old man aid Yeh-Shen. She is far from helpless, and she exhibits good sense as well as a kind heart, which, of course, wins her the prince in the end. The striking illustrations provide an aesthetic antidote to children's stereotypic concepts of beauty.

MacGregor, E. *Miss Pickerell Goes to Mars.* Illus. by P. Galdone. McGraw-Hill, 1951. (Ages 9–12.) Miss Pickerell is an old woman who travels from one exciting adventure to another, all over the universe. She is much brighter than most of the males and accomplishes more than most people. There is a long series of Miss Pickerell books.

MacLachlan, P. *Arthur, for the Very First Time.* Illus. by L. Bloom. Harper, 1980. (Ages 9–12.) Arthur and Moira enjoy a close friendship, albeit a bumpy one. Moira is active, strong, and adventuresome. Arthur is a writer and an observer, reflective and sensitive. The two help each other in times of emotional stress and benefit enormously from each other's strengths. The supporting characters in this involving story are also free of gender stereotypes and strong in their own right. The plot revolves around Arthur's extended visit with his great aunt and uncle on their farm while his parents are away. The anticipated birth of a new sibling for Arthur, as well as the fact of Moira's remaining in her grandfather's custody, also figure in the story.

MacLachlan, P. *Sarah, Plain and Tall.* Harper, 1987. [See Family Constellations]

MacLachlan, P. *The Sick Day.* Illus. by W. P. Du Bois. Pantheon, 1979. (Ages 5–8.) Emily and her father spend some loving time together while Emily is sick with a bad cold and her mother is at work. Emily's father is tender, nurturing, and fun.

Manson, C. *The Crab Prince.* Illus. by the author. Holt, 1991. (Ages 7–10.) This story is based on an Italian folktale. It has some traditional elements such as a wedding as the happy ending, but the two protagonists do not fall in love at first sight. The young woman rescues the prince by using her natural talents as well as her brains.

Markham, M. M. *The April Fool's Day Mystery.* Illus. by P. Estrada. Houghton Mifflin, 1991. (Ages 7–10.) The twins in this story are intelligent, independent girls whose interests defy female stereotypes. The female culprit also helps to blast stereotypes. Although there are boys in the class who throw spitballs while girls giggle and another boy who runs around scaring girls with a rubber spider, the twins' behavior contributes much to the notion of gender equity.

Maury, I., translated by A. Muñoz. *My Mother and I Are Growing Strong/Mi Mama y Yo Nos Hacemos Fuertes.* Illus. by S. Speidel. New Seed, 1978. (Ages 5–8.) [See Family Constellations]

Mayer, M. *Noble-Hearted Kate.* Illus. by W. Pels. Bantam, 1990. (Ages 10 and up.) The story combines the legend of Tam Lin with several other tales. Kate and Meghan are stepsisters, beautiful and devoted to one another. The girls are courageous and generous, a refreshing change from the stepsister stereotypes in so many fairy tales. The characters are respectfully portrayed and the illustrations are lovely.

McFarland, R. *Coping with Sexism.* Rosen, 1990. (Ages 10 and up.) Straight talk augmented by vignettes about sexism and how to deal with it. The author helps readers identify and react appropriately to sexist behavior and language. Males and sexism are also included as a topic in this informative and balanced book.

McGovern, A. *Half a Kingdom.* Illus. by N. Langner. Warne, 1977. (Ages 7-10.) Signy, a poor peasant girl, rescues Prince Lini from the evil trolls. When they marry, they decide to rule jointly and make the kingdom a more democratic place.

McKee, D. *Snow Woman.* Illus. by the author. Lothrop, Lee & Shepard, 1987. (Ages 4-8.) This tongue-in-cheek exploration of gender roles and language centers around two children, a brother and sister who want to build a snowman. "Snowperson," the father corrects, so the children build two snow people, a man and a woman, who run away together. The children decide to build a gender-neutral "snow bear" next. The father cooks and cleans, the mother does carpentry and sports close-cropped hair, and the children dress alike. The whimsical illustrations complement the story, which is sure to provoke interesting discussions (e.g., why is "snow woman" a permissible term while "snowman" is not?).

McPherson, S. S. *I Speak for the Women: A Story about Lucy Stone.* Illus. B. Liedahl. Carolrhoda, 1992. (Ages 9-12.) In swiftly moving narrative, the author chronicles the life of this remarkable outspoken defender of human rights. The details of her marriage to Henry Blackwell, himself an ardent feminist, provide a model for equity, mutual respect, and love.

McPherson, S. S. *The Workers' Detective: A Story about Dr. Alice Hamilton.* Illus. by J. Schulz. Carolrhoda, 1992. (Ages 9-12.) The life of this extraordinary woman who exposed lead and other occupational hazards in American factories and became a pioneer in industrial medicine. Her work with the Department of Labor, close relationship with Jane Addams, antiwar activity, appointment as the first female faculty member at Harvard, and personal struggles against gender discrimination are all recounted in a lively and accessible narrative.

Mellor, B., and Hemming, J. *Changing Stories.* Illus. by J. Lydbury. ILEA English Center, 1984. (Ages 8-10.) Among the fairy tales included here are several versions of *Red Riding Hood*, each presenting a different perspective. The slim book contains analyses and activities for children to become more aware of the messages implicit in the way fairy tales are written. The stories are presented unedited; the commentary precedes and follows each section.

Meltzer, M. *Mary McLeod Bethune: Voice of Black Hope.* Illus by S. Marchesi. Penguin, 1987. (Ages 9-12.) One of a series of biographies of noteworthy women called "Women of Our Time," this well written and researched account details the life of the educator who paved the way for black people to become active in national government and education. Ms. McLeod was the first child in the family of fourteen to be born free. She grew to become a founder of a college and a lifelong activist for the rights of African Americans.

Meltzer, M. *Tongue of Flame: The Life of Lydia Marie Child.* Crowell, 1965. (Ages 12 and up.) A well-written account of the life and times of Lydia Maria Child, who fought for such causes as abolition, women's rights, and rights of Native Americans. This book is one of the excellent series of biographies entitled "Women of America."

Merriam, E. *Boys and Girls, Girls and Boys.* Illus. by H. Sherman. Holt, Rinehart & Winston, 1972. (Ages 3-8.) An unpretentious book showing children, boys and girls alike, of various ethnic heritages, exploring, being active, and enjoying life.

Merriam, E. *Daddies at Work,* revised ed. Illus. by E. Fernandes. Simon & Schuster, 1989. (Ages 3-6.) This book shows men working at all sorts of jobs (e.g., doctors, nurses, construction workers, laundromat operators) and nurturing and playing with their children. The text highlights similarities and differences among fathers. The illustrations show characters of different races.

Merriam, E. *Mommies at Work,* revised ed. Illus. by E. Fernandes. Simon & Schuster, 1989. (Ages 3-6.) Beginning with jobs that all mothers do such as tying shoelaces, giving baths, and tucking children into bed, the book then shows some of the other jobs women can have, from driving trucks to working in ice cream parlors to being doctors. The text dispels stereotypes and reassures children whose mothers work outside the home that their mommies love them. The illustrations show a multiethnic cast of characters.

Merrill, J., adaptor. *The Girl Who Loved Caterpillars.* Illus. by F. Cooper. Philomel, 1992. (Ages 7-10.) This unusual tale from twelfth-century Japan features Izumi, a young girl who refuses to conform to the conventions of her time but prefers to play with boys of low social standing and collect caterpillars and seeds. Izumi does not marry, and she is happy with herself and enjoys her life. Izumi's parents do not approve of her interests, but they do not forbid her to pursue them. The illustrations convey well the tone of the story, but they are drawn from material that appeared centuries after the time of this story, and some of the houses depicted are Chinese rather than Japanese.

Merrill, S. *Washday.* Illus. by the author. Seabury, 1978. (Ages 5-8.) A little girl describes the fun her family shares on washday. Everyone joins in to help, even Papa. Cooperation is the rule as Papa makes cocoa while Mama builds a fire. In all the illustrations, Papa is shown helping with the children or the housework. This book could be used as a tool to discuss the importance of a family working together and sharing responsibilities.

Minard, R., ed. *Womenfolk and Fairy Tales.* Illus. by S. Klein. Houghton Mifflin, 1975. (Ages 7-10.) Females are the major characters in all the stories in this book. In general, they exhibit such qualities as intelligence, courage, and integrity. The introduction is a valuable addition to the tales.

Mitchell, J. S., ed. *Free to Choose: Decision-Making for Young Men.* McGraw-Hill, 1974. (Ages 12 and up.) Good advice to young men from a number of authors, ministers, psychologists, and other professionals interested in helping young people grow up in a liberated society.

Moore, E. *Grandma's House.* Illus. by E. Primavera. Lothrop, Lee & Shepard, 1985. (Ages 5-8.) [See Aging]

Murrow, L. K. *Dancing on the Table.* Illus. by R. Himler. Holiday House, 1990. (Ages 8-12.) [See Aging]

Nathan, D. *Women of Courage.* Illus. by C. Cather. Random House, 1964. (Ages 10 and up.) Biographies of five brave women: Susan B. Anthony, women's rights crusader; Jane Addams, social reformer who worked for the poor; Mary McLeod Bethune, educator of black children; Amelia Earhart, daring aviator; and Margaret Mead, anthropologist searching for the "secrets of human nature."

Naylor, P. R. *Shiloh.* Dell, 1991. (Ages 9-12.) This Newbery Award winner features an eleven-year-old boy whose sensitivity to animals and relationships with people are outstanding features of his personality. The plot revolves around Marty's rescue of a dog from its abusive owner.

Neilson, W., and Neilson, F. *Seven Women: Great Painters.* Chilton, 1969. (Ages 12 and up.) Serious critique of seven famous painters, from Angelica Kauffmann to Georgia O'Keeffe.

New Day Films. *Heroes and Strangers.* New Day Films, 1991. (Ages 12 and up.) Touching accounts of the feelings of adult children and their fathers, reflecting the loss they experience because society has pressured fathers to take a negative role in rearing their children.

O'Dell, S. *Island of the Blue Dolphins.* Houghton Mifflin, 1960. (Ages 10 and up.) Karana, a young Native-American girl, is alone on her home island after her people have left and her brother has been killed by wild dogs. She manages her own survival courageously for many years until at last she is rescued.

Oneal, Z. *A Long Way to Go.* Illus. by M. Dooling. Viking, 1990. (Ages 8–11.) Lila's grandmother is jailed for demonstrating in Washington with other suffragists. Eight-year-old Lila becomes passionately involved, at her level, with the suffragist movement. Her persuasive skills are so strong that she even convinces her antagonistic father to permit her to march in a parade with her grandmother. The author makes the era and the cause come alive and conveys the flavor and furor of the World War I era.

Paterson, K. *Bridge to Terabithia.* Illus. by D. Diamond. Crowell, 1977. (Ages 9–12.) [See Death]

Paterson, K. *The King's Equal.* Illus. by V. Vagin. Harper, 1992. (Ages 7–10.) Rosamund proves to be more than the king's equal in beauty, intelligence, and wealth. She rules the kingdom humanely and wisely while the king takes a year to mature and learn some important lessons. The illustrations and text combine to produce a beautiful and thought-provoking story about the nature of true beauty, intelligence, and wealth.

Paterson, K. *Lyddie.* Lodestar, 1991. (Ages 11 and up.) Lyddie is only thirteen years old, but she feels responsible for her mother and siblings' welfare, especially since their father has deserted them. She goes to work at a mill in Lowell, Massachusetts, to earn enough money to sustain her family's farm. The lack of concern for women's rights or for workers in general all figure into the plot. In the end, Lyddie manages to turn tragedy into triumph of spirit.

Paulsen, G. *The River.* Delacorte, 1991. (Ages 11 and up.) In this sequel to *Hatchet* (1987), Brian once more finds himself forced to survive in the wilderness. His determination and native abilities again help him to overcome all obstacles. His character has expanded and his perceptions are those of a clear-minded, sensitive person, unafraid to express his feelings and appreciation of life and of other people. Another such character can be found in Paulsen's *The Voyage of the Frog,* in which fourteen-year-old David survives a storm at sea in his sailboat. He too evidences emotions that are free of gender constraints.

Peavy, L., and Smith, U. *Dreams into Deeds: Nine Women Who Dared.* Scribner, 1985. (Ages 10 and up.) The authors have attempted, through their research, to recreate the childhoods of these nine women, all of whom have been named to the National Women's Hall of Fame. The women are activists, scientists, athletes, and performers. The stories also include the events of the women's adult years. The authors invite readers to be dreamers and to become "the doers of tomorrow."

Peavy, L., and Smith, U. *Women Who Changed Things.* Scribner, 1983. (Ages 12 and up.) Included are a mountain climber, a medical inspector, a psychologist, a social worker, a journalist, an educator, an astronomer, and a woman who founded an organization of craftspeople that provided jobs for many other women. None of these women were world-famous in their time, but each of them has an interesting story and provides an excellent model for young readers.

Perl, L. *Molly Picon: A Gift of Laughter.* Illus. by D. Ruff. Jewish Publication Society, 1990. (Ages 9-11.) The popular and lively Jewish entertainer's life reads like a Horatio Alger story. Ms. Picon's rise from ghetto child to internationally renowned performer is meticulously chronicled.

Pfeffer, S. B. *The Beauty Queen.* Doubleday, 1974. (Ages 12 and up.) A girl is coerced by her mother to enter beauty contests. She wins titles but after much thought, she realizes that being a beauty queen has no real meaning for her; she rejects her titles and the values they represent.

Phelps, E. J. *The Maid of the North: Feminist Folk Tales from around the World.* Illus. by L. Bloom. Holt, Rinehart & Winston, 1981. (Ages 11 and up.) A collection of tales from the oral tradition of many countries. Approximately seventeen different heritages are represented. The heroes are resourceful, intelligent, active, courageous, and self-confident. The author has provided an introduction describing the sources for the tales.

Phelps, E. J. *Tatterhood and Other Tales.* Illus. by P. B. Ford. Feminist Press, 1978. (Ages 8-12.) A collection of traditional tales from Norway, England, China, and other countries. Each tale portrays a witty and resourceful woman who actively sets about to determine her own fate.

Powell, M., and Yokubinas, G. *What to Be?* Illus. by R. Miodock. Children's Press, 1972. (Ages 5-8.) A little girl tries to decide what to be when she grows up. Her choices are varied. She considers everything from lumberjack or astronaut to dancer or beautician. The book offers good choices for girls, even for boys. It shows the many professions in which women can be involved.

Pryor, B. *Lottie's Dream.* Illus. by M. Graham. Simon & Schuster, 1992. (Ages 7-10.) Lottie longs to live by the ocean. For most of her life she is defined by her roles: daughter, so she must accompany her family westward; wife, so she stays where her husband wants to live; mother, so she stays with her children and raises them. When her husband dies, despite the warnings and importunings of her friends, children, and grandchildren, Lottie moves to a place near the ocean. She is not isolated; from time to time her grandchildren come to visit, but she is an entity unto herself and she is happy.

Rappaport, D. *American Women: Their Lives in Their Words.* Crowell, 1990. (Ages 12 and up.) Told through the voices of women from American colonial history to contemporary times. Women who were slaves, Ann Hutchinson, Catherine Beecher, Sarah Hale, and such notable women as Sojourner Truth, Margaret Sanger, Eleanor Roosevelt, Jacqueline Cochran, and Margaret Mead are quoted. The book ends with interviews with modern teenagers who express their vision of a future with fewer restrictions due to gender.

Rappaport, D. *Living Dangerously.* Harper, 1991. (Ages 8-12.) Stories of six women who risked death to perform extraordinarily hazardous deeds like going over Niagara Falls in a barrel, climbing mountains, hunting elephants, deep sea diving, and running marathons. The women come from different ethnic backgrounds: The one who went over the falls was 63 years old. In each story, the women defied great odds and persevered beyond human expectation. The author supplies an appendix of 23 women adventurers with a brief description of their accomplishments.

Reimold, M. G. *My Mom Is a Runner.* Illus. by S. Dorris. Abingdon, 1987. (Ages 3-6.) John's mother is a competitive athlete who runs every day to keep in shape and often enters races. Sometimes the boys run with her. The book's photographs show the family in a variety of settings. John takes a great deal of pride in his mother and sees her as a role model. This book shows a woman in a nontraditional gender role who is still in a supportive relationship with her children.

Reit, S. *Behind Rebel Lines: The Incredible Story of Emma Edmonds, Civil War Spy.* HBJ, 1988. (Ages 8-11.) An admiring, swiftly moving story of the woman who masqueraded as a man in order to serve the Union cause during the Civil War.

Rich, G. *Firegirl.* Illus. by C. P. Farley. Feminist Press, 1972. (Ages 6-10.) A girl ambitious to become a fire fighter learns what it takes to realize this goal.

Rogers, P., and Rogers, E. *Zoe's Tower.* Illus. by R. B. Corfield. Simon & Schuster, 1991. (Ages 5-7.) In this simple story illustrated with beautiful watercolors, a little girl named Zoe leads the reader down paths through woods and fields to her favorite spot to be alone, an old, crumbling stone tower. Zoe is an independent little girl who is unafraid of spiders, crows, or being alone and whose mother gives her the freedom to explore.

Rose, D. L. *Meredith's Mother Takes the Train.* Illus. by I. Trivas. Whitman, 1991. (Ages 3-6.) In a simple rhyming text appropriate for preschoolers, the author tells the story of Meredith and her single mother and how they spend one Friday—Meredith at daycare and her mother at the office. Although both are busy, they take time to think of one another. Mom is not a stereotype. She is a busy, hard working woman who makes time for her much-loved child.

Sachs, M. *Call Me Ruth.* Doubleday, 1982. (Ages 9 and up.) Ruth and her mother emigrate from Russia to New York City to join Ruth's father who has finally saved enough money to send for them. Ruth loves America from the moment she arrives; her mother hates it. The father is sick and soon dies. The mother becomes active in the Labor Movement, causing enormous embarrassment to her daughter. Ruth is a bright, academically talented child who works hard at school, loves to read, and is considered a model child. The author presents several points of view clearly and sympathetically. She also conveys an accurate historical view of early twentieth-century labor and immigrant issues.

San Souci, R. D. *Cut from the Same Cloth: American Women of Myth, Legend, and Tall Tale.* Illus. by B. Pinkney. Philomel, 1993. (Ages 8 and up.) This unusual collection of stories of female American folk heroes includes legends from African Americans, Native Americans, and Anglo Americans. The reader is introduced to such diverse characters as Molly Cottontail, the wife of Brer Rabbit and a trickster in her own right; Bess Call, sister of strongman Joe Call, who lifts oxen with one hand and wrestles strangers in her brother's absence; and Hiiaka, a strong, wise, and brave Hawaiian goddess. In all, fifteen myths are included in this collection. The tales are well told, and Brian Pinkney's scratchboard illustrations dramatically depict each protagonist.

Sawyer, R. *Roller Skates.* Illus. by V. Angelo. Viking, 1936. (Ages 9-12.) Lucinda is the lively, bouncy hero of this story. The episodes take place in upper-class old New York. Lucinda is unusual for her time but beautifully in tune with today.

Scott, A. H. *Someday Rider.* Illus. by R. Himler. Clarion, 1989. (Ages 6-9.) Kenny wants to learn how to ride a horse and help with the chores associated with riding skill. His mother teaches him, and the satisfying outcome is that mother, Kenny, and father set out together with the other ranch hands for the cattle roundup.

Scott, C. J. *Kentucky Daughter.* Clarion, 1985. (Ages 12 and up.) [See Abuse]

Seed, S. *Saturday's Child: 36 Women Talk about Their Jobs.* O'Hara. 1973. (Ages 11 and up.) Thirty-six women who have had successful careers in architecture, theatre, law, carpentry, science, and so on talk about their training, how they chose their jobs, and how their jobs affect their families.

Sills, L. *Inspirations: Stories about Women Artists*. Whitman, 1989. (Ages 10 and up.) Four artists, Faith Ringgold (author and illustrator of the Newbery Honor book *Tar Beach*), Georgia O'Keeffe, Frida Kahlo, and Alice Neel are profiled, and samples of their work are reproduced in this interesting and valuable book. A companion book, *Visions: Stories about Women Artists* (1993), profiles Mary Cassatt, Betye Saar, Leonora Carrington, and Mary Frank.

Smith, S. *Wren to the Rescue*. HBJ, 1990. (Ages 12 and up.) High fantasy involving four courageous and spirited girls and boys. Wren, who has the gift of magic, actively aids in the rescue of her friend Tess. No gender roles are stereotyped in this adventure.

Speare, E. G. *The Witch of Blackbird Pond*. Houghton Mifflin, 1958. (Ages 9–12.) Ki Tyler, orphaned as a young teenager, decides to leave her native island of Barbados to live with her maternal aunt, Puritan uncle, and two female cousins. She has been educated and encouraged to lead an active life. The role of the female in Colonial days, as well as the impact of politics and religion, is dramatically described in this book. The women are individuals, as are all the characters.

Staples, S. F. *Shabanu: Daughter of the Wind*. Knopf, 1989. (Ages 12 and up.) The story is set in Pakistan, and the details of the nomadic culture are vividly conveyed. The plot is intricate but never confusing. Shabanu and her sister have been matched with two brothers. Shabanu is pleased with her betrothal and believes that she can maintain her spirited personality even after her marriage. Tragedies intervene, and Shabanu is promised to a wealthy landowner with several wives. She must choose what she will do: jeopardize her family's safety to escape from the marriage or marry and lose her opportunity for self-fulfillment. Her choice should provoke much discussion and argument by young readers. Each character is well drawn and believable.

Steelsmith, S. *Elizabeth Blackwell: The Story of the First Woman Doctor*. Illus. by J. Kerstetter. Parenting, 1987. (Ages 5–8.) This biography for very young readers is simply but not condescendingly written. Dr. Blackwell emerges as a real person working hard to achieve her goals.

Steptoe, J. *Mufaro's Beautiful Daughters*. Illus. by the author. Lothrop, Lee & Shepard, 1987. (Ages 8–10.) Two sisters, both stunningly attractive, one selfish and mean-spirited, the other kind and loving, vie for the hand of the king. Of course the virtuous sister wins. The illustrations demonstrate the strength and beauty of the people and the land. Incidentally, the message is communicated that the comeliness of these two women is palpable and needs not be European in standard.

Stevens, B. *Deborah Sampson Goes to War*. Illus. by F. Hill. Carolrhoda, 1984. (Ages 6–9.) [See War and Peace]

Stren, P. *There's a Rainbow in My Closet*. Illus. by the author. Harper, 1979. (Ages 8–10.) [See Aging]

Sufrin, M. *Payton*. Illus. with photos. Scribner, 1988. (Ages 11 and up.) The biography of Walter Payton, who, despite his reputation as a football star, is nicknamed "Sweetness." The story maintains a fine balance between Payton as a person and Payton as a superhero.

Thomas, M.; Steinem, G.; and Pogrebin, L. C. *Free to Be . . . You and Me*. McGraw-Hill, 1974. (Ages 6 and up.) A collection of stories, poems, and songs dealing with people's potential to become whatever they want to become.

Tobias, T. *Marian Anderson*. Crowell, 1972. (Ages 7–10.) This biography of Marian Anderson is written in simple language with many illustrations and large print. The text details the magnificent singer's childhood interest in music and the encouragement she received from her family, as well as the obstacles she faced as a black woman in her professional career.

Torre, B. L. *The Luminous Pearl: A Chinese Folktale.* Illus. by C. Inouye. Orchard, 1990. (Ages 7 and up.) Princess Mai Li, the intelligent and beautiful daughter of the Dragon King, is permitted by her father to select her husband. After rejecting many suitors, she sets the conditions for finding a man who is honest and brave. The illustrations do not depict ancient China, but the story transmits traditional Chinese values.

Van Woerkom, D. *The Queen Who Couldn't Bake Gingerbread.* Illus. by P. Galdone. Knopf, 1975. (Ages 5–8.) An adaptation of a German folk tale about a king in search of the perfect wife—one who bakes gingerbread, darns socks, and cures his loneliness. She must be beautiful, too. The princesses he interviews cannot bake gingerbread but can bake other beautiful things. The queen he picks is wise and has a mind of her own. In the end, the king bakes the gingerbread himself.

Vare, E. A. *Adventurous Spirit: A Story about Ellen Swallow Richards.* Illus. by J. Hagerman. Carolrhoda, 1992. (Ages 8–10.) One of the series "Creative Minds," this book provides details about Richards, the first woman accepted into M.I.T. and the founder of the American Home Economics movement. Dr. Richards emerges as a woman who persevered against heavy odds and did so with dignity and strength.

Viorst, J. "And Then the Prince Knelt Down and Tried to Put the Glass Slipper on Cinderella's Foot." In *If I Were in Charge of the World and Other Worries.* Illus. by L. Cherry. Atheneum, 1981. (Ages 7–10.) In this poem, Cinderella has second thoughts about marrying a prince she hardly knows.

Voigt, C. *Dicey's Song.* Atheneum, 1982. (Ages 9 and up.) [See Family Constellations]

Voigt, C. *Seventeen against the Dealer.* Atheneum, 1989. (Ages 12 and up.) Dicey has grown up and maintained her fierce independence of spirit, as well as her way of life. She works hard at her boat-building business, but unfortunately, her trusting nature leads her to be betrayed by a man who steals all her money. She and Jeff maintain their love for each other and plan to marry. Their relationship is one of mutual respect and affection.

Walsh, J. P. *Grace.* Farrar, Straus & Giroux, 1991. (Ages 12 and up.) Based on an event that took place in 1838, the story tells of Grace Darling and her father in their heroic efforts to save the survivors of a shipwreck. Although Grace becomes the object of public adoration, the townspeople excoriate her and her father, accusing them of acting only for money. The valiant deed haunts her for the rest of her life and is the indirect cause of her death. The book is written in a vivid style.

Walter, M. P. *Justin and the Best Biscuits in the World.* Illus. by C. Stock. Lothrop, Lee & Shepard, 1986. (Ages 8–10.) Justin learns from his grandfather that "woman's work" is human work. The grandfather teaches Justin how to maintain an orderly house and how to bake biscuits. Most of all, he helps Justin to acquire self-esteem and pride in his accomplishments.

Wandro, M., R.N., and Blank, J. *My Daddy Is a Nurse.* Illus. by I. Trivas. Addison-Wesley, 1981. (Ages 4–8.) With accompanying remarks by a helpful adult, this book can help change some preconceptions about gender-role careers. For those children who are not burdened by these stereotypes, the book can be a useful reinforcement. It tells of ten fathers who work as nurses, weavers, flight attendants, dental hygienists, librarians, and other jobs generally associated with women workers.

Ward, S. G. *What Goes Around Comes Around.* Illus. by the author. Doubleday, 1991. (Ages 5 and up.) [See Aging]

Warren, R. *A Pictorial History of Women in America.* Crown, 1975. (Ages 10 and up.) A useful overview of the role of women in America's development. The book focuses on the women rather than the historical context.

Weidt, M. N. *Stateswoman to the World.* Illus. by L. M. Anderson. Carolrhoda, 1991. (Ages 8–10.) Part of the "Creative Minds" series, this biography reports not only the important work of Eleanor Roosevelt but also the details of her unhappy childhood, difficulties with her imperious mother-in-law, and agony over her husband's infidelity. It is frank about her relationship with her husband. It is also admiring and respectful of Eleanor Roosevelt's accomplishments and leadership. Like the others in this series, the book calls its subject by her first name while calling most of the men by their surnames, a slight flaw but one worthy of noting.

Wetterer, M. K. *Kate Shelley and the Midnight Express.* Illus. by K. Ritz. Carolrhoda, 1990. (Ages 7–10.) Based on an actual event, this easy-to-read book tells of the heroic actions of Kate Shelley, a fifteen year old living in Iowa in the mid-1890s, who risked her own life to warn the railroad of a fallen bridge. The account is rousing, and the story treats Kate as a real person rather than an idol.

White, E.B. *Charlotte's Web.* Illus. by G. Williams. Harper, 1952. (Ages 7–12.) [See Death]

Whitmore, A. *The Bread Winner.* Houghton Mifflin, 1990. (Ages 8–11.) Sarah is too perfect to be true, but the story of how she saves her family from the poorhouse by means of her astute business sense, combined with her ability to bake delicious bread, makes for entertaining and fast-paced reading. The Great Depression and its effects on families are well portrayed. The resolution of the family's problems, while idealized, is plausible.

Wilder, L. I. *Little House in the Big Woods* (1932) and *Little House on the Prairie* (1935). Illus. by H. Sewell. Harper. (Ages 7–11.) The first two books in a series about a girl growing up with her family and leading an interesting frontier life. The characters, who actually lived, are accurately portrayed. They display courage and strength.

Williams, J. *Petronella.* Illus. by F. Menstra. Parents Magazine, 1973. (Ages 5–8.) Petronella, the youngest of three children, sets off to seek her fortune and rescue a prince. She finds a prince, but it turns out he is really just a parasite dependent on the enchanter at whose house he is staying. Petronella ends up marrying the wise, kind enchanter rather than the nitwit prince.

Williams, V. B. *Music, Music for Everyone.* Illus. by the author. Greenwillow, 1984. (Ages 7–10.) The women in this book, in *A Chair for My Mother* (1982), and in *Something Special for Me* (1983) support one another emotionally. The mother is the wage-earner, and the other family members help in various ways. A positive and healthy picture is painted.

Winthrop, E. *A Very Noisy Girl.* Illus. by E. Weiss. Holiday House, 1991. (Ages 4–8.) Elizabeth is a very noisy girl. She jumps on furniture, bangs her drum, runs around the house, and slams doors. When her mother sends her to her room to quiet down, she emerges pretending to be a dog, a very quiet one. Her mother plays along with the fantasy. After a while, the mother sends the "dog" off to find Elizabeth, who is much noisier but much less boring. The mother is an active participant in her daughter's play and fantasies. No father is present.

Worth, R. *The American Family.* Illus. by R. Sefcik. Watts, 1984. (Ages 12 and up.) [See Family Constellations]

Yolen, J. *Dove Isabeau.* Illus. by D. Nolan. HBJ, 1989. (Ages 12 and up.) A bloody tale of evil enchantment and hard-won victories. The hero is a beautiful young girl who is turned into a monster. The spirit of her dead mother helps to restore her and her prince to their true shapes.

Yolen, J. *Dragon's Blood.* Delacorte, 1982. (Ages 12 and up.) The young male and female protagonists of this fantasy gain independence by means of their wits and perseverance. Both are sensitive people, willing to take risks to accomplish their goals. The story is rich in adventure, interweaving setting, plot, and character. The sequel, *Heart's Blood,* is the second of the *Pit Dragon* trilogy.

Yolen, J. *The Emperor and the Kite.* Illus. by E. Young. World, 1967. (Ages 5-8.) Loyal Djeow Seow rescues her father, the emperor, who has been captured by evil men and locked in a high tower. Written in a poetic style, this is a story of a girl's love, courage, and ingenuity.

Yolen, J. *The Girl Who Cried Flowers and Other Tales.* Illus. by D. Palladini. Crowell, 1974. (Ages 9-12.) Three of these five tales have unconventional female protagonists. One contains a wise and frostily silent queen; one has a woman who takes upon herself the burden of designing the world's fate; one presents a woman destroyed by her desire to please.

Yolen, J. *The Girl Who Loved the Wind.* Illus. by E. Young. Crowell, 1972. (Ages 5-8.) Danina is kept from the outside world by her father who wants to protect her from all sad things. But despite the garden wall, Danina hears the wind's voice and eventually accepts the wind's challenge to discover the world for herself.

Yolen, J. *The Hundredth Dove.* Illus. by D. Palladini. Schocken, 1977. (Ages 12 and up.) Tales with the flavor of the oral tradition peopled with characters who defy stereotypes. Not all end happily, and most of them contain pain and sorrow; but the beauty of the language and the internal logic of the storylines make this a collection to ponder on.

Yolen, J. *The Magic Three of Solatia.* Illus. by J. Noonan. Crowell, 1974. (Ages 10 and up.) Sianna is a wise, strong, and active hero; and she retains all these qualities from childhood into womanhood. These imaginative stories sustain a poetic and folkloric quality that is very satisfying.

Yolen, J. *Pirates in Petticoats.* Illus. by L. Vosburgh. David McKay, 1963. (Ages 10 and up.) An engagingly written series of descriptions of female pirates.

Yolen, J. *Tam Lin.* Illus. by C. Mikolaycak. HBJ, 1990. (Ages 9-12.) A woman is the hero of this vivid retelling of the ancient Scottish ballad. Jennet is stubborn, courageous, and determined to claim her birthright, as well as her prince.

Zolotow, C. *The Summer Night.* Illus. by B. Shecter. Harper, 1974. (Ages 5-8.) When a little girl cannot sleep, her father tries all kinds of remedies for her sleeplessness and finally accompanies her on a walk. The father is tender and understanding.

Zolotow, C. *William's Doll.* Illus. by W. P. duBois. Harper, 1972. (Ages 3-8.) William likes sports and playing with trains, but he also wants a doll. His father, brother, and friends (male) object, but Grandmother gets him a doll and explains that he can practice for the time when he becomes a father. This book serves as the basis for much discussion.

chapter 9

Heritage

$\mathbf{A}$ teacher in a suburb of a large city received new books for the class library. She selected some containing a variety of characters representing different heritages and set them in random order on a table. She then noted, somewhat to her surprise because she had not planned this as an experiment, that children gravitated to the books describing their own individual heritages. Their behavior was not unique. Given the opportunity, most of us choose, at least sometimes, to read about ourselves or some extensions of ourselves. That is not to say that fantasy and experiences other than our own are not important; fantasy reinforces, validates, and helps us to confront our emotions.

When any segment of society is excluded from its literature, the implication is thereby conveyed that the group is without value. Color, religion, and national origin constitute an important portion of any person's makeup. Culture is also significant; it is often described as part of the environment and the particular ways in which a group practices its rituals. Further, individual family trees must be included. Witness the popularity of the television series *Roots* and its effect on the nation. Interest in one's own personal roots is an extension of the need for validating a group's heritage.

For many years, stories for children implied that all successful families, neighborhoods, and people were Christian, white, middle class, and suburban. This situation clearly could not continue in a society committed to moving away from racism. Children who were neither Caucasian nor middle class were made to feel invisible. They were told by their omission that they were too unimportant to mention. They were unvalued. Fortunately, more and more excellent authors and illustrators have responded to the call to acknowledge the nation's and the world's diversity.

The United States is not yet a utopia: People are still ignorant of others' cultures and beliefs, certain that their own heritages are superior or so insecure about their own identities that they act negatively and demean others because of religion, color of skin, or national origin.

Unfortunately, stereotypes (oversimplified, standardized generalizations that adhere to any member of a group without regard to individuals and their differences) are still used to foster and maintain divisions among people. Even so-called positive stereotypes are detrimental because they deny human variation. (Not all Chinese people are math whizzes, nor do all African Americans have rhythm.)

Those of us involved with children have a special responsibility. What criteria should be considered to build a library? How can racist attitudes in books be handled? How can we help children to become aware of connotations and innuendos in the books they read? What is the place of the classics? What about popular fantasies, novels, and even works of so-called nonfiction that are rife with racist ideas? How can progress be maintained in openness and world-mindedness? How can acts of omission be recognized?

To address these questions, the first task is to cultivate self-awareness. Only then can we recognize how others react to certain words or labels and how they feel about themselves and their world. We can compare different modes of response, backgrounds, and values. Cultural differences may be difficult for some people to understand and appreciate; but the more people are encouraged to value their own diversity, the more they should be able to value those of others. Respect and admiration should lead to a sense of comfort and joy that eventually invite the cooperation that is an ultimate aim of human relations. *Knowledge about one's own heritage* and characteristics and the problems imposed by society are essential for learning and growth. *Tolerance of oneself and one's people* is important as a next step. *Acceptance and valuing* must follow for true self-pride to grow. Finally, the ability to make one's own decisions comfortably results in a sense of *independence and collegiality.* The pattern must be repeated with each new situation and practiced consistently.

No person can be said to have reached a state of total awareness. Some may still be at the point where culturally different people are either invisible, "strange," or frightening. The fact that books in the past excluded most non-Caucasian people has exacerbated this problem. Too many children have been unable to find themselves in books. They have not been able to identify with male or female heroes or even with ordinary children who simply "belong." Nancy Larrick brought this appalling gap to the attention of children's book publishers and the public in her important and influential article in the *Saturday Review* of September 11, 1965, called "The All-White World of Children's Books." In recent years, more and more culturally diverse books have been published. A first step, then, in working toward nonracist and antiracist classrooms and libraries is to stock them with books that include a variety of people, cultures, points of view, lifestyles, and situations.

People are where they are, not where they should be. They can be helped to take next steps; it is not feasible to force them to make leaps. Meanwhile, each person can continue to advance in attitudes and behaviors.

Try This

Select three books for young children that you believe demonstrate a good level of cultural awareness and valuing. List the qualities that support your judgment. Find one way each of the books could have done an even better job. Do the same with three books for older children. Compare your observations with those of a peer.

SUGGESTED CRITERIA

How can books help readers become more aware and respectful of other cultures and differences? What criteria can help not only to locate racist inferences but also to recognize positive gains? Many individuals and groups have provided sets of criteria. No list is complete, nor should it be used as a template for judging the value of each book. Eventually each reader must compile a personal inventory. Since few books can adhere to every criterion, the whole class or library collection must be considered in the light of completeness, fairness, literary quality, perspective, and accuracy.

Characters of different heritages should be three-dimensional and beyond stereotypes. This, of course, is an important literary consideration when portraying any character, but ethnic clichés are often casually inserted into books. It is essential that readers be taught to recognize them.

Try to find books written from an authentic cultural perspective. As Rudine Sims points out in *Shadow and Substance,* "There is a difference between being talked *to* and being talked *about.*" Members of a particular group should be able to see themselves mirrored in literature with as many facets of their heritage as possible presented and developed. This can occur only if the books in a classroom, home, or library contain a number of heritages.

Literature should indicate that in any population, people, even those with a common heritage, differ in lifestyle, economic condition, personality, interests, and abilities.

The specific heritage of characters should reflect the care the author takes about detail. For example, wherever possible, the particular African country from which a person or group came should be identified. A general reference to Africa is insufficient. So too with Asians. Look for the name of the Native American nation and the setting of a story. The origin of a Spanish-speaking person should be included. He or she should not simply be called Latino, Latina, or Hispanic. A lack of specificity can communicate that there are no distinctions among people or that the author either is ignorant of them, does not care about them, or is not demonstrating respect for the particular person or group.

In books describing a general setting or community, characters should occupy positions of authority or status apart from their heritage. The norm should not be that a white character is the boss or supervisor or that a person of color or a female is relegated to a menial or lesser position. Even with minor characters of little importance to the story, the message about roles and heritage is internalized by young readers.

Standards, aspirations, relationships, and viewpoints should result from the story line and character development, not from preconceptions about specific groups. White, middle-class children should not automatically set the norms for behavior and lifestyle.

Nor should assimilation be the goal or happy outcome for an ethnic or linguistic population. The "melting pot" is no longer the operative metaphor for American society. Today, the idea of a tossed salad, stew, or mosaic, conveys the idea of retaining, valuing, and respecting individual characteristics while forming a cohesive larger community.

Victims or martyrs should not always be members of one particular group, nor should one group always supply the heroes.

When stories take place in cities or in geographic areas where a variety of people live and work, the characters should reflect this range. Omission of any part of a multicultural population should be noted, and readers should be invited to discuss the reasons for it.

The language of any book is an important factor in its quality as well as its impact. The cadences and vocabulary of a particular regional or ethnic group are important features of that group. Literature should reflect the linguistic richness of a culture. Dialect should not be used as a differentiating mechanism with negative intent. Talented authors convey through their characters' language the music of authentic speech. Characters should also be named authentically.

Language should avoid insulting or demeaning implications. Authors should not use such adjectives as *strange, primitive,* or *savage* to describe cultural differences. These differences should be affirmed, encouraged, and valued; they should appear as integral parts of the characters, not as labels. Note that an overly idealized description is just as detrimental to understanding and appreciation as one that is negative.

The terminology identifying a group should be respectful. For example, *African American* rather than *Negro* or *black* is currently preferred by most spokespeople in key African-American organizations. *Latino (Latina),* which connotes a wider group than *Hispanic* (referring only to people from Spain) is preferable. This criterion is difficult. To some people, the request for a particular term is an annoyance and is branded "political correctness." Furthermore, the labels are a source of dispute, even among the individuals and the groups in question. Nevertheless, it is a mark of respect to attempt to discern the preferred mode of address and reference and use it. Just as it is no longer a contentious matter to call adult females *women* rather than *girls* or *ladies,* so too authors should show the same regard for people's heritage. Vintage works and books set in the past reflecting the language of their time can be used to show the contrasts between then and now.

Even works of fiction should report history accurately. Because historic portrayal depends on the perspective and background of the author, several books about the same event or famous person should be available to young readers. This will help counteract the effects of some authors who consider battles won by people of European origin "victories" and those won by Native Americans "massacres."

Most good authors write from experience. They illuminate and extend their perceptions through research and imagination. Above all, their talents as storytellers and their sensitivity to people enhance their writing. Authentic books, no matter what the age of the intended audience or the genre of the literature, contain nuances reflecting the flavor of the heritage. This is a quality difficult to achieve and rare in authors whose primary experiences lie outside those of the group depicted. It is always a good idea to check authenticity and accuracy by consulting other resources.

In books of folklore, the complexity of the symbols and the messages should be conveyed accurately. Some stories—as is true of any attempt to set down in writing what has been part of the oral literature—are obscure and badly told. Again readers should search for the author's credentials. Some tales are sacred to a particular group. A person familiar with the origins of the tale would be able to caution readers about violating taboos and would know which tales were appropriate to tell.

Illustrations figure importantly in the impact of books. In some books, only the illustrations give readers clues about the ethnic heritage of the characters. Good illustrations avoid stereotypes, tokenism, quaintness, and demeaning implications. They are accurate and respectful of their subject.

Try This

Select three books for young children (preschool to age eight) and three books for older children (eight to twelve). Use the Bibliography at the end of this chapter as a source if you wish. Analyze the books for evidence of a nonracist approach. For example, try to find specific evidence of nonstereotypic illustrations. In examining the story line, try to find examples of situations where all people have constructive power. List the books you have found and the positive characteristics you have discovered.

It is important to be able to recognize both the positive and the negative aspects of any book, filtering one's observation through such qualities as literary excellence, the effectiveness of the story, the side effects of the message, and the universality of the human experiences described. The mood of the story, the author's ability to cause the reader to empathize with the characters—in short, the overall impact of the book—must always be considered. The more knowledgeable readers are, the more able they will be to determine whether an author has presented historical, anthropological, and emotional truth.

What steps can authors take to provide the reading public with fewer racist books? First, they must examine their own racial biases and fantasies before presenting them in print. Their words are read by many children and adults. Their ideas are received, internalized, and acted upon. Their impact is enormous. Although it is a truism not to believe all that is in print, disbelief is suspended when a writer is powerful, particularly when readers are immersed in fantasy. Then the messages seep into readers' systems without their having weighed or even recognized the information.

Authors who care about combating racism present characters in a varied and unstereotypic fashion. They base their work on research or life experience and try to examine it with a diagnostic eye, looking for balanced images for a variety of people. They try to weed out inaccuracies that would foster racist attitudes and responses in their readers.

On their part, readers can communicate to publishers and authors both positive and negative criticisms. They can examine their own perceptions, compare them with those of others, ask for validation, and be alerted when they find themselves so enthralled by a book that they do not actively question the author's intent and methodology. While recognizing positive factors, they must keep their minds open for negative implications and act to overturn them.

Books are currently published with a variety of audiences in mind. Some books attempt to educate "outsiders," and are at the earliest level of fostering awareness. Some seek to inform the reader about long-neglected and little-known history. A fairly large body of books deals with constructing and reinforcing a sense of pride and positive self-image for children whose culture is depicted while at the same time helping uninformed readers to develop awareness and appreciation of others' qualities and contributions. Differences are cherished rather than discouraged in the best of these books.

PEOPLING THE COUNTRY

The United States of America was populated in a number of different ways. Historians and archaeologists speculate that the first settlers came, probably from Asia, about 40,000 years ago across the land bridge that then existed. This migration continued, and most of these people traveled south, following herds of wild game. It is estimated that migrating groups of people reached the southern tip of South America about 10,000 years ago. At about the same time, the northern land bridge became submerged, so subsequent explorers or settlers had to come by sea. There is some evidence in pottery and games played by ancient groups to indicate that people from Japan, China, and India may have made contact of some sort with people of the Americas thousands of years ago.

By the time Christopher Columbus reached the West Indies, many different peoples lived in North, Central, and South America. Some groups farmed, others fished, and still others hunted. There were artisans, engineers, and astronomers. The Aztecs of central Mexico, who inhabited great stone cities, had developed a complex civilization, including writing and a calendar. Mayans and Incas also were skilled craftspeople, scientists, and builders. The Inca Empire, perhaps 16 million people, was larger than any kingdom in Europe at the time.

The indigenous peoples of the Americas were the first victimized ethnic group on this continent, beginning with Columbus and continuing with later European explorers, settlers, and governments. Although many of the European immigrants who sought religious freedom had themselves been oppressed for their beliefs, they were incapable of seeing Native Americans as people with their own legitimate cultures. Fearful and contemptuous of the people who already inhabited the country, they viewed them for the most part as less than human. Their religion was considered pagan and therefore illegitimate. Because of this superior feeling on the part of the colonists, their disregard for the rights of the American Indians was not considered persecution. By converting the "heathens" to the true religion of Christianity, they felt that they were repaying helpfulness on the part of Native Americans with the greatest kindness of all: initiation into European culture and beliefs.

Texts and works of fiction have conveyed the image of the intrepid pioneer fighting valiantly against all odds to "settle" the land. Americans have not been encouraged to think about the people whose lands were usurped or those who were pressed against their will into the service of the settlers.

After the colonists had established their settlements and more and more of them kept coming, the indigenous people recognized that they were being pushed out of their homes and that there would be no abating of the European encroachment. Before the American Revolution, their lands were protected to some extent by the English Crown. Even after the colonists won the war, it was considered unlawful to take land without either purchasing it or making some attempt at treaties. Although the Northwest Territory Ordinance and the Articles of Confederation insured the rights of the American Indians to their own government and property, by 1800 Congress was beginning to demand native loyalty to the government of the United States.

In 1804, the infamous removal of the Cherokee from their lands was made "legal" under the provisions of the Louisiana Purchase. The Cherokee Nation, which had conformed in every way to U.S. government demands and expectations, was nevertheless forced to relinquish all lands and possessions. Soon after, other indigenous peoples were ordered removed to the West. What they could not carry was confiscated, and they were forced to endure killing marches across many miles. Torn from their well-established patterns of life, they were forced to try farming land that was almost totally barren. Some were set down in swamp lands, where many succumbed to fever. Those who survived found it almost impossible to endure the hostile conditions of the new lands. They were removed time and time again, whenever it was discovered that their land contained lead or gold deposits or anything remotely useful. Those who did not die of disease or starvation were subject to military harassment.

President Andrew Jackson's attitude and behavior toward Native Americans disregarded their legal and human rights. In 1832, when Chief Justice of the Supreme Court John Marshall ruled in favor of the Cherokee Nation and declared the occupation of Indian land to be illegal, Jackson refused to enforce the ruling. In effect, he told Marshall to enforce it himself if he could.

In 1887, the Allotment Act permitted the United States to divide all Indian lands into small allotments and make all acreage that remained after the Indians had received their "shares" available to white settlers. At this point, there were only about 250,000 native people remaining in the United States, where once there had been more than a million. Most were contained in the land reserved for them alone (reservations) but subject to U.S. law.

Meanwhile, in 1867, the United States purchased Alaska. Russia had practiced a policy of abuse there for almost a century. Aleut, Yupik, Athapaskan, Tlingit, Haida, and Tsimshian were pressed into forced labor, coerced into becoming Christians, exported to Russia as servants, and decimated by diseases such as smallpox, chicken pox, measles, influenza, and tuberculosis. The exploitation of Alaska's resources compounded the serious economic situation that confronted the indigenous peoples. When Alaska was made a state in 1959, Alaskan natives were made official citizens of the United States. As a result, native children were forced to go to schools, many of them far distant from their homes. Children were taken from their families and sent to live in government or Catholic missionary boarding schools. Like their counterparts across the lower United States, children in these schools were forbidden to speak their own language or practice their native religion. Communities were eroded, and traditional ways of life were subverted.

When oil was discovered on the Alaskan North Slope in 1968, the issue arose of how to respond to the claims of native peoples. In 1971, the Alaska Native Claims Settlement Act (ANCSA) established twelve geographic corporations (irrespective of tribial or clan divisions). Alaskan natives born before 1971 are members of their regional corporation. Those born after 1971 are not shareholders. Native corporations are under pressure to parcel out the land so that it may be sold to companies wanting to "develop" it.

Despite concentrated external efforts to assimilate all native peoples, an era of change has begun. Native Americans are again practicing once-forbidden religious rites and speaking their own languages. A knowledge of and respect for the customs and beliefs of tribal ancestors are being communicated in schools and communities. Young people are being encouraged to write about their heritage, and many tribal newspapers and publications have appeared across the country. Native peoples' associations whose membership is composed largely if not exclusively of Native Americans are gaining in influence. Indigenous peoples' voices are being heard in Congress, the news media, and books. Native Americans are relying on their own abilities and leadership as they more and more take control of their own affairs.

Try This

Find histories of indigenous American peoples in encyclopedias and history texts. Compile traditional descriptions of the removal to "Indian territory." Then do the same with any of the books written after 1965 from a Native American perspective. Analyze the differences in factual presentation. Do the same with the Battle of Little Big Horn and the massacre at Wounded Knee.

With the various Spanish incursions of the fifteenth century and continuing with English, Dutch, French, and Portuguese conquests in the next several centuries, the population of the Americas became a mix of native peoples and Europeans—soldiers, religious sects fleeing oppression, farmers, and fur trappers—and African slaves brought by Spanish settlers to the Caribbean beginning in 1517. The importation of slaves from Africa, mostly from countries on the west coast, introduced a large body of people who had not come here for profit, comfort, or adventure—had not, in fact, come here of their own free will. Their alienation was further exacerbated by the fact that they spoke many different languages, came from divergent cultures, and practiced diverse religions.

The development of sugar and coffee plantations in Central and South America in the seventeenth century accelerated the slave trade to enormous proportions. In 1619, a Dutch ship brought the first African slaves to Virginia. By about 1700, there were approximately 80,000 people of African origin in the colonies. Although abolitionist sentiment was present in the English colonies in the mid-eighteenth century, the cultivation of tobacco and rice nevertheless instigated the wholesale importation of Africans for forced labor. The invention of the cotton gin in 1793 made the dreadful institution of slavery much more economically advantageous and widespread. By 1860 there were almost four million slaves in the United States.

In 1862, Lincoln signed the Emancipation Proclamation freeing all slaves in the rebel states on January 1, 1863. Congress had already ended slavery in the territories and in the District of Columbia with the Confiscation Acts of 1861 and 1862. The Fifteenth Amendment, declaring that all men have the right to vote, was added to the Constitution in 1870 (women did not gain this right until 1920), but many local restrictions were placed on voter registration. It was not until 1957 that Congress passed an act creating a Commission on Civil Rights and affirming the fifteenth amendment by permitting the challenge of certain states' voting restrictions. Three years earlier, in 1954, the Supreme Court decreed that "separate but equal" was discriminatory and ordered schools to desegregate. The 1964 Civil Rights Act forbade discrimination in schools and public accommodations. This same year, Dr. Martin Luther King, Jr., was awarded the Nobel Peace Prize in recognition of his work in nonviolent protest.

Spaniards came to the Americas first as conquerors and then as settlers. They brought African slaves to help do the hard work of cultivating the land and mining precious minerals. From 1819 to 1898, the United States acquired land controlled by Spain through a series of purchases and military conquests. Although the Roman Catholic religion and the Spanish language are links (Note, however, that Brazilians speak Portuguese) and there are other similarities of custom and style, each of the Latino groups is also different from the others in heritage, customs, culture, lifestyle, outlook, appearance, and even vocabulary and accent. It is important to acknowledge that within each group there is also wide diversity. The Latino population of the United States includes 13.5 million from Mexico, 2.7 million from Puerto Rico, 1 million from Cuba, and 5 million from all other Latin American countries.

In 1917, Puerto Ricans were granted American citizenship without any plebiscite of their own. Economic hardship on the island and unrestricted entry to the United States because of citizenship motivated thousands of Puerto Ricans to migrate to the mainland to seek work and better financial conditions. Many go back and forth from the island to the mainland, and about one-third resettle in Puerto Rico permanently.

Of the other Latino populations, Cubans are most readily welcomed into the United States when they claim political asylum. The million Cubans here in 1993 are concentrated mostly in Florida and are part of a vocal and active community.

In 1980 the press to admit people escaping from Vietnam, Laos, and Cambodia impelled Congress to pass the Refugee Act allowing thousands to enter. Although this act was intended to correct the imbalance of political forces affecting acceptance of refugees and introduce more neutral standards, according to the *World Refugee Survey of 1992* (U.S. Committee for Refugees) 99.8 percent of the refugees admitted to the United States since 1980 have come from Communist countries or from Arab countries hostile to the United States. This pattern is virtually identical to the one that existed before passage of the 1980 Refugee Act.

Since colonial times, waves of people have come voluntarily to search for religious or political freedom, to escape from wars or oppression, or to seek opportunities for economic advancement. Europe in the seventeenth century was an oppressive place in many ways, with religious persecution and harsh punishments for people who could not pay their debts. Most European immigrants of the colonial period came from England, Wales, or Ireland. However some people from Belgium, Sweden, Norway, and Finland, and others from Holland also established settlements. French Huguenots arrived at this time, as well as Dutch, Spanish, and Portuguese Jews.

Five million people emigrated from western Europe between the 1820s and the 1850s. They doubled the existing population. In Ireland, two factors figured strongly in a surge of immigration: the conversion of farmland to sheepgrazing land (because the sale of wool was more profitable than the sale of produce) and the potato blight, which destroyed a significant source of food and led to terrible famine. Many Irish people became domestic servants and laborers on canals, roads, and railroads. During this time, many people from southern Germany and the German-Swiss areas came for economic reasons and settled in great numbers in the Midwest and in Pennsylvania. They favored occupations such as butcher, carpenter, shoemaker, and other skilled entrepreneurial work. In this same period, people continued to come from Great Britain. Some of them opened such commercial enterprises as textile mills and pottery factories.

Starting in the mid-nineteenth century, Chinese immigrants arrived on the West Coast in response to the need for laborers to build railroads and work in mines. By 1880, approximately 105,000 Chinese laborers lived in the United States. They were generally not treated kindly, and they were often victims of violence and hatred. After the Civil War, new waves of immigrants, mostly from western Europe, moved into the country and settled in the lands west of the Mississippi to aid in the development of settlements and the wresting of land from the indigenous peoples.

In 1882, sentiment against Chinese immigrants reached such proportions that the Chinese Exclusion Act (the first antiimmigration act to be passed in the United States) suspended Chinese immigration for the next ten years. It was followed by more exclusionary laws that were not repealed until 1943. Japanese immigrants were not banned, and from 1885 to the turn of the century, Japanese emigrated in large numbers, mostly to Hawaii and California. In 1890, about 2,000 Japanese lived in the United States. In 1907, because of pressure exerted by people afraid of losing their jobs to low-paid Japanese laborers and because of an irrational fear of a "Yellow Peril," the United States and Japan negotiated what was euphemistically called a "Gentlemen's Agreement." The Japanese government agreed to forbid laborers to emigrate to the United States for a period of two years.

Anti-Japanese sentiment accelerated in the twentieth century and reached a height at the onset of World War II when internment camps were constructed. From 1942 to 1945, the United States imprisoned more than 110,000 Japanese Americans in these camps, almost the entire Japanese-American population, many of them citizens. Only recently has Congress officially admitted wrongdoing and begun to plan for reparations. With Hawaii's becoming the fiftieth state in 1960 came greater acceptance of Japanese people. The 1990 Census reported that there are almost 850,000 Japanese Americans living in the United States. This represents a 21 percent increase since 1980.

Not until the late nineteenth century did immigrants from southern and eastern Europe arrive. The availability of jobs in the United States was the major attraction for these people; and newly developed steamship lines permitted travel to the American continent at very low cost. Italians, Poles, Czechs, Lithuanians, Finns, and Croats came, largely for economic reasons. Many Jews fled Russia as a result of the *pogroms* (organized annihilation of entire settlements of Jews) and because of virulent and violent anti-Semitism in the other countries of Europe. Turks, Armenians, and people from the Balkans also came to escape religious and ethnic persecution.

A common experience for most working-class immigrant groups in the twentieth century was to encounter suspicion, resentment, and rejection from people who had come before them. U.S. immigration laws reflected these negative attitudes. A literacy requirement for citizenship was imposed on all new immigrants, and restrictions were toughened against Asian immigration. In 1924 the Johnson-Reed Act limited immigration from each country to 2 percent of the number in the United States in 1890, with the total not to exceed 150,000. This act was intended to sharply limit "undesirable" populations from immigrating in great numbers.

In 1965, the quota system was eliminated. In its place, variable ceilings were set annually for immigrants from North and South America and from the rest of the world. By 1991, the United States was accepting more immigrants and refugees than all other countries combined: about 700,000 each year, about 140,000 of them being refugees. Most now come from Asia, Latin America, and the Middle East.

The 1990 Census counted over 7 million Asian Americans (doubling the 1980 number), about 22 million Latino people (a 50-percent increase over 1980), about 2 million Native Americans, including Inuits and Aleuts (a 25-percent increase in ten years), and about 30 million African Americans (a very slight increase). Whites constitute 80% of the population and number about 200 million (a 3-percent decline). The predictions about the changing demographics of the United States are coming to fruition. It is expected that the Asian population will increase tenfold and Latinos threefold in the next fifty years and that by 2070 Caucasians will probably be a minority. It is all the more important, therefore, that children's literature reflect as many hues, backgrounds, and cultures as possible, so as to provide both mirrors and windows for young people as well as for adults.

DISCUSSION OF CHILDREN'S BOOKS

This chapter looks primarily at works of fiction. Nonfiction abounds, and it is important for children to read it, but its size and scope are too enormous to be confined to one chapter. Indeed, the fiction is so extensive as to permit only a sampling to be reviewed here. The intent is to provide a format and frame for the reader to continue to critically examine the literature and to make constructive judgments.

Folktales

The realm of oral literature is rich and wide. Until recently, libraries and classrooms have had unbalanced collections of folklore, with little or no indication of the existence of sources other than Europe. As a result, children of all races have been deprived of the imaginative, colorful, and rich heritage derived from Asia, Africa, and North and South America. They have remained ignorant of the interrelationships throughout all folk literature, the universality of many of the themes of folk tales and myths, and the effect of societies and cultures upon one another. As a result of increased insight, libraries and classrooms are being stocked with more of a variety. Children are beginning to ask about their own and others' backgrounds and to value diversity in a way that was not possible before. Many African, Asian, and European folktales are available, some with gorgeous illustrations. Brian Pinkney won a Caldecott honor for his illustrations of *The Dark Thirty,* African-American folktales compiled by Patricia McKissack. *The Orphan Boy,* Tololwa M. Mollel's retelling of a Tanzanian Maasai tale, is dramatically illustrated by Paul Morin. Anything by Leo and Diane Dillon or by Ed Young is a treat for the eyes and evidences a careful and respectful rendering of the culture, (e.g., in Katherine Paterson's *The Tale of the Mandarin Ducks,* a Japanese folktale, and *Yeh Shen: A Cinderella Story from China,* by Ai-Ling Louie).

Folktales appeal to readers of all ages, but careful selection is required. Some stories are too difficult for very young readers to handle by themselves. Others, because of their sexual content, are meant for adults only. Some adaptations, because of ignorance on the part of the reteller, do not accurately reflect the intent of the tales, and some are so watered down for young readers that they lose their special stylistic qualities and degenerate into little more than easy-to-read exercises.

Well-written folktales compiled for children are most effective and enjoyable when read aloud. Teachers do well to read these tales regularly to their classes as a steady diet. They can augment the curriculum in almost any subject area. Discussions about the differences and similarities among countries and peoples provide material for many research projects, lessons, and other classroom activities. Folktales are also an informative way of learning about customs and features of other lands.

More members of various ethnic groups indigenous to various locales have been setting down traditional tales as they have heard them so that their special qualities will be communicated in print. Writers outside a culture who value folk literature and take the time and effort to research the tales properly and convey them respectfully also play an important part in making these tales available to children. Joyce Cooper Arkhurst's *The Adventures of Spider: West African Folk Tales* introduces Spider, that mischievous, magical, amusing, amazing character. The author maintains a respectful attitude toward the stories and the customs described in them. The style of the writing is clear and smooth and abounds in cleverness and good humor. Spider's adventures are detailed in myth-like stories and in less complex folk tales. Most anthologies of African tales contain at least several episodes about Spider.

Verna Aardema is an acknowledged expert in African tales. *Bimwili and the Zimwi,* a Swahili story, and *Bringing the Rain to Kapiti Plain,* from Kenya, are two of her many lively and respectful retellings. Paul Goble's brilliant illustrations and renderings of Native-American stories are sanctioned by many native people. Among his many books are the *Iktomi* series of trickster tales from the Plains nations. They are lightheartedly told and precisely illustrated, using many details of tribal life and customs.

Explanatory tales abound in all cultures, many of them reflecting people's understanding of creation. Animals and magical creatures inhabit still other stories. Recognizing the different origins of the various tales, collectors and retellers have appropriately identified them according to the group from which they came. One such work is *Skunny Wundy: Seneca Indian Tales,* by Arthur C. Parker, himself a Seneca. The Seneca belong to the Iroquois Nation, and these tales convey the special qualities attributed to animals by the Iroquois.

Joseph Bruchac's *Iroquois Stories: Heroes and Heroines, Monsters and Magic* contains an invaluable introduction that helps readers understand the importance of respecting the sacredness of certain tales by not setting them into print. Bruchac's retellings are meant to be read aloud and are true to the oral tradition. Another of Bruchac's excellent collections, *Return of the Sun: Native American Tales from the Northeast Woodlands,* contains tales from such groups as the Onondaga, Abenaki, Oneida, Anishinabe, Seneca, and Penobscot.

Other collections describe Zuni ways (Kristina Rodanas's *Dragonfly's Tale* is one in which the kindness of two children earns a lasting reward for the entire village from the Corn Maidens), Papago and Pima myths, Paiute, Algonquin, Hopi, Kiowa, and many other individual tribal customs and beliefs. James Houston has retold some Inuit tales in a respectful manner. *Tikta'Liktak* is one such story, telling how the seal spirits help a young hunter survive.

Folklore belonging to Puerto Rico is not easily available in English. One anthology, edited by Kal Wagenheim, includes stories, some based on folk tales, by well-known Latino writers. This book, *Short Stories from Puerto Rico,* published in English by the Institute of Puerto Rican Culture, is a worthy purchase for any classroom or library. For younger children, *Juan Bobo and the Pig* is a folktale retold in English by Bernice Chardiet. Many more such books are needed. The Children's Book Press has been active in publishing a number of Latin American folktales with Spanish and English texts. Manlio Argueta's *The Magic Dogs of the Volcano: Los Perros Magicos de los Volcanes* is Salvadoran; *Atariba and Niguayona* by Harriet Rohmer and Jesus Guerrero Rea is indigenous Puerto Rican. Robert Baden has retold *And Sunday Makes Seven,* a story set in Costa Rica containing the universal folkloric elements of the clever and kindly poor man winning over the greedy rich man. Alma Flor Ada is one of the few authors of children's literature with a Latino perspective. She was born in Cuba and lived in Spain and Peru before settling in California. Her focus on action rather than description and her communication of the values and qualities of the culture makes her books notable. *The Gold Coin* tells of a man who is twisted in body and spirit until he is transformed by honest hard work and caring, decent people. While the tale is not necessarily confined to Central American people, it conveys the flavor of the culture and the setting. This is her first English publication.

Chinese folk and fairy tales are better represented in children's books than those of other Asian populations. *Yeh-Shen: A Cinderella Story from China,* retold by Ai-Ling Louie, beautifully introduces this forerunner of the European versions of *Cinderella.* Diane Wolkstein respectfully retells the story of the moon goddess in *White Wave.* In both books, the illustrations heighten the impact of the story. *The Fourth Question,* retold by Rosalind C. Wang, demonstrates the virtues of loyalty to one's word and kindness to strangers. For older readers, Lawrence Yep's *The Rainbow People* and *Tongues of Jade* offer brilliant insights into the beliefs and culture of Chinese Americans.

Some Japanese folktales are being published. Besides Paterson's *The Tale of the Mandarin Ducks, The Girl Who Loved Caterpillars* by Jean Merrill, is an interesting retelling of a twelfth-century story in which a young girl is decidedly not bound by stereotypical expectations. The happy ending is not that she gets married and lives happily ever after.

Other Asian sources include *Sir Whong and the Golden Pig,* a retelling of a Korean trickster tale by Oki S. Han. *The Brocaded Slipper and Other Vietnamese Tales,* by Lynette Dyer Vuong, provides a sampling of five fairy tales from Vietnam akin to Cinderella, Thumbelina, Rip Van Winkle, the Frog Prince, and the

Goose Girl. *Nine-in-One, Grr! Grr!,* by Blia Xiong (adapted by Cathy Spagnoli), is a Hmong tale explaining why the world is not overrun by tigers.

Awarding the Nobel Prize for literature to Isaac Bashevis Singer, who wrote in Yiddish, reflected the quality of books including the folklore and flavor of the Jewish population. Singer's *The Power of Light: Eight Stories for Hannukah* is one of many collections of exquisitely told tales of miracles, realities, and, above all, people Singer created from his store of Jewish oral tradition and from his own imagination. Marilyn Hirsch has retold a story that communicates Orthodox Jewish values in *Joseph Who Loved the Sabbath.* It demonstrates the power of diligence and piety over avarice and trickery and the importance of the sabbath, the holiest of days in the Jewish calendar. Howard Schwartz and Barbara Rush have compiled *The Diamond Tree: Jewish Tales from Around the World,* an unusual multicultural collection of stories from such places as Iraq, Yemen, Morocco, and Babylon, as well as eastern Europe.

Collections of folk tales from various sources can help fill in the gaps when tales from some groups are underrepresented. Virginia Hamilton's *The Dark Way* offers the opportunity to sample tales from Ireland, Kenya, India, Italy, Greece, and Haiti, among others. The annotated bibliography and the lists of the individual heritages contain more titles and examples of stories from Iceland, India, Norway, Italy, Russia, and other places.

Try This

Find and compare folktales from different countries that contain the following elements:

1. A simpleton who wins out over his or her smarter siblings
2. A beast who is transformed into a prince or princess
3. A hero who is a trickster
4. A series of three tasks required for the hero (male or female) to win a prize
5. A child abandoned at birth who grows up to become the ruler of a country

Discuss the implications of your findings.

Poetry

Poetry anthologies have become somewhat more inclusive and contemporary in their selections, and a number of writers have set their stories for young readers in verse. *Through Our Eyes,* collected by Lee Bennett Hopkins, represents children of many cultures and races and includes experiences of children growing up in the 1990s. Many parts of the world are represented in a wide-ranging collection of poets and poetry, *Life Doesn't Frighten Me at All,* by John Agard. An interesting multicultural, multinational compilation is bound together by the theme of time in Ruth Gordon's *Time Is the Longest Distance. This Same Sky: A Collection of Poems from Around the World,* compiled by Naomi Shihab Nye, demonstrates the commonality of emotions of all people. A map shows readers where the poems originated.

Arnold Adoff's poetry includes *All the Colors of the Race,* which honors the feelings and perceptions of a biracial child; and *In for Winter, Out for Spring,* a joyful portrait of an African-American family over the course of a year. Eloise Greenfield and Lucille Clifton consistently provide poetry that touches the heart and provides accurate portraits of African-American children and their families. Greenfield's *Under the Sunday Tree,* set in the Bahamas, reflects a universal view of childhood. Her *Honey, I Love and Other Love Poems* is a palpable celebration of African-American beauty and interaction. Clifton's recently reissued series of books about Everett Anderson sensitively and poetically convey life issues every child faces.

Lulu Delacre has captured Latin American rhythm and verse in her collections of games and songs, among them *Arroz con Leche.* Demi has selected and beautifully illustrated a collection of Japanese poems about the seasons, called *In the Eyes of the Cat.* However, more books of poetry representing Asian cultures, a wider variety of European heritages, and more Latino traditions are needed. Poetry should be included as part of many story hours and readalouds. Ashley Bryan, a talented artist, writer, and story teller, includes poetry as a regular feature of his presentations and persuades many hundreds of children, teachers, and librarians to embrace more poetry.

Nonfiction

What kind of information are children receiving about themselves and people different from them? Although units on Native Americans and African Americans are common from elementary grades through college, not every classroom uses a variety of materials beyond conventional texts so as to convey an accurate notion of the history and diversity of these peoples. Rey Mickinock, author and member of the Ojibwa nation, points out that even talented illustrators include inaccuracies in their pictures. They dress characters in inappropriate and incorrect costumes and mix tribal characteristics. He describes many errors, oversights, and misconceptions conveyed to the young reading public by authors and illustrators ignorant of such details. This is true of all heritages. Japanese people are shown eating with Chinese-style chopsticks, a supposedly Jewish bakery is shown with bread in its window during Passover, animals in Alaska that inhabit vastly different regions of the state are shown together.

Multicultural studies are becoming more prevalent in elementary and middle school curriculums. Teachers and librarians are seeing to it that children are exposed to many cultures represented in a wide variety of genres by people with different perspectives. It is important to engage children in research, critical thinking, and awareness of differences so that they will be prepared to live in an increasingly multicultural society.

Some authors who can help in this endeavor are Milton Meltzer, Russell Freedman, Walter Dean Myers, James Haskins, and Patricia and Frederick McKissack. Their biographies and histories help young readers to organize information, become aware of the special contributions of people from different cultures and heritages, learn facts that have been suppressed by textbooks, and appreciate the special part each group played in the building of American society. Books such as *Black Music in America,* by Haskins; the entire "Great African Americans" series of biographies by the McKissacks; illustrated histories like *Buffalo Hunt,* by Freedman; and historical commentary such as *The Chinese Americans, The Black Americans, Hispanic Americans,* and *All Times, All Peoples: A World History of Slavery,* as well as such biographies as *Mary McLeod Bethune,* by Meltzer, all help to reveal history and illuminate the present. Laurence Yep's memoir of his childhood, *The Lost Garden,* effectively informs readers about Chinese Americans and their culture in a personalized, immediate fashion.

Younger children, too, can begin to appreciate and understand diversity and locate the universals of human experience. Picture books such as *Talking Walls,* by Mary Burns Knight, and *Bread Bread Bread,* by Ann Morris, take simple themes and explore them through a multicultural and international filter. Both books, and others of this sort, are well illustrated and entertainingly and informatively convey images of one world and its many customs.

Fiction

In fiction for the older child, more varied protagonists are appearing. Moreover, there is a greater sense of this country's multiethnic nature. Although many gains have been made, more are needed. Hardly any authors except Nicolasa Mohr and Gary Soto are writing novels about the Latino population. Mohr's stories of life in New York City's barrio, exemplified in *Going Home* and *Felita,* provide strong portraits of Puerto Ricans living in two worlds, making constant adjustments to the conflicts between their heritage and the exigencies of daily life in a sometimes hostile environment. Soto's *Taking Sides* deals with the pressures in the life of a Mexican-American adolescent after he moves from a San Francisco barrio to a suburban town. He must decide what he will do when his new school team competes against his old one in basketball. The internal conflict is well depicted, and his decision is good. Ernesto T. Bethancourt's *The Me inside of Me* emphasizes the importance of appreciating the major character's Mexican-American heritage. Lulu Delacre's picture book, *Vejigante Masquerader,* conveys the joyousness of the *carnaval* celebration in Ponce, Puerto Rico. Unfortunately, there is not enough quality fiction available to reflect the Latino population.

Asian Americans are represented more by their folklore than by contemporary fiction. A notable exception is Paul Yee's *Tales from Gold Mountain: Stories of the Chinese in the New World,* which tells of Chinese immigrants to the New World, which includes all of North America. A sense of ironic justice pervades the stories, and they unfailingly reflect the hardships and challenges the immigrants endured. The sense of tradition, including respect for religion; the work ethic; and the value of loyalty to family, friends, and one's word, is strong and authentic. Lawrence Yep's works, such as *Child of the Owl, Sea Glass,* and *The Star Fisher,* also reflect contemporary realistic fiction about Chinese Americans.

Other than books revealing the painful period when Japanese Americans were interned in camps (these books are mentioned in the chapter on War and Peace), little fiction can be found about contemporary Japanese Americans. *How My Parents Learned to Eat,* by Ina R. Friedman, is a light-hearted account for young children about how two people very much in love with each other struggle to learn each other's ways. The story, which involves a Japanese woman and an American man, is set in Japan. Another story for this age level is *Aki and the Fox*, by Akiko Hayashi. The simple story line uses a train ride taken by Aki to see her grandmother as the backdrop for displaying a Japanese setting. Allen Say's work, notably *The Bicycle Man*, provides realistic and respectful portraits of real people engaging in real activities. From Yoshiko Uchida, probably the leading contemporary author of fiction about Japanese Americans for the 9- to 12-year-old reader, came *A Jar of Dreams, The Best Bad Thing*, and *The Happiest Ending*, which describe a Japanese-American family's life and interactions. They provide a potent example of how the younger generation learns to value their heritage.

Only a few Cambodian, Vietnamese, Thai, Laotian, or Hmong people appear in novels for young readers. To say that Asian-American populations are sorely underrepresented in fiction would be to grossly understate the case. This area in children's literature needs new authors and illustrators. The same is true of Arabian Americans and other peoples of the Middle East. Elsa Marston Harik points out in her article, "The Mid East in Fiction for Young Readers," that while there are several books about Israel and many books about Jewish Americans, there are hardly any about any of the other populations and cultures in and from that part of the world.

African Americans have fared better in recent years; they appear in many meritorious works. A prolific group of African-American writers continues to contribute quality fiction for all age levels. They include Virginia Hamilton, Walter Dean Myers, Julius Lester, Lucille Clifton, Joyce Hansen, Angela Johnson, Irene Smalls-Hector, Eleanora Tate, Mildred Taylor, Mildred Pitts Walter, Sharon Bell Mathis, Rosa Guy, Patricia McKissack, and Faith Ringgold.

For younger readers, *Uncle Jed's Barbershop*, by Margaree King Mitchell, with superb illustrations by James Ransome, tells the story of Sarah Jean's favorite relative, Uncle Jedediah Johnson, her granddaddy's brother. He is an itinerant barber whose life dream is to own his own shop. The family, which lives in the South during the Depression, is part of a larger African-American community. Although he is frugal and saves money regularly, Uncle Jed has to postpone buying his shop because he helps Sarah Jean's family pay for her emergency surgery. After he has accumulated more money, the banks fail and his money is lost again. Finally, at age 79, he opens his shop and everyone celebrates with him. Each of the characters connects visually and emotionally with the others; the bond is plain to see. James Ransome's father always aspired to have his own barber shop and achieved his dream late in his life, so the story could have been his as well.

Also for the younger reader, artist and author Faith Ringgold's *Tar Beach* provides a good story about an African-American family. The setting is New York City in the 1930s. The illustrations bring to life the rich fantasies the young protagonist, Cassie, creates, and information emerges about both family and African-American history. Cassie is also the name of the protagonist in Mildred Taylor's series of books for older children about the Logan family. In Depression years in Mississippi, the family serves as an example of strength in their community. In addition to being vivid, swift-moving stories, the books (*Song of the Trees, Roll of Thunder, Hear My Cry, Let the Circle Be Unbroken, The Friendship, Mississippi Bridge*, and *The Road to Memphis*) help overcome stereotypic thinking about African Americans. They also serve as strong portraits of an era and setting that may have been reported differently in history books.

Virginia Hamilton's portraits in such books as *The House of Dies Drear; M.C. Higgins, the Great; Cousins; Sweet Whispers; Brother Rush;* and *Zeely* (to mention but a few) also serve to show the richness of character and the multidimensional aspects of African Americans. Walter Dean Myers is another African-American writer who helps readers transcend stereotypes. His settings are usually urban, and his characters are often young people in difficult circumstances. *Motown and Didi: A Love Story* and *Scorpions* (see War and Peace) are among the many books in which he tells complex stories that hold readers' attention while at the same time unveiling important social issues.

Immigrants from eastern Europe can be found in a number of books. Much fiction describes the sometimes harrowing trip across the ocean, often accompanied by descriptions of the abuses of Ellis Island. In *Letters from Rifka,* Karen Hesse accurately conveys the anguish of family members when one child is sent back to Russia because she has contracted ringworm. Like many immigrants, this family is fleeing persecution and views America as the golden paradise. In contrast, Roslyn Bresnick-Perry's *Leaving for America* focuses on the pain of leaving the old country and family to face an unknown future in the new land. *Land of Hope,* by Joan Lowery Nixon, features three young women from different religious backgrounds and countries who meet on the ship to Ellis Island and whose families look forward to a better life in the New World.

More books have been published about Jews and the Jewish immigrant experience than about other European heritages such as Irish, Polish, Italian, or Scandinavian, although some books can be found that exemplify each of these groups (see listings in the Bibliography). It is important to affirm the diversity within every group so as to avoid stereotypes. It is not difficult to find examples of Jews who are secular, religious, traditional, revolutionary, urban, rural, rich, or poor. Books with Jewish characters also run the gamut from historical reflections to novels set in modern times.

Barbara Cohen's *The Christmas Revolution* exposes a difficult issue for American Jews and other people who do not practice Christianity. In this story, twins Emily and Sally attend a predominantly Christian elementary school. They have never given much thought to their Judaism or to what it means to practice other people's rituals until one year when Simeon, an Orthodox classmate, refuses to participate in the Christmas festivities. Emily realizes that she too has always felt uncomfortable singing carols and drawing Santas, and she decides to go along with Simeon's boycott. Sally has a solo in the Winter Festival, however, and she feels differently. When the school Christmas tree is knocked down, Emily and Simeon are blamed. Emily and Sally's best friends ostracize them and behave with unmerciful cruelty until the real culprits are discovered. At the end, the sisters invite their friends to their family Hannukah party. Adults may wish to raise such questions (if young readers do not think of them themselves) as why the burden of understanding is placed on the Jewish children, why no adults intervene on their behalf, and why scapegoating is tolerated in the school environment, as well as what the place is of separation of church and state.

Children can compare religious or cultural practices; critique books according to the criteria listed in this chapter; do research on contemporary groups; examine the causes of bigotry; and make recommendations for eliminating racial, cultural, and religious bias. With the current availability of materials about many different people and with an increasingly affirming societal attitude toward diversity, caring adults will be able to provide children with the basis for healthful and constructive attitudes toward themselves and others.

REFERENCES

Heritage

Abel, M. B. "American Indian Life as Portrayed in Children's Literature." *Elementary English* 50 (Feb. 1973): 202–208. One of the earliest historical overviews of the variety of children's books concerning Native Americans, this article points out the poor quality of most illustrations.

Ada, A. F. and Zubizarreta, R. *Language Arts through Children's Literature.* Children's Press, 1989. A teacher's guide to creating a multicultural language arts program through children's literature. Activities for developing oral, written, and artistic development by using multicultural and bilingual books from *Children's Book Press* are explored.

Allen, A. A. *Library Services for Hispanic Children.* Oryx, 1987. Lists of valuable references for finding materials for the Spanish-speaking population and books for children that contain Latino characters or culture.

Anderson/Sankofa, D. A. *Kwanzaa: An Everyday Resource and Instructional Guide.* Gumbs & Thomas, 1992. A detailed and sequential approach to learning about Kwanzaa. The introduction is followed by two units of activities.

Anti-Defamation League of B'nai B'rith. "What to Tell Your Child about Prejudice and Discrimination." ADL and National Parent Teacher Association, 1989. This brief pamphlet contains information for responding to children's questions and comments on prejudice and noting how children learn prejudice.

Arnez, N. N. "An Annotated Bibliography of Selected Non-Racist Books for Black Children." *Negro Educational Review* 32 (July–October 1981). Reports that books by black authors are more likely to describe African-American characters in vivid and genuine fashion than those by white authors. Recommends that black parents purchase and encourage the reading of books by authors of their heritage. Supplies an annotated list of seventeen good African-American children books.

Asian American Children's Book Project. "How Children's Books Distort the Asian American Image." *Bridge* 4 (July 1976): 5–7. Including criteria for analyzing books on Asian Americans, this article points out stereotypes, myths, and misrepresentations.

Au, K. H. *Literacy Instruction in Multicultural Settings.* HBJ, 1993. Methods for improving reading and writing among students of diverse backgrounds from kindergarten through high school. Describes cultural and linguistic differences, providing information not only for bilingual classrooms but also for students of Native-American, African-American, Asian-American, and Latin-American heritage.

Banks, J. A. *An Introduction to Multicultural Education.* Allyn and Bacon, 1994. This definitive text includes definitions, a historical perspective, and a theoretical structure for multicultural education.

Banks, J. A. "Multicultural Literacy and Curriculum Reform." *Education Horizons* 69 (Spring 1991): 135–140. Recognizes the strong need for curriculum reform to incorporate multiculturalism. Discusses controversial issues such as the curricular canon and special interest groups. Differentiates between cultural and multicultural literacy.

Banks, J. A. *Multiethnic Education: Theory and Practice,* 3rd ed. Allyn and Bacon, 1994. Focusing on teaching strategies and curriculum, this volume contains a storehouse of information on how to incorporate ethnicity into the curriculum.

Barry, A. L. "Teaching Reading in a Multicultural Framework." *Reading Horizons* 31 (1990): 39–48. A general overview of the "why, when and how" of choosing multicultural literature. Presents a critical look at basal readers and offers some alternatives for classrooms, such as culturally diverse trade books.

Beilke, P. F., and Sciara, F. J. *Selecting Materials for and about Hispanic and East Asian Children and Young People.* Shoe String, 1986. Recommends that generic terms such as "Hispanic American" be avoided when possible for the more specific, such as "Mexican American," "Cuban American," or the like. Good discussion of criteria to avoid stereotyping and promote authenticity.

Berkman, P., Pearce, A., and Baxter, E. "Crossing the Pacific: Books about Japan and Japanese-Americans." *The Children's Book Bag* 1 (1993). A diverse annotated book list is presented, including picture books, as well as beginner, intermediate, and advanced reading lists.

Bigelow, B. "Once upon a Genocide . . . A Review of Christopher Columbus in Children's Literature." *Rethinking Schools* 5 (Oct./Nov. 1990): 1, 7–9, 12. An extensive examination of biographies of Christopher Columbus, particularly in light of the Native-American experience.

Boehnen, E., and Kruse, G. M. *Multicultural Children's and Young Adult Literature.* University of Wisconsin: Coop Children's Book Center, 1988. An annotated listing of books that include people of color. Themes such as "seasons and celebrations" and "issues in today's world" are included.

Bracken, J., Wigutoff, S., and Baker, I. *Books for Today's Young Readers: An Annotated Bibliography of Recommended Fiction for Ages 10–14.* Feminist Press, 1981. Descriptions and analyses of books for older readers. Gender, ethnicity, acculturation and racism, peer friendships, and special needs are among the categories specified. Helpful discussion and format.

Brown, D. *Bury My Heart at Wounded Knee.* Holt, 1971. History of United States relations with Native Americans written from a point of view sympathetic to the indigenous people. Shocking details of atrocities, lies, and betrayals on the part of the United States.

Bruner, K. E. "Stereotypes in Juvenile Historical Fiction." *School Library Journal* 35 (Spring 1988): 124–125. Outlines damaging stereotypes in many "classics" of children's literature, with emphasis on African-American and Native-American images.

Bryan, A. "On Poetry and Black American Poets." *Horn Book Magazine* 55 (Feb. 1979): 42–49. Black poets are quoted to illustrate the point that in describing the multifaceted black experience in this nation they speak not only to black Americans but to all humanity. Poetry crosses the barriers of age, sex, and race, allowing the dreams, joys, and pains of one person, one people to be felt by all people.

Caduto, M. J., and Bruchac, J. *Keepers of the Animals.* Illus. by J. Kahionhes. Fulcrum 1991. Contains Native-American animal stories and wildlife activities on the subjects of creation, celebration, vision, and survival. Includes maps showing cultural and tribal locations in North America.

Cai, M. "A Balanced View of Acculturation: Comments on Lawrence Yep's Three Novels." *Children's Literature in Education* 23 (June 1992): 107–118. Three novels of Lawrence Yep are provided as models for respectfully portraying an ethnic group, in this case Chinese Americans. Stresses the need for literature to undo harmful stereotypes.

Celebrating the Dream. New York Public Library Office of Young Adult Services, 1990. An annotated listing of young adult books celebrating African-American heritage on the topics of fiction, art, photography, music, dance, film, theater, poetry, sports, and life in the United States, Africa, and South Africa.

Chan, I. "The Use of Folktales in the Development of Multicultural Lit. for Children." *TESL-Talk* 15 (Winter-Spring 1984): 19-28. Discusses the rationale for children's multicultural literature. Emphasizes ensuring authenticity of folktales and other children's stories about different heritages.

Chang, M. A. "The Chinese Experience: China and Chinese-Americans in Children's Literature." *The Children's Book Bag* 1 (1992). Contains an annotated bibliography on children's books portraying authentic Chinese experiences.

Charles, J. "Celebrating the Diversity of American Indian Literature." *The ALAN Review* 18 (Spring 1991): 4-8. Confirms the importance of diversity in Native-American literature. Also included are themes surrounding Native-American literature such as identity formation, discrimination, mixed-blood ancestry, and reaffirmation of American Indian cultural and spiritual systems.

Children's Literature Association Quarterly 16 (Summer 1991). This entire issue focuses on cross-culturalism. Specific articles include "Tell Him about Vietnam: Vietnamese-Americans in Contemporary American Children's Literature," by J. Susina.

Clark, R., and Heller, C. E. "Quilt Connections." *Teaching Tolerance* 2 (Spring 1993): 38-45. Explains how the versatile theme of quilting can be used to teach history, build intergenerational and interdependent relations, and promote ethnicity in the classroom.

Council on Interracial Books for Children. *Bulletin* 14 (Nos. 1 and 2, 1983). Special issue on Puerto Ricans in children's literature and history texts: a ten-year update.) Contains articles by Sonia Nieto, Sharon Wigutoff, Iris Santos-Rivera, Jan Hernandez-Cruz, Analda Colon-Munoz, and others critiquing material on Puerto Rico and Puerto Ricans. Includes criteria and analyses.

Council on Interracial Books for Children. *Guidelines for Selecting Biasfree Textbooks and Storybooks.* The Council, 1980. A useful manual for teaching children about bias in the books they read.

Cox, J., and Wallis, B. S. "Books for the Cajun Child—Lagniappe or a Little Something Extra for Multicultural Teaching." *Reading Teacher* 36 (Dec. 1982): 263-266. A valuable resource not only for teachers in the French-speaking Acadian community but also for teachers who care that their children be exposed to as many cultures as possible.

Deane, P. "Black Characters in Children's Fiction Series Since 1968." *Journal of Negro Education,* Vol. 58, No. 2, 1989, pp. 153-162. A look at the role of African Americans within the popular Bobbsey Twins, Nancy Drew, Hardy Boys, and Sweet Valley High series. The author describes positive trends, including the attempt to portray characters realistically with unique personalities.

Deloria, V., Jr., *Custer Died for Your Sins.* Macmillan, 1969. Controversial, personal, and impressive. Deloria is a Standing Rock Sioux. His opinions and interpretations of current and past events compel the reader to raise many questions.

Feder-Feitel, L., et al. "How Teachers Can Help Stop Racism." In *Creative Classroom,* Children's Television Workshop, 1992. A diverse collection of lesson plans (kindergarten to grade six) designed to combat racism and resolve conflicts.

Fisher, L. "All Chiefs, No Indians: What Children's Books Say about American Indians," *Elementary English* 51 (Feb. 1974): 185-189. An excellent analysis of the clichés, stereotypes, and distortions presented in children's books that deal with Native Americans. Fisher recommends a number of books that she judges to be better than most in fostering healthy attitudes in the reader.

Fuchs, L. "Gold from the South: Hispanic Literature." Paper presented at the Annual Meeting of the National Council of Teachers of English, March 14-16, 1991. Describes the serious problem of how frequently Latino immigrants drop their cultural heritage because of the extreme prejudice and discrimination against them. The author finds a "woeful ignorance" of Latin American life. Discusses the important and relevant role of children's stories in passing culture down.

Galda, L., and Cox, S. "Books for Cross-Cultural Understanding." *The Reading Teacher* 44 (April 1991): 580-587. Detailed annotations of children's literature representing many heritages, organized by geographic location or cultural identity. The author suggests systematic study and integration into "focus units."

Gast, D. K. "The Dawning of the Age of Aquarius for Multiethnic Children's Literature." *Elementary English* 47 (May 1970): 661-665. An influential article listing different approaches to beware of in children's books dealing with the black experience.

Global Beat: A List of Multicultural Books for Teenagers. New York Public Library Office of Young Adult Services, 1992. An extensive annotated listing of multicultural and multinational books for young adults.

Gould, S. J., and King, D. "Exploring the Intellectual and Cultural Roots of Racism and Antisemitism." *Facing History and Ourselves News,* Spring 1992. Traces the roots of "biological determinism" and the destructive consequences of beliefs that some races are superior to others.

Hamilton, V. "Ah, Sweet Rememory." *Horn Book Magazine* 57 (Dec. 1981): 633-640. The award-winning author discusses the way her heritage has informed her fiction. All her books are influenced by the journey of black people through America, "the dream of freedom tantalizingly out of reach."

Hannigan, T. P. "Traits, Attitudes, and Skills That Are Related to Intercultural Effectiveness and Their Implications for Cross-Cultural Training: A Review of the Literature." *International Journal of Intercultural Relations* 14 (1990): 89-111. A scholarly look at important criteria for a cross-cultural study of literature. These include the issues of adjustment, adaption, acculturation, assimilation, and effectiveness.

Harik, E. M. "The Mid East in Fiction for Young Readers." *Children's Reading Round Table Bulletin,* Jan-Feb, 1991, pp. 3-7. The author shares her finding that young readers are not being offered a balance of both Arab and Israeli images and information. A listing of children's books is given at the end.

Harris, V. J. "Multicultural Curriculum: African American Children's Literature." *Young Children* 46 (Jan. 1991): 37-44. In the context of early childhood education, the author presents the need for authentic African-American children's literature. She applauds the growing national social consciousness.

Harris, V. J., ed. *Teaching Multicultural Literature in Grades K-8.* Christopher-Gordon, 1992. A compilation of articles, each containing a discussion of the current status of a heritage within children's literature and suggested criteria for choosing and presenting quality books.

Hearne, B. "Respect the Source: Reducing Cultural Chaos in Picture Books, Parts 1 & 2." *School Library Journal* 39 (Jul. & Aug. 1993): 22-27, 33-37. This two-part lucid, even-handed presentation of the issues involved in recreating folklore for children includes discussions of authenticity, accuracy, scholarship, quality of illustrations, feminist concerns, and what constitutes folklore. Hearne urges authors to cite sources and provide commentary via source notes.

Heltshe, M. A. *Multicultural Explorations: Joyous Journeys with Books.* Teacher Ideas Press, 1991. Thorough units of study on specific areas such as Hawaii, Japan, Kenya, Brazil, and Australia with the purpose of providing elementary students with an increased knowledge of geography and multicultural experiences.

Henderson, E. B. "The Black Athlete: Emergence and Arrival." *International Library of Negro Life and History.* Association for the Study of Negro Life and History, 1968, pp.

70-83. A clarifying perspective on Jackie Robinson, discrediting myths of his passivity and portraying him as a fierce competitor with a determined, defiant spirit.

Hudson, W., and Hudson, C. W., eds. *Black History Activity and Enrichment Handbook.* Just Us Books, 1990. Concisely presents ideas, activities, and games on African-American history and culture. Themes include ancient African kingdoms, slavery, civil rights, and combating racism.

Hughes, L., Meltzer, M., and Lincoln, C. E. *A Pictorial History of Black Americans,* 5th rev. ed. Illus. with photos and historical reproductions. Crown, 1983. Organized in chronological order, beginning in 1619, this remarkable compendium includes a look at slavery and its aftermath. It brings the reader up to the early 1980s—a treasure trove of information and insights.

Jenkins, E. C., and Austin, M. C. *Literature for Children about Asians and Asian Americans.* Greenwood, 1987. Materials include folk and contemporary literature from China, Japan, Korea, and Southeast Asia. The criteria for selection serve as an excellent guide. Some of the books on the list are not authentic or respectful. Nevertheless, with some monitoring of the materials, this reference is a helpful resource.

Johnson, D. *Telling Tales.* Greenwood, 1990. Examines three critical and historical contributions to African-American children's literature. Emphasizes the need for authors to be African Americans or have extensive knowledge and appreciation for African-American history and culture.

Jones, M., Jr. "It's a Not So Small World." *Newsweek,* Sept. 9, 1991, pp. 64-65. Examines the impact of multiculturalism in education on children's books. Affirms that all children need to see themselves in books or have occasion to learn about a different ethnic group in an enjoyable manner.

Journal of Negro Education 59 (Fall 1990). This issue contains several articles by such scholars as V. Harris and R. S. Bishop emphasizing the need for multicultural children's literature (particularly African American) as a tool for empowerment.

Kalisa, B. G. "Africa in Picture Books: Portrait or Preconception." *School Library Journal* 36 (Feb 1990): 36-37. Insightful criticisms of the portrayal of Africans in children's books published between 1960 and 1980. Misconceptions are revealed. A recommended list is provided of more positive and respectful books.

Kendall, F. E. *Diversity in the Classroom: A Multicultural Approach to the Education of Young Children.* Teachers College Press, 1983. Explains not only how to begin a multicultural program in the classroom but also how to extend these teachings into the family with strategies for parents to help combat racism.

King, E. W., Chipman, M., and Cruz-Janzen, M. *Educating Young Children in a Diverse Society.* Allyn and Bacon, 1994. Focusing on early childhood education, the authors demonstrate the importance of helping teachers of young children bring them a positive perspective on diversity. Combining theory with practice, the authors convey a personal perspective, as well as a scholarly approach to the issues.

Klein, B. T., ed. *Reference Encyclopedia of the American Indian,* 5th ed., vol. 1. Todd, 1990. A thorough listing of government agencies, museums, libraries, associations, courses, government publications, magazines, periodicals, and other resources on the Indians of North America. Several thousand entries are included in the extensive bibliography.

Kruse, G. M., and Horning, K. T. *Multicultural Lit for Children and Young Adults.* University of Wisconsin, Coop Children's Book Center, 1991. A thorough annotated bibliography that contains Native-American, Latin-American, African-American, and Asian-American children's literature.

Kuipers, B. J. *American Indian Reference Books for Children and Young Adults.* Libraries Unlimited, 1991. An extensive reference containing methods and materials for the study of Native Americans in the classroom. Includes an evaluative checklist, information on publishers, cross-curricular study, and an annotated bibliography of nonfiction, myths, and legends.

Ladd, J. "Global Education and Children's Literature." In *Children's Literature: Resource for the Classroom,* edited by M. K. Rudman. Christopher Gordon, 1993. Contains a section called "Teaching Through Themes Common to All Humans." Offers titles of books as well as activities.

Language Arts 70 (March 1993). This entire issue focuses on the theme of multiculturalism and the language arts. Selecting appropriate books, examining personal perspectives, and understanding the image of the child are discussed.

Larrick, N. "The All-White World of Children's Books." *Saturday Review,* Sept 11, 1965, pp. 63–85. A seminal article that was the first to present a powerful argument against stereotypes in children's books. The author helps the reader to recognize subtle negative implications in books and expresses hope that publishers will take heed.

Latimer, B. I., ed. *Starting out Right: Choosing Books about Black People for Young Children.* Wisconsin Department of Public Instruction, 1972. Presents sixteen criteria for books involving African Americans. Several chapters discuss the issues involved in books for children. The authors annotate more than 200 books according to their criteria. The authors suggest several ways of effecting change. Still useful despite its age.

Laurain, B. "Finding Inner Self through Native American Literature." *The Leaflet, Journal of the New England Association of Teachers of English* 91 (Spring 1992); 25–31. In an issue devoted entirely to teaching to confront racism, this article discusses the importance of language to help Native Americans find their own identities.

Library Trends 41 (Winter 1993). Includes an excellent article by K. P. Smith outlining the history of the concept of multiculturalism. An informative and provocative piece by K. E. Vandergrift uses feminist theory to examine multicultural literature for young people. C. J. Collins supports African-American literature as a tool for change in the lives of young adult African Americans; and A. B. Hirschfelder stresses the importance of accuracy and authenticity in children's books about Native Americans.

Lindgren, M. V. *The Multicolored Mirror: Cultural Substance in Lit for Children and Young Adults.* HighSmith, 1991. Selected writings on multiculturalism from the eighth children's and young adult literature conference in 1991, cosponsored by the University of Wisconsin and the Madison School of Education. Includes such authors as Kathleen T. Horning, Ginny Moore Kruse, Walter Dean Myers, Elizabeth Fitzgerald Howard, and Rudine Sims Bishop.

Loer, S. "A Reading Rainbow." *The Boston Globe,* Nov. 30, 1992. Reaffirms the view that children's literature should reflect all heritages and cultures. Emphasis is placed on interdependence among all groups. Includes an annotated bibliography.

MacCann, D. "Multicultural Books and Interdisciplinary Inquiries." *The Lion and the Unicorn* 16 (June 1992): 43–56. Explains how multicultural literature is one attempt to bring equity and social justice into education by its interdisciplinary approach of "social history, pluralistic aesthetics, and antiracist librarianship."

MacCann, D., and Richard, O. "The Japanese Sensibility in Picture Books for Children." *Wilson Library Bulletin,* Oct. 1990, pp. 23–27. A unique look at authentic Japanese art in picture books and the aesthetic value it adds to the child's reading of the book. An interesting and informative history of this art is included.

MacCann, D., and Woodard, G. *Cultural Conformity in Books for Children.* Scarecrow, 1977. Discusses racism and stereotypes in children's literature. Includes excerpts from articles dealing with these subjects.

MacCann, D., and Woodard G., eds. *The Black American in Books for Children: Readings in Racism.* Scarecrow, 1985. Essays on racism by renowned authors and theorists on the African-American perspective. Subtopics include racism in twentieth-century fiction and biography, in contemporary picture books, and in publishing.

Manna, A. L., and Brodie, C. S. *Many Faces, Many Voices: Multicultural Literary Experiences for Youth.* Highsmith, 1992. For some years, the annual V. Hamilton conference has been devoted to promoting all heritages equally. This compilation of papers from previous conferences includes presentations on Appalachia, the Jewish-American experience in children literature, the African-American folktale, and the Latino identity struggle in this country.

Martinez, M., and Nash, M. F. "Talking about Children's Literature (Bookalogues)." *Language Arts* 67 (Oct. 1990): 599–606. Three questions addressing multicultural literature with answers by V. Harris, K. Short, and Yetta Goodman. An annotated bibliography of children's books is included.

May, J. P. "To Think Anew: Native American Literature and Children's Attitudes." *Reading Teacher* 36 (April 1983): 790–794. Discusses a course of study used with gifted fifth and sixth graders, using literature to help dispel negative impressions of Native Americans.

McCunn, R. L. "Chinese Americans: A Personal View." *School Library Journal* 34 (June–July 1988): 50–51. Stereotypes are explored, as well as the exclusion of Chinese Americans from many aspects of our society, including children's literature. The author warns that many of these stereotypes will remain unless more accurate, respectful, realistic contemporary literature becomes available.

Mickinock, R. "The Plight of the Native American." In *Issues in Children's Book Selection.* Bowker, 1973. The author, a member of the Ojibwa Nation, discusses and corrects the inaccuracies and misconceptions printed in many children's books. He recommends several books for their accuracy and usefulness.

Miller-Lachmann, L. *Our Family, Our Friends, Our World: An Annotated Guide to Significant Multicultural Books for Children and Teenagers.* Bowker, 1992. A critical source for multicultural books including native, African, Latino, European, Asian, and American heritages. Books for new immigrant groups from areas such as South and Central America, the Middle East, the Caribbean, and Eastern Asia are also explored. Literature ranges from preschool level to grade 12.

Multicultural Review 2 (March 1993). Articles such as "Good and Bad Books about Latino/a People and Culture for Young Readers," by Isabel Schon; "Selected African-American Bibliography," compiled by Glenderlyn Johnson; and "Selecting Books for and about Native Americans for Young People," compiled by Peter McDonald.

National Conference of Christians and Jews. *The Human Family* (formerly *Books for Brotherhood*). The Conference, 1992. An annual listing of books selected "on the basis of their contribution to the search for community in a pluralistic society."

Native Peoples 6 (Winter 1993). Aesthetically and authentically portrays the arts and lifestyles of Native Americans. In this issue, research on the Hopi is presented.

Nieto, S. *Affirming Diversity: The Sociopolitical Context of Multicultural Education.* Longman, 1992. One chapter, "Multicultural Education and School Reform," defines the characteristics of multicultural education as being antiracist, basic, important to all students, and pervasive, including education for social justice, education as process, and critical pedagogy.

Neito, S. "Self-Affirmation or Self-Destruction: The Image of Puerto Ricans in Children's Literature Written in English." In *Images and Identities: The Puerto Rican in Two World Contexts,* edited by Asela Rodriguez de Laguna. Transaction Books, 1987. An eye-opening account of the extreme paucity of Puerto Rican children's literature compared to the volume of children's literature available. Also explored are specific criteria to watch for in books, such as racism; sexism; and stereotypical physical features, settings, and language.

Norton, D. E. "Teaching Multicultural Literature in the Reading Curriculum," *The Reading Teacher* 44 (Sept. 1990): pp. 28–40. In using the Native American heritage as a model, the author presents a five-step sequenced approach to studying multicultural children's literature for middle school, high school, and college students.

O'Flaherty, W. D. *Other People's Myths.* Macmillan, 1988. Describes many types of myths, as well as their historical and cultural perspective and importance.

Pang, V. O., Colvin, C., Tran, M., and Barba, R. H. "Beyond Chopsticks and Dragons: Selecting Asian-American Literature for Children." *The Reading Teacher* 46 (Nov. 1992): 216–225. Recommends guidelines for evaluating the quality of Asian-American literature, including historical accuracy, positive and sensitive portrayal of characters, authentic illustrations, and a culturally pluralistic theme.

Perez-Selles, M. E., and Barra-Zuman, N. C. *Building Bridges of Learning and Understanding: A Collection of Classroom Activities on Puerto Rican Culture.* Regional Laboratory for Educational Improvement of the Northeast and Islands, New England Center for Equity Assistance, 1990. Offers curricular instruction and activities on Puerto Rican culture, including the island's history, geography, climate, migration, legends, and traditions, as well as information on the Taino.

Perry, T., and Fraser, J. W. *Freedom's Plow: Teaching in the Multicultural Classroom.* Routledge, 1993. A compilation of essays on strategies for designing multicultural curriculum by restructuring existing school curriculum.

Peterson, Bob. "Columbus and Native Issues in the Elementary Classroom." *Rethinking Schools Special Edition* (1991) 16–20. Discusses how to work with the Columbus curriculum to produce accurate information on Native Americans. Shows how a fifth grade class was able to break down many of the stereotypes of American Indians.

Pineiro de Riciera, F. *A Century of Puerto Rican Children's Literature.* Rio Piedras: University of Puerto Rico Press, 1987. A history of children's literature in Spanish in Puerto Rico from 1876 to 1978. Includes a discussion of folklore, poetry, and trends in the twentieth century and highlights certain illustrators who are fine artists.

Pugh, S. L., and Garcia, J. "Portraits in Black: Establishing African American Identity through Nonfiction Books." *Journal of Reading* 34 (Sept. 1990): 20–25. Affirms the need for multicultural curricula for all students and rationale for teaching from nonfiction tradebooks. Raises important questions about the unequal distribution of material across different occupations and suggests an agenda for future expansion in the arena of nonfiction for young readers.

Ramsey, P. G. "Beyond 'Ten Little Indians' and Turkeys: Alternative Approaches to Thanksgiving." *Young Children,* Sept. 1979, pp. 576–580. Traditions of feasts, harvests, and hunting are explored, with emphasis on similarities to and differences between Native and European Americans. Since to many Native Americans, Thanksgiving symbolizes the loss of land and freedom, suggestions are made for encouraging respectful language and appropriate, educationally sound activities.

Rasinski, T. V., and Padak, N. "Multicultural Learning through Children's Literature." *Language Arts* 67 (Oct. 1990): 576–580. Supports the curriculum model by James A. Banks for integrating multiculturalism into the curriculum. Shows how multicultural children's literature naturally fits.

Rochman, H. *Against Borders: Promoting Books for a Multicultural World.* American Library Association, 1993. The purpose of this book is to promote multiculturalism by using literature to explain or exemplify various aspects of culture, lifestyles, and beliefs. Junior and senior high students are the target audience.

Rollock, B. *Black Authors and Illustrators of Children's Books.* Garland, 1988. A biographical compilation of African-American authors and illustrators, complete with many photographs.

Rollock, B., ed. *The Black Experience in Children's Books,* New York Public Library, 1989. An extensive list of books relating to black people. Annotations are informative. The list is regularly updated.

Roney, R. C. "Multiethnicity in Children's Fiction." *Social Education* 50 (Oct. 1986): 464–470. Uses literature webs to teach multiethnicity. Included are activities for grades K-3 and 4-6, with sample webs and an extensive bibliography.

Rudman, M. K. "Multicultural Children's Literature: The Search for Universals." In *Children's Literature: Resource for the Classroom,* 2nd ed. Christopher Gordon, 1993. Discusses the responsibility to dispel stereotypes by identifying similarities among all peoples. Extensive annotated bibliography.

St. Clair, J. "Recreating Black Life in Children's Literature." *Interracial Books for Children Bulletin* 19 (1989): 7-11. A historical look at African-American children's literature concluding that all children have the right to unbiased images.

Schneider, E., Allen, N., and Walaszek, A. "Dispelling Prejudices with Multicultural Literature: A Developmental Perspective." Paper presented at the Massachusetts Chapter 1 Conference, Hyannis, May 14, 1992. Numerous activities for children ages three to eight for developing a sense of self, acknowledging others' differences, and eliminating prejudices.

Schon, I. *A Hispanic Heritage: Series II and III.* Scarecrow, 1988. The author is respected in the area of Latin-American history and culture in children's literature. Annotated lists of books spanning the K-12 curriculum are provided.

Schon, I. "Reading the World-Mexico." *Book Links,* March 1993, pp. 45-49. An annotated listing of high quality Mexican-American children's literature. Picture books, fiction, folklore, biographies, and informational books are noted. Also in this issue by the same author is "Classroom Connections—Latino Books." (pp. 50-53).

Shannon, G. "Making a Home of One's Own: The Young in Cross-Cultural Fiction." *English Journal* 77 (Sept. 1988): 14-19. Discusses the character of the "cross-cultural child" in four novels. Identifies four stages cross-cultural children go through in developing an identity, the ideal being self-respect.

Sims, R. *Shadow and Substance: Afro-American Experience in Contemporary Children's Fiction.* National Council of Teachers of English, 1982. A clear and persuasive consideration of 150 books of contemporary realistic fiction about African Americans, classifying them into four categories: social context, melting pot, reflections of African-American experience, and work by the image makers.

Sims, R. "Strong Black Girls: A Ten-Year-Old Responds to Fiction about Afro-Americans." *Journal of Research and Development in Education* 16 (1983): 21-28. An interesting look at African-American children's literature from a scholarly perspective, using a categorization system similar to that described in the author's *Shadow and Substance.* The article also includes an interview with a ten-year-old African-American girl which confirms the belief that children need to read about characters who share their experiences, values, aspirations, and above all, culture.

Slapin, B.; Seale, D.; and Gonzales, R. *How to Tell the Difference: A Checklist for Evaluating Native American Children's Books.* Oyate, 1989. Criteria for analyzing children's literature containing Native American references. This helpful list draws attention to examples of disrespectful language, stereotypical images, tokenism, historical distortions, and the roles of women, children, and elders in the community, to name a few.

Slapin, B. and Seale, D., eds. *Through Indian Eyes: The Native Experience in Books for Children.* New Society, 1992. A compilation of articles and poems, plus an annotated bibliography of children's books, that respectfully and authentically represents Native Americans. This work is a collaborative effort including the advice and knowledge of many native people across North America.

Stensland, A. L. *Literature by and about the American Indian.* National Council of Teachers of English, 1979. Describes guides for curriculum planning for teaching Native American literature. Includes an annotated bibliography.

Stover, L. "Exploring and Celebrating Cultural Diversity and Similarity through Young Adult Novels." *The ALAN Review,* Spring 1991, pp. 12–15. Cross-cultural studies that emphasize similarities, as well as differences, illuminate an understanding of others and foster self-awareness and introspection. Included is a bibliography.

Tanyzer, H., ed. *Reading, Children's Books, and Our Pluralistic Society.* International Reading Association and Children's Book Council, 1972. Although this monograph is more than 20 years old, the topics are still highly relevant, with many notable authors and critics such as Nancy Larrick, Virginia Hamilton, David Elkind, and Ruth Kearney Carlson.

Trousdale, A. M. "A Submission Theology for Black Americans: Religion and Social Action in Prize-Winning Children's Books about the Black Experience in America." *Research in the Teaching of English* 24 (May 1990): 117–140. Analyzes four award-winning children's books, three by white authors and one by a black author. Concludes that only *Roll of Thunder, Hear My Cry,* by the African-American author, avoids an inaccurate and demeaning portrayal of black culture and religion.

Tye, K. A., ed. *Global Education: From Thought to Action.* Association for Supervision and Curriculum Development, 1990. Part I presents the context of global education, and Part II contains ideas for the implementation.

Wagoner, S. A. "Mexican-Americans in Children's Literature since 1970." *Reading Teacher* 36 (Dec. 1982): 274–279. Concludes that much improvement is needed in literature about the Mexican American. Includes an annotated list of books that are, in general, recommended and includes specific comments on their quality of presentation.

Warren, J., and McKinnon, E. *Small World Celebrations.* Illus. by Marion Hopping Ekberg. Warren, 1988. Significant holidays celebrated by different heritages around the world, including Lei Day (Hawaiian), Diwali (Indian), Kwanzaa (African American), Winter Festival (Russian), and Chinese New Year. Suggestions for lessons on music, science, art, language arts, movement, and food.

Weatherford, J. *Indian Givers: How the Indians of the Americas Transformed the World.* Fawcett Columbine, 1988. The author, an anthropologist, details the impact of Native Americans on our society today. Medical, agricultural, ecological, and governmental contributions are explored. The sequel, *Native Roots* (1991) focuses on native North American peoples.

Wood, K. D., and Avett, S. G. "Bookalogues: Talking about Children's Literature." *Language Arts* 70 (Jan. 1993): 60–65. The theme is the positive effects of working together to improve racial relationships and self-esteem and to welcome diversity. An annotated bibliography (primary, intermediate, and advanced reading levels) reflects these qualities.

Yep, Lawrence. "The Ethnic Writer as Alien." *Bulletin of the Council on Interracial Books for Children* 10 (1979): 10-11. The author reflects on the influence of his heritage on his writing.

RESOURCES

Afro-American Cultural Foundation. 10 Fiske Place, Suite 204-206, Mt. Vernon, NY 10550. Works to improve the self-esteem of and attitudes toward African Americans through lectures, seminars, and workshops.

Afro-Hispanic Institute. 3306 Ross Pl., N.W., Washington, DC 20008. Promotes the study of African American–Latino literature and culture.

Amherst Educational Publishing. 30 Blue Hills Road, Amherst, MA 01002. Publishes multicultural curriculum materials, including a multicultural resource calendar.

Anti-Defamation League of B'nai B'rith. 823 United Nations Plaza, New York, NY 10017. Publishes materials about and advocates multicultural understanding.

Asia Media Publications. Greenshower Corp., 10937 Klingerman St., S. El Monte, CA 91733. Publishes a catalog of multicultural and multilingual children's books.

Asia Resource Center, P.O. Box 15275, Washington, DC 20003. Publishes and distributes books, videos, slideshows, and newsletters and provides guest lecturers on the peoples and cultures of Asia.

Asia Society, The. 725 Park Avenue, New York, NY 10021. Publishes *Japan through Children's Literature: A Critical Bibliography,* by Yakuki Makino, with a foreword by Betty M. Bullard.

Aspira of America. 1112 16th St., N.W., Washington, DC 20036. Works with Latino youth, primarily Puerto Ricans. Services include counseling, tutoring, college guidance, and cultural activities.

Association of Jewish Libraries c/o National Foundation for Jewish Culture, 330 Seventh Ave, 21st Floor, New York, NY 10001. Publishes "Jewish Children's Books Too Good to Miss: 1985-1990."

Children's Book Press. 6400 Hollis St., Suite 4, Emeryville, CA 94608. Publishes bilingual stories from Central and Latin America and books about Asians and African Americans.

Council for Indian Education. 517 Rimrock Road, Billings, MO 59102. "Dedicated to improving the education of Native American children." Publishes books and conducts inservice training for teachers.

Edit Cetera Co. 528 Belair Way, Nashville, TN 37215. Publishes *Black Images in Contemporary Children's Books,* by J. Lambert, an annotated bibliography of 100 recommended books.

Interracial Family Alliance. P.O. Box 16248, Houston, TX 77222. Promotes public support for and acceptance of interracial families through articles, videotapes, social activities, and workshops.

Interracial-Intercultural Pride. 1060 Tennessee St., San Francisco, CA 94107. Maintains a library and a speaker's bureau and publishes a bimonthly newsletter, *I-Pride,* to support interracial and intercultural families.

Mexican American Legal Defense and Education Fund. 28 Geary St., N.W., San Francisco, CA 94108. Legal services for Mexican Americans and other Latino groups in the areas of immigration, bilingual education, and employment.

National Association for Asian and Pacific American Education c/o ARC Assoc., 310 8th St., Suite 220, Oakland, CA 94607. Works to unify communities, promotes multicultural and bilingual education in the United States, holds workshops and support services.

National Association for Vietnamese American Education. 3206 Wynford Dr., Fairfax, VA 22031. An organization of educators promoting the education and welfare of Vietnamese Americans. Holds annual conference and publishes newsletter.

Native American Authors Distribution Project. The Greenfield Review Press, 2 Middle Grove Rd., P.O. Box 308, Greenfield Center, NY 12833. This 1990 Summer book list specializes in books by American Indian writers, with over 250 publications covering all genres.

Network of Educators' Committees on Central America. P.O. Box 43509, Washington, DC 20010-9509. A network of teachers throughout the country working for communication and understanding between North and Central American teachers and students. Some projects include *Caribbean Connections: Classroom Resources for Secondary Schools and Workshops on Teaching about Nicaragua and El Salvador.*

Praxis Publications. P.O. Box 9869, Madison, WI 53715. Publishes the *1989 Guide to Multicultural Resources,* which includes Asian, African, Latino and Native American resources.

Puerto Rican/Latino Educational Roundtable. Hunter College, 695 Park Ave., Room E-1434, New York, NY 10021. Provides services for Puerto Rican–Latino students within the New York Public School System. Bilingual education, adult literacy, and affirmative action are some of its goals.

Teaching Tolerance. 400 Washington Avenue, Montgomery, AL 36104. A semiannual magazine "dedicated to helping teachers promote intercultural understanding in the classroom." Free for teachers; to receive a copy, send a request on school stationery. Free curriculum kits are available upon principal's request.

Visions Foundation. 1538 9th St., N.W., Washington, DC 20001. Promotes understanding of African-American culture. Conducts programs on societal contributions of African Americans.

BIBLIOGRAPHY

If a book has a special focus, it is identified in brackets following the bibliographic entry. For a listing of titles arranged by specific heritage, write to the author at 224 Furcolo Hall, UMASS, Amherst, MA 01003.

Aardema, V. *Bimwili & the Zimwi.* Illus. by S. Meddaugh. Dial, 1985. (Ages 4–8.) [African/Tanzanian] Bimwili, a Swahili child, encounters a Zimwi, a devilish spirit who kidnaps her and forces her to sing while she is trapped inside his drum. Through her own wits and with some help from her family, she escapes and sends the Zimwi back to the sea from which he came. Family and communal life are background for the story.

Aardema, V. *Bringing the Rain to Kapiti Plain.* Illus. by B. Vidal. Dial, 1981. (Ages 4–8.) [African/Kenyan] In the same pattern as "The house that Jack built," this cumulative traditional rhyme tells how Ki-Pat brought rain to the drought-stricken Kenyan plains. The illustrations convey much information about this part of Africa.

Aardema, V. *Tales from the Story Hat.* Illus. by E. Fax. Coward, McCann, 1960. (Ages 8–10.) [African American] All but one of these well told and illustrated stories are based on folklore, much of which came from Africa. Notes on the stories and a glossary contain useful information.

Aardema, V. *Who's in Rabbit's House?* Illus. by L. and D. Dillon. Dial, 1977. (Ages 4–8.) [African/Masai] An intruder in rabbit's house frightens away all the animals by his grandiose threats and enormous voice. Only the frog is clever enough to outwit the villain, who turns out to be nothing more than a caterpillar. The format of the book is a play, presented by Masai actors wearing animal masks. The masks are the invention of the illustrators, but all other details, as well as the story, are typical of the Masai.

Aaseng, N. *Carl Lewis: Legend Chaser.* Lerner, 1985. (Ages 8-10.) [African American] Engagingly written, this upbeat biography is both factual and inspiring. Carl Lewis is a talented young man, and his family is supportive and exemplary. They do not seem to be romanticized or overblown. Good models are provided for young readers. This biography is one of a series about African-American athletes and other notable people.

Abdul, R. *The Magic of Black Poetry.* Illus. by D. Burr. Dodd Mead, 1971. (Ages 12 and up.) [African American] A collection of poetry written by black people all over the world—some anonymous, many of them notable living poets—across a great span of years. A section describing the poets is included.

Acuna, R. *A Mexican American Chronicle.* American, 1971. (Ages 12 and up.) [Mexican American] Providing a different view of the Spanish "conquerors" and an extensive study of Indian civilizations in Mexico, the book discusses contemporary problems facing Mexican Americans. Acuna's *The Study of Mexican-Americans: The Men and the Land* (1969) does the same for readers ages 6 to 9.

Ada, A. F. *The Gold Coin.* Illus. by N. Waldman. Atheneum, 1991. (Ages 5-9.) [Central American] A miserable, twisted, nasty thief becomes a healthy, productive man who appreciates honest labor, kindness, and the beauty of the natural world. The illustrations convey the Central-American setting.

Adams, B. J. *The Picture Life of Bill Cosby.* Illus. with photos. Watts, 1986. (Ages 7-10.) [African American] A simplified account of the famous entertainer's life and accomplishments. The point is well made that Cosby is also an educator, philanthropist, and spokesperson for many good causes.

Adams, E. B., reteller. *Blindman's Daughter.* Illus. by D. H. Choi. Seoul International, 1981. (Ages 6-8.) [Korean] Chung, an obedient and loving daughter to Mr. Shim, who is blind, sacrifices her own life to cure her father. Chung is magically rescued from the sea, marries a prince, and is reunited with her father. Korean and Confucian virtues of filial loyalty, affection, and sacrifice are brought out in this folk tale in both Korean and English.

Addy, S. H. *A Visit with Great-Grandma.* Illus. by L. Halverson. Whitman, 1989. (Ages 5-8.) [Czechoslovakian] [See Aging]

Adler, D. A. *Jackie Robinson: He Was the First.* Illus. by R. Casilla. Holiday House, 1989. (Ages 7-10.) [African American] Robinson broke barriers and brought the unfairness of segregation and prejudice to the attention of the American public. Although he bore the indignities and physical onslaughts of bigoted people when in the public eye as a ball player, he also fought for his rights and maintained his dignity.

Adler, D. A. *A Picture Book of Martin Luther King, Jr.* Illus. by R. Casilla. Holiday House, 1989. (Ages 5-8.) [African American] An excellent chronology in terms young readers can understand. The climate and political context are conveyed, as well as the details of the great peacemaker's life.

Adoff, A. *All the Colors of the Race.* Illus. by J. Steptoe. Lothrop Lee and Shepard, 1982. (Ages 5 and up.) [Biracial] A celebration of the elements that combine to form the biracial and bireligious heritage of the child narrator. Self-pride, compassion, and understanding mark the poetry and illustrations.

Adoff, A. *Black Is Brown Is Tan.* Illus. by E. A. McCully. Harper, 1972. (Ages 3-8.) [Biracial] [See Family Constellations]

Adoff, A., ed. *Black Out Loud*. Illus. by A. Hollingsworth. Macmillan, 1969. (Ages 9 and up.) [African American] Modern poems by African Americans of consistently high quality.

Adoff, A. *Hard to Be Six*. Illus. by C. Hanna. Morrow, 1991. (Ages 4–6.) [Universal/biracial] [See Family Constellations]

Adoff, A., ed. *I Am the Darker Brother*. Illus. by B. Andrews. Macmillan, 1968. (Ages 12 and up.) [African American] Poems about the African-American experience by African-American poets.

Adoff, A. *In for Winter, Out for Spring*. Illus. by J. Pinkney. HBJ, 1991. (Ages 6–10.) [Universal/African American] Poems celebrating a child's good feelings about herself and her African-American family include everyday events within a framework of the changing seasons. The illustrations convey joy and liveliness.

Adoff, A. *Malcolm X*. Illus. by J. Wilson. Crowell, 1970. (Ages 7–10.) [African American] In simple language, the book details Malcom X's life, what he believed, and what happened to him. The heroic quality of his life emerges dramatically.

Adoff, A. *My Black Me: A Beginning Book of Black Poetry*. Dutton, 1971. (Ages 8 and up.) [African American] Excellent compilation of poetry by many black poets dealing largely with African-American identity, families, history, and pride. A brief description of each poet is included.

Adrine-Robinson, K., ed. *Black Image Makers*. New Day, 1988. (Ages 9–12.) [African American] Stories of significant African Americans: Phillis Wheatley, poet; Henry Highland Garnet, abolitionist leader; Frances E. W. Harper, writer; William Howard Day, activist; and Paule Marshall, writer, are dramatically told. The illustrations are the work of three African-American eighth-graders from the Cleveland public schools. Although the typeface makes the reading somewhat difficult, the narratives are compelling enough to overcome this problem.

Agard, J., compiler. *Life Doesn't Frighten Me at All*. Holt, 1989. (Ages 12 and up.) [Universal/multicultural] Some of the poems are by well-known writers such as W. B. Yeats or Nikki Giovanni, but most are by people ranging from grade school students and reggae singers to physicists. There's even one by Nelson Mandela's daughter Zinzi, written when she was twelve. The poets' cultures are as diverse as their occupations; every part of the world is represented in this eclectic but unified collection.

Albert, B. *Where Does the Trail Lead?* Illus. by Brian Pinkney. Simon & Schuster, 1991. (Ages 6–9.) [Universal/African American] [See Family Constellations]

Alexander, L. *The Fortune Tellers*. Illus. by T. S. Hyman. Dutton, 1992. (Ages 7–10.) [Universal/Cameroon] A young carpenter takes over for a missing fortune-teller and dispenses common sense. He becomes immensely popular and wealthy and finds true love. Although this story, combining many folkloric elements, could have been set anywhere, Hyman's brilliant illustrations capture the color, patterns, dress, and details of a village in Cameroon, her son-in-law's home country.

Allen, T. *The Whispering Wind: Poetry by Young American Indians*. Doubleday, 1972. (Ages 10 and up.) [Native American] Fourteen works by Native American poets, who are described in introductory remarks before each section. Much of the poetry is directly about the experience of being a Native American.

Allison, D. W. *This Is the Key to the Kingdom*. Illus. by the author. Little, Brown, 1992. (Ages 5–8.) [Universal/African American] The traditional chant is adapted for this story about a young African American girl who lives in the inner city. Her imagination takes her to a lush, multicultural world filled with warmth and opulence. When she returns to reality, she manages to make someone else's life a little warmer and happier. The child is not an object of pity; she serves as an excellent model for coping with hard reality in an unusual way.

Almonte, P., and Desmond, T. *The Facts about Interracial Marriages.* Crestwood, 1992. (Ages 9-12.) [Biracial] A nonjudgmental book detailing ways of coping with prejudice against interracial marriages. Case studies are provided.

Ancona, G. *Pablo Remembers: The Fiesta of the Day of the Dead.* Lothrop Lee and Shepard, 1993. (Ages 7-10.) [Mexican] Pablo misses his grandmother, who died two years ago. The three-day fiesta celebrating the day of the dead helps him feel that she is near. The author-illustrator is of Mexican heritage, and he respectfully depicts the celebration in both text and brilliant color photos.

Ancona, G. *Powwow.* Illus. by the author. HBJ, 1993. (Ages 7 and up.) [Native American/ Crow] Vividly counteracting the notion that native customs and celebrations are a thing of the past, the author-illustrator provides stunning color photos of a contemporary powwow (Crow Fair in Crow Agency, Montana, the largest powwow held in the United States) accompanied by a personalized explanatory text. The powwow's reality is further underscored as Ancona introduces the reader to young Anthony Standing Rock and his family and friends.

Anzaldua, G. *Friends from the Other Side: Amigos del Otro Lado.* Illus. by C. Mendez. Children's, 1993. (Ages 7-10.) [Mexican American] The story tells of Prietita, a young Chicana, who befriends Joaquin and his mother, illegal immigrants living in poverty in an old shack on the Mexican-American border. An herb woman is the trusted adult who hides the mother and son from the border guards. More a political statement than a work of literature; but the combination of illustrations and topic will certainly arouse discussion among young readers.

Argueta, M. *The Magic Dogs of the Volcano: Los Perros Magicos de los Volcanes,* translated by S. Ross. Illus. by E. Simmons. Children's, 1990. (Ages 5-8.) [Salvadoran] Charmingly illustrated and told, this text in English and Spanish tells of the *cadejos,* or magical dogs, of El Salvador. The cadejos vanquish an army of lead soldiers sent by a family of heartless brothers who want to destroy the magic and oppress the villagers.

Arkhurst, J. C. *The Adventures of Spider: West African Folk Tales.* Illus. by J. Pinkney. Little, Brown, 1964. (Ages 7-11.) [African/West African] These stories from Liberia and Ghana provide a swiftly moving introduction to Spider (also known as Anansi). Spider is a clever trickster who usually outwits his foes but sometimes entraps himself. The stories explain natural phenomena and include details of African foods, work, and customs. See also *More Adventures of Spider* (1972).

Ashabranner, B. *An Ancient Heritage: The Arab-American Minority.* Illus. by P. S. Conklin. Harper, 1991. (Ages 12 and up.) [Arab American] The author defines the population as "people who speak Arabic as a native language," names some famous Arab Americans (Doug Flutie, Dr. Michael DeBakey, John Sununu, Ralph Nader, and Christa McAuliffe, among others), and frankly discusses complex political and social problems. The photos and text portray the people's diversity, as well as their similarity.

Avery, C. E. *Everybody Has Feelings.* Illus. by the author. Open Hand, 1992. (Ages 5 and up.) [Universal/Multicultural] The book's black-and-white photos of children, from toddlers to teenagers, in both rural and urban settings form its substance. The sparse text, in both Spanish and English, simply labels the wide-ranging feelings of the children: loneliness, liking to be alone, excitement, anger, and mixed feelings.

Awiakta, M. *Rising Fawn and the Fire Mystery.* Illus. by B. Bringle. St. Luke's, 1983. (Ages 8-12.) [Native American/Choctaw] [See Adoption and Foster Care]

Baden, R. *And Sunday Makes Seven.* Illus. by M. Edwards. Whitman, 1990. (Ages 7-10.) [Latino/Costa Rican] A charming story containing universal elements of folk tales but unmistakably Latino in flavor. Set in Costa Rica, it tells of a kind but poor man who is given a reward by a coven of witches because of his rhyme-making. His rich and nasty cousin attempts to profit from the witches, but he is punished instead. This satisfying tale also teaches the days of the week and numbers from one to seven in Spanish.

Baer, E. *This is the Way We Go to School.* Illus. by S. Bjorkman. Scholastic, 1990. (Ages 5-8.) [Universal/Multicultural] Rhymed verse introduces readers to the modes of transportation used by twenty-two children all over the world to go to school. A world map is labeled with the countries mentioned. The illustrations not only add spice to the poetry but also turn the book into a guessing game of each child's location.

Bang, M. *The Paper Crane.* Illus. by the author. Greenwillow, 1985. (Ages 6-9.) [Japanese] An adaptation of a Japanese folktale expressing the value of kindness to strangers. In this retelling, a stranger helps a kindly restaurant owner increase business by giving him a magical crane whose dancing attracts many customers to the restaurant. After the restaurant's success is assured, the stranger reclaims his bird. The pictures of the origami crane and the dancing patrons of the restaurant illustrate the artist's vision of a multicultural society.

Bang, M. *Ten, Nine, Eight.* Illus. by the author. Greenwillow, 1983. (Ages 4-6.) [Universal/African American] [See Family Constellations]

Banks, S. H. *Remember My Name.* Illus. by Birgitta Saflund. Roberts Rinehart, 1993. (Ages 9-12.) [Native American/Cherokee] One of a series of books published in collaboration with the Council for Indian Education, this story dramatically tells of Agin'agili (Annie Rising Fawn] and her family's struggles against the encroachment and cruelty of the State of Georgia and the federal government in the early and mid-nineteenth century. Stereotypes are overturned as the reader learns of a well-established and affluent Cherokee community at New Echota, some of whom owned slaves. Annie's uncle frees his slaves before he and his family are forced into captivity and relocation.

Barrie, B. *Lone Star.* Delacorte, 1990. (Ages 10-12.) [Jewish American] Jane Miller, whose family are Orthodox Jews, is unhappy in their new home, particularly because she feels so different from her Christian classmates. Jane's confrontation with her Jewishness, the issues of acceptance or rejection of one's heritage, the conflict between the traditional and the modern, and the larger questions raised by the world situation in 1944 transcend the book's flaws.

Barry, R. *Ramon and the Pirate Gull.* Illus. by the author. McGraw-Hill, 1971. (Ages 5-8.) [Puerto Rican] Ramon, a young boy living in Ponce, Puerto Rico, sights a rare gull, captures it, and returns it to the Marine Research Station in San Juan. The story shows that Puerto Rico is more than beaches and agriculture.

Baylor, B. *God on Every Mountaintop.* Illus. by C. Brown. Scribner, 1981. (Ages 9-12.) [Native American/Southwest] Sacred myths of the Native Americans of the southwest, well told and illustrated. Sources are included for further study.

Begay, S. *Ma'ii and Cousin Horned Toad: A Traditional Navajo Story.* Illus. by the author. Scholastic, 1992. (Ages 5-8.) [Native America/Navajo] Greed overtakes Coyote, and he is punished. This traditional tale is authentically told and superbly illustrated. The explanatory note and glossary are informative.

Belpre, P. *Once in Puerto Rico.* Illus. by C. Price. Warne, 1973. (Ages 8-11.) [Puerto Rican] Authentic Puerto Rican tales, including historical and animal stories.

Belpre, P. *Santiago.* Illus. by S. Shimin. Warne, 1969. (Ages 5-8.) [Puerto Rican] Santiago, who now lives in New York, must adjust to new friends, as well as a new setting. His empathic teacher and mother respond to his strong longing for his former home in Puerto Rico and for his pet hen Selina. The illustrations and writing are sympathetic and respectful.

Belting, N. M. *Moon Was Tired of Walking on Air.* Illus. by W. Hillenbrand. Houghton Mifflin, 1992. (Ages 9-12.) [Native American/South American] Fourteen South American Indian myths describing the creation of the earth and other natural phenomena, including "How the Birds Got New Beaks and Men Got Teeth," "Ghosts and Souls," and "Why Rainbow is Bent." Arising out of the oral tradition, these myths explore nature's critical importance in cultures indigenous to South America.

Benitez, M. *How Spider Tricked Snake.* Illus. by D. Sierra. Raintree, 1989. (Ages 5-8.) [Jamaican] A familiar tale describing the dangers of pride, in which Spider outwits sly, slippery Snake. The story has a light, humorous tone.

Bennett, N. *Halo of the Sun.* Illus. by J. Running. Northland, 1987. (Ages 12 and up.) [Native American/Navajo] Tales of the Navajo culture with emphasis on the arts of weaving and story-telling. The author lived for eight years on a reservation before collaborating with Navajo weaver T. Bighorse, to write this book.

Berkow, I. *Hank Greenberg: Hall-of-Fame Slugger.* Illus. by M. Ellison. Jewish Publication Society, 1991. (Ages 8-10.) [Jewish American] Hank Greenberg was the first Jew to be elected to the Baseball Hall of Fame. He played for the Detroit Tigers at a time when there was rampant, overt anti-Semitism in the country. His story invites many questions on assimilation, prejudice, and internalized oppression.

Bernstein, J. E. *Dmitry, a Young Soviet Immigrant.* Illus. by M. J. Bernstein. Clarion, 1981. (Ages 7-10.) [Jewish American/Russian American] Photos and text present a clear picture of Dmitry and his family, recent immigrants from the Soviet Union. They struggle with their identities as Jews; their difficult financial situation; isolation from family and friends; and new expectations, language, and customs. The book ends on an encouraging note.

Berry, J. *Ajeemah and His Son.* Harper, 1992. (Ages 11 and up.) [Jamaican] Ajeemah and Atu, his eighteen-year-old son, are wrenched from their unnamed homeland in Africa and forced into slavery in Jamaica. New names are imposed on them, and the son is killed for his refusal to acquiesce to subservience. Ajeemah makes a new life for himself, especially after 1838 when slavery is abolished in Jamaica. This provocative story invites discussion and further research.

Berry, J. *A Thief in the Village and Other Stories.* Orchard, 1987. (Ages 12 and up.) [Jamaican] A collection of nine stories about life in Jamaica, including one about a girl who flouts convention by wanting to own and ride her own bicycle. The characters, language, and setting are authentic and vivid.

Bethancourt, T. E. *The Me Inside of Me.* Lerner, 1985. (Ages 10-12.) [Mexican American] Social pressures, class boundaries, and self-identity are explored in the story of seventeen-year-old Alfredo Flores, young, middle class, and of Latino heritage, who unexpectedly becomes very wealthy. What Alfredo learns in the end is that money and prestige cannot bring happiness and fulfillment in life. In Alfredo's case, he rediscovers pride and respect for his Latino heritage.

Bider, D. *A Drop of Honey.* Illus. by A. Kojoyian. Simon & Schuster, 1989. (Ages 6-9.) [Armenian] [See Siblings]

Bierhorst, J. *Lightning Inside You and Other Native American Riddles.* Illus. by L. Brierley. Morrow, 1992. (Ages 10 and up.) [Native American] Riddles about the human body and the natural world make up this unique Native-American collection, translated from twenty different languages. Descriptions of special customs and rituals, as well as information on specific indigenous nations, are included.

Bird, P. "Harlem 1960 and 1968." In *I Heard a Scream in the Street,* edited by N. Larrick. Dell, 1970. (Ages 10 and up.) [African American] The difference in self-pride in the African-American population is illustrated in this two-part comparison between 1960, when "the whiter you are the better you are," and 1968, the beginning of the realization that "black is beautiful."

Blaine, M. *Dvora's Journey.* Illus. by G. Lisowski. Holt, 1979. (Ages 8–11.) [Jewish American] For Jews in Russia at the turn of the century, life was difficult and dangerous. Twelve-year-old Dvora and her family daringly cross the border to escape to America.

Blanc, E. S. *Berchick.* Illus. by T. Dixon. Volcano, 1989. (Ages 7–9.) [Jewish American] The setting is a Jewish homestead in Wyoming at the beginning of the century, combating the stereotype that Jews live only in cities. The story involves Mama and an orphaned colt, Berchick, which is sold to a horse dealer from whom he eventually escapes. The black-and-white illustrations capture the emotions and dignity of the people and their surroundings. The story reflects the author's own family background.

Bode, J. *Different Worlds: Interracial and Cross Cultural Dating.* Watts, 1989. (Ages 12 and up.) [Biracial/multicultural] [See Sex and Sexuality]

Bode, J. *New Kids on the Block: Oral Histories of Immigrant Teens.* Watts, 1989. (Ages 12 and up.) [Multicultural] Adolescents from eleven countries tell what it is like to come to the United States as immigrants. Something of each person's culture is included, as is a description of each teen's mode of adjustment.

Bontemps, A., ed. *American Negro Poetry.* Hill & Wang, 1963. (Ages 10 and up.) [African American] A valuable and diverse selection of African-American poetry across a span of many years. Biographical descriptions of the poets are included.

Boyd, C. D. *Circle of Gold.* Scholastic, 1984. (Ages 10–12.) [African American] [See Death]

Bradman, T., and Browne, E. *Wait and See.* Illus. by E. Browne. Oxford, 1987. (Ages 5–8.) [Universal/Biracial] [See Family Constellations]

Bresnick-Perry, R. *Leaving for America.* Illus. by M. Reisberg. Children's, 1992. (Ages 7–10.) [Immigrant/Jewish] The young narrator and her mother left their *shtetl* in Russia to join her father in America. She is filled with excitement and hope for the future but also heartbroken that she may never see her friends and family. The reader experiences with the main character the palpable loss of community, family, and culture in the decision to come to America.

Brown, D. *Tepee Tales of the American Indian.* Illus. by L. Mofsie. Holt, 1979. (Ages 8 and up.) [Native American] Native American folk tales and myths representing more than two dozen nations. The illustrator is a Native American. Brown provides a short introduction at the beginning of each section.

Brown, T. *Chinese New Year.* Illus. by F. Ortiz. Holt, 1987. (Ages 7–10.) [Chinese American] Set in San Francisco, this book is an informative photo essay on how some Chinese-American families celebrate the New Year. The black-and-white photos indicate a sense of the involvement of the people and the artifacts of the celebration, but the color photo on the cover conveys the excitement of the festivities.

Brown, T. *Hello, Amigos.* Illus. by F. Ortiz. Holt, 1986. (Ages 6–10.) [Mexican American] Through a fine combination of black-and-white photos and simple noncondescending text, the reader gets to know about Frankie Valdes and his life in San Francisco. Frankie's birthday is described, complete with piñata and other Mexican-American customs. Some Spanish words and a glossary are included.

Browne, V. *Monster Slayer.* Illus. by B. Whitethorne. Northland, 1991. (Ages 7–9.) [Native American/Navajo] Both the author and illustrator are of Dine (Navajo) heritage, adding authenticity to this folktale of human wit conquering the supernatural.

Bruchac, J. *The Faithful Hunter: Abenaki Stories.* Illus. by Kahionhes. Greenfield Review, 1988. (Ages 8–12.) [Native American/Abenaki] A number of these stories tell of Gluskabe, the creator of humans and designer of many natural phenomena. Like all this author's work, the tales are entertaining and satisfying. Other tales of the Abenaki retold by this author include *The Wind Eagle and Other Abenaki Stories.*

Bruchac, J. *The First Strawberries: A Cherokee Story.* Illus. by A. Vojtech. Dial, 1993. (Ages 6–10.) [Native American/Cherokee] Tells how the creation of strawberries saved the marriage of the first man and woman. Angered by her husband's lack of understanding, the woman leaves her husband. The sun helps him by creating a variety of berries to tempt the woman to slow down. She cannot resist the strawberries, and she and her repentant husband are reunited. Respect and understanding are the themes of the story. The illustrations are as beautiful, flowing, and respectful as the text.

Bruchac, J. *Hoop Snakes, Hide Behinds and Side-Hill Winders: Tall Tales from the Adirondacks.* Illus. by T. Trujillo. Crossing, 1991. (Ages 8 and up.) [Adirondacks] Tall tales, including some about Bill Greenfield: part fool, part superhero, part prodigious yarn-spinner. All the stories give a sense of the lifestyle of the people who lived in the Adirondacks in the nineteenth century.

Bruchac, J. *Return of the Sun: Native American Tales from the Northeast Woodlands.* Illus. by G. Carpenter. Crossing, 1990. (Ages 7–11.) [Native American/Northeast Woodland] Many of these stories depict the intimate relationship with nature that peoples of the northeast woodlands experienced. Included are trickster tales, magical transformations, and stories that satisfyingly reward the virtuous and punish the wicked. Bruchac's introduction explains the derivations of the tales and his respectful practice of retelling only those stories that have already been set down in print. See also *Iroquois Stories,* illustrated by Daniel Burgevin, (1985) and *The Boy who Lived with the Bears.* Society for the Study of Myth and Tradition, 1990.

Brusca, M. C., and Wilson, T. *The Blacksmith and the Devils.* Illus. by M. C. Brusca. Holt, 1992. This version of a popular Latin American folktale is adapted from a retelling by don Segundo Sombra, an Argentine gaucho. It tells how a poor blacksmith outwits all the devils in hell and lives lavishly for many years. Unfortunately, he is excluded from heaven and must forever wander the earth. The illustrations add to the fun.

Bryan, A. *Lion and the Ostrich Chicks.* Illus. by the author. Atheneum, 1986. (Ages 7–10.) [African] Lively retellings of four tales from the Masai, Bushmen, Hausa, and Angolan peoples. The prose is musical in its movement; the illustrations complement the text admirably.

Bryan, A. *Sing to the Sun.* Harper, 1992. (Ages 5 and up.) [African American] Original poems, accompanied by brightly colored paintings filled with movement, celebrate being alive. Family pride, the joy and power of nature, and a valuing of heritage are all ingredients.

Bryan, A. *Turtle Knows Your Name.* Illus. by the author. Atheneum, 1989. (Ages 5–8.) [Caribbean] Upsalamana Tumpelarado lives with his grandmother, whose name is even longer than his. The importance and mysticism of names is developed in this delightful tale for younger readers. Caribbean customs, including some special foods, enhance the story, as do the illustrations.

Bryan, A. *Walk Together Children, Black American Spirituals.* Illus. by the author. Atheneum, 1974. (Ages 6 and up.) [African American] Striking illustrations accompany the 24 songs (music included) in this valuable book. Two additional volumes, contributing more songs, are equally attractive: *I'm Going to Sing: Black American Spirituals, Volume Two* (1982) and *All Night, All Day: A Child's First Book of African American Spirituals* (1991).

Bunin, C., and Bunin, S. *Is That Your Sister?* Illus. by S. K. Welch. Pantheon, 1976. (Ages 6–12.) [Biracial] [See Adoption]

Bunting, E. *Summer Wheels.* Illus. by T. B. Allen. HBJ, 1992. (Ages 7–10.) [Universal/African American] [See Aging]

Bunting, E. *The Wall.* Illus. by R. Himler. Clarion, 1990. (Ages 5–9.) [Universal/Latino] [See War and Peace]

Burgie, I. *Caribbean Carnival: Songs of the West Indies.* Illus by F. Lessac. Tambourine, 1992. (Ages 5–8.) [Caribbean] The notes by R. Guy explaining some of the links to Caribbean cultures add a significant feature to this pleasant compilation of songs, some traditional, some composed by the author.

Burt, O. *Black Women of Valor.* Illus. by P. Frame. Messner, 1974. (Ages 9–11.) [African American] [See Gender Roles]

Cameron, A. *The Most Beautiful Place in the World.* Illus. by T. B. Allen. Knopf, 1988. (Ages 8–10.) [Guatemalan] [See Aging]

Cameron, A. *The Stories Julian Tells.* Illus. by A. Strugnell. Knopf, 1981. (Ages 7–10.) Also *More Stories Julian Tells* (1986), *Julian, Secret Agent* (1988), and *Julian, Dream Doctor* (1990). [African American] [See Siblings]

Carlson, L. M., and Ventura, C. L., eds. *Where Angels Glide at Dawn: New Stories from Latin America.* Illus. by J. Ortega. Lippincott, 1990. (Ages 10 and up.) [Latin America] Stories from South and Central America, Cuba, and Puerto Rico, each different in genre and tone but capturing some element of the nation of its origin. Political issues, what it is like to go "home" from the barrios of New York, economic contrasts, and a measure of the supernatural are some of the ingredients.

Carlson, V., and Witherspoon, G. *Black Mountain Boy: A Story of the Boyhood of John Honie.* Illus. by A. Tsinajinnie. Navajo Curriculum Center, 1968. (Ages 10 and up.) [Native American/Navajo] The story is told in the first person by John Honie, a Navajo medicine man whose values come through clearly in his account of his boyhood. An excellent book for discussing the building of a positive self-image.

Carlstrom, N. W. *Light: Stories of a Small Kindness.* Illus. by L. Desimini. Little, Brown, 1990. (Ages 9–12.) [Universal/Multicultural] Stories from different cultural settings (Haiti, Mexico, New York City, and Guatemala) describe kindness; mystical events; and universal aspects of faith, determination, and confronting adversity.

Chaikin, M. *Hanukkah.* Illus. by E. Weiss. Holiday, 1990. (Ages 5–8.) [Jewish American] A historical background of Hanukkah, focusing on the celebration of freedom and the fight against oppression, refraining from comparisons with other holidays such as Christmas.

Chaikin, M. *I Should Worry, I Should Care.* Illus. by R. Egielski. Harper, 1979. (Ages 7–10.) [Jewish American] The ambience of a working-class Jewish family in Brooklyn comes through strongly in each of the books about Molly, spanning the time period from the 1930s through World War II. Jewish foods, customs, and language figure as part of the setting. *Finders Weepers* (1980), *Getting Even* (1982), *Lower! Higher! You're a Liar!* (1984), and *Friends Forever* (1988) are the other books in this well-written series.

Chardiet, B. *Juan Bobo and the Pig.* Illus. by H. Meryman. Walker, 1973. (Ages 5–9.) [Puerto Rican] A classic folk tale of the simpleton, found in many cultures, retold here in a savory style.

Choi, S. N. *Echoes of the White Giraffe.* Houghton Mifflin, 1993. (Ages 10 and up.) [Korean] [See War and Peace]

Choi, S. N. *Halmoni and the Picnic.* Illus. by K. M. Dugan. Houghton Mifflin, 1993. (Ages 6–9.) [Korean-American] Halmoni, Yunmi's grandmother, has a difficult time adjusting to

American customs. Yunmi and her friends invite her to chaperon their class picnic. The entire class, including the teacher, show great respect and admiration for Halmoni. Imbedded in the story is a respectful unfolding of Korean customs of raising children, etiquette, clothing, and food.

Choi, S. N. *Year of Impossible Goodbyes.* Houghton Mifflin, 1991. (Ages 10 and up.) [Korean] [See War and Peace]

Cisneros, S. *The House on Mango Street,* 2nd ed. Arte Publico, 1988. (Ages 10 and up.) [Mexican American] Reflections, musings, and memories of Esperanza, a Mexican-American girl growing up in poverty. She describes her family, friends, some painful events, and some aspirations. Although her life is hard, she retains her sensitivity and a belief in herself as a writer and a survivor.

Clark, A. N. *Circle of Seasons.* Illus. by W. T. Mars. Farrar, Straus, and Giroux, 1970. (Ages 8–11.) [Native American/Pueblo] The author was a teacher in schools for Native Americans for many years. This book tells of the Pueblo Indians and their celebrations of different seasonal ceremonies, including Christian ones.

Clark, A. N. *Little Herder in Autumn.* Illus. by H. Denetsosie. Ancient City, 1988. (Ages 6–9.) [Native American/Navajo] The finely crafted story is told in both English and Navajo from the point of view of the little girl who is "the little herder." The text is gracefully supplemented by the drawings of the Navajo illustrator.

Clark, A. N. *Sun Journey: A Story of Zuni Pueblo.* Illus. by P. T. Sandy. Ancient City, 1988. (Ages 8–10.) [Native American/Zuni] Ze-do, a ten-year-old Zuni boy, returns from school and relearns the ways of his people. The illustrator is Zuni, and the author is a well-respected ally of native peoples. The grandfather is an excellent model for young readers to encounter, and Ze-do's relationship with him is warm and loving. The dilemma of living in two worlds is confronted at the end, when Ze-do must return to the government school.

Clifton, L. *Don't You Remember?* Illus. by E. Ness. Dutton, 1973. (Ages 5–8.) [African American] [See Siblings]

Clifton, L. *Three Wishes,* rev. ed. Illus. by M. Hays. Bantam, 1992. (Ages 5–8.) [Universal/African American] Told in the cadences of black English, the story builds on the classic tales of three wishes and how they are spent. Lena's wishes all come true, and the reader is invited to speculate about whether magic was involved. Readers may want to engage in the game of "If I had three wishes, I'd . . . "

Climo, S. *The Korean Cinderella.* Illus. by R. Heller. Harper, 1993. (Ages 7–10.) [Korean] Many of the classic elements are included in this version: Pear Blossom endures the abusive behavior of her stepmother and stepsister, and she loses her sandal, which then becomes the means for the magistrate-prince to find her. She does not have a fairy godmother, but she does enlist the aid of magical creatures. The author researched the half-dozen Korean Cinderella versions and combined three variations for this retelling.

Coerr, E. *Chang's Paper Pony.* Illus. by D. K. Ray. Harper, 1988. (Ages 6–9.) [Chinese American] The easy-to-read format provides young children access to historical information about Chinese immigrants in the mid-nineteenth century. Chang is lonely and wants a pony as a companion and pet. His grandfather, with whom he lives, is loving but unable to help him. With the help of a friendly prospector, Chang finds enough gold to buy a pony. Values of honesty and acceptance are presented in the story.

Cohen, B. *The Christmas Revolution.* Lothrop Lee and Shepard, 1987. (Ages 9–12.) [Jewish American] Emily and Sally are twins in the fourth grade at a predominantly Christian public school. They never gave much thought to their Judaism and what it means to practice other people's rituals until the year when Simeon, an Orthodox classmate, refuses to participate in the Christmas festivities. The book can spark discussion about sensitivity to the "outsider's" perspective.

Cohen, B. *Molly's Pilgrim.* Illus. by M. J. Deraney. Lothrop Lee and Shepard, 1983. (Ages 6–8.) [Jewish American] Molly's classmates tease her because she is different from them. Her mother and teacher use a doll that looks like Molly's mother to show that Molly's family, who are refugees, are really modern-day pilgrims.

Cohen, N. *Jackie Joyner-Kersee.* Illus. by B. Hamann. Time Magazine, 1992. (Ages 10–12.) [African American/Universal] A biography of a remarkable athlete, "up close and personal." Joyner's close connections to her family, her drive, and even her insecurities are revealed in this fact-filled book.

Conlon-McKenna, M. *Under the Hawthorne Tree.* Illus. by D. Teskey. Holiday House, 1990. (Ages 10–12.) [Irish] Despite the almost unbelievably virtuous and heroic characters of the three child protagonists and because this story provides a detailed and grim look at the effects of the potato famine and disease on the Irish people in the 1840s, readers will understand better the wave of Irish immigration and the heritage that Irish people brought with them to this country. The sequel, *Wildflower Girl* (1992), continues the story, focusing on Peggy, the youngest child. Despite a somewhat overblown style, the history revealed here makes the book worth reading.

Cooper, M. L. *Playing America's Game: The Story of Negro League Baseball.* Dutton, 1993. (Ages 9–12.) [African American] A fascinating and detailed account, beginning with the last half of the nineteenth century and lasting into the mid-twentieth century. Because black baseball players were banned from the major leagues, they formed their own very successful leagues. Ironically, integration of African-American players into the major leagues killed Negro baseball.

Courlander, H., and Dofl, A. *Hat-Shaking Dance and Other Tales from the Gold Coast.* Illus. by E. Arno. Harcourt, Brace & World, 1957. (Ages 8–12.) [African/Ashanti] Ashanti stories, most about Anansi, very well told. The endnotes give interesting background information.

Coutant, H. *First Snow.* Illus. by V. Mai. Knopf, 1974. (Ages 5–8.) [Vietnamese American] [See Death]

Cox, C. *Undying Glory: The Story of the Massachusetts 54th Regiment.* Scholastic, 1991. (Ages 10 and up.) [African American] [See War and Peace]

Crew, L. *Children of the River.* Delacorte, 1989. (Ages 9–12.) [Cambodian American] Sundara fled Kampuchea with her aunt and uncle and their children, leaving behind her parents and siblings. The dilemma of honoring one's heritage while adapting to new demands and mores is well conveyed here. The plot becomes overinvolved when Sundara and Jonathan, a football hero too good to be true, fall in love; but the story is competently told. There is so little written about the Cambodian American population that despite its flaws the book is worth including.

Crews, D. *Bigmama's.* Greenwillow, 1991. Illus. by the author. (Ages 5–8.) [Universal/African American] [See Family Constellations]

Crowder, J. L. *Tonibah and the Rainbow.* Navajo translation by C. Tohtsonie and J. Wilson, Sr. Illus. by the author. Upper Strata Ink, 1986. (Ages 7–10.) [Native American/Navajo] Although the text lacks fluidity and connectedness, the photographs of contemporary Navajo life and the factual, respectful recounting of events in the community make this book valuable. The story tells of the cooperation of the entire community (men, women, and children) in rebuilding a hogan destroyed by fire.

Davis, B. *Black Heroes of the American Revolution.* HBJ, 1976. (Ages 8–11.) [African American] The book provides interesting facts, such as "At least five thousand black men served on the patriot side during the [American] Revolution," and describes many of them.

Davis, O. *Escape to Freedom: A Play about Young Frederick Douglass.* Trumpet Club special edition, 1992. (Ages 9–12.) [African American] The triumphant escape from slavery and rise to success of the remarkable Frederick Douglass. The play format engagingly captures the spirit of the times and the man.

Davis, O. *Langston.* Delacorte, 1982. (Ages 12 and up.) [African American] This description of the famous African-American poet Langston Hughes also includes some of his writing. The play format invites readers to actively participate in its drama.

Delacre, L. *Arroz Con Leche.* Illus. by the author. Scholastic, 1989. (Ages 5–8.) [Latin American] This collection of Latin-American songs and chants in Spanish contains English translations, musical scores, and colorful illustrations. Puerto Rico, Mexico, and Argentina are represented, with themes such as animals, work, love, and marriage. Footnotes describe games that go with some of the songs: Children can be invited to add sections to this book, based on their own family heritages of songs and chants.

Delacre, L. *Las Navidades: Popular Christmas Songs from Latin America.* Illus. by the author. Scholastic, 1990. (Ages 6–10.) [Puerto Rican/Latin American] Most of the songs are from Puerto Rico. Explanatory descriptions of the customs accompanying the songs. The musical arrangements provided in the back of the book are simple enough for people with minimal musical ability to play and sing.

Delacre, L. *Vejigante Masquerader.* Illus. by the author. Scholastic, 1993. (Ages 6–10.) [Puerto Rican] Ramon wants to be included in the festivities of *Carnaval,* the pre-Lenten festival celebrated in Ponce, Puerto Rico. He manages to buy a mask, and he sews his own costume. This sample of Puerto Rican heritage is worthy of attention. The book is written in both Spanish and English, and the illustrations accurately convey the customs. Directions are included for making the *papier-mâché* masks.

Demi. *The Empty Pot* Illus. by the author. Holt, 1990. (Ages 5–8.) [Chinese] This adaptation of a Chinese folktale is meant to teach the value of honesty. Whichever child can grow the most beautiful flower from the emperor's special seed will be heir to the throne. The emperor reveals that the seeds were all sterile and Ping was the only child honest enough to bring him an empty pot, so he wins. Demi's artwork makes this a captivating book.

Demi. *In the Eyes of the Cat: Japanese Poetry for All Seasons.* Translated by T. Huang. Illus. by the author. Holt, 1992. (Ages 5 and up.) [Japanese] Seasonal poetry by a number of noted Japanese poets. The illustrations aptly convey a sense of the Japanese reverence for nature.

Demi. *The Magic Boat.* Illus. by the author. Holt, 1990. (Ages 8–12.) [Chinese] This tale, so popular in China that it was made into a children's movie the 1960s, is retold engagingly in this elegantly illustrated book. Chang is not only virtuous, kind, and industrious but also clever and self-respecting. He does not permit the wicked prime minister and greedy emperor to deprive him of the magic boat that is rightfully his.

Denenberg, B. *Nelson Mandela: No Easy Walk to Freedom.* Scholastic, 1991. (Ages 11 and up.) [African/South African] Just as much a history of contemporary South Africa as it is a biography of Nelson Mandela, the book tells of the evil consequences of apartheid, the political infighting and divisions continuing to the present time, and the story of Mandela and his rise to leadership.

De Paola, T. *The Legend of the Bluebonnet.* Illus. by the author. Putnam, 1983. (Ages 5–8.) [Native American/Comanche] Based on Comanche lore, this is the story of an orphaned girl who sacrifices what she loves best to save her people. The decision is the girl's alone; it is an active and heroic act that she performs.

Dooley, N. *Everybody Cooks Rice.* Illus. by P. J. Thornton. Carolrhoda, 1991. (Ages 6–8.) [Multicultural] In this harmonious multicultural neighborhood all of the families are industrious, loving, and open hearted. Despite the idyllic setting, the story retains a realistic tone. Eight rice recipes from all over the world are included.

Dorris, M. *Morning Girl.* Hyperion, 1992. (Ages 9 and up.) [Caribbean] Morning Girl and her brother Star Boy belong to a community of people, the Tainos, who value hospitality, avoidance of conflict, and courtesy. As the story builds, the reader comes to know the family and community and to feel a strong bond of affection with them. At the end, when Columbus and his men arrive, the reader knows that the Tainos will all be destroyed. An excerpt from Columbus's journal ends the book so that readers see the difference between the European invaders' perspective and that of the peaceful indigenous Tainos.

Dorros, A. *Abuela.* Illus. by E. Kleven. Dutton, 1991. (Ages 5–8.) [Latin American] Rosalba, a Latina girl, spends time with her loving *abuela* (grandmother). She imagines that they fly above New York City. Many Spanish phrases worked into the reading are listed in a glossary. Colorful mixed-media collages augment the text.

Dorros, A. *Tonight is Carnaval.* Illus. with *arpilleras* sewn by the Club de Madres Virgen del Carmen of Lima, Peru. Dutton, 1991. (Ages 7–10.) [Peruvian] The young Peruvian narrator tells of his impatience while awaiting *Carnaval,* the annual three-day celebration before Lent. This will be his first year as an active participant, playing his *quena* (flute) in the parade. Illustrations take the form of *arpilleras,* cloth applique collages (a traditional Peruvian folk art usually used as wall hangings) made by a women's collective in Lima. An appendix shows how these are made.

Ehlert, L. *Moon Rope* (*Un laza a la luna*). Spanish translation by A. Prince. Illus. by the author. HBJ, 1992. (Ages 4–8.) [Peruvian] This story from Peru, written in both Spanish and English, explains the origins of the Man in the Moon and why moles like to hide underground. The author's collage illustrations are striking.

Ekoomiak, N. *Arctic Memories.* Illus. by the author. Holt, 1990 (first U.S. publication). (Ages 7–10.) [Native American/Inuit] Included are descriptions of the igloo, games, ice fishing, some ancient beliefs, and Christian celebrations. The text is written in both English and Inuktitut, the Inuit written language developed by the Crees and used by missionaries to translate the Bible. The stylized paintings are spectacular.

Esbensen, B. J. *Ladder to the Sky.* Illus. by H. K. Davie. Little, Brown, 1990. (Ages 5–8.) [Native American/Ojibway] A creation story explaining how pain and death came to people because of their disobedience. The story includes the tempering provision of healing herbs and special people capable of applying them.

Falwell, C. *Shape Space.* Illus. by the author. Clarion, 1992. (Ages 4–6.) [Universal/African American] A lively young African-American girl dances with all types of colorful geometrical shapes she finds in a toy box. She forms the triangles, semicircles, rectangles, circles, and squares into toys, clothing, a playmate, and even a village. A creative way to explore the concept of shapes. Too often concept books exclude any group but Caucasians. This one is a book balancing addition to a library.

Feelings, M. *Jambo Means Hello.* Illus. by T. Feelings. Dial, 1974. (Ages 5–10.) [African] The simple text in the format of an alphabet book. Each letter has a word, its definition, and a more complete explanation of the customs associated with it. For example, after the definition of *arusi* (a wedding), the author explains how weddings are celebrated.

Feelings, M. *Zamani Goes to Market.* Illus. by T. Feelings. Seabury, 1970. (Ages 6–9.) [African/Kenya] [See Family Constellations]

Ferris, J. *What Are You Figuring Now?* Illus. by A. Johnson. Carolrhoda, 1988. (Ages 8–10.) [African American] As a free black man living in the mid-1700s, Banneker accomplished major feats in astronomy, surveying, mathematics, and owning and managing his own farm. He was known and respected by George Washington and Thomas Jefferson for his ingenuity and perseverance. The author has created a comprehensive biography of this talented man who defied stereotypes. Other well-written biographies of African Americans by Ferris include *Arctic Explorer: The Story of Matthew Henson* (1989) and *Walking the Road to Freedom: A Story about Sojourner Truth* (1988).

Finkelstein, N. H. *The Other 1492: Jewish Settlement in the New World.* Scribner's, 1989. (Ages 10 and up.) [Jewish/Sephardic] Details the expulsion of the Jews from Spain in 1492, their arrival in Portugal and Holland, and their subsequent emigration to Brazil, Cuba, and North America. Although the book is nonfiction, it provides a dramatic picture of the spirit of the Jewish people, as well as the tribulations they endured. Historical paintings and charts illustrate the text.

Folsom, F. *The Life and Legend of George McJunkin: Black Cowboy.* Nelson, 1973. (Ages 10 and up.) [African American] McJunkin was a competent cowboy, as well as a naturalist, meteorologist, and rancher. He undertook many responsibilities and discharged them well. An interesting, well-researched account of his life.

Fontenot, M. A. *Clovis Crawfish and the Big Betail.* Illus. by S. R. Blazek. Pelican, 1988. (Ages 5–8.) [Cajun/French American] All the Clovis Crawfish stories, set in the bayous of Louisiana, convey information about Cajun language and culture. Each has a story line that deals with people helping people, and each contains a song in French that children can learn. Translation of the Cajun words is woven into the text, as is information about animals, the bayou setting, and cultural details. See also *Clovis Crawfish and . . . the Spinning Spider; the Curious Crapaud; Michele Mantis; Etienne Escargot; the Singing Cigales; the Orphan Zo-Zo; Petit Papillon; His Friends.*

Fox, P., reteller. *Amzat and His Brothers: Three Italian Tales Remembered by Floriano Vecchi.* Illus. by E. A. McCully. Orchard, 1993. (Ages 7–10.) [Italian] The tales contain fools, tricksters, and the same ingredients as stories from other European folklore such as greedy brothers and animal friends. They are humorously told and move swiftly.

Freedman, R. *Buffalo Hunt.* Illus. Holiday House, 1988. (Ages 10 and up.) [Native American/Plains] Illustrated with paintings made by such artist-adventurers as George Catlin and Karl Bodmer in the era when many buffalo roamed the plains. This book not only provides information about the buffalo and its demise but also tells how white people encroached on native lands.

Freedman, R. *Children of the Wild West.* Clarion. 1983. (Ages 12 and up.) [Native American] This photographic history, with accompanying text, of the nineteenth-century American West spotlights the children of pioneer families, as well as Native American boys and girls. Described are the journeys westward, frontier schools, and the injustices wrought on Native Americans. The remarkable photos make this time period come alive.

Friedman, I. R. *How My Parents Learned to Eat.* Illus. by A. Say. Houghton Mifflin, 1984. (Ages 5–8.) [Japanese American] An engaging story of how the narrator's parents, one Japanese and one American, learned to adapt to each other's ways.

Fullen, M. K. *Pathblazers.* Illus. by S. Waldman. Open Hand, 1992. (Ages 8–12.) [African American] Succinct accounts of eight African Americans whose lives and work made a difference in this world. Included are Septima Clark, Jester Hairston, Josephine Baker, Gwendolyn Brooks, Thurgood Marshall, James Forman, Andrew Young, and Barbara Jordan.

Garland, S. *The Lotus Seed.* Illus. by T. Kiuchi. HBJ, 1993. (Ages 6–10.) [Vietnamese] A Vietnamese family is forced to flee their home because of war. The grandmother brings with her to the United States a precious lotus seed that symbolizes life and hope as a remembrance of her country of origin. The extraordinary illustrations extend the emotional impact of the story and provide a historical context, as well as a feeling for the different settings of Vietnam and the United States.

Garne, S. T. *One White Sail.* Illus. by L. Etre. Green Tiger, 1992. (Ages 3–6.) [Caribbean] Watercolors and rhymed verse comprise this Caribbean counting book from one to ten. Boats, homes, fishing, and music are illustrated.

Gay, K. *The Rainbow Effect: Interracial Families.* Watts, 1987. (Ages 12 and up.) [Interracial/American] [See Family Constellations]

Geras, A. *My Grandmother's Stories.* Illus. by J. Jordan. Knopf, 1990. (Ages 8–12.) [Universal/Jewish American] As with most folktales, the lessons and themes are universal, but the tales retain their own individuality. The author is a talented writer. The tales deal with the value of generosity, as well as cleverness. Several tell of the well-known fools of Chelm. All reflect the wisdom and warmth of the grandmother.

Gerson, M. J. *Why the Sky Is Far Away.* Illus. by C. Golembe. Little, Brown, 1992. (Ages 6 and up.) [Nigerian] The author worked for two years in Nigeria with the Peace Corps; the illustrator researched Nigerian folk art and incorporated motifs and patterns into the artwork. The result is a well-told story, visually elegant, and applicable to today's focus on ecology. It tells of the sad results of people's greed and wastefulness.

Gerstein, M. *The Mountains of Tibet.* Illus. by the author. Harper, 1987. (Ages 7–10.) [Tibetan] After living a long and contended life, a dying woodcutter is given the choice of becoming part of heaven or being reincarnated. Thus begins a series of choices of what the man will become in his new life. He finally decides to live on the same planet, in the same country where he has already lived. The one difference is that he now wants to return as a female. The story, which emphasizes the cyclical nature of life, was inspired by the Tibetan Book of the Dead. The illustrations echo the cyclical message of the text.

Ginsburg, M. *The Twelve Clever Brothers and Other Fools.* Illus. by C. Mikolaycak. Lippincott, 1979. (Ages 7–10.) [Eurasian] These tales demonstrate that every culture has its share of fools and tricksters. The collection also reveals how varied the people from the former Soviet Union are, with such differing sources as Armenian, Veps, Chuvash, Tatar, Latvian, Moldavian, and Assyrian peoples.

Giovanni, N. *Spin a Soft Black Song,* rev. ed. Illus. by G. Martins. Farrar, Straus and Giroux, 1985. (Ages 7–12.) [African American] Poetry reflecting the experiences, thoughts, and feelings of African-American children. Some are humorous, some serious.

Girard, L. W. *We Adopted You, Benjamin Koo.* Illus. by L. Shute. Whitman, 1989. (Ages 6–10.) [Multicultural] [See Adoption and Foster Care]

Gleeson, B. *Anansi.* Illus. by S. Guarnaccia. Simon & Schuster, 1992. (Ages 5–8.) [Jamaican] The setting and dialect are Jamaican. Anansi, the hero-trickster who sometimes becomes the victim of his own tricks, is the protagonist in the two tales recounted here. Designed to be read along with an accompanying tape from Rabbit Ears Productions, the narrative flows musically.

Goble, P. *Buffalo Woman.* Illus. by the author. Bradbury, 1984. (Ages 8–10.) [Native American/Plains] Because of his respect for the buffalo, the hero is permitted to marry Buffalo Woman, a supernatural being. After his wife and child leave to escape the persecution of his unthinking relatives, the husband is transformed into a young buffalo bull. As is usual with this sensitive storyteller and artist, the text and the pictures are respectful, informational, and aesthetically pleasing.

Goble, P. *Death of the Iron Horse.* Illus. by the author. Bradbury, 1987. (Ages 9-12.) [Native American/Cheyenne] In a departure from his usual folk stories, the author-artist tells how a Union Pacific train is derailed by a group of Cheyenne. Told from a Cheyenne perspective, the story includes the death of the trainmen, as well as a pictorial view of a massacred encampment of native people.

Goble, P. *Dream Wolf.* Illus. by the author. Bradbury, 1990. (Ages 5-8.) [Native American/Plains] Two children who have wandered too far from their people spend the night in a wolf's den. The next morning, the wolf guides them to their camp. The story, which reflects the reverence the Plains people have for wolves, is told respectfully and illustrated with accurate detail.

Goble, P. *The Gift of the Sacred Dog.* Illus. by the author. Bradbury, 1980. (Ages 7-10.) [Native American/Sioux] Tells of the coming of the horse (the sacred dog) because of a brave young boy who seeks to help his people. Poetically told and pictured.

Goble, P. *Her Seven Brothers.* Illus. by the author. Bradbury, 1988. (Ages 9-12.) [Native American/Sioux] A young woman embroiders exquisite designs on seven sets of men's clothing for seven brothers who live in a faraway land. To escape persecution, the young woman and her buffalo brothers escape to the sky where they can now be seen as the Big Dipper constellation. Sioux designs are faithfully and aesthetically rendered.

Goble, P. *Iktomi and the Berries.* Illus. by the author. Orchard, 1989. Also see *Iktomi and the Buffalo Skull* (1991), *Iktomi and the Ducks* (1990), and *Iktomi and the Boulder* (1988). (Ages 5-8.) [Native American/Plains] The Iktomi stories are all designed for oral performance. Iktomi is a trickster. Like his counterparts in other cultures, he is sometimes clever, sometimes foolish. He can be mischievous or helpful. The tales begin and end with a ritual introduction and conclusion and are written with a tongue-in-cheek playfulness. The illustrations are brilliant and respect the origins of the tales.

Goble, P. *Star Boy.* Illus. by the author. Bradbury, 1983. (Ages 7-10.) [Native American/Blackfoot] Based on Blackfoot tipi designs, the illustrations accompany a *pourquoi* tale explaining why the people annually build a Sun Dance lodge, round as the earth and sky.

Goffstein, M. B. *Family Scrapbook.* Illus. by the author. Farrar, Straus, and Giroux, 1978. (Ages 8-11.) [Jewish American] [See Family Constellations]

Gogol, S. *Vatsana's Lucky New Year.* Lerner, 1992. (Ages 9-12.) [Laotian American] Vatsana, a twelve-year-old Laotian-American girl, is menaced by a bully who hates all Asian people, ostensibly because his father was wounded in the war in Vietnam. Her friend Becky and her family help her to take pride in her heritage and to find a place for herself in American society.

Gold, S., and Caspi, M. M. *The Answered Prayer and Other Yemenite Folktales.* Illus. by M. Wunsch. Jewish Publication Society, 1990. (Ages 8 and up.) [Jewish/Yemenite] This book captures tales that might otherwise have been lost because of the lack of a written tradition in the Yemenite community. The stories echo themes from other cultures yet retain a distinctiveness.

Golenbock, P. *Teammates.* Illus. by P. Bacon. HBJ, 1990. (Ages 7-10.) [African American] Only a few books describe the ordeal Jackie Robinson suffered in order to break the color barrier in professional baseball. This story is augmented by photos and illustrations helping young readers to understand what life was like in the America of the 1940s, especially for Americans of African heritage. It also movingly portrays the simple act of friendship that earned Pee Wee Reese the reputation of being a fair-minded and loyal teammate to Jackie Robinson. Why did Branch Rickey require that Jackie Robinson avoid responding angrily to ugly racist behavior? Why did other white ball players tolerate abuse against their teammate? These and other questions could be explored as a result of reading this story.

Gordon, R. *Time Is the Longest Distance.* Harper, 1991. (Ages 12 and up.) [Multicultural] An international anthology of selected poems (all English translations) dealing with the universal constancy of time. Featured works include Yiddish, Hebrew, French, Italian, Chinese, Japanese, American, German, Spanish, Russian, and Persian heritages.

Gordy, B., Sr. *Movin' Up.* Harper, 1979. (Ages 12 and up.) [African American] This autobiography of the founder of Motown Records was completed shortly before his death at the age of 90. It was written from a series of taped sessions during which "Pop" Gordy reminisced about his life. The essence of his personality and energy is evident.

Graham, L. *Hungry Catch the Foolish Boy.* Illus. by J. Brown, Jr. Crowell, 1973. (Ages 7–10.) [African American] The Prodigal Son retold in Liberian English. There is a satisfying rhythm to the words, and the illustrations are dramatically simple. Graham, a minister's son born in New Orleans, has retold other Bible stories in this style: *David He No Fear* and *Every Man Heart Lay Down.*

Graham, L. *John Brown: A Cry for Freedom.* Illus. with photos. Crowell, 1980. (Ages 11 and up.) [African American] A biography of this controversial figure making the case that he had deep religious convictions about freeing slaves rather than taking the view of historians that he was wild and insane. This account does not, however, portray him as a saint.

Graham, L. *Whose Town?* Crowell, 1969. (Ages 12 and up.) [African American] David Williams, eighteen years old, is an intelligent, quiet young African American who wants to go to medical school after college. Tragic events deprive his father of a job, and David gets into trouble with the police. In the end, David graduates from high school with a college scholarship, but a bright future is not totally assured. Discussions in the book about black power and what course of action to take are useful. This is a sequel to *North Town* and *South Town,* which also tell about David Williams and the struggles he and his family must endure.

Greenberg, K. E. *Magic Johnson: Champion with a Cause.* Illus. with photos. Lerner, 1992. (Ages 8 and up.) [African American] [See Special Needs]

Greenfield, E. *Africa Dream.* Illus. by C. Byard. Harper, 1977. (Ages 6–8.) [African American] An African-American child dreams that she travels to long-ago Africa to the village of her ancestors. There she is welcomed by her extended family. Although the author does not specify where in Africa the dream takes place, the child's fantasy of reconnecting with her roots is powerful. The black-and-white drawings contribute to the dreamlike feeling of the narrative.

Greenfield, E. *Honey, I Love and Other Love Poems.* Illus. by D. and L. Dillon. Crowell, 1978. (Ages 7–10.) [African American] Inspired by everyday experiences, these sixteen poems are slices in the life of a young African-American child. Black vernacular is used naturally and resonantly. The illustrations are affirming.

Greenfield, E. *Mary McLeod Bethune.* Crowell, 1978. (Ages 7–10.) [African American] Explains in simple language how a little girl with a burning desire to read grew up to start numerous schools for African Americans in the South at the turn of the century.

Greenfield, E. *Paul Robeson: The Life and Times of a Free Black Man.* Illus. by G. Ford. Crowell, 1975. (Ages 6–9.) [African American] Not just a recounting of facts, this biography in story format is written for young readers. The author adds her own perspective on the injustices wrought against African Americans.

Greenfield, E. *Under the Sunday Tree.* Illus. by A. Ferguson. Harper, 1988. (Ages 6-10.) [Bahamian] Short poems evoking many aspects of Bahamian life (fishing, sailboat racing, market day, and riding a donkey) are side by side with the universal memories of childhood. The paintings receive and deserve equal billing with the text. Their stylized forms and bright patches of color capture a child's view with strength and joyfulness.

Greenfield, E., and Little, L. J. *Childtimes: A Three-Generation Memoir.* Illus. by J. Pinkney and with photos from the author's family albums. Crowell, 1979. (Ages 10 and up.) [African American] Poetic memoirs of three strong African-American women, their times, and their families. The book makes the people and their eras come alive.

Gridley, M. E. *Indian Tribes of America.* Illus. by L. Wolf. Hubbard, 1973. (Ages 11 and up.) [Native American] A useful reference to help differentiate among the different nations and appreciate their special qualities. The author conveys a sense of the contributions each group made and of the heritage behind each.

Griego, M. C.; Bucks, B. L.; Gilbert, S. S.; and Kimball, L. H., selectors and translators. *Tortillitas Para Mama and Other Nursery Rhymes.* Illus. by B. Cooney. Holt, 1981. (Ages 5-8.) [Central American] A pleasingly illustrated collection of nursery rhymes sung or chanted by people from various Spanish-speaking communities in the Americas.

Grifalconi, A. *Osa's Pride.* Illus. by the author. Little, Brown, 1990. (Ages 5-8.) [African] Jewel-like colors illuminate the text in this third book in the series of stories about the villages of round and square houses. In this story, her grandmother helps Osa to see how her behavior has driven away her friends. She then sets Osa on the right trail to regain peace of mind. Also see *The Village of Round and Square Houses* (1986) and *Darkness and the Butterfly* (1987).

Grode, P. *Sophie's Name.* Illus. by S. O. Haas. Kar-Ben Copies, 1990. (Ages 4-7.) [Jewish American] [See Family Constellations]

Grunsell, A. *Let's Talk about Racism.* Watts, 1991. (Ages 10 and up.) [Multicultural] This book defines such words as *racism, prejudice, stereotype,* and *apartheid,* including historical references. Using terms and examples that can be understood and discussed by students in grades 4 to 6, the author reviews how racism first affects the individual and then expands world wide. She includes Nazi Germany and South Africa as examples.

Guirma, F. *Tales of Mogho: African Stories from Upper Volta.* Macmillan, 1971. (Ages 8-10.) [African/Mossi] Interlaced with words of the Mossi people in the More language, the words of a creation myth and of other tales passed along by storytellers are set down here in print for the first time. A glossary is provided.

Gurko, M. *Theodore Herzl: The Road to Israel.* Illus. by E. Weihs. Jewish Publication Society, 1988. (Ages 9-12.) [Jewish] A readable and frank biography of the father of modern Zionism. Rising widespread anti-Semitism caused Herzl to become involved with the movement to find a homeland. This biography focuses on Herzl's life and style rather than on his intellectual or philosophical vision.

Guy, R. *The Friends.* Delacorte, 1989. (Ages 12 and up.) [African American] Phylissia and Ruby Cathy and their parents are recent arrivals from the West Indies. It is a difficult adjustment for them, particularly since Mrs. Cathy is dying. Phylissia finds a friend in Edith Jackson, but this friendship does not compensate for the obstacles imposed by urban problems, sibling competition, and an angry and violent father.

Haber, L. *Black Pioneers of Science and Invention.* HBJ, 1970. (Ages 10-14.) [African American] Each chapter begins with a biographical account of an inventor and proceeds with a detailed description of his invention. Benjamin Banneker, G. W. Carver, Granville T. Woods, Garrett A. Morgan, David Hale Williams, Charles Richard Drew, and others are included.

Hale, S. J. *Mary Had a Little Lamb.* Illus. by B. McMillan. Scholastic, 1990. (Ages 4-8.) [Universal/African American] This retelling of the popular nursery rhyme is illustrated with photos of an African-American child. Teachers can invite their students to illustrate other poems or nursery rhymes using their own pictures or photos of their class.

Hall, M. *"T" is for terrific/("T" es por terrifico).* Design by D. Figen. Open Hand, 1989. (Ages 5-10.) [Spanish/American] Written by a talented elementary school student, this creative Spanish and English alphabet book uses words that begin with the same first letter such as "guitarra" and "guitar". Included in the back of the book is a pronunciation guide for both English and Spanish words.

Hamilton, V. *Anthony Burns: The Defeat and Triumph of a Fugitive Slave.* Knopf, 1988. (Ages 12 and up.) [African American] The story of Anthony Burns, an escaped slave who was caught and returned to his master then set free again after being bought by an African-American minister and his friends. The author communicates the cruelties of the torture and degradation practiced by slave owners. Burns's case influenced state laws; he was the last fugitive slave ever seized in Massachusetts.

Hamilton, V. *The Bells of Christmas.* Illus. by L. Davis. HBJ, 1989. (Ages 8-10.) [African American] [See Special Needs]

Hamilton, V. *Cousins.* Philomel, 1990. (Ages 10-12.) [African American] [See Family Constellations]

Hamilton, V. *The Dark Way: Stories from the Spirit World.* Illus. by L. Davis. HBJ, 1990. (Ages 10 and up.) [Multicultural] The stories originate in many diverse countries. Hamilton's research is impeccable, her explications are informative, and her retellings are dramatic and absorbing. Witches, enchantments, and spirits abound here.

Hamilton, V. *Drylongso.* Illus. by J. Pinkney. HBJ, 1992. (Ages 8-10.) [African American] After a three-year period of drought, a wall of a dust storm invades Lindy's family's home, sweeping in front of it a tall boy named Drylongso. The family takes care of the boy; and in return, he gives them seeds and finds an underground spring. Then he leaves. Lindy, who loves having him as a temporary brother and a permanent friend, mourns his departure but benefits from all he has taught her. The pictures and text combine to convey a palpable sense of the drought and the relief at finding water. The language calls to be read aloud.

Hamilton, V. *The House of Dies Drear.* Illus. by E. Keith. Macmillan, 1968. (Ages 10 and up.) [African American] An African-American family moves from North Carolina to Ohio. The father is a college professor. They rent a large historic house that was once a station on the Underground Railroad and a repository of a fabulous underground cavern full of treasures. Mysterious characters, ghosts, and a sense of history pervade this adventure story, instilling African-American pride. The sequel, *The Mystery of Drear House* (1987) continues the story.

Hamilton, V. *The Magical Adventures of Pretty Pearl.* Harper, 1983. (Ages 11 and up.) [African American] Drawing on roots in African mythology, this story creates a mystical fantasy in which Pretty Pearl and her brother, John de Conquer, cross the ocean to be with their enslaved people. Other folkloric figures such as John Henry appear, and there is some interaction with Cherokee people. The author's personal involvement with the story is evident, especially in the end when the characters take on the name of Perry (her ancestors) who not only survived, but prospered.

Hamilton, V. *M. C. Higgins, the Great.* Macmillan, 1974. (Ages 12 and up.) [African American] [See Family Constellations]

Hamilton, V. *Many Thousand Gone: African Americans from Slavery to Freedom.* Illus. by L. and D. Dillon. Knopf, 1993. (Ages 10 and up.) [African American] Stirring vignettes of individual struggles to overcome slavery spanning the years 1671 to 1863. This work of nonfiction, with its direct, understated language, is compellingly eloquent. The illustrations are fit companions to the prose.

Hamilton, V. *Paul Robeson, The Life and Times of a Free Black Man.* Harper, 1974. (Ages 12 and up.) [African American] A well-written account of this talented and controversial man.

Hamilton, V. *The People Could Fly.* Illus. by L. an D. Dillon. Knopf, 1985. (Ages 6 and up.) [Multicultural] These folktales "were once a creative way for an oppressed people to express their fears and hopes to one another." The origins of the stories range from North and South America to Africa and Europe. Each story is followed by Hamilton's insightful commentary on its origins and meanings.

Hamilton, V. *The Time-Ago Tales of Jahdu.* Illus. by N. Hogragian. Macmillan, 1973. (Ages 7-10.) [African American] Lee Edwards is a young African American whose baby-sitter, Mama Luka, tells him stories of Jahdu, a magical young boy. The stories are aimed at helping African-American children develop and maintain a sense of self-pride and positive ambition. The character of the storyteller is well captured. Also see *Time-Ago Lost: More Tales of Jahdu* (1973).

Hamilton, V. *Zeely.* Illus. by S. Shimin. Macmillan, 1967. (Ages 10-12.) [African American] Elizabeth and her brother vacation at their uncle's farm. There they meet a strikingly beautiful girl named Zeely. Six and one-half feet tall, a descendant of the Watusi, she helps Elizabeth learn to take pride in herself.

Han, O. S., and Plunkett, S. H., adapters. *Sir Whong and the Golden Pig.* Illus. by O. S. Han. Dial, 1993. (Ages 5-9.) [Korean] Although somewhat awkwardly told, this folktale from Korea in which a trickster is outwitted by the wise and generous Sir Whong has clever characters and a satisfying ending. The culture is well portrayed.

Han, S. *The Rabbit's Judgment.* Illus. by Y. Heo. Holt, 1994. (Ages 7-10.) [Korean] This adaptation of a Korean folktale poses a number of moral dilemmas for young readers. It is the tale of a tiger who cannot change his basic nature, a man who perhaps foolishly performs and act of kindness, and a clever rabbit who saves the man's life. This retelling (in both Korean and English) raises issues of condemning one person for the sins of the group. The illustrations are stylized and dramatic. The author lives in Seoul, and the illustrator is of Korean heritage.

Hansen, J. C. *The Gift-Giver.* Walker, 1980. (Ages 10 and up.) [African American] Amir, almost too perfect to be true, is sensitive to others, quietly determined, nonviolent, never self-pitying, strong, and loving. When he is forced to move to another state, his best friend Doris is bereft. The positive sense of African-American community is one of the strengths of this book. In *Yellow Bird and Me* (1986), the sequel, Doris misses Amir so much that it is difficult for her to function. At Amir's urging, Doris learns to help another boy, Yellow Bird, who has a learning disability; and this makes her more content.

Hansen, J. *Out from This Place.* Walker, 1988. (Ages 9-12.) [African American] Three young people, Easter, Obi, and Jason, have been together for a number of years—slaves to Mr. and Mrs. Jennings. This book focuses on Easter and her successful journey to freedom. It chronicles the years 1862-1865. This is the sequel to *Which Way Freedom?* (1986), which is told from Obi's perspective during the same period of time. The key to both books is the strong sense of the right of every person to be free.

Harris, J. C., adapted by V. D. Parks and M. Jones. *Jump! The Adventures of Brer Rabbit.* Illus. by B. Moser. HBJ, 1986. (Ages 8–12.) [African American] This book, together with *Jump Again! More Adventures of Brer Rabbit* (1987) and *Jump on Over! The Adventures of Brer Rabbit and His Family* (1989), contains lively retellings of fifteen African-American folktales featuring Brer Rabbit, Brer Fox, and Brer Wolf. The character of Uncle Remus, who told these stories in Harris's original 1880 collection, does not appear in these adaptations; thus the stories stand on their own. They are told in the dialect of the rural south, which adds an authentic feeling, and are dramatically illustrated by Barry Moser.

Hart, P. S. *Flying Free: America's First Black Aviators.* Illus. with photos. Lerner, 1992. (Ages 10 and up.) [African American] The presentation of exciting adventures, societal and technical pioneers, and an understanding of the context of the times both in the African-American and Caucasian communities make this accessible book a gem for young readers.

Harvey, B. *Immigrant Girl, Becky of Eldridge Street.* Illus. by D. K. Ray. Holiday, 1987. (Ages 7–10.) [Immigration/Jewish] [See Family Constellations]

Haskins, J. *Black Dance in America: A History Through Its People.* Crowell, 1990. (Ages 12 and up.) [African American] With its companion book, *Black Music in America: A History through Its People* (1987), this provides not only a cultural history but also an understanding of the political and emotional importance of dance and music to African Americans.

Haskins, J. *Against All Opposition: Black Explorers in America.* Walker, 1992. (Ages 12 and up.) [African American] A comprehensive look at African-American explorers who have generally been excluded from history books. York, who saved Lewis and Clark's famous expedition; Stephan Darantez (Estevanico), who explored Mexico; and some of the people of African descent who traveled with Columbus are profiled. This book helps dissolve stereotypes and counters inaccurate historical accounts.

Haskins. J. *Bill Cosby: America's Most Famous Father.* Walker, 1988. (Ages 9–13.) [African American] Lots of detail is integrated into the story of this versatile, multitalented man. His function as a role model for African Americans is appropriately highlighted. Other biographies of remarkable African Americans by this author include *Katherine Dunham* (Coward-McCann, 1982); *Lena Horne* (Coward-McCann, 1983); and *Thurgood Marshall: A Life for Justice* (Holt, 1992).

Haskins, J. *Get On Board: The Story of the Underground Railroad.* Scholastic, 1993. (Ages 12 and up.) [African American] A thoroughly researched account of the workings of the Underground Railroad focusing on African Americans' involvement in their own liberation. The stories of individuals include not only the details of their escape but also accounts of what happened to them afterwards.

Haskins, J. *One More River to Cross: The Stories of Twelve Black Americans.* Scholastic, 1992. (Ages 10 and up.) [African American] A wide range of outstanding African Americans is included here, some well known, others perhaps not as familiar to school children, like Madam C. J. Walker (first American woman to become a millionaire), Romare Bearden (artist), Eddie Robinson (football coach), and Ronald McNair (astronaut). Their tribulations as well as their triumphs are included.

Haskins, J. *Outward Dreams: Black Inventors and Their Inventions.* Walker, 1991. (Ages 11 and up.) [African American] Describes in some detail the inventions of several black men and women. The appendix lists almost 400 inventions of black men and women between 1834 and 1900 as evidenced by the patents they filed.

Havill, J. *Jamaica's Find.* Illus. by A. S. O'Brien. Scholastic, 1986. (Ages 5-7.) [Universal/ African American] Jamaica, an African-American girl, finds a stuffed dog in the park. Although she does not want to return it, she locates its rightful owner, Kristin, who is overjoyed to get it back. For further adventures of Jamaica and her family, see *Jamaica Tag-Along* (1989) [See Siblings] and *Jamaica and Brianna* (1993). [See War]

Havill, J. *Treasure Nap.* Illus. by E. Savadier. Houghton Mifflin, 1992. (Ages 4-6.) [Mexican American] Alicia's mother soothes her from the heat of summer and tells about her great grandmother and her Mexican heritage. The valuing of heritage is transmitted here. The continuity of the family is also conveyed, as Alicia still carefully and appreciatively plays with her great-great-grandfather's *serape* (shawl), *pito* (flute), and bird cage.

Hayes, S. *Happy Christmas, Gemma.* Illus. by J. Ormerod. Lothrop Lee and Shepard, 1986. (Ages 4-6.) [Universal/African American] [See Siblings]

Hayashi, A. *Aki and the Fox.* Illus. by the author. Doubleday, 1991. (Ages 5-9). [Japanese] A whimsical adventure about a young Japanese girl and her toy fox, Kon, given to her by her grandmother when she was born. When Kon is torn, Aki travels to grandmother's by train to have Kon repaired. Along the way, they encounter some unexpected adventures that almost end in disaster for the little fox. The author-illustrator, who lives in Tokyo, depicts an authentic cultural perspective.

Heide, F. P. *The Day of Ahmed's Secret.* Illus. by T. Lewin. Lothrop Lee and Shepard, 1990. (Ages 6-8.) [Universal/Arab/Egyptian] The reader journeys with Ahmed, a young boy in Egypt, as he delivers gas canisters and meets vendors. When the day ends, Ahmed returns to his home and family and shares a secret: He has learned to write his name. Ahmed is proud of his responsibility and importance to the community. He is proud of his family and home and loves his city. All this is conveyed through rich illustrations and a well-written text.

Heide, F. P., and Gilliland, J. H. *Sami and the Time of the Troubles.* Illus. by T. Lewin. Clarion, 1992. (Ages 7-10.) [Lebanese] [See War and Peace]

Heidish, M. *A Woman Called Moses.* Houghton Mifflin, 1976. (Ages 12 and up.) [African American] This biography of Harriet Tubman goes beyond most simplified versions written especially for younger readers. It is told through the voice of Harriet herself as she looks back over her long life. Such famous figures as John Brown, Frederick Douglass, and William Lloyd Garrison are encountered in the book so that readers gain a sense of history.

Heller, L. *The Castle on Hester Street.* Illus. by the author. Jewish Publication Society, 1982. (Ages 5-8.) [Jewish American] Julie's grandfather regales her with stories about his youthful adventures. After each of these tales, Julie's grandmother sets the record straight with what really happened. Woven into the family's bantering is an appreciation of the hardships this immigrant couple encountered both in Europe and as newcomers to America.

Henderson, N., and Dewey, J. *Circle of Life: The Miccosukee Indian Way.* Illus. by D. Pickens. Messner, 1974. (Ages 8-10.) [Native American/Miccosukee] A close look at the history and customs of the Miccosukee, who now control their own education and culture, teach and practice their own ways, and manage their own economic affairs. The respectfully written book expresses optimism and dignity.

Hesse, K. *Letters from Rifka.* Holt, 1992. (Ages 10 and up.) [Immigrant/Jewish] Rifka, a twelve-year-old Russian Jew escaping the Pogroms in 1919, becomes separated not only from her homeland but from her family as well, first when she comes down with typhus in Poland and again when she is detained at Ellis Island because she has ringworm. On Ellis Island, where she proves herself to be intelligent, resourceful, and hard working, she finally is permitted to rejoin her family.

Heyman, A. *Exit from Home.* Crown, 1977. (Ages 12 and up.) [Jewish/Russian] A Russian Jewish boy from a pious family moves away from his religion and becomes active in the Revolution of 1905. He escapes to America. The book is one of the few that points out the conflict between secularism and religion for Jews.

Highwater, J. *Many Smokes, Many Moons: A Chronology of American Indian History through Indian Art.* Lippincott, 1978. (Ages 12 and up.) [Native American] Beginning with a creation story, the text offers an informative history of the native peoples of North America. Photos of Native Americans illuminate and extend the reader's enjoyment.

Highwater, J. *Moonsong Lullaby.* Illus. by M. Keegan. Lothrop Lee and Shepard, 1981. (All Ages.) [Native American/Cherokee] Vibrant photos of the activities of a Cherokee camp and its setting. The words of the song affirm the positive quality of native life.

Hill, Kirkpatrick. *Toughboy and Sister.* McElderry, 1990. (Ages 8–12.) [Native American/Athapaskan] [See Siblings]

Hirsch, S. C. *Famous American Indians of the Plains.* Illus. by L. Bjorklund, Rand McNally, 1973. (Ages 12 and up.) [Native American/Plains] Lavishly illustrated with paintings by famous artists as well as drawings by Bjorklund, tells about the accomplishments, customs, and circumstances of the Plains Indians.

Hirschfelder, A. B., and Singer, B. R., eds. *Rising Voices: Writings of Young Native Americans.* Scribner, 1992. (Ages 11 and up.) [Native American] B. Singer, a member of the Santa Clara Pueblo, has taught Native American studies. A. Hirschfelder has written many articles and books about native people. The essays and poems, from numerous published and unpublished sources, are written by native people from Maine to Alaska. The writing spans many years from the late nineteenth century to the present; and the authors, although all are young, voice different opinions and feelings. The strength of tradition is strongly manifested, as is the will to overcome adversity.

Hoberman, M. A. *Fathers, Mothers, Sisters, Brothers: A Collection of Family Poems.* Illus. by M. Hafner. Joy Street, 1991. (Ages 7–10.) [Universal] [See Family Constellations]

Hodges, M. *The Fire Bringer: A Paiute Indian Legend.* Illus. by P. Parnell. Boston: Little, Brown, 1972. (Ages 7 and up.) [Native American/Paiute] Elegantly told and illustrated story of how the coyote and a Paiute boy brought fire to people.

Hoffman, M. *Amazing Grace.* Illus. by C. Binch. Dial, 1991. (Ages 5–8.) [African American] When Grace's class plans a production of Peter Pan, she wants to be Peter even though her classmates tell her she can't because she's black and she's a girl. Her mother and grandmother, who are extremely supportive, demonstrate that she can be anything she wants to be. Grace wins the audition and does a wonderful job as Peter. This is an affirming story of a confident, talented child. The illustrations contain an unfortunately insensitive rendering of Grace, supposedly as Hiawatha, in a war bonnet.

Hoig, S. *People of the Breaking Day: The Southern Cheyenne Today.* Illus. with photos and old prints. Dutton, 1992. (Ages 11 and up.) [Native American/Cheyenne] The author has lived near the former Cheyenne reservation for many years; and the careful research he presents in this book includes the testimony of many members of the Cheyenne nation. He chronicles their history, including the loss of their land, and discusses their relationship with other nations, especially the Arapaho. Although many southern Cheyenne today live in poverty, others are teachers, doctors, artists, and lawyers. Their pride, strength, and struggle to maintain their cultural identity are described.

Never condescending, demeaning, or overly glorifying, Hoig paints a realistic picture of a culture determined to survive.

Holt, D. *The ABC's of Black History.* Illus. by S. Bhang, Jr. Ritchie Ward, 1985. (Ages 9–12.) [African American] For each letter of the alphabet, the author, who is an African-American teacher, gives the name of an African American who achieved much and contributed to the struggle for freedom. An impressive array of contemporary and historical heroes is presented.

Hooks, W. H. *The Ballad of Belle Dorcas.* Illus. by B. Pinkney. Knopf, 1990. (Ages 8–10.) [African American] Sorcery helps Belle retain a beyond-the-grave relationship with her husband Joshua, who has been killed by slave-catchers. The drama is heightened by Brian Pinkney's powerful scratchboard illustrations. The pain of slavery and the triumph of the spirit are demonstrated.

Hooks, W. H. *Peach Boy.* Illus. by J. Otani. Bantam, 1992. (Ages 5–8.) [Japanese] A simply told and easy-to-read version of the well-known Japanese folktale about the child found in a peach by an aging couple. He grows to be a hero who vanquishes the wicked *oni* monsters.

Hopkins, L. B. *This Street's for Me.* Illus. by A. Grifalconi. Crown, 1970. (Ages 7–9.) [Universal] City poems conveying a sense of the moods and activities of the city, with nicely integrated illustrations.

Hopkins, L. B., ed. *Through Our Eyes.* Illus. by J. Dunn. Little, Brown, 1992. (Ages 4–7.) [Multicultural] Poems and photos describing the experiences of children growing up in the 1990s. Issues such as identity formation, peer pressure, sibling interaction, biracial children, abandonment, and the latch-key child are explored. Children of many different heritages are represented in both the photos and the poetry.

Hopkins, L. B., ed. *Don't You Turn Back.* Illus. by A. Grifalconi. Knopf, 1969. (Ages 11 and up.) [African American] The title comes from a line in a poem called "Mother to Son." It stresses the positive determination of African Americans to endure. The poems in this collection reflect this courage.

Hopkins, L. B., ed. *On Our Way: Poems of Pride and Love.* Illus. by D. Parks. Knopf, 1974. (Ages 8 and up.) [African American] Twenty-two poems by African Americans singing of the black experience. A beautiful collection, visually as well as poetically.

Hopkinson, D. *Sweet Clara and the Freedom Quilt.* Illus. by J. Ransome. Knopf, 1993. (Ages 6–10.) [African American] This book provides a basis for even the youngest of children to appreciate the inventiveness and courage required for slaves to escape into freedom. Clara, a young slave, uses her skills to construct a quilt that serves as a map of an escape route to Canada. Her story is a celebration of the human spirit and an alterative to the image of the abused, passive, pitiful slave. The paintings palpably communicate the characters' emotional connections with one another and demonstrate the illustrator's personal investment in the story.

Hort, L. *How Many Stars in the Sky?* Illus. by J. E. Ransome. Tambourine, 1991. (Ages 5–8.) [Universal/African American] [See Family Constellations]

Houston, J. *Akavak.* Illus. by the author. HBJ, 1990. (Ages 10 and up.) [Native American/Inuit] (See Aging)

Houston, J. *Tikta'Liktak.* Illus. by the author. HBJ, 1990. (Ages 10 and up.) [Native American/Inuit] The importance of learning Inuit traditions and practices is conveyed in this tale of a young hunter carried out to sea who survives with the aid of the seal spirits. This retelling of an Inuit legend is respectful and accurate in its reporting of Inuit customs.

Hou-Tien. *The Chinese New Year.* Holt, 1976. (Ages 6–12.) [Chinese] Describes the many days of celebration that signify the end of winter and the coming of spring, including the Little New Year, the Chinese New Year, and the Lantern Festival or Feast of the First Full Moon.

Howard, E. F. *Chita's Christmas Tree.* Illus. by F. Cooper. Bradbury, 1989. (Ages 6–9.) [Universal/African American] Set in Baltimore, the author's birth place, the story is a celebration of family closeness, traditions, and love. Many stereotypes are overturned: The African American family is affluent (the father is a physician). Nowhere is there a hint of didacticism, but the values of the close-knit family are apparent in both the text and the illustrations. The city of Baltimore in the early years of the twentieth century provides a rich tableau in which to set the story. See also *Aunt Flossie's Hats (and Crab Cakes Later)* (1991) and *The Train To Lulu's* (1988), which contain the same setting and appeal.

Howard, V. *A Screaming Whisper.* Illus. by J. Ponderhughes. Holt, 1972. (Ages 12 and up.) [African American] Howard is an African-American poet. Her poem "For My Children" could be used as guide to writers. In it, she says, "My children are unique, my children have names."

Howard, V. "Monument in Black." In *The Voice of the Children,* edited by J. Jordan and T. Bush. Holt, 1970. (Ages 9–12.) [African American] The poet suggests honoring African Americans on coins and with statues. She alludes to the many black soldiers who died for our country in Vietnam and have not been recognized.

Hoyt-Goldsmith, D. *Cherokee Summer.* Photos by L. Migdale. Holiday House, 1993. (Ages 6–10.) [Native American/Cherokee] Color photos provide a personalized view of Bridget, a contemporary Cherokee girl, her family, and her community. Bridget enjoys taking part in the activities of her people, demonstrating that the culture and traditions of the Cherokee are respected and flourishing.

Hoyt-Goldsmith, D. *Hoang Anh: A Vietnamese-American Boy.* Illus. by L. Migdale. Holiday House, 1992. (Ages 8–12.) [Vietnamese American] Illustrated with colorful photos, this slim book describes the family's daring escape by boat from Vietnam, traditional Vietnamese cooking, and the annual Tet festival. Hoang Anh is proud of his heritage and wants to learn more about it. A map, a glossary, and a pronunciation guide are provided.

Hoyt-Goldsmith, D. *Pueblo Storyteller.* Illus. by L. Migdale. Holiday House, 1991. (Ages 8–10.) [Native American/Pueblo] Through photos and first-person narrative, the book explores the everyday life of April, a ten-year-old Cochiti Pueblo girl. It shows how the people make bread and pottery and how they celebrate their culture through dance and dress.

Hoyt-Goldsmith, D. *Totem Pole.* Illus. by L. Migdale. Holiday House, 1990. (Ages 10 and up.) [Native American/Tsimshian] Narrated by young David Boxley, a member of the Eagle clan of the Tsimshian Nation, this is an account of his father's continuation of the traditional practice of totem pole carving in the Northwest. The text and the color photographs help dispel the "vanished race" myth all too prevalent in some children's literature.

Hudson, C. W., and Ford, B. G. *Bright Eyes, Brown Skin.* Illus. by G. Ford. Just Us, 1990. (Ages 2–5.) [African American] A simple rhyming text celebrating the beauty of black children. The setting is a preschool in which energetic, self-confident, affectionate, and outgoing children interact.

Hudson, W. *Pass It On: African American Poetry for Children.* Illus. by F. Cooper. Scholastic, 1993. (Ages 5–8.) [African American] An introduction to such important poets as

Langston Hughes, Nikki Giovanni, Gwendolyn Brooks, and Eloise Greenfield, among others. The illustrations will help attract the youngest of readers.

Hungry Wolf, B. *The Ways of My Grandmother.* Morrow, 1980. (Ages 12 and up.) [Native American/Blackfoot] Like all good oral histories, the book contains stories, accounts of daily life, myths and legends, and informative passages on the history and customs of the author's people, the Blackfoot.

Hurmence, B. *A Girl Called Boy.* Clarion, 1982. (Ages 9-12.) [African American] Transported into the era of slavery, Boy (Blanche Overtha Yancey) appreciates the traditions, intelligence, strength, and beauty of her family background. The device of time travel is plausible here, and the story provides an excellent context for the message.

Hurmence, B. *Tancy.* Clarion, 1984. (Ages 12 and up.) [African American] After emancipation, Tancy leaves the plantation where she has lived all her life and searches for her mother, who was sold when Tancy was very young. Tancy becomes a teacher and finally finds her mother. She also finds her vocation and a man whom she can respect and love. Postemancipation feelings and events are candidly described.

Hurwitz, J. *Once I Was a Plum Tree.* Morrow, 1980. (Ages 8-12.) [Jewish American] Gerry Flam's family name was once Pflamenbaum, or "Plumtree." They have become assimilated, even somewhat alienated from their Jewish background. Gerry finally finds the opportunity to learn about her heritage from a family who are escapees from the Holocaust.

Hurwitz, J. *The Rabbi's Girls.* Illus. by P. Johnson. Morrow, 1982. (Ages 8-12.) [Jewish American] Carrie's father is a rabbi, and the family has moved from one congregation to the next. The story takes place in 1923 in Ohio. The family endures anti-Semitism, illness, and finally, the death of the father; but the tone is one of hope and determination, and the strength of the characters emerges as the overriding element.

Huynh, Q. N. *The Land I Lost: Adventures of a Boy in Vietnam.* Illus. by V. Mai. Harper, 1982. (Ages 9-12.) [Vietnamese] Only on the last two pages of this book does war enter into the story, and then it is the war between the French and the Vietnamese, who are led by Ho Chi Minh. The author tells of his family and friends and the life they led before the war. Customs, beliefs, and adventures are described in the context of a dearly loved community and lifestyle.

Igus, T.; Ellis, V. F.; Patrick, D.; and Wesley, V. *Book of Black Heroes, Volume II: Great Women in the Struggle.* Just Us, 1991. (Ages 10 and up.) [African American] [See Gender Roles]

Isadora, R. *At the Crossroads.* Illus. by the author. Greenwillow, 1991. (Ages 4-8.) [African/South African] [See Family Constellations]

Isadora, R. *Ben's Trumpet.* Illus. by the author. Greenwillow, 1979. (Ages 6-10.) [African American] Ben pretends he has a horn and plays splendid music in his imagination. A professional trumpet player helps turn his fantasies into reality.

Isadora, R. *Over the Green Hills.* Illus. by the author. Greenwillow, 1992. (Ages 4-8.) [African/South African] [See Family Constellations]

Jenness, A. *Families: A Celebration of Diversity, Commitment, and Love.* Illus. by the author. Houghton Mifflin, 1990. (Ages 8 and up.) [Universal] [See Family Constellations]

Jenness, A., and Rivers, A. *In Two Worlds: A Yup'ik Eskimo Family.* Illus. by A. Jenness. Houghton Mifflin, 1989. (Ages 9-12.) [Native American/Yupik] [See Family Constellations]

Johnson, A. L. "A Black Poetry Day." In *Black Out Loud: An Anthology of Modern Poems by Black Americans,* edited by A. Adoff. Illus. by A. Hollingsworth. Macmillan, 1970.

(Ages 6–12.) [African American] The poet wants a day to celebrate black poets and, ultimately, all areas of achievement by African Americans.

Johnson, A. *Tell Me a Story, Mama*. Illus. by D. Soman. Orchard, 1989. (Ages 5–8.) [African American] The child knows very well what stories she wants, and her clever and nurturing mother permits her to fill in most of the details while at the same time contributing to the interaction with her own well-placed comments. The illustrations of the African American family enhance the work.

Johnson, A. *When I Am Old with You*. Illus. by D. Soman. Orchard, 1990. (Ages 5–8.) [Universal/African American] [See Aging]

Johnson, D. *What Will Mommy Do When I'm at School?* Illus. by the author. Macmillan, 1990. (Ages 5–8.) [Universal/African American] [See Family Constellations]

Johnson, J. W. *Lift Every Voice and Sing*. Illus. by E. Catlett. Walker, 1993. (Ages 6 and up.) [African American] Strong illustrations accompany the inspirational words of what has come to be known as the national anthem for African Americans.

Jones, H. *Coyote Tales*. Illus. by L. Mofsie. Holt, 1974. (Ages 8–12.) [Native American] Coyote, a trickster, is a recurrent character in Native American tales, which are similar in many ways to the African tales of Spider. The illustrations (by a Native American illustrator) are excellent.

Jones, H., ed. *The Trees Stand Shining: Poetry of the North American Indian*. Illus. by R. A. Parker. Dial, 1971. (Ages 6 and up.) [Native American] Chants, songs, and poems of Native Americans which express an observation of and respect for the natural world. Each is credited with the nation of origin. The illustrations are respectful and accurate.

Joseph, L. *An Island Christmas*. Illus. by C. Stock. Houghton Mifflin, 1992. (Ages 5–8.) [Trinidadian/Tobagoan] Rosie and her brother Ragboy prepare for Christmas on the islands of Trinidad and Tobago. They gather sorrel to make juice, prepare currant cakes and aloe pies, make presents for their family, and paint and decorate the guava branch they use as a Christmas tree. Parang bands roam the streets, and neighbors join in the festivities. Readers may enjoy comparing this Christmas celebration with those of the United States and others.

Joseph, L. *A Wave in Her Pocket*. Illus. by B. Pinkney. Clarion, 1991. (Ages 8–10.) [Trinidadian] The scratchboard illustrations make a fine accompaniment to these stories from the author's homeland of Trinidad. The storyteller heritage carried on by "Tantie," the author's aunt, includes scary as well as funny and touching stories. In all of them the reader is privileged to join the large, loving family. Rich Trinidadian traditions are embodied in the stories rather than tacked on artificially.

Kanawa, K. T. *Land of the Long White Cloud*. Illus. by M. Foreman. Arcade, 1989. (Ages 8–10.) [Native New Zealand/Maori] Tales of Maui, Te Kanawa (the great Waikato chief), and other heroes of Maori culture. The author retells the tales she heard when she was growing up. The illustrations are dramatic.

Katz, J. B., ed. *This Song Remembers: Self Portraits of Native Americans in the Arts*. Houghton Mifflin, 1980. (Ages 12 and up.) [Native American] A well-researched and designed book of written and artistic representations of Native Americans as they view themselves. A good cross-section of cultures and work are included.

Katz, W. L. *Black Indians: A Hidden Heritage*. Illus. with photos. Atheneum, 1986. (Ages 12 and up.) [Native American/African American] This work of nonfiction explores the alliances of African Americans and Native Americans that have occurred throughout U.S. history. Many Indian nations have adopted both blacks and whites. The Seminoles in Florida, for example, gave refuge to runaway slaves, and many intermarriages occurred. This book, which chronicles such episodes from the time of Columbus, helps dispel myths.

Katz, W. L. *The Black West.* Open Hand, 1987. (Ages 12 and up.) [African American] An encyclopedic work revealing the important part African Americans played in the development of the West. Included in the contents are women, cowboys, explorers, and soldiers, both infantry and cavalry, as well as other categories. This is a resource to be dipped into time and again.

Katz. W. L. *Breaking the Chains: African-American Slave Resistance.* Atheneum, 1990. (Ages 12 and up.) [African American] An important account of slaves' resistance. This chronicle makes clear how erroneous is the stereotype that slaves were either passive or happy in their condition.

Keegan, M. *Pueblo Boy: Growing up in Two Worlds.* Illus. with photos. Cobblehill, 1991. (Ages 6–10.) [Native American/Pueblo] Timmy Roybal, whose Indian name is Agoyo-Paa (Star Fire), is ten years old and lives in the San Ildefonso Pueblo in New Mexico. He rides a bike, shoots pool, and uses computers at school; but he also participates in tribal dances and ceremonies and is learning the oral tradition of his people. He is a happy, well-adjusted child with a strong community and extended family. Ceremonies, clan affiliations, kiva worship, and other aspects of Pueblo life are accurately and respectfully portrayed.

Kendall, R. *Eskimo Boy: Life in an Inupiaq Eskimo Village.* Illus. by the author. Scholastic, 1992. (Ages 7–10.) [Native American/Inupiaq] Despite the title, this book is an authentic account of life in the native Alaskan village of Shishmaref. The color photographs graphically take readers to visit seven-year-old Norman Kokeok and his family. Norman's schooling includes learning the Inupiaq language and carving soapstone. Misinformation is corrected: Alaskan natives do not live in igloos; they live in houses. Customs and daily life are respectfully reported. A valuable and attractive book.

Kherdian, D. *Feathers and Tails: Animal Fables from around the World.* Illus. by N. Hogrogian. Philomel, 1992. (Ages 5–8.) [Multiracial] Twenty-one stories from many countries outside western Europe. The variety goes well beyond traditional fables and includes trickster tales, myths, and other genres, many humorously told.

Kherdian, D. *Root River Run.* Illus. by N. Hogrogian. Carolrhoda, 1984. (Ages 10 and up.) [Armenian American] Third in the trilogy of the author's autobiographical novels of his Armenian heritage, this one focuses on David himself. He vividly shows how it feels to grow up in a close-knit community within the larger non-Armenian community. Prejudice, pride, and family interactions are all ingredients of this worthy end-piece to its two acclaimed precursors, *The Road from Home: The Story of an Armenian Girl* (1979), and *Finding Home* (1981).

Kimmel, E. A., reteller. *Anansi and the Moss-Covered Rock.* Illus. by J. Stevens. Holiday House, 1988. (Ages 6–10.) [African/West African] Anansi stories are an important part of the African-American heritage. In some, Anansi is a hero; in others a villain; but he is always a trickster. In this tale, Anansi is bested by a shy creature, the little bush deer. Anansi is drawn as a realistic spider with no distinguishing features. The other animals are anthropomorphic and modern (Turtle wears sunglasses, for example.) Also see *Anansi Goes Fishing* (1992), in which Anansi tries to outsmart Turtle and which explains why spiders spin webs.

Kimmel, E. A. *Boots and His Brothers.* Illus. by K. B. Root. Holiday House, 1992. (Ages 6–10.) [Norwegian] This Norwegian folktale tells of three brothers who set off to find their fortune. Peter and Paul are large and greedy, and Boots is small and generous. Through patience and kindness, Boots obtains the magical means to perform the tasks.

He receives his weight in gold and becomes heir to the kingdom. This version is toned down from some others (Peter and Paul are merely chased away, not beheaded).

Kliment, B. *Ella Fitzgerald*. Chelsea House, 1988. (Ages 10-14.) [African American] An admiring but not fatuous biography of the popular singer, this is part of the "Black Americans of Achievement" series, with an introductory essay by Coretta Scott King. Black-and-white photos provide an excellent image of the times. As with the other volumes in this excellent series, there is a chronology and a recommended list for further reading.

Knight, M. B. *Talking Walls*. Illus. by A. S. O'Brien. Tilbury House, 1992. (Ages 6-10.) [Universal] Using as examples the Great Wall of China, the Lascaux Caves, Mahabalipuram's Animal Walls, the Vietnam Veterans Memorial, the Berlin Wall, and others, this unique book examines the history, purposes, and meaning of walls to each culture. Included in the back is a complete index of each wall's history and a labeled world map.

Knutson, B. *How the Guinea Fowl Got Her Spots*. Illus. by the author. Carolrhoda, 1990. (Ages 5-8.) [Swahili] This Swahili story of friendship is a creation tale as well. It explains that the cow gave the guinea fowl camouflaging milky spots because the guinea fowl frequently saved the cow from the lion. The text and illustrations work well together.

Knutson, B. *Why the Crab Has No Head*. Illus. by the author. Carolrhoda, 1987. (Ages 5-8.) [African/Zaire] This retelling of a tale from the Bakongo people of Zaire sings with a cadence and carefully crafted lyric. The strong and wise female creator suitably punishes the crab for his arrogance at thinking he is the most important creature she has created. The story moves well; the language is simple but strong; the stylized black-and-white illustrations contain borders with geometric designs that frame the text.

Kouzel, D. *The Cuckoo's Reward (El Premio del Cuco)*. Illus. by E. Thollander. Doubleday, 1977. (Ages 5-8.) [Central American/Mayan] Told in both English and Spanish, the story is an adaptation of a Mayan legend explaining why the cuckoo lays her eggs in other birds' nests.

Kraus, J. H. *Tall Boy's Journey*. Illus. by K. Ritz. Carolrhoda, 1992. (Ages 6-9.) [Korean American] A sensitive look at the feelings a young Korean boy when he first comes to the United States to be adopted by a white American couple. Customs and their conveyed meanings are central here, and the book helps readers to understand how people from other cultures feel upon sudden immersion into a strange new environment.

Kuklin, S. *How My family Lives in America*. Illus. with photos. Bradbury, 1992. (Ages 6-10.) [Multicultural] Sanu, Eric, and April, three children with multiethnic backgrounds, tell of the daily routines and special celebrations unique to their individual heritages. The theme of food is used throughout the book, with recipes included. Photos highlight each child's culture.

Kusugak, M. A. *Baseball Bats for Christmas*. Illus. by V. Krykorka. Annick, 1990. (Ages 6-9.) [Native American/Inuit] A memory of 1955, when the author lived in a tiny community of fewer than 100 people in Repulse Bay on the Arctic Circle. He remembers one Christmas time when the pilot who was their only connection to the rest of the world brought spindly trees the children used to make baseball bats. Through the story a nostalgic sense of everyday life and community interaction in this remote place is conveyed.

Kwon, H. H. *The Moles and the Mireuk*. Illus. by W. Hubbard. Houghton Mifflin, 1993. (Ages 7-10.) [Korean] A mole father wants to find the most powerful being in the universe to marry his beloved daughter. After visiting the sky, the sun, the clouds, the wind, and the great stone Mireuk in his valley, he finally finds her a suitable husband. This whimsical, beautifully illustrated traditional Korean folktale is almost identical to the Hopi tale *The Mouse Couple,* by Ekkehart Malotki, with which it invites comparison.

Lacapa, M. *The Flute Player.* Illus. by the author. Northland, 1990. (Ages 7-10.) [Native American/Apache/Hopi] Michael Lacapa is a gifted storyteller, artist, and educator whose Apache-Hopi heritage informs his craft. Drawn from the oral tradition of the White Mountain Apache, the story tells of the love between a young Apache flute player and a young woman. The lovers die before they can be united, but the sound of his flute blowing through the trees always remains. The story helps dispel stereotypes of "unfeeling stoicism" on the part of the Apache people. Because this is a pourquoi tale, an explanatory myth, the death and disappearance of the young lovers should not be read literally as death and suicide but as an expression of how nature and people are intertwined.

Langone, J. *Spreading Poison: A Book about Racism and Prejudice.* Little, Brown, 1993. (Ages 11 and up.) [Multicultural] A factual, passionate indictment of bigotry in its many forms. The author specifically addresses prejudice against African Americans, Jews, Native Americans, various immigrant groups, women, and homosexuals.

Langstaff, J. *Climbing Jacob's Ladder.* Illus. by A. Bryan. Macmillan, 1991. (Ages 7-12.) [African American] A companion to *What a Morning!: The Christmas Story in Black Spirituals* (1987), the books provide a brief textual explanation of the songs. The illustrations convey a sense of joy and celebration. Musical notation is included for each song.

Lankford, M. D. *Hopscotch around the World.* Illus. by K. Milone. Morrow, 1992. (Ages 8-12.) [Multicultural] Variations of the game of hopscotch from 17 countries throughout the world. Included with each description are directions and a full-page illustration of children playing the game.

Lasky, K. *The Night Journey.* Illus. by T. S. Hyman. Warne, 1981. (Ages 11 and up.) [Jewish American] Rachel's great-grandmother tells her stories about life long ago in czarist Russia and how cruelly Jews were treated in those times. The book is full of the language and customs of Jewish families.

Lawrence, J. *The Great Migration.* Harper, 1993. (Ages 8-11.) [African American] The stark illustrations dramatically depict the movement of African Americans from the South to the northern United States in the early and middle parts of the twentieth century. Searching for a better life in the industrial North, the emigrants encountered racism and difficult living conditions; but on the whole they were better off than they had been in the South. Lawrence shares the story as his parents told it to him. The poem, "Migration," by W. D. Myers, is included.

Lawrence, J. *Harriet and the Promised Land.* Verses by R. Kraus. Simon & Schuster, 1993. (Ages 6-10.) [African American] J. Lawrence is an African-American artist. His stark paintings, accompanied by Kraus's verses, powerfully convey a sense of Harriet Tubman's heroism.

Lee, J. M. *Silent Lotus.* Illus. by the author. Farrar, Straus, and Giroux, 1991. (Ages 6-9.) [Cambodian] [See Special Needs]

Lee, J. M. *Toad Is the Uncle of Heaven.* Illus. by the author. Holt, 1985. (Ages 6-9.) [Vietnamese] Reminiscent of other cultures' cumulative tales and animal-helper tales, the story explains why Toad is a symbol of rain for the Vietnamese people. Several unlikely companions accompany Toad to see the King of Heaven in order to plead for rain. After a number of angry encounters, the King finally accedes to the request. The tale is illustrated and retold from the author's heritage.

Lee, M. G. *Finding My Voice*. Houghton Mifflin, 1992. (Ages 12 and up.) [Korean American] Ellen Sung, the only Asian American in her school (her family is from Korea), spends her last year of high school juggling academics, gymnastics, and a social life while trying to meet her parents' high expectations. With the support of friends, Ellen learns to stand up for herself in her own quiet way, gaining the respect of her parents and some of her previously hostile peers. This thought-provoking book is well written.

Lester, J. *Black Folktales*. Illus. by T. Feelings. Grove, 1969. (Ages 6-10.) [African/American] Powerful retelling of tales from Africa, the South, and urban America. The illustrations are excellent.

Lester, J. *The Knee-High Man and Other Tales*. Illus. by R. Pinto. Dial, 1972. (Ages 3-8.) [African American] Tales from times of slavery containing trickery and competition.

Lester, J. *Long Journey Home: Stories from Black History*. Dial, 1972. (Ages 12 and up.) [African American] Deeply involving accounts of people who have not appeared in many history books, demonstrating that many African Americans were the source of their own freedom. Some are angry, some are triumphant, some end tragically. Based on historical research, the stories are amplified by the author.

Lester, J. *This Strange New Feeling*. Dial, 1982. (Ages 11 and up.) [African American] Three love stories with slaves as protagonists, testimony to the power of the human spirit and the resolve for freedom. Eloquently written and based on fact, the stories dramatize the quest for freedom.

Lester, J. *To Be a Slave*. Illus. by T. Feelings. Dial, 1968. (Ages 12 and up.) [African American] Written in the words of slaves and former slaves and spanning a time period from their transportation from Africa to after Emancipation, this book tells what it means to be slave. Lester's comments guide the reader to a deeper understanding of the time and the people. A bibliography provides sources of additional information. A forceful, well-constructed, and important book.

Levine, A. A. *All the Lights in the Night*. Illus. by J. E. Ransome. Tambourine, 1991. (Ages 5 and up.) [Jewish/Russian] A story of two Jewish brothers who escape from Russia to Palestine during the Hanukkah season. The themes of freedom and hope make this a story that can be appreciated by all cultures while gaining some insight into Jewish traditions.

Levine, E. *Freedom's Children: Young Civil Rights Activists Tell Their Own Stories*. Putnam, 1993. (Ages 11 and up.) [African American] The years from 1955 to 1965 were key in the American civil rights movement. In this dramatic presentation in their own words, 30 African Americans tell of their participation in the events that marked their fight against injustice.

Levine, E. *I Hate English!* Illus. by S. Bjorkman. Scholastic, 1989. (Ages 6-9.) [Chinese American] Mei Mei feels uprooted from her home and is terrified that if she learns English she will lose her identity and her affiliation with her Hong Kong Chinese roots. She understands English but resents it. The ending indicates that Mei Mei will continue to speak both languages and will be encouraged to maintain her culture of origin while at the same time adding new customs and experiences. The turnaround is a bit too abrupt and easy, but the point comes across.

Levinson, R. *Watch the Stars Come Out*. Illus. by D. Goode. Dutton, 1985. (Ages 5-8.) [Immigrant] Narrated through the perspective of a young girl, the story describes the voyage she and her brother take to join their parents in the United States. They arrive at Ellis Island and eventually reach their new home in the Lower East Side of Manhattan. The illustrations convey the fear, sadness, excitement, and hope on the part of the hundreds of immigrants on the ship.

Levoy, M. *Shadow Like a Leopard.* Harper, 1981. (Ages 11 and up.) [Puerto Rican] To prove his worth to a street gang, fourteen-year-old Ramon Santiago robs an old man, Arnold Glasser, at knife point. Glasser is an artist; Ramon is a poet. The two form an alliance and help each other find a way out of their problems. Both are strong, intelligent, talented, and unwilling to conform to what others want them to be.

Levoy, M. *The Witch of Fourth Street and Other Stories.* Illus. by G. Lisowski. Harper, 1972. (Ages 6–10.) [Multicultural] Eight stories about people from various countries living in the Lower East side of Manhattan in the early 1900s. All share the dream of a better life for themselves and their children. The stories and pictures engage children while instructing them about the feelings and customs of each group.

Lewis, R. *All of You Was Singing.* Illus. by E. Young. Atheneum, 1991. (Ages 6 and up.) [Native American/Aztec] A poetic retelling of the Aztec myth of the coming of music to the earth. Following the god Tezcatlipoca's request, Wind journeys to the sun and brings back musicians and music to break the silence of the earth. Ed Young's stunning illustrations use Aztec designs and move from the abstract to the realistic.

Lewis, R. *In the Night, Still Dark.* Illus. by E. Young. Atheneum, 1988. (Ages 9–12.) [Hawaiian] This poetic secular version of a Hawaiian creation myth is a variation of *The Kumulipo* from Maria Leach's *In the Beginning: Creation Myths around the World.* The paintings take us from deep night into the light of the new day. Like other folktales, this myth invites multicultural comparisons.

Lewis, R., ed. *Out of the Earth I Sing.* Norton, 1968. (All ages.) [Native American] Commanding illustrations and photos of original artwork by the people represented by the poetry complement the many Native American songs, chants, and poems included here.

Linden, A. M. *One Smiling Grandma: A Caribbean Counting Book.* Illus. by L. Russell. Dial, 1992. (Ages 4–6.) [Caribbean] Rhythmic and fun, this counting book serves to introduce objects and images of the Caribbean to young children.

Lomas Garza, C., as told to H. Rohmer. *Family Pictures (Cuadros de Familia).* Illus. by the author. Children's, 1990. (Ages 5–8.) [Mexican American] [See Family Constellations]

Lord, B. B. *In the Year of the Boar and Jackie Robinson.* Harper, 1984. (Ages 8–12.) [Chinese American] Shirley Temple Wong and her mother have just come to Brooklyn to join Shirley's father. Shirley, who is bright, feisty, imaginative, and cares deeply about people, has trouble learning English and has to face some antagonistic classmates. The triumphant moment when she is introduced to her idol, Jackie Robinson, is believable, as is the rest of the action. Chinese customs are part of the story, and the conflict between traditional and modern values is well presented.

Lotz, K. E. *Can't Sit Still.* Illus. by C. Browning. Dutton, 1993. (Ages 4–8.) [Universal/ African American] A young African-American girl describes the sights, sounds, and rhythms of her life in the city as it changes through the four seasons. Richly colored illustrations wonderfully complement the simple, poetic text.

Louie, A., adaptor. *Yeh-Shen: A Cinderella Story from China.* Illus. by E. Young. Philomel, 1982. (Ages 8 and up.) [Chinese] [See Gender Roles]

Lutzeier, E. *The Coldest Winter.* Holiday House, 1991. (Ages 10 and up.) [Irish] This story tells about the potato blight and the massive exodus of people from Ireland to the United States in the mid-nineteenth century. Eamonn and his family, like many other poor Irish families, have been evicted from their home. Kate Burke, whose family is fairly well-to-do, befriends Eamonn and his family and finally enables them to emigrate to America. Although the plot has some holes in it and most of the characterization is somewhat shallow, background knowledge is provided here for understanding the bitterness between England and Southern Ireland.

Lyons, M. E. *Letters from a Slave Girl: The Story of Harriet Jacobs.* Macmillan, 1992. (Ages 11 and up.) [African American] The author has drawn heavily on Harriet Jacobs's autobiography for this fictionalized account of her life, using transcriptions of interviews with former slaves to create the dialect of her invented letters. The dialect is sometimes a distraction, but it does not diminish the power of the story.

Lyons, M. E. *Sorrow's Kitchen.* Scribner, 1990. (Ages 12 and up.) [African American] A detailed account, Zora Neale Hurston, a tempestuous and controversial figure. Her life was not easy, but many of her problems were self-inflicted. Her extraordinary talent was not as recognized as it should have been during her lifetime. This book treats her fairly and respectfully.

Maher, R. *Alice Yazzie's Year.* Illus. by S. Gammell. Coward, McCann, and Geoghegan, 1977. (Ages 7-10.) [Native American/Navajo] In poetic form and language, the author tells of the setting, culture, and activities experienced by Alice Yazzie, a Navajo girl, throughout the year. Instructive notes about Navajo ways of life end the book.

Mahy, M. *The Seven Chinese Brothers.* Illus. by J. and M. Tseng. Scholastic, 1990. (Ages 8-10.) [Chinese] [See Siblings]

Malotki, E. *The Mouse Couple.* Illus. by M. Lacapa. Northland, 1988. (Ages 7-10.) [Native American/Hopi] This faithful retelling of a Hopi tale not only provides the reader with a good story but also supplies rich information about the values and customs of the Hopi people. The story, almost identical to that of *The Moles and the Mireuk,* by Molly H. Kuan, tells of a mouse couple who so value their adopted daughter that they want the most powerful being in the world to marry her. With the advice of the sun, clouds, north wind, and the spirit of the butte, they find a suitable husband. The design-laden illustrations add to the authenticity.

Manson, C. *The Crab Prince.* Illus. by the author. Holt, 1991. (Ages 7-10.) [Italian] [See Gender Roles]

Manushkin, F. *Latkes and Applesauce: A Hanukkah Story.* Illus. by R. Spowart. Scholastic, 1990. (Ages 4-7.) [Jewish] Among the elements here are a strong sense of family interdependence, tradition, and the possibility of miracles occurring in ordinary people's lives. A poor family rescues a dog and a cat who, in the end, make it possible to celebrate Hanukkah with *latkes* (potato pancakes) and applesauce. The author provides a synopsis of the story of Hanukkah, a recipe for *latkes,* and instructions for the traditional game of dreidels.

Margolies, B. A. *Rehema's Journey.* Illus. by the author. Scholastic, 1990. (Ages 7-10.) [Tanzanian, East African] Rehema, a nine-year-old Tanzanian girl, spends a week with her father traveling to the game park where he works. Along with Rehema, the reader sees several cultures, a modern city, wild animals, and a marketplace and learns about life in a village.

Martel, C. *Yagua Days.* Illus. by J. Pinkney. Dial, 1976. (Ages 5-9.) [Puerto Rico] Adan's parents take him for a visit to his relatives in Puerto Rico where he has a joyous time with his extended family. He appreciates the beauty of the land and the diversity and caring of the people.

Martin, R. *The Rough-Face Girl.* Illus. by D. Shannon. Putnam, 1992. (Ages 7-10.) [Algonquin] This Cinderella variant filled with imagery and metaphor has three sisters vying for the love of the Invisible Being. Two of the sisters are beautiful but cruel and deceitful. The rough-faced girl is scarred from her fire-tending duties, but she is inventive and kind. She is able to see the Invisible Being and becomes his wife.

Marzollo, J. *Happy Birthday, Martin Luther King.* Illus. by J. B. Pinkney. Scholastic, 1993. (Ages 5-9.) [African American] Directed to young children, the language is sometimes oversimplified, but the book provides the important events of King's life, as well as a picture of American society at the time. Pinkney's scratchboard illustrations are dramatic and dignified.

Mathis, S. B. *Listen for the Fig Tree.* Viking, 1974. (Ages 12 and up.) [African American] [See Special Needs]

Mathis, S. B. *Sidewalk Story.* Illus. by L. Carty. Viking, 1971. (Ages 8–11.) [African American] Nine-year-old Lilly Etta Allen helps her friend Tanya overcome the effects of being evicted. She calls the newspapers, contacts a sympathetic reporter, and saves the day.

Mayerson, E. W. *The Cat Who Escaped from Steerage.* Scribner, 1990. (Ages 8–10.) [Jewish American/Immigrant] Chanah is adventuresome, assertive, and bright. Upon landing on Ellis Island she helps prevent her young cousin from being sent back to Poland. She also saves the life of a mangy cat. The persuasively written story makes it clear that life in steerage was miserable and dangerous.

Mayo, G. W. *Earthmaker's Tales: North American Indian Stories about Earth Happenings.* Illus. by the author. Walker, 1989. (Ages 8–10.) [Native American] In this book and its precursor, *Star Tales: North American Indian Stories about the Stars* (1987), each tale's origin and a description of the people associated with the story are provided before the actual telling. The author further details the specific sources of each tale, including the person who first set it into print. The stories—short and well told— represent a variety of native groups across the United States and Canada.

McClester, C. *Kwanzaa: Everything You Always Wanted to Know But Didn't Know Where to Ask.* Illus. by various African-American artists. Gumbs & Thomas, 1985. (Ages 10 and up.) [African American] This informative little book, a guide to the celebration of Kwanzaa, as well as its history and principles, explains how Kwanzaa was created in 1966 by Dr. Maulana "Ron" Karenga, an African-American scholar, as an African-American cultural holiday of unity.

McConkey, L. *Sea and Cedar: How the Northwest Coast Indians Lived.* Illus. by D. Tait. Madrona, 1973. (Ages 10 and up.) [Native American] Respectfully tells of the traditional customs of the Northwest Coast Indians. The interference of the white man is described at the end.

McKissack, P. C. *The Dark Thirty: Southern Tales of the Supernatural.* Illus. by B. Pinkney. Knopf, 1992. (Ages 10 and up.) [African American] Each of the tales or poems from times of slavery to the present involves something supernatural and also includes information about African-American history and lifestyles. Several stories tell of grievous wrong and even murder, but all end with justice accomplished. The book won the 1993 Coretta Scott King Award and a Caldecott Honor.

McKissack, P. C. *Flossie and the Fox.* Illus. by R. Isadora. Dial, 1986. (Ages 6–10.) [African American] Written in the rich, colorful dialect of the rural South as it was told to the author by her grandfather, this whimsical story tells how Flossie, a young African-American girl, outsmarts a clever fox and safely delivers a basket of eggs to a nearby farm. Flossie is strong, quick witted, and self-assured; and the story is funny and engaging.

McKissack, P., and McKissack, F. "Great African Americans" series. Enslow, 1991. (Ages 7–10.) [African American] Titles in the series, by the same authors, include *Mary McLeod Bethune: A Great Teacher* (1991), *Carter G. Woodson: The Father of Black History* (1991), *Louis Armstrong: Jazz Musician* (1991), *Marian Anderson: A Great Singer* (1991), *Langston Hughes: Great American Poet* (1992), *Zora Neale Hurston: Writer and Storyteller* (1992), *Jesse Owens: Olympic Star* (1992), *Sojourner Truth: A*

Voice for Freedom (1992), and *Martin Luther King, Jr.: Man of Peace* (1991). These biographies introduce younger children to the lives and accomplishments of many African Americans, some very well known and others who should be. The practice of highlighting certain terms (such as "dance hall" and "trumpet" in the book about Louis Armstrong) and defining them in a glossary is somewhat arbitrary and distracting, but the information is appropriate and well selected. An index is included in each.

McKissack, P. *A Million Fish . . . More or Less.* Illus. by D. Schutzer. Knopf, 1992. (Ages 5–8.) [African American/Cajun] Before Hugh Thomas goes fishing, Papa-Daddy and Elder Abbajon recount one of their numerous tall tales. Hugh Thomas catches "a million fish . . . more or less," and returns home with a tall tale of his own about how he was cheated out of them. Legendary creatures from the Bayou, like Atoo the grand-père of all alligators, play roles in this comical adventure tale with a strong regional flavor.

McKissack, P. C. *Mirandy and Brother Wind.* Illus. by J. Pinkney. Knopf, 1988. (Ages 6–10.) [African American] Mirandy wants to attend the annual cakewalk dance contest with the wind as her partner and must find a way to capture him. Though Mirandy's family is Christian and doesn't approve, the determined, spirited country girl seeks advice from a conjure woman. The ending neatly brings the reader back from the supernatural to the real treasures of the community. McKissack, always a pleasure to read, revels in the richness of African-American culture, handles the language with authenticity and style, and communicates her love and respect to her readers.

McKissack, P. C. *Nettie Jo's Friends.* Illus. by S. Cook. Knopf, 1989. (Ages 6–8.) [African American] Nettie Jo, an African-American girl, is to be the flower girl at her cousin's wedding. She needs a needle to sew a suitable dress for her doll. She helps three animal friends who are in trouble; but they seem to have no time to return the favor. Just when she has given up hope and returns sadly home, Rabbit, Fox, and Panther come by to thank her and bring her a needle. The text is written in African-American dialect, and the warm illustrations nicely complement the story.

McLuhan, T. C. *Touch the Earth.* Illus. with photos. Promontory, 1971. (Ages 10 and up.) [Native American] A collection of writings and sayings of Native Americans accompanied by stirring photographs. This is an authoritative book, obviously the result of considerable research.

McMullan, K. *The Story of Harriet Tubman, Conductor of the Underground Railroad.* Illus. by S. J. Petruccio. Dell, 1991. (Ages 8–10.) [African American] Including many details of Harriet Tubman's growing-up years, this story reveals how quick witted and creative she was and fills in gaps that other books for young children have not discussed, particularly about Harriet Tubman's life after being a conductor. She helped newly liberated slaves adjust to their freedom, assisted in training them to develop ways of earning a living, and worked as a nurse and a spy in the Union Army. The author researched the topic extensively, producing a comprehensive and swiftly moving book.

Meltzer, M. *All Times, All Peoples: A World History of Slavery.* Illus. by L. E. Fisher. Harper, 1980. (Ages 8–12.) [Multicultural] [See War and Peace]

Meltzer, M. *The Amazing Potato.* Harper, 1992. (Ages 8–12.) [Multicultural] In a chronological approach, Meltzer presents eye-opening facts about this amazing vegetable, from the Spanish conquistadors to the Irish famine to McDonald's french fries.

Meltzer, M., ed. *The American Promise: Voices of a Changing Nation.* Bantam, 1990. (Ages 12 and up.) [Multicultural] Arranged by themes, this provocative look at American history from 1945 to the present shows the profound changes of the last half of the decade. The content includes women's rights and environmental movements, changes in Eastern Europe since the Cold War, and the changing U.S. economy. The author provides background information, but most of the history is told through essays and anecdotes by people who directly experienced or participated in the events.

Meltzer, M. *The Black Americans: A History in Their Own Words 1619-1983.* Crowell, 1984. (Ages 12 and up.) [African American] Personal accounts by slaves and former slaves, abolitionists, unlettered as well as highly educated African Americans, famous persons, and lesser-known individuals. Meltzer identifies each speaker and sets the context. An index assists in locating specific people, topics, and events.

Meltzer, M. *The Chinese Americans.* Illus. with photos. Crowell, 1980. (Ages 10 and up.) [Chinese American] With his customary sensitivity and expertise, the author describes the history, trials, and accomplishments of the Chinese people in America.

Meltzer, M. *The Hispanic Americans.* Illus. with photos. Crowell, 1982. (Ages 11 and up.) [Latino American] The focus is on the backgrounds, as well as the current positions, of Puerto Ricans, Mexicans, and Cubans in the United States. Photos and personalized anecdotes enhance this readable and informative book.

Meltzer, M. *Hunted Like a Wolf: The Story of the Seminole War.* Farrar, Straus, and Giroux, 1972. (Ages 12 and up.) [Native American/Seminole] An informative account of the Seminoles of Florida, their relationship with African Americans, and their resistance to white encroachment on their land. The treachery of the U.S. government is clear.

Meltzer, M. *Remember the Days: A Short History of the Jewish American.* Illus. by H. Dennerstein. Doubleday, 1974. (Ages 10 and up.) [Jewish American] An informative account of Jews in America from 1654 to contemporary times. The origin of the term *anti-Semitism* and explanations of the sources of stereotyping behavior help to illuminate the history, not only of Jewish Americans but also of the United States in general.

Merrill, J., adaptor. *The Girl Who Loved Caterpillars.* Illus. by F. Cooper. Philomel, 1992. (Ages 7-10.) [Japanese] [See Gender Roles]

Mills, L. *The Rag Coat.* Illus. by the author. Little, Brown, 1991. (Ages 8 and up.) [Appalachian] Minna's new coat is very special to her since it was made by the kind-hearted Quilting Mothers from her small Appalachian mining town. Although the other children make fun of her, Minna finds the strength to face them and share with them each piece of history in her rag coat. An endearing story of a child's inner strength and the loving support often found within small communities.

Mitchell, A., ed. *Strawberry Drums.* Illus. by F. Lloyd. Delacorte, 1989. (Ages 9 and up.) [Multicultural] Includes poems of the West Indies, England, and the American Midwest. A section encourages children to write their own poetry and gives hints for doing so. The poems are light and free of conflict.

Mitchell, B. *Down Buttermilk Lane.* Illus. by J. Sandford. Lothrop Lee and Shepard, 1993. (Ages 5-8.) [Amish] The illustrations and text combine to provide a nonjudg-mental, factual, respectful look at contemporary Amish life. Details of food, clothing, activities, and family are beautifully and warmly presented. The effect is one of intimacy and well-being.

Mitchell, B. *Shoes for Everyone: A Story about Jan Matzeliger.* Illus. by H. Mitchell. Carolrhoda, 1986. (Ages 8-10.) [African American] This gifted inventor revolutionized the shoe industry by designing a machine for "lasting" a sole onto the rest of the shoe. Matzeliger, a biracial immigrant from Surinam, had difficulty at every stage of the game and in fact had to sell the rights to most of the profits for his invention. His determination comes through clearly in this account without making him seem overly heroic.

Mitchell, M. K. *Uncle Jed's Barbershop.* Illus. by J. Ransome. Simon & Schuster, 1993. (Ages 6-10.) [African American] Jedediah Johnson is an itinerant barber whose life dream is to own his own shop. The family lives in the South during the Depression where they are part of a larger African-American community. At age 79, he opens his shop, and everyone celebrates with him. The illustrations are particularly striking, and the story is engagingly told.

Mohr, N. *Felita*. Illus. by R. Cruz. Dial, 1979. (Ages 9-12.) [Puerto Rican] Because of the bigotry eight-year-old Felita and her family encounter when they move away from the barrio, they return to a place where they know they have a supportive community. Felita's grandmother helps her to respect her Puerto Rican heritage. In *Going Home* (Bantam, 1986), Felita, now twelve, experiences hostility when she visits Puerto Rico. Through perseverance, she finally makes friends and brings home a different perspective of her native land and a better sense of her own identity.

Mollel, T. M. *The King and the Tortoise*. Illus. by K. Blankley. Clarion, 1993. (Ages 8-10.) [Cameroon] A witty tale of cleverness. When the tortoise undertakes the king's challenge to make a robe of smoke, everyone, including the reader, is surprised at his success (even though the robe never actually gets constructed.) The page borders depict designs from the Cameroon.

Mollel, T. M. *The Orphan Boy*. Illus. by P. Morin. Clarion, 1990. (Ages 6-10.) [Tanzanian] This Masai story from the author's homeland affirms the importance of keeping one's word and overcoming curiosity. Some other universal themes include the longing to become a parent and the inevitable separation of the child from the parent when the time has come. The illustrations shimmer with inner light and demonstrate the artist's familiarity with the pasture lands of Tanzania, as well as his respect for the culture of his people.

Mollel, T. M. *The Princess Who Lost Her Hair*. Illus. by C. Reasoner. Troll, 1993. (Ages 6-10.) [Akamba/Kenyan] This folktale from the Akamba people of East Africa contains many universal themes. A vain, greedy princess loses her beautiful hair. With the intervention of a beggar boy and through her own growing ability to nurture, she regains her hair and marries the young beggar. The stylized illustrations nicely complement the story.

Mollel, T. M. *A Promise to the Sun*. Illus. by B. Vidal. Little, Brown, 1992. (Ages 5 and up.) [African/Masai] This Masai story explains why Bat never ventures out in daylight. It is a tale of broken promises and guilt over not accomplishing a task.

Montejo, V., trans. by W. Kaufman. *The Bird Who Cleans the World and Other Mayan Fables*. Curbstone, 1991. (Ages 10 and up.) [Guatemalan/Mayan] The author grew up in Guatemala, and his first language was the Mayan language of Jakaltek, from which these stories were translated. All the stories convey a moral. Many are creation tales. Although the presentations are somewhat uneven, the tales are, in general, well told.

Morey, J. N., and Dunn, W. *Famous Asian Americans*. Illus. with photos. Dutton, 1992. (Ages 11 and up.) [Asian American] Profiles of fourteen prominent Americans of Filipino, Japanese, Chinese, Korean, Vietnamese, and Cambodian heritage are included in this well-researched volume. Connie Chung, the TV newscaster; Jose Aruego, the children's book author and illustrator; and Ellie Onizuka, an astronaut who died in the Challenger explosion, are a few of the people introduced here. The profiles include the subjects' feelings about their heritage and a discussion of barriers they have encountered. A history of Asian immigration to the United States is included in the preface.

Morris, A. *Bread Bread Bread*. Illus. by K. Heyman. Scholastic, 1989. (Ages 4-9.) [Multicultural] Breads from many cultures and countries are pictured. An index includes 29 ways people eat bread all over the world. Other books in this series with the same format include *Hats Hats Hats* (1989), *Loving* (1990), and *On the Go* (1990) about different ways people travel. The format is an excellent model for children to design their own integrated studies of other universal topics.

Musgrove, M. *Ashanti to Zulu: African Traditions.* Illus. by L. and D. Dillon. Dial, 1976. (Ages 7–10.) [African] A unique alphabet book describing the traditions of many African peoples, utilizing native language. It was awarded a Caldecott Medal.

Myers, W. D. *Brown Angels: An Album of Pictures and Verse.* Harper, 1993. (Ages 7–10.) [African American] The author has collected hundreds of photographs of African-American children from past generations. He uses the photos as the basis for a series of poems of varying moods and images. Apparent in all the pages is the valued individuality of each child and the genuine love and respect of the author for his subjects.

Myers, W. D. *Malcolm X: By Any Means Necessary.* Scholastic, 1993. (Ages 9–12.) [African American] A multidimensional view of the life of this complex and dynamic man. Illustrated with photos, not only the person but the events of the time come alive for the reader.

Myers, W. D. *Motown and Didi: A Love Story.* Viking, 1984. (Ages 11 and up.) [African American] Didi is a strong, attractive young African-American woman who surmounts many challenges. She receives help from Motown, another survivor, who has trodden a less conventional path than Didi but whose values are similar and clear. A sense of the importance of appreciating one's heritage, an absorbing plot, three-dimensional characters, and a satisfying love story are some of the components of this excellent book.

Myers, W. D. *The Mouse Rap.* Harper, 1990. (Ages 10–12.) [African American] [See Family Constellations]

Myers, W. D. *Now Is Your Time! The African American Struggle for Freedom.* Harper, 1991. (Ages 11 and up.) [African American] Myers personalizes the history of African Americans by describing individuals like Abdal Rahman Ibrahima, Ida B. Wells, Dred Scott, James Forten, Frederick Douglass, and other noteworthy people of African heritage. In closing, Meyers brings the reader up to date and includes a note on his research and his intent in writing the book.

Myers, W. D. *Scorpions.* Harper, 1988. (Ages 12 and up.) [African American/Puerto Rican] [See War and Peace]

Nathiri, N. Y., compiler. *Zora!: Zora Neale Hurston, A Woman and Her Community.* Illus. with photos. Sentinel Communications, 1991. (Ages 12 and up.) [African American] The compiler grew up in Eatonville, Florida, the oldest incorporated municipality founded by African Americans, where Hurston and her family resided for a time. An obituary by John Hicks is reproduced in the first part of the book. The author includes the only group interview ever conducted with Zora's close relatives, brought together to clarify some of the facts about Zora's life and death. Another selection contains an essay by Alice Walker on Zora and her life. An album of color photos enlivens the text.

Newlon, C. *Famous Puerto Ricans.* Dodd Mead, 1975. (Ages 12 and up.) [Puerto Rican] Carmen Maymi, Roberto Clemente, Luis Pales Matos, Herman Badillo, Concha Melendez, and La Familia Figueroa are among the accomplished people described here. Readers should be encouraged to do further research and compile their own lists of notable Latinos.

Newth, M. *The Abduction.* Farrar, Straus, and Giroux, 1989. (Ages 13 and up.) [Inuit] Osuqo and Poq, two young Greenland Inuits, are kidnapped and brought to Norway where they are treated with fearsome cruelty as their captors try to Christianize and "civilize" them. Their native culture and tents are the sustaining elements in their survival. In time, Christine, the daughter of one of the sailors, helps them to escape. The author, although not native herself, treats the Inuit characters with dignity and accuracy. Though harsh, this is a historical account of the treatment Inuits received at the hands of some Christian Europeans.

Nixon, J. L. *Land of Hope.* Bantam, 1992. (Ages 9-12.) [Immigrant] Rebekah, Rose, and Kristin come from different countries, cultures, and religions; but they become friends on the ship coming to Ellis Island. Rebekah and her family are the main characters in this volume, but the immigrants all share the same sorts of aspirations and tribulations.

Nomura, T. *Grandpa's Town.* Illus. by the author. Kane/Miller, 1989. (Ages 5-8.) [Japanese] [See Aging]

Norman, H. *How Glooskap Outwits the Ice Giants and Other Tales of the Maritime Indians.* Illus. by M. McCurdy. Little, Brown, 1989. (Ages 8-10.) [Native American/Maritime] In simple narrative prose, the author retells some of the stories of the Eastern Maritime Indians, including the Abenaki and Micmac nations. The tales include how Glooskap created humans, protected them from evil forces, and eventually chose to live apart from them. Black-and-white wood engravings illustrate the text.

Norman, H. *Who-Paddled-Backward-with-Trout.* Illus. by E. Young. Little, Brown, 1987. (Ages 6-9.) [Native American/Cree] A young Cree boy, named Trout-with-Flattened-Nose because of his clumsiness, longs for a new name. In keeping with the traditions of his people, he sets out to earn one. He does, in fact, earn a new name, though not at all the one he expected.

Nye, N. S., ed. *This Same Sky: A Collection of Poems from around the World.* Bradbury, 1992. (Ages 12 and up.) [Multicultural] Contains 161 poems from many countries in a variety of styles demonstrating universal emotions. The map, indexes, and notes on the poets provide information for further exploration. A valuable book.

O'Connor, J. *Jackie Robinson and the Story of All-Black Baseball.* Illus. by J. Butcher. Random House, 1989. (Ages 7-9.) [African American] This book is important because it chronicles the little-known history of the Negro Leagues. Aimed at a young audience, it contains many facts, as well as an enthusiastic attitude about this group.

O'Connor, K. *Dan Thuy's New Life in America.* Illus. with photos. Lerner, 1992. (Ages 8-12.) [Vietnamese American] Thirteen-year-old Dan Thuy Huynh and her family are refugees. Through photos and text this book tells of the situation in Vietnam that caused the family to flee, defines "refugee," and describes their life and the adjustments they have made. The difficulty of preserving one's own cultural traditions in a new land is effectively discussed.

Ochs, C. P. *When I'm Alone.* Illus. by V. J. Redenbaugh. Carolrhoda, 1993. (Ages 4-6.) [Universal/African American] A high-spirited African-American girl explains in verse, incidentally counting from ten to one, how numerous animals (aardvarks, turtles, lions, camels, and hippos among them) have created the mess in her room.

Okomoto, J. D. *Molly by Any Other Name.* Scholastic, 1990. (Ages 12 and up.) [Biracial] [See Adoption and Foster Care]

Orr, K. *My Grandpa and the Sea.* Illus. by the author. Carolrhoda, 1990. (Ages 5-8.) [St. Lucia] [See Aging]

Osofsky, A. *Dreamcatcher.* Illus. by E. Young. Orchard, 1992. (Ages 4-8.) [Native American/Ojibway] A day in the life of an Ojibway family as they fish and pick berries. The big sister weaves a dreamcatcher, a small hoop with a web inside it, to hang from the baby's cradleboard to catch and keep away bad dreams and let only good dreams through. The lyrical text is complemented by the soft pastel illustrations.

Ozaki, Y. T. *The Japanese Fairy Book.* Illus. by K. Fujiyama. Tuttle, 1970. (Ages 8 and up.) [Japanese] Classic tales, including "Momotaro" and "The Tongue-Cut Sparrow" told in a lively manner. Most of the stories have happy endings that are all the more satisfying because they come about by cleverness or kindness.

Page, S. *A Celebration of Being: Photographs of the Hopi and Navajo.* Illus. by the author. Northland, 1989. (Ages 10 and up.) [Native American/Hopi and Navajo] The author and photographer lived with native people. Her stunning photos and simple text, quoting heavily from named and anonymous Hopi and Navajos, show that these two different and sometimes antagonistic nations have much in common. She dispels stereotypes, discusses the white-dominated society, and is always respectful.

Palmer, E. *Everything You Need to Know about Discrimination.* Rosen, 1990. (Ages 8–10.) [Multicultural] Information about discrimination because of religion, sex, race, age, and condition of ability. History and definitions are supplied, along with anecdotes about what some people did when they found themselves victims of discrimination.

Parker, A. C. *Skunny Wundy: Seneca Indian Tales,* new ed. of 1926 version. Illus. by G. Armstrong. Whitman, 1970. (Ages 8 and up.) [Native American/Seneca] These animal tales are somewhat reminiscent of the Anansi stories of Africa. Skunny Wundy is a magical, clever character. (Mighty hunters are called Skunny Wundy, as are good story tellers.) The author, a Seneca Indian, was an anthropologist and museum director.

Parks, R., with Haskins, J. *Rosa Parks: My Story.* Dial, 1992. (Ages 12 and up.) [African American] An inspiring story through which readers can understand the quiet dignity and courage of this remarkable woman, as well as the details of the historic bus boycott and the fight for human rights.

Paterson, K. *The Tale of the Mandarin Ducks.* Illus. by L. and D. Dillon. Dutton, 1990. (Ages 8–11.) [Japanese] Loyalty and open-heartedness, combined with a little bit of magic, overcome greed and cruelty in this splendidly illustrated retelling of a popular Japanese folktale. A wicked lord captures a mandarin duck and abuses it. He then tries to execute a Samurai and a tender-hearted kitchen maid for setting the duck free. The human pair are rescued by means of magical intervention by the ducks in the form of messengers from the emperor. The emperor's edict is difficult to believe, but the rest of the story works very well.

Patrick, D. L. *Red Dancing Shoes.* Illus. by J. E. Ransome. Tambourine, 1993. (Ages 4–8.) [Universal/African American] A little girl is given a pair of shiny red dancing shoes by her grandmother. She is so excited that she wants to show them off to the whole neighborhood. In her enthusiasm, she falls and gets them dirty and scuffed, but a little polish saves the day. The characters are African American within a closely knit community and a loving extended family.

Paul, P. *You Can Hear a Magpie Smile.* Elsevier/Nelson, 1980. (Ages 9–12.) [Mexican] A new doctor learns to value the ancient ways of healing in a remote Mexican village. The child, Lupe, will grow up to be respectful of both old and new ways.

Paulsen, G. *The Crossing.* Orchard, 1987. (Ages 12 and up.) [Mexican American] The border between Mexico and the United States serves in this story as a spiritual, as well as physical, barrier to be crossed. Robert, a man who has been severely emotionally damaged by his experiences in the Vietnam War, helps young Manny to cross illegally into the United States. Robert dies in the end, but there is hope for Manny.

Pellegrini, N. *Families Are Different.* Illus. by author. Crowell, 1978. (Ages 9 and up.) [Multicultural] [See Adoption and Foster Care]

Pellowski, A. *First Farm in the Valley: Anna's Story.* Illus. by W. Watson. Philomel, 1982. (Ages 10 and up.) [Polish American] The third in the series of stories about a community of Polish Americans who settled in Latsch Valley, Wisconsin, in the late nineteenth and early twentieth centuries (the others are *Willow Wind Farm: Betsy's Story* [1981] and *Winding Valley Farm: Annie's Story* [1982]). The stories focus particularly on one family, modeled from the author's own, and follow them through four generations. Although this book is last in the series, chronologically it takes place first.

Pelz, R. *Black Heroes of the Wild West.* Illus. by L. D. Piana. Open Hand, 1990. (Ages 8–12.) [African American] This slim book briefly outlines the stories of nine people of African-American heritage who figured in the history of the western part of the United States. The sketches are brief, but they provide a base for children's further research.

Pena, S. C. *Tun-Ta-Ca-Tun.* Illus. by N. Pena. Arte Publico, 1986. (Ages 8 and up.) [Latino] Designed to foster an appreciation of the literature and heritage of the Latino peoples, this collection of poetry and stories presented in English and Spanish reflects the everyday life and interests of Latino children. The poems, collected from the Spanish-speaking population in Houston, are for the most part fun and light-hearted, with no particular theme. The stories, by several authors, are particularly strong in their inclusion of Puerto Ricans. *Kikiriki* (1981) is the companion book.

Perl, L. *Piñatas and Paper Flowers: Holidays of the Americas in English and Spanish.* Illus. by V. de Larrea. Spanish by A. F. Ada. Clarion, 1983. (Ages 7–10.) [Latino] Aimed at the non-Latino reader, this is a comprehensive compendium of holiday customs.

Perl, L. *Puerto Rico: Island between Two Worlds.* Morrow, 1979. (Ages 12 and up.) [Puerto Rican] A cornucopia of information is packed into this book about every aspect of Puerto Rico. It is clear that the author feels that it is a place worth learning about and visiting.

Peters, R. M. *Clambake: A Wampanoag Tradition.* Illus. by J. Madama. Lerner, 1992. (Ages 8–11.) [Native American/Wampanoag] The photographs help the text convey its special-occasion atmosphere as a boy and his grandfather prepare a feast to honor an elder. The details of the preparation accurately represent the Wampanoag tradition.

Philip, N. *Fairy Tales of Eastern Europe.* Illus. by L. Wilkes. Clarion, 1991. (Ages 9–13.) [Eastern European] Twenty-two stories from many Eastern European countries, containing a variety of folk-themes. The tales are told respectfully without losing any of their complexity.

Pinkney, B. *Max Found Two Sticks.* Illus. by the author. Simon & Schuster, 1994. (Ages 5–8.) [African American] Max is not in a talkative mood, but he communicates well by making music with two sticks he has found, tapping out a rhythm on his thighs, his grandfather's bucket, his sisters' hatbox, some empty bottles, and the trash cans. The activities and interactions of his family members are revealed as Max plays his music. The essence of the neighborhood also becomes one of the important elements of this well-designed book.

Pinkney, G. J. *Back Home.* Illus. by J. Pinkney. Dial, 1992. (Ages 6–9.) [African American] [See Family Constellations]

Polacco, P. *Just Plain Fancy.* Illus. by the author. Bantam, 1990. (Ages 5–8.) [Amish] In a story that demonstrates how children grow to understand their heritage through questioning and exploring, a little Amish girl has her desire for "something fancy" satisfied by the chance discovery and nurturing of a peacock's egg. The language conveys the flavor of the Amish people's talk and the illustrations portray their customs and dress.

Polacco, P. *Mrs. Katz and Tush.* Illus. by the author. Bantam, 1992. (Ages 5–8.) [Jewish American/African American] Mrs. Katz, a Jewish immigrant from Poland with no surviving family in the United States, is befriended by Larnel and his mother, African-American neighbors. Larnel learns about the similarities in the histories of their people. This is a thoughtful story of an intergenerational, interracial friendship. Although the author-illustrator errs in showing a Jewish bakery full of breads and cakes on Passover, the book is generally respectful of Jewish traditions and culture and makes use of Yiddish words in the text.

Polacco, P. *The Keeping Quilt*. Illus. by the author. Simon & Schuster, 1988. (Ages 7-10.) [Russian Jewish/Immigrant] The author traces the history of her quilt made of articles of clothing, including the babushka and dress her great grandmother wore on her trip from Russia to the United States. The quilt has served as a *huppa* (wedding canopy) at three generations of weddings, a Sabbath table cloth, and in many other instances. The author plans to give it to her own daughter one day. The illustrations are in black and white, except for the quilt, which is always shown in full color. This special book could encourage children to learn about their own family histories.

Porte, B. A. *I Only Made up the Roses*. Greenwillow, 1987. (Ages 10-12.) [Biracial] [See Family Constellations]

Porter, A. P. *Jump at de Sun: The Story of Zora Neale Hurston*. Lerner, 1992. (Ages 10 and up.) [African American] In the process of describing this talented, unusual woman, the author makes vivid the town of Eatonville, the times of the Harlem Renaissance, and the social context. Hurston is not idealized or romanticized. This biography is note-worthy not only for its subject matter but also for its value as a work of literature. The photos enliven the story.

Porter, A. P. *Kwanzaa*. Illus. by J. L. Porter. Carolrhoda, 1991. (Ages 5-8.) [African American] A comprehensive, simple, informational presentation of the holiday, its origins, and its rituals.

Porter, C. F. *The Day They Hanged the Sioux and Other Stories from Our Indian Heritage*. Chilton, 1964. (Ages 12 and up.) [Native American] Nine stories of outstanding Native Americans. An appendix includes some selected folklore told to the author by contemporary young Native Americans. A perspective of history from a native point of view.

Raynor, D. *My Friends Live in Many Places*. Illus. by the author. Whitman, 1980. (Ages 6-10.) [Multicultural] Pictures of people from around the world engaged in playing, mourning, studying, working, celebrating, and eating. Although there are few photos from South America or Africa and none from Australia or the Arctic regions, if care is taken to supply additional resources, the excellent quality of the photos and the variety of lifestyles shown can add to children's understanding of world unity and diversity.

Red Hawk, R. *A, B, C's the American Indian Way*. Illus. with photos. Sierra Oaks, 1988. (Ages 4-8.) [Native American] An informative book made even more interesting by photographs gleaned from many sources. The author is a Wyandot.

Reddix, V. *Dragon Kite of the Autumn Moon*. Illus. by J. and M. Tseng. Lothrop Lee and Shepard, 1991. (Ages 5-8.) [Taiwanese] One year, Grandfather is too sick to build a kite. Tad-Tin owns a magnificent dragon kite with lantern eyes that Grandfather made for him when he was born and they flew together on Tad-Tin's birthday every year. When he lets it go, it comes to life and effects the magical cure Tad-Tin had hoped for. The illustrations and author accurately convey the cultural details of life in rural Taiwan.

Regguinti, G. *The Sacred Harvest: Ojibway Wild Rice Gathering*. Illus. by D. Kakkak. Lerner, 1992. (Ages 9-12.) [Native American/Ojibway] Color photos underscore the accurate portrayal of a young boy's responsibilities in learning how to participate in his community's rituals. It is important for readers to understand that these traditions continue.

Rhee, N. *Magic Spring: A Korean Folktale*. Putnam, 1993. (Ages 7-10.) [Korean] This Korean folktale is retold with an excellent narrative style. The story is a variant of tales in which a childless couple magically acquires a child. This one has a wonderful twist:

the hard-working and faithful couple redeem a greedy and selfish neighbor by raising him as their son when he has overindulged at the fountain of youth. The author-illustrator was born and raised in Korea.

Ringgold, F. *Tar Beach.* Illus. by the author. Crown, 1991. (Ages 7–10.) [African American] The stunning illustrations magically transport both readers and Cassie Louise Lightfoot on her fantasy flight over the newly completed George Washington Bridge and the city where Cassie and her family live. Incorporated into the narrative is the unfairness of her father's exclusion from the union because he is not Caucasian, even though he is a most skilled and agile high-beam construction worker. In the sequel, *Aunt Harriet's Underground Railroad in the Sky* (1992), Cassie's younger brother Be Be flies on a magical railroad whose conductor is Harriet Tubman. The journey that ensues takes the children and readers through a history lesson whose illustrations are far more exciting than the text. Faith Ringgold is a recognized artist and quiltmaker.

Rochman, H., ed. *Somehow Tenderness Survives: Stories of Southern Africa.* Harper, 1988. (Ages 12 and up.) [South African] [See War and Peace]

Rodanas, K. *Dragonfly's Tale.* Illus. by the author. Clarion, 1991. (Ages 8 and up.) [Native American/Zuni] This Ashiwi Zuni folktale is set in a prosperous village where the residents squander their corn harvest to prove their wealth to their neighbors. The Corn Maidens punish them by bringing a terrible drought that ends when these gods reward two children for their earlier kindness. The carefully rendered illustrations capture details of Zuni pueblo life, from the dance to summon the Corn Maidens to the clay bread ovens and the geometric designs on the pottery.

Rodriguez, C. *César Chavez.* Illus. with photos. Chelsea House, 1991. (Ages 9–12.) [Mexican American] A well-written, respectful book presenting an honest view of César Chavez as a human being with problems, concerns, dignity, and an overwhelming commitment to bettering the lives of people from his socioeconomic and ethnic background. The book is well researched and contains many black-and-white photos.

Rohmer, H.; Chow, O.; and Vidaure, M. Spanish trans. by R. Zubizarreta and A. F. Ada. *The Invisible Hunters (Los cazadores invisibles).* Illus by J. Sam. Children's, 1987. (Ages 8–10.) [Miskito/Nicaraguan] This legend from the Miskito Indians of Nicaragua documents the first contact between the indigenous people and the outside world. It relates how three brothers who were magically granted invisibility violate their promise never to sell their meat or hunt with guns. As a result, they are forced to remain invisible and are banished from the village. This lively retelling in Spanish and English, illustrated with multimedia collages, has a rhythm reflecting its oral tradition.

Rohmer, H., adaptor. Spanish trans. by A. F. Ada and R. Zubizarreta. *The Legend of Food Mountain (La montana de alimento).* Illus. by G. Carrillo. Children's, 1982. (Ages 8–10.) [Aztec] A mythic reminder that food and its sources must be respected by people. This story, in Spanish and English, derived from Aztec legends, tells of the bringing of food to the ancient people by Quetzalcoatl, aided by a giant red ant and despite the interference of the rain dwarves.

Rohmer, H., and Guerrero R., J., adaptors. Spanish trans. by R. Zubizarreta. *Atariba and Niguayona.* Illus. by C. Mendez. Children's 1988. (Ages 8–10.) [Taino/Puerto Rican] The story, one of the few available about the Taino, the indigenous people of Puerto Rico, tells of Niguayona's successful search for the magic caimoni tree whose fruit saves the life of his playmate and eventual partner Atariba. The illustrations are stunning in their vibrant colors and stylized but accurate depictions of Taino life and culture. The text is in English and Spanish.

Rohmer, H., and Willson, D., adaptors. Spanish trans. by R. Zubizarreta and A. F. Ada. *Mother Scorpion Country.* Illus. by V. Stearns. Children's, 1987. (Ages 8–10.) [Miskito/ Nicaraguan] This retelling in Spanish and English is reminiscent of the Orpheus and Eurydice myth. Naklili accompanies his beloved wife Kati to Mother Scorpion Country, the land of the dead, because he cannot bear to be parted from her. He follows her instructions and is killed by a poisonous snake so that he can legitimately dwell with his beloved in the land of the dead, which, incidentally, is ruled by a powerful and wise woman. The illustrations create an appropriately mystical mood.

Rosario, I. *Idalia's Project ABC.* Illus. by the author. Henry Holt, 1981. (Ages 4–7.) [Latino] The author handles well the challenge of designing an alphabet book that simultaneously represents each letter of the alphabet in two languages. An example of the author's thoughtful selection is shown in *L* for litter and, in Spanish, the corresponding *L* for *limpieza* (cleanliness) picturing children cleaning up a vacant lot.

Rosen, M. *How the Animals Got Their Colors.* Illus. by J. Clementson. HBJ, 1992. (Ages 8 and up.) [Multicultural] Nine brief folktales from New Guinea, India, Uganda, Australia, and China telling each culture's versions of why animals look the way they do. All are boldly illustrated with colorful collages. End notes for each tale describe the animal referred to in the story and a bit about the culture from which the story comes.

Rosen, M., ed. *South and North, East and West: The Oxfam Book of Children's Stories.* Illus. by many artists. Candlewick, 1992. (Ages 7–10.) [Multicultural] Twenty-five engaging tales, including some rarely seen, from such places as Bangladesh, Malta, and Cyprus. Illustrators of note have generously added their talents. The varied collection benefits all readers who are searching for stories beyond North America and western Europe.

Rosenberg, M. B. *Living in Two Worlds.* Illus. by G. Ancona. Lothrop Lee and Shepard, 1986. (Ages 10 and up.) [Biracial] [See Family Constellations]

Roughsey, D. *The Rainbow Serpent.* Illus. by the author. Gareth Stevens, 1988. (Ages 6–8.) [Australian] A creation myth. The story line is a little confusing and the characters are different from most conventional folktale characters, but children can get a flavor of the culture of the people indigenous to Australia and compare different creation tales.

Roy, J. *Soul Daddy.* Gulliver, 1990. (Ages 12 and up.) [Biracial] [See Family Constellations]

Ruby, L. *This Old Man.* Houghton Mifflin, 1984. (Ages 12 and up.) [Chinese American] [See Adoption and Foster Care]

Rushmore, H., and Hunt, W. R. *The Dancing Horses of Acoma and Other Acoma Indian Stories.* Illus. by W. R. Hunt. World, 1963. (Ages 12 and up.) [Native American/Acoma] These stories, some including the magical characters Spider Woman and Spider Boy, were told to the author by Wolf Robe Hunt. Most are well told and clear, despite many complicated details. The author is respectful of the old traditions, and the illustrations are excellent.

Sales, F. Trans. by M. Simont. *Ibrahim.* Illus. by E. Sariola. Lippincott, 1989. (Ages 6–10.) [Moroccan] Ibrahim tends his father's stall in the market in Marrakesh. When his friend Hassan announces that he is leaving the city to become a nomad in the desert and find freedom, Ibrahim is torn between the market life he loves and the lure of the unknown in the desert. He stays in Marrakesh, eventually taking over his father's business, and becomes a storyteller as well.

Samuels, V. *Carry Go Bring Come.* Illus. by J. Northway. Macmillan, 1988. (Ages 4–8.) [Universal/African American] [See Family Constellations]

San Souci, R. D. *The Boy and the Ghost.* Illus. by J. B. Pinkney. Sion & Schuster, 1989. (Ages 8–11.) [African American] In this African American variation on a familiar folk theme, a poor boy brave enough to spend the night in a haunted house is rewarded by the ghost for his courage. He is given the house and half of its treasure and is told to give the rest to the poor. Pinkney's illustrations show a boy more amused than frightened as the ghost appears one piece at a time.

San Souci, R. D. *Larger Than Life*. Illus. by A. Glass. Delacorte, 1991. (Ages 6–10.) [American] John Henry, Old Stormalong, Slue-Foot Sue, Pecos Bill, Strap Buckner, and Paul Bunyan figure in these tall tales of American folk heroes. Children may discuss what characteristics the heroes share and which of these remain positive values today, and they may compare these heroes with those of other cultures.

San Souci, R. D. *The Talking Eggs*. Illus. by J. Pinkney. Scholastic, 1989. (Ages 6–8.) [African American/Creole] Like other folktales, this story of two sisters, one bad, one good, with the mother favoring the bad child, contains a tapestry of details and a number of archetypal ingredients. Obedience and generosity are the virtues to be admired. The Creole setting and contemporary realistic artwork (which earned the book a Caldecott Honor) distinguish this version from its European counterparts.

Sandin, J. *The Long Way to a New Land*. Illus. by the author. Harper, 1981. (Ages 5–8.) [Swedish/Immigrant] Detailed illustrations add to the information about the emigration of a Swedish family to America in the last half of the nineteenth century.

Sandoval, R. *Games Games Games*. Illus. by D. Strick. Doubleday, 1977. (Ages 5 and up.) [Mexican American] A delightfully illustrated description of traditional games played by children of Mexico and in the contemporary barrios of California.

Say, A. *The Bicycle Man*. Illus. by the author. Parnassus, 1982. (Ages 5–9.) [Japanese] The author recalls an incident from the days when he was growing up during the American occupation of Japan. The story tells of the friendly visit and bicycle-riding prowess of two American soldiers.

Say, A. *El Chino*. Illus. by the author. Houghton Mifflin, 1990. (Ages 7–11.) [Chinese American] The biography of Bong Way "Billy" Wong, a Chinese American who became a famous bullfighter in Spain. Although he experienced discrimination, he was able to achieve his goal through determination and the support of his family. He was originally billed as a novelty act, but in the end his skill at this dangerous sport brought him success. The book presents his triumph a bit too abruptly, but it is useful for combatting stereotypes and affirming the power of determination.

Say, A. *Grandfather's Journey*. Illus. by the author. Houghton Mifflin, 1993. (Ages 7–11.) [Chinese American] This story of belonging to two cultures and loving two lands is told sparingly but movingly. The grandson describes how his grandfather settled in California. After he married and had a daughter, he returned to the land of his youth, but he always missed California. When the grandson grows up, he too journeys to California and settles there. He understands his grandfather's feelings because when he is in one place he misses the other. The paintings portraying the people and the settings earned the book the 1994 Caldecott Award.

Schaffer, P. *Chag Semeach! (Happy Holiday) A Jewish Holiday Book for Children*. Illus. with photos. Tabor Sarah, 1986. (Ages 5–8.) [Jewish] The simple text provides brief descriptions of many Jewish celebrations as seen through children's eyes. Black-and-white photos help dispel stereotypes by showing Jews of all ages, some with disabilities, and of varying racial backgrounds.

Schlak, C. H., and Metzger, B. *Martin Luther King, Jr.: A Biography for Young Children*. Illus. by J. Kastner. Gryphon House, 1990. (Ages 3–6.) [African American] A simple introduction to the life of this hero focuses on how much like other children young Martin was and how it was his dream that all people would love and help each other.

Schmidt, D. *I Am a Jesse White Tumbler.* Illus. by the author. Whitman, 1990. (Ages 7–11.) [African American] The Jesse White Tumbling Team, originally formed in the housing projects in Chicago, performs at professional sporting events across the country and all over the world. The author's color photos capture the remarkable talents of these young people.

Schroeder, A. *Ragtime Tumpie.* Illus. by B. Fuchs. Little, Brown, 1989. (Ages 6–10.) [African American] This fictionalized biography of African American entertainer Josephine Baker shows her as a spirited little girl, nicknamed Tumpie, who wants to dance to the kind of ragtime and jazz her estranged daddy played. Despite her stepfather's disapproval but with her mother's encouragement, Tumpie wins a dance contest. Fuchs's glowing illustrations capture Tumpie's exuberance and the atmosphere of the setting.

Schwartz, A. *And the Green Grass Grew All Around: Folk Poetry from Everyone.* Illus. by S. Truesdell. Harper, 1992. (Ages 5 and up.) [Multicultural] More than 250 poems and chants transmitted via oral tradition through the ages and across many cultures are captured in print. The commentary interspersed with the rhymes adds to readers' knowledge.

Schwartz, D. M. *Supergrandpa.* Illus. by B. Dodson. Lothrop Lee and Shepard, 1991. (Ages 5–8.) [Swedish] [See Aging]

Schwartz, H., and Rush, B. *The Diamond Tree: Jewish Tales from around the World.* Illus. by U. Shulevitz. Harper, 1991. (Ages 7–10.) [Jewish/Multicultural] Fifteen Jewish tales from as long ago as the third century, originating in countries such as Turkey, Iraq, Yemen, and Morocco. Some are versions of such familiar tales as Thumbelina; others have "fool" themes.

Shannon, G. *Stories to Solve: Folktales from around the World.* Illus. by P. Sis. Beech Tree, 1985. (Ages 8–10.) See also *More Stories to Solve: Fifteen Folktales from around the World* (1989). [Multicultural] Each brief tale ends with a problem for readers to solve. For example, in a story where there is a test to discover which flower is real among many artificial flowers, the reader is invited to guess how King Solomon did it. (He opened the window and let a bee fly in.)

Shelby, A. *Potluck.* Illus. by I. Trivas. Orchard, 1991. (Ages 4–7.) [Multicultural] A rollicking alphabet book is the vehicle for a multicultural feast, with each item especially chosen to contribute to a variety of ethnic and culinary flavors. ("Ben brought bagels" and "The triplets turned up with tacos.") Not all ethnic groups are represented, but the book provides a model for young readers to replicate and build upon. The illustrations could have been more detailed and accurate, but they're fun and not disrespectful.

Shelby, A. *We Keep a Store.* Illus. by J. Ward. Orchard, 1990. (Ages 5–8.) [African American] [See Family Constellations]

Shepard, A. *Savitri: A Tale of Ancient India.* Illus. by V. Rosenberry. Whitman, 1992. (Ages 6–10.) [Indian] In this retelling of an Indian myth from the Mahabharata (an ancient Hindu epic) Savitri, through cleverness and determination, wins back her husband Satyavan's life and also her father-in-law's sight and the kingdom he had lost.

Sierra, J. *The Elephant's Wrestling Match.* Illus. by B. Pinkney. Dutton, 1992. (Ages 5–8.) [Cameroon] This folktale from the Bulu people of Cameroon tells how the mighty elephant, after defeating the rhino, crocodile, and leopard, was beaten by the tiny bat in a wrestling match. The monkey announces the winner of each match using a talking drum (a tradition explained in an end note) giving a rhythmic feeling to this respectful retelling.

Singer, I. B. *The Power of Light: Eight Stories for Hannukah.* Illus. by I. Lieblich. Farrar, Strauss, and Giroux, 1980. (Ages 8 and up.) [Jewish American] Each of these masterly stories tells of a miracle and provides ethical as well as dramatic content. Imbedded in the tales is much about Jewish tradition.

Singer, I. B. *Stories for Children.* Farrar, Strauss and Giroux, 1984. (Ages 9–12.) [Jewish] Selected from several anthologies and single-story volumes of Singer's work, these stories include fools from Chelm, pious children and adults, sinners, wise people, and tricksters. Even without illustrations, the words provide an extensive look into Eastern European Jewish culture.

Singer, M. *Nine O'Clock Lullaby.* Illus. by F. Lessac. Harper, 1991. (Ages 5–8.) [Multicultural] Brightly colored pictures alive with movement illustrate various cultures and locations around the world at a given moment in time: 9 P.M. in Brooklyn; 10 P.M. in Puerto Rico; 3 A.M. in Zaire and Switzerland, and so on. Children learn about time as well as culture.

Sloat, T., reteller. *The Eye of the Needle.* Illus. by the author. Dutton, 1990. (Ages 5–8.) [Yupik] Teri Sloat relates this whimsical Yupik tale, as told to her by Betty Huffman, about a child with a prodigious appetite. Amik, who lives with his grandmother, sets off to hunt for the first time. He catches and eats progressively larger animals until he eats a whale. He is then so full that he returns home with nothing to show for his hunt. He is too fat to fit through the door, so his grandmother magically draws him into the house through the eye of her needle, releasing the animals he has swallowed, thus providing food for the whole village for a long time.

Smalls-Hector, I. *Irene and the Big, Fine Nickel.* Illus. by T. Geter. Little, Brown, 1991. (Ages 6 and up.) [African American] [See War and Peace]

Smalls-Hector, I. *Jonathan and His Mommy.* Illus. by M. Hays. Little, Brown, 1992. (Ages 4–7.) [Universal/African American] [See Family Constellations]

Sneve, V. D. H., ed. *Dancing Teepees.* Illus. by S. Gammell. Holiday House, 1989. (Ages 6 and up.) [Native American] The editor, a Sioux, has selected traditional and contemporary poetry (including a few pieces of her own), representing native youth throughout North America. Each author is credited with his or her tribal affiliation. Evident is the respect for children and nature within the customs and beliefs of many Native American nations.

Sneve, V. D. H. *Jimmy Yellow Hawk.* Illus. by O. Lyons. Holiday, 1972. (Ages 12 and up.) [Sioux] These adventures of a young modern Sioux living on a South Dakota reservation convey a sense of the mixture of old ways and new.

Sneve, V. D. H. *When Thunders Spoke.* Illus. by O. Lyons. Holiday, 1974. (Ages 12 and up.) [Native American] Norman Two Bull lives with his parents in the Dakota reservation. His family is conflicted over how to live in modern times as native people. In the end, it seems that Norman, while still respecting the traditions of his people, will use whatever new ways are appropriate for his success. Excellent illustrations; well-written text.

Sobol, H. L. *We Don't Look like Our Mom and Dad.* Illus. by P. Agre. Coward McCann, 1984. (Ages 6–9.) [Biracial] [See Adoption and Foster Care]

Soto, G. *Baseball in April.* HBJ, 1990. (Ages 12 and up.) [Mexican American] Eleven realistic stories featuring young Mexican Americans in California and focusing on a wide range of emotions and dilemmas about growing up. The stories promote values such as honesty, education, and hard work. They are well written and funny. Except for the characters' names and the occasional insertion of Spanish into the dialogue, the characters could be from any culture.

Soto, G. A *Fire in My Hands.* Scholastic, 1990. (Ages 12 and up.) [Mexican American] Reflective poems about the author's life growing up with a Mexican-American heritage.

Some of the selections reveal the author's feelings about parenthood, but most represent his adolescent years.

Soto, G. *Neighborhood Odes*. Illus. by D. Diaz. HBJ, 1992. (Ages 8 and up.) [Mexican American] A collection of delightful poems celebrating life in a Mexican-American neighborhood. Many are universal in theme, but all have the feeling of a Latino neighborhood, and some are explicitly about Mexican-American experiences. A glossary is provided for some of the Spanish words.

Soto, G. *The Skirt*. Illus. by E. Velasquez. Delacorte, 1992. (Ages 9–12.) [Mexican American] [See Family Constellations]

Soto, G. *Taking Sides*. HBJ, 1991. (Ages 11 and up.) [Mexican American] Lincoln Mendoza likes his new junior high school and neighborhood, but he feels like an outsider. His loyalties are tested when he must compete on his new school's basketball team against his old school's team. He decides that by playing for himself and doing his best he will win either way. Soto deals with the mother's non-Latino boyfriend, a racist coach, peer pressure, loyalty, single parenting, and socioeconomic issues and culture within a Latino setting. Spanish words are interspersed in the text, and a glossary is provided.

Stanek, M. *I Speak English for My Mom*. Illus. by J. Friedman. Whitman, 1989. (Ages 5–9.) [Mexican American] Lupe, a Mexican-American girl, provides emotional support to and serves as an interpreter for her Spanish-speaking mother, who has a difficult time adapting to life in the United States. In the end, she encourages her mother to enroll in English classes in order to get a better job. The mother has overcome many obstacles and taken many risks. The book addresses a real situation for many children of immigrants who must grapple with learning English.

Stanek, M. *We Came from Vietnam*. Illus. by W. F. McMahon. Whitman, 1985. (Ages 7–10.) [Vietnamese] The Nguyen family, Vietnamese immigrants to the United States, left their homeland as "boat people" after the communist takeover. The similarities, as well as differences, between life in rural Vietnam and life in urban Chicago are described, and the author tells of the family's challenges upon arrival. A strong community is shown, and the children are seen as adjusting well to their new lives.

Staples, S. F. *Shabanu*. Knopf, 1989. (Ages 12 and up.) [Pakistani/nomadic/Muslim] [See Gender Roles]

Steichen, E. *The Family of Man*. Prologue by C. Sandburg. Museum of Modern Art, 1955. (All ages.) [Multicultural] This book brings home the point that we all are, in fact, part of the human family. Through verse and pictures, the author illustrates common experiences all people share: birth, happiness, grief, and many more.

Steptoe, J. *Baby Says*. Illus. by the author. Lothrop Lee and Shepard, 1988. (Ages 3–7.) [African American] [See Siblings]

Steptoe, J. *Mufaro's Beautiful Daughters*. Illus. by the author. Lothrop Lee and Shepard, 1987. (Ages 8–10.) [African] [See Gender]

Stiles, M. B. *James the Vine Puller*. Illus. by L. Thomas. Carolrhoda, 1992. (Ages 5–8.) [Brazilian] This trickster tale came to Brazil by way of Africa. James, a turtle, is frustrated because the elephant, king of the forest, refuses to let him eat any of the food growing there. Whale, the king of the sea, refuses to share any of the ocean's bounty either. James tricks them into a tug-of-war that ends in a stalemate, after which each opponent agrees to permit James free rein.

Stock, C. *Halloween Monsters*. Illus. by the author. Bradbury, 1990. (Ages 4–6.) [Universal/African American] A young child fears going out trick-or-treating until his mother assures him that there are no monsters, only children dressed in costume.

The family is African American, thus including this population in a universal U.S. children's celebration.

Stolz, M. *Storm in the Night.* Illus. by P. Cummings. Harper, 1988. (Ages 5-8.) [Universal/African American] [See Aging]

Strangis, J. *Grandfather's Rock.* Illus. by R. Gamper. Houghton Mifflin, 1993. (Ages 6-9) [Italian] [See Aging]

Strickland, D. S., ed. *Listen Children: An Anthology of Black Literature.* Illus. by L. and D. Dillon. Bantam, 1982. (Ages 8-12.) [African American] Poetry, essays, and excerpts from larger works are included here by such excellent writers as Eloise Greenfield, Gwendolyn Brooks, Virginia Hamilton, Maya Angelou, Langston Hughes, Lucille Clifton, Alice Childress, and others. Although the range of topics and styles is enormous, all entries touch upon the African-American experience.

Surat, M. M. *Angel Child, Dragon Child.* Illus. by V. Mai. Scholastic, 1983. (Ages 5-9.) [Vietnamese American] Ut and her family came to the United States from Vietnam but could not afford to have the mother join them. Ut is teased mercilessly by Raymond, a classmate. The principal cleverly requires him to interview Ut and write her story. The principal then rallies the student body to raise money for Ut's mother to come.

Sussman, S. *Hanukkah: Eight Lights around the World.* Illus. by J. Friedman. Whitman, 1988. (Ages 7-10.) [Jewish] In an unusual format, the author takes the reader through the eight nights of Hanukkah, celebrated in a different location across the world. The special characteristics of the different countries are presented, as well as the different ways Jews around the world celebrate the same holiday. Children may be surprised to learn that there are Jewish communities in such countries as Mexico, Argentina, and India.

Swentzell, R. *Children of Clay: A Family of Pueblo Potters.* Illus. by B. Steen. Lerner, 1992. (Ages 7-10.) [Santa Clara Pueblo] [See Family Constellations]

Syme, R. *Geronimo, the Fighting Apache.* Illus. by B. F. Stahl. Morrow, 1975. (Ages 8-12.) [Apache] This biography, sympathetic to Geronimo and the Apache, is drawn from many documents. Quotations from Geronimo and his contemporaries convey a sense of authenticity.

Tate, E. E. *The Secret of Gumbo Grove.* Watts, 1987. (Ages 10-12.) [African American] When Raisin Stackhouse begins to uncover the past of families living in Gumbo Grove by cleaning up the town's old cemetery, she faces her family's antagonism and the ire of several members of the community. Prominent people are afraid that their family skeletons (literally) will prove to be embarrassing. Truth and openness, coupled with a valuing of heritage, win out. The story conveys an understanding of how to conduct primary research. It is too bad Raisin's parents are so narrow and punitive throughout her historical hunt. They seem otherwise too aware to succumb to internalized oppression.

Tate, E. E. *Thank You, Dr. Martin Luther King.* Bantam, 1990. (Ages 10-12.) [African American] A young southern black girl, Mary Elouise, comes to terms with her internalized negative feelings about African Americans with the help of her grandmother, Big Momma, and a charismatic drama and dance teacher who gives her a part in the school Black History Week play. Mary Elouise's teacher is ignorant and racist, and her mother retains some unfortunate attitudes about skin color. Although the ending occurs a bit too abruptly and idealistically, it is nevertheless satisfying.

Taylor, M. *The Gold Cadillac.* Dial, 1987. (Ages 9-12.) [African American] [See Family Constellations]

Taylor, M. D. *The Road to Memphis.* Dial, 1990. (Ages 10 and up.) [African American] A sixth book in the series about the Logans that dramatically and authentically conveys a sense of the struggles and passion of this African-American family in Mississippi during the Great Depression. The other books are *Song of the Trees* (1975), *Roll of Thunder, Hear My Cry* (1976), *Let the Circle Be Unbroken* (1981), *The Friendship* (1987), and *Mississippi Bridge* (1990). This latest book, which takes place in 1941, includes a romantic interlude for Cassie, now grown up. The series blasts the passive, downtrodden stereotype of African Americans and sustains a message of strength, togetherness, intelligence, and determination.

Taylor, S. *All-of-a-Kind Family Downtown,* new ed. Illus. by B. and J. Krush. Follett, 1988. (Ages 8-12.) [Jewish American] [See Family Constellations]

Temple, F. *Taste of Salt: A Story of Modern Haiti.* Orchard, 1992. (Ages 13 and up.) [Haitian] Set in Haiti just after Jean-Bertrand Aristide was elected president, this is the story of Djo and Jeremie, teenage victims of poverty and the violence perpetrated by the Tenton Macoute, Duvalier's private army. They tell about their lives and struggles. Both Jeremie and Djo are well developed and complex people, though the minor characters are less fully explored. The violence is graphic, making this appropriate only for mature readers; but the author admirably captures the terror and hope in modern Haiti.

Thomas, I. *Lordy, Aunt Hattie.* Illus. by T. di Grazia. Harper. (Ages 4-8.) [African American] A loving, poetic glance at growing up in the Deep South. The child, Jeppa Lee, and her Aunt Hattie engage in a conversation that demonstrates their warmth, affection, and positive sense of self. Other worthwhile works by this author are *My Street's a Cool Morning Street* (1976), *Walk Home Tired, Billy Jenkins* (1974) [See Siblings], and *Willie Blows a Mean Horn* (1981).

Thomas, J. C., ed. *A Gathering of Flowers: Stories about Being Young in America.* Harper, 1990. (Ages 12 and up.) [Multicultural] Such competent authors as Jeanne Wakatsuki Houston, Joyce Carol Thomas, Kevin Kyung, and Gary Soto relate some aspect of growing up in a particular community in America. Each story carries a sense of a special culture or heritage and reflects the author's own background.

Thompson, V. L. *Hawaiian Myths of Earth, Sea and Sky.* Illus. by M. Kahalewai. University of Hawaii Press, 1966. (Ages 10 and up.) [Hawaiian] This volume, along with *Hawaiian Legends of Tricksters and Riddlers* (1969) and *Hawaiian Tales of Heroes and Champions* (1971), contain Hawaiian myths and folklore full of magic, shape shifters, spirits, gods, and heroes. The tales are well researched, respectfully told, and perfect for reading aloud. Many are suitable for younger children, but others contain violence and should be screened first by adults to judge the appropriateness for the intended audience. Background information on the tales is provided, along with a glossary and pronunciation guide.

Thum, M. *Exploring Black America: A History and Guide.* Atheneum, 1975. (Ages 10 and up.) [African American] Combines an informative and comprehensive historical account of African Americans in the United States with a guide to places of historical and cultural significance. A valuable, well-constructed resource.

Tobias, T. *Isamu Noguchi: The Life of a Sculptor.* Illus. with photos. Crowell, 1974. (Ages 7-11.) [Japanese American/biracial] Too few books portray notable Japanese Americans. This account tells of Noguchi's development, not only as a sculptor but also as a person who confronts being the son of a Japanese father and white American mother.

Tompert, A. *Bamboo Hats and a Rice Cake.* Illus. by Demi. Crown, 1993. (Ages 7-10.) [Japanese] In this tale adapted from Japanese folklore, an old man who demonstrates his kindness in several ways is rewarded by Jizo, a divinity who is the protector of children. Each page of this aesthetic and compellingly illustrated book is accompanied by characters from the Japanese alphabet, incorporated into the text and explained in the margins. Thus, in addition to the pleasure readers receive from the story itself, they also enjoy the rebus-like game with the Japanese characters.

Torre, B. L. *The Luminous Pearl: A Chinese Folktale.* Illus. by C. Inouye. Orchard, 1990. (Ages 7 and up.) [Chinese] [See Gender Roles]

Trezise, P. *The Peopling of Australia.* Illus. by the author. Milwaukee: Gareth Stevens, 1987. (Ages 6-10.) [Indigenous Australian] The messages conveyed are that the indigenous peoples of Australia revered the land and one another for thousands of years. Then Europeans came who lacked respect for the land and subjugated the people. A glossary defines unfamiliar and specialized terms.

Trimble, S. *The Village of Blue Stone.* Illus. by J. O. Dewey. Macmillan, 1990. (Ages 10-12.) [Native American/Anasazi] Archaeology, anthropology, and oral tradition enlighten this description of life in an Anasazi village through a calendar year. The story is told through vignettes about various individuals, each seen in the context of the society. The afterword focuses on one archaeologist who is himself a member of Acoma Pueblo people and therefore a descendent of the Anasazi. Readers are helped to understand that even today Anasazi culture gives meaning to the lives of the Pueblo Indians.

Turner, F., ed. *Puerto Rican Writers at Home in the USA.* Open Hand, 1991. (Ages 12 and up.) [Puerto Rican] An anthology containing poems, short stories, and autobiographical sketches about Puerto Rican history and culture. Although this is not exclusively intended for a juvenile audience, readers age twelve and up may enjoy reading any of the selections in this impressive collection.

Turner, G. T. *Take a Walk in Their Shoes.* Illus. by E. C. Fox. Dutton, 1985. (Ages 9-12.) [African American] Brief but balanced biographies of fourteen African Americans who deserve recognition. Some, such as Rosa Parks and Martin Luther King, Jr., are well known. Others, such as Maggie Lena Walker, America's first woman bank president, and Garrett Morgan, inventor of the stoplight, deserve to be better known. In addition to the biographies, short skits are provided for readers to perform.

Uchida, Y. *The Invisible Thread.* Messner, 1991. (Ages 10-12.) [Japanese American] This well-known author contributes her memoirs of growing up in the United States and being sent with her family to Topaz internment camp in Utah. Her narrative makes an impact devoid of bitterness or recrimination.

Uchida, Y. *A Jar of Dreams.* Atheneum, 1981. (Ages 9-12.) [Japanese American] Rinko and her family struggle economically during the Depression years, which are the backdrop for this story about learning to value one's heritage. *The Best Bad Thing* (1983) and *The Happiest Ending* (1985) continue the story of this close-knit, caring Japanese-American family.

Uchida, Y. *The Magic Listening Cap: More Folk Tales from Japan,* new ed. Illus. by the author. Berkeley, 1987. (Ages 8 and up.) [Japanese] This is the second book of folk tales (the first is *The Dancing Kettle*) containing themes of magic, obedience, and kindness rewarded, and cleverness respected. The retellings are entertaining and absorbing.

Volkmer, J. A. Spanish by L. A. Schatschneider. *Song of the Chirimia.* Illus. by the author. Carolrhoda, 1990. (Ages 8-10.) [Mayan/Guatemalan] King Clear Sky's beloved daughter Moonlight loves Black Feather, a young, impoverished folk singer. He can marry Moonlight if in three months he can make music as well as the birds. He succeeds with the aid of the Great Spirit of the Woods who helps him to make a *chirimia* (flute). The bold geometric paintings convey a sense of the traditions and colors of Guatemala.

Vuong, L. D. *The Brocaded Slipper and Other Vietnamese Tales.* Illus. by V. Mai. Harper, 1982. (Ages 8-10.) [Vietnamese] Variants of Cinderella, Thumbelina, the Frog Prince, and even Rip Van Winkle appear in this collection of complex and magical tales. The Cinderella story, which contains a magical fish and its bones, is similar to the Chinese version, *Yeh-Shen.*

Vuong, L. D. *The Golden Carp and Other Tales from Vietnam.* Illus. by M. Saito. Lothrop Lee and Shepard, 1993. (Ages 9-12.) [Vietnamese] Another engaging and beautifully retold collection of stories from Vietnam. The virtues of loyalty, hard work, generosity, and love that transcends outward appearances are among those portrayed in the tales. Strong women, compassionate men, and characters respectful of themselves and each other people these stories.

Vyong, L. D. *Sky Legends of Vietnam.* Illus. by V. Mai. Harper, 1993. (Ages 10-12.) [Vietnamese] Six stories accompanied by explanatory notes from the author explaining various celestial phenomena. Although most of the stories have origins in other areas of Asia, they are also part of Vietnamese folklore. Most of the stories caution against going back on one's word and daring to antagonize heavenly spirits. Although the stories are clearly told, the abstract concepts in most of them make this a compilation for older readers to enjoy and understand.

Wade, B. *Little Monster.* Illus. by K. Kew. Lothrop Lee & Shepard, 1992. (Ages 4-7.) [Universal/African American] [See Siblings]

Wagenheim, K., ed. *Short Stories from Puerto Rico.* Institute of Puerto Rican Culture, 1978. (Ages 12 and up.) [Puerto Rican] This valuable collection of stories contains several derived from the oral tradition, some concerned with contemporary times, and some that reflect historical themes.

Walker, P. R. *Pride of Puerto Rico. The Life of Roberto Clemente.* HBJ, 1988. (Ages 10 and up.) [Puerto Rican] Although this biography is somewhat romanticized, it succeeds in presenting the story of Roberto Clemente as a talented, principled man, beloved by Puerto Ricans and other fans. Racism and its impact are mentioned but not deeply examined. Clemente's family figure strongly.

Walter, M. P. *Justin and the Best Biscuits in the World.* Illus. by C. Stock. Lothrop Lee and Shepard, 1986. (Ages 8-10.) [African American] [See Gender Roles]

Walter, M. P. *Mariah Keeps Cool.* Bradbury, 1990. (Ages 7-11.) [Universal/African American] [See Family Constellations]

Walter, M. P. *Mississippi Challenge.* Bradbury, 1992. (Ages 12 and up.) [African American] Facts mount inexorably to demonstrate Mississippi's cruel oppression of African Americans. The book also discloses how African Americans heroically fought this oppression.

Wang, R. C. *The Fourth Question.* Illus. by J. Chen. Holiday House, 1991. (Ages 7-10.) [Chinese] Yee-Lee seeks an answer from a wise man about why he is so impoverished. He also promises to ask the wise man questions that an old woman, an old man, and a dragon need answered. When he meets the wise man he finds that he may ask only three questions. Because of his compassion for others' needs and loyalty to his word, he earns rewards far beyond his expectations. These virtues are an important part of many Chinese tales.

Waters, K., and Slovenz-Low, M. *Lion Dancer: Ernie Wan's Chinese New Year.* Illus. by M. Cooper. Scholastic, 1990. (Ages 5-9.) [Chinese American] Ernie Wan, a six-year-old Chinese-American boy, performs the Lion Dance in the annual Chinese New Year parade in New York's Chinatown. He and his family and friends are shown eating, rehearsing, blessing the new costumes, and finally parading amidst the smoke of firecrackers. Information about the details of this annual celebration is included here, and the color photos help the reader to share Ernie's excitement.

Watkins, Y. K. *Tales from the Bamboo Grove.* Illus. by J. and M. Tseng. Bradbury, 1992. (Ages 7-10.) [Japanese] Each of these traditional stories communicates a moral but it is always presented in the context of the story. Irony characterizes some, bearing out the warning, "Beware of making wishes: they may come true." The tales are eloquently told.

Wells, R. *A to Zen.* Illus. by Yoshi. Picture Book Studio, 1992. (Ages 8 and up.) [Japanese] Presented in the format of an alphabet book and illustrated with magnificent paintings on silk, this book introduces the reader to many elements of Japanese culture. Both traditional and contemporary items are included. The book is presented back to front, with detailed explanations in English and Japanese for each element.

Whelan, G. *Goodbye, Vietnam.* Knopf, 1992. (Ages 9-12.) [Vietnamese] Mai and her family flee their native Vietnam to Hong Kong. The somewhat traditional mother, the father who is mechanically talented, the grandmother who is a respected healer and the least eager to migrate, the physician whose concern for her people overrides her personal comfort, and the children, perhaps most of all, engage the reader's attention and empathy.

Wilkinson, B. *Ludell.* Harper, 1975. (Ages 10 and up.) [African American] Also see *Ludell and Willie* (1977) and *Ludell's New York Time* (1980). Ludell is a bright, competent, passionate young woman who was raised in the South by her strict but loving grandmother. Ludell and Willie, the boy next door, are inseparable companions. When her grandmother dies and Ludell is taken to New York by her mother, she maintains her relationship with Willie.

Williams, J. S. *And the Birds Appeared.* Illus. by R. Y. Burningham. University of Hawaii Press, 1988. (Ages 4-8.) [Hawaiian] Once Maui, a young boy living on the island of Hawaii, was the only person who could see the birds. One day, a stranger comes to Hawaii and brags about how much more beautiful it is in his homeland. Maui commands the birds to appear, thus settling the quarrel. Since then, the birds have been visible to all. This folk tale is colorfully illustrated and introduces the reader to Hawaiian vocabulary, flora, and fauna.

Williams, S. A. *Working Cotton.* Illus. by C. Byard. HBJ, 1992. (Ages 6-9.) [African American] Shelan and her family arrive at the cotton fields before dawn. The work is gruelling, as evidenced by the sweat on the character's faces, but the children still find time to play. The illustrations show a strong African-American family doing the best they can.

Williams, V. B. *"More More More," Said the Baby.* Illus. by the author. Greenwillow, 1990. (Ages 4-6.) [Multicultural] [See Family Constellations]

Wilson, B. K. *The Turtle and the Island.* Illus. by F. Lessac. Lippincott, 1978. (Ages 5-9.) [Papua New Guinea] This retelling of a traditional folk tale from Papua New Guinea is accompanied by colorful illustrations. It tells of a turtle exploring the depths of the ocean who finds a lonely man living in a submerged cave. She brings him to the island she has constructed and finds him a wife. Together the man and woman populate New Guinea.

Wilson, B. P. *Jenny.* Illus. by D. Johnson. Macmillan, 1990. (Ages 5-8.) [African American] Jenny is reminiscent of the young narrator in Eloise Greenfield's *Honey I Love.* She is generous in sharing her feelings about her parents' divorce; her relationships with her teacher, friends, and family members; her fears; and her pleasures. Her loving extended African-American family communicates well.

Winter, J. *Klara's New World.* Illus. by the author. Knopf, 1992. (Ages 5-8.) [Swedish American/Immigrant] A touching and realistic story about a family's emigration from Sweden to the United States in the second half of the nineteenth century. Jeanette Winter is the daughter of Swedish immigrants, and her familiarity with the situation lends authenticity to the story. The family's sadness at leaving their home is well captured, as are the details of their arrival at Castle Garden and subsequent travel to the Midwest. Their filing of a claim and settling on the land seem a little too effortless, but this does not damage the impact of the story.

Wolfson, E. *From Abenaki to Zuni: A Dictionary of Native American Tribes.* Illus. by W. S. Bock. Walker, 1988. (Ages 10 and up.) [Native American] Descriptions of 68 Native American nations, carefully researched, accurate, and concise. The text is supplemented with hundreds of black-and-white drawings. Religious practices are described in the present tense, affirming that the traditions are still practiced in some form. Some of the suggested readings should be carefully perused; they are less respectful and accurate than one would want.

Wolkstein, D. *Oom Razoom.* Illus. by D. McDermott. Morrow, 1991. (Ages 7-10.) [Russian] A complicated but satisfying retelling of the victory of loyalty and faithfulness over greed and power. The beautiful and clever Olga helps her husband become wealthy and outwit the wicked king.

Wolkstein, D. *White Wave: A Chinese Tale.* Illus. by E. Young. Crowell, 1979. (Ages 7 and up.) [Chinese] The Moon Goddess visits and befriends a poor young man, and he is appropriately grateful. The illustrations enhance the text.

Wood, T., with W. N. Afraid of Hawk. *A Boy Becomes a Man at Wounded Knee.* Illus. with photos. Walker, 1992. (Ages 9-12.) [Native American/Oglala Lakota] To mend the sacred hoop of their nation, every year for five years the Lakota retrace the path taken almost one hundred years ago by Big Foot and his people on the way to their deaths at Wounded Knee. Wanbli Numpa Afraid of Hawk, eight years old, decides to participate in the last year (1990). The story of his journey is told here in his words.

Xiong, B. Adapted by C. Spagnoli. *Nine-in-One, Grr! Grr!* Illus. by N. Hom. Children's, 1989. (Ages 6-8.) [Hmong/Laotian] Tiger, who has no cubs yet, is tricked by a bird into changing her special song to "One-in-nine, Grr! Grr!" and having only one cub every nine years (rather than nine every year). This is why, the Hmong say, the world is not overrun with tigers. The illustrations are evocative of the stunning embroidery of the Hmong people.

Yacowitz, C. *The Jade Stone.* Illus. by J. Chen. Holiday House, 1992. (Ages 5-8.) [Chinese] When the emperor orders the great stone-carver, Chen, to carve him a dragon from a piece of jade, Chen cannot comply because the jade stone tells him it must be carved into a sculpture depicting three fish. The emperor at first wants to punish Chen but realizes that the sculpture is a masterpiece and was, indeed, what the jade was meant to become. The story demonstrates the mystical power of art and the sacred commitment of the artist.

Yagawa, S. Translated by K. Paterson. *The Crane Wife.* Illus. by S. Akaba. Mulberry, 1987. (Ages 5-8.) [Japanese] Feathery illustrations combine with a fine retelling of the classic story of the crane who becomes human and stays with her husband until he violates his word not to observe her as she is weaving. Similar in theme to *The Orphan Boy* and many other folk tales from various cultures, the ideas of keeping one's word and of valuing creatures that are beyond human conception are presented in a context appropriate to the heritage.

Yarbrough, C. *Cornrows.* Illus. by C. Byard. Coward, McCann, and Geoghegan, 1979. (Ages 5-9.) [African American] As Mama and Great-Grammaw braid the children's hair into cornrows, they tell of the meaning of the designs of the cornrows and present some of the tradition and richness of African American history.

Yashima, T. *Crow Boy.* Illus. by the author. Viking, 1955. (Ages 5–8.) [Japanese]Chibi's schoolmates tease him because he is shy and different from them. A new teacher encourages him to express his talents, and all his peers appreciate him at last. *Umbrella* (1958) provides a universal story of a young Japanese-American child wanting to use her new umbrella, waiting impatiently for rain.

Yee, P. *Tales from Gold Mountain: Stories of the Chinese in the New World.* Illus. by S. Ng. Macmillan, 1989. (Ages 10 and up.) [Chinese American] The author, who has settled in Canada, writes of Chinese immigrants to the "New World" and includes all of North America. Each tale has an element of the supernatural, with intervention by ghosts and gods. The plight of the immigrants, particularly those laboring for whites, is vividly described, always with a sense of compassion and a maintenance of the laborors' dignity.

Yellow Robe, R. *Tonweya and the Eagles and Other Lakota Tales.* Illus. by J. Pinkney. Dial, 1979. (Ages 9–12.) [Native American/Lakota Sioux] The author tells stories she heard from her father, Chano, about his boyhood. The tales celebrate events in Chano's life or use animals to impart a moral. The theme of love and respect for all things is replayed continuously.

Yep, L. *Child of the Owl.* Harper, 1977. (Ages 12 and up.) [Chinese American] Casey must stay with her grandmother in Chinatown after living an assimilated and transient existence with her gambler-father. In the story, Casey at last values her heritage.

Yep, L. *Dragon of the Lost Sea.* Harper, 1982. (Ages 11 and up.) [Chinese] Based upon an old Chinese myth, the story follows a shape-changing dragon and her companion Thorn, a human boy, in their adventures to combat evil. The other titles in this series are *Dragon Steel* (1985), *Dragon Cauldron* (1991), and *Dragon War* (1992).

Yep, L. *Dragonwings.* Harper, 1975. (Ages 12 and up.) [Chinese American] Telling the story of one family's emigration from China to America, the author creates special characters who become universal reflections of many people.

Yep, L. *The Lost Garden.* Simon & Schuster, 1991. (Ages 10 and up.) [Chinese American] The author's memoir of growing up in San Francisco in a Chinese-American family and community. His honest portrayal of his ambivalent feelings about his heritage and culture reflects the attitudes of many people trying to find their identities in a society that is not sympathetic to diversity. At the same time, Yep lovingly conveys the richness and positive features of the Chinese-American experience.

Yep, L. *Sea Glass.* Harper, 1979. (Ages 12 and up.) [Chinese] Craig Chin cannot fit into any of the worlds he has been forced to live in. His peers, family, and community look at him with displeasure, except for Uncle Quail, who takes him into yet another world.

Yep, L. *The Star Fisher.* Morrow, 1991. (Ages 11 and up.) [Chinese American] Set in the 1920s in a small West Virginia town, this is the story of fifteen-year-old Joan Lee. The treatment of prejudice and its resolution are described realistically and persuasively.

Yep, L. *Tongues of Jade.* Illus. by D. Wiesner. Harper, 1991. (Ages 9–12.) [Chinese American] Originally gathered in California in the 1930s from Chinese laborers living in Chinatown, these are stories that nurtured the men far from home. They clung to them as part of their tradition and culture. Most of the tales include the supernatural. All invoke lessons of morality, loyalty, generosity of spirit, and respect for elders. *The Rainbow People* (1989), taken from the same sources, focuses on some facets of Chinese life in America.

Yep, L., ed. *American Dragons: Twenty-Five Asian American Voices.* Harper, 1993. (Ages 12 and up.) [Asian American] Stories by different authors of Chinese, Korean, Japanese,

Vietnamese, Thai, and Tibetan heritage illuminating the experience of growing up in America and grappling with the differences in cultures.

Yolen, J. *The Lullaby Songbook.* Illus. by C. Mikolaycak. Music arr. by A. Stemple. HBJ, 1986. (Ages 7-12.) [Multicultural] A collection of lullabies from many cultures attesting to the fact that the universal ingredients of repetition, nonsense, and rhythmic melodies exist in lullabies around the world.

Yolen, J., ed. *Favorite Folktales from around the World.* Pantheon, 1986. (Ages 10 and up.) [Multicultural] More than 40 cultures are represented in this volume of 160 tales categorized under such headings as "Tricksters, Rogues and Cheats"; "Heroes: Likely and Unlikely"; "Death and the World's End"; and ten other sections of equally intriguing topics.

Young, B. E. *Harlem: The Story of a Changing Community.* Messner, 1972. (Ages 8-10.) [African American] The history of Harlem from early Dutch times to 1970. The author is African American.

chapter 10

Special Needs

Everyone has special needs and deserves respect, sensitivity, and appropriate behavior from others. This chapter deals with children's literature containing characters who have physical or emotional disabilities, as well as unusual intellectual, artistic, or physical abilities. Almost any person might fit into one of the categories discussed here.

The United Nations designated the year 1981 as "The International Year of Disabled Persons." During this year, public awareness and sensitivity were aroused. Buildings and streets were made accessible to people in wheelchairs; devices aiding people whose hearing or sight are impaired were added to public institutions such as libraries and schools. Awareness continues to grow: the Americans with Disabilities Act, passed on July 26, 1991, to be phased in through 1994, requires employers to "reasonably accommodate the disabilities of qualified applicants or employees." Any physical or mental impairment that substantially limits a major life activity comes under this law.

Laws in several states provide for special education for exceptional children. In 1975, the United States Congress enacted Public Law 94-142. Aimed at correcting some of the problems that children with special needs had encountered in the public schools, this law, also known as the Education for All Handicapped Children Act, requires that disabled children be placed in the least restrictive educational environment. That is, children must be incorporated into regular classrooms whenever possible (mainstreamed) and provided with educational plans most suitable for them. No educational plan is implemented until parents have approved it.

This law also prohibits the detrimental labeling of children with special needs. Language is an important factor in any movement. Describing people by their characteristics and behavior is preferable to viewing them as captives of their condition with no other distinguishing attributes. Wherever possible, language should be specifically descriptive of a behavior or condition. A person should be described as someone with epilepsy rather than "an epileptic." If it is known that someone has Down syndrome, that term is preferable to "mentally retarded." If a general term must be used, at present, "developmentally disabled" is preferred. The word "disability" is preferred to "handicap." "Differently abled" and "challenged" are moving into the lexicon, some people preferring this terminology and others protesting that it denies reality. Joan Tollison comments in her "Open Letter," "It might be possible to draw a parallel between [the terms] 'handicapped' and 'Negro,' between 'disabled' and 'black,' and between 'cripple' and 'nigger'" (p. 19). Barbara Baskin and Karen Harris state in *Notes from a Different Drummer* that "a *disability* is a reality, for example, the loss of vision. The restrictions and opportunities imposed by society determine whether or not the disability becomes a *handicap*." "Cripple," "retard," and other terms depriving people of their dignity should be avoided.

Adults working with children must face their own feelings and prejudices. How can anyone change negative attitudes without admitting their existence? Only after individuals are able to confront their fears, ignorance, and superstitions and build on knowledge, comfort, and positive experiences can they help children cope with their feelings toward people with special needs and differences. Movies, television, newspapers, and books often reinforce stereotypes and inaccuracies simply because the writers have not taken the trouble to study their topic extensively enough. Many informative resources are available free of charge to increase awareness.

Try This

Answer the following questions. Add others that will help test your knowledge. Find out how you can expand your current information.

How much help does a disabled person need?

How should help be offered?

How do people with special needs feel about being with people who are different from themselves?

How do people with special needs feel about talking about their particular conditions?

Can people who use wheelchairs engage in sexual intercourse?

How can respectful curiosity be shown to individuals in discussing their specific disabilities?

How can physically limited people become part of the work force?

Are communications disabilities the same as intellectual limitations?

Do people with disabilities develop super powers in other functions?

What is the best learning environment for a child with special needs, and how can this be determined?

What aspects of a child's life are affected by his or her special need, and which ones have nothing to do with the special need?

What agencies offer information about particular special needs?

> What laws has my state passed that affect people with disabilities?
>
> What percentage of the population of my state, my community, or the entire country is disabled?

Many people are uncomfortable when they are with others who are noticeably different from themselves. Some individuals with special needs, through no choice of their own, may be excluded from the rest of society. This situation is especially unfair and hurtful.

"Typical" children, too, are victims of certain misconceptions that prevail about people who look different. They are often afraid to talk to or even stand near people with disabilities because they imagine the condition is contagious. Even adults become anxious about their own physical well-being when they are faced with someone else's condition. Just as someone's death makes people aware of their own mortality, a disability reminds them of their vulnerability. Sometimes this makes people empathic, sometimes it causes them to be fearful.

SUGGESTED CRITERIA

Social psychologists tell us that stereotypes of disabled people are maintained because groups that are unlike the cultural majority are isolated and given few opportunities to develop intimate relations with others. What is more, they are rewarded for living up to others' images of them and punished in subtle ways for breaking out of the mold. They are expected to be helpless, sweet-natured (or constantly complaining), asexual, passive, and uninterested in anything but their own conditions. Good authors do not perpetuate these stereotypes.

Books should focus on what the characters with special needs *can* do rather than creating a deficit model and dwelling on what they cannot do.

Ideally, people with special needs should appear as major and minor characters in approximately the same proportion as they occur in real life. They should be as fully dimensional as the other characters, with the same flaws, strengths, problems, feelings, and responses. They should also be varied in their race, economic background, social class, religion, age, and lifestyle, and be represented in different genres such as poetry, fiction, folktales, nonfiction, adventure tales, and fantasy.

In many folk and fairy tales, people who are smaller or larger than standard size or who do not conform to current norms of beauty are used as devices to frighten and menace the child protagonists. Some stories have a character with a patch over one eye or a wooden leg as a signal that he or she is wicked. Good literature avoids these clichés.

Although for the most part differently abled people are no longer comic foils, many books portray them as the butts of the other characters' bad humor. This ugly behavior does happen in real life. When it occurs in a book, young readers should be invited to think about the effect of this demeaning behavior both on the bully and on the differently abled person. The author should convey that this behavior is not acceptable.

Sometimes a disability is portrayed as something that can be either overcome or made to disappear through positive thinking, prayer, or hard work. This attitude does disabled people an incredible injustice and insinuates that they are the cause of their own conditions. It presents an unrealistic fantasy that cures can be effected just from wishing them to occur or from "good" behavior.

Readers should look for books in which disabled people are respected, not pitied. Pity can be a dehumanizing reaction. (Note how often someone says, "Poor *thing*" in referring to someone who is pitiable.) Stories inviting sympathy, compassion, and empathy reflect more respect for the individual.

Books should contain information acknowledging the enabling effects of equipment such as wheelchairs, hearing aids, glasses, and prosthetic devices. Characters should not be described as "wheelchair-bound" but rather may be said to "use wheelchairs."

Characters should be worthy of attention in their own right, capable of helping themselves and others, coping with their situations.

Gifted people are also often turned into stereotypes such as mad scientists and social outcasts—spoiled, conceited, weak, unathletic, unpopular, unattractive, and emotionally disturbed. Try to note when these false images occur and take steps to rectify them. Characters may, of course, be nasty, conceited, or isolated if the plot and interaction with the other characters logically call for these qualities.

Gifted individuals should be described in a balanced, nonstereotypic manner. A talent should be part of a character's overall makeup, not something unnatural, superimposed, or existing on its own. Giftedness should be valued, not ridiculed.

Characters with special needs should not always be "loners." They should not lack sexual involvement, social interactions, normal feelings, or desires. Differently abled people belong to families, they can maintain close friendships, and they are capable of loving relationships. Their desires and sexuality do not differ from those of the general population, and books should reflect this fact.

Beware when disabled people, no matter how old they are, are looked upon and treated as children. Their capabilities, maturity, and sexuality should not be ignored in favor of a protective, patronizing attitude. They should not be sheltered from bad news, hard work, and other realities of everyday existence.

Authors should avoid forcing characters with special needs to become heroes to be accepted. This is a literary cliché. An analogy may be drawn to the treatment of females who sometimes (in books as well as life) in order to gain acceptance must be the first of their sex to accomplish something (the first woman doctor, judge, astronaut). So too it is with differently abled people: they must save someone's life, be superheroic or super-competent. They are not permitted to have ordinary flaws or be typical, nonspectacular people. That again is an unfair expectation.

People with special needs are individuals. They are as different from one another as they are from the rest of the population (e.g., there is no one quintessential blind person). They have complex personalities, and they are capable of many activities. They can be angry, pleasant, nasty, loving, and irritable in the same proportions as anyone else, and literature should portray them in this balanced way.

What is the person's view of him or herself? If it is negative, what has caused this? What changes occur in the course of the story to help modify this attitude? Good literature provides answers to these questions.

Accuracy is particularly important when an author is describing the behavior of a character with special needs. Generalities or invented characteristics mislead readers and cause them either to develop unrealistic expectations or to misunderstand the consequences of a specific condition.

Settings should be described accurately. Institutions are rarely either ideal havens or torture chambers. With the current emphasis on placement in regular schools and halfway houses, most people with special needs are now likely to have settings outside an institution. If "special" classes or schools are described in a book, it should be made clear that there are good reasons for removing the children from their chronological peers and placing them in specially designed environments.

Books of quality avoid the automatic equating of physical attributes with personality traits or intellectual ability. A person who is physically attractive need not be empty headed ("beautiful but dumb"); a person with a spinal malformation need not be wicked or dishonest.

Books should avoid the cop-out of killing off the character with special needs. Too often this occurs when authors do not know how to handle the relationships and circumstances surrounding people with special needs. Thus the characters who die a martyr's death, in an accident or as a result of an illness, can be remembered fondly and sadly but not confronted. This kind of unrealistic plot gives the impression that their very presence is a problem that can be solved only by their disappearance. This negative literary strategy is also used in some books to avoid coping with gay characters or people of color.

Violence or tragedy should not automatically be a by-product of disability but should occur as the realistic result of an action of the plot, nor should they be linked exclusively with a differently abled person.

It is important to notice the attitudes of typically abled characters toward the differently abled. How does the author indicate what the desired behavior should be? If the attitude of a character toward disabilities is disrespectful and negative, how is the reader informed of this? If these attitudes change for the better, how realistic is this change? Facts embedded skillfully into a work of fiction accomplish much more than moralizing. For example, if it is shown that a person who is effective at his or her job also happens to have disabilities, then young readers are more likely to assume that people with special needs can be competent at their work.

Interaction with people with special needs is the best way to counteract negative preconceptions. Becoming conscious of the stereotypes or lack of them in books children read also contributes to better relationships in their daily lives.

Try This

Look for books in which there are characters who have special needs.

1. List the characters and their conditions.
2. Describe their personalities; compare them to their typical peers. (Note the language used to describe the characters with special needs.)

3. Discuss how the story would be affected if the condition were removed.
4. Discuss how the action would change if other characters had the special condition.
5. What happens to the differently abled characters at the end of the story? Comment on the appropriateness of the ending.

DISCUSSION OF CHILDREN'S BOOKS

Learning

Learning disabilities should not be confused with intellectual impairment. Children who cannot succeed in schoolwork though they are mentally competent are often diagnosed to have learning disabilities. They can have visual or auditory perception problems or difficulty with muscular coordination. When the difficulty is associated with reading, the condition is often called *dyslexia* (specific language disorder). This is always a controversial diagnosis. Some experts believe that most "learning disabilities" are in fact the result of poor or improper teaching methods. Whatever the cause, the treatment is usually the same: Students are encouraged to find physical ways of getting meaning from written symbols. Children often engage in activities involving their muscles or sense of touch. Good teachers also try to find materials and topics that interest these children so they will be drawn into the reading process through their own volition rather than by external pressure.

In *Kelly's Creek,* by Doris Buchanan Smith, Kelly is in a special program where he must practice meaningless perceptual exercises. He hates to do them, and he does not benefit from them. He would much rather play in the creek that runs near his house, where he has a friend who values him and where he can do things he enjoys. He displays special knowledge about pond life and demonstrates that he is mentally competent, even if he cannot read.

Several important lessons can be learned from this book. Although motor skills often are involved in helping children overcome learning disabilities, the most important ingredient in the learning process is motivation. It is essential to pair educational materials with the interests of the child. Small successes build on one another, and self-esteem follows and contributes to the overall success of the program. Kelly's school experience is limiting rather than enhancing because it focuses on mechanical exercises rather than on giving personal meaning to learning.

Joe Lasker's *He's My Brother,* about Jamie, whose family understands and helps him deal with his learning disabilities, brings up other factors, such as peer acceptance and the value of someone's positive qualities.

Not many stories include characters with learning disabilities. Some books containing this topic demean the children who are having difficulty, distort their behaviors, or treat the issue as a mysterious malady that cannot be overcome. Readers of these books can verify the accuracy of the details and discuss some alternative treatment for the characters.

Rose Blue's *Me and Einstein* helps children recognize that dyslexia has little, if anything, to do with a person's potential for success or with innate ability. The author points out that famous people such as Winston Churchill, Thomas Edison, Woodrow Wilson, and Albert Einstein probably had this condition. The book deals with the dilemma of a bright, motivated boy for whom reading is an ordeal. He wants help, but does not know how to ask for it because he does not know what is wrong. He expends a great deal of energy trying to hide his condition; and because he is so bright, he manages to do so until he reaches the fourth grade. Then he reacts to his teacher's accusation that he is simply not trying hard enough by getting into trouble. Eventually he enrolls in a special program for children with learning disabilities. For some people, this is an unsatisfactory solution; they prefer that such a problem be handled within the context of the regular classroom. It must also be recognized that not all teachers are capable of devoting the extra time and energy to children with special needs. In those cases, it might be preferable to provide outside help until the regular classroom can supply an individualized and appropriate program.

Neurological Conditions

Other conditions too often confused with intellectual disability are cerebral palsy and epilepsy. Although these impairments affect muscular control, they do not hamper thought. A frustrating concomitant is the lack of control over the muscles that work the speech organs, sometimes making it difficult for people with cerebral palsy to be understood.

Let the Balloon Go, by Ivan Southall, describes the condition from the perspective of John, a twelve-year-old Australian boy who attempts to demonstrate both to his overprotective mother and to the rest of the world that despite his disorder he is capable of doing many things for himself. For younger children, *About Handicaps,* by Sara Bonnett Stein, helps to validate "normal" children's feelings about themselves and about children with disabilities. Joe, Matthew's playmate, is pictured as a child with cerebral palsy. Matthew learns how to respond to Joe and to deal with his own fears when his father recognizes that Matthew is having difficulties and lovingly and sensitively helps him handle them. The book's excellent photographs enhance the text. As with other books in the "Open Family" series, a simultaneous text is provided for adults' use. Books such as *Epilepsy,* by Alvin Silverstein and Virginia B. Silverstein, clarify and define what epilepsy is and what it is not.

Intellect

The language of disability is nowhere more complicated than in the realm of the intellect. Intellectual impairment results from congenital conditions such as Down syndrome, brain tissue anomalies, chromosomal disorder, or prenatally acquired infections. Disorders of growth, ingestion of lead, serious brain damage, poor nutrition, tumors, and certain degenerative diseases also cause this condition, which is demonstrated by subnormal intellectual functioning.

Until the advent of laws providing for the mainstreaming of children with special needs into the regular classroom wherever possible, children with intellectual disabilities were often shut off from any contact with other youngsters. They were labeled either "trainable" or "educable." The former meant that they had very low IQ scores (usually under 55, but always depending on the capacity of a program to handle a specified number of students) and were not expected to know how to do very much more than the minimal tasks of self-care. "Educable" children scored somewhere between 55 and 80 (depending on a program's requirements) and could be taught to do minimal academic and functional tasks. Labeling usually had the detrimental effect of holding back these students from achieving what they could. It was assumed that their limitations were of such magnitude that they could never take care of themselves or function in "normal" society. Today, the focus is on what they can do, and many books are available to help other children understand and respond constructively to them.

One gem of a book that deals with this topic is Lucille Clifton's *My Friend Jacob,* which tells of the friendship between Sam, an eight-year-old African-American child, and Jacob, a white seventeen year old with limited intellectual capacities. They share a mutually rewarding friendship and help their mothers understand the quality of their relationship. Jake is not labeled in the text; the illustrations are sensitively drawn to indicate that Jake probably has Down syndrome. This book helps set aside stereotypes and build understanding.

In another excellent book, *Making Room for Uncle Joe,* Ada B. Litchfield personalizes the current practice of closing state hospitals and relocating their former residents into halfway houses or other facilities. In this story, Joe, who has Down syndrome, is the mother's younger brother. Beth, Dan, and Amy are anxious about how Uncle Joe's coming to live with them will affect their lives. Beth, the eldest, is particularly resentful of Uncle Joe's arrival. Amy, the youngest, is the most welcoming. The story demonstrates the difficulties and benefits for everyone, including Uncle Joe, of the relocation. It is an excellent example of how a loving and supportive family confronts a challenge and handles it well. The author respects everyone's feelings and point of view and indicates, without romanticizing the situation, how much a part of the family a developmentally disabled person can become.

In *Welcome Home, Jellybean,* by Marlene Shyer, Neil, the narrator is younger than his sister Geraldine (Jellybean), who has lived in an institutional setting since she was an infant because her parents felt unable to deal with her intellectual disability. When the mother finally cannot cope any longer with her guilt and insists on bringing Geraldine home, life changes considerably for the entire family. Neil feels embarrassment, anger, pride, love, and a variety of ambivalent emotions. Neil's father is so angry and frustrated that he eventually moves out of the house. In the end, it looks as though Geraldine, Neil, and their mother will make a good life for themselves. The strengths of this story lie in the vivid descriptions of Geraldine's behavior and in Neil's growing understanding of her needs and his ability to nurture.

Readers and helping adults may benefit from discussing the dilemma faced by many families when their child's condition mandates an institutional setting. Sometimes home care is not feasible, and the family should be helped to avoid guilt when their decision is made for everyone's benefit.

Physical Conditions

Mobility.   The range of disabilities resulting in impairment of mobility is wide. In some individuals, conditions such as cerebral palsy, spastic diplegia, spina bifida, polio, scoliosis, juvenile rheumatoid arthritis, and spinal cord injuries may impede walking and other sensorimotor tasks only moderately. In other people, these same conditions and others can require them to use wheelchairs, crutches, braces, prosthetic devices, or canes to move around.

Accessibility is a major problem for people whose mobility is impaired. Curbs; narrow door openings; stairs; gravel paths; slopes that are too steep; faulty illumination; doors that are difficult to open; and inconveniently placed facilities such as telephones, toilets, drinking fountains, light switches, handles, and knobs can be formidable obstacles.

Attitudinal barriers are sometimes more difficult to overcome than physical. One book that helps dispel fears and false notions is *Don't Feel Sorry for Paul,* by Bernard Wolf. Paul wears prosthetic devices that help him ride horseback and engage in ordinary everyday activities. The photos help satisfy a nondisabled child's desire to look closely at a prosthetic device without being rude. *About Handicaps,* by Sara Bonnett Stein, also demonstrates how a prosthesis works. Another work of nonfiction, *What Do You Do When Your Wheelchair Gets a Flat Tire? Questions and Answers about Disabilities,* edited by Douglas Biklen and Michele Sokoloff, contains questions asked by able-bodied children and answered by disabled children. It includes not only factual responses but also the emotional responses of these children. The photos portray a range of disabilities and a variety of children from different backgrounds.

In Virginia Hamilton's *The Bells of Christmas,* the main character, Jason, has great respect for his father. "He was only different to me because he was such a fine carpenter and woodworker," says Jason. The fact that the father has mobility difficulties is a part of the plot but not the overriding characteristic of the father's personality.

For younger readers, many books, among them Eloise Greenfield's *Darlene,* show that a wheelchair need not be a deterrent to enjoyment of life. *The Balancing Girl,* by Bernice Rabe, describes a classroom where a girl who uses a wheelchair demonstrates her abilities and engages in all sorts of activities. *Someone Special, Just like You,* by Tricia Brown, shows photos of young children with various impairments all functioning in much the same manner that typical children do. This book, aimed at young readers, demonstrates the universality of emotions and responses irrespective of condition of ability. *Our Teacher's in a Wheelchair,* by Mary Ellen Powers, demonstrates graphically the capabilities of an excellent day-care teacher who leads a very active life although he uses a wheelchair to get around.

It is important for children to read books in which the disabled characters learn to help themselves rather than depend totally on others. A competent woman who can demonstrably take care of herself and maintain an active life although she spends most of her time in bed is depicted in *Grandma Drives a Motor Bed,* by Diane Johnston Hamm. In *Run, Don't Walk,* by Harriet Savitz, two teenagers help to educate and persuade their community to stop discriminating against disabled people. Savitz is also the author of *Wheelchair Champions,* describing real people who have gained prowess in various sports. This book lists organizations and publications dealing with sports for people who use wheelchairs.

What If You Couldn't . . . ?, by Janet Kamien, is directed at nondisabled children to help them empathize with disabled people. In conjunction with some materials from the Children's Museum of Boston, the activities in this book can spark many others. Simulations such as wearing a sling on one arm or both arms or using crutches or a wheelchair while attempting to accomplish tasks such as cleaning a room, playing a game, or moving from one place to another across some barrier stimulate discussion and additional activities.

Hearing. People with hearing impairments do not necessarily live in a silent world. Hearing disorders can involve the distortion or muffling of sounds as well. Sometimes a hearing aid can totally control a disability; sometimes it serves as a partial corrective; at other times it would do no good at all.

A child with a hearing problem can go undiagnosed for a long time because of the mistaken impression that the child is "slow." The signs of a hearing disorder include frequent colds and infections, runny or inflamed ears, distorted speech, rubbing or pulling on the ears, use of gesture rather than speech, frequent requests for repetition of statements by others, talking too loudly, and seeming inattention may all be behaviors of a child who has a hearing disability. If a hearing disorder is suspected, the child should be referred to a specialist.

A person who has a hearing impairment is not necessarily deprived of the ability to enjoy conversations, music, and other pleasures related to speech and sound. Deaf people can often dance, play musical instruments, and sing.

One controversy concerning the education of people with hearing disabilities involves the issue of whether or not to use sign language. Some experts believe that only oral communication permits deaf people to function in the hearing world. They argue that if sign language is taught, people grow to rely solely on it as a means of communication and never become fluent talkers. Others argue that a combination of lip-reading, speech, and signing provides "total" communication for hearing-impaired people and constitutes the ideal program of instruction. Still others advocate signing as the "normal" and exclusive mode of communication. A powerful drama, *Children of a Lesser God,* by Mark Medoff, explores this controversy and presents the issues as comparable to those facing any activist group that tries to win recognition from society.

Most books about this disability are nonfiction. Some of them, like *Handtalk: An ABC of Finger Spelling and Sign Language,* by Remy Charlip, Mary Beth Miller, and George Ancona, teach how to communicate without oral speech. This book is delightfully illustrated and conveys a sense of joy in the process. Others, like *Claire and Emma,* by Diana Peter, and *I Have a Sister, My Sister Is Deaf,* by Jeanne Peterson, discuss the everyday life of a deaf child while imparting information about hearing disorders and how to manage them.

In some works of fiction, a deaf character is made to be mysterious, afflicted by God, or abnormal in ways that exceed what can realistically be expected of a hearing-disabled person. Sometimes the deaf character is a nonperson, a foil for the other characters. In contrast, in Emily Hanlon's *The Swing,* Beth, an eleven-year-old girl who has been deaf since birth, demonstrates courage, insight, and a sense of her own talents and limitations. She is treated naturally by the other characters and is portrayed well by the author. Margaret, the fourteen-year-old protagonist in Barbara Corcoran's *A Dance to Still Music,* has many problems and suffers from a sense of isolation. She runs away to escape from what she believes to be an uncaring mother and the unwelcome prospect of "banishment" to a school for deaf children. At the end of the book a wonderful woman (who is almost too good to be true) helps her acknowledge and resolve her problems. Incidental factual information about hearing disabilities is well integrated into this novel.

Speech. Communication is an essential part of human interaction. The usual mode of interacting with others is speech. People with hearing impairments often find it difficult to be understood because they cannot hear the speech sounds they make. If someone has been deaf from birth, it is difficult to learn to speak. A person like Helen Keller is admired for surmounting the difficulties resulting from multiple disabilities, particularly those affecting her ability to communicate.

Children's books that convey this sense of overcoming the problem while still retaining the disability are important for both disabled and nondisabled readers. Not everyone can be a genius or become famous. With understanding and help from others, however, most people can manage to make their thoughts and feelings known.

Speech problems can be as extensive as total muteness; they also include more common concerns such as stuttering, lisping, and other minor disorders. Most children's books covering this topic feature characters who are mute. In some of the books, such as E.B. White's *Trumpet of the Swan,* the disability is the primary focus of the plot. In this story, Louis is a swan who uses a trumpet to substitute for his voice and thereby finds success. In Jane Yolen's *Dragon's Blood,* the dragon is deliberately bred to be mute because the lack of a raucous cry is a great advantage to a fighting beast; but this dragon can communicate in a special way with a limited number of people: She transmits her feelings and thoughts through her mind.

Frank Jupo's *Atu, the Silent One* tells of a young hunter, an African Bushman, who is mute. He communicates through his paintings both to his peers and to future generations. Although he cannot tell his people's stories orally, his talent as an artist accomplishes something that speech cannot. The uncle in Meindert DeJong's *Journey from Peppermint Street* is another mute person who speaks eloquently through gesture and writing and emerges as a strong, sensitive, and admirable character.

Aaron, the mute twelve-year-old boy in Paul Fleischman's *The Half-a-Moon Inn,* achieves self-responsibility through a harrowing adventure. His thoughts and behavior communicate vividly to his audience.

Books about speech problems other than muteness are difficult to find. Although some books contain characters who have difficulty with speech or who stutter, either the disabilities are not described accurately or it is implied that the problem is a figment of the character's imagination. The "defects" disappear as soon as other events make the plot take an upward turn. In some of the stories, the character's speech returns or is improved after he or she has performed some remarkable task, saved someone's life, or developed an amazing talent. As is the case in so many of these areas of disability, many more books are needed that knowledgeably and sensitively portray disabled characters integrated into well-constructed plots.

Vision.   Although some people have no vision at all and neither see nor sense light, most visually impaired people have at least some sight. Some people can see only distorted images; others can see only at certain distances. There are many aids for people with sight dysfunction: corrective lenses help a large percentage; surgery is performed successfully on most cataracts and detached retinas and is used to provide corneal transplants. The development of the Braille alphabet and of "talking books" has been a boon to people who want to enjoy the pleasures of reading. Trained guide dogs have also liberated many visually disabled people from dependence on others.

Vision is an important factor in school success, and teachers and parents should be alert to the signals of visual problems. They should watch for signs of eyestrain or eye fatigue such as squinting or frowning, red or watery eyes, frequent headaches, or rubbing of the eyes. Also significant are the practices of holding reading material very close to the face or very far away and copying incorrectly from a chalkboard or another piece of paper. Other signs of trouble are double or blurred vision, frequent eye infections, and awkward movement (bumping into things, tripping, spilling liquids when pouring). Sometimes children are unaware that they are not seeing as clearly as they should; sometimes they are aware and want to hide it. Symptoms of this situation can include children's seeming fearful or irritable, having problems making friends, and appearing reluctant to engage in new activities.

Many authors have included blind characters as major elements in their stories, both fiction and nonfiction, for young, middle grade, and older children. One book that can be appreciated by children of all ages is Jane Yolen's *The Seeing Stick.* In this moving story, told in poetic language rich in sensory images, with illustrations that extend the text, an old man journeys to the palace of the emperor to teach the blind princess Hwei Ming to "see." By means of the carvings on his stick, the old man helps Hwei Ming to use her sense of touch to visualize the details of the stories he tells her. Eventually she learns this technique so well that she teaches it to the blind children of her kingdom. It is only at the end of the story that we are informed that the old man too is blind.

Another sensitively written story about a competent blind person is Patricia MacLachlan's *Through Grandpa's Eyes.* In it, John and his grandfather enjoy each other's company and John acquires new dimensions of perception because of his talented grandfather. *Mom Can't See Me,* by Sally Hobart Alexander, is a work of nonfiction that demonstrates vividly by means of the text and especially through the beautiful black-and-white photos by George Ancona how competent and strong a person with no vision can be. The author is herself blind. She has written the story from the perspective of her nine-year-old daughter and honestly portrays the difficulties, as well as the triumphs, of living in a family where the mother is blind.

Yet another superbly competent blind person appears in Sharon Bell Mathis's powerful novel for older children, *Listen for the Fig Tree.* Muffin, the sixteen-year-old protagonist, has become blind over a period of years. She has prepared for this condition by her father, another very strong character. After the father is killed, Muffin's mother falls apart; and it is up to Muffin to maintain their household. She is emotionally supported by a close-knit black community. The descriptions of each character, as well as Muffin's ability to cope with everyday routines, are flawlessly handled by the author in this sometimes painful but always inspiring book.

Children can invent their own stories about visual problems. An alert adult can sense many anxieties by actively listening to the stories children invent.

Emotions

Emotional problems afflict all of us at one time or another. Literature would be dull indeed if characters in stories always behaved in rational, dispassionate, logical ways. The occasional outburst or slump is part of normal functioning, and it would be an enormous disservice to children to label such behavior aberrant or demand professional treatment for it. In contrast, emotional dysfunction, which can range from depression to dissociation from reality, can be severely disabling and require therapy or even hospitalization. Books can help readers distinguish between temporary upsets and deeply rooted problems. They should also communicate that a serious problem often has a physiological base or results from some intensely stressful or unusual psychological or situational factor.

In most books an emotionally distraught character is seen through the eyes of a narrator. One notable exception to this practice is *I Can Hear the Mourning Dove,* by James Bennett. The entire story is narrated by Grace Braun, a young woman who has been hospitalized for emotional problems, in a voice that clearly communicates the protagonist's feelings and thoughts and gives the reader an understanding of what it means to be emotionally disabled.

If a book is well crafted, seriously disturbed characters invite empathy from the part of the reader. Sometimes a character seeks a fantasy world for solace: Fran Ellen, in Marilyn Sachs's *The Bears' House,* tries to cope with a harsher world by escaping into the fantasy of the toy bears' house her teacher brought into the classroom. In Virginia Hamilton's *The Planet of Junior Brown,* Junior leaves the pain of this world for a safer, utopian planet. Naomi, who has seen her father beaten to death by Nazis, runs back into silence when Alan, her friend and protector, engages in a bloody fist fight with an anti-Semitic bully in Myron Levoy's masterly novel *Alan and Naomi.* These are all powerful tales of human suffering and interaction that deal with intimate relationships and the quest for acceptance and security; they are literary works of quality rather than clinical examinations of mental illness.

Specific symptoms of emotional dysfunction are described in some books: Florence Parry Heide's protagonist in *Growing Anyway Up* performs elaborate rituals to make her private world safe; Alexandra's journal in Patricia Windsor's *The Summer Before* details her feelings and observations.

In some stories, the mother of the protagonist experiences emotional problems so severe that they cause her to be unable to function. In *The Bears' House,* Fran Ellen's mother has lapsed into an almost catatonic stage because of the desertion of her husband. Her condition precipitates the trauma for her children. They try desperately to maintain their household, take care of the baby, and stay together; but in the end, they are taken into charge by a social worker who will try to place them in appropriate homes. In Cynthia Voigt's *Homecoming,* their mother's mental collapse causes Dicey and her siblings to search for a safe haven. The sequel, *Dicey's Song,* won the Newbery Award. There are some books in which fathers are emotionally disturbed, but for some reason these stories are not of as high a quality as those where the mothers are disabled.

Some characters have temporary emotional problems or problems that are not quite as severe. Trissy, in Norma Fox Mazer's *I, Trissy,* loses her sense of proportion and behaves in a destructive fashion; but she returns to balance by the end of the book. In *Chloris and the Creeps,* by Kin Platt, Chloris seems to be relinquishing her obsessive, false image of her father, and the reader hopes that her behavior will change for the better by the time the story has ended.

When it is clear that a character is emotionally dysfunctional, the behavior must be accurately described and not lightly "cured." Children should be invited to discuss which behaviors fall within the realm of normalcy and which require professional attention.

Special Categories

People with serious chronic illnesses, as well as gifted and talented people, have substantial special needs and require particular understanding and attention on the part of helping adults. They are therefore included in this chapter.

Serious Illness.   Diabetes, asthma, leukemia, cancer, Alzheimer's disease, AIDS, and other physical conditions that sometimes can be controlled by medicine but always affect a person's life can be found in a number of books. The same criteria apply to these books as to other books involving physical disabilities. It is important to remember that the characters should have lives outside their illness and exhibit their own distinctive personalities. Their stories should contain more than the symptoms and treatments of their physical conditions. In books where the characters have diabetes, asthma, or other treatable conditions, it is unfortunate to find the situation kept as a guilty secret as though it were something to be ashamed of. An open discussion could dispel some of the misconceptions surrounding these health problems. A helpful book, *You Can't Catch Diabetes from a Friend,* by Lynne Kipnis and Susan Adler, defines and explains the condition.

Another plot element that may invite readers' discussion deals with characters who have particular illnesses but forget or refuse to take their medicine. They know what to do and how to do it, but they neglect to do so, and someone else in the story must rescue them. This is the case in Ron Roy's *Where's Buddy?*; but in the end Buddy proves to be responsible and more capable of caring for himself than his overprotective parents thought.

Some illnesses, such as leukemia, cancer, Alzheimer's disease, and AIDS, are less controllable by the individual who suffers from them and necessitate hospitalization and extensive medical treatment. The process of treatment, as well as a complete description of the effects of the disease, are well presented by Jason Gaes, the six-year-old author of *My Book for Kids with Cansur.* Hope is the key element in this book, as it is in *On with My Life,* by Patti Trull. In *Understanding AIDS,* Ethan Lerner details, by means of a number of different stories, the various aspects of AIDS, including how it can be contracted and what its ramifications are. The effects of the relentless progress of Alzheimer's disease are movingly portrayed in *Always Gramma,* by Vaunda Micheaux Nelson.

Each illness has implications for societal response. They are expensive, debilitating, frightening, and, particularly with Alzheimer's disease and AIDS, without any known cure. In all these cases, individuals can live for many years with the disease but its effects are extensive, not only on the person who is afflicted but also on family and friends. With AIDS, an additional concern is how to handle people's fears that they will contract the disease by casual contact. As this disease becomes more prevalent, the general public is less apt to ostracize people with AIDS; but it is still an issue to be reckoned with. More and more books are acknowledging these problems and trying to deal with them in story form. It is important for helping adults to look for books that are developmentally appropriate and accurate and refrain from sensationalism or romanticization.

Giftedness.   Although intellectual, artistic, creative, or leadership talents are not disabilities, gifted people do have special needs; they are sometimes treated in destructive ways by the rest of society. Most heroes in fantasies and fairy tales are gifted in one way or another; but it is more difficult to find children in stories about everyday life who are gifted and whose talents are respected, not instruments that invite punitive behavior.

The *Encyclopedia Brown* series by Donald Sobol is excellent for showing a child who is valued for his cleverness. Ramona, the creative little girl in Beverly Cleary's series of books, is another bright child who is in no way scorned or feared. On the other hand, Madeleine L'Engle's *Time* trilogy contains a number of wonderfully gifted characters, including Charles Wallace, a young boy whose extraordinary intelligence is perceived by some of the general public as "weird" and "retarded." L'Engle's series of books about the Austin family portrays unusually gifted people who are admirable, loving, and balanced. In the thousands of books published in recent years, it is rare to find a balanced, fair portrayal of an intellectually gifted person. Perhaps biographies of gifted contributors to society could be used to counter the message that giftedness is either nonexistent or unappealing.

Books also contain descriptions of characters who are gifted in ways other than intellectual. Taro Yashima's *Crow Boy* has outstanding powers of observation and mimicry; Nancy Garrett has extrasensory perception in Lois Duncan's *A Gift of Magic*. Marcia Simon's young male protagonist in *A Special Gift* is a talented dancer; a mute boy in Glen Rounds's *Blind Outlaw* is remarkably gifted with animals. Minna Pratt is a talented cellist in Patricia MacLachlan's *The Facts and Fictions of Minna Pratt*.

Books that provide a sensible and positive perspective on giftedness that seems reasonable in the context of the story avoid derogatory stereotypes (thick glasses, fragile health, unpopularity with peers, arrogant self-interest, emotional imbalance) and represent a great variety of characters, heritages, and talents.

REFERENCES

Special Needs

Academic Therapy Publications. *Directory of Facilities and Services for the Learning Disabled.* Academic Therapy, 1991. The resources named in this comprehensive directory are listed geographically as well as alphabetically.

Americans with Disabilities Act. U.S. Equal Employment Opportunity Commission, 1991. Pamphlets explain the law and its implications for employers and employees, including how to determine if one has an "impairment that substantially limits a major life activity," employees' rights, employers' obligations, and how to determine what accommodations are reasonable for an employer to make.

Anderson, H. "Don't Stare, I'll Tell You Later!" *The Exceptional Parent,* Dec. 1980, pp. 14-18. Discusses how to explain a person's disability to children. Lists helpful suggestions for parents in order to promote empathy and understanding on the part of children who are not disabled. The author was born with cerebral palsy.

Anderson, M. F. *Hospitalized Children and Books: A Guide for Librarians, Families, and Caregivers.* Scarecrow, 1992. Story hour themes, poetry writing, developmental bibliotherapy, and procedures for reading aloud to the young patient are discussed.

Ayrault, E. W. *Growing up Handicapped: A Guide to Helping the Exceptional Child.* Seabury, 1977. The author, born with cerebral palsy, is a clinical psychologist working primarily with disabled people and their families. She contributes information and helpful suggestions to parents and other adults interested in working with disabled children. Her advice is practical; she is aware of the pitfalls of overprotection and ignorance.

Baskin, B. H., and Harris, K. H. *Notes from a Different Drummer.* Bowker, 1977. A guide to more than 300 juvenile fiction titles promoting the understanding and acceptance of the disabled. The second volume, *More Notes from a Different Drummer* (1984), describes an additional 348 books.

Bauer, C. J. "Books Can Break Attitudinal Barriers toward the Handicapped." *The School Counselor* 32 (Mar. 1985): 303-306. The author contends that books about children with disabilities can foster a beneficial social climate among all children.

Carlin, M. F.; Laughlin, J. L.; and Saniga, R. *Understanding Abilities, Disabilities, and Capabilities: A Guide to Children's Literature.* Libraries Unlimited, 1991. More than 45 disabling conditions are listed, described, and rated for students in grades K-12, demonstrating that while the literature addressing children with special needs has increased, not all books deal with the issues appropriately.

Corman, C. "Bibliotherapy: Insight for the Learning-Handicapped." *Language Arts* 52 (Oct. 1975): 935-937. Annotated bibliographies are provided to complement the author's plea for the use of classroom guidance through books.

Council on Interracial Books for Children. *Bulletin* 8 (Nos. 6, 7, 1977). (Special issue on "Handicapism in Children's Books.") Contains many articles and reviews of books pertaining to attitudes toward disabled people as evidenced in children's books.

Council on Interracial Books for Children. *Bulletin* 11 (Nos. 1, 2, 1980). (Special issue on "American Sign Language/Hearing Impairment in Children's Materials.") Articles focus on how deaf people are portrayed in children's books and include self-perceptions by hearing-impaired authors.

Council on Interracial Books for Children. *Bulletin* 13 (Nos. 4, 5, 1982). (Special issue: "Handicapism in Children's Books: A Five Year Update.") This issue updates the previous examination of materials and provides thoroughly annotated entries of recommended materials, as well as criticisms of items containing negative stereotypes and attitudes.

Cunningham, C. *Down's Syndrome: An Introduction for Parents,* revised ed. Brookline, 1988. A reassuring and informative volume on all aspects of living with a child who has Down syndrome. The author provides excellent arguments to support his views on the benefits of mainstreaming.

Dobo, P. J. "Using Literature to Change Attitudes toward the Handicapped." *The Reading Teacher* 36 (Dec. 1982): 290-292. Lists sources of literature to help children without disabilities overcome fear and grow to accept their peers with disabilities.

Ferguson, A. M. *Children's Literature—For All Handicapped Children,* ERIC Document Reproduction Service, 1981. Fourteen children's books are included in a discussion of children with disabilities. Designed for teachers.

Fine, J. *Afraid to Ask: A Book for Families to Share about Cancer.* Lothrop Lee and Shepard, 1986. The author offers information to young people about many types of cancer and its related emotional problems.

Frasier, M. M., and McCannon, C. "Using Bibliotherapy with Gifted Children." *Gifted Child Quarterly* 25 (Spring 1981): 81-85. Annotated list of books containing gifted children who solve their particular problems.

Friedberg, J. B.; Mullins, J. B.; and Sukiennik, A. W. *Portraying Persons with Disabilities.* Bowker, 1992. Nonfiction titles are provided, with reading levels preschool through young adult, portraying people and situations that can educate readers about human differences.

Gavron, S. "Surviving the Least Restrictive Alternative." *Strategies,* Jan. 1989, pp. 5-8. Discusses information physical education teachers must have to establish a positive classroom atmosphere for children with disabilities.

Gerber, P. J., and Harris, K. B. "Using Juvenile Literature to Develop Social Skills in Learning Disabled Children." *The Pointer* 27 (Summer 1983): 29-32. Recognizing that children with learning disabilities may lag behind in social skills, the authors discuss components of good books and include a list of recommended titles.

Gold, Janet T. "That's Me! The LD Child in Literature." *Academic Therapy* 18 (May 1983): 609-617. Books about children with learning disabilities can foster self-esteem in children with similar learning problems. A listing of recommended books is included.

Grandin, T., and Scariano, M. M. *Emergence: Labeled Autistic.* Arena, 1986. In this fascinating autobiography, Grandin, a woman who has overcome her autism to complete a Ph.D. and pursue a successful career, talks about her life and what it means to have autism.

"HIV and AIDS." *Book Links* 2 (Nov. 1992): 11-15. Books pamphlets, coloring books, and videos about AIDS are listed to facilitate teachers', librarians', and parents' selection.

Hopkins, C. J. "Developing Positive Attitudes toward the Handicapped through Children's Books." *Elementary School Journal* 81 (Sept. 1980): 34-37. Identifies materials for regular elementary school classrooms to create awareness of the abilities of disabled children. Lists a number of recommended children's books.

Howe-Cousar, C. "Instructing Gifted Middle School Readers." New England League of Middle Schools, 1990. The pamphlet discusses instructional choices and other information for regular education teachers of gifted children. A book list is included.

Interagency Committee on Learning Disabilities. "Learning Disabilities: A Report to the U.S. Congress." Washington, D.C.: 1987. Reveals the prevalence of learning disabled children in the United States.

Karolides, N. J. *Focus on Physical Impairments: A Reference Handbook.* ABC-CLIO, 1990. Provides information about nine physical conditions including visual impairment, hearing impairment, cerebral palsy, muscular sclerosis, and neuromuscular dysfunction and how learning is affected by the condition, as well as an annotated list of books for children.

Kronick, D. "Children's Books and Games: More Doing Books." *Academic Therapy* 21 (May 1986): 623-627. An annotated list of books about children with learning disabilities.

Kronick, D. "Children's Books, Games, and Literature for the Learning Disabled." *Academic Therapy* 20 (Nov. 1984): 241-245. Books that can be used to promote social awareness are discussed.

Lass, B., and Bromfield, M. "Books about Children with Special Needs: An Annotated Bibliography." *The Reading Teacher* 34 (Feb. 1981): 530-533. Criteria for selection of books are clearly stated, with a rationale provided. Books are discussed and recommended.

Levert, S. *AIDS: In Search of a Killer.* Messner, 1987. The author talks about AIDS and implications of the deadly virus.

Litton, F. W.; Banbury, M. M.; and Harris, K. "Materials for Educating Nonhandicapped Students about Their Handicapped Peers." *Teaching Exceptional Children* 13 (Fall 1980): 39-43.

Lukawevich, A. "Three Dozen Useful Information Sources on Reading for the Gifted." *The Reading Teacher* 36 (Feb. 1983): 542-548. An annotated bibliography of resources for use in the classroom with gifted children. Included are articles and books on various aspects of the teaching of reading.

Marozas, D. S., and May, D. C. *Issues and Practices in Special Education.* Longman, 1988. Raises practical, ethical, and legal issues affecting special education.

McQueen, K., and Fassler, D. "Children's Books about AIDS." *Children's Literature in Education* 20 (Sept. 1989): 183-190. The authors confront fear, confusion, and misconceptions with a listing of book reviews about AIDS for school-age children.

Mellon, C. A. "Evaluating the Portrayal of Disabled Characters in Juvenile Fiction." *Journal of Youth Services in Libraries* 2 (Winter 1989): 143-150. The author, mother of a child with a disability, contends that reviewers may reinforce myths by excusing lower literary quality in fiction containing "stories of the less fortunate." Recommended fiction is included and described.

Mellon, C. A. "Exceptionality in Children's Books: Combining Apples and Oranges." *School Library Journal* 35 (Oct. 1989): 46-47. Criticizes the practice of lumping all children with disabilities under one label and discusses good and bad aspects of books for children about disabilities.

Perske, R. *New Life in the Neighborhood: How Persons with Retardation or Other Disabilities Can Help Make a Good Community Better.* Abingdon, 1988. A discussion of the issue of people with developmental and other disabilities moving into mainstream neighborhoods and society. Educates readers about the capabilities of people with handicaps and shows that communities can be cohesive when everyone is seen as "people first."

Polette, N. and Hamlin, M. *Exploring Books with Gifted Children.* Libraries Unlimited, 1980. Provides guidelines for working with gifted children, discusses programs and materials, approaches to instruction, and suitable books.

Pyne, C. S.; Campbell, S.; and Gross, L. "Books for Blind and Physically Handicapped Children." *Book List* 87 (Nov 1990): 670-672. Compiled by three children's librarians, the article describes about 50 children's book titles for preschool to junior high school age. The books are available for loan in the form of records, cassettes, and braille through the Library of Congress.

Quackenbush, M., and Nelson, M., with Clark, K. *The AIDS Challenge: Prevention Education for Young People.* Network, 1988. An encyclopedic compendium of articles on how to educate adolescents about AIDS prevention.

Quackenbush, M., and Villarreal, S. *Does AIDS Hurt?" Educating Young Children about AIDS.* Network, 1988. The authors advocate comprehensive health education in schools and at home. They offer specific answers to questions children might ask.

Quicke, J. *Disability in Modern Children's Fiction.* Brookline, 1985. Astute critiques of a number of children's books, both positive and negative, containing characters with special needs.

Renzulli, J. S. *The Enrichment Triad.* Creative Learning, 1977. An important model of curriculum construction for gifted students. Renzulli is a major proponent of education for the gifted.

Robertson, D. *Portraying Persons with Disabilities.* Bowker, 1992. A lengthy annotated bibliography of children's and young adult fiction follows a discussion about the need to carefully and honestly depict children with disabilities.

Schwartz, A. V. "Books Mirror Society: A Study of Children's Materials." *Bulletin of the Council on Interracial Books for Children* 11 (Nos. 1, 2, 1980): 19–24. An extensive evaluation of books dealing with deafness and hearing-impaired characters. Criteria are established and used as a filter for the evaluation. Most books are found wanting, but some are recommended.

Slapin, B. *Books without Bias: A Guide to Evaluating Children's Literature for Handicapism.* Squeaky Wheels, 1990. Books featuring children with disabilities are listed, annotated, and reviewed with an astute eye for the author's perspective.

Stanovich, K. E., and Stanovich, P. "Speaking for Themselves: A Bibliography of Writings of Mentally Handicapped Individuals." *Mental Retardation* 17 (April 1979): 83–86. Annotated listing of articles and books, written by people with some condition of mental disability.

Stark, L. S. "Understanding Learning Disabilities through Fiction." *School Library Journal* 32 (May 1986): 30–31. The author advises that books about children with learning disabilities be chosen critically and carefully. Selected fiction about children with learning disabilities is included.

Teasley, A. B. "YA Literature about AIDS: Encountering the Unimaginable." *The ALAN Review* 20 (Spring 1993): 18–23. Following a brief introduction regarding the status of the AIDS epidemic in the young adult population, the author provides an annotated bibliography of both fiction and nonfiction books for young adults. He also includes resources for adults and some video and audiotapes.

Tway, E. "The Gifted Child in Literature." *Language Arts* 57 (Jan. 1980): 14–20. Excellent overview of how the gifted child is portrayed in children's books. Analyses of books are thorough and informative.

Weiss, A. B. "Using Picture Books to Teach Literary Elements to the Disabled Reader." *The Pointer* 27 (Fall 1982): 8–10. Discusses how carefully selected books can help remotivate discouraged children with learning disabilities.

West, N., ed. "Educating Exceptional Children." *Annual Edition.* Dushkin, 1982. One of a series of *Annual Editions,* each a compendium of informative articles on a particular topic. This volume contains 48 articles on mainstreaming, strategies for helping children understand their disabled peers, and educating disabled as well as gifted children.

RESOURCES

American Association for Gifted Children. Duke University, 01 West Duke Bldg., Campus Dr., Durham, NC 27708. Works to help gifted children reach their potential and use their talents to benefit others. Encourages cooperation of community and professional groups for understanding their needs and problems.

American Civil Liberties Union. 132 W. 43rd St., New York, NY 10036. The ACLU has published a series of books on disability rights, the mental patient, teachers, and developmentally delayed individuals.

American Deafness And Rehabilitation Association. P.O. Box 251554, Little Rock, AR 72225. Promotes development and understanding of deaf people, rehabilitation, and scientific research.

American Diabetes Association. P.O. Box 25757, 1660 Duke St., Alexandria, VA 22314. Educates the public in the early recognition and treatment of diabetes and promotes and funds research and care programs.

American Foundation for the Blind. 15 W. 16th Street, New York, NY 10011. (800) AFB-LIND. Development, maintenance, and improvement of services for blind and visually impaired people. Offers consulting and referral services.

American Printing House for the Blind. 1839 Frankfort Ave., P.O. Box 6085, Louisville, KY 40206-0085. Publishes literature in Braille, large type, and recorded computer disc and manufactures educational aids for visually impaired students.

Association for Retarded Citizens of the United States. 500 E. Borter St., Suite 300, Arlington, TX 76010. Works to promote services, research, public understanding, and legislation for developmentally disabled persons and their families.

Burt Harrison & Co. P.O. Box 732, Weston, MA 02193. Distributes a multimedia program sensitizing elementary school children to what it is like to have a disability. The kit, "What If You Couldn't," can be rented from Boston Children's Museum, 300 Congress St., Boston, MA 02210-1034.

Center on Human Policy. Syracuse University, 200 Huntington Hall, 2nd Floor, Syracuse, NY 13244-2340. A policy, research, and advocacy organization involved in the national movement to insure rights of people with disabilities. Publishes a variety of reports and resources on the integration of people with severe disabilities into community life.

Council for Exceptional Children. 1920 Association Dr., Reston, VA 22091. Champions the right of exceptional individuals to full educational opportunities and provides information to teachers, parents, and others.

Directory of Organizations Interested in the Handicapped. People to People Committee for the Handicapped, P.O. Box 18131, Washington, D.C. 20036.

Disability Rights Education and Defense Fund. 2212 6th St., Berkeley, CA 94710. Seeks to educate the public and policymakers in order to further the civil rights of people with disabilities. Provides information on legislation, provides training for legislators, lawyers, and judges.

Epilepsy Foundation of America. 4351 Garden City Dr., Landover, MD 20785. Supports medical, social, rehabilitation, legal, employment, education, research, and advocacy programs and provides information for people with epilepsy, their families, and interested individuals.

The Exceptional Parent. 296 Boylston St., Third Floor, Boston, MA 02116. A magazine aimed at parents of children with disabilities.

Federation of Children with Special Needs. 95 Berkley St., Suite 104, Boston, MA 02116. Provides information on special education laws and resources and how to obtain related services. Operates a project to increase parent involvement in the health care of children with disabilities.

Gifted Child Quarterly. 1426 Southwind, Westlake Village, CA 91361. A magazine dedicated to the education of gifted and talented children.

Journal for the Education of the Gifted. School of Education, Ruffner Hall, Room 103, University of Virginia, Charlottesville, VA 22903. Aimed at teachers of gifted and talented children.

March of Dimes Birth Defects Foundation. 1275 Mamaroneck Ave., White Plains, NY 10605. Promotes prevention of birth defects by focusing on maternal and child health issues. Offers public and professional health education and community service programs to improve maternal and neonatal health.

Muscular Dystrophy Association of America. 3561 E. Sunrise Dr., Tucson, AZ 85718. Offers professional and public education and information programs, as well as services for those with this disease.

National Association for Hearing and Speech Action. 10801 Rockville Pike. Rockville, MD 20852. (800)638-8255. Provides educational information and referrals on language and hearing disabilities.

National Association of the Deaf. 814 Thayer Ave., Silver Spring, MD 20910. Protects the civil rights of people with hearing impairments in the areas of employment and elimination of communication barriers. Promotes legislation and programs that benefit the deaf.

National Association of Retarded Children. 420 Lexington Avenue, New York, NY 10017. Furnishes information regarding developmentally disabled children.

National Center for Law and the Deaf. Gallaudet College, 800 Florida Avenue, N.E., Washington, DC 20002. Provides information and publishes a newsletter for legal information regarding the deaf and education.

National Center for Stuttering. 200 E. 33rd Street, New York, NY 10016. (800) 221-2483. Furnishes information to parents of children who stutter and publishes *Annual Review of Published Literature.*

National Down's Syndrome Society. 146 East 57th Street, New York, NY 10022. Provides information and resource material on Down Syndrome.

National Easter Seal. 70 E. Lake St., Chicago, IL 60601. Establishes and conducts programs that serve people with disabilities. Publishes and disseminates information on services for the disabled.

National Federation for the Blind. 1800 Johnson Street, Baltimore, MD 21230. Federation of state and local organizations that seeks complete equality and integration of the blind into society. Offers scholarships, conducts seminars, and distributes information.

National Information Center. P.O. Box 1492, Washington, DC 20013. Publishes the periodical *News Digest* free of charge. Also distributes free information packets.

National Institute of Neurological Disorders and Stroke. National Institute of Health, Information Center, 900 Rockville Pike, Bethesda, MD 20014. (800) 999-5599. Conducts and supports research and training on causes, prevention, diagnosis, and treatment of neurological disorders and stroke.

National Multiple Sclerosis Society. 733 3rd Ave., New York, NY 10017. Supports research into the cause, treatment, and cure of multiple sclerosis. Provides services for persons with MS and related diseases.

National Society to Prevent Blindness. 500 E. Remington Rd., Schaumburg, IL 60173. Services include support of glaucoma screening, vision testing, industrial safety, and data collection on causes of blindness and defective vision.

Recording for the Blind. 20 Roszel Road, Princeton, NJ 08540. Provides computerized books, audiotape, and library reference services.

Special Olympics International. 1350 New York Ave., N.W., Suite 500, Washington, DC 20004. Disseminates information on organization of programs and participation of athletes.

United Cerebral Palsy Association. 7 Pemme Plaza, Suite 804, New York, NY 10001. Sponsors professional and public education in the prevention and management of cerebral palsy.

U.S. Department of Health and Human Services. Office of Human Development, President's Committee on Mental Retardation, Washington, DC 20201. Publishes "The Problem of Mental Retardation," and other information on special needs and disabilities.

BIBLIOGRAPHY

The items in this bibliography are listed in alphabetical order by author, not sorted according to specific needs. If a book has a special focus it is identified in brackets following the bibliographic entry. Also, each subtopic is listed in the index so that separate lists can be constructed. Many of the books mention more than one special need. Readers may benefit from applying the criteria noted in the chapter to any book dealing with special needs. For a listing of titles arranged by special needs, write to the author at 224 Furcolo Hall, UMASS, Amherst, MA 01003.

Adams, B. *Like It Is: Facts and Feelings about Handicaps from Kids Who Know.* Illus. by J. Stanfield. Walker, 1979. (Ages 8–12.) [General] Photos and text describe children with a variety of disabilities. Presented from the perspective of a disabled person speaking to the public.

Adler, C.S. *Good-bye Pink Pig.* Putnam, 1985. (Ages 10 and up.) [Emotional] Amanda spends much of her time dwelling in fantasy. Her "perfect" mother, who is beautiful, elegant, and mindful of all the necessary ingredients for success, turns out to be the disturbed person. Amanda's friend Libby and her grandmother Pearly help Amanda come to the point where she can relinquish her fantasy life and manage well in the real world.

Adler, D. A. *A Picture Book of Helen Keller.* Illus. by J. and A. Wallner. Holiday House, 1990. (Ages 5–8) [Vision, hearing, gifted] Without idealizing or glorifying her, the author details important facets of Helen Keller's life. The language is simple but not condescending.

Alexander, S. H. *Mom Can't See Me.* Illus. by G. Ancona. Macmillan, 1990. (Ages 7–10.) [Vision] Narrated from the perspective of the author's nine-year-old daughter Leslie, the book describes the family, which must make accommodations because of the mother's blindness but which also engages in challenging activities like running a rope course, paddling a canoe, and riding a tandem bicycle. The photos accompanying the text make this an outstanding and exemplary look at a "can do" situation.

Allan, M. E. *View beyond My Father.* Dodd Mead, 1978. (Ages 12 and up.) [Vision] A blind girl growing up in Britain in the 1930s fights her parents' stifling overprotectiveness to gain a measure of independence.

Amadeo, D. M. *There's a Little Bit of Me in Jamey.* Illus. by J. Friedman. Whitman, 1989. (Ages 8–10.) [Serious illness/leukemia] Brian, the narrator, is Jamey's older brother. The story leads up to Brian's donating bone marrow so that Jamey's leukemia may be arrested. Details of Jamey's illness and hospitalization are presented factually and in context. Unfortunately, although the reader is made aware of Brian's feelings and personality, the reader learns little about Jamey other than his illness.

Anders, R. *A Look at Mental Retardation.* Illus. by M. Forrai. Lerner, 1976. (Ages 7–11.) [Intellectual] The text and photos describe problems faced by mentally disabled people.

Andrews, J. F. *The Flying Fingers Club.* Kendall Green, 1988. (Ages 8–10.) [Hearing, learning] Donald, a child with learning disabilities, teams up with Matt, who is hearing impaired, to solve mysteries in this somewhat didactic but worthwhile story of a friendship between children with special needs in a mainstreamed classroom setting.

Arnold, C. *A Guide Dog Puppy Grows Up.* Illus. by R. Hewett. HBJ, 1991. (Ages 8-11.) [Vision] An unsentimental, factual account of the training of guide dogs and their masters. The color photos nicely illustrate the process.

Aseltine, L.; Mueller, E.; and Tait, N. *I'm Deaf and It's Okay.* Illus. by H. Cogancherry. Whitman, 1986. (Ages 7-10.) [Hearing] The story is told from the perspective of a deaf child. His negative feelings are revealed and dealt with. The book ends with his looking forward to the future when he can be in more control of his environment and behavior.

Bahr, M. *The Memory Box.* Illus. by D. Cunningham. Whitman, 1992. (Ages 8-10.) [Serious illness/Alzheimer's] Zach's grandfather has learned that he has Alzheimer's disease and decides to construct a memory box so that family memories will be preserved. The grandmother participates and together they write their memories and accumulate photos and souvenirs. The symptoms of the disease are clearly spelled out in the course of the touching story. The focus is on dealing with the situation, not dwelling on the sadness but acknowledging it, as well as the strength of the family's love and its preservation of the happy memories.

Bates, B. *Tough Beans.* Illus. by L. Morrill. Holiday House, 1988. (Ages 8-11.) [Diabetes] The story describes symptoms, as well as the treatment, of Nat's diabetes; but this is not the only aspect of Nat that we see. He has friends, encounters a bully, resolves the conflict, and finally feels as though he has taken charge of his life. It is unfortunate that the doctor in this story does not know how to tell Nat about diabetes and its implications. The nurse is somewhat helpful, but it would have been more informative and comforting to young readers to know that most hospitals conduct orientation sessions for patients and their families about how to administer injections, what to eat, the symptoms of excess insulin, and how to cope with the condition.

Bennett, J. *I Can Hear the Mourning Dove.* Houghton Mifflin, 1990. (Ages 12 and up.) [Emotional] Grace is hospitalized for a psychotic condition and receives excellent treatment. Her thoughts and feelings are presented to the reader in a dramatic first-person narrative that never lets the reader's attention wander. The issues of death, attempted suicide, and emotional disability and its treatment are all authentically presented in the context of a gripping story. The author is an experienced professional in the field of mental health. The characters are believable in behavior as well as words. The therapist is not godlike, although she is understanding and insightful; the patients have personalities in addition to their problems, and the ending is not an unrealistic panacea.

Bergman, T. *Finding a Common Language: Children Living with Deafness.* Illus. by the author. Gareth Stevens, 1989. (Ages 7-10.) [Hearing] See also: *Seeing in Special Ways: Children Living with Blindness* (1989), *On Our Own Terms: Children Living with Physical Disabilities* (1989), *One Day at a Time: Children Living with Leukemia* (1989), *We Laugh, We Love, We Cry: Children Living with Mental Retardation* (1989). Bergman, a noted Swedish photographer, provides documentation of children with special needs, each book focusing on a different disability or serious illness. The focus is on abilities rather than limitations. In each book, a helpful section is provided that answers common questions and provides a list of resources.

Bernstein, J. E., and Fireside, B. J. *Special Parents, Special Children.* Illus. by M. J. Bernstein. Whitman, 1991. (Ages 8-12.) [General] Members of four families in which one or both parents have a disability discuss their lives. All the children are "typical" and discuss the impact on their lives of having a disabled parent. One father is blind, another uses a wheelchair. In another family, both parents are dwarves; and in the fourth, both parents are hearing impaired. The photos show the families engaging in all sorts of activities. The straightforward, unsentimentalized text addresses concerns, demonstrates adaptations, and shows the parents leading full lives and fulfilling their parental responsibilities.

Bess, C. *Big Man and the Burn-Out.* Houghton Mifflin, 1985. (Ages 12 and up.) [Emotional, sickle cell anemia] [See Sex and Sexuality]

Biklen, D., and Sokoloff, M. *What Do you Do When Your Wheelchair Gets a Flat Tire? Questions and Answers about Disabilities.* Human Policy, 1978. (Ages 7-11). [General] Children with various disabilities tell what it is like to be disabled, answer questions about their disabilities, explain how they get around, what their likes and dislikes are, and how they want others to treat them.

Birdseye, T. *Just Call Me Stupid.* Holiday House, 1993. (Ages 8-11.) [Learning] Patrick is bright and talented. He has a vivid imagination, plays both chess and soccer well; but he cannot read, even though he is now in fifth grade. His father, who has left his mother and him, was abusive when he was living with them. His mother works hard as a waitress; and she is studying nursing. Patrick's life looks up when Celina moves next door and becomes his friend. The story demonstrates the inefficacy of unrelated exercises and phonics for a child with problems learning to read. A sympathetic teacher and Celina between them help Patrick find the key to his own learning. The story is somewhat predictable and pat, but it makes its important points well.

Blue, R. *Me and Einstein.* Human Sciences, 1979. (Ages 8-12.) [Learning] Bobby has dyslexia, a reading problem that some famous people (among them Thomas Edison, Winston Churchill, Woodrow Wilson, and Albert Einstein) have also had. The story makes it clear that Bobby is a bright, competent boy and that appropriate instruction will help him.

Blume, J. *Deenie.* Dell, 1977. (Ages 8-12.) [Scoliosis] Thirteen-year-old Deenie has always avoided contact with disabled people. When she finds she has scoliosis and must wear a confining brace for four years, she has a rough time adjusting to the situation; but her view of disabled people changes.

Booth, Z. *Finding a Friend.* Illus. by T. Breeden. Windswept House, 1987. (Ages 4-6.) [Intellectual/Down syndrome] Andy and Mike, who has Down syndrome, are friends. Mike can join Andy in many games, although sometimes his actions annoy his companions. It is too bad that the cliché of heroic action intrudes on the story (Mike helps to rescue Andy from a cave by getting help for him); but Mike has established himself as a good friend before the rescue; and his behavior doesn't magically make everyone love him. The book provides a positive model of how children of differing abilities can be friends.

Brightman, A. J. *Like Me.* Little, Brown, 1976. (Ages 5-8.) [Intellectual] Narrated by a child who has Down syndrome, this photo story invites sympathetic understanding on the part of nondisabled children.

Brightman, A. J., and Storey, K. S. *Ginny's Backyard.* Illus. by A. J. Brightman. Human Policy, 1978. (Ages 6-9.) [Dwarfism] Ginny, a twelve-year-old girl with dwarfism, talks about her hopes, frustrations, friendships, and the impact of her condition on her life.

Brown, T. *Someone Special, Just like You.* Illus. by F. Ortiz. Holt, 1982. (Ages 4-8.) [General] The book is filled with photos of children with a variety of disabilities engaged in activities children universally enjoy, such as eating ice cream, listening to stories, and playing on the playground. The simple text focuses on similarities rather than differences. A multicultural group of children is shown. An annotated bibliography of books about disabilities for children and adults is included.

Butler, B. *Light a Single Candle.* Dodd Mead, 1964. (Ages 12 and up.) [Vision] In learning to accept her newly sightless condition and lead a full life, fourteen-year-old Cathy

Wheeler must overcome not only obstacles such as doors and curbs but also people's prejudices and fears. Through her own determination and the help of her very supportive family and friends, Cathy manages to get through her initial depression, as well as a semester at a dismal school for the blind. The author, who is blind, vividly describes how Cathy learns to have confidence in herself, get around with her guide dog Trudy, make many friends, and achieve success in her classes at the public high school.

Byars, B. *The Summer of the Swans.* Illus. by T. CoConis. Viking, 1971. (Ages 10 and up.) [Intellectual] Fourteen-year-old Sara feels responsible for Charlie, her developmentally disabled younger brother. She also resents him and feels guilty about this. Charlie's thoughts and feelings are described in a sensitive way. In the end, a friend helps Sara resolve her feelings.

Calvert, P. *Picking up the Pieces.* Scribners, 1993. (Ages 12 and up.) [Physical] Megan's spine was injured in a motorcycle accident, and she now uses a wheelchair and depends on her family to tend to her needs. She is self-pitying and resentful, not a gracious or resigned sufferer; and she makes her family unhappy by what she says and does. When she reluctantly goes to the lake cottage her family has rented every summer, she encounters a young man and his family who help her put things into a different perspective. The author incorporates specific details of the challenges people with spinal injuries must conquer, including skin sores, bathroom difficulties, and the minute planning that must accompany every move away from home. Harris, their young summer neighbor, is a little too good to be true; but the story and characters are compelling, and the situations are presented realistically.

Carter, S. and Clayton, L. *Coping with Depression.* Rosen, 1990. (Ages 12 and up.) [Emotional] Straight talk about causes and different manifestations of depression and what can be done about it. Anecdotes about real people are interlaced with information and advice.

Cassedy, S. *Lucie Babbidge's House.* Crowell, 1989. (Ages 9–12.) [Emotional] [See Adoption and Foster Care]

Charlip, R.; Miller, M. B.; and Ancona, G. *Handtalk: An ABC of Finger Spelling and Sign Language.* Illus. by G. Ancona. Four Winds, 1980. (All ages.) [Hearing] Many ways people can talk without using their voices: finger spellings (making words by letter with the finger) and signing (using hands to convey a picture for a word or idea). Color pictures show children how it is done. A striking, accessible introduction to signing.

Clark, L. "Charles." In *A Flock of Words,* collected by D. MacKay. Illus. by M. Gill. Harcourt, Brace & World, 1970. (Ages 12 and up.) [Vision] Although his parents despair because of his blindness, Charles uses other senses to become a marvelous pianist.

Cleary, B. The *Ramona* series. Illus. by A. Tiegreen and L. Darling. Morrow, 1975–1983. (Ages 8–12.) [Gifted] [See Gender Roles]

Cleaver, V., and Cleaver, B. *Me Too.* Lippincott, 1973. (Ages 12 and up.) [Intellectual] [See Siblings]

Clifford, E. *I Hate Your Guts, Ben Brooster.* Houghton Mifflin, 1989. (Ages 8–10.) [Gifted] Ben Brooster is a nine-year-old genius, and his older cousin Charlie resents his talents. Although Ben behaves in an arrogant manner, the author permits us to see that he is a lonely and vulnerable little boy at times. Each of the characters captures our sympathy in this lightly told, somewhat zany and entertaining mystery. The message finally is that we need to understand that everyone's feelings are valid.

Clifford, E. *Leah's Song.* (Original title *The Man Who Sang in the Dark.*) Illus. by M. B. Owens. Houghton Mifflin, 1987. (Ages 9–12.) [Vision] Leah and her little brother Daniel rely strongly on each other after their father's death. Their economic circumstances, as well as their emotional stability, are shaky. Their neighbor, a blind man, at first inadvertently frightens Leah, but eventually he gains both her confidence and her mother's love. The ending is romantic but satisfying. The characters grapple with their real problems and solve them believably.

Clifton, L. *My Friend Jacob*. Illus. by T. DiGrazia. Dutton, 1980. (Ages 6-10.) [Intellectual] The story describes the relationship between an eight-year-old black child, Sam, and Jacob, who is fourteen years old, white, and intellectually disabled, probably with Down syndrome. The children teach and learn from each another and demonstrate a loving and understanding friendship.

Cohen, B. *The Long Way Home*. Illus. by D. de Groat. Lothrop Lee and Shepard, 1990. (Ages 8-10.) [Serious illness/breast cancer] Sally's mother is undergoing chemotherapy for breast cancer. The mother's situation has affected the entire family; and Sally is reacting with the most negative outward show of emotion. Friendship, how to handle a bully, the family's practice of some Jewish rituals, the value of storytelling, and the importance of confronting one's fears are some of the ingredients in the story.

Cohen, M. *See You Tomorrow, Charles*. Illus. by L. Hoban. Greenwillow, 1983. (Ages 5-8.) [Vision] Charles, who is visually disabled, joins the first grade. He and the other children learn a great deal about each other and come to respect each other's abilities. This same multiethnic classroom is featured in other Cohen-Hoban books.

Corcoran, B. *Axe Time, Sword Time*. Atheneum, 1976. (Ages 12 and up.) [Learning] Elinor, coming of age in the 1940s, struggles hard against her reading disability. Her story shows what such a problem meant at a time when little was known about this condition.

Corcoran, B. *A Dance to Still Music*. Atheneum, 1974. (Ages 10 and up.) [Hearing] Margaret feels it is the end of her world when she becomes deaf as a teenager. She runs away, and is befriended by Juie, an amazingly patient, noble character. Finally Margaret becomes willing to enter a program especially for deaf people.

Cowen-Fletcher, J. *Mama Zooms*. Illus. by the author. Scholastic, 1993. (Ages 3-6.) [Mobility] A little boy and his mother joyfully play together imagining that her wheelchair is a train, a wagon, and a spaceship. An excellent model of a capable, loving parent with a disability who responsibly cares for her child.

Crofford, E. *Frontier Surgeons: A Story about the Mayo Brothers*. Illus. by K. Ritz. Carolrhoda, 1989. (Ages 8-10.) [Gifted] In noncondescending language, the author helps readers become acquainted with this gifted pair of brothers. Their family and upbringing played a major role in their success. They were gifted youngsters whose parents expected them to take responsibility early in their lives.

Curtis, P. *Cindy, a Hearing Ear Dog*. Illus. by D. Cupp. Dutton, 1981. (Ages 7 and up.) [Hearing] Not a work of literature, but a factual account of the training of a dog to be an interpreter of sounds for hearing-impaired people. The book would be even more informative if it included information about which hearing-impaired people benefit most from the services of these dogs. The photos are appealing.

Curtis, P. *Greff: The Story of a Guide Dog*. Illus. by M. Bloom. Lodestar (Dutton), 1982. (Ages 9 and up.) [Vision] Illustrated with descriptive and appealing black-and-white photographs, this book details the training of a guide dog.

Davidson, M. *Louis Braille, the Boy Who Invented Books for the Blind*. Hastings House, 1971. (Ages 9-12.) [Vision] Blinded at the age of three, Louis Braille is helped by the village priest to go to the Royal Institute of Blind Youth in Paris. At fifteen, he perfects the raised-dot alphabet that enables blind people to read with their hands. His brief life is devoted to helping others with his disability.

Davidson, M. *Helen Keller's Teacher.* Four Winds, 1965. (Ages 9-12.) [Gifted, vision] The story of Annie Sullivan, poor, orphaned, and severely visually disabled, whose studies at the Perkins Institute enabled her to teach Helen Keller. Annie's grim childhood and Helen's amazing accomplishments are realistically described in this true story of extraordinary determination.

De Angeli, M. *The Door in the Wall.* Illus. by the author. Doubleday, 1950. (Ages 9-12.) [Mobility] Set in medieval times when the bubonic plague was rampant. Ten-year-old Robin's legs are impaired. Aided by monks, he learns to read, write, whittle, and use crutches.

Dejong, M. *Journey from Peppermint Street.* Harper, 1968. (Ages 8-11.) [Speech, hearing] Uncle Siebren is mute. His nephew is afraid of him at first but soon appreciates his gentleness and strength. Uncle Siebren communicates wonderfully with his hands and in writing.

Delton, J., and Tucker, D. *My Grandma's in a Nursing Home.* Illus. by C. Robinson. Whitman, 1986. (Ages 7-10.) [Serious illness/Alzheimer's] When Jason first goes to visit his beloved grandmother in her nursing home, it seems like a lonely, scary, sad place. The picture of the nursing home is realistic, and the progressive symptoms of Alzheimer's disease shown by the grandmother are accurate. It is a shame that Jason wasn't better prepared for what to expect before his first visit, but the story provides a fine model for overcoming anxiety and forming intergenerational friendships.

Dinner, S. H. *Nothing to Be Ashamed Of: Growing up with Mental Illness in Your Family.* Lothrop Lee and Shepard, 1989. (Ages 10 and up.) [Emotional] Lots of no-nonsense information and advice about how to help young people take charge of their lives, even when a member of their family is suffering from a mental illness. Topics covered in this book include mood and anxiety disorders, as well as posttraumatic stress disorder, Alzheimer's disease, and eating disorders.

Dixon, P. *May I Cross Your Golden River?* Atheneum, 1975. (Ages 12 and up.) [Serious illness] [See Siblings]

Duncan, L. *A Gift of Magic.* Little, Brown, 1971. (Ages 10 and up.) [Gifted] Nancy Garrett has extrasensory perception. Her gift causes her anxiety and grief at first, but she learns to control and value herself.

Fanshawe, E. *Rachel.* Illus. by M. Charlton. Bradbury, 1975. (Ages 5-8.) [Mobility] Rachel uses a wheelchair. She goes to a regular school and does many of the things nondisabled children do. The emphasis is on what Rachel can do, not what she cannot do. The theme of accepting people with differences is well presented.

Fassler, D. *One Little Girl.* Human Sciences, 1969. (Ages 5 and up.) [Learning] Laurie has a learning problem. When attitudes change on Laurie's part and that of the adults around her, everyone becomes happier.

Fassler, D., and McQueen, K. *What's a Virus, Anyway?: The Kids' Book about AIDS.* (Also translated into Spanish.) Waterfront, 1990. (Ages 5-8.) [Serious illness/AIDS] For the youngest of readers, this workbook-type presentation outlines simply and clearly what the AIDS virus is and how it manifests itself. It makes a strong plea for understanding people who have AIDS.

Fassler, J. *Howie Helps Himself.* Illus. by J. Lasker. Whitman, 1975. (Ages 5-8.) [Mobility] Howie, a child who uses a wheelchair, at first relies on others to wheel him around. The book recounts various aspects of his home and school life, but concentrates on Howie's frustrations because he is unable to control his own wheelchair. Howie tries and strains to make his wheels move. At last, he turns himself around as his dad comes to pick him up from school and succeeds in wheeling himself.

Fleischman, P. *The Half-a-Moon Inn.* Illus. by K. Jacobi. Harper, 1980. (Ages 10 and up.) [Speech] Aaron is mute. His mother helps him to accept his need for independence. He endures extreme hardships but eventually overcomes them. The muteness is not just a device, and Aaron is a full character.

Fleming, A. *Welcome to Grossville.* Scribner, 1985. (Ages 8-11.) [Serious illness/cystic fibrosis] Michael's adjustment to his parents' divorce and to the family's forced relocation is made more difficult when he encounters a bully who frightens him into remaining close to home for quite some time. Ralph, a boy with cystic fibrosis introduces Michael to the pleasures of bird watching and provides an excellent example of how to make and keep friends.

Forrai, M. S., and Pursell, M. S. *A Look at Physical Handicaps.* Illus. by the authors. Lerner, 1976. (Ages 5-8.) [Mobility] Excellent black-and-white photos and a simple text convey the message. Handicaps are defined and explained in terms of causes, and special ways of adjusting to them are shown.

Friis-Baastad, B. *Don't Take Teddy.* Scribner, 1967. (Ages 10-12.) [Intellectual] Mikkel is determined not to let anyone put his developmentally disabled brother Teddy into an institution. The Norwegian boys are very close, and Mikkel accepts much responsibility for caring for Teddy. He even leads him through the mountains to his uncle's cabin to keep him from being sent away. Eventually, Mikkel's parents enter Teddy into a special day school near their home. The ending is ideal but not unrealistic.

Gaes, J. *My Book for Kids with Cansur.* Illus. by T. and A. Gaes. Melius and Peterson, 1987. (Ages 4-7.) [Serious illness/cancer] Written in his own spelling by six-year-old Jason, this book is the story of how he won his battle with cancer. It communicates his fears and provides some avenues for emotional support for other children who are experiencing or who fear this disease.

Galvin, M. M.D. *Otto Learns about His Medicine.* Illus. by S. Ferraro. Magination, 1988. (Ages 4-6.) [Neurological/hyperactive] The analogy is made between a child who is hyperactive and a car whose motor goes too fast. The book is designed to dilute the negative implications of taking medicine to control behavior. The metaphor becomes a little heavy handed, and the didacticism outweighs the literary merit; but the overall effects are positive because of the useful information.

Garfield, J. B. *Follow My Leader.* Viking, 1957. (Ages 9-12.) [Vision] When a firecracker explodes, Jimmy loses his sight. With a guide dog, he learns to do things he had thought impossible.

Garrigue, S. *Between Friends.* Bradbury, 1978. (Ages 10 and up.) [Intellectual] Ten-year-old Jill has just moved to New England. She befriends a developmentally disabled girl, Dede, who lives on her street, because she is lonely and all the other neighbors her own age are away on summer holidays. Jill likes Dede and becomes interested in how much developmentally disabled children can do (although at first she is very uncomfortable with them).

Gehret, J. *The Don't-Give-Up Kid and Learning Differences.* Illus. by S. A. DePauw. Verbal Images, 1990. (Ages 6-9.) [Learning] Alex is a determined child who loves to invent things and keeps trying until he finds solutions to his problems. With the help of a psychologist, the resource room teacher, and the patient support and encouragement of his parents, he learns to apply this same perseverance to overcoming his difficulty with reading and paying attention. Alex learns that others, including his idol,

Thomas Edison, have struggled with learning disabilities. Although the text is didactic in intent, Alex is an engaging character, and his story is reassuring.

George, J. C. *Julie of the Wolves.* Illus. by J. Schoenherr. Harper, 1972. (Ages 12 and up.) [Gifted] [See Gender Roles]

Giff, P. R. *Watch Out, Ronald Morgan!* Illus. by S. Natti. Puffin, 1985. (Ages 6-8.) [Vision] When Ronald has trouble cutting straight lines, reading, and catching balls, his teacher realizes that he is having trouble seeing. He is excited about his new glasses; but he is frustrated when they fail to make him a "super kid" who never makes mistakes and instantly becomes a great ball player. His teacher helps him to understand what his glasses can and cannot do for him and assures him that he is a super kid anyway.

Gilson, J. *Do Bananas Chew Gum?* Lothrop Lee and Shepard, 1980. (Ages 10-12.) [Learning] Sam, who is in sixth grade, has a severe learning disability. He learns that he cannot hide from his problems, comes to realize that he is not stupid (as he had believed), and begins to discover his learning strengths. Sam is not defined by his disability. He has a full range of emotions and interests. He is also a good friend, able to give advice to his peers. The reader discovers that learning disabilities come in all varieties and that all learners have both strengths and needs.

Girard, L. W. *Alex, the Kid with AIDS.* Illus. by B. Sims. Whitman, 1991. (Ages 8-10.) [Serious illness/AIDS] Although not much is imparted about AIDS, the reader learns that children with serious illnesses need to be treated like other children and not as if their condition is their only characteristic.

Glenn, M. "Ernest Mott." In *Class Dismissed! High School Poems.* Illus. by M. Bernstein. Clarion, 1982. (Ages 12 and up.) [Emotional] Ernest has managed to control his feelings after several years of therapy and drugs, but he is afraid to be mainstreamed "back to people who still have fear in their faces."

Glenn, M. *My Friend's Got this Problem, Mr. Candler.* Illus. by M. J. Bernstein. Clarion, 1991. (Ages 11 and up.) [General] A collection of poems from the perspective of a high school counselor seeing a variety of students with many issues and concerns.

Glenn, M. "Nancy Soto." In *Class Dismissed! High School Poems.* Illus. by M. Bernstein. Clarion, 1982. (Ages 12 and up.) [Emotional] Nancy suffers from excruciating shyness. Her inability to speak out loud in class is a major source of pain and embarrassment for her.

Gravelle, K., and John, B. A. *Teenagers Face to Face with Cancer.* Messner, 1986. (Ages 11 and up.) [Serious illness/cancer] The young people's initial shock at finding that they have cancer, their treatments, their surgery (including amputation), and the types of cancer are discussed. Emotions are addressed throughout. The book provides hope, offering a substantial section on planning for the future. Coming to terms with possible death is also explored. The teens' self-reflections are eloquent. A glossary and bibliography are included.

Greenberg, J. *No Dragons to Slay.* Farrar, Straus, and Giroux, 1983. (Ages 12 and up.) [Serious illness/cancer] Tommy goes through the stages of denial, anger, and depression when he discovers that he has cancer. His family never comes to terms with his illness, but he does. This is not a didactic, single-issue book. Tommy's relationships with his friends and mentors form an important part of the story.

Greenberg, K. E. *Magic Johnson: Champion with a Cause.* Illus. with photos. Lerner, 1992. (Ages 8-11.) [Serious illness/AIDS] A well-paced biography of the talented basketball star that focuses on his handling of the fact that he contracted the AIDS virus. His work in educating about AIDS has been important.

Greenfield, E. *Darlene*. Illus. by G. Ford. Methuen, 1980. (Ages 5-8.) [Mobility] This slim picture book effectively shows that there is much a girl who uses a wheelchair can enjoy.

Guthrie, D. *Grandpa Doesn't Know It's Me: A Family Adjusts to Alzheimer's Disease*. Illus. by K. K. Arnsteen. Human Sciences, 1986. (Ages 4-8.) [Serious illness/Alzheimer's] The specific details of Alzheimer's are woven into the story as part of young Elizabeth's memories. She also remembers happy times with her grandfather. The book ends with the grandfather living with his children. Questions children are likely to ask are answered honestly, and information is incorporated into the story as well.

Hamilton, V. *The Bells of Christmas*. Illus. by L. Davis. HBJ, 1989. (Ages 8-10.) [Mobility] The father in this African-American family is physically disabled with a leg injury. Though the story takes place in 1890, not many years after the end of slavery in America, and the family are sharecroppers, they are self-sufficient achievers: The mother has her own sewing business, and the father is a capable woodcarver and carpenter who does not let his disability hinder his productivity.

Hamilton, V. *The Planet of Junior Brown*. Macmillan, 1971. (Ages 12 and up.) [Emotional, appearance] Junior Brown is a very fat (almost 300 pounds), very unhappy young man. His friend Buddy has created a community of homeless children by finding abandoned buildings for them to live in. Junior moves out of his destructive home setting into Buddy's place. As with all of Hamilton's books, the writing is exceptional, and the characters are African American.

Hamilton, V. *Sweet Whispers, Brother Rush*. Philomel, 1981. (Ages 12 and up.) [Illness, intellectual] A masterly story about an African-American family, past and present, and a young girl's coming of age. Tree, fourteen years old, is protective of her seventeen-year-old brother Dabney (Dab), who is "slow" and "different." Brother Rush, a handsome ghost, appears to Tree and tells about the family's past, including the emotional neglect of Dab by their mother. Dab has a rare illness and eventually dies. When Tree recovers from her mourning, she begins to accept her own womanhood.

Hamm, D. J. *Grandma Drives a Motor Bed*. Illus. by C. Robinson. Whitman, 1987. (Ages 6-8.) [Mobility] Josh enjoys spending time with his grandmother who is physically disabled. He is fascinated by her motor-driven bed, which can sit her up or raise her legs. Grandma takes care of herself as well as she can and understands Josh's curiosity about her disability. The grandmother has many friends who come to visit and remains sexually attractive to her husband. The cause of her disability and her prognosis are unclear; but although she is frustrated at times, she makes the best of her situation. It helps that she is surrounded by people who love her.

Hanlon, E. *The Swing*. Bradbury, 1979. (Ages 9-12.) [Hearing] The two main characters are Emily, a hearing-disabled eleven-year-old, and Danny, a thirteen year old having a difficult time recovering from his father's death. The two lock horns in this well-written story dealing with how to be an individual in a society that demands conformity. The information about hearing loss and its effects is accurately woven into the story.

Hansen, J. *Yellow Bird and Me*. Clarion, 1986. (Ages 8-10.) [Learning] [See Heritage]

Hausherr, R. *Children and the AIDS Virus: A Book for Children, Parents, and Teachers*. Clarion, 1989. (Ages 7-10.) [Serious illness/AIDS] A good combination of factual and personalized representation. One of the children with AIDS described here contracted it through a blood transfusion, the other was born with the virus because her mother was infected. Both have survived with the disease for several years, so the tone of the book is generally positive, suitable for its young audience.

Hearn, E. *Good Morning Franny, Good Night Franny*. Illus. by M. Thurman. Women's Educational Press, 1984. (Ages 5-8.) [Mobility] Franny is an active child who sometimes

gets into trouble because she is not careful to avoid bumping into people as she whizzes through her multicultural neighborhood in her wheelchair. This outgoing, exuberant child becomes friendly with Ting, a young Asian girl. At the end of the story, Ting
moves away, but she has left an indelible greeting in the park, wishing Franny a good
morning and a good night. (Finding this message on a Toronto sidewalk inspired the
author to write the book.) The wheelchair is an incidental prop in the story, but it helps
young readers erase some stereotypes.

Heide, F. P. *Growing Anyway Up.* Lippincott, 1976. (Ages 10 and up.) [Emotional] Florence
has an elaborate system for protecting herself from further emotional harm. Her Aunt Nina,
a wholesome, loving woman, helps her to establish a more stable perspective.

Henriod, L. *Grandma's Wheelchair.* Illus. by C. Chevalier. Whitman, 1982. (Ages 4-7.)
[Mobility] Although Grandmother uses a wheelchair to get around, she can accomplish
many tasks, and she loves four-year-old Thomas. The author conveys information as part
of the story line—how the grandmother gets in and out of the wheelchair and how it
sometimes malfunctions. What is communicated best is that the two lovingly enjoy and
help each other.

Hermes, P. *What If They Knew?* Dell, 1980. (Ages 9-12.) [Epilepsy] Beginning fifth grade
in a new school is difficult for Jeremy, who suddenly becomes concerned about keeping her epilepsy secret. By the end of the school year, after an epileptic episode, her
friends and family persuade her of their good intentions, and she becomes more self-
sufficient. Although the book is somewhat flawed (layer upon layer of secrets unrealistically intrude on the plot), the points made are pertinent to the topic.

Hildick, E.W. *The Case of the Invisible Dog.* Illus. by L. Weil. Macmillan, 1977. (Ages 8-
12.) [Gifted] All the McCurtle mysteries involve a group of bright youngsters who use
their imaginations and intelligence to solve mysteries.

Hirsch, K. *My Sister.* Illus. by N. Inderieden. Carolrhoda, 1977. (Ages 5-8.) [Intellectual]
The book covers a wide range of feelings and situations where a developmentally disabled child might make things difficult for a family. The child narrator accepts his
sister; other people are not always so tolerant. The story ends with the brother knowing that no matter how much he wishes, his sister will never lose her disability. He
accepts her as she is.

Holland, I. *Dinah and the Green Fat Kingdom.* Lippincott, 1978. (Ages 8-10.) [Appear-
ance/cerebral palsy] Dinah is twelve years old and has been overweight for several years.
Her family, especially her mother, has launched an intensive campaign to make her lose
weight. She is helped both to accept herself and to lose weight by a nun who is a
nutritionist at a school for children with special needs. Her puppy, her father, and
Sebastian, a boy with cerebral palsy who is very good with animals and very intelligent, also contribute to her changed self-image.

Holmes, B. *The First Seeing Eye Dogs.* Contemporary Perspectives, 1978. (Ages 8-10.)
[Vision] The history of The Seeing Eye, a school for blind people and guide dogs. The
resistance to guide dogs in many places, public and private, is also detailed.

Hull, E. *Alice with Golden Hair.* Atheneum, 1981. (Ages 10 and up.) [Intellectual] Developmentally disabled, Alice lives in an institution. She obtains a resident job in a nursing home where she handles her responsibilities well.

Hunt, N. *The World of Nigel Hunt.* Garrett, 1967. (Ages 12 and up.) [Intellectual] The diary
of Nigel Hunt, a British child with Down syndrome. His physician and his father provide prefactory comments.

Hyde, M. O., and Forsyth, E. H. *AIDS: What Does It Mean to You?* Walker, 1987. (Ages 12
and up.) [Serious illness/AIDS] Historical perspective, information about research,

profiles of people with AIDS, and an intelligent discussion of the controversies surrounding this disease are well presented.

Jordan, M. *Losing Uncle Tim.* Illus. by J. Friedman. Whitman, 1989 (Ages 8-10.) [Serious illness/AIDS] Dan's beloved uncle Tim is dying of AIDS. Dan is angry and confused but is reassured after an enlightening conversation with his dad. When Uncle Tim dies, Dan is comforted by the knowledge that they have told each other of their love and have said their good-byes. Dan's father conveys good, clear information about AIDS.

Jupo, F. *Atu, the Silent One.* Illus. by the author. Holiday, 1967. (Ages 5-8.) [Speech, gifted] Atu, a young African Bushman, lived before the era of recorded history. He is mute, but through his talent as an artist, he is able to leave a beautiful graphic record of his people's activities and customs.

Kamien, J. *What If You Couldn't . . . ? A Book about Special Needs.* Scribner, 1979. (Ages 6-12.) [General] Approaches six disabilities from the "what if you couldn't?" perspective. A good adjunct to the Boston Children's Museum activities to help nondisabled children experience, to a limited extent, how it feels to be disabled.

Katz, B., and Katz, J. *Black Woman.* Pantheon, 1973. (Ages 10 and up.) [Gifted] Lucy Terry Prince (1730-1821), an eighteenth-century slave, seeks education and legal redress for her family through the courts.

Kent, D. *Belonging.* Dial, 1978. (Ages 12 and up.) [Vision] Meg is blind. She is also self-sufficient and refuses to conform to the preconceptions of peers and adults. The author conveys how Meg feels and functions. Excellent sensitivity to the physical perceptions of visually disabled people is imbedded into a good story.

Kerr, M.E. *Night Kites.* Harper, 1986. (Ages 12 and up.) [Serious illness/AIDS] [See Sex and Sexuality]

Kipnis, L., and Adler, S. *You Can't Catch Diabetes from a Friend.* Illus. by R. Benkof. Triad, 1979. (Ages 7-11.) [Diabetes] Using a series of photos and simple but specific text, the book follows the experiences of several children with diabetes through their daily routines. The children are of different ages and backgrounds, but they all handle their condition competently.

Kosof, Anna. *Why Me?: Coping with Family Illness.* Watts, 1986 (Ages 11 and up.) [Serious illness] The author focuses on how families cope with cancer, heart disease, accidents, and birth defects. In each case, we are brought into the family with viewpoints expressed by all involved. The author acknowledges that illness affects each person's life in different ways and supplies constructive emphasis.

Krementz, J. *How It Feels to Fight for Your Life.* Illus. by the author. Little, Brown, 1989. (Ages 10 and up.) [Serious illness] Each segment is narrated by a young person who is grappling bravely with a condition such as asthma, heart disease, spina bifida, leukemia, juvenile rheumatoid arthritis, aplastic anemia, lupus, epilepsy, cancer, cystic fibrosis, kidney disease, diabetes, and physical trauma, such as burns or gunshot wounds. The photos enable the reader to connect with the narrator and his or her situation.

Krisher, T. *Kathy's Hats: A Story of Hope.* Illus. by N. B. Westcott. Whitman, 1992. (Ages 5-9.) [Serious illness/cancer] When Kathy is treated for cancer, her hair falls out, and she wears a hat to cover her baldness. Kathy is concerned about how her classmates will react to her and decides to put a favorite teddy bear pin on her hat. Her friends and family respond by giving her other pins. Her collection helps her to feel better about wearing her hat. The book ends on a hopeful note: Kathy's treatments are over, and her cancer has apparently gone into remission. The book is based on a true story about the author's daughter, which makes it even more useful for children who may be in similar circumstances.

Laird, E. *Loving Ben.* Delacorte, 1988. (Ages 10-12.) [Hydrocephalus] Anna has an especially loving relationship with her baby brother, Ben. Because Ben is hydrocephalic, his appearance is a shock to many people when they first see him. The family's joy of loving the child and noting his progress, their mixed feelings at having to change their lifestyle because of Ben, the discomfort of having to deal with strangers' pity and revulsion, and their grief at Ben's death are well handled.

Landau, E. *We Have AIDS.* Watts, 1990. (Ages 12 and up.) [Serious illness/AIDS] The deadly disease is dramatically portrayed through first-person accounts by teenagers of their ordeal with AIDS. Interspersed is factual information about the virus and its means of transmission.

Larsen, H. *Don't Forget Tom.* Crowell, 1978. (Ages 5-7.) [Intellectual] Using photos of Tom and his family, the book informs young readers about developmental disability. Some of Tom's difficulties are mentioned in a tactful manner; He is not toilet trained, and he sometimes gets angry or sad about things he cannot do. The approach is realistic and appropriate. The original version was written in Danish.

Lasker, J. *He's My Brother.* Illus. by the author. Whitman, 1974. (Ages 6-9.) [Intellectual] Jamie gets teased for being a slow learner. Becka, his older sister, bakes brownies for him and treats him kindly. Sometimes his brother is impatient but plays with him to make up for it. Jamie is good with babies and animals. The family is loving and patient with him. Mildred and Joe Lasker write at the end that they hope "this book will enable other Jamies and their families to identify with the experiences shown and take comfort."

Lee, J. M. *Silent Lotus.* Illus. by the author. Farrar, Straus, and Giroux, 1991. (Ages 6-9.) [Speech, hearing] A child who can neither speak nor hear wins fame as a court dancer. The setting is ancient Kampuchea, but the story is universal. The child's disabilities are not magically cured; her life is rich and fruitful.

Le Guin, U. K. *Very Far Away from Anywhere Else.* Atheneum, 1976. (Ages 11 and up.) [Gifted] Owen, a talented seventeen-year-old with identity problems, finds facing home, school, and daily life very difficult. Through his relationship with Natalie, a creative and talented musician, he begins to find himself and learns to deal with life.

L'Engle, M. *A Ring of Endless Light.* Farrar, Straus, and Giroux, 1980. (Ages 11 and up.) [Gifted] This fourth book in the Austin family series focuses on Vicky. Her family is staying on the island where her grandfather lives. He is dying. Vicky and her brother John become close friends in this story. Vicky also discovers that she has the gift of communicating with dolphins. The book is an investigation of love, life, and coming to terms with death.

L'Engle, M. *A Wrinkle in Time.* Farrar, Straus, and Giroux, 1962. (Ages 10 and up.) [Gifted] The father, a scientist, has vanished; and now an eerie midnight visitor leads two of his children and a friend in search through a "wrinkle in time." Charles Wallace's intellect and depth of understanding and Meg's math ability are outstanding. The rest of the family is also talented. Other books in the time trilogy are *A Wind in the Door* (1973) and *A Swiftly Tilting Planet* (1978).

Levine, E. S. *Lisa and Her Soundless World.* Human Sciences, 1974. (Ages 6-8.) [Hearing] The book introduces Lisa, an eight-year-old deaf girl. Hearing aids, instruction in lip-reading, sign language, and finger spelling, help her to communicate.

Levoy, M. *Alan and Naomi.* Harper, 1977. (Ages 10 and up.) [Emotional] [See War and Peace]

Litchfield, A. B. *Making Room for Uncle Joe.* Illus. by G. Owens. Whitman, 1984. (Ages 6-8.) [Intellectual/Down syndrome] Uncle Joe, who has Down syndrome, has lived in a state school most of his life. When the school closes, he comes to stay with his sister and her family. The youngest child takes to Joe right away, but the older children are embarrassed and resentful at his presence. He misses his friends and familiar routine. Gradually, they adjust to one another, and Joe becomes a loved and valued member of the family.

Little, J. *From Anna.* Illus. by J. Sandin. Harper, 1972. (Ages 9–12.) [Vision] Anna's vision problem is discovered after she and her family emigrate to Canada from Nazi Germany. Because of her disability, Anna has been awkward and clumsy; she has therefore been rejected by others. She becomes competent once her visual impairment is attended to. The sequel, *Listen for the Singing* (1977), adds the blindness of Anna's oldest brother to the problems the family must face.

London, J. *The Lion Who Had Asthma.* Illus. by N. B. Westcott. Whitman, 1992. (Ages 3–6.) [Asthma] Sean's imagination allows him to be a hippo, a lion, a tree-eating giant, and an airplane pilot when he uses his nebulizer mask after an asthma attack. The colorful pictures and imaginative text could be reassuring for a child with this condition.

Lowry, L. *A Summer to Die.* Illus. by J. Oliver. Houghton Mifflin, 1977. (Ages 10 and up.) [Serious illness/leukemia] [See Siblings]

Mack, N. *Tracy.* Illus. by H. Kluetmeier. Raintree, 1976. (Ages 5–8.) [Cerebral palsy] The book follows Tracy, who has cerebral palsy, through a day in school and at home. She rides a bike, works at a desk, slides on the playground slide, and turns a jump rope. The excellent photographs include pictures of Tracy receiving therapy using her wheelchair.

MacLachlan, P. *The Facts and Fictions of Minna Pratt.* Harper, 1988. (Ages 10 and up.) [Gifted] Minna is a bright, observant, imaginative, and musically talented young woman whose intelligent, if somewhat unconventional, family understands her, supports her emotionally, and grants her unconditional love. She is a well-balanced, friendly person, not a freak in any way. Her relationship with an equally gifted young man is one of mutual liking and respect.

MacLachlan, P. *Through Grandpa's Eyes.* Illus. by D. Ray. Harper, 1979. (Ages 6–9.) [Vision] When John spends time with his blind grandfather, he learns to appreciate nature while discovering how to use all his senses. Both grandparents are seen as productive, creative people. The grandmother sculpts, the grandfather plays the cello. The grandparents love each other and enjoy their lives.

Mathis, S. B. *Listen for the Fig Tree.* Viking, 1974. (Ages 12 and up.) [Vision] Muffin Johnson, an extraordinarily competent young woman, is blind. She manages all the details of housekeeping, sews, shops, and maintains excellent relationships with people. Her mother, almost destroyed over the death of the father, is frequently in an alcoholic stupor. Muffin takes care of her with remarkable facility. The support of the African-American community is a strong part of the book.

Mazer, N. F. *I, Trissy.* Delacorte, 1971. (Ages 9–12.) [Gifted, emotional] [See Divorce]

McKenzie, E. K. *Stargone John.* Illus. by W. Low. Holt, 1990. (Ages 8–10.) [Vision] John doesn't talk much; he hates school; his teacher is punitive and incompetent; and he remains illiterate until he becomes friendly with a retired teacher, Miss Mants, who is now elderly and blind. By the end of the story, John has demonstrated that he is as capable of learning as any other child, especially when his teacher is responsive and kind.

McKillop, P. A. *The Riddle-Master of Hed.* Atheneum, 1976. (Ages 10 and up.) [Gifted] Morgan, a prince of Hed, tries to be a simple prince, but he is drawn into riddles and mysterious adventures which he must use his head to solve.

McKinley, R. *The Blue Sword.* Greenwillow, 1982. (Ages 11 and up.) [Gifted] Harry Crewe, an unusually tall, strong, and intelligent young woman, is the protagonist of this fantasy adventure.

Meyer, C. *Killing the Kudu.* Macmillan, 1990. (Ages 12 and up.) [Mobility] Alex was accidentally shot and left paraplegic seven years ago at age eleven. The focal point of the story is his unfolding relationship with Claire, his grandmother's *au pair* for the summer. Alex has never thought he might be capable of a sexual relationship with a woman; Claire changes all that. This issue is frankly and sensitively handled. The book challenges stereotypes of people with disabilities. Alex wants to go to college, he swims at the beach, and he learns to ride behind his cousin on a motorcycle.

Miklowitz, G. D. *Good-bye Tomorrow.* Delacorte, 1987. (Ages 12 and up.) [Serious illness/AIDS] Alex acquired HIV during a blood transfusion after an automobile accident and has developed AIDS-related complex (ARC). His doctor explains the difference between this and AIDS and points out that he must be careful to avoid infections. Alex then must deal with his illness and its impact on his friends, family, and teachers. For a while it looks as though Alex will be ostracized, but his closest friends stand by him, and the reader can hope for the best. The author includes many details about AIDS and ARC within the context of the story. Although the term *ARC* is no longer used, the issues raised in the story remain valid.

Mills, C. *After Fifth Grade, the World!.* Macmillan, 1989. (Ages 8–10.) [Gifted] Heidi is a resourceful fifth grader, gifted in math and passionately opinionated. When she sets out to reform the world, especially her mean teacher, she discovers with her father's help that she can accomplish more by understanding others than warring with them. A fast-paced story with humor that hits the mark without being demeaning.

Mitchell, J. S. *See Me More Clearly: Career and Life Planning for Teens with Physical Disabilities.* HBJ, 1980. (Ages 12 and up.) [General] Specific disabilities are described and discussed to help people with these disabilities learn survival skills and become self-supporting. Topics such as sexuality are also included.

Neimark, A. E. *A Deaf Child Listened.* William Morrow, 1983. (Ages 12 and up.) [Hearing] Although Thomas Gallaudet was not himself deaf, he made it his calling to help people who were. He pioneered in the education of hearing-impaired people, especially in the area of sign language. This biography is deeply respectful and admiring of its subject but does not descend into overidealization.

Nelson, V. M. *Always Gramma.* Illus. by K. Ubler. Putnam, 1988. (Ages 6–10.) [Serious illness/Alzheimer's] A young girl remembers wonderful times with her grandmother, as well as the changes the family undergoes as Gramma's Alzheimer's disease progressively worsens. Although Gramma is now in a nursing home and unable to care for herself or recognize her family, her granddaughter still visits and loves her.

O'Brien, R. C. *Mrs. Frisby and the Rats of NIMH.* Atheneum, 1971. (Ages 8–10.) [Gifted] The doctors at NIMH create a race of super intelligent rats who can read labels on medicine bottles and instructions on how to open their cages. The dilemma and responsibilities of intelligence are explored.

O'Dell, S. *Island of the Blue Dolphins.* Houghton Mifflin, 1960. (Ages 10 and up.) [Gifted] Karana, a young Native-American girl, is alone on her home island after her people have left and her brother has been killed by wild dogs. She survives on her own for many years until at last she is rescued.

Ominsky, E. *Jon O: A Special Boy.* Prentice-Hall, 1977. (Ages 5–8.) [Intellectual/Down syndrome] The photos provide a graphic representation of the manifestations of Down syndrome. The text describes the family interactions and feelings.

O'Neal, Z. *The Language of Goldfish*. Viking, 1980. (Ages 11 and up.) [Emotional] Carrie's psychotherapy helps her to return to a reality where she can handle the demands upon her to grow up and cope with her overanxious mother. She discovers talents in herself that she had not seen before, and she and the reader learn that life is very complex but manageable.

O'Neill, M. "The Milk Man's Little Boy." In *People I'd Like to Keep*. Illus. by P. Galdone. Doubleday, 1964. (Ages 6-12.) [Hearing] Using the voice of a young child, the poet is delighted on milk-bill day. He accompanies his father, the milkman, who speaks on his fingers "with lightning speed and dazzling grace," as the son translates for the customers. A positive, joyous poem.

O'Neill, M. "Mimi's Fingers." In *Fingers Are Always Bringing Me News*. Illus. by D. Bolognese. Doubleday, 1969. (Ages 6-9.) [Visual] Mimi is a well-adjusted blind girl who experiences the world with her sensitive fingers. In the last line of the poem, Mimi acknowledges her disability as she asks the reader to "tell me about blue?"

Ostrow, W., and Ostrow, V. *All about Asthma*. Illus. by B. Sims. Whitman, 1989. (Ages 8-10.) [Asthma] Although this book is informative and written from a personal perspective, it does have an aspect that teachers and parents may want to address. The child-narrator, albeit humorously, blames his mother for passing asthma on to him. The mother and child are coauthors of this book, and their intention is undoubtedly to make young asthma sufferers feel knowledgeable and comfortable about their condition. Nevertheless, the mother may feel guilty about her genetic problem, and the child may feel resentful. It would be unfortunate if young readers caught this attitude of blame and guilt. With this caveat, the book is useful, especially since there are so few books about asthma.

Pankow, V. *No Bigger Than My Teddy Bear*. Illus. by G. Connelly. Abingdon, 1987. (Ages 4-7.) [Premature baby] [See Siblings]

Paterson, K. *The Great Gilly Hopkins*. Crowell, 1978. (Ages 9 and up.) [Gifted] [See Adoption and Foster Care]

Peter, D. *Claire and Emma*. Illus. by J. Finlay. Day, 1977. (Ages 6-9.) [Hearing] Claire and Emma are sisters who were born deaf. The book, illustrated with color photos, explains details of the condition, including the use of hearing aids, difficulty of communication, and procedures for helping the sisters function in a hearing world.

Peterson, J. W. *I Have a Sister, My Sister Is Deaf*. Illus. by D. Ray. Harper, 1977. (Ages 5-8.) [Hearing] Told from the perspective of the sister of a deaf child. The narrator describes how other people react to her sister and how she feels about her sister's condition.

Phipson, J. *A Tide Flowing*. Atheneum, 1981. (Ages 11 and up.) [Mobility] Mark's problems with his family are seemingly insurmountable until his disabled friend Connie helps him.

Pirner, C. W. *Even Little Kids Get Diabetes*. Illus. by N. B. Westcott. Whitman, 1991. (Ages 6-8.) [Diabetes] In a nonthreatening way, the narrator of the story, a child about five years old who has diabetes, tells how she was diagnosed and how the illness has affected her life. She describes her feelings about the frequent blood tests, insulin shots, dietary restrictions, and family fears. The book can reassure children with diabetes and children who know someone with diabetes that they can lead normal, active lives.

Platt, K. *The Boy Who Could Make Himself Disappear*. Chilton, 1968. (Ages 12 and up.) [Speech, emotional] [See Abuse]

Platt, K. *Chloris and the Creeps*. Chilton, 1973. (Ages 12 and up.) [Emotional] [See Divorce]

Powers, M. E. *Our Teacher's in a Wheelchair*. Illus. by the author. Whitman, 1986. (Ages 5-8.) [Mobility] This book, illustrated with photos, describes the life of Brian Hanson, who teaches in a day-care center. He is paraplegic as a result of a sports injury. The book primarily focuses on what Brian can do rather than on what he cannot: he rides subways, eats at restaurants with friends, cooks at home, and drives a car. His frustrations with his disability are discussed but not overemphasized. The photos give children an opportunity to stare and ask questions of a helpful adult if they need to.

Rabe, B. *The Balancing Girl.* Illus. by L. Hoban. Dutton, 1981. (Ages 5–8.) [Mobility] Margaret is talented at balancing things: blocks, books on her head, dominoes, and herself on braces, with crutches. She also can get around pretty well in her wheelchair. The story revolves around Tommy's jealousy of Margaret's ability and what really constitutes a disability.

Rabe, B. *Margaret's Moves.* Scholastic, 1987. (Ages 8–12.) [Mobility] In this sequel to *The Balancing Girl,* Margaret displays her sense of humor and stubborn determination to succeed. Margaret, who was born with spina bifida, is occasionally frustrated by her limitations, but for the most part she is confident and happy. She is not coddled or overprotected. It's refreshing to see a portrayal of a disabled character who is encouraged to be as independent as she can.

Rabe, B. *Where's Chimpy?.* Illus. by D. Schmidt. Whitman, 1988. (Ages 5–8.) [Intellectual/Down syndrome] The photos nicely accompany the well-written text of a simple story with deep implications. Misty is a child with Down Syndrome. When her father is getting ready to put her to sleep, she notices that her stuffed chimpanzee is missing and asks for him. The father asks Misty to recall where she's been that day and accompanies her in the search for the toy but lets her find her own way. He is remarkably flexible and patient. At last Chimpy is found, and Misty helps her dad locate his glasses so he can read her a bedtime story. The model of parenting here is excellent for any family to emulate. No need to describe Down syndrome or talk about how to treat children with this condition; the story and pictures say it all.

Raskin, E. *Spectacles.* Illus. by the author. Atheneum, 1968. (Ages 4–7.) [Vision] A lighthearted, imaginative reflection of what happens when a nearsighted child gets glasses. The fantasy creatures she is used to seeing suddenly become ordinary people and objects when her vision is corrected. Readers who wear glasses can add their own blurry recollections to the story.

Richmond, S. *Wheels for Walking.* Atlantic Monthly, 1983. (Ages 13 and up.) [Mobility] Sally's world changes when a car crash leaves her paralyzed from the chest down. The book chronicles the teenager's experience in the hospital and rehabilitation center as she slowly regains some function and comes to terms with her limitations. The story is a fictional recounting of the author's own experiences. For mature readers only; the language and subject matter are graphic.

Robinson, V. *David in Silence.* Lippincott, 1966. (Ages 12 and up.) [Hearing] A working-class industrial town in England provides the setting for this sensitive novel about David, a deaf teenager trying to settle in a new town with a hearing group of friends. The reader is made aware of all the tools David has at his disposal; lip-reading, special schooling, and sign language are all integral but not overpowering parts of his life. The author has done her research well but keeps technicality to a minimum. A warm and upbeat book about a special group of young people who learn with and from each other.

Rogers, A. *Luke Has Asthma, Too.* Illus. by M. Middleton. Waterfront, 1990. (Ages 4–7.) [Asthma] Specific, informative, and reassuring, this little book helps young readers lose some fear of asthma, while also helping children who do not know anything about the condition to empathize with children who have the condition. A useful resource list is included.

Rogers, J. *Dinosaurs Are 568.* Illus. by M. Hafner. Dell, 1988. (Ages 5-7.) [Gifted] Raymond is a very bright child who refuses to go to kindergarten because there is nothing there to challenge him. When it is time for first grade, he quickly becomes the class dinosaur expert. He is jealous when a bright girl who is also interested in dinosaurs joins the class, but he soon learns that there is more than enough attention and praise to go around. The adults in his life support his talents and give him resources to pursue his interests.

Rosenberg, M. B. *Finding a Way.* Illus. by G. Ancona. Lothrop Lee and Shepard, 1988. (Ages 8-12.) [General] Describes the lives of three children who have siblings with special needs. One has a brother with spina bifida, one has two siblings with asthma, and the third has a brother with diabetes. The children with disabilities and the relationships between the children are portrayed in a balanced manner. The anger and frustration of the "typical" children at the extra attention their siblings receive and the added expectations of them are acknowledged, but rewarded moments are seen as well. Information is provided about the disabilities. The book is written from the perspective of the able-bodied, but the view points of the children with disabilities are also evident.

Rosenberg, M. B. *My Friend Leslie.* Illus. by G. Ancona. Lothrop Lee and Shepard, 1983. (Ages 5-8.) [General] Leslie has multiple handicaps. This photographic essay depicts her fellow kindergartners as helpful and mutually respectful; they enjoy one another's company.

Rosofsky, I. *My Aunt Ruth.* Harper, 1991. (Ages 12 and up.) [Serious illness, diabetes, mobility] The story provides a compelling look at some of the consequences of improper attention to diabetes. Aunt Ruth, a beautiful and talented actor, must learn to cope with two prosthetic legs; diabetes caused her to lose her legs. (Aunt Ruth was a smoker.) Aunt Ruth recovers and goes on with her life, having learned some important lessons.

Rostkowski, M. I. *After the Dancing Days.* Harper, 1984. (Ages 11-14.) [Serious injury] [See War and Peace]

Rounds, G. *Blind Outlaw.* Holiday House, 1981. (Ages 7 and up.) [Speech, vision] A mute boy, talented in working with animals, tames a blind wild horse. The step-by-step progress of the horse, led by the patient boy, results in an evocatively beautiful story.

Roy, R. *Move Over, Wheelchairs Coming Through!.* Illus. by R. Hausherr. Clarion, 1985. (Ages 8-12.) [Mobility] Profiles of seven children who use wheelchairs because of such conditions as spina bifida or cerebral palsy. Adaptive equipment designed to give the children maximum independence is discussed and shown in photos. The children talk about their lives, school, hopes, and frustrations in this readable text supplemented with the author's commentary and explanations. List of further readings is included.

Roy, R. *Where's Buddy?* Illus. by T. Howell. Clarion, 1982. (Ages 8-11.) [Diabetes] Buddy is seven years old and has diabetes. On the day that Mike, his older brother, is in charge of him, Buddy disappears. Mike finds him trapped in a cave; and although Buddy has not taken his medicine, it is clear to the reader that he knows what regimen is required and can cope with his condition.

Sachs, M. *The Bears' House.* Illus. by L. Glanzman. Doubleday, 1971. (Ages 9-12.) [Emotional] [See Siblings]

Sachs, M. *Dorrie's Book.* Illus. by A. Sachs. Doubleday, 1975. (Ages 9-12.) [Gifted] Dorrie is bright but self-centered; and until her siblings are born, she is a pampered only child. Her giftedness is mentioned throughout the book. Reactions of adults to gifted children are depicted somewhat realistically. Her educational program is mentioned but not specifically described. Fortunately, her teacher is flexible and responsive. This book is well written and very funny in parts.

Sakai, K. *Sachiko Means Happiness.* Illus. by T. Arai. Children's, 1990. (Ages 5–8.) [Serious illness/Alzheimer's] Young Sachiko's grandmother, also named Sachiko, has Alzheimer's disease. She does not know her family and believes she is five years old. Young Sachiko is sent to entertain her and becomes angry and frustrated until she figures out that she can help her grandmother by playing along with her fantasies. She learns how to accept her grandmother's limitations and communicate her love.

Savitz, H. M. *Run, Don't Walk.* Watts, 1979. (Ages 12 and up.) [Mobility] Two disabled teenagers fight for their rights when their high school imposes barriers, both physical and emotional. They are strong and independent people who display adolescent vulnerabilities.

Savitz, H. M. *Wheelchair Champions: A History of Wheelchair Sports.* Illus. with photos. Crowell, 1978. (Ages 9–12.) [Mobility] A factual account of the athletes and events that comprise wheelchair competition.

Selden, B. *The Story of Annie Sullivan, Helen Keller's Teacher.* Illus. by E. McKeating. Dell, 1987. (Ages 8–10.) [Vision] The teacher is the focus of this biography rather than her famous student. Annie Sullivan was, in her own way, as remarkable as Helen Keller. She devoted her life to her student but managed to live fully nevertheless. The similarities of temperament and intellect between the two women are evident here, although Annie was much more self-effacing than Helen. The story of how both women coped with their disabilities is so remarkable that it would be difficult for a book about these two women not to be fascinating. The implications for societal provision of access to people with special needs come through.

Shapiro, P. G. *Caring for the Mentally Ill.* Watts, 1982. (Ages 11 and up.) [Emotional] A brief overview of emotional dysfunction, how it is treated, what resources are available, and legal rights of the "mentally ill."

Sharmat, M. *Nate the Great.* Coward, McCann, and Geohegan, 1972. (Ages 6–8.) [Gifted] Another child detective who is bright, capable, and fun.

Shyer, M. F. *Welcome Home, Jellybean.* Scribner, 1978. (Ages 8–12.) [Intellectual] Twelve-year-old Neil's life changes completely when his parents bring his thirteen-year-old sister Geraldine home to stay after she has spent nearly all her life in an institution for the developmentally disabled. Neil endures fights at school, Geraldine's disruptive behavior, and his father's departure from home. Neil develops compassion for his sister and acknowledges her small accomplishments. The story ends hopefully.

Silverstein, A., and Silverstein, B. *Epilepsy.* Lippincott, 1975. (Ages 11 and up.) [Epilepsy] Dispels myths and defines and describes the condition. Helps to clarify what it is and what it is not.

Simon, M. L. *A Special Gift.* HBJ, 1978. (Ages 10–13.) [Gifted] Simon has written a deeply probing novel about a boy's coming to terms with himself, his determined but unsteady shaping of values and friendships, and his acceptance of his love for dancing as a special gift rather than a problem.

Simon, S. *Einstein Anderson, Science Sleuth, Shocks His Friends.* Viking, 1980. (Ages 9–12.) [Gifted] Like the *Encyclopedia Brown* series, these stories revolve around a bright young boy who uses logic and facts to solve mysteries. Anderson's solutions are all based on scientific information.

Slepian, J. *The Alfred Summer.* Macmillan, 1980. (Ages 11 and up.) [Intellectual] Lester, who has cerebral palsy, narrates this story about friendship. Alfred is intellectually disabled and epileptic. Myron is overweight. Clair, a "typical" child, completes the group. When Alfred has a seizure, Lester finds strength and coordination he didn't know he possessed to help Alfred.

Slote, A. *Hang Tough, Paul Mather.* Lippincott, 1973. (Ages 9-12.) [Leukemia] Paul is twelve years old and has leukemia. The descriptions of his reactions to medication are graphic, but the book essentially conveys a hopeful message. The boy's devotion to baseball carries him through some of the bad times with his illness and treatment.

Smith, D. B. *Kelly's Creek.* Illus. by A. Tiegreen. Crowell, 1975. (Ages 7-12.) [Learning] Kelly has a learning disability. At home and in school, he feels like a failure. His only true friend is Philip, a college biology student doing an ecological study of the creek behind Kelly's house. At the creek Kelly feels intelligent and whole. Finally, with Philip's help, his interest in and knowledge of water life are recognized and valued.

Smith, G. *The Hayburners.* Delacorte, 1974. (Ages 10 and up.) [Intellectual] Joey is a developmentally disabled adult who does odd jobs. He nurtures a calf so that it becomes a prizewinner; and in the process, he leads young Will and his family to value him. Readers might speculate about how the family would feel about Joey if the calf did not win a prize.

Snyder, Z. K. *Libby on Wednesday.* Delacorte, 1990. (Ages 10 and up.) [Gifted, cerebral palsy] [See Family Constellations]

Sobol, D. J. *Encyclopedia Brown Carries On.* Illus. by I. Ohlsson. Four Winds, 1980. (Ages 8-11.) [Gifted] All books in this series depict a bright young boy who is valued by his parents and peers for his intelligence. The stories permit the reader to try to solve the mysteries along with Encyclopedia Brown, thus challenging their problem-solving skills.

Sobol, H. L. *My Brother Steven Is Retarded.* Illus. by P. Agre. Macmillan, 1977. (Ages 8-11.) [Intellectual] A sensitive book told from the perspective of the eleven-year-old sister of a developmentally disabled boy. The photos bring the reality of the family situation close to the reader.

Southall, I. *Let the Balloon Go.* Illus. by I. Ribbons. St. Martin's, 1969. (Ages 9-12.) [Cerebral palsy] John is a twelve-year-old Australian boy. He has cerebral palsy and has been overprotected by his mother. The plot involves John's slow and painful bid for more independence.

Stein, S. B. *About Handicaps.* Illus. by D. Frank. Walker, 1974. (Ages 6-9.) [General] Good photos, explanatory material for adults, and a text for children tell the story of Matthew and his friend Joe, who has cerebral palsy. Matthew's fears are explored, and questions are answered with understanding. The book's photos show the workings of an artificial arm and hand.

Sullivan, M. B., and Bourke, L., with S. Regan. *A Show of Hands: Say It in Sign Language.* Illus. by L. Bourke. Addison-Wesley, 1980. (Ages 6-10.) [Hearing] Conveys a positive attitude about sign language and its use. Depicts a wide variety of people with hearing impairment, some of them famous.

Teague, S. *The King of Hearts' Heart.* Little Brown, 1987. (Ages 11 and up.) [Intellectual/brain damage] Harold and Billy are neighbors, inseparable until a head injury leaves Billy developmentally disabled at the age of four. Now, at thirteen, Billy idolizes Harold and follows him everywhere. Harold coaches Billy in track for the International Special Olympics. Although Billy does not win, both boys are ready to compete next year. They have matured considerably, and their friendship has been strengthened.

Ter Haar, J. *The World of Ben Lighthart.* Dell, 1977. (Ages 11 and up.) [Vision] As the result of an accident, Ben Lighthart, about to enter high school, loses his sight. In the hospital and later at home, Ben begins the journey through anger, fear, and darkness to find a new life.

Thesman, J. *The Last April Dancers.* Houghton Mifflin, 1987. (Ages 12 and up.) [Emotional] Cat's father commits suicide on her sixteenth birthday, and she feels guilty because she and her father had an argument that day. The issue of mental illness is dealt with accurately and within the context of the story. The message is conveyed that it is dangerous to pretend that there is nothing wrong in hopes that bad feelings will go away.

Thiele, C. *Jodie's Journey.* Harper, 1988. (Ages 10 and up.) [Serious illness/rheumatoid arthritis] Jodie's dreams of being a champion horseback rider are shattered when the pains in her joints turn out to be rheumatoid arthritis, a debilitating illness that leaves her in severe pain, using a wheelchair until she is old enough for joint-replacement surgery. In the Afterword we see Jodie several years later, still in chronic pain but leading a fulfilling life that includes pursuing a career and helping young girls interested in horses. Jodie's heroism in a fire, though based on fact, adds an unnecessary melodramatic burden to the story; nevertheless the value of the book survives.

Trull, P. *On with My Life.* Putnam, 1983. (Ages 12 and up.) [Serious illness/cancer] This impressive true story tells of an adolescent's struggle with a sarcoma that cost her a leg. The author has become a hospital worker with young cancer patients. Down to earth and honest, she communicates the family's shock, her own feelings, and her uphill battle for entry into the study of occupational therapy. She helps the reader understand the trauma of cancer and the courageous sense of adventure that comes from coping with it.

Voigt, C. *Dicey's Song.* Atheneum, 1982. (Ages 9 and up.) [Emotional] [See Family Constellations]

Voigt, C. *Izzy, Willy-Nilly.* Atheneum, 1986. (Ages 12 and up.) [Mobility/amputation] Izzy, a junior in high school and a member of the "in" crowd, loses the lower part of her right leg as a result of an auto accident in which her date was driving drunk. Izzy has to learn to deal with friends' deserting her, feelings about her date's drinking, and her own suddenly changed view of life. She is forced to explore her own prejudices about disabilities and to face the stereotypes her friends still hold. With great sensitivity and well-researched accuracy, Voigt explores the pain and success of Izzy's adjustment.

Wahl, J. *Jamie's Tiger.* Illus. by T. de Paola. HBJ, 1978. (Ages 4–7.) [Hearing] Jamie becomes deaf from German measles. With information about lip reading and sign language, this book can serve as a textbook about deafness for the very young, both hearing and hearing impaired.

White, E.B. *The Trumpet of the Swan.* Illus. by E. Frascino. Harper, 1970. (Ages 9 and up.) [Speech] Louis, a cygnet, is born without a voice. Louis's determination enables him to provide for himself in life.

White, P. *Janet at School.* Crowell, 1978. (Ages 5–8.) [Mobility] A five-year-old child with spina bifida finds her own ways of doing things. A straightforward, caring account of her daily life.

Wolf, B. *Anna's Silent World.* Illus by the author. Lippincott, 1977. (Ages 8–10.) [Hearing] Born deaf, Anna is able to function well, thanks to firm family support, special training, and sound-amplifying technology.

Wolf. B. *Connie's New Eyes.* Illus. by the author. Lippincott, 1976. (Ages 10–12.) [Vision] Connie, a young blind woman, and Blythe, the seeing-eye dog who helps her carry on her life, manage very well together.

Wolf, B. *Don't Feel Sorry for Paul.* Illus. by the author. Lippincott, 1974. (Ages 8 and up.) [Mobility] Paul Jockimo has malformed hands and feet and wears prostheses on his right arm and both legs. This determined seven year old worked hard learning to use these prostheses. Paul can run, write, play ball, and do many other activities that nondisabled children can do. He has even won ribbons competing in horse shows. His supportive family, doctors, therapists, and technicians have assisted him. The author's full-page black-and-white photos demonstrate the prostheses.

Wrighton, P. *A Racehorse for Andy.* HBJ, 1968. (Ages 9 and up.) [Intellectual] Set in Australia, this beautifully written story tells of Andy, a developmentally disabled young man, and his circle of friends. Andy's friends include him in their games. When he is tricked into thinking he has bought a racetrack, his friends intervene. All is righted in the end, with no one the loser and Andy's dignity intact.

Yashima, T. *Crow Boy.* Illus. by the author. Viking, 1955. (Ages 3-5.) [Gifted] A picture book story of Chibi (Tiny Boy), who has the ability to observe and record minute details about crows and thus wins the admiration of his peers.

Yolen, J. *The Boy Who Had Wings.* Illus. by H. Aichinger. Crowell, 1974. (Ages 5-8.) [Gifted] Aetos, a Greek boy, is born with wings. He is rejected by his family and forbidden to use his wings. One day, he must use them to save his father's life. He then loses them forever. An allegory about how people view the gifted. Sparks much discussion and debate.

Yolen, J. *Dragon's Blood.* Delacorte, 1982. (Ages 12 and up.) [Speech, gifted] [See Gender Roles]

Yolen, J. *The Seeing Stick.* Illus. by R. Charlip and D. Marselis. Crowell, 1977. (Ages 5-8.) [Vision] The emperor's daughter learns to "see" by touching a carved stick. The wise old man who brings her the stick is also blind. The young princess and the old man work together to help other blind people. Beautifully told and illustrated, this book is a treasure.

Zhensun, Z., and Low, A. *A Young Painter: The life and paintings of Wang Yani—China's Extraordinary Young Artist.* Illus. with photos. Scholastic, 1991. (Ages 9-12.) [Gifted] This story tells of a remarkable child prodigy whose paintings have caused her to be referred to as "The Picasso of China."

chapter 11

Abuse

In contemporary American society, abuse in all its forms has become a major problem. More and more instances of child molestation, family violence involving children, sexual abuse, and substance abuse, with its frequent accompaniment of physical abuse, fill the news media. These problems are not relegated to lower socioeconomic groups; middle and upper class families have been severely affected by the rise in violence and drug and alcohol abuse. Another problem increasingly apparent in middle-class families, eating disorders, is viewed as addiction and, therefore, abuse of food. This chapter examines how these various categories of abuse are treated in children's literature.

PHYSICAL AND EMOTIONAL ABUSE

Historically, emotional and physical child abuse has been a fact of life that few people found worthy of notice or thought to change. Not until the late nineteenth century, with the advent of child advocacy groups, were children considered to be anything but their parents' property. In 1962 the term "battered child syndrome" was coined by Ruth and C. Henry Kempe in an article in *The Journal of the American Medical Association.* Since that time national and state legislation has mandated the reporting of abuse and guaranteed informers anonymity and immunity from prosecution. Each state has its own definitions, sometimes as part of the legal system, sometimes embedded in the civil system and social justice agencies. For example, Massachusetts defines abuse as "the nonaccidental commission of any act by a caretaker which causes substantial risk of harm or threat of harm to a child's well-being." Massachusetts regulations also include "the commission of a sex offense against a child as defined by the criminal laws of the Commonwealth." Serious emotional injury (anxiety, depression, or withdrawal) can accompany physical or sexual abuse.

Parents Anonymous, a volunteer organization for adults who recognize that they are or have the potential to be abusive, works to help these parents improve their interaction with their children and their skills in parenting. It is now considered important to help the abuser as well as the child. This stance is not without controversy, especially when children are returned to abusive parents after a period of time and counseling.

According to the National Committee for the Prevention of Child Abuse, more than 2.9 million cases of child abuse were reported in 1992, and an estimated 1,261 children died of abuse in that year alone. Although the number of reported cases has risen dramatically, it may be that incidence itself is not increasing. Certainly, people are more willing to report cases now because they have broader information about what constitutes abuse, laws require professionals to report abuse, and provision of services for abusers as well as victims has increased.

Abusers are most likely to be a child's parents. Victims of family violence seem to be at a higher risk of becoming abusers; parents who were themselves subject to severe physical punishment as children are more than twice as likely to inflict such treatment on their own children. These facts make the issue of educating children to recognize and report abuse even more compelling. Emotional abuse and neglect may not leave visible scars on children, but they are nevertheless behaviors to be reckoned with.

SEXUAL ABUSE

In most cases, sexual abuse is defined as "an act of a person (adult or child) which forces, coerces, or threatens a child to have any form of sexual contact or to engage in any type of sexual activity at his or her direction." Any inappropriate handling of a person's private parts constitutes sexual abuse. Seventeen percent of all reported abuse cases are sexual. This amounted to 500,000 children in 1992. Although most of the victims are female, in the last national incidence study (1988) it was found that 22 percent of the child victims of sexual assault were boys. The perpetrator is most likely to be someone the child knows and trusts.

One controversial factor is the lack of accurate reporting of rape because victims are afraid to subject themselves to the pain of interrogation and allegations of seduction. It should be pointed out that there is no acceptable rationale for considering "consent" as a factor when children under the age of sixteen are involved.

Another controversy is fueled by the fear that children invent some incidents of purported sexual abuse and falsely accuse people. Daycare providers have been particularly involved in this controversy. At present, experts disagree about whether this is a significant consideration. Some written materials help parents to approach the subject with children so as not to impose invented situations but invite children to report the facts without embellishment. There have been cases of alleged lying on the part of children, but for the most part, professionals agree that children should be listened to and their stories should be respectfully investigated.

Try This

Answer these questions to the best of your ability. Discuss the answers with a partner after referring to references in the bibliography.

1. Is rape a sexual act?
2. Can children unwittingly entice an adult to commit a sexual assault?
3. Will telling children about their right to refuse the touches of adults make them disrespectful of their elders?
4. How can adults warn children about sexual assault without paralyzing them with fright?
5. What is the difference between good secrets and bad secrets?

For adults and children to best protect themselves, they must become more acquainted with accurate information about the nature and consequences of sexual assaults. One of the most common problems for children occurs when supposedly loving adults ask them to keep sexual acts secret. It is important to help a child differentiate between harmful secrecy and something that will turn out to be a pleasant surprise. Secrets can be guilt laden and negative, especially if they are accompanied by threats of retribution if they are disclosed. Children must learn to differentiate between a secret that is potentially threatening to their safety and a surprise that will eventually be aired to please someone. They must understand that they are permitted to break promises of secrecy, even if it means that an adult may be punished as a consequence.

SUBSTANCE ABUSE

More people are addicted to alcohol and tobacco than to any other chemicals. Alcohol, tobacco, marijuana, heroin, cocaine, amphetamines, barbiturates, and other mood-altering drugs have invaded the population, even though there have been widespread publicity and educational campaigns to warn people of their dangers. Steroids, drugs used to enhance physical stamina, are also very dangerous. Sometimes misleading statements from well-intentioned but ill-informed adults serve to attract rather than deter children's experimenting with drugs. Programs to help youngsters raise their self-esteem and enhance their decision-making abilities are far more effective than scare tactics.

In 1956 The American Medical Association classified addiction as a disease. This means that a person is not evil or sinful if he or she abuses a substance. People with this disease need to seek and maintain treatment. People with addictions usually evidence certain behaviors as they progress through their disease, denying that they are addicted, blaming others, and often violently expressing anger against people who are innocent of wrongdoing. At times they distort reality or invent "facts," especially when they cannot remember what really took place. They are generally resistant to any recommendations for change.

One of the most difficult realizations for friends and families of addicts is that they can do little to change an addicted person's behavior. Sometimes they make excuses, cover up, or pretend that nothing is wrong. This is called co-addiction, codependence, or enabling behavior because it does not help the loved one to understand that he or she must seek treatment.

Children of addicts tend to have low self-esteem and to engage in behaviors that can cause other people to reject them. They are often frightened of people in authority, and they can become loners. They seek others' approval, and they are frightened by criticism and anger, rarely standing up for themselves. They often deny their own feelings, although they are constantly fearful of being abandoned. All these characteristics affect their ability to make and keep friends. They feel out of control.

Research demonstrates that twelve-step programs such as those offered by Alcoholics Anonymous, Narcotics Anonymous, or Overeaters Anonymous are the most effective means of self-help and recovery for victims of substance abuse. The steps include acknowledging the problem, seeking help, making amends, assisting other people who have the same difficulty, and accepting a spiritual power greater than the individual alone. Sometimes people delay entering a program until it is made clear that no one will continue to enable the addiction, that addicts will be expelled from the family or fired from a job if they refuse help. Some people need medical care and detoxification in a medical facility before they can begin the lifelong process of recovery. In any case, the motivation must come from within the individual person.

Eating disorders are addictions because victims of these disorders are out of control and abuse food. They cannot healthfully abstain from all food, but they must acquire the skills of moderating the amount of food they eat.

Anorexia nervosa, bulimia nervosa, and compulsive overeating occur more in females than males, most often in the teenage or early adult years. Anorexia is a condition wherein people starve themselves and often exercise excessively under a compulsive drive to lose weight. Sometimes anorexia begins with a diet that rages out of control because of factors having nothing to do with eating. People with anorexia generally consider themselves to be fat even when their body weight is dangerously low.

Bulimia involves eating large amounts of food and purging afterward, usually through vomiting. People with bulimia share certain characteristics of people with anorexia: they are usually high achievers who feel unworthy and have distorted images of their own bodies. Eating disorders are often manifested by people who want to control their lives in a dramatic way. As is the case with all addiction, media and societal expectations play a large role in leading people into self-abusive behavior.

Children's literature can be effective as one means of helping children to see that they are not alone, that their friends may be experiencing some of these problems, and that they are capable of taking ownership of their lives.

SUGGESTED CRITERIA

Books about physical, emotional, or sexual abuse should never blame the victim.

A collection should be balanced, with at least some books identifying the abuser as someone known to the victim rather than a stranger.

Books on addiction or abuse should reflect the fact that abusers and addicts represent all classes, all economic and social backgrounds, and both genders. The norm should not be that they are poor and non-Caucasian.

Care should be taken to differentiate rape and other sexual abuse from loving or sexual behavior. Abusive handling should not be confused with "fondling" or loving and affectionate touching.

In books about substance abuse, oversimplifying by "just saying no" is not enough to help young readers understand how to avoid drug addiction.

Happy endings that occur without hard work and knowledgeable interaction make for poor literature and convey harmful messages. Easy solutions are not helpful or realistic.

Scare tactics that threaten children with dire punishment are not helpful. Extreme consequences of drug or alcohol abuse (e.g., one puff of marijuana leading to heroin addiction) may cause children to disbelieve everything an author says, even the accurate information.

The person with an addiction should not be an object of amiable acceptance, a freak, or a dehumanized object of scorn or pity. The caricature of the happy or jovial drunkard is harmfully stereotypic.

Drinking or taking drugs should not be presented as admirable social behavior. Abstainers should not be portrayed as killjoys or prudes.

People suffering from addiction should not be portrayed as evil, violent, or nasty. Their humanity should be acknowledged.

People with addictions should not be identified by their illness. "Person with anorexia" is preferable to "the anorexic"; the author needs to make clear that addiction is only one of the character's traits. As in all good literature, characters should be fully fleshed out.

Recovery should always be seen as a complex long-term process, always in a state of becoming, never totally accomplished. ("One day at a time" is the motto of most recovery programs.)

Young people should not be put into the position of rescuing their addicted families or friends. Professional help and programs are the recourse, not one child's heroic efforts.

People should not be made to feel that they must accomplish their recovery in isolation. Support should be modeled.

Books should include information to help readers recognize whether they are victims of abuse.

Wherever possible, alternative ways of getting help should be suggested.

Graphic scenes of abuse and violence should be kept to a minimum.

Some books should contain models of how people were able to break the cycle of abuse.

Try This
Select five criteria from the above list. Read any book in the Bibliography. Critique the book according to the criteria. Add criteria of your own.

DISCUSSION OF CHILDREN'S BOOKS

Physical and Emotional Abuse

Sexual, physical, and emotional abuse are the topics of several books for preadolescent and older children. This painful, delicate issue is more prevalent in real life than has been previously suspected. Sometimes reading one of these books can help a young person recognize that he or she is a victim of abuse and alert him or her to seek help. In Louise Moeri's *The Girl Who Lived on the Ferris Wheel,* Til, the young protagonist, is not quite sure that she is being abused until her mother almost kills her. She keeps wondering if her mother is simply punishing her the way other children's parents do. She talks with a friend about this question and begins to suspect that her mother is not a normal parent. In the end, she determines that she will never again be victimized or forced into a situation that is too painful for her to bear.

Victims of child abuse almost always feel that they must be to blame in some unknown way. They fear that the abuse is in their imagination, that their punishment is deserved. They are ashamed of their bruises and try to hide them from others. They often protect the abuser, who in many cases is a parent. Harvey, one of the foster children in *The Pinballs,* by Betsy Byars, lies about the fact that his father ran him down with a car while in a drunken stupor, breaking both his legs. Til does not tell about her mother's abuses, for fear that something worse will happen if she does. Hildy, the abused teenager in the poem "Hildy Ross," by Mel Glenn, does not want to "turn in" her father, even though he beats her.

Sometimes the parent is a substance abuser who hurts the child only when under the influence of alcohol or drugs. Often, the parent is emotionally disturbed, unaware of the ramifications of his or her abusive act. Will, the severely battered boy in Michelle Magorian's *Good Night, Mr. Tom,* is confused about his mother's irrational behavior and disoriented when he reaches the loving, healthful environment of the countryside far away from London. When he returns to his mother, he almost dies as a result of her insane brutality and must be rescued by outsiders. Occasionally the parents are portrayed as well-intentioned people who cannot cope with the realities and expectations of ordinary existence. Almost always, the abuser himself or herself has been a victim of abuse.

It is difficult for a book to free itself of the violence and hysteria surrounding this topic. Because abuse is the major theme of the book, the plot often verges on melodrama. One rare book, Virginia Hamilton's *Sweet Whispers, Brother Rush,* not primarily about abuse, is exquisitely written. It deals with many issues as it tells a compelling story. It hints at what appears to be abusive behavior on the part of the mother and manages to convey a sense of the mother's confusion and despair that lead her to confine her child to his bed and leave him, eventually, to the ministrations of his younger sister. Vy, the mother, is neither disturbed nor a substance abuser. Her character and behavior are complex. The reader does not hate her but empathizes with her. Dabney, her son, has a congenital illness that impairs his intellect and claims his life at an early age. Like the others, he is a unique character. If this book is read with a concern for child abuse, it may help make readers aware of the pitfalls of easy answers and pat explanations. Social service agencies currently try to help abusive parents rather than condemning them.

A number of nonfiction books offer advice and information about how to recognize abuse and what to do about it. One book that provides an introduction is *Family Violence: How to Recognize and Survive It,* by Janice E. Rench. The author provides succinct answers to questions about definitions and signs of abuse, lists specific characteristics of abusive people, offers some ideas about causes, and tells how to get help. Many forms of abuse are included; and although the topics are painful, the author is careful not to become melodramatic or lurid. She includes a comprehensive section on self-esteem, pointing out its importance in resisting and avoiding abuse. Margaret Hyde's *Know about Abuse* contains much more extensive information about abusive behavior. It, too, indicates the necessity of recognizing, reporting, and dealing with abusive behavior. The author uses examples of a number of abused children to make her points.

Sexual Abuse

Both works of nonfiction mentioned above include sections on sexual abuse. Incest, unwelcome touching, and forced disrobing are examples of sexual abuses. It is estimated that one girl in three and one boy in six experience some sort of sexual abuse before they reach eighteen years of age. Since this problem is so widespread, it is necessary to help children understand how to prevent abuse or, at the very least, recognize and report it. Young women and men must understand that rape is any unwanted intercourse. A helpful book, *Everything You Need to Know about Date Rape,* by Frances Shuker-Haines, refutes such false notions as these: Rape only happens with strangers; victims mean yes when they say no; and it is the victim's fault if he or she wore provocative clothing.

For young children, *Who Is a Stranger and What Should I Do?,* by Helen Cogancherry, advises how to prevent strangers from abusing them. The rules the author provides are clear and helpful. *I Like You to Make Jokes with Me, but I Don't Want You to Touch Me,* by Ellen Bass, assures young readers that they will be believed and their wishes will be respected when it comes to preventing abuse.

Incest is one of the most difficult topics to present without sensationalism, in either fiction or nonfiction. Ellen Howard succeeds in *Gillyflower.* In the story, Gilly's father rapes her repeatedly, always cautioning her to keep this their secret. She experiences all the symptoms and behaviors associated with victims of sexual abuse such as retreating into another identity, isolating herself from peers, and suspecting that the abuse is her fault. She does not reveal the "secret" until she becomes afraid that her father has also raped her younger sister. A new friend gives her the courage to report the situation, and her mother acts appropriately to protect her children and to see to it that the father gets help. The important message of most books containing this painful topic is that the victim is never to blame.

Substance Abuse

Although a number of books for adolescents deal with the issue of substance abuse, the topic is often either presented in a heavy-handed nonliterary fashion or mentioned as a factor in a character's behavior pattern without being fully explored. Unfortunately, substance abuse and physical and emotional abuse often go hand in hand. Even if there is no overt bodily hurt, the emotional pain endured by the family of a substance abuser is equivalent to, and often deeper than, physical bruises.

In Eve Bunting's *A Sudden Silence,* an intoxicated woman driver is responsible for the death of a young man. Her husband and her daughter conspire to try to "protect" her from public embarrassment, enabling her to avoid taking responsibility for her behavior.

Laughter in the Background, by N. B. Dorman, graphically details the moment-to-moment experience of living with an alcoholic parent. Marcie tries to compensate for her mother's alcoholism by gorging herself on food. She is obese, unhappy, friendless, and trapped until she takes matters into her own hands and asks to be removed from her house. The book leaves us without much hope for her mother, but support groups and the help of loving and competent foster parents bring Marcie to a point where we know she will continue to progress to stability and success.

In the books that include the daughter of an alcoholic mother, the daughter often takes responsibility for what is traditionally regarded as the mother's role. The father in these stories is generally irresponsible, weak, and ready to blame anyone but himself for the situation. All the books described in this section have these ingredients. It is to be hoped that more varied stories will eventually counteract what seems to be an emerging stereotype.

Laurie, the sixteen-year-old daughter in Jane Claypool Miner's *Why Did You Leave Me?* is one such character. The story emphasizes her reaction to her alcoholic mother's return after two years, part of that time spent in a special treatment center. Laurie finds it difficult to relinquish her caretaking position and feels anger, jealousy, and resentment, as well as self-pity. She behaves in a self-defeating fashion throughout most of the book. In the end, a nineteen-year-old woman, herself a recovering alcoholic, helps her move from her negative stance. Her mother regularly attends Alcoholics Anonymous, and evidently she is likely to be successful in overcoming her drinking problem.

The efficacy of support groups is also demonstrated in C. S. Adler's *With Westie and the Tin Man.* Greg has been in prison, partly because he has acted out against his mother's alcoholism. When he returns and finds his mother and her partner, also a recovering alcoholic, successful in business together, both of them regularly attending AA, he does not know how to behave. He has been so accustomed to reacting to her addiction that it is difficult for him to relinquish his former enabling role. The support system and the interaction with his mother and her partner help Greg to function as an individual and to enjoy his mother's recovery.

Most children's books dealing with drugs other than alcohol are nonfiction. One notable exception is *Motown and Didi,* by Walter Dean Myers. Didi's brother Tony is addicted to heroin; and no matter what Didi does, she cannot protect him from himself. The climate of the mean streets of the city forms the backdrop for this dramatic story. The power of self-esteem and love is what saves Didi and Motown; since Tony has neither, he dies.

Susan and Daniel Cohen's *What Can You Believe about Drugs: An Honest and Unhysterical Guide for Teens* avoids the pitfalls of overstating the case against moderate drug use while still warning of the dangers of addiction. Rhoda McFarland does the same in *Coping with Substance Abuse.* She also discusses how to avoid enabling friends and family in their addictions.

Many books contain a young protagonist who has "fallen into evil ways," and become addicted to drugs or alcohol. Most of these stories are written to a formula: they portray shallow characters whose parents do not understand them; whose friends are wild and only out for a good time; and who succumb to the temptations of drugs, alcohol, and crime but are rescued by some loving person. Adolescents may enjoy these stories as escapist adventure tales, but they are not likely to gain insight or information from them. Readers should try to find books where the characters are more than vehicles for a message and where the information is accurate and clearly conveyed. Substance abuse is a serious social problem, and young people should be able to acquire helpful advice through the medium of literature, as well as responsible agencies and adult helpers.

Eating disorders are another form of substance abuse. Although eating disorders differ from other forms of substance abuse because people must eat, this problem nevertheless shows many characteristics of any other addiction. In all eating disorders, self-image and self-esteem are key. Again, most books about this problem are nonfiction. *Toughing It Out,* by Joan L. Oppenheimer, at first glance looks like a romance novel; but its content and structure provide substance, and each of the characters is three dimensional. It is one of the few works of fiction that address this problem. The story involves a young woman whose seemingly innocent dieting turns into an obsession, and finally into anorexia. Like many people with food addictions, Jennifer combines elements of bulimia and anorexia. She gets help through group and individual counseling, but only after being hospitalized. The seriousness of the condition is demonstrated when one of her friends, also suffering from anorexia, dies.

Jennifer's family is somewhat stereotypic in their responses and interactions, but they are recognizable as people with their own issues. Jennifer's treatment does not mention Overeaters Anonymous as an aid in her lifelong recovery process, but a number of works of nonfiction provide information about this group. In *Why Are They Starving Themselves: Understanding Anorexia Nervosa and Bulimia,* Elaine Landau stresses the importance of joining support groups for ongoing help and building self-esteem. She also presents information about the specifics of the diseases.

In all cases of abuse and addiction, society plays a large part in setting the conditions for potential abuse. Television, cinema, popular magazines, and many books glorify exploitative sex, convey the impression that the practices and perceptions of drug use are automatic and acceptable, that thinness is the ideal body condition, and that there are easy ways to gain popularity and success. Until educators, parents, and people responsible for packaging these messages change their priorities, children will continue to be confused about appropriate sexual behavior, attracted to artificially induced highs, and vulnerable to binge-and-purge eating habits. Frank discussions of literature presenting recommendations counter to these messages can help.

REFERENCES

Abuse

Adams, C., and Fay, J. *No More Secrets: Protecting Your Child from Sexual Assault.* Impact, 1981. A product of the King County Rape Relief Center, this little book counteracts misinformation by providing facts. For example, 85 percent of the time an assault is committed by someone the child knows. It gives clues and indicators that warn of possible sexual attacks and recommends activities that help teach prevention. It teaches how to listen carefully to what children say. It also supplies advice about what to do should a sexual attack take place.

Baggett, C. "The Specter of Child Abuse in Realistic Fiction for Children." *Catholic Library World* 56 (April 1985): 371-374. After a brief discussion of the nature and extent of child abuse in American homes, the author discusses sixteen books on this topic.

Bartimole, C. R., and Bartimole, J. E. *Teenage Alcoholism and Substance Abuse: Causes, Consequences and Cures.* Fell, 1987. A short but informative resource for parents on how to recognize if their children are abusing drugs. It also contains information about what drugs are, their classification (narcotics, sedative-hypnotics, stimulants, etc.) and actions that parents and schools can take in response to abuse and for its prevention.

Bourne, R., and Newberger, E. H. *Critical Perspectives on Child Abuse.* Heath, 1979. Thirteen essays presenting an analytic approach to practice and policy, as well as theory of child abuse. Each essay views the issue from a different perspective. Excellent introduction and overview.

Breton, M. "Resocialization of Abusive Parents." *Social Work* 26 (March 1981): 119-122. Recommends procedures for working with parents who abuse their children and holds out hope that they can be helped to become nurturing parents. Acknowledges inadequacy of resources to deal with this problem.

Campbell, J. D. "Children of Alcoholics." *Learning88* 16 (March 1988): 45-48. Startling statistics (There are "7 million American children of alcoholic parents.") and distressing conditions are disclosed. Several books containing useful information are described, and classroom strategies are recommended. Also supplied are lists of books and of supportive and informational organizations.

Cantrell, L. *Into the Light: A Guide for Battered Women.* Franklin, 1986. An excellent guide to understanding the issue of woman battering. Good questions to guide the reader, good resources for follow up.

English, J.; Pyles, A. A.; and Wicker, A. *Drug Education through Literature: An Annotated Bibliography for Grades K-6.* Northwest Regional Educational Laboratory, 1991. Annotated bibliography on literature supportive of drug education that may be used across the curriculum. Fiction and poetry are listed. Activities are also suggested.

Fassler, D. G. "Children's Books about Alcoholism." *Childhood Education* 63 (Feb. 1987): 188-94. Criticizes books that treat the problem in a frightening or overly dramatic fashion, employ sensationalism, or mislead the reader. Author supplies a list of questions for judging if a book is suitable.

Finkelhor, D. *Stopping Family Violence: Research Priorities for the Coming Decade.* Sage, 1988. A detailed discussion of reports indicating the priorities for research needed to help stop abuse. Substantive questions are raised.

Freeman, J. *How to Drug-Proof Kids: A Parent's Guide to Early Prevention.* Illus. by T. Flanagan. Think Shop, 1989. A helpful guide, especially for teachers. The author resists the temptation to say "just say no." She provides thought-provoking activities, useful information, and many recommendations for further resources. She is respectful both of her audience and of the difficulty of the task of preventing drug abuse.

Gelinas, D. J. "The Persisting Negative Effects of Incest." *Psychiatry* 46 (Nov. 1983): 312-332. The author details statistics on the prevalence of incest in the United States. She discusses the short- and long-term psychological manifestations of the aftereffects of such abuse and the implications for psychotherapy. She demonstrates that incest has a devastating effect on a larger portion of American society than previously suspected.

Gelles, R. J., and Straus, M. A. *Intimate Violence: The Causes and Consequences of Abuse in the American Family.* Simon & Schuster, 1988. Reports the results of research about domestic violence in the United States. The authors counter many stereotypes by demonstrating that there is no statistical difference between black and white families in abusive violence toward children. They also conclude that abused women are not more masochistic than other women. They observe that abuse may stem from a feeling of isolation from family and community, but they also indict "discipline" that condones spankings and beatings.

Handelman, G. "Child Abuse! The Nuclear Family Explodes." *Columbia,* Feb. 1983, pp. 31-36. A sympathetic discussion of how parents who abuse their children need help to learn how to rehabilitate themselves and their children.

Hart-Rossi, J. *Protect Your Child from Sexual Abuse: A Parents Guide.* Parenting, 1984. This brief, informative companion to "It's My Body," by Lori Freeman, includes statistics about child abuse and activities designed to help people understand their own sense of comfort with others in terms of touch, to encourage the telling of feelings, and to facilitate the disclosure of any sexual abuse.

Hearne, B. "Problems and Possibilities: U.S. Research in Children's Literature." *School Library Journal* 34 (Aug. 1988): 27-31. An overview of some of the criticisms and studies of children's books that deal with abuse. A plea is made for more research and analysis.

Hollander, S. K. "Coping with Child Sexual Abuse through Children's Books." *Elementary School Guidance and Counseling* 23 (Feb. 1989): 183-193. The author urges education of young children about sexual abuse, arguing that ignorance is dangerous. She recommends bibliocounseling (the use of books before a problem has emerged) and provides guidelines for how to integrate children's books on this subject into school programs. She describes sixteen works of nonfiction for children.

Karlin, A., and Bruneau, O. "Child Abuse: Helping Children through Bibliotherapy." ERIC Document Number ED268487. March 1985. Discusses the application of literature as therapy to help abused children and educate all children about abuse.

Karolides, N. J., and Karolides, M. "Eating Disorders and Overtraining." In *Focus on Fitness: Reference Handbook,* pp. 343-418. ABC-CLIO, 1993. This chapter includes a discussion of obesity, bulimia, and anorexia. The authors focus on the symptoms, causes, and health risks of each disorder. A short annotated bibliography at the end of the chapter lists both fiction and nonfiction for children.

Loontjens, L. *Talking to Children/Talking to Parents about Sexual Assault.* Network, 1984. One of the many valuable resources from the King County Rape Relief Center, this book provides step-by-step presentations for different age groups on how to educate children about sexual assault.

Omizo, S. A., and Michael, M. "Eating Disorders: The School Counselor's Role." *School Counselor* 39 (Jan. 1992): 217-224. The authors offer suggestions for school counselors on responding to students who may be at risk for bulimia or anorexia.

Pardeck, J. T. "Children's Literature and Child Abuse." *Child Welfare* 69 (Jan.-Feb. 1990): 83-88. Bibliotherapy and the specific problems of working with abused children are discussed. A dozen books for use with abused children are briefly described. Follow-up activities such as art and writing projects are recommended.

Perez, K. *Using Young Adult Literature to End Discrimination against Mental Illness.* ERIC Document Accession No. ED293133, 1988. Annotated bibliography of young adult literature on topics such as anorexia, drugs, and alcohol. Also includes suggestions for activities.

Phelps, L., and Bajorek, E. "Eating Disorders of the Adolescent: Current Issues in Etiology, Assessment, and Treatment." *School Psychology Review* 20 (1991): 9-22. Review of literature on bulimia and anorexia in adolescents. Strategies are suggested to assist students who may be at risk for these disorders.

Pita, D. D. *Addictions Counseling.* Continuum, 1992. Applicable to different kinds of addiction, this book offers detailed strategies for assisting the person who is addicted. The author has combined the ideas of twelve step programs with those of rational emotive therapy in her approach.

Rudman, M. K.; Gagne, K. D., and Bernstein, J. E. *Books to Help Children Cope with Separation and Loss,* 4th ed. Bowker, 1993. Contains more than 40 titles and annotations on children's literature dealing with abuse.

Ryan, S. M. "Disorders and Teens: Anorexia and Bulimia." *The ALAN Review* 20 (Spring 1993): 62-63. In this brief article, the authors touch on the causes of eating disorders and the role of teachers in responding to girls who may have trouble with either bulimia or anorexia. They provide suggestions for relevant books, both fiction and nonfiction.

Sanford, L. T. *The Silent Children: A Parent's Guide to the Prevention of Child Sexual Abuse.* Doubleday, 1980. Teaches parents of children seven years of age and older how to warn their children about sexual abuse. Gives an overview of child molestation and incest and provides exercises for parents to use with children.

Schwebel, R. *Saying No Is Not Enough: Raising Children Who Make Wise Decisions about Drugs and Alcohol.* Newmark, 1989. A guide for parents, educators, and counselors regarding drug abuse in children. Offers practical suggestions for working with children.

RESOURCES

Al-Anon Family Group Headquarters. P.O. Box 862, Midtown Station, New York, NY 10018. (800) 356-9996 For relatives and friends of individuals with alcohol problems. Operates Alateen for members 12-20 years of age whose lives have been affected by someone else's drinking problem.

Alcoholics Anonymous World Services. 475 Riverside Drive, New York, NY 10163. AA provides group support for individuals recovering from alcoholism using the twelve-step recovery model.

Alcohol Research Information Service. 1106 E. Oakland, Lansing, MI 48906. Collects and disseminates information regarding alcohol; its manufacture, sale, and use; and its relation to health in the United States. Provides pamphlets and teaching materials.

American Academy of Child and Adolescent Psychiatry. PO Box 96106, Washington, D.C. 20090-6106. Provides brief, informative "fact sheets" on topics such as "Teenagers with Eating Disorders"; "Teens: Alcohol and Other Drugs"; and "Child Sexual Abuse."

American Council for Drug Education. 204 Monroe Street, Suite 110, Rockville, MD 20850. Disseminates information and research on marijuana, cocaine, and other psychoactive drugs. Provides resource information kits.

American Anorexia/Bulimia Association. 418 E. 76th Street, New York, NY 10021. An information and referral service, as well as an organizer of self-help groups for people with anorexia or bulimia and their families.

American Humane Association. 63 Inverness Drive E., Englewood, Colo. 80112. (800) 227-4645 Works in area of child abuse and neglect. Provides evaluation, research, training, and information. Publications include a curriculum on prevention and pamphlets on identification.

ANAD—National Association of Anorexia Nervosa and Associated Disorders. Box 7, Highland Park, IL 60035. A resource center for facts and research on the disorder, methods of prevention, and types of treatment and their effectiveness. Provides referral and children's services, as well as early detection programs.

ANRED—Anorexia Nervosa and Related Eating Disorders. PO Box 5102, 1255 Hillyard, Eugene, OR 97405. Collects and distributes information on eating disorders; provides support groups, referrals, and counseling. Conducts educational seminars. Publishes a monthly newsletter, *Alert.*

Child Abuse and Neglect. This journal regularly contains articles on various aspects of abuse.

Children of Alcoholics Foundation. P.O. Box 4185, Grand Central Station, New York, NY 10163-4185. Educates the public about children of alcoholics and alcohol abusers.

International Association of Eating Disorders, 123 NW 13th Street, No. 206, Boca Raton, FL 33432. Provides education and information on eating disorders, as well as establishing and developing curricula.

King County Sexual Assault Resource Center. PO Box 300, Renton, WA 98057. Publishes materials on recognizing and preventing sexual abuse and assisting victims. Pamphlets and catalogs are available. (Many in English, Spanish, Cambodian, and Lao).

Narcotics Anonymous. P.O. Box 9999, Van Nuys, CA 91409. Groups of individuals help others seeking recovery from addiction. Applies twelve-step approach to aid recovery.

National Association for Children of Alcoholics. 31582 Coast Hwy., Suite B, South Laguna, CA 92677. Supports and serves as a resource for COAs of all age groups.

National Commission for Prevention of Child Abuse. 332 South Michigan Ave., Suite 1250, Chicago, IL 60604-4357. Provides informational materials and statistics on child abuse.

National Council on Child Abuse and Family Violence. 1155 Connecticut Ave., N.W., Suite 300, Washington, DC 20036. (202) 429-6695. Collects and distributes information regarding child abuse, domestic violence, and elder abuse. Concerned with the intergenerational nature of family abuse; seeks to support early prevention programs and assistance to victims of violence.

National Federation of Parents for Drug-Free Youth (NFP). 11159 B South Town Square, St. Louis, MO 63123. Network of parent groups formed to combat drug use.

National Woman Abuse Prevention Project. 1112 16th Street, N.W., Suite 920, Washington, DC 20036. (202) 857-0216. Seeks to increase public awareness through educational programs on the recognition and prevention of domestic violence.

Overeaters Anonymous, P.O. Box 92870, Los Angeles, CA 90009. Local groups across the country meet to share their experiences in hopes of easing their disease of overeating. Uses twelve-step approach.

Parents Anonymous. 520 S. Lafayette, Suite 316, Los Angeles, CA 90057. (800) 421-0353; in CA (800) 352-0386. Support for parents who fear that they may be abusers. Help for parents to get along better with their children.

Target. 11724 N.W. Plaza Circle, Kansas City, MO 64195-0626. (800) 366-6667. Provides information to schools, individuals, and organizations to help students deal with tobacco, alcohol, and other drugs.

TOVA—The Other Victims of Alcoholism. PO Box 1528, Radio City Station, New York, NY 10101. Provides public information and education about the less visible victims of alcoholism, as well as focusing on alcoholism's impact on society.

BIBLIOGRAPHY

If a book has a special focus it is identified in brackets following the bibliographic entry. For a listing of titles arranged by type of abuse, write to the author at 224 Furcolo Hall, UMASS, Amherst, MA 01003.

Adler, C. S. *With Westie and the Tin Man.* Macmillan, 1985. (Ages 12 and up.) [Substance] On his release from jail, Greg finds that his mother and her friend, both recovering alcoholics, are successfully in business together. At first Greg feels displaced and confused; but as time goes on, he comes to value his mother's newfound health and her friend's help. Greg's progress is believable, and the facts about recovering from addiction are woven into the story.

Anders, R. *A Look at Alcoholism.* Lerner, 1978. (Ages 7–11.) [Substance] A very "sobering" book in language young children can understand.

Anderson, D., and Finne, M. *Margaret's Story: Sexual Abuse and Going to Court.* Illus. by J. Swofford. Dillon, 1986. [Sexual] A fictionalized account that tells in detail the preparations for and actual experience of a child testifying in court in a sexual abuse case. Parents, social worker, and lawyer form a support team for the child. The book provides an excellent model.

Anderson, D., and Finne, M. *Robin's Story: Physical Abuse and Seeing the Doctor.* Illus. by J. Swofford. Dillon, 1986. (Ages 7–10.) [Physical] An alert teacher notices bruises on Robin's face and refers the child to a social worker, who in turn refers her to a doctor and on to child protective services. Robin and her family are helped to end the abuse.

Austrian, G. *The Truth about Drugs.* Doubleday, 1971. (Ages 12 and up.) [Substance] A description of drug usage, effects, and history and the reasons people take them, documented with case histories. Useful glossary included in this reasoned view.

Avi. *Sometimes I Think I Hear My Name.* Pantheon, 1982. (Ages 11 and up.) [Emotional] Conrad's aunt and uncle try to protect him from finding out that his divorced parents really do not want him. When both his parents demonstrate that they are incapable of giving him love and security, he returns to his aunt and uncle, finally accepting his situation and himself. Part of the plot involves Conrad's relationship with a lonely, angry, and rejected young girl whose upper-class parents are emotionally abusive.

Bass, E. *I Like You to Make Jokes with Me, but I Don't Want You to Touch Me.* Illus. by M. Betz. Lollipop Power, 1985. (Ages 3–8.) [Sexual] When the supermarket clerk Jack comes too close to Sara, his tickling and teasing become frightening. Jack means no harm, but he is not adequately cognizant of boundaries between people. Sara's mother helps her confront Jack with her discomfort. Jack understands and they resolve the situation. A good job on an underexplored subject that deserves mention.

Benedict, H. *Safe, Strong, and Streetwise: Sexual Safety at Home, on the Street, on Dates, on the Job, at Parties, and More.* Little, Brown, 1987. (Ages 12 and up.) [Sexual] Stresses the necessity for teenagers to retain control over their own bodies and actions. Lots of specific hints are given for warding off muggings, sexual attack, and date pressure. General precautions are also included.

Berger, G., and Berger, M. *Drug Abuse A–Z.* Enslow, 1990. (Ages 11 and up.) [Substance] A helpful dictionary of terminology associated with drugs and drug use. Slang phrases, as well as medical and pharmacological terms, are defined.

Bernstein, S. C. *A Family That Fights.* Illus. by K. Ritz. Whitman, 1991. (Ages 5–9.) [Physical, emotional] The book realistically describes an abusive family in which the father regularly beats and abuses his wife. The children live in constant fear that he will hurt them too, and the mother tries to cover up and deny the fact of the abuse. The book does not end happily; the abusive environment is not changed. An afterword gives young readers specific advice on how children can help themselves in similar circumstances and includes advice to abused adults.

Birdseye, T. *Tucker.* Holiday House, 1990. (Ages 9–12.) [Substance, neglect] Eleven-year-old Tucker Renfro lives with his alcoholic father. Duane Renfro's alcoholism and its debilitating effects on his ability to function might cause the reader to wonder why he was granted custody of his son. On the other hand, he is not an abusive alcoholic; and the story provides a good model of the effects of the disease when it does not lead to violence and physical abuse. The ending is somewhat hopeful, but not unrealistically so.

Bode, J. *Rape: Preventing It; Coping with the Legal, Medical, and Emotional Aftermath.* Watts, 1979. (Ages 12 and up.) [Sexual] Using case histories and extensive interview material, this book discusses rape as a "social problem." The author looks at the legal, medical, and emotional aftermath of rape and gives practical information on preventive and protective measures. Very informative and eye-opening.

Bunting, E. *A Sudden Silence.* HBJ, 1988. (Ages 10 and up.) [Substance] Bry Harmon is killed by a hit-and-run driver, partly because he is deaf and cannot hear the oncoming car, but mostly because the driver is drunk. Bry's brother Jesse feels guilty because he was walking with Bry the night of the accident and could not save his brother's life. Through assiduous investigation, he discovers that the killer is the alcoholic mother of a young woman he is involved with emotionally. Throughout his investigation, he acquires much information about alcoholism and its effects. The book is dramatic and suspenseful, and the plot shows how relationships are damaged because of substance abuse.

Byars, B. *The Pinballs.* Harper, 1977. (Ages 9–12.) [Physical] Three foster children, or "pinballs" as Carlie labels them, are sent to stay with the Masons. Each of the three has a problem that must be confronted, discussed, and accepted. Harvey has been run over by his drunken father, and Carlie has been sexually abused. A well-written, sensitively handled story.

Caines, J. *Chilly Stomach.* Illus. by P. Cummings. Harper, 1986. (Ages 5–8.) [Sexual] The contrast between good feeling and discomforting touches is presented directly and simply. Young readers can understand Sandy's feelings and behavior in avoiding her uncle. When she decides to tell her parents, they are sympathetic and helpful.

Childress, A. *A Hero Ain't Nothing but a Sandwich.* Coward, McCann, and Geoghegan, 1973. (Ages 12 and up.) [Substance] A novel that pulls no punches and offers no easy solutions probes the problems of Benjie, a thirteen-year-old Harlem boy well on his way to becoming a heroin addict. The book tells the story from Benjie's point of view, with comments from his mother, stepfather, and pusher friends.

Cleaver, V., and Cleaver, B. *Hazel Rye.* Lippincott, 1983. (Ages 11 and up.) [Emotional] Hazel's mother has deserted her and her father, who expresses his love by keeping Hazel isolated from anyone but him. His abuse is insidious and emotional rather than physical (although she is neglected physically). Hazel's awakening is incomplete but realistic at the end, and there is hope that she will overcome her father's influence.

Cohen, S., and Cohen, D. *A Six-Pack and a Fake I.D.: Teens Look at the Drinking Question.* Evans, 1986. (Ages 12 and up.) [Substance] Without moralizing, the authors examine the role of alcohol in society. They offer practical advice to adolescents on how to deal with peer pressure and how to get professional help when it is needed.

Cohen, S., and Cohen, D. *What Can You Believe about Drugs: An Honest and Unhysterical Guide for Teens.* Evans, 1988. (Ages 12 and up.) [Substance] The authors communicate that drugs, in and of themselves, are not devils, but there are excellent reasons not to abuse them.

Cole, B. *The Goats.* Farrar, Straus, and Giroux, 1987. (Ages 12 and up.) [Peer] [See War and Peace]

Cullen, R. V. *Sometimes You Just Have to Tell Somebody.* Illus. by E. Antonucci. Paulist Press, 1992. (Ages 5–7). [Alcohol] Patti's father has a drinking problem, and Patti has no one to talk with until she opens up to her teacher who puts her in touch with a counselor with whom Patti can air her problems.

Daugherty, L. B. *Why Me? Help for Victims of Child Sexual Abuse (Even if They Are Adults Now).* Mother Courage, 1984. (Ages 12 and up.) [Sexual] Stories about children who have been abused, with graphic descriptions and not always happy endings, make this a book that readers under twelve would probably find frightening. Basic questions, such as "What is sexual abuse?" and "What is incest?" are answered. Much of the book consists of narratives in the words of victims. In fact, the book is directed to victims to communicate to them that they are not alone, that the abuse was not their fault, and that even now they can do something to overcome their negative feelings.

Dayee, F. S. *Private Zone.* Illus. by M. M. Horosko. Franklin, 1982. (Ages 3–9.) [Sexual] A dispassionate presentation of what a young child needs to know to prevent or report sexual assault. Included is information on symptoms in children's behavior that indicate they may have been sexually assaulted, as well as advice on what to do if it occurs and a listing of additional books on the subject.

Dorman, N. B. *Laughter in the Background.* Elsevier/Nelson, 1980. (Ages 11 and up.) [Substance, food, sexual] Marcie's mother is an alcoholic. Marcie is obese and slovenly. She seems helpless to do anything about her situation until she is almost raped by one of her mother's boyfriends. Then she takes charge of her own life and demands to be taken out of her mother's custody. She emerges as a strong young woman who will overcome her problems.

Due, L. A. *High and Outside.* Harper, 1980. (Ages 12 and up.) [Substance] Niki is a seventeen-year-old star athlete and honor student who, from both her parents' and her teachers' point of view, has everything a teenager could want or need. This is a modern family in which mother and father are called by their first names and Niki partakes in their daily ritual of cocktails. From the first few pages, the reader is aware that Niki is a lonely and desperate girl who drinks too much. Niki tries to commit suicide but decides "If I liked my wrist enough not to cut it anymore, maybe I could learn to like the rest of me." The story ends with Niki accepting the help of Al-Anon.

Erlanger, E. *Eating Disorders.* Lerner, 1988. (Ages 9–12.) [Food] An excellent and informative book citing startling statistics about the wide incidence of these diseases in contemporary society. The use of Victorian illustrations distracts from the up-to-date information, but that is a small flaw.

Fox, P. *The Moonlight Man.* Bradbury, 1986. (Ages 12 and up.) [Substance] Catherine's parents are divorced. Her father, a writer, is a charming man, as well as an alcoholic. He lies, cheats, and acts irresponsibly, but he can be loving and wonderful. The dialogue, characterizations, and plot compel the reader's attention. Although this is no clinical case study, it is as authentic as any text and has the advantage of being clothed in the truth of story.

Freeman, L. *Loving Touches: A Book for Children about Positive, Caring Kinds of Touches.* Illus. by C. Deach. Parenting, 1986. (Ages 3–5.) [Sexual, physical] Focusing on positive kinds of touching, this book can serve as a preparation for children to understand the differences between loving and abusive touches.

Gale, N. "Bobby's First Poem." In *Pick Me Up,* edited by W. Cole. Macmillan, 1972. (All ages.) [Sexual] Because children don't always recognize tickling as an early potential form of sexual abuse, this poem, read aloud, may be useful in introducing this awareness.

Gallagher, V., with Dodds, W. F. *Speaking Out, Fighting Back.* Madrona, 1985. (Ages 12 and up.) [Sexual] Portraits of women who have overcome their childhood history of sexual abuse and become successfully functioning adults. Consequences of abuse are presented, and professional help is described.

Girard, L. W. *My Body is Private.* Illus. by R. Pate. Whitman, 1984. (Ages 4–6.) [Sexual] A gentle, accurate discussion for young children of what kinds of behaviors are acceptable and what kinds are not. Talking to children and listening to them is important in the prevention of abuse and in reacting appropriately to attempts at abuse.

Girard, L. W. *Who Is a Stranger and What Should I Do?* Illus. by H. Cogancherry. Whitman, 1985. (Ages 6–10.) [Physical, sexual] Excellent guidelines for young people on how to deal with strangers. Rules are recommended, and reasons for them are supplied.

Glenn, M. "Hildy Ross." In *Class Dismissed! High School Poems.* Illus. by M. Bernstein. Clarion, 1982. (Ages 12 and up.) [Physical] Hildy is an abused teenager with ambivalent feelings about her father. Even though he beats her, she "can't see turning him in."

Glenn, M. "Rhonda Winfey." In *Class Dismissed! High School Poems.* Illus. by M. Bernstein. Clarion, 1982. (Ages 12 and up.) [Substance] Rhonda is under constant stress: for good grades, college entrance, first place. She depends on Valium to see her through the "jungle" that is high school.

Grosshandler, J. *Coping with Alcohol Abuse.* Rosen, 1990. (Ages 12 and up.) [Substance] Written as a reference guide for teens, this book provides an overview of alcoholism and the skills needed to cope with it. The author includes information on counseling and alcohol treatment centers.

Hall, L., and Cohn, L. *Dear Kids of Alcoholics.* Illus. by R. E. Lingenfelter. Gurze, 1988. (Ages 7–10.) [Substance] Told in the first person by the young son of an alcoholic, the story is a step-by-step description of the progress of the child's father from abusive to recovering alcoholic. An intervention is also meticulously described, where family members and friends confront the father. Although the story is designed to inform people about this condition, the details are well integrated into the plot, and the reader's attention and sympathy are always with the boy.

Hall, L. *The Boy in the Off-White Hat.* Scribner, 1984. (Ages 11 and up.) [Sexual] Shane is nine years old. Burge, a visitor and suitor to his mother sexually abuses him and terrorizes him into continuous submission. Shane takes on a new persona, refusing to call himself by his own name. In the guise of his alter ego, he reports the abuse to a friend; and it is discovered that Burge has a record of molestation. The story effectively communicates the important of helping children to express their fears and learn to stand up for their rights.

Halvorson, M. *Cowboys Don't Cry.* Delacorte, 1985. (Ages 11 and up.) [Substance] Shane's father is an alcoholic whose wife was killed in an accident when he was driving drunk. Finally another near-fatal accident shocks the father into deciding to take hold of his life. Shane is a strong character who tries very hard not to support his father's alcohol abuse while at the same time continuing to love him.

Hamilton, V. *Cousins.* Philomel, 1990. (Ages 10–12.) [Bulimia] [See Family Constellations]

Hamilton, V. *Sweet Whispers, Brother Rush.* Philomel, 1981. (Ages 12 and up.) [See Special Needs]

Harris, J. *Drugged Athletes: The Crisis in American Sports.* Four Winds, 1987. (Ages 11 and up.) [Substance] Society's constant invitation to use all sorts of drugs is one of the factors mentioned here for the use of steroids. Each chapter is interesting and informative and brings up other issues of concern dealing with athletes and their exploitation.

Hautzig, D. *Second Star to the Right.* Greenwillow, 1981. (Ages 12 and up.) [Anorexia nervosa] Leslie is bright, athletic, and eager to please, especially her mother, who is a Holocaust survivor. In her zeal to lose weight (and hating herself and any notion that she will mature into womanhood), she almost starves herself to death. After denying that she has anorexia nervosa, she ultimately begins her slow climb back to health.

Holland, I. *Dinah and the Green Fat Kingdom.* Lippincott, 1978. (Ages 8–10.) [Obesity] [See Special Needs]

Howard, E. *Gillyflower.* Atheneum, 1986. (Ages 12 and up.) [Sexual] Gilly retreats to a fantasy world to escape the secret that her father has regularly been abusing her sexually. Gilly thinks it is her fault. She tells her mother only when she fears that her father will now begin to abuse her younger sister. To her credit, the mother immediately moves out with both daughters, and the father receives help.

Hunt, I. *The Lottery Rose.* Scribner, 1976. (Ages 10 and up.) [Physical] Georgie has been abused all his seven years. He slowly begins to heal emotionally and eventually establishes a loving and permanent relationship with a woman whose life has been full of tragedies. Although the book contains some clichés, its language and power are extraordinary.

Hyde, M. O. *Cry Softly! The Story of Child Abuse.* Westminster, 1980. (Ages 10 and up.) [Physical] Helps children and concerned adults understand that child abuse is present in families at all socioeconomic levels. Provides a list of organizations that help abusive parents as well as their children.

Hyde, M. O. *Know about Abuse.* Walker, 1992. (Ages 10 and up.) [Physical, sexual, emotional] Lots of plain, straight talk and facts about all sorts of abuse. The author sets the record straight on the necessity to report abuse and to understand that abuse is never the victim's fault.

Hyde, M. O. *Know about Alcohol.* Illus. by B. Morrison. McGraw-Hill, 1978. (Ages 9 and up.) [Substance] Simple description of alcohol, its use, and abuse. Information about Alcoholics Anonymous, plus resources for further information.

Hyde, M. O. *Sexual Abuse: Let's Talk about It,* rev. ed. Westminster, 1987. (Ages 11 and up.) [Sexual] The author helps young readers differentiate between good and harmful touching and explains how children can protect and help themselves.

Johnsen, K. *The Trouble with Secrets.* Illus. by L. J. Forsell. Parenting, 1986. (Ages 5–8.) [Sexual] A practical set of situations detailing which secrets are OK to keep, and which are not.

Kolodny, N. J. *When Food's a Foe.* Little, Brown, 1987. (Ages 12 and up.) [Food] The book discusses the importance of a positive self-image and self-esteem, helping the reader to identify potential problems in these areas. It defines anorexia and bulimia, their symptoms and possible causes. Kolodny provides an informative self-help section and recommends taking a personal inventory so as to develop greater self-awareness. The importance of acknowledging that there is a problem and information about how to find a therapist are also included. The author reassures people with eating disorders that they are not alone.

Kurland, M. L. *Coping with Family Violence.* Rosen, 1987. (Ages 12 and up.) [Physical, substance] Anecdotes and stories demonstrate that abusers come in many sizes and shapes and can be any relationship to the victim. Siblings, parents, teachers, coaches, and even friends are on the list. The major message is that people who are being abused must seek professional help.

Landau, E. *Child Abuse: An American Epidemic.* Messner, 1984. (Ages 11 and up.) [Physical, sexual] Tells of the depth of the problem of child abuse in our country and helps the adolescent audience to understand that seeking help is not betraying their parents. The tone is factual and resists hysteria.

Landau, E. *Why Are They Starving Themselves? Understanding Anorexia Nervosa and Bulimia.* Messner, 1983. (Ages 11 and up.) [Food] Descriptions of the illnesses and speculation about why they occur are offered here. Also included is information about methods of treatment, including self-esteem building.

Lee, E. E. *Breaking the Connection.* Messner, 1988. (Ages 11 and up.) [Substance] The author discusses how social pressure plays a role in enticing children into drug addiction. She describes treatment centers and self-help programs and includes a list of resources.

LeShan, E. *When Grownups Drive You Crazy.* Macmillan, 1988. (Ages 11 and up.) [Sexual, physical] Although the title is lighthearted, some of the problems are serious. Sexual abuse, parents who are out of control because of alcohol abuse, and parents who gravely anger or embarrass their children are described in this book of helpful advice. LeShan focuses on how young readers can help themselves.

MacLean, J. *Mac.* Houghton Mifflin, 1987. (Ages 12 and up.) [Sexual] After being sexually abused by a physician during a routine examination, Mac breaks up with his girlfriend, starts having fights at school, and in general feels as though his life is ruined. A counselor helps Mac let go of his guilt and rage and provides him with strategies for rebuilding his self-image and his life. The story is well written, but the language and details may be hard for children under twelve.

MaGorian, M. *Good Night, Mr. Tom.* Harper, 1981. (Ages 12 and up.) [Physical] Willie Beech is at first disoriented when he is sent to the country with other evacuated city children. He has been abused by his mother to the point where he has no conception of what a normal relationship is. He meets with understanding and affection. Finally, he is rescued from near death by Mr. Tom, his elderly benefactor.

Mann, J. S. *The Good Drug and the Bad Drug.* Illus. by L. Sivet. Evans, 1970. (Ages 8–12.) [Substance] A primer on the effects of drugs on our bodies. The emphasis is on basic biology. The book is nicely illustrated.

Mathis, S. B. *Listen for the Fig Tree.* Viking, 1974. (Ages 12 and up.) [Substance, sexual] [See Special Needs]

Mathis, S. B. *Teacup Full of Roses.* Viking, 1972. (Ages 12 and up.) [Substance] Three brothers in this African-American family love each other. The eldest, who is fatally addicted to drugs, is his mother's favorite; but only the middle brother survives. This story palpably demonstrates the impossibility of helping addicted people unless they want to help themselves.

McFarland, R. *Coping with Substance Abuse.* Rosen, 1987. (Ages 12 and up.) [Substance] This wide-ranging book discusses many important factors in drug abuse, including addicted parents. The author explores codependency issues and gives advice on how to avoid becoming part of the problem.

Meinke, P. "This Is a Poem to My Son Peter." In *Don't Forget to Fly,* collected by P. Janeczko. Bradbury, 1981. (Ages 10 and up.) [Physical] A different perspective is presented in this poem about a father apologizing to his son for beating him. The anguish of the father is evident in his admission that the child was the victim of his need to inflict pain.

Miner, J. C. *A Day at a Time.* Crestwood House, 1982. (Ages 9–13.) [Substance] Ellen and her mother are in denial about the severity of the father's alcoholism until he becomes violent. Ellen calls the police, and her father is sent to three weeks in a detoxification unit. During this time, her mother joins Al-Anon and begins to take control of her life. She relinquishes her guilt and begins to learn how to cope. Finally, after her father is released from treatment but again gets drunk (and this time becomes violent towards her), Ellen agrees to go to Alateen meetings. The gender-stereotypical illustrations are unfortunate, and the narrative is somewhat didactic, but the author is successful in her portrayal of a troubled family beginning recovery.

Miner, J. C. *Why Did You Leave Me?* Scholastic, 1980. (Ages 12 and up.) [Substance] Laurie's mother has spent some time in a special treatment center for alcoholics. When she returns, Laurie feels anger, jealousy, and resentment, as well as self-pity. In the end, she moves from her negative stance with the help of a nineteen-year-old woman who is a recovering alcoholic. Her mother regularly attends Alcoholics Anonymous, and it appears that she will be successful in handling her drinking problem.

Moeri, L. *The Girl Who Lived on the Ferris Wheel.* Dutton, 1979. (Ages 10 and up.) [Physical, emotional] Til's father visits with her every Saturday and takes her to an amusement park, where they ride the ferris wheel. Til is afraid to tell him that she hates the ride to the point where it gives her nightmares. She is also afraid to tell anyone that her mother physically abuses her. When Til realizes that her mother is seriously disturbed and that she herself is in danger of her life, she finally gets help.

Myers, W. D. *Motown and Didi: A Love Story.* Viking, 1984. (Ages 11 and up.) [Substance] [See Heritage]

Oppenheimer, J. *Francesca, Baby.* Scholastic, 1976. (Ages 12 and up.) [Substance] Francesca's mother is an alcoholic. Francesca and her sister protect their mother from outsiders and cut themselves off from any social contact because they are ashamed. Finally they get help from Al-Anon and force their mother to help herself.

Oppenheimer. J. *Toughing It Out.* Crosswinds, 1987. (Ages 11 and up.) [Food] The story is a fictionalized case study of a young woman who develops anorexia nervosa. Jennifer's condition is detailed step by step. Jennifer is helped by a series of interventions: her friend reports her behavior to the school nurse, who in turn tells Jennifer's parents, who take her to a competent physician. Jen is hospitalized, and the whole family goes to therapy sessions. Facts about this disorder dramatically imbedded in the novel will probably convey more to young readers than a nonfiction treatise.

Osborne, M. P. *Last One Home.* Dial, 1986. (Ages 11 and up.) [Substance] Bailey feels that her world is falling apart because of all the changes occurring in her family, and she cannot tolerate it. She begins behaving like a child with tantrums instead of a twelve year old. She gets drunk and obtains the help she needs. Her behavior is consistent with that of other children of alcoholics. It is fortunate that her father has married a woman who understands her problems.

Otto, M. *Never, No Matter What.* Illus. by C. Clarke. Women's, 1988. (Ages 3-7.) [Physical] The message is that abused women must extricate themselves and their children from abusive situations. By telling the story of Mark, his mother, and his little sister Sara, the book provides an example of an abused family who sought and received help.

Otto, M. *Tom Doesn't Visit Us Anymore.* Illus. by J. Waples. Women's, 1987. (Ages 3-5.) [Sexual] A good model of what a child should do if he or she is being abused by an adult, even if that adult is a previously trusted family friend. The parents react appropriately, and the message is clear.

Parrot, A. *Coping with Date Rape and Acquaintance Rape.* Rosen, 1988. (Ages 12 and up.) [Sexual] Myths are debunked and the message is communicated that males, as well as females, can be raped. Different categories of rapists are described. The importance of acknowledging an expanded definition of rape is emphasized, so that both men and women will understand the concepts of date-rape and accepting no as an answer.

Paulsen, G. *The Foxman.* Nelson, 1977. (Ages 12 and up.) [Physical, emotional] Carl was fifteen when he was removed from his abusive parents' house to live with his aunt and uncle in northern Minnesota. The story is one of survival, emotional and physical, on the part of both Carl and an elderly man, called the Foxman, who was horribly mutilated in World War I. The Foxman helps Carl become independent and strong and to see how cruel war is. Readers empathize with rather than pity the characters.

Platt, K. *The Boy Who Could Make Himself Disappear.* Chilton, 1968. (Ages 12 and up.) [Physical] Roger is an abused child, unloved and unwanted by his sadistic, selfish parents, who are divorced. Although he has totally lost touch with reality by the end, he at last has a friend who cares for him and who holds out hope that he can make a new life for himself. As with many of Platt's books, the writing is excellent and the situation is painful. Readers should be warned of the explicit abuse scenes.

Powell, E. S. *Daisy.* Illus. by P. J. Thornton. Carolrhoda, 1991. (Ages 5-12.) [Physical, emotional] Daisy lives with her father, who calls her names and hits her. When a new tutor at school sees some bruises and asks her about them, Daisy finally tells someone what is happening. With the help of her teacher and principal, she is put into a foster home where she is happy to be safe from the abuse. She is still concerned about her father.

Reading, J. P. *The Summer of Sassy Jo.* Houghton Mifflin, 1989. (Ages 11 and up.) [Substance/alcohol] Sara Jo is spending the summer with her estranged mother Joleen, who abandoned the family when Sara Jo was five. Joleen is a recovering alcoholic. She has got her life together and wants to win her daughter back. Joleen is not excused for the pain she caused by abandoning her family, but her situation is explained by the fact that she was an extremely depressed alcoholic who could not even take care of herself. She sought treatment and continues to go to A.A. meetings years later.

Rench, J. E. *Family Violence: How to Recognize and Survive It.* Lerner, 1992. (Ages 10 and up.) [Physical, sexual] Each chapter contains a brief but specific description of a form of family abuse. The contents include physical, emotional, sexual, elder, sibling, and domestic abuse. The last chapter discusses the importance of self-esteem and recommends some strategies for improving it. A list of resources and hotlines completes this informative, simply stated book.

Reynolds, M. *Telling.* Peace Venture, 1989. (Ages 12 and up.) [Sexual] The story focuses on a twelve-year-old girl being molested by the man for whom she babysits. Cassie confides in her cousin Lisa, who tells her parents. Cassie's abuser leaves town after he is caught assaulting a second twelve-year-old girl. Cassie begins seeing a therapist who helps her understand what happened and work through her guilt and the feeling that she might have somehow asked for it.

Rogak, L. A. *Steroids: Dangerous Game.* Lerner, 1992. (Ages 11 and up.) [Substance] Aimed at aspiring athletes, the book is divided into chapters that discuss the definition, use, abuse, and dangers of anabolic steroids. Each chapter begins with a vignette about steroid use then continues with factual information to help readers decide to stay away from them. Although the writing is at times a little heavy-handed, the book provides useful information.

Rosenberg, M. B. *Not My Family: Sharing the Truth about Alcoholism.* Bradbury, 1988. (Ages 7 and up.) [Substance] A collection of fourteen stories about both children and adults who have experienced alcoholism within their families. The author includes a list of organizations that provide assistance or information.

Sachs, M. *A December Tale.* Doubleday, 1976. (Ages 11 and up.) [Physical] Myra and Henry Fine have been placed in the home of an abusive woman and her dysfunctional family. Myra feels that she hates her brother Henry. She thinks that if Henry were not around, her father would permit her to come home. When Henry is beaten so brutally that Myra fears for his life, she realizes that she loves him and finally takes hold of their situation. The major message in this unrelievedly painful but well-written book is that abused children must take their fate into their own hands and not permit themselves to be abused.

Scott, C. J. *Kentucky Daughter.* Clarion, 1985. (Ages 12 and up.) [Sexual] Mary Fred leaves her rural home to live with her aunt and uncle in order to get a good education. Her English teacher molests her, and she has the good sense to report this to the principal. The story not only brings out the importance of a supportive family, it also deals with coping with abuse from adults and peers and the feelings of being different and ashamed of one's background.

Shuker-Hines, F. *Everything You Need to Know about Date Rape.* Rosen, 1990. (Ages 12 and up.) [Sexual] The author points out that date rape is such a hidden topic, sometimes a man does not understand that he has raped a woman, and there are even occasions when a woman does not realize that what has happened to her is rape. The definition of rape is given as "forced sex." The author clarifies and expands on the definition and helps readers overcome misinformation. She also gives helpful advice on how to prevent date rape.

Shulman, J. *Focus on Cocaine and Crack.* Illus. by D. Neuhas. 21st Century, 1990. (Ages 8–12.) [Substance] Provides information to children on cocaine and crack about the effect they have on the mind and body.

Silverstein, A., and Silverstein, V. B. *Alcoholism.* Lippincott, 1975. (Ages 11 and up.) [Substance] Comprehensive description of alcoholism: its history, physiological effects, manifestations, treatment, and implications.

Stevens, S. *The Facts about Steroids.* Crestwood House, 1991. (Ages 8–12.) [Substance] A balanced look at steroids, why people choose to use them, and the health problems they can cause. It avoids relying on scare tactics but does not mince words when describing the effects of these potentially dangerous drugs. It points out alternatives, such as exercise and diet.

Stolz, M. *The Edge of Next Year.* Harper, 1974. (Ages 12 and up.) [Substance] A moving story of the devastating effects of a mother's death on her family. The husband becomes an alcoholic, and the two boys try to fend for themselves. In the end, there is hope that the father will recover.

Taylor, B. *Everything You Need to Know about Alcohol.* Rosen, 1989. (Ages 11 and up.) [Substance] Provides information about alcohol and alcoholism. Brief vignettes illustrate the issues raised.

Taylor, D. B., and Taylor, P. M. *Coping with a Dysfunctional Family.* Rosen, 1990. (Ages 12 and up.) [Physical, emotional] Case histories help to offer practical strategies for coping with various forms of abuse.

Thesman, J. *When the Road Ends.* Illus. by R. Wisnewski. Houghton Mifflin, 1992. (Ages 10 and up.) [Physical] [See Adoption and Foster Care]

Woolverton, L. *Running Before the Wind.* Houghton Mifflin, 1987. (Ages 10 and up.) [Physical, emotional] Kelly bears the brunt of her father's abusive behavior; her mother and sister are cowed by his violence. When the father dies, Kelly is torn between relief and anguish over the death of a man she sometimes enjoyed and loved.

chapter 12

War and Peace

War as a concept is relatively easy to deal with; most people agree that it is ugly, destructive, frightening, and evil. But when it comes to interpersonal and group disputes and actual war within and among nations, when real issues must be confronted and decisions must be made whether to engage in armed conflict or intervene where it seems that human rights are being violated, the matter becomes much more complicated and murky. For children, peer relationships and problems getting along with others are akin to the concerns that emerge on a global level. They may see their arguments as black and white, while caring and impartial outsiders may be able to discern areas for potential compromise and cooperation.

Apartheid and its violent consequences, social instability in Central and South America, brutal aftereffects of the breakup of the former Soviet Union, revolution and starvation in Asia and Africa, terrorism, the volatile climate in the Middle East, and ultimately the peace-making negotiations attendant upon all these events are part of contemporary children's everyday environment. This chapter is not only about global or international war and peace. It concerns how people behave with each other and how communities are built or destroyed. It also looks at competition, bullying, and friendship in order to explore how individual relationships can serve as modes for the acquisition and demonstration of peace-making and peace-keeping skills.

Complications arise when we move beyond the generalized realm of war as a concept. Then we encounter a sometimes tangled web of issues including causes, individual concerns, power struggles, ethical decisions, and conduct during war. Historically, the incursions of the United States against Native populations were considered justified by settlers who wanted the indigenous people's land. Battles won by natives were "massacres"; but those in which Native Americans were defeated were "victories." To some people, the Spanish-American War was a nakedly imperialistic seizure of land by the United States. To others it was the rescue of land from Spanish dictatorial control. World War I was considered the war to end all wars, and a righteous cause to some people. To opponents, it was interference in European politics. Korea and Vietnam were the sites of conflicts many Americans believed we should have avoided, while others considered it our obligation to defend these countries from Communist domination.

Today's children, living in an era of so many controversial armed conflicts, probably have been exposed to a wider variety of responses to war than were children growing up during the time of World War II, when there was widespread (though not unanimous) support for American involvement. Those who dissented were often labeled traitors, fascists, or cowards.

Feelings about a specific war can run very high, particularly while the conflict is raging. National response is greatest when our own soldiers are involved, but we also react emotionally when people with whom we are concerned, even indirectly, are engaged in war. The issues become very complex, depending on the level of the relationship between us and the warring nations. Sides are drawn; arguments are presented for and against the combatants as well as the issues; action is proposed.

Just as there is concern about how nations can negotiate and settle disputes peacefully, so it is for individuals. Children can learn to be mediators and peacemakers. Even in kindergarten there are programs that focus on what children can do for themselves and for one another to lessen competition and encourage cooperation.

In order to encourage the kind of constructive decision making necessary for a healthy society, children should be exposed to the complexities of moral and political issues. Young children may not comprehend all the ramifications of specific situations, but they can understand the processes of escalation and competition. They can perceive the ambiguity, as well as the logic, of what is right or fair. Their daily interactions, on a scaled-down level, invite the same sorts of decisions political leaders must handle for their countries.

SUGGESTED CRITERIA

Books, especially those purporting to be realistic, should provide evidence that the causes of wars are not simple. One issue or incident is rarely the entire reason that armed conflict has ensued.

An effective book dealing with war should present some indication of the difficulty of viewing any confrontation in absolute terms. When only one side is right, the story usually becomes less effective than its author intended.

Books extolling the glory of battle are likely to be propaganda if they do not also reveal war's bloody and mundane aspects.

Some authors fear that young children cannot understand complexity. They therefore write in oversimplified terms rather than risk confusing their readers. Children can handle many ideas at one time. They can follow subplots and sort out characters. Another criterion, therefore, for a book about war is that it contain enough detail and depth to convey a sense of the many facets of war, the participants, and the historical events.

Books should try to avoid inflammatory language or propaganda. In works of nonfiction terms such as *massacre, sneaky, cowardly, noble-hearted, patriotic,* or *heroic* signal a prejudicial attitude on the author's part. In fiction, the author also needs to take care in the use of language with powerful emotional connotations. Teachers can instruct children how to recognize and deal with bias; it is a detriment to literary quality, as well as historical balance.

Although overly gruesome details or gratuitous violence are not advisable, books should not trivialize the realities of war.

Peace should not seem to be achieved totally or suddenly.

Problems do not evaporate because a war is over. Authors should acknowledge this by indicating what yet remains unresolved.

Solutions should be presented in understandable and believable terms. Even in fantasies, the resolution should be plausible.

Plot and character should carry the message. Even in books for young children, details should be accurate and story lines should be logical.

In the case of bullies, children should be shown finding a solution if possible. However, adults should intercede appropriately.

Most books should avoid the clichéd ending where the bully becomes the victim's best friend.

Most books should avoid the overused literary device wherein the victim overcomes the bully by physical force, improbably converting the bully to a nonviolent person.

To qualify as a friend or a member of the group, a character should not be required to save someone's life or commit other heroic acts.

The format of the book should signal the appropriate developmental level of the reader. In general, picture books should not be so grisly, violent, or sophisticated as to confuse, frighten, or overwhelm young readers.

Authors should recognize that young children need concrete references. Too many abstract concepts should be avoided.

Historical facts should be well researched and show evidence of consultation with a variety of sources and perspectives.

Facts and opinion should be distinguishable.

Illustrations and writing should be of high quality, free of stereotypes, sentimentality, or cliché.

Enemies and allies should be presented in perspective as human beings with virtues and flaws. They should not solely be combatants.

Try This

Examine three books about a specific war, such as the American Civil War or the World War II. How does each author treat the "enemy"? How human are the characters? What are set forth as the causes of the war? How complex are these causes? How unanimous are the opinions of all the "good" characters? Compare the three books. How much more insight or information do you think you gained about the war because you consulted more than one source?

DISCUSSION OF CHILDREN'S BOOKS

With the breakup of Communist governments and the resulting dissipation of the Cold War, there has been an enormous shift in literature, as well as the popular press, away from the fear of a nuclear holocaust, even though nations are still capable of producing nuclear weapons. The literature now focuses more on providing a world view of how nations may learn to live in peace with one another, or a least understand the various factors that are at play in international relations.

Books describing interpersonal dissension, group clashes, and wars can be written from a number of perspectives, among them those that take sides and present the history in a selective manner so as to blame one side and totally exonerate the other. Some authors personalize the conflict, choosing one family or one specific group of people to convey the effects of war more intimately and therefore more concretely. A number of books deal with friendships, smooth and rough, with the strife resolved in a variety of ways.

BOOKS FOR YOUNG CHILDREN

Allegories and Picture Books

Many books written for very young children concentrating on the theme of war are attempts at allegory. Their usual intent is to show that war is meaningless and hurtful. Unfortunately, in a preponderance of these books the construction of the plot is so absurd or untenable that the reader, no matter how young, is tempted to relegate the lesson to the ranks of often-heard but seldom-heeded proverbs and wise sayings. Recognizing the truism, they divorce it from real-life behavior. A notable exception is *Terrible Things: An Allegory of the Holocaust,* by Eve Bunting. In this story, suitable for young children but compelling enough to interest adults, the woodland creatures accept without question the systematic annihilation of the other species, one by one. They even try to accommodate to the loss: "Those birds were too noisy. . . . There's more space in the trees now." In the end, when even the white rabbits, the last survivors, have been captured and removed, the littlest white rabbit, who escapes, sadly vows to tell creatures in other forests about what has happened here. He hopes they will listen to his message that the animals could have banded together, protected one another, and prevented the catastrophe.

In some picture books, the authors portray the pain and discomfort of war and illustrations complement this intent, but peace comes through a simplistic solution. These need to be compared to reality.

One book that lends itself to debate and investigation is *Drummer Hoff,* by Barbara Emberly. The colorful, bold illustrations by her husband Ed are essential to the book, which won the Caldecott Award in 1968. Details and subtleties within both the illustrations and the plot bear repeated examination. The story is simple: A band of soldiers assembles and fires a cannon. The refrain, "But Drummer Hoff fired it off," is repeated throughout. The text describes the military preparations carried on by each of the soldiers, starting with the general. A two-page spread of the actual firing is impressive. At the end, the cannon is left in a field of grass and flowers, a haven for grasshoppers, spiders, and birds.

The refrain seems to indicate that firing the cannon is a grand event and that Drummer Hoff is to be envied. But a close inspection of the soldiers reveals that the powder man has a wooden leg and that one soldier has only one eye. The text, coming from an old folk rhyme, could be interpreted as nonsense, as prowar in celebrating the act of the drummer, or as antiwar in that all the upper-echelon soldiers pass the burden of responsibility for the act of destruction onto the drummer.

Young children may need help noticing some of the details of this intricate book. They can be invited to discuss why the cannon is all by itself in the field without any people around it at the end. They might be asked how they would feel if they were the drummer. Those readers particularly interested in things military can assemble a hierarchical listing of ranks and analyze the importance of the task according to rank.

Kjell Ringi has designed an allegory that works well. *The Winner* has no text whatsoever; the story is told entirely through the illustrations. The plot, in which two characters trying to outdo each other with increasingly elaborate costumes and weapons are finally destroyed, communicates the dangers of escalation and competition. It demonstrates that the acquisition of powerful weapons destroys everyone. In this case, a dragon is the ultimate weapon that eventually eats its master. Children of any age, and adults as well, can learn from this book. The illustrations are colorful and amusing. The arms race begins innocuously and ends in disaster. Perhaps the absence of words is one of the greatest advantages of the book; it ensures that each reader will insert vocabulary appropriate and manageable at his or her level. The ending is not happy, even for the dragon, because now there is no one left to eat and he is all alone. The people do not spring magically back to life. They are dead.

This book could provide the stimulus for some extensive thought and investigation of the problems inherent in waging war. Children can write their own text or dictate the words to an adult. They can construct puppets and perform the story in front of an audience.

Several authors have attempted to help children deal with conflict and competition with their peers. By extension, this interpersonal friction can be looked at as a model of problem solving on a larger scale. Crosby Bonsall's *Mine's the Best* is a very easy to read book describing an argument between two boys who are carrying identical balloons. Each believes his balloon is best. The balloons are destroyed as the argument grows heated. At that point, a girl walks by with a balloon identical to theirs. Quickly, the former enemies align with each other and say, "Ours was the best." The analogy is not unlike that of countries at war becoming allies when new adversaries appear.

Three other books—*The Hating Book,* by Charlotte Zolotow; *Let's Be Enemies,* by Janice May Udry; and *I Am Better Than You,* by Robert Lopshire— describe arguments between friends and their eventual resolution. These books may not have been designed to carry a message beyond that of children and their disagreements, but if a group of children and a teacher are talking about war and conflict among nations, this sort of book is perfect as an introduction or even as a case in point when analyzing the more complex international situations. On the other hand, it is equally important to address the incidents for what they are and focus on the immediate matter of children maintaining peace in their own personal relationships.

The Hating Book is about a misunderstanding in which one child mistakes what she hears her friend say. Until the error is cleared up, the friendship is on rocky ground. The child's mother keeps suggesting that her daughter ask her friend directly why she is behaving in such an unfriendly way. When at last the girl takes her mother's advice, the misunderstanding dissolves. Nations do not function so directly and easily, but at least this serves as a model for peaceful behavior for children.

Let's Be Enemies is somewhat different. Two boys are friends, but one is angry because of the other's constant bossy behavior. John becomes so angry at James's behavior that he goes to his house to declare that they are no longer friends, whereupon James also declares his enmity for John. Strangely enough, with no seeming intervention, John invites James to go roller-skating and James offers John a pretzel. Perhaps this does happen when children quarrel, but they should be encouraged to exercise judgment and recognize rational behavior. Why should they be friends if they mistreat each other?

I Am Better Than You involves two lizards who look exactly alike to the reader. One of them, Sam, is determined to prove that he is the best lizard there is. He is very competitive and quarrelsome. Pete, the other lizard, is a perfect model of even temperament and good fellowship. Finally, after it is shown that Sam is no better but is, in fact, somewhat silly, Pete and Sam resume their friendship. Pete's behavior could be used as an example of how to avoid wars, or at least arguments.

Addie Lacoe's *Just Not the Same* features triplets whose patient and inventive mother tries to mediate among them when each wants her own way. They finally learn to cooperate when they receive a puppy for a gift, even though it is not the same as if each had her own dog.

Books about friendships and their maintenance, such as the *Frog and Toad* series, by Arnold Lobel, and the *George and Martha* series, by James Marshall, are entertaining stories that also model how individuals with very different personalities, strengths, and needs can get along together. Sometimes the going is bumpy, but with enough good will, tolerance for idiosyncrasies, and a willingness to let go of peeves, a strong friendship can be preserved.

History

There are fewer books for younger children that relate to actual wars than there are books that deal with war in general. Nathaniel Benchley has contributed an easy-to-read book about the American Revolutionary War called *Sam the Minuteman*. The young boy, Sam, helps his father fight at the Battle of Lexington. Benchley does an excellent job of communicating the fear and anger caused by the incidents of the battle. By graphically showing Sam's reactions when his friend is wounded, he personalizes the experience of war for young children. Sam's ideals take second place to his immediate responses. Although bravery is valued, Benchley makes it clear that raw survival sometimes has nothing to do with heroism. The book manages an excellent balance between recognizing that the war had a cause and showing that war itself is a gruesome experience. Nothing much is said about the British side, but there is enough in this book to start some thoughtful inquiry about the different shades of justification for warfare.

The Revolutionary War, the Civil War, and World War II are well represented in literature, especially for older children. But one war this author had never heard of is the subject of a book by Betty Baker called *The Pig War.* It describes a real war that took place in 1859 off the coast of the state of Washington, where there was a small island whose rightful ownership was disputed. Both the British and the Americans claimed possession. American farmers lived there, as did a small detachment of British soldiers. The conflict erupted when a small display of patriotism escalated into a grand display of power. In the end, the armies sent to fight ate up so much of the island's produce that the regular inhabitants became disgusted and sent both armies away. They decided to live in peace with one another until at last ownership was given to the United States. The story sounds too good to be true, but the author assures us of its authenticity. Children can begin a correspondence with her through the publisher and can send to the Washington State Historical Society to investigate the Pig War. Research skills could be practiced to good advantage by using this book as a starter.

The Holocaust cannot generally be brought to the developmental level of a five-to-eight year old. As was mentioned earlier, Eve Bunting's *Terrible Things* brings allegory to the subject in terms that children can understand. David Adler has written *The Number on My Grandfather's Arm,* intended for this age group, focusing on a child's curiosity about the tattoo indicating his grandfather's incarceration in a concentration camp. The story is told as gently as possible and serves as an introduction to the Holocaust while focusing on the importance of listening to people and respecting their feelings, as well as their experience.

Ken Mochizuki's *Baseball Saved Us* brings another painful experience—the internment of Japanese Americans during World War II—to the attention of young readers. The story focuses on the cooperative construction of a baseball field as an indicator of how the human spirit is capable of constructive energy and activity, even in times of extraordinary hardship.

Poetry

Nursery rhymes and nonsense verses for young children mention war more often than is at first apparent. Usually the pageantry and excitement of war in general are mentioned in these verses. The first section of one collection, *Drums and Trumpets,* compiled by Leonard Clark, is called "Here Come Processions." Martial poems of homage comprise most of the selections, but a Thomas Hardy poem, "Men Who March Away," hints at the futility of war and the lack of comprehension on the part of the people who fight about why they are there.

A deeply moving book of poetry was selected from the archives of the State Jewish Museum in Prague by Hana Volavkova. *I Never Saw Another Butterfly* contains children's drawings and poems from the Terezin concentration camp. All the young poets represented in this book were destroyed by the war. Their camp was a way-station to extermination centers, and they knew this; but their poetry speaks more of the joy of life than of a fear of, or preoccupation with, death. They express hope, love, and determination to survive. This powerful antiwar book does not preach against war and does not moralize. It conveys its strong message because of the information the reader brings to the poetry. It is therefore a book that knowledgeable adults should share with others and encourage children to read so that the strength of the message can be reinforced.

Although Eve Bunting's *The Wall* does not describe the fighting in Vietnam, its touching story of a father and son who visit the memorial in Washington, D.C., communicates the grief that this and any other war engenders.

BOOKS FOR OLDER CHILDREN

Beginning at a personal level, books such as *Blubber,* by Judy Blume; *The Hundred Dresses,* by Eleanor Estes; and *The Goats,* by Brock Cole, serve as examples of children forming groups and scapegoating others. In none of these books is there evidence of any adult intervention. In *Blubber,* Jill is the narrator. Wendy is the thoroughly unlikable ringleader whose latest object of persecution is Linda, ostensibly because Linda is somewhat overweight. Jill finally summons up the inner strength to break away from Wendy's influence, only to find herself the new victim of the gang. Rather than being grateful to Jill, Linda joins Wendy and the other children in their tormenting behavior. Because Wendy is never confronted about her behavior and because the children unquestioningly follow her leadership, significant discussion would have to accompany the reading of this story. Children can be invited to provide various solutions to Jill's and Linda's dilemmas.

The Hundred Dresses offers a somewhat more thoughtful resolution to the problem of exclusion and subjecting children to ridicule. This Newbery Honor book is a classic that retains its freshness and relevance today. It is the story of Maddie and her friends who torment a girl named Wanda because she is different from them (she is Polish), is poor, comes from a different part of town, and wears the same dress to school every day. The behavior is precipitated when Wanda says she has one hundred dresses in her closet. It turns out that Wanda has drawn the dresses on her closet walls and that she is a talented artist. Maddie never gets the opportunity to apologize for her behavior because Wanda and her family move away before the dresses are discovered. Maddie's regret at not being able to make amends leads her to promise herself that she will never again participate in bullying behavior.

The Goats begins with a disturbing enactment of what is evidently an acceptable ritual of scapegoating on the part of a group of youngsters at a summer camp. The two hapless victims manage to survive their ordeal, and the story deals with much more than this single incident; but it is important for children to discuss what they would do if they were confronted with a kind of mob hysteria involving the persecution of others. In this story, the two victims become friends and provide a model of how cooperation and collaboration can overcome adversity.

Every book about friendship is a book about peace. *Always and Forever Friends,* by C. S. Adler, demonstrates that friendships are not necessarily built on similarities but can flourish when they are based on trust and understanding. *Bridge to Terabithia,* by Katherine Paterson, portrays a friendship between two young people that transcends differences, social pressure, and even death. Cynthia Voigt's series of books about the Tillerman family and their friends supports the importance of friendship, particularly in times of emotional difficulties. In Patricia MacLachlan's *Arthur, for the Very First Time,* Moira and Arthur demonstrate that working out difficulties can help in the process of maturing and developing a sense of self.

It is critical for children to understand that maintaining friendships involves active work, just as the global effort to bring about and preserve peace requires constant effort, understanding, and willingness to listen and adapt. Problem solving that uses means other than violence, a willingness to live with ambiguity, a genuine respect for others' values and customs, and a commitment to a global community should be modeled in books, as well as in life, so that our goal of world peace can be achieved.

In contrast to books written for the very young, most of the books about war written for older children are specific and based on fact. The bulk of the work falls under the category of historical fiction, but there are fantasies such as the Narnia series, by C.S. Lewis, containing descriptions of battles and wars that symbolize the conflict between good and evil. The message of these works is that violence and bloodshed are justified when the cause is virtuous. Lewis does not guarantee that good will triumph, but he avers that the fight is worth it.

History (Fiction and Nonfiction)

For older children, most books about war involve young heroes of both sexes so as to arouse interest and empathy in the readers. Some stories, such as Anne Frank's *Diary,* are true accounts told in the first person. These books, which carry enormous impact, are generally the ones that readers remember best after a long period of time. Children need to recognize that although certain elements of war are universal, each war has its own individual complexities and issues. The intent in dealing with these books is to affect future attitudes and behavior. Teachers and librarians should follow through on the children's reading with questions, discussions, and recommendations for further readings.

Revolutionary War

The Colliers' *My Brother Sam Is Dead,* a Newbery honor book and a finalist for the National Book Award, leaves the reader with the intriguing question of whether this war was absolutely necessary for the founding of the United States as an independent nation. The authors help readers to view the American Revolution as a personal tragedy for some people, communicating that it was not the splendid patriotic event depicted in many books and films. *The Fighting Ground,* by Avi, conveys the same message about this war. Each of these books focuses on a young boy's experiences and on the differing views held by members of their families and communities.

Civil War

Most books about the Civil War take a stance that the North was totally virtuous while the South had no redeeming arguments. The war is usually described as a wrenching one for our country, but it is seldom explained that both sides had their villains, as well as their heroes.

Irene Hunt's *Across Five Aprils*—more about people than it is about war—concerns a family living in southern Illinois at the time of the Civil War. In this story, the "good guys" are not always on the "right" side.

For Jethro, who is nine years old, war is an exciting idea. He believes that it will solve all problems and demonstrate the validity of the Union. He anticipates the thrill of battle and the satisfaction of overcoming an enemy.

Bill, an admirable and likable character, decides to fight against Northern arrogance and hypocrisy, even though he knows that no side is in the right. His reflections help the reader understand that what the history books depict as a clearcut cause is not, after all, that simple.

Across Five Aprils was a Newbery Honor Book in 1965. Very well written, it uncovers many levels of emotion and behavior in wartime. It helps students compare different accounts of battles, causes of war, and issues in order to begin to construct a balanced, informed view. It also indicates that the end of the war is not triumphant but full of agony and anxiety over the future of the nation.

Shades of Gray by Carolyn Reeder, explores issues through the eyes of a boy, Will Page, who is forced to live with his pacifist uncle after his parents, who supported the Confederacy, are dead. Will's growing understanding of the deeper dilemmas involved in war and its aftermath forms the basis for the story.

World War I

There are not nearly as many books about this war as there are about World War II. Classics such as *All Quiet on the Western Front*, by Erich Maria Remarque, focus on the futility and senselessness of war. A poignant section in a book of nonfiction, *War in the Trenches*, by Stewart Ross, reveals the extraordinary brief period of fraternization that occurred, mostly between British and German troops, on Christmas Eve, 1914. From time to time, the author inserts quotations from solders' journals and writing to indicate how individuals felt. He also includes cartoons, newspaper clippings, and photographs to communicate the atmosphere of the times. The book clearly demonstrates the complexity of the causes and the devastating effects of the war. The world was shocked by the extent and pain of this conflict, and probably the best literature to emerge about this war took the form of poetry expressing that emotional response.

As indicated in the Poetry section, Edward Sel Hudson's *Poetry of the First World War* dramatically depicts how terrible it was to fight in the war. Many fine poets contributed to this collection, and each poem is illustrated with a photograph from The Imperial War Museum in Great Britain. In some instances, the photos are more shocking, revealing, and painful than the words.

World War II

Almost above all others, this war had the support of most of the country. Books about World War II focus on the experiences of people in other countries, since that is where the battles were fought. *The Summer of My German Soldier*, by Bette Greene, however, centers on Patty, a desperately unhappy and lonely twelve-year-old Jewish girl in a small Southern town. When German prisoners of war are brought to the town, Patty befriends one of them. Her parents are emotionally abusive to her. Ruth, the African-American maid, cook, and house-keeper, is Patty's only friend.

The German soldier is a likable, intelligent, nonviolent young man. The reader hopes he will escape; but he is caught, despite Patty's help, and killed. He does not fit the pattern of the German that Americans were taught to recognize.

The book discloses some little-known facts about prisoners of war held in the United States. It also humanizes the enemy and demonstrates that not all German soldiers were Nazis. This is all the more important since many books about this war concentrate on the "rightness" of the Allied side and the bestiality of the Nazis, with no conflicting issues raised. They do not address any of the abstract questions that pertain to war in general. When is it right to kill or maim? When both sides believe that they are right, who can say where crimes lie? World War II in particular seems to invite only one answer. No matter what the conclusions, the process of inquiry and investigation contributes to greater clarity of thought and perspective.

Holocaust

It is difficult for children to conceive of as monumentally evil an undertaking as the planned elimination of an entire people. Gypsies and other "undesirables" also were marked for extermination, but the Jewish population was the prime target. Because it is so difficult to believe that such an event was permitted to occur, it is all the more important that Holocaust curricula and books be provided for children to read and understand.

One exemplary planned curriculum on genocide focuses on the Holocaust. Designed for adolescents, the materials of Strom and Parsons's *Facing History and Ourselves: Holocaust and Human Behavior* can be adapted to other age levels. Books are recommended and information is provided for a variety of sessions probing historical, psychological, economic, and political factors.

Some books on this topic deal specifically with children and their lives. Judith Kerr's *When Hitler Stole Pink Rabbit* describes a family who escapes from Germany just before Hitler's election. Their father is an anti-Nazi journalist. The family is Jewish, although they have not practiced the religion actively. They go to Switzerland, where they are physically safe, but where they unhappily encounter anti-Semitism. They then move to France and ultimately to England. Not a horror story, this book details the small everyday discomforts and large fears occasioned by Hitler's takeover. It provides an interesting perspective for readers who have been exposed only to the tragic Anne Frank.

A story quite similar to Anne Frank's *Diary* and also based on fact, is Johanna Reiss's *Upstairs Room*. It has a different ending: The people hidden away from the Germans emerge alive at the end of the war. This book describes the individual actions of people who risk their own lives to save other people, not in active combat but through acts of quiet courage. These are ordinary people who believe they are responsible for others and become important heroes of this war. At Yad Vashem, the institution in Jerusalem dedicated to the study and documentation of the Holocaust, there is a beautiful tree-lined path called "The Path of the Righteous." Each of the trees represents a non-Jewish person or family who risked their lives to protect Jews. Milton Meltzer's *Rescue: The Story of How*

Gentiles Saved Jews in the Holocaust provides ample testimony to the inspiring courage of such people as Joop and Wil Westerweel, Andre and Magda Trocme, Raoul Wallenberg, Oskar Schindler, and Anna Simaite. Many other individuals are mentioned in this book, along with the rulers and the general populations of countries such as Bulgaria and Denmark.

Books like *Lisa's War,* by Carol Matas, bring to life the valiant and successful efforts of the Danish people, in concert with the Jews themselves, to prevent the annihilation of the Danish Jews. This book reveals some little-known information, as well as a balanced view of what really happened in Denmark. It presents both the Jews and the Danes as varied individuals, neither saints nor devils, working together to combat the Nazi edict.

One of the most devastatingly effective books on the Holocaust is *Friedrich,* by Hans Peter Richter, written from the perspective of a non-Jewish German boy. Perhaps the most powerful part of the book is the unadorned chronology appended to the text, recounting the regulations put into effect against the Jews. The sadistic thoroughness of the Nazi oppression is exemplified by such regulations as those forbidding Jews to keep pets, go to barbershops, or use public phones. This story does not have a happy ending; few stories about the Holocaust do. But children become involved in the action and with the characters and think about the implications of the message long after they close the book.

Another story that does not end happily but keeps the reader glued to its pages is *Alan and Naomi,* by Myron Levoy. The story takes place in New York City in the 1940s. Naomi, who saw her father brutally beaten to death by Nazis in her native France, is seriously emotionally disabled. Now she and her mother have moved into the apartment house where Alan and his family live. For a while it seems that Alan will help her to adjust to normal living, but a vicious anti-Semitic remark provokes Alan to become involved in a fistfight, and Naomi relapses. The book ends with questions about the meaning of life, as well as the causes of hatred and how to respond to hateful language.

Some books (like *Lisa's War*) help to offset the stereotype that all Jews were passive victims. *Uncle Misha's Partisans,* by Yuri Suhl, tells of an actual band of Jewish guerrillas who wrought much damage on the German army. One of the partisans is a young boy named Mottele. He is also the subject of a book by Gertrude Samuels called *Mottele.* Both books are designed for students no younger than ten or eleven years of age. The stories are not pretty, but they are true, and their message is important for young people to learn.

The necessity of telling the story to children comes through clearly in Jane Yolen's *The Devil's Arithmetic.* In it, Hannah is reluctant to go to her grandfather's seder because she feels distanced from the experiences her grandfather and great-aunt endured during the Holocaust. When she herself lives the nightmare (through the magic of time travel), she emerges with a deeper appreciation of her heritage and of the necessity to prevent such a calamity from ever happening again. Another book that deals with the effect of children's understanding what happened during the Holocaust is Gary and Gail Levine Provost's *David and Max.* David's grandfather Max encounters an old friend who he thought was killed in the concentration camps. It turns out that the man was so guilt-ridden about his survival that he took a new name, identity, and life, and categorically denied ever having been his former self. This leads Max to tell David about his experiences in a concentration camp.

Many journals have been published in the past ten years, perhaps because people realize that if they do not reveal their stories now, the stories may never be told. These first-hand accounts underscore the horror, but they also carry with them a sense of hope that the world has changed as a result of recoiling from the atrocities of the Holocaust. Books such as *To Life,* by Ruth Minsky Sender; *Gideon,* by Chester Aaron; *Stolen Years* and *Struggle,* by Sara Zyskind; and *I Am a Star,* by Inge Auerbacher, personalize the events and move them to a more individual level.

Korean War

Pearl S. Buck's *Matthew, Mark, Luke and John* tells about the plight of abandoned children after the Korean War. They are offspring of G.I.s and Korean women. The author explains that Koreans consider children to belong to the father and his family; therefore these children are outcasts. Unable to withstand the social pressure, some of the mothers desert the children.

This book tells about four of these children, each with a distinctive personality, who fortuitously band together for survival. It neither deals with causes nor take sides but recounts the effects of any war on the people after the war is over. The story has a somewhat pat happy ending: the children are all adopted. If students want to explore further the problems resulting from the impact of American military presence in foreign countries, they can research newspaper and magazine accounts.

Sook Nyul Choi, the author of the autobiographical *Year of Impossible Goodbyes,* describes her family's tribulations at the hands of the occupying Japanese forces in northern Korea during World War II and at the beginning of the Korean conflict. Another story taken from real life and set in the same place and time is Yoko Kawashima Watkins's *So Far from the Bamboo Grove.* The author and some of her family, Japanese by birth, escape North Korean soldiers who are angry that Japanese people have occupied their country. The story describes a little-known series of circumstances stemming from the war. Very little else, other than Richard Edwards's factual account, *The Korean War,* tells about this war.

Vietnam War

In contrast to World War II, the contest in Vietnam was probably the least popular of any American foreign involvement. Margot C. Mabie's *Vietnam, There and Here* manages to provide a thorough and even-handed picture of the context, as well as the specifics, of this hotly debated war. She offers both the "Doves'" and the "Hawks'" positions, complete with rationales. Unfortunately, most books have neglected a balance of views and thus do not prepare children to make their own decisions about this or any other war.

Walter Dean Myers's *Fallen Angels* presents the war "up close and personal," as seen through the eyes of seventeen-year-old Richie Perry. His interactions with his comrades, a group of young men from various backgrounds, demonstrate the ordinary discomforts of the war, as well as the extraordinary pain and fear it engenders. In comparison, *My Name Is San Ho,* by Jayn Pettit, relates the experiences of a young Vietnamese boy who suffers the loss of his home and family until he can rejoin his newly remarried mother in the United States. His story continues to his eventual settling in Philadelphia, with all its new customs. He is confronted with racist behavior, but he is most impressed by the absence of the devastation of war.

Ironically, one of the most positive results of this conflagration is the memorial commemorating it. In *Always to Remember: The Story of the Vietnam Veterans Memorial,* Brent Ashabranner gives a brief, balanced history of the war then tells of how the Vietnam Veterans Memorial Wall came about. By sharing some of the notes visitors to the wall have left there, he provides an account certain to touch each reader personally. Eve Bunting's *The Wall,* listed in the section for young children, can also be used with older students. The wall figures prominently in *Park's Quest,* by Katherine Paterson. Park cannot begin to heal his hurt over his father's death until he physically visits the wall to see his father's name inscribed on it.

Poetry

The poems included in the section for young readers are appropriate for older ones as well. The writings of the doomed children in the concentration camp invoke an even deeper response when understood by more mature readers. Some preteens can even handle Kenneth Patchen's bitter war poetry. Many of our most renowned poets have written several poems about war, some of them pointing to the eventual glory of battle. Julia Ward Howe's "Battle Hymn of the Republic" grew to be the most popular marching song of the Civil War.

In popular music, many poems are the lyrics of songs that decry war. Several describe war as bloody and meaningless. Folk songs such as "Johnny Has Gone for a Soldier" speak of the agonies of war and its aftermath. A reading of *The Judy Collins Songbook* will unearth antiwar songs, as will *The Joan Baez Songbook.* "Where Have All the Flowers Gone?" by Pete Seeger, is based on a traditional Russian folk song. Both pro- and anti-war perspectives are available both in verse and in longer works of fiction and nonfiction. How the teacher or librarian uses them can be of utmost importance.

Some poetry has emerged as a result of specific wars. Edward Sel Hudson's *Poetry of the First World War* is a heart-rending commentary on war. In Mel Glenn's *Class Dismissed! High School Poems,* the poem "Song Vu Chin" reflects the feelings of a young Vietnamese immigrant remembering the horrors of war in his country and resenting the ignorance of his current classmates. His perspective can cause young people untouched by war and knowing violence only vicariously to consider their responsibilities in this world.

General Nonfiction

Subject Guide to Children's Books in Print lists many books of nonfiction about each war and war in general. Albert Carr's *A Matter of Life and Death* is addressed to the minds of young people, as well as their emotions. Carr makes a distinction between "death patriotism" and "life patriotism." The first requires the death of one's enemies; the other aims at improving one's country. Using the Spanish-American War as an example of how our country has dealt with war, he describes several ways in which the war could have been averted. He also details several other wars. Although he offers no concrete ideas for avoiding war in the future, he does recommend that young people make their opinions known to their legislative representatives. This is a clearly written book that makes readers aware of the complexities of international relationships and of the necessity for responsible personal and public behavior.

In looking at any factual accounts of wars, a reader is cautioned to examine more than one point of view. Questions should be raised, not only for purposes of criticism but also for analysis. If readers of all ages acquire the habit of actively questioning what they read and if that process is valued by people they respect, one of the more important goals of responsible education is accomplished. Besides examining and evaluating history texts, students should read and compare accounts of a war from the perspectives of different countries. As they watch for the author's attitude toward war in general, they should try to determine if and where that point of view intrudes. Is war considered a patriotic, sublime enterprise? Is it viewed as exclusively evil, never with just and ample cause? Are wars differentiated one from the other? How is the reader's decision-making ability enhanced as a result of reading the book? Are peaceful alternatives suggested?

Peace

Very few children's books are written with the imbedded concept of peacemaking as an active part of the plot. Several works of nonfiction, however, do address the issues directly. Although *Peace Begins with You,* by Katherine Scholes, is like a small sermon, its message is beautifully presented. The author offers the concept of peace as an active entity needing nurturing rather than a vacuum existing between wars. Laurie Dolphin has written two nonfiction books that demonstrate the possibilities of peace between people of different, and even warring, nations: *Georgia to Georgia: Making Friends in the U.S.S.R.* and *Neve-Shalom/Wahat Al-Salam: Oasis of Peace.* Specific projects bind together the children and people of such disparate places as Atlanta, Georgia and Georgia, in the former Soviet Union, and such hostile factions as Israelis and Arabs in Israel.

War is ugly; it kills. There are other ways, better ways, of solving the world's problems. But as long as war continues to occur, we must try to learn as much as we can about its causes and effects, using information rather than propaganda. Perhaps one day we will have the ability to avoid it and to resolve our conflicts in less disastrous fashions. In the meantime, it would be beneficial if people learned more about how to cooperate with one another at a more personal and local level.

REFERENCES

War and Peace

Ashton, P. T., ed. *Journal of Teacher Education* 42 (Jan.-Feb., 1991). The theme of this volume is "Educating for a Global Society." It discusses the inclusion of global education across the curriculum.

Bauer, Y. "They Chose Life: Jewish Resistance in the Holocaust." American Jewish Committee, 1973. This pamphlet traces the various forms of Jewish resistance and counteracts the stereotypes of the passive victim.

Butler, F. "The Theme of Peace in Children's Literature." *The Lion and the Unicorn,* June 1990, pp. 128–138. Discusses many children's books that contain within them conflict and peaceful resolution on the personal, family, communal, national, or international levels; sometimes on several levels in the same story.

Carlsson-Paige, N., and Levin, D. E. *Who's Calling the Shots? How to Respond Effectively to Children's Fascination with War Play and War Toys.* New Society, 1990. This helpful book discusses children's developmental levels of play. It provides activities for parents to join with their children, recommendations for toys and materials, and strategies to help children develop constructive attitudes and values of peace.

Carpenter, L. "You Can Be a Peacemaker." *Parade Magazine,* Aug. 26, 1990, pp. 17–18. Describes the multitude of local and national organizations trying to make peace less a dream and more a reality.

Chatton, B., and Tastad, S. "The American Revolution: 1754–1783." *Book Links,* May 1993, pp. 7–12. Topics include "What makes a revolution right?" and causes and effects of the war. Biographies of American leaders are recommended. The basic thesis is that students should be aware that attitudes have changed over time and learn to form their own. A thorough annotated bibliography accompanies the article.

Cheatham, A. "Annotated Bibliography for Teaching Conflict Resolution in Schools." National Association for Mediation in Education. 1989. The bibliography is divided into three large sections, each containing brief annotations of children's books, manuals, and workbooks for adults, and various materials of an instructional nature, all aimed at helping children become successful at conflict resolution.

Cloud, K., et al. *Watermelons, Not War: A Support Guide for Parenting in the Nuclear Age.* New Society, 1984. A wonderful resource for teachers and parents examining the realities of nuclear power, alternatives, and many suggestions for taking action.

Cooney, R., and Michalowski, H., eds. *The Power of the People: Active Nonviolence in the United States.* New Society, 1987. A compilation of readings on the history of the nonviolence movement from 1650 to the present. Beginning with Chief Seattle's message and including the various civil rights, women's, and labor movements, among others, the book is a comprehensive resource. It lists organizations and contains a bibliography.

Cordova, J. M. T. "Reflections on Conflict Management as an Empowering Process for Students . . . and for Me." *ESR Journal* (1990): 50–61. Training consists of "active listening, communication, and problem-solving skills," which has greatly helped teachers. Skills taught to the students emphasize the need for communication over physical violence.

Council on Interracial Books for Children. *Bulletin* 13 (Nos. 6 & 7, 1982). (Special issue on militarism and education.) Contains a number of articles critiquing materials, including children's books and textbooks, that deal with the topic of war.

Dawidowicz, L. S. *The War against the Jews: 1933–1945.* Bantam, 1976. Shows how the destruction of the Jews figured in Hitler's goals and with what demonic energy his policies carried out that aim.

Derevensky, J. L. "Introducing Children to Holocaust Literature: A Developmental-Psychological Approach." *Judaica Librarianship* 4 (Fall 1987–Winter 1988): 53–54. Using Piaget's work as a base, the author recommends the presentation of concrete material about the Holocaust, preferably from a child's perspective, cautioning that it is only after age eleven that children can understand the enormity of the event. Urges multiple exposures to different literary media.

Diakiw, J. Y. "Children's Literature and Global Education: Understanding the Developing World." *The Reading Teacher* 43 (Jan. 1990): 296–300. Indicates how research has shown that young children are developmentally ready for global issues and that children's literature constitutes a "powerful medium." Describes how children assimilate new information when it is presented in the form of a story.

Drew, N. *Learning the Skills of Peacemaking.* Jalman, 1987. This activity guide for elementary-age children consists of a three-stage process of understanding that peace begins with the individual, moves to an awareness of others that supports diversity, and concludes with discussing solutions for world conflict.

Educational Leadership 50 (Sept. 1992). The entire issue is devoted to solving conflicts peaceably and building communities for learning.

Eiss, H. "Materials for Children about Nuclear War." Paper presented at the Eighteenth Annual Meeting of the Popular Culture Association, March 23–26, 1988. Discusses several children's books, from picture books to young adult novels, dealing with war and the potential for inviting thoughts about world peace.

Farish, T. "If You Knew Him Please Write Me." *School Library Journal* 35 (Nov. 1988): 52–53. Describes the importance of novels as a source on the Vietnam War. Discusses a few in detail.

Farnham, J. F. "Holocaust Literature for Children: The Presentation of Evil." *University of Hartford Studies in Literature: Journal of Interdisciplinary Criticism* 18 (1986): 55–61. The author suggests that despite the risks "there is a moral and social imperative for presenting the Holocaust to children." He supports the position that it is important to present evil in the literature but to be certain to include an affirmation of the worth of living. Given this stance, the author describes several children's books that meet these requirements.

Fassler, J., and Janis, M. "Books, Children and Peace," *Social Education* 49 (Sept. 1985): 493–497. An annotated listing for the primary grades of children's books that emphasize peaceful solutions to difficult problems.

Freeman, L. A. "Children and War." *The Children's Book Bag* 3 (1991). This pamphlet centers around the theme of how the Persian Gulf War has profoundly affected children's awareness of war. The author recommends that each book be read carefully before use with children, considering each child's age and maturity. The annotated bibliography includes picture books and books for intermediate and advanced readers.

Gallagher, A. F. "In Search of Justice: The Thousand-Mile Walkathon." *Social Education* 52 (Nov.–Dec. 1988) 527–530. The medium of children's literature is used here as an important approach to teaching justice and developing different perspectives to deal with complex global issues.

Harrison, B. "Howl like the Wolves." In *Innocence and Experience.* Lothrop Lee and Shepard, 1987. The author poses the question: "How can children's books adequately convey the human tragedy of the Holocaust and the devastation of Hiroshima and Nagasaki in World War II?" She then presents a detailed account of many books that succeed.

Hawkes, G. W. "What about the Children?" Parents and Teachers for Social Responsibility, 1984. The booklet raises important questions concerning the threat of nuclear war and the responsibility placed on adults for future generations.

Hennen, T. J., and Stanton, V. C. "Let There Be Peace: An Annotated Bibliography of Anti-War Literature and Realistic Fiction about War." *Language Arts* (Jan. 1977): 66–70. The compilers of this bibliography recommend books that present a realistic portrayal of the effects of war, particularly on children. Aimed at junior high students.

Hopkins, S., and Winters, J. *Discover the World.* New Society, 1990. A creative curriculum guide on teaching the values of peace with themes such as fostering an awareness of others, conflict management, global awareness, appreciation of the environment, and celebrations.

Kalb, V. "Literature as a Personal Approach to the Study of the Holocaust." *School Library Media Quarterly* 17 (4): 213–214. Critiques several children's books about the Holocaust. The author's thesis is that literature helps to build awareness, initiate discussion, and promote further research, ultimately leading to greater knowledge and understanding. She believes that children should study literature on the Holocaust so that history will not repeat itself.

Kennemer, P. K. *Using Literature to Teach Middle Grades about War.* Oryx, 1993. Designed to serve as an instructional resource, the book provides a selected chronology, a list of recommended books (each with a short paragraph describing its contents), a sample lesson plan, suggested questions and activities, and a glossary about four wars: World War I, World War II, the war in Vietnam, and the Gulf war.

Kimmel, E. A. "Confronting the Ovens: The Holocaust and Juvenile Fiction." *The Horn Book Magazine,* Feb. 1977, pp. 84–91. Discusses some issues authors of juvenile fiction must consider in writing about the Holocaust. Highlights some books that deal with different aspects such as resistance, refugees, occupation, and heroics.

Kreidler, W. J. "Conflict Resolutionland: A Round-Trip Tour." *ESR Journal* (1990): 41–45. Describes three conflict situations: win–win, win–lose, and lose–lose. Suggests steps for conflict management and a win–win resolution by taking the perspective of the other person.

Kreidler, W. J. *Creative Conflict Resolution.* Scott, Foresman, 1984. Contains specific strategies for elementary students to resolve arguments and fights. Some suggestions include "Cooling off," "Mediation," "Reflective Listening," and "Role Playing" to name a few.

Kreidler, W. J. *Elementary Perspectives 1. Teaching Concepts of Peace and Conflict.* Educators for Social Responsibility, 1990. The theme and vision of peace are woven throughout this book even in discussing enemies and war. Contains activities and ideas for integrating peace and conflict issues, community building, stereotypes, prejudice, and societal problems into the curriculum.

Lantieri, L., and Roderick, T. "A New Way of Fighting: Resolving Conflict Creatively." *ESR Journal* (1990): 46–49. Describes the success and effectiveness of the mediation program begun in 1985 in the New York City Public Schools.

Law, N. R. "Children and War." Association for Childhood Education International, 1973. This position paper on war was adopted in 1971. In essence it advocates teaching children about war so they will be upholders of peace and respecters of all human life.

Luvmour, S., and Luvmour, J. *Everyone Wins! Cooperative Games and Activities.* New Society, 1990. Games and activities designed to foster friendship and cooperation both in and out of the classroom. Some goals are to build a child's self-esteem and to cross both social and cultural barriers. Every entry suggests numbers of participants, ideal location, appropriate age level, and level of difficulty.

MacCann, D. "Militarism in Juvenile Fiction." In *How Much Truth Do We Tell the Children?* edited by B. Bacon. MEP, 1988. Criticism of a number of children's books about war. The author decries the propagandistic tone used by many writers of children's books in glorifying war and maintaining stereotypes.

Mallea, K. "Educating for Peace." *Middle School Journal* (Nov. 1985): 11-13. The plea is made to educate children "for peace and not against war," emphasizing that peace is more than simply the absence of war. Some suggestions for implementation include encouraging cooperation instead of competition, supporting critical and creative thinking, and promoting nonviolence and techniques for conflict resolution.

Marinak, B. "Books in the Classroom: The Holocaust." *The Horn Book Magazine,* May-June 1993, pp. 368-373. A book-by-book description of how to implement a unit of study on the Holocaust in an elementary classroom. The author points out that children need to be taught about this subject, not through memorizing dates in a textbook, but by children's literature and "real accounts."

McAllister, P. *You Can't Kill the Spirit.* New Society, 1988. A useful resource appropriate for advanced young readers as well as adults, this book traces the history of women's contributions to the peace movement and nonviolent activism around the world.

McGinnis, J. "A Methodology for Educating for Peace and Justice." *Interracial Books for Children Bulletin* 19 (1, 2): 8-11. A down-to-earth approach to understanding peace and justice issues. The author's stance is that in order to teach about peace one has to live it first. This article is an excerpt from the book, *Peace and Justice,* developed by the Institute for Peace and Justice in St. Louis.

McMath, J. S. "Young Children, War, and Picture Books." *Day Care and Early Education* 19 (Winter 1991): 10-13. An annotated listing of ten picture books that deal sensitively with the subjects of war and peace. Emphasizes that reading aloud well-written books containing successful conflict resolution strategies is an essential companion to TV programs, the main source of information for children.

Miedzian, M. *Boys Will Be Boys: Breaking the Link Between Masculinity and Violence.* Doubleday, 1991. A thorough analysis of how boys are systematically trained to be violent in our society. Some topics discussed are the theory of "real men," the role of fathers, the effects of war and the military, and the dangerous influence from the media, especially the music industry.

Orlick, T. *The Second Cooperative Sports and Games Book.* Pantheon, 1982. Contains cooperative games and activities from around the world.

Paterson, K. "Living in a Peaceful World." *The Horn Book Magazine.* Jan.-Feb. 1991, pp. 32-38. Emphasizes making peace a more concrete concept for children. The author recommends children's literature that sensitively develops these themes as an excellent place to start. Many books are discussed in detail.

Perrone, V. "Peace Studies." *Insights into Open Education* 18 (Jan.-Feb. 1986): 1-6. A reasoned discussion of what it means to study peace. The author recommends that war studies be transformed so as to emphasize an understanding of what war means and how peace and nonviolence can be achieved. Several books are praised for their impact against war.

Posner, M. W. "Echoes of the Shoah: Holocaust Literature." Part I, *School Library Journal* 34 (Jan. 1988): 36-37; Part II, idem 34 (Feb. 1988): 30-31. The author makes connections between the Holocaust and other large-scale oppression such as apartheid, religious conflict in India, and the denying of refuge to boat-people. She recommends a gradual approach to teaching the Holocaust to children and reviews several articles that discuss how to do this. In Part II, the author provides an annotated list of children's books about the Holocaust.

Prutzman, P.; Stern, L.; Burger, M. L.; and Bodenhamer, G. *The Friendly Classroom for a Small Planet.* Illus. by D. McMurray, New Society, 1988. A teacher's reference book designed for understanding the roots of conflict. Activities include affirming diversity and fostering cooperation in the classroom.

Pytowska, E. I., and Willett, G. P. *Empowerment Bibliography.* Savanna, 1987. A section of this multicultural bibliography contains books on self-affirmation and empowerment through friendship.

Reardon, B. A. *Comprehensive Peace Education: Educating for Global Responsibility.* Teacher's College Press, 1988. Offers a practical scholarly guide for peace and conflict resolution. Distinguishes between negative peace (gained through war and violence) and positive peace (human rights and global justice).

Rudman, M. K.; Gagne, K. D.; and Bernstein, J. E. *Books to Help Children Cope with Separation and Loss,* 4th ed. Bowker, 1993. This reference work lists more than 130 titles and annotations on war.

Rudman, M. K., and Rosenberg, S. "Confronting History: Holocaust Books for Children." *The New Advocate* 4 (Summer 1991): 163–178. A comprehensive discussion of the varying perspectives of the Holocaust as portrayed in children's literature. A book list is included.

Schwarcz, J. H., and Schwarcz, C. "The Threat of War and the Quest for Peace." In *The Picture Book Comes of Age.* American Library Association, 1991. An extensive look at how literature for children handles war. The authors discuss the importance of presenting this issue in picture books. They brilliantly analyze and critique the illustrations of several books on this topic.

Sherman, U. F. "Why Would a Child Want to Read about That: The Holocaust Period in Children's Literature." In *How Much Truth Should We Tell the Children?* edited by B. Bacon. MEP, 1988. Discusses what should be included in a study of Holocaust literature in order to be comprehensive. Mentions the difficulty of dealing with evil and points out that literature confronts life-and-death decisions. Seventeen books on the Holocaust are described.

Strom, M. S., and Parsons, W. S. *Facing History and Ourselves: Holocaust and Human Behavior.* International Education, 1982. An extensive, well-designed curriculum for adolescents to investigate and learn from a study of the Holocaust. Genocide of Armenians, as well as Jews, is discussed in this book.

Taxel, J. "The American Revolution in Children's Books: Issues of Race and Class." In *How Much Truth Do We Tell the Children?* edited by B. Bacon. MEP, 1988. Examines messages about race and class that appear in 32 children's novels about the American Revolutionary War. Demonstrates that many books give a biased and inaccurate picture.

Wade, R. C. *Joining Hands: From Personal to Planetary Friendship in the Primary Classroom.* Zephyr, 1991. The importance of promoting friendship in the classroom is extended to the world. Emphasis is placed on cooperation, communication, conflict resolution, friendship in children's books, and class projects such as a friendship quilt and games from around the world. Designed primarily for preschool to second grade.

Walter, V. A. *War and Peace: Literature for Children and Young Adults.* Oryx, 1993. Critical and literary perspectives on how children respond to books. The bulk of the book contains an annotated listing of children's books and resources for adults about war. A briefer section includes books about conflict resolution and peace.

Webster-Doyle, T. *Tug of War.* Illus. by R. Cameron. Atrium, 1990. Attempts to help young people understand the causes and sources of conflict such as societal expectations of "winning." Examines conditioned behaviors such as prejudice, stereotyping, and scapegoating with activities on how to deal with propaganda.

Yolen, J. "An Experiential Act." *Language Arts* 66 (March 1989): 246-251. The author discusses her book, *The Devil's Arithmetic,* and hopes that readers will "remember as if they had been there." She eloquently reflects on the Holocaust and places the book into a historical context.

Zack, V. "It Was the Worst of Times: Learning about the Holocaust Through Literature." *Language Arts* 68 (Jan. 1991): 42-48. A fifth grade teacher who describes working with a group of students as they read through Yolen's *The Devil's Arithmetic.* She relates the students' reactions to the book to questions this experience raises about the use of Holocaust literature with children.

Zeece, P. D., and Graul, S. K. "Children Learning about War: Children Living with Peace." *Day Care and Early Education,* Winter 1991, pp. 5-9. Based on current research from the Gulf War, the authors link a child's perceptions of war to cognitive and social-emotional development and provide activities in dramatic play, art, and communication to impart feelings of safety and comfort to children when dealing with the topic.

RESOURCES

Beyond War. Dept. P, 222 High St., Palo Alto, CA 94301. Provides services and volunteers in 40 states and 6 countries.

Center for Conflict Resolution. 731 State Street, Madison, WI 53703. Publishes *A Manual for Group Facilitators,* addressing issues for facilitators such as crisis intervention, conflict resolution, creative problem solving, and the like, in the context of a workshop.

Children's Creative Response to Conflict Program. P.O. Box 271, Nyack, NY 10960. Publishes *The Friendly Classroom for a Small Planet* to help improve children's skills in conflict resolution, respect for diversity, and cooperation.

Educators for Social Responsibility. 23 Garden Street, Cambridge, MA 02138. "Seeks to make social responsibility an integral part of education." Publishes a pamphlet, "Dealing with Differences: Conflict Resolution in Our Schools" and the journal, *Educating for Social Responsibility.*

National Coalition on Television Violence. P.O. Box 2157, Champaign, IL 61820. Publishes a pamphlet on the harmful effects of war cartoons and war toys, which can increase violence in children.

National Peace Institute Foundation. Dept. P, 1424 16th St., N.W., Suite 602, Washington, DC 20036. Reference source for peace and conflict-resolution groups.

Parents and Teachers for Social Responsibility. Box 517, Moretown, VT 05660. Publishes "What about the Children?" a booklet on nuclear war.

Peace Development Fund. 44 N. Prospect St. P.O. Box 270, Amherst, MA 01004. Supports community involvement in peace and justice projects for educating the public on current governmental and military policies.

Peacemakers, Inc. Dept. P, P.O. Box 141254, Dallas, TX 75214. Serves as an educational resource for promoting peaceful resolutions in schools. Also publishes a newsletter on peace initiatives worldwide.

20/20 Vision. Dept. P, 69 S. Pleasant St., Suite 203, Amherst, MA 01002. Promotes environmental and social institutions over military and defense budget priorities. Puts concerned citizens in contact with policy makers.

BIBLIOGRAPHY

If a book has a special focus it is identified in brackets following the bibliographic entry. For a listing of titles arranged by specific topic, write to the author at 224 Furcolo Hall, UMASS, Amherst, MA 01003.

Aaron, C. *Alex, Who Won His War.* Walker, 1991. (Ages 10-12.) [World War II] An adventure story raising questions about how war makes enemies of people who might otherwise be friends. Based on an account of German spies who actually landed near New York City during World War II, the story centers on Alex, who gets involved with some German spies and must deal with some serious ethical issues before he is finally extricated from the dangerous situation.

Aaron, C. *Gideon.* Lippincott, 1982. (Ages 11 and up.) [Holocaust] Although fiction, the first-person narrative persuades the reader of its authenticity. Gideon becomes a member of the resistance both in the Warsaw ghetto and in the Treblinka concentration camp. Affirms the human ability to endure.

Aaseng, N. *Robert E. Lee.* Lerner, 1991. (Ages 8-10.) [Civil War] In an informal, anecdotal style, this biography provides a personalized account of the Civil War. Lee's stellar reputation is confirmed. Despite fighting for the South he is acknowledged as a decent person and an "enemy" who is not narrowly defined as such.

Abells, C. B. *The Children We Remember.* Illus. with photos. Greenwillow, 1986. (Ages 7 and up.) [Holocaust] The photos of children who were victims of the Holocaust are sufficient to sustain interest. The short phrases accompanying each photo are heart breaking in their matter-of-factness. The cadence and imagery raise the text to the level of poetry.

Ackerman, K. *The Tin Heart.* Illus. by M. Hays. Atheneum, 1990. (Ages 8-10.) [Civil War] Along the Ohio River at the time of the Civil War, two girls, Flora and Mahaley, each wears half of a tin heart necklace to demonstrate their friendship. Mahaley's father uses his ferry boat to transport slaves to freedom. Flora's father supports the South. The girls know it will be a long time before they see one another again, but they are sure their friendship is secure. Except for an appearance by Flora's mother to serve cocoa, adult women are absent; politics seems to be a man's domain. The girls' friendship supersedes all other concerns; the war is secondary in their thoughts.

Adler, C. S. *Always and Forever Friends.* Clarion, 1988. (Ages 9-12.) [Friendship] As a newcomer, Wendy tries to cultivate the friendship of one girl who is incapable of a sincere relationship. At last Wendy and Honor, an African-American girl who at first glance is very different from Wendy, become good chums. Wendy's apparent lack of perception can spark readers' advice-giving.

Adler, D. A. *The Number on My Grandfather's Arm.* Illus. by R. Eichenbaum. Union of American Hebrew Congregations, 1987. (Ages 5-9) [Holocaust] Assisted by photos, this is a skillful telling of a story deemed by many adults to be too horrible for children's ears. The grandfather's account of his experiences and losses during the Holocaust is important, particularly in light of Holocaust survivors' reluctance to burden their families with the details. The point is made that people should not be ashamed of their experiences or remain victims of their own memories.

Adler, D. A. *A Picture Book of Anne Frank.* Illus. by K. Ritz. Holiday House, 1993. (Ages 7-9.) [Holocaust] Despite the somewhat distorted illustrations, this slim book provides younger readers with an accessible account of the life of Anne Frank. It does not dwell on pain or atrocities; but Anne's joys, frustrations, hopes, and tragic death are communicated.

Adler, D. A. *We Remembered the Holocaust*. Holt, 1989. (Ages 10 and up.) [Holocaust] Interspersed with photographs and interviews of people who experienced life in Germany from 1933 through the war years, the book offers a realistic portrait of pre-war and Holocaust Germany. The pervasive feeling is one of disbelief and dismay that a group of people who had been such a vital part of the fabric of the country could be so thoroughly turned upon and victimized.

Armstrong, L. *How to Turn War into Peace*. Illus. by B. Basso. HBJ, 1979. (Ages 5-8.) [Peace] A child's guide to resolving conflict. A little girl and her friend resolve their argument without loss of dignity or sense of self-worth.

Ashabranner, B. *Always to Remember: The Story of the Vietnam Veterans Memorial*. Illus. by J. Ashabranner. Dodd Mead, 1988. (Ages 10 and up.) [Vietnam] In addition to a history of the war and of the contest for who would create the memorial, the author and his daughter include examples of memorabilia and messages left at the wall by grieving relatives and friends and by empathic visitors.

Ashabranner, B., and Ashabranner, M. *Into a Strange Land: Unaccompanied Refugee Youth in America*. Illus. with photos. Putnam, 1987. (Ages 11 and up.) [General] [See Adoption and Foster Care]

Atkinson, L. *In Kindling Flame: The Story of Hannah Senesh, 1921-1944*. Lothrop Lee and Shepard, 1985. (Ages 12 and up.) [Holocaust] Hannah Senesh was passionate, difficult to get along with, strong-willed, and convinced that she was destined for a special mission in life. She emigrated to Israel, then returned to her native Hungary as a partisan fighting the Nazis. Here she was imprisoned and executed at age 23. Because she was a writer, many records attest to her feelings and observations about the world, the war, and herself.

Auerbacher, I. *I am a Star: Child of the Holocaust*. Illus. by I. Bernbaum. Simon & Schuster, 1986. (Ages 12 and up.) [Holocaust] One of only thirteen people to survive Terezin concentration camp from her original transport of twelve hundred, the author provides a moving combination of general and personal history expressed through strong rhyming poetry, photos of the her town and family, and stark drawings.

Avi. *The Fighting Ground*. Illus. by E. Thompson. Lippincott, 1984. (Ages 11 and up.) [American Revolution] Jonathan, thirteen years old, fights in a battle in the Revolutionary War. Counter to his expectations, he finds it bloody and inglorious. The book never discusses the merits of either side or indicates the causes or issues, but it is a telling indictment against war.

Baker, B. *The Pig War*. Illus. by R. Lopshire. Harper, 1969. (Ages 5-8.) [Peace] The story takes place on an island off the state of Washington in 1859. Both Americans and British are stationed there because neither country knows to whom the island belongs. Some trespassing pigs throw the island into a minor turmoil, which is then logically and non-violently settled. Because the book is based on a historical incident, the ending is all the more satisfying.

Bauer, M. D. *Rain of Fire*. Clarion, 1983. (Ages 11 and up.) [World War II] The story draws parallels between children's interactions and nations at war. The community, particularly the group of children with whom Steve is friendly, supports war. Steve's older brother Matthew, who has returned from fighting in World War II, is morose and shaken by his experiences. To impress his friends, Steve joins them in a series of violent acts.

The book reveals the damage that can occur when children are left confused about the disparity between adults' words and their behavior.

Beatty, P. *Charley Skedaddle*. Morrow, 1987. (Ages 11 and up.) [Civil War] This story dramatizes the complexity and futility of war. Charley is a drummer boy in the Union army. During a battle he is so traumatized when he shoots a man that he runs away. He wanders into the home of an old woman with whom he stays and whose life he saves when she has an accident, proving his courage and his character. The author's notes demonstrate the extent of her research.

Beatty, P. *Turn Homeward, Hannalee*. Morrow, 1984. (Ages 9-12.) [Civil War] Hannalee Reed, a young millworker, has been forcibly removed to the North by Union soldiers. She is an admirable and attractive character whose heroism and ability to endure personal hardship are remarkable but believable. For her further adventures, see *Be Ever Hopeful, Hannalee* (1988).

Beatty, P. *Who Comes with Cannons?* Morrow, 1992. (Ages 9-12.) [Civil War] The pacifist role of the Quakers is well portrayed in this story set in North Carolina during the Civil War. Truth Hopkins, an orphan living with her uncle and his family, discovers that they are a station on the underground railroad. Truth's two cousins are conscripted into the Confederate Army. One brother escapes; the other is captured and imprisoned in the North. The only flaw in this otherwise well-crafted book is the contrived rescue of the imprisoned brother, involving President and Mrs. Lincoln.

Benard, R., editor. *A Short War between Trains: An Anthology of War Short Stories by American Writers*. Delacorte, 1991. (Ages 12 and up.) [General] Stories about war by such well-known American writers as Eudora Welty, Stephen Crane, Ambrose Bierce, Irwin Shaw, Philip Roth, and Bernard Malamud. For the more mature reader, these stories deal with American wars in chronological order beginning with the Civil War. Benard's intention is that the stories "serve as antidotes to propaganda."[1]

Benchley, N. *Sam the Minuteman*. Harper, 1969. (Ages 3-8.) [American Revolution] It is unusual to have a book on this topic that is accessible to the youngest of readers. Sam is reluctant to participate with his father in the Battle of Lexington until his friend is wounded. Sam then fights wildly to avenge his friend, remembering only afterward the humane ideals he supposedly believes in.

Bergman, T., translated by M. Swirsky. *Along the Tracks*. Houghton Mifflin, 1991. (Ages 12 and up.) [World War II] In this survival tale, Yankele, a Polish Jewish child has been separated from his family during their escape from the Nazis. He remains alive and is miraculously reunited with his parents and sister. The suffering brought about not by direct atrocities but by hunger separation, cold, and the small cruelties of strangers makes this a painful experience for the reader.

Bergman, T., translated by H. Halkin. *The Boy from over There*. Houghton Mifflin, 1988. (Ages 10 and up.) [After World War II] Avram, a Holocaust survivor now in Israel, has been emotionally damaged by being in hiding for most of his young years, seeing his father killed, and not knowing what has happened to his mother. He and Rina, another child whose father has been killed in the war, share the conviction that their missing parents will one day return. They finally accept reality and learn to bear their loss.

Berleth, R. *Samuel's Choice*. Illus. by J. Watling. Whitman, 1990. (Ages 8-10.) [American Revolution] Although the story is somewhat slow moving, it conveys a sense of what it was like to be a slave during the time of the American Revolution. Set in New York and narrated by Samuel, a young African-American slave, the book not only discloses historical events but also examines issues surrounding fighting for one's freedom and what that freedom means.

Bernbaum, I. *My Brother's Keeper: The Holocaust through the Eyes of an Artist*. Illus. by the author. Putnam, 1985. (Ages 9 and up.) [Holocaust] The author's aim is to prevent such a tragedy as the Holocaust from recurring and to teach the lesson of being one's brother's keeper. The book displays six symbol-laden paintings focusing mainly on the Warsaw Ghetto, inspired by newspaper and archival photos.

Blume, J. *Blubber*. Bradbury, 1974. (Ages 8 and up.) [Bullies] Linda is slightly overweight but not really obese. She has become the object of ridicule for Wendy, a bully and class ringleader. The other children go along with Wendy's cruelty for reasons that are unclear. No adults intervene. A discussion of the behavior of the children, as well as the outcome of this story, would be helpful.

Bosch, C. W. *Bully on the Bus*. Parenting, 1988. (Ages 5–9.) [Bullies] Not a work of literature but a well-crafted "choose your own solution" book. Children are invited to select from a number of viable responses to dilemmas involving conflict. The book avoids clichés of becoming best friends with the bully or besting him or her in a fight.

Bunting, E. *Terrible Things: An Allegory of the Holocaust*. Illus. by S. Gammell. Jewish Publication Society, 1989. (Ages 5 and up.) [Holocaust] The forest creatures are all destroyed by the "Terrible Things," species by species. Only Little Rabbit remains to tell the story. In a gripping allegory, not only of the Holocaust but also of any attempt to "divide and conquer," the author and illustrator combine to demonstrate the necessity of cooperation with one's fellows.

Bunting, E. *The Wall*. Illus. by R. Himler. Clarion, 1990. (Ages 5 and up.) [Vietnam] A little boy and his father visit the Vietnam Veterans Memorial. The boy feels honored but saddened to find his grandfather's name engraved there. The illustrations convey the powerful emotion this monument brings to its observers, especially those who have lost loved ones in the war. The family is of Mexican-American heritage.

Caple, K. *Fox and Bear*. Illus. by the author. Houghton Mifflin, 1992. (Ages 4–7.) [Conflict resolution] In each of the stories, Fox and Bear, who are best friends, engage in some sort of competition and manage either to compromise or to prove their point. On occasion, there is a sense of one-upmanship, but for the most part they settle their differences amicably.

Carr, A. *A Matter of Life and Death*. Viking, 1966. (Ages 12 and up.) [General] A history of many American wars, their possible prevention, and their individual and social implications. Also included is a discussion of patriotism and the necessity of considering alternatives to war.

Carter, J. *Talking Peace: A Vision for the Next Generation*. Dutton, 1993. (Ages 12 and up.) [Conflict resolution] In topics ranging from the Camp David talks on the Middle East to the ways food and medicine are used as weapons in war, the former president discusses the difficult and important process of active peace-making and recommends personal involvement on the part of young people.

Caseley, J. *Silly Baby*. Illus. by the author. Greenwillow, 1988. (Ages 5–7.) [Conflict resolution] [See Siblings]

Chaikin, M. *A Nightmare in History: The Holocaust 1933–1945*. Illus. with photos and prints. Clarion, 1987. (Ages 10 and up.) [Holocaust] Detailing the history of the Holocaust, including information about Hitler's boyhood and background, the book provides a picture of the elaborate plans the Nazis concocted for the extermination of the Jews. The extensive bibliography will help young researchers.

Choi, S. N. *Year of Impossible Goodbyes*. Houghton Mifflin, 1991. (Ages 10 and up.) [World War II] Sookan and her family endure cruel treatment at the hands of the occupying

Japanese forces in northern Korea during World War II. After the Japanese are replaced by the Russians, the family is separated; but eventually all of them are reunited in Seoul. *Echoes of the White Giraffe* (1993) follows Sookan and her family from their displacement in Pusan back to their home in Seoul. The book offers a vivid picture of the restrictions and expectations placed on women in traditional Korean society. Both books personalize the history of Korea and provide an informative context.

Clark, L., ed. *Drums and Trumpets.* Illus. by H. Copley. Dufour, 1962. (Ages 10 and up.) [General] Poetry for young people dealing with war: some of its glories, some of its despairs.

Climo, S. *King of the Birds.* Illus. by R. Heller. Harper, 1988. (Ages 6–9.) [Conflict resolution] In this pourquoi tale, the birds conquer chaos and settle their battle over who should be their king. He turns out to be the wren, who wins through a combination of cleverness and tenacity. The sources for the story come from European variants, as well as a Chippewa tale. Children may enjoy arguing over the logic of the contest and its winner and may discuss the ways the conflict was resolved.

Coerr, E. *Sadako and the Thousand Paper Cranes.* Illus. by E. Young. Putnam, 1993. (Ages 10 and up.) [World War II, nuclear war] Sadako Sasaki was twelve years old when she died of leukemia as a result of the atomic bombing of Hiroshima. This revised edition stresses her love of life and her exuberant, active nature. It is painful to learn of her leukemia and to witness her struggle for life as she folds the complicated origami paper cranes, an ancient symbol of peace and hope in Japanese tradition. Since her death, she has become a folk hero for Japanese children, and there is now a monument to her in Peace Park, in Japan. The pastel illustrations are drawn from the images the artist created for a video of the story, narrated by Liv Ullmann. *The Day of the Bomb,* by K. Bruckner, (E.M. Hale, 1962) tells the same story.

Cole, B. *The Goats.* Farrar, Straus, and Giroux, 1987. (Ages 12 and up.) [Bullies] Preadolescents and outcasts, Laura and Howie find each other as a result of the bullying and abusive behavior of their fellow campers. Their parents are neglectful though not intentionally unkind. Because of their friendship and the strength they draw from it, the realistic ending gives readers hope that the two characters will be better able to deal with the world in general and with their families in particular.

Collier, J. L., and Collier, C. *My Brother Sam Is Dead.* Four Winds, 1974. (Ages 12 and up.) [American Revolution] Tim is the narrator of the story, set in the Revolutionary War era. His brother Sam and his father (as well as other characters in the story) are killed, but not in battle. The ugliness and hardship of war are clearly presented. Neither side is favored. The authors suggest that readers consider whether the war was necessary.

Collier, J. L., and Collier, C. *War Comes to Willy Freeman.* Delacorte, 1983. (Ages 9–12.) [American Revolution/Slavery] Willy, a young black former slave has been freed because her father served in the Revolutionary army. She witnesses her father's death at the hands of British soldiers and discovers that her mother has been taken prisoner by British soldiers and brought to New York. Willy dresses as a boy and searches for her mother. Eventually, she must cope with her mother's death and with an attempt to return her to slavery. Her bravery and survival strategies are commendable. The book provides a close look at the ugliness of any war and raises some disturbing questions about African-American involvement in the Revolution.

Cowan, L. *Children of the Resistance.* Hawthorn, 1969. (Ages 12 and up.) [World War II] A collection of stories about young people in eight Nazi-occupied countries, including Germany, who actively aided the resistance during World War II. While the book does not glorify war, it does value resistance and support the necessity for retribution. The stories, told as great adventures, occasionally take the form of simulated diaries.

Cox, C. *Undying Glory: The Story of the Massachusetts 54th Regiment.* Scholastic, 1991. (Ages 10 and up.) [Civil War] Photos and quotations from newspapers, letters, and personal accounts add to the authenticity of this report. The all-black regiment was formed with a young white colonel at its head. Frederick Douglass was one of the primary recruiters, and two of his sons enlisted in the regiment, as did Sojourner Truth's grandson. The story is composed of facts building on facts to create a vivid image of a group of brave, dedicated, and competent men fighting against many odds.

Creighton, J. *The Weaver's Horse.* Illus. by R. Creighton. Annick, 1991. (Ages 7–10.) [General] Lord Henry returns from the war to find that his brother has commandeered his castle and possessions and sold his beloved horse. Weary of war and violence, Henry has made a solemn vow of peace, so he leaves his brother and finds work as a weaver. The eventual reunion with his cherished horse figures strongly in the story. Although he is plagued by thoughts and dreams of excruciating violence, with the help of his cousin, a healer, Henry learns to conquer his rage and turn his feelings into creative work. He eventually earns a reputation as a wonderful weaver.

Crew, L. *Children of the River.* Dell, 1989. (Ages 12 and up.) [See Heritage]

Dank, M. *Red Flight Two.* Delacorte, 1981. (Ages 12 and up.) [General] This well-written adventure tale presents the dilemmas of leadership in war. Who should be exposed to the most risk to save the most lives? What is the responsibility of people not in command when they feel that their superior officers are making incorrect judgments?

Davis, B. *Black Heroes of the American Revolution.* HBJ, 1976. (Ages 10–12.) [American Revolution] [See Heritage]

Davis, D. S. *Behind Barbed Wire.* Dutton, 1982. (Ages 12 and up.) [World War II] A fully researched and detailed account of the internment of Japanese Americans during World War II.

Deford, D. H., and Stout, H. S. *An Enemy among Them.* Houghton Mifflin, 1987. (Ages 10 and up.) [American Revolution] The story conveys the feelings of the German-speaking community in Pennsylvania about the Hessian mercenaries hired by the British to fight against the colonists. It also demonstrates that some Hessian soldiers were not the beasts they were reported to be in U.S. history books. People's common humanity emerges, even in times of war and even between enemies.

Degens, T. *The Game on Thatcher Island.* Viking, 1977. (Ages 11 and up.) [General] Harry is flattered when a group of older boys invites him to participate in their game of war on Thatcher Island. His pleasure disappears when the game takes a terrifying turn. This well-written adventure story helps young readers think about the implications of war games.

Degens, T. *Transport 7-41-R.* Viking, 1974. (Ages 12 and up.) [World War II] A thirteen-year-old girl travels from the Russian sector of defeated Germany to Cologne on a transport carrying returning refugees in 1946. Readers become involved with other passengers and their suspenseful journey. The ravages of war are communicated well.

Denenberg, B. *Nelson Mandela: No Easy Walk to Freedom.* Scholastic, 1991. (Ages 12 and up.) [Apartheid] A chronology and narrative of Nelson Mandela's role in fighting apartheid in South Africa. Some of the history of the country is given, including the bloody warfare between the Zulus and the Boers. Although the author admires Mandela, he does not romanticize him. Readers are left to draw their own conclusions about controversial issues.

DePaolo, P. *Rose and the Yellow Ribbon*. Illus. by J. Wolf. Little, Brown, 1992. (Ages 5-8.) [Friendship] Rosie and Lucille are best friends. When Rosie's favorite ribbon disappears, she suspects that Lucille has stolen it. Lucille is irate at this accusation, and the two girls begin a bitter fight. After a couple of days Rosie becomes lonely for Lucille's company and decides to permit her to keep the ribbon. Before she can tell this to Lucille, the ribbon is found. (A bird has used it in her nest.) Rosie apologizes, and the two girls resume their friendship. The story provides a model of an interracial friendship (Rosie is black and Lucille is white) and highlights the importance of trust between friends.

Dolphin, L. *Georgia to Georgia: Making Friends in the U.S.S.R.* Illus. by E. A. McGee. Tambourine, 1991. (Ages 8-10.) [Conflict resolution] A special transatlantic link exists between children of Atlanta, Georgia, and those of the former Soviet Republic of Georgia through the work of Project Peace Tree. By communicating and sharing customs, hobbies, and dreams, these children experience and discover the many similarities among people.

Dolphin, L. *Neve-Shalom/Wahat Al-Salam: Oasis of Peace*. Illus. by B. Dolphin. Scholastic, 1993. (Ages 7-10.) [Arab-Israeli conflict, Peace] A photo essay about a special school in Israel where Arab and Israeli children speak one another's languages, learn about one another's religions, and become friends. The color photos dramatically demonstrate the similarities and the possibilities for peace between the two peoples.

Donnelly, J. *A Wall of Names*. Illus. with photos. Random House, 1991. (Ages 7-10.) [Vietnam] Designed to be easily read, this slim book attempts to explain the war in Vietnam and provides a history of the memorial. The photos convey a sense of the wall and its impact on visitors.

Dr. Seuss. *The Butter Battle Book*. Illus. by the author. Random House, 1984. (Ages 5-8.) [General] The Yooks butter their bread on top and the Zooks butter it on the bottom. Otherwise they are identical. Their fight over these buttering practices escalates to a war. At the end of the story, a Yook and a Zook stand on either side of a wall, each with a powerful bomb in his hand. Although this allegory is meant to represent the futility and inanity of escalating arms races and global confrontation, it is so oversimplified it loses much of its impact. The similarity of the combatants could have been a powerful message had it been highlighted or articulated. Nevertheless, the notion comes across that two nations are brought to the brink of destruction over an unimportant issue.

Emberley, B. *Drummer Hoff*. Illus. by E. Emberley. Prentice-Hall, 1967. (Ages 3-8.) [General] A folk rhyme about loading and firing a cannon. After the cannon blasts, flowers gradually surround it and birds come to nest in the barrel. The illustrations depict the deformed and maimed victims of war in bright, cartoon-like images. The book conveys an antiwar message, but adults will need to help children analyze this book in order to come to the intended conclusion.

Estes, E. *The Hundred Dresses*. Illus. by L. Slobodkin. Scholastic, 1944. (Ages 6-9.) [Bullies] Wanda is teased by the children because she is poor and looks and behaves differently from the others. In the end, the narrator, Maddie, resolves that she will never again stand silent when someone is being unjustly treated. Although the book was written fifty years ago, the feelings of the children and the nature of the plot fit the present day.

Finkelstein, N. H. *Remember Not to Forget: A Memory of the Holocaust*. Illus. by L. and L. Hokanson. Watts, 1985. (Ages 9-12.) [Holocaust] The author writes poetically of his conviction that the world must never forget the Holocaust. The book offers a historical overview, starting from A.D. 70, when the Jewish capital of Jerusalem was destroyed, sending the Jews into the diaspora. The history concludes with a description of the Yad Vashem Memorial and the Yom Hashoa annual day commemorating the victims of the Holocaust. Simple woodcuts support the narrative well.

Fitzhugh, L., and Scoppettone, S. *Bang Bang You're Dead.* Illus. by L. Fitzhugh. Harper 1969. (Ages 5–8.) [Conflict resolution] Two groups of boys battle for possession of a hill as a playground for make-believe wars. They mutually agree that real violence is no fun and settle their disputes cooperatively.

Forbes, E. *Johnny Tremain.* Illus. by L. Ward. Houghton Mifflin, 1943. (Ages 12 and up.) [American Revolution] The romanticized but well-written story of a boy living at the time of the American Revolution. Set against the background of war, Johnny's story is the main focus of the book.

Frank, A. *Diary of a Young Girl.* Modern Library, 1952. (Ages 12 and up.) [Holocaust] The now-classic diary of a thirteen-year-old Jewish girl who spent two years with her family in hiding from the Nazis during the occupation of Holland. She describes her feelings and daily events and gives a sense of the aura of the times.

Frankel, M. E., with Saideman, E. *Out of the Shadows of Night: The Struggle for International Human Rights.* Delacorte, 1989. (Ages 12 and up.) [Peace] A history of the international human rights movement. It praises individuals and groups for their involvement in peace making, and highlights possibilities for future advances.

Freedman, R. *Lincoln: A Photobiography.* Clarion, 1987. (Ages 10 and up.) [Civil War] This well-researched biography of Abraham Lincoln, so engrossing it almost reads like a novel, deserved its Newbery Medal. The complex issues of governing the country during wartime are explored. Lincoln's own personal background is revealed in great detail. Then follows a sampling of Lincoln's writings, a list of historical Lincoln sites, a bibliography, and an index.

Friedman, I. R. *The Other Victims: First-Person Stories of Non-Jews Persecuted by the Nazis.* Houghton Mifflin, 1990. (Ages 10 and up.) [Holocaust] This book contributes perspectives of non-Jewish people persecuted by the Nazis. It is important to know that in addition to six million Jews, five million non-Jews were killed because of Hitler's edicts. Not all targeted groups are represented by personal narrative, but the accounts included here convey a sense of the dimensions of the terror of those times.

Gauch, P. L. *This Time, Tempe Wick?* Illus. by M. Tomes. Coward, McCann, and Geoghegan, 1974. (Ages 7–11.) [American Revolution] The young hero is unusual in size, strength, and behavior. Tempe outwits some disgruntled soldiers by hiding her horse in her bedroom.

Giff, P. R. *The War Began at Supper: Letters to Miss Loria.* Illus. by B. Lewin. Dell, 1991. (Ages 7–11.) [Gulf war] One of few books for children written about the 1991 war in the Persian Gulf. It is told in the format of letters to a favorite student-teacher who has moved away. Although the characters are somewhat shallow and some of the conflicts are resolved too easily, this book touches on important issues, including the discrimination suffered by Arab-Americans during the war, and acknowledges the confusion, fear, and frustration young children feel when a war is going on.

Gilmore, K. *Remembrance of the Sun.* Houghton Mifflin, 1986. (Ages 14 and up.) [Middle East] The story is based on the author's experience in Iran during the late 1970s. Jill, an American girl, and Shaheen, an Iranian boy, both talented musicians, fall in love. He is committed to revolution against the Shah; she deplores violence. The book could serve as motivation for young readers to research the complex issues of Iran and the current situation in the Middle East.

Glenn, M. "Song Vu Chin." In *Class Dismissed! High School Poems.* Illus. by M. Bernstein. Clarion, 1982. (Ages 11 and up.) [Vietnam War] This young Vietnamese immigrant vividly remembers the horrors of war he witnessed in his native land and sardonically refers to his current schoolmates as belonging to "America, home of the ignorant."

Green, C. J. *The War at Home.* McElderry, 1989. (Ages 10-12.) [World War II] [See Family Constellations]

Green, D. H. *The Lonely War of William Pinto.* Little, Brown, 1968. (Ages 10 and up.) [American Revolution] Despite the patriotic fervor of his father and brother, William, a Jewish boy in Connecticut, cannot feel loyal to the Revolution. The book describes the vicious anti-Semitism of that time and shows how some Jews tried to dispel it by becoming super-American.

Greene, B. *The Summer of My German Soldier.* Dial, 1973. (Ages 12 and up.) [World War II] In Arkansas during World War II, twelve-year-old Patty befriends a German POW and helps him escape. He is caught and killed; Patty is questioned and sent to reform school. Patty's family are the only Jews in town, which compounds her problems.

Greenfield, E. *Koya DeLaney and the Good Girl Blues.* Scholastic, 1992. (Ages 10-12.) [Friendship] Koya and her sister Loritha are both friendly with Dawn until Loritha and Dawn have a falling out. Koya tries hard to make peace and is distraught when she is teased and derided for her "goodness." The would-be peacemaker is accused of denying any feelings of anger, and the complex process of maintaining friendships is opened for examination.

Hansen, J. *Which Way Freedom?.* Walker, 1986. (Ages 9-12.) [Civil War] [See Heritage]

Hardy, T. "The Man He Killed." In *Cavalcade of Poems.* edited by G. Bennett and P. Molloy. Scholastic, 1968. (Ages 10 and up.) [General] The poet reflects on the irony of having to kill a person in battle whom under any other circumstances he would have befriended, thus raising the issue of the dehumanization of war.

Haskins, J. *Resistance: Profiles in Nonviolence.* Doubleday, 1970. (Ages 11 and up.) [Peace] A series of biographical sketches follows an introduction that discusses the precepts of nonviolence.

Hautzig, E. *The Endless Steppe.* Crowell, 1968. (Ages 11 and up.) [World War II] A fictionalized autobiography about the exile of Jews from Poland to Siberia during the period before the Nazis invaded Poland. A gripping story and the details of one family's survival despite dehumanizing conditions help readers to empathize with victims of any oppression.

Havill, J. *Jamaica and Brianna.* Illus. by A. S. O'Brien. Houghton Mifflin, 1993. (Ages 5-8.) [Conflict resolution] Jamaica and her friend Brianna have a misunderstanding and settle it by communicating clearly and honestly with each other. Their friendship means a lot to each of them.

Heide, F. P., and Gilliland, J. H. *Sami and the Time of the Troubles.* Illus. by T. Lewin. Clarion, 1992. (Ages 7-10.) [Middle East] In better times Sami, a young boy in war-torn Lebanon, can go outside to play, shop, and go to school; but during the fighting, he must stay in his uncle's basement with his family. His father was killed. The family supports one another through this "time of troubles." Sami remembers a day long ago when the children rose up in protest, and he would like to try this tactic again. The book is dramatically illustrated and sensitively written. The author raises conflicting feelings over children's war play. Adults will need to do much explaining here because the book does not explicitly state what the fighting is about.

Hesse, K. *Phoenix Rising.* Holt, 1994. (Ages 10 and up.) [Nuclear accident] The author has provided a carefully crafted, personal story based on the nightmare of a nuclear accident. Although global war is not as looming a prospect as it once was, the incidents at Chernobyl and Three Mile Island make this story all too possible. By focusing on the human elements rather than making the story a diatribe, the author's impact is even greater. Readers identify with all the characters, especially Nyle, the protagonist, who must cope with loss after loss. The issue of including people with special needs is brought into the story in the person of Muncie, Nyle's friend whose physical development is dwarfed. The relationships among the characters, the moral strength of the grandmother, and the real issues that erupt after a nuclear accident are all woven into this moving and effective story.

Hest, A. *Nana's Birthday Party.* Illus. by A. Schwartz. Morrow, 1993. (Ages 5–8.) [Conflict resolution] Maggie and her cousin Brette compete with each other regularly, especially each year when they vie to see who will make their nana the best birthday present. Maggie is a writer, and Brette is an artist; each is jealous of the other's talents. This year, however, they decide to collaborate and make a book. They know it will be the best gift ever, and the activity makes them closer friends.

Hoehling, M. U. *Girl Soldier and Spy.* Messner, 1960. (Ages 12 and up.) [Civil War] The biography of a young woman who disguises herself as a male and joins the Union Army during the Civil War.

Houston, J. W., and Houston, J. *Farewell to Manzanar.* Houghton Mifflin, 1973. (Ages 12 and up.) [World War II] Details seven-year-old Jeanne Wakatsuki's experiences growing up in one of the largest of the internment camps for Japanese Americans during the World War II.

Hudson, E. S., editor. *Poetry of the First World War.* Illus. with photos. Lerner, 1990. (Ages 12 and up.) [World War II] A forceful collection of poetry demonstrating the sadness, waste, ugliness, and irony of war. Many of the photos were taken from the collection of the Imperial War Museum in Britain. Brief biographies of the poets, most of whom fought in World War I, are included.

Hunt, I. *Across Five Aprils.* Follett, 1964. (Ages 12 and up.) [Civil War] This story of the hardships of a family living in a border state during the Civil War helps readers to understand that war is complex. The author demonstrates that people are individuals with good and bad characteristics no matter what their politics.

Hurwitz, J. *Anne Frank: Life in Hiding.* Illus. by V. Rosenberry. Jewish Publication Society, 1988. (Ages 12 and up.) [Holocaust] While the book does not deliver Anne's story with the emotional impact of her own diary, it nevertheless is a good companion piece to Anne Frank's diary, providing background information about Anne and her family and informing readers how she died.

Jampolsky, G. G., editor. *Children as Teachers of Peace.* Celestial Arts, 1982. (Ages 4 and up.) [Peace] This moving collection of children's artwork and poetry on the theme of peace was written by children and intended for adults, but it is appropriate for use with any age group. Teachers may want to use this book as a model for creating a similar work with their own students.

Jones, R. C. *Matthew and Tilly.* Illus. by B. Peck. Dutton, 1991. (Ages 5–8.) [Friendship] Like most friends, Matthew and Tilly occasionally argue and hurt each other's feelings. After one of their disagreements, each child tries to play alone but does not enjoy it. They each apologize and resume their close friendship. The illustrations provide an urban setting for the story. The friendship is biracial: Matthew is white and Tilly is black. It is also good to see a friendship between a boy and a girl without gender-linked activities or characteristics.

Kasza, K. *The Rat and the Tiger.* Illus. by the author. Putnam, 1993. (Ages 5-8.) [Conflict resolution] Rat, who always gets the short end of any bargain, is the victim of Tiger's destructive urges. One day when he speaks up and threatens to end the friendship, Tiger promises to behave in a fair and reasonable manner. The two friends together face a problem at the end when a rhinoceros moves onto the block. It is made clear that it is necessary to communicate to your friends when you feel that you have a grievance.

Kerr, J. *When Hitler Stole Pink Rabbit.* Coward, McCann, and Geoghegan, 1972. (Ages 8 and up.) [Holocaust] A German Jewish family escapes just before Hitler comes to power. They go first to Switzerland, then to France, then to England. The impact is somewhat softened because although the family are refugees they seem not to suffer unduly.

Kerr, M. E. *Gentlehands.* Harper, 1978. (Ages 11 and up.) [Holocaust] Buddy does not know why his mother has been estranged from her father for so many years. He comes to know and love his grandfather who appreciates music and art, lives in a cultured (almost aristocratic) setting, and is kind and gentle to animals. To Buddy's horror, it is revealed that his grandfather was once a feared and hated concentration camp torturer who is still involved with other Nazi war criminals. Questions about the nature of torturers can be raised here.

Knight, M. B. *Who Belongs Here? An American Story.* Illus. by A. S. O'Brien. Tilbury House, 1993. (Ages 7-10.) [Cambodian Civil War] Interspersed with the story of Nary, who escaped from his native Cambodia with his grandmother and lived in a refugee camp in Thailand before reaching the United States, is a running commentary about refugees, the history of immigration, and the contributions made by diverse populations to the United States. The illustrations convey more of an emotional flavor than the factual text.

Kuchler-Silberman, L. *My Hundred Children.* Laurel-Leaf, 1987. (Ages 12 and up.) [Holocaust] Trying to find a reason to go on living after her family died in the Holocaust, Kuchler-Silberman directed a postwar orphanage for 100 Jewish children who survived in Poland. She and her charges encountered continuing aggressive anti-Semitism, in which the authorities would neither take responsibility for them nor permit them to leave the country. This first-person narrative tells how the author finally was permitted to leave Poland for safer Czechoslovakia.

Lacoe, A. *Just Not the Same.* Houghton Mifflin, 1992. (Ages 5-8.) [Conflict resolution] A clever mother, with the occasional assistance of the father, teaches her triplet daughters how to compromise and cooperate. The dilemmas are real: Who will get the top bunk? Who will sit in the front seat of the car? Who will own the puppy? The solutions are not satisfying to the children until they realize that it is up to them to make a sharing situation work.

Landau, E. *Terrorism. America's Growing Threat.* Lodestar, 1992. (Ages 11 and up.) The author identifies elements of terrorist movements and myths associated with them, such as the erroneous assumption that all terrorists are "suicidal maniacs." In the chapter dealing with domestic terrorists, the author investigates organizations like the Ku Klux Klan and the Skinheads, whose membership has expanded by ten times since 1986. The author avoids sensationalism and writes factually.

Landau, E. *The Warsaw Ghetto Uprising.* New Discovery, 1992. (Ages 11 and up.) [Holocaust] Shortly before Passover 1943, the Jews of the Warsaw Ghetto learned that the Nazis were about to destroy the entire ghetto and all its inhabitants as "a birthday gift" for Hitler. The Jews' subsequent uprising demonstrated their fierce bravery and determination. The rest of the world showed callous indifference by not intervening.

Lattimore, D. N. *The Flame of Peace*. Illus. by the author. Harper, 1987. (Ages 6–9.) [General war] The author has combined traditional elements of folklore with Aztec mythology to create this original tale of Two Flint, an Aztec boy who brings the flame of peace to his people, ushering in decades of peace. The colorful, symbol-filled illustrations are reminiscent of the frescos found in Aztec ruins in Mexico.

Lawrence, L. *Children of the Dust*. Harper, 1985. (Ages 12 and up.) [Nuclear war] The deprivation and terror of the aftermath of a nuclear blast are chillingly conveyed in this engrossing story. A new group evolves that has learned from the mistakes of the past and will build a functional self-constructive new world. There are lessons to be learned here, and they are all the more powerful because the story is so well crafted.

Leitner, I., with Leitner, I. A. *The Big Lie: A True Story*. Illus. by J. Pedersen. Scholastic, 1992. (Ages 9–12.) [Holocaust] Although the story depicts the author's experience in Auschwitz and subsequent camps, the language she uses is so simple and direct that the book is suitable for children in the third grade. Even when describing death and degradation, the tone is matter-of-fact and calm, devoid of self-pity or bitterness. The near miracle that the author and three of her siblings were eventually reunited with their father provides a positive ending to the ordeal. The charcoal illustrations are a fitting accompaniment to the text.

Levitin, S. *Journey to America*. Atheneum, 1970. (Ages 9–12.) [Holocaust] Lisa's family plans to escape the Nazis by emigrating to America. Their decision is difficult, complicated by the fact that their father must go first. The children and their mother stay for a while in Switzerland, where two of them are subjected to terrible treatment in a foster care facility. Finally, they are reunited in America.

Levoy, M. *Alan and Naomi*. Harper, 1977. (Ages 10 and up.) [Holocaust] A beautifully written story of the attempts of a young American boy, Alan, to help his friend, Naomi, recover from her traumatic ordeal in the Holocaust. Naomi remains in a catatonic state until Alan helps her gradually relate to other children and go to school. A violent incident spurred by an anti-Semitic ruffian sends her back into an emotional crisis.

Lewis, C.S. *The Last Battle*. Macmillan, 1956. (Ages 10 and up.) [General war] The end of the battle between the forces of Good and Evil, the theme throughout the Narnia series. The book is an allegorical account of the end of the world, Judgment Day, and entrance into heaven.

Lifton, B. J. *Children of Vietnam*. Illus. by T. Fox. Atheneum, 1972. (Ages 10 and up.) [Vietnam war] Interviews with and pictures of children who survived the battles and massacres in Vietnam. A powerful description of individual suffering, confusion, fear, and sorrow.

Lifton, B. J. *Return to Hiroshima*. Illus. by E. Hosoe. Atheneum, 1970. (Ages 10 and up.) [World War II, nuclear war] A pictorial view of the damage and destruction of Hiroshima by the atomic bomb during World War II and the subsequent rebuilding of the city.

Lobel, A. *Frog and Toad Are Friends*. Illus. by the author. Harper, 1970. (Ages 4 and up.) [Friendship] Along with its companions, *Frog and Toad Together, Days with Frog and Toad,* and *Frog and Toad All Year,* each story demonstrates the solid friendship between Frog and Toad. Despite Toad's neuroses and Frog's occasional insensitivity, the two characters accommodate each other's needs and enjoy each other's company.

Lopshire, R. *I Am Better Than You*. Illus. by the author. Harper, 1968. (Ages 5–8.) [Conflict resolution] A competition between two identical lizards where one of them declines to fight, thus averting a war. A useful book to teach the effects of competition, escalation, and boasts. Solutions other than violence are suggested here.

Lowry, L. *Number the Stars*. Houghton Mifflin, 1989. (Ages 10 and up.) [Holocaust] In this winner of the 1989 Newbery Award, Annemarie and her family take part in the rescue of Danish Jews. The book demonstrates the power of a people's refusal to collude with the Nazis. Readers never get to know the Jewish characters very well; this is really not their story. It is told from the perspective of a ten-year-old Danish Christian girl. Annemarie's family is courageous and highly principled.

Mabie, M. C. *Vietnam, There and Here*. Holt, 1985. (Ages 12 and up.) [Vietnam War] The author has provided a thorough, thoughtful, accurate, even-handed presentation. The book moves from 2879 B.C. to the present time, detailing and presenting rationales for the positions of both the "doves" and the "hawks." Although the material is challenging, the book is worth the effort.

MacLachlan, P. *Arthur, for the Very First Time*. Illus. by L. Bloom. Harper, 1980. (Ages 9-12.) [Friendship] [See Gender Roles]

Marshall, J. *George and Martha*. Illus. by the author. Houghton Mifflin, 1972. (Ages 4-7.) [Friendship] Like every other volume in the *George and Martha* series, the stories reveal how George and Martha, two hippopotamuses, continuously reestablish their friendship. Sometimes one plays tricks on the other; sometimes one forgets to show concern for the other's feelings. But always they see the error of their ways, and set the matter right without much fuss.

Martin, A. *Rachel Parker, Kindergarten Show-off*. Illus. by N. Poydar. Holiday House, 1992. (Ages 5-8.) [Conflict resolution] Olivia is a bright, confident kindergartner, proud of being the only child in her class who can read. Then Rachel moves in next door. At first Olivia is pleased to have a classmate living so close, but she becomes jealous when she learns that Rachel can read too. The friendship dissolves into competition until their perceptive teacher finds a way to help them learn to cooperate. A nice model of conflict resolution made even better by the fact that the friendship is interracial (Olivia is black and Rachel is white.)

Maruki, T. *Hiroshima No Pika*. Illus. by the author. Lothrop Lee and Shepard, 1982. (Ages 10 and up.) [World War II, nuclear war] Although the illustrations make this appear to be a picture book, it is not directed at very young readers. The story and pictures graphically detail the effects of the nuclear bomb. The translation of the title is "Hiroshima's Flash." A powerful antiwar statement.

Marx, T. *Hanna's Cold Winter*. Illus. by B. Knutson. Carolrhoda, 1993. (Ages 5-9.) [World War II] This heartwarming fictionalized account tells how the Hungarian people successfully campaigned to save the Budapest Zoo's beloved hippos during the World War II. Despite bitter cold and food shortages, the hippos, who eat straw, were able to survive because the residents of Budapest donated more than nine thousand straw slippers, doormats, and hats. Compare this with *Faithful Elephants*, by Yukio Tsuchiya.

Matas, C. *Lisa's War*. Scribner, 1987. (Ages 10 and up.) [Holocaust] During the Holocaust, Lisa, a twelve-year-old Danish Jew becomes actively involved in the resistance. Many Jews anticipate the impending disaster; a number refuse to believe the Nazis have evil intent. Some are likable; others are not. The Christian Danes too differ strongly from one another. Most are sympathetic to the Jews, but a few use the opportunity to extort money from the people they ferry to Sweden and even collude with the Nazis. This story makes it clear that the Jewish Danes were not sheeplike martyrs who relied solely on their Christian benefactors to rescue them.

Meltzer, M. *Ain't Gonna Study War No More: The Story of America's Peace Seekers.* Harper, 1985. (Ages 12 and up.) [Peace] Meltzer highlights conscientious objection to war. Most of the book deals with the United States from Revolutionary times up to the present. Notable war resistors are profiled. A bibliography is included.

Meltzer, M. *All Times, All Peoples: A World History of Slavery.* Illus. by L. E. Fisher. Harper, 1980. (Ages 8-12.) [Slavery] Tracing the history of slavery from ancient times to the present, the author informs readers that there are currently ten million slaves in various places of the world (counting political prisoners who are forced to labor against their will). He ends with a plea for action on the part of the free world.

Meltzer, M. *The American Revolutionaries.* Crowell, 1987. (Ages 11 and up.) [American Revolution] The setting and emotional climate of the war and its effects on the soon-to-be nation. Men and women, old and young people from all walks of life, as well as both sides of the war, are represented by their own writing and by newspaper accounts and other documents in this cohesive document of people's feelings and experiences during the time of the American Revolution. Meltzer introduces each account by identifying the author and setting a context for what he or she has to say.

Meltzer, M. *Never to Forget: The Jews of the Holocaust.* Harper, 1976. (Ages 11 and up.) [Holocaust] Based on careful research and documentation, this excellent, readable book provides a comprehensive history of the persecution of the Jews by the Nazis. Included are excerpts from diaries, letters and poems of the concentration camp prisoners. The book demands that the reader ponder the moral issues of war and persecution.

Meltzer, M. *Rescue: The Story of How Gentiles Saved Jews in the Holocaust.* Harper, 1988. (Ages 12 and up.) [Holocaust] Inspiring stories of individual non-Jews across Europe who sheltered Jews, brought them food, helped them escape, provided for their children, and served as couriers and gatherers of news. Both clergy and some rulers resisted Nazi edicts and successfully thwarted annihilation of the Jews of their countries. These people of conscience demonstrated that in an evil time and place goodness was still possible.

Meltzer, M. *Voices from the Civil War.* Crowell, 1989. (Ages 12 and up.) [Civil War] Little-known events such as the draft riots in New York City and across the North are described here. The author's comments illuminate the events and amplify the original writings.

Merrill, J. *The Pushcart War.* Illus. by R. Solbert. Scott, 1964. (Ages 9-12.) [General] An allegory of how wars begin, escalate, and end. Colorfully and imaginatively told, the story is the pseudo-history of a war between the trucks and pushcarts of New York City. Causes, strategies, and battles are described in this humorous but thoughtful book.

Mills, C. *After Fifth Grade, the World!* Macmillan, 1989. (Ages 8-10.) [Conflict resolution] Heidi is a resourceful fifth grader, gifted in math and passionately opinionated. She sets out to reform the world, especially her mean teacher; but with her father's help, she discovers that she can accomplish more by understanding others than by warring with them. A fast-paced story with humor that hits the mark without being demeaning.

Mochizuki, K. *Baseball Saved Us.* Illus. by D. Lee. Lee & Low, 1993. (Ages 7-10.) [World War II] Narrated by Shorty, the young protagonist, this story reveals one of the self-preservative activities initiated by Japanese Americans interned in camps. Shorty's father sparks a project to build a baseball field in the desert where their camp is located. After the war Shorty continues to play baseball and still encounters racism. No easy answers here, but a testimony to human ability to overcome impossible conditions. The author's parents were interned in Minidoka camp in Idaho during the war.

Moore, E. *Whose Side Are You On?*. Farrar, Straus, and Giroux, 1988. (Ages 9–11.) [Bullies] At first Barbra is a spoiled, self-centered child who thinks that her poor grades and mishaps are everyone's fault but hers. She is a member of a small clique of girls who scapegoat another girl in the class. As the story progresses, Barbra begins to appreciate what friendship means and to understand the consequences of her own behavior. Included in the story are the problems of being a twin, the issue of abandonment, and the sense of pride in being a member of an African-American community.

Moore, M. *Our Future at Stake: A Teenager's Guide to Stopping the Nuclear Arms Race.* New Society, 1985. (Ages 12 and up.) [Peace] Potential problems of nuclear armament are seen through the eyes of young people ages thirteen through sixteen.

Murphy, J. *The Boys' War.* Clarion, 1990. (Ages 12 and up.) [Civil War] Because an estimated 250,000 to 420,000 boys sixteen year old and younger may have fought in the Civil War, procedural changes were enacted to prevent such young people from ever again enlisting in the American Army. The author narrates in the third person but makes liberal use of the first-hand accounts and letters of the young soldiers.

Murphy, J. *The Long Road to Gettysburg.* Illus. by the author. Clarion, 1992. (Ages 9–12.) [Civil War] The author personalizes this bloody battle by drawing strongly upon the writings of two boys (one eighteen years old and one fifteen) who fought in the Battle of Gettysburg. Humane gestures are included along with the brutality and ugliness of the fighting.

Myers, W. D. *Fallen Angels.* Scholastic, 1988. (Ages 12 and up.) [Vietnam War] Richie Perry, a tough young New Yorker, narrates the story of a group of young people stationed in Vietnam. The language and action are rough, but mature readers will be moved by the voices of these young soldiers and the human issues they encounter.

Myers, W. D. *Scorpions.* Harper, 1988. (Ages 12 and up.) [Gangs] Twelve-year-old Jamal Hicks's older brother Randy is in jail for a gang-related murder. Jamal and his best friend Tony are lured into taking Randy's place in his street gang, the Scorpions, and running drugs to pay for a court appeal. This graphic portrayal of gang life by a gifted author is an important exploration of a neglected subject.

Naidoo, B. *Journey to Jo'burg: A South African Story.* Illus. by E. Velasquez. Lippincott, 1986. (Ages 11 and up.) [Apartheid] Naledi, thirteen, and her brother Tiro, nine, fetch their mother from Johannesburg in order to save the life of their baby sister. They learn about the spirit of a people determined one day to eliminate apartheid. In the end, their journey completed and their sister on the road to health, they vow to fortify themselves for the long struggle ahead. In the sequel, *Chain of Fire* (1990), children who engage in a peaceful march are attacked by soldiers, an outspoken leader is killed in cold blood, and teenagers who protest are jailed and tortured. These books are potent indictments of apartheid and a call to young readers to be counted in the fight for freedom for all the world's people.

Neimark, A. E. *One Man's Valor: Leo Baeck and the Holocaust.* Lodestar, 1986. (Ages 10 and up.) [Holocaust] As Chief Rabbi of Berlin during the Nazi era, Baeck chose to stay in Germany and use his influence to help others escape. He spent more than two years in a concentration camp. Baeck saved thousands of people from death. This book is part of the Jewish Biography series.

Nelson, T. *And One for All.* Watts, 1989. (Ages 11 and up.) [Vietnam War] Geraldine Brennan, her older brother Wing, and Sam are close friends; but the Vietnam War threatens to tear them apart. The reconciliation between Geraldine's father and Sam happens a bit too easily; but for the most part, the action and characters are believable. They dramatically illustrate some of the difficult, divisive issues that surrounded the U.S. response to the Vietnam war.

Nicholson, M., and Winner, D. *Raoul Wallenberg.* Stevens, 1989. (Ages 12 and up.) [Holocaust] Wallenberg was born into a family of great wealth and position in Sweden. He succeeded in rescuing 100,000 Hungarian Jews before he disappeared after his arrest by Soviet soldiers. He was an exemplar of what can be done in the face of seemingly overwhelming odds.

Ofek, U. *Smoke over Golan: A Novel of the 1973 Yom Kippur War in Israel.* Illus. by L. Bloom. Harper, 1979. (Ages 10 and up.) [Middle East conflict] Written in the form of memoirs of a ten-year-old Israeli boy, this account of the twelve days of the war focuses mostly on the need for people to live together peacefully and to build rather than destroy.

Oppenheim, S. L. *The Lily Cupboard.* Illus. by R. Himler. Harper, 1992. (Ages 6–8.) [Holocaust] Set in Holland, this book for younger readers is the story of Miriam, a Jewish girl taken to the countryside to live with a Dutch family. Miriam must hide in a secret cupboard if the German soldiers come but refuses to go into the cupboard without her rabbit. When she is not discovered, she tells the relieved family that she had to care for the rabbit the way they cared for her. This heartwarming story portrays unsung heroes.

Orgel, D. *The Devil in Vienna.* Dial, 1978. (Ages 11 and up.) [Holocaust] Inge, a thirteen-year-old Jewish girl, narrates the story in the form of a diary. Lieselotte, whose father is a violent Nazi, is Inge's best friend. Despite her forced membership in the Hitler Youth, she remains loyal to Inge. Inge and her family finally escape.

Orlev, U. *The Island on Bird Street,* trans. by H. Halkin. Houghton Mifflin, 1983. (Ages 12 and up.) [Holocaust] Eleven-year-old Alex is in hiding alone in the ruins of a bombed-out house in the Warsaw Ghetto. His mother has disappeared, but he hopes that his father, who has been taken away by the Germans, will return. The details of Alex's everyday activities, the dangers he is exposed to, his final reunion with his father, and their escape into the forest to fight with the partisans make exciting, as well as inspiring, reading.

Patchen, K. *First Will and Testament.* Padell, 1948. (Ages 12 and up.) [General] Passionate and angry poetry, much of it concerning war.

Paterson, K. *Bridge to Terabithia.* Illus. by D. Diamond. Crowell, 1977. (Ages 9–12.) [Friendship] [See Death]

Paterson, K. *Park's Quest.* Lodestar, 1988. (Ages 11 and up.) [Vietnam War] Park's father died in the Vietnam war. His mother is estranged from her husband's family and refuses to talk to Park about his father. Park journeys to the Vietnam Veterans Memorial wall and takes sustenance from seeing his father's name there. Many issues emerge here, including the toll that separation exacts in any war.

Paulsen, G. *The Foxman.* Nelson, 1977. (Ages 12 and up.) [World War I] [See Abuse]

Paulsen, G. *The Monument.* Delacorte, 1991. (Ages 12 and up.) [General] Rocky, a biracial adolescent adopted by a couple from Bolton, Kansas, learns what it means to be an artist from Mick, an alcoholic and contentious but deeply talented artist hired by the town to construct a memorial to honor veterans of the Vietnam war. The focus here is on how to commemorate any war. It is mostly about the power of art to raise people above themselves, to stir them, and to make them think.

Perez, N. A. *The Slopes of War: A Novel of Gettysburg.* Houghton Mifflin, 1984. (Ages 11 and up.) [Civil War] This Canadian author has managed to convey an authentic sense of how people felt during the American Civil War. He portrays soldiers and officers on both the Confederate and Union sides. Southerners are seen here to be as much the victims of the war as Northerners. The issues are not glossed over, and the human condition overrides the battle lines.

Pirtle, S. *An Outbreak of Peace.* New Society, 1987. (Ages 13 and up.) [Peace] A group of students creates an art display for peace. The students are admirable models as they organize their activity without adult intervention. They learn to listen to one another and respect one another's differences as well as strengths.

Pople, M. *The Other Side of the Family.* Holt, 1988. (Ages 12 and up.) [World War II] [See Aging]

Posell, E. *Homecoming.* HJB, 1987. (Ages 11 and up.) [Russian Revolution] Olya tells of the terrifying circumstances her middle-class Jewish family endured during the Russian Revolution. The father flees to America in fear of his life; the mother dies of starvation. With the aid of former servants and kind strangers, the six children finally escape to join their father in the United States. The writing is uneven, and there are puzzling questions, but the impact of the story is strong, and this little-known aspect of the revolution is important.

Pringle, L. *Nuclear War: From Hiroshima to Nuclear Winter.* Illus. with photos. Enslow, 1985. (Ages 10 and up.) [Nuclear war] The history of nuclear war from the beginnings of World War II. Pringle discusses survivors in Japan and takes readers to a hypothetical city and shows what would happen in a limited nuclear war with today's more powerful weapons.

Provost, G., and Levine-Provost, G. *David and Max.* Jewish Publication Society, 1988. (Ages 9–12.) [Holocaust] David's grandfather, Max, reveals the story of his experiences in the Holocaust. Bernie, a long-lost friend of Max's has hidden his past and taken on a new identity. Both Max and Bernie feel guilty that they survived but deal with this in different ways. Their behavior and David's response to it can be helpful in demonstrating the effects this tragic period in history continues to have on later generations.

Quinlan, P. *Planting Seeds.* Illus. by V. Krykorka. Annick, 1988. (Ages 4–6.) [General] Rachel is fortunate that her parents are understanding of and responsive to her fears of violence. The metaphors of planting seeds and of hands holding the earth are presented in understandable language and images.

Ramati, A. *And the Violins Stopped Playing: A Story of the Gypsy Holocaust.* Watts, 1986. (Ages 11 and up.) [Holocaust] Young Roman and his father are among the leaders of the Gypsies, who recognize the Nazi threat but are eventually interned in concentration camps where they witness the slaughter of others of their heritage. In total, 500,000 Gypsies were killed in the Holocaust.

Rardin, S. L. *Captives in a Foreign Land.* Houghton Mifflin, 1984. (Ages 10 and up.) [Terrorism] Six children are held captive by Muslims in an attempt to force the U.S. government to abandon all nuclear weapons. The children become the instruments of their own rescue. Some of them find that their captors are not inhuman beasts; all are changed forever.

Ray, D. K. *My Daddy Was a Soldier: A World War II Story.* Illus. by the author. Holiday House, 1990. (Ages 7–10.) [World War II] Jeannie tells of her experience as a child of a soldier who is fighting overseas in World War II. She describes her mother joining the work force as a welder, ration stamps, air raid drills, a friend's brother returning home with only one leg, and especially the loneliness and fear she and her mother feel knowing that her father is engaged in battle. The book, illustrated with soft pencil drawings, authentically conveys the feelings of an American child during this war.

Reeder, C. *Shades of Gray.* Macmillan, 1989. (Ages 10–12.) [Civil War] Will Page, an orphan whose family fought on the side of the South in the Civil War, must now live with an uncle who refused to fight on either side. Will bitterly resents his uncle's stance and displays his anger openly, as do the people of the community who were once his uncle's friends. His uncle's steadfast courage, ability to accomplish tasks, ethical attitude toward all people, and consummate kindness to him finally combine to help Will understand that pacifism is not treachery or cowardice and that war is more complex than it first appears.

Reiss, J. *The Upstairs Room.* Crowell, 1972. (Ages 10–12.) [Holocaust] Annie and her family are Jews. They spend several years in hiding in Holland, but most of the family survive. The story tells of the courage not only of the Jews but also of the Dutch Christians who risked their lives to help them. In the sequel, *The Journey Back* (1976), the author brings to readers' attention the hard truth that recovery after the war does not have a fairytale ending. Anti-Semitism is still evident in the community; the years in hiding have left their mark, and the world still needs mending.

Reit, S. *Behind Rebel Lines.* HBJ, 1988. (Ages 8–11.) [Civil War] Sarah Emma Edmonds was one of an estimated four hundred women who posed as men to fight in the Civil War. Originally from Canada, Emma (as she wanted to be called) fled from an abusive father to Michigan and enlisted in the Union Army as Frank Thompson. On occasion the book is confusing because the author sometimes calls Emma by her male names (Frank and Cuff) and refers to her as he. However, the story is engaging, and the facts are well researched.

Remarque, E. M. *All Quiet on the Western Front.* Little, Brown, 1929. (Ages 12 and up.) [World War I] A classic story about the senselessness of war tells of the battles of World War I through the eyes of a group of German soldiers.

Richards, A. "A War Game." In *I Heard a Scream in the Street,* edited by N. Larrick. Dell, 1970. (Ages 11 and up.) [General] Calling war "uniformed murder," the poet mourns the killing of children.

Richter, H. P. *Friedrich.* Holt, 1970. (Ages 10 and up.) [Holocaust] Told from the perspective of a German boy whose friendship with a Jewish boy is destroyed by the war. The chronology at the end of the book is chilling in its specifics of anti-Jewish laws and actions.

Ricther, H. P. *I Was There.* Holt, 1962. (Ages 10 and up.) [World War II] An autobiographical story of the induction of two boys into the youth corps in Germany in World War II. The book deals with their confusion over many issues of war.

Ringi, K. *The Stranger.* Random House, 1968. (Ages 3–7.) [Conflict resolution] A giant stranger causes fear in a land of tiny people. When the people make war on the giant, he cries, flooding the land until the people float to his face level. There they talk easily and make friends. Face-to-face communications provide a model for real-life problem solving.

Ringi, K. *The Winner.* Harper, 1969. (Ages 3–9.) [General] A story about escalation and competition. The story deals with the ultimate absurdity of war. Although there are no words in this book, the powerful message could extend to readers well beyond age nine.

Roberts, M. *Stephanie's Children.* Victor Gollancza, 1969. (Ages 12 and up.) [French Revolution] A book dealing with the effect of the Reign of Terror on individuals and families in France during the Revolution.

Rochman, H., editor. *Somehow Tenderness Survives: Stories of Southern Africa.* Harper, 1988. (Ages 11 and up.) [Apartheid] Short stories written by South Africans of different heritages and perspectives, all opposing apartheid.

Rogasky, B. *Smoke and Ashes: The Story of the Holocaust.* Illus. with photos. Holiday House, 1988. (Ages 12 and up.) [Holocaust] Hitler's rise to power in the context of long-standing anti-Semitism. Other areas of focus include the late, inadequate response of the United States and the United Kingdom and the resurgence of anti-Semitism in the 1980s. Attention is given to rebellion and resistance by Jews and non-Jews.

Rosen, R., and McSharry, P., editors. *Apartheid: Calibrations of Color.* Rosen, 1991. (Ages 12 and up.) [Apartheid] A rich collection of stories, essays, and photos attesting to the evils of apartheid and celebrating the black South-African spirit. The introduction is by Archbishop Desmond Tutu. Included is the work of twelve prominent authors, all of whom are antiapartheid activists.

Rosen, R., and McSharry, P. *Teenage Soldiers, Adult Wars.* Rosen, 1991. (Ages 12 and up.) [General] Each writer is profiled before the presentation of his or her work. The stories describe young soldiers in Russia, Vietnam, Israel, Lithuania, Ireland, Nicaragua, Zimbabwe, Lebanon, China, the Persian Gulf, and Poland. The political message is strong.

Ross, S. *War in the Trenches.* Bookwright, 1991. (Ages 10 and up.) [World War I] Part of the "Witness History" series, this book communicates through photographs, newspaper clippings, quotations from soldiers and leading figures of the time, and short chunks of narrative what the war was like for the British soldiers in the field. An earlier work, *The Origins of World War I* (1989), provides more general information about the war.

Rossel, S. *The Holocaust: The Fire That Raged.* Watts, 1989. (Ages 12 and up.) [Holocaust] Chronicles Hitler's rise to power and his use of anti-Semitism and racism as effective tools. The necessity to examine the past and be on guard for warning signs in the future is emphasized, and the issue of accountability of the German people and government is discussed. The final message is that the only way to ensure prevention of another holocaust is through education, communication, and vigilance.

Rostkowski, M. I. *After the Dancing Days.* Harper, 1986. (Ages 11 and up.) [World War I] Annie joins her father in his work with victims of World War I and pays special attention to a young veteran who has serious burn wounds. Community attitudes toward war victims and the desire to forget the war figure in actions of the characters.

Sachs, M. *A Pocket Full of Seeds.* Illus. by B. F. Stahl. Doubleday, 1973. (Ages 9–12.) [Holocaust] Nicole and her family are French Jews. She is the only one to escape capture by the Nazis. Readers are left knowing that Nicole will survive, but sharing her anxiety and grief for her family.

Samuels, G. *Mottele.* New American Library, 1977. (Ages 12 and up.) [Holocaust] For mature readers, the gripping story of Mottele, a young Jewish boy who joins the Partisans fighting the Nazis.

Savin, M. *The Moon Bridge.* Scholastic, 1992. (Ages 9–12.) [World War II] Ruthie and Mitzi, a Japanese American, become friends. As the war continues, anti-Japanese behavior escalates. Finally, Mitzi and her family are removed to an internment camp. The two friends try to maintain contact through letters, but lose touch. After the war, Mitzi and Ruthie meet again, but each has changed, and their relationship can never again be what it was.

Schami, R. *A Hand Full of Stars.* 1987. (Ages 12 and up.) [Middle East] Spanning four years, this personal narrative details the daily life, feelings, and interactions of a young Syrian boy growing up in Damascus after World War II. His journal helps us to see what caused him to become a resistor to the oppressive government.

Scholes, K. *Peace Begins with You.* Illus. by R. Ingpen. Little, Brown, 1989. (Ages 7–10.) [Peace] Presents peace on a personal, interpersonal, and societal level and attempts to make connections between large-scale and small-scale disagreements. Methods of conflict resolution, both positive (compromise, tolerance) and negative (war, tension) are explored. Children are encouraged to begin working for peace by examining themselves, their relationships, and their ways of solving problems.

Schur, M. R. *The Circlemaker.* Dial, 1994. (Ages 11 and up.) [Conflict resolution] Two Jewish boys who have been antagonists since they were little are now forced to rely on each other for their survival as they try to escape conscription into the czar's army. They undertake a danger-fraught journey from the Ukraine into Hungary.

Sender, R. M. *The Cage.* Macmillan, 1986. (Ages 11 and up.) [Holocaust] At age 16, Riva, who lives in Poland, becomes the legal guardian of her three younger brothers. Her older siblings have been sent to Russia for protection; her mother has been taken by the Nazis. Their Christian neighbors, once close friends, have turned against them and aided the Nazis in pillaging their home. She survives, as do her siblings. A sequel, *To Life* (1988) begins the day the Germans abandoned Auschwitz and looks at the lives of the Jewish survivors immediately after the war. It details their desperate search for family and the still-present anti-Semitism in Poland. *The Holocaust Lady* (1992) tells of Riva's contemporary family and her efforts as a teacher to help children learn about the Holocaust so that it will never again happen.

Siegal, A. *Grace in the Wilderness: After the Liberation, 1945-1948.* Farrar, Straus, and Giroux, 1985. (Ages 12 and up.) [Holocaust] Piri and her sister Iboya, concentration camp survivors, are sent to Sweden, where they attend school and try to resume a normal life. In some ways, this story is even more powerful than its precursor, *Upon the Head of a Goat* (1981). The book includes tales of atrocities, but what dominates is the victory of the human spirit.

Singer, I. B. "The Power of Light." In *The Power of the Light.* Illus. by I. Lieblich. Farrar, Straus, and Giroux, 1980. (Ages 9 and up.) [Holocaust] David and Rebecca, young survivors of the Warsaw ghetto, take courage from the light of a Hanukkah candle and escape into the forest where they join the Partisans. Eventually they settle in Israel and marry. This story is the only factual one in Singer's book.

Sone, M. I. *Nisei Daughter.* University of Washington Press, 1979. (Ages 12 and up.) [World War II] A moving and authentic personal account of a Japanese-American family's internment during World War II.

St. Germain, S. *The Terrible Fight.* Illus. by D. Zemke. Houghton Mifflin, 1990. (Ages 5-8.) [Conflict resolution] Becky and Molly, next-door neighbors, are best friends until a small fight escalates. Finally, both girls independently come to the conclusion that their friendship is worth more than their petty fight.

Steele, W. O. *The Perilous Road.* HBJ, 1958. (Ages 8-12.) [Civil War] Told from the point of view of Chris, a young Southern boy who feels that the Confederate side is right, the story shows how he learns a powerful lesson about right and wrong and the ugliness of war.

Stevens, B. *Deborah Sampson Goes to War.* Illus. by F. Hill. Carolrhoda, 1984. (Ages 6-9.) [American Revolution] Strong and tall, 21-year-old Deborah dressed as a man and joined the army as Robert Shurtleff. Only at the close of the war was Deborah's identity revealed. An afterword tells about her later life, including marriage, children, and becoming the first woman lecturer in the United States to speak about her war experiences.

Suhl, Y. *Uncle Misha's Partisans.* Four Winds, 1973. (Ages 10 and up.) [Holocaust] Inspired by an actual event, the story describes Jewish partisans in the Ukraine. The hero is

Mottele, orphaned by the Nazis, who joins a band of partisans. Although the book in some ways justifies revenge and violence, it also portrays the ugliness of war. It presents a little-known fact of war, that of the active Jewish resistance.

Temple, F. *Taste of Salt: A Story of Modern Haiti.* Orchard, 1992. (Ages 12 and up.) [Haiti] Set in Haiti just after Jean-Bertrand Aristide was elected president, this is the story of Djo and Jeremie, teenage victims of poverty and the violence perpetrated by the Tarton Macoute, Duvalier's private army. The violence is graphic, making this appropriate only for mature readers, but the author admirably captures the hope and terror of life in modern Haiti.

Toll, N. S. *Behind the Secret Window: A Memoir of a Hidden Childhood during World War Two.* Dial, 1993. (Ages 11 and up.) [Holocaust] Using her diary as a foundation, the author recreates the years of World War II in Poland when she and her mother were hidden by a Polish couple. The author is also an artist, and she includes samples of the drawings she made when she was in hiding with her mother.

Trivas, I. *Annie . . . Anya: A Month in Moscow.* Illus. by the author. Orchard, 1992. (Ages 5–8.) [Friendship] Five-year-old Annie is unhappy at the prospect of spending a month in Moscow where her parents are participating in an exchange program. She sulks for the first days in a Russian day care center and refuses to participate until she is introduced to Anya. They become good friends, and soon Annie is learning Russian and discovering that the children in Moscow are much like her friends at home. In the end, the two girls vow to keep in touch.

Tsuchiya, Y. *Faithful Elephants.* Illus. by T. Lewin. Bantam, 1988. (Ages 9–12.) [World War II] An upsetting story about the decision to kill all the large animals in the Tokyo Zoo out of fear that they will escape into the general population if the zoo is bombed. The agonized zoo keeper starves them to death. The story is true. Zoos all over the world had to decide what to do with their large animals, and many of them also destroyed them. The simple, direct style of the telling adds to the impact of the story.

Turner, A. *Katie's Trunk.* Illus. by R. Himler. Macmillan, 1992. (Ages 7–10.) [American Revolution] Katie, a member of a Tory family, hides in her mother's wedding trunk to escape being caught by marauding rebels. One of the rebels is a neighbor who discovers her hiding place but does not give her away. Katie and her family are grateful that even in time of war some people remember their humanity and behave accordingly.

Uchida, Y. *Journey to Topaz: A Story of Japanese-American Evacuation.* Scribner, 1971. (Ages 9–12.) [World War II] After Pearl Harbor is attacked, Yuki and her family are forced to go to an "aliens" camp in Utah along with many other Japanese Americans. The story tells of their internment, where they endure terrible deprivation but maintain their dignity and their family ties. In the sequel, *Journey Home* (1978), the family attempt to reconstruct their lives after their release from the camp. Readers may be motivated to investigate this shameful period in American treatment of Japanese Americans.

Udry, J. M. *Let's Be Enemies.* Illus. by M. Sendak. Harper, 1961. (Ages 5–8.) [Friendship] Two boys who were once close friends fight. They never settle their conflict, but resume their friendship nevertheless. Discussions of this book can lead to suggestions for resolving personal conflicts.

Vigna, J. *Nobody Wants a Nuclear War.* Illus. by the author. Whitman, 1986. (Ages 5–8.) [Nuclear war] Two young children are frightened at the thought of nuclear war. Their mother acknowledges their feelings and describes actions of people around the world to ensure that there will never be a nuclear war. The children decide to construct a propeace banner and send a picture of it to the president of the United States. They vow to continue to work for peace throughout their lives.

Vinke, H. *The Short Life of Sophie Scholl.* Harper, 1984. (Ages 12 and up.) [Holocaust] This is one of the few books for young readers about the German teenage underground movement called the White Rose. Although the movement failed, it remains a symbol of courage and sanity in a time when these qualities were in too short supply. The author interviewed the two surviving members of Sophie Scholl's family, as well as friends, and he uses their voices in addition to Sophie's diaries, letters, photos, and drawings to help tell the story.

Volavkova, H. *I Never Saw Another Butterfly (Children's Drawings and Poems from Terezin Concentration Camp, 1942-1944).* McGraw-Hill, 1962. (All ages.) [Holocaust] Though Terezin was a waystation to an extermination camp, these poems deal with life, happiness, and freedom. A powerful indictment of war.

Vos, I., translated by T. Edelstein and I. Smidt. *Hide and Seek.* Houghton Mifflin, 1991. (Ages 12 and up.) [Holocaust] In terse sentences designed to sound like the words and thoughts of Rachel, an eight-year-old Jewish child in Nazi-dominated Holland in the early 1940s, the dread and outrage of the Holocaust unfold. The exquisite torture of edicts that banned Jews from owning bicycles and forbade them to sit on public benches is brought out through the narrative. Rachel and her immediate family survive, but at what cost? A sequel, *Anna Is Still Here* (1993), follows up on the family after the war.

Wallin, L. *In the Shadow of the Wind.* Bradbury, 1984. (Ages 11 and up.) [Civil War] Caleb McElroy is a white adolescent who befriends Creek Indians in his community in Alabama in 1835. The story is a bloody and somber tale of raids on Creek settlements and of deceit and betrayal. Caleb rescues Pine Basket and her mother from captivity. He and Pine Basket are married; and when the Civil War comes, he joins the Union army. Some of the facts about the Indian slave holdings and the arguments about the settlement of the Oklahoma Territory may be new to young readers. This book makes history come alive.

Watkins, Y. K. *So Far from the Bamboo Grove.* Lothrop Lee and Shepard 1986. (Ages 12 and up.) [World War II] Yoko, her sister, and her mother flee from North Korea to their native Japan after World War II. It is a dangerous journey, and they narrowly escape capture by North Korean soldiers. The mother dies; but the two young women manage to survive. The epilogue tells us that the girls' father returned from a Siberian prison camp six years later.

Williams, M. *Crocodile Burning.* Dutton, 1992. (Ages 12 and up.) [Apartheid] The crocodile, a symbol of fear and evil in South Africa, forms a powerful and recurring metaphor in this novel. Seraki wins a role in an antiapartheid musical chosen for a Broadway run. By organizing the cast members and confronting the dishonest director (with the help of a lawyer), Seraki is able to negotiate a fair contract for the cast. He learns a great deal about the many forms oppression can take and emerges a stronger person for it. The story never resorts to gratuitous violence. The author is a white South African.

Yolen, J. *All Those Secrets of the World.* Illus. by L. Baker. Little, Brown, 1991. (Ages 6–9.) [General] A personalized reflection from a child's point of view of daddy going off to war, staying away for a long time, and finally returning. Details of everyday living at home contrast with the abstraction and distance of war, helping children understand the real effects of separation.

Yolen, J. *The Devil's Arithmetic.* Viking, 1988. (Ages 10 and up.) [Holocaust] Hannah is annoyed at having to go to her grandparents' house in the Bronx for the Passover *seder*. She feels a special kinship with her Aunt Eva, for whose dear friend she was named; but she feels no real connection with the rest of her family or, for that matter, with the Jewish people. During the part of the *seder* where she is asked to symbolically open the door for the prophet Elijah, she steps back in time into the *shtetl* of her grandparents during the Holocaust. When she is permitted to avoid the ovens, she substitutes herself for her friend Rivka (later Eva) and dies in her place. At that point, she reenters the present and returns to the *seder* table, knowledgeable and forever a part of her people. The authenticity of the Yiddish phrases and customs helps involve the reader. The author, a master storyteller, has used not only her personal experience but also her impeccable research skills to weave a tale that is potent and unforgettable.

Zalben, J. B. *The Fortuneteller in 5B.* Holt, 1991. (Ages 10-12.) [Holocaust] [See Aging]

Ziefert, H. *A New Coat for Anna.* Illus. by A. Lobel. Knopf, 1986. (Ages 7-10.) [World War II] Set in the aftermath of World War II and based on a true story, this book tells of the inventiveness and determination of Anna's mother in seeing to it that her daughter has a warm new coat for the winter by enlisting the cooperation of farmers and craftspeople. Too often war is thought of in terms of battles and victories. Here is an accurate and accessible accounting of how people rebuild afterward.

Zeinert, K. *The Warsaw Ghetto Uprising.* Millbrook, 1993. (Ages 12 and up.) [Holocaust] The author tells in unemotional language about the Jews' removal to ghettos, the systematic deportation to concentration camps of 300,000 Jews from the Warsaw Ghetto, and finally the plan to burn the Ghetto and kill all the remaining Jews. The uprising in Warsaw stands as a symbol of Jewish resistance in the Holocaust.

Zolotow, C. *The Hating Book.* Illus. by B. Shecter. Harper, 1969. (Ages 3-8.) [Conflict resolution] Two girls who are friends have a misunderstanding but settle it in a peaceful fashion. This story makes a good discussion starter on the topic of personal conflict.

Appendixes

APPENDIX A: RESOURCES FOR TEACHING A LITERATURE-BASED CURRICULUM

Altwerger, B.; Edelsky, C.; and Flores, B. M. "Whole Language: What's New?" *The Reading Teacher* 41 (Nov. 1987): 144-154. The authors describe whole language and provide definitions for frequently used terms.

Atwell, N. *In the Middle: Writing, Reading, and Learning with Adolescents.* Boynton/Cook, 1987. The author describes how her views about student writing have changed, the connection between writing and reading, and the processes she has used in her classroom. Includes examples of student writing.

Atwell, N. *Side By Side: Essays on Teaching to Learn.* Boynton/Cook, 1991. Continues the author's exploration of the reading and writing process began in *In the Middle*. Looks at such topics as the teaching of poetry, special education students, teaching critical thinking skills, and teacher research.

Barchers, S. L. *Creating and Managing the Literature Classroom.* Teacher Ideas Press, 1990. A detailed guide for setting up a "literate classroom." Provides suggestions for materials, where to obtain them, and how to use them.

Booklinks: Connecting Books, Libraries, and Classrooms. American Library Association. A bimonthly journal describing books linked by themes, suggestions for stimulating discussions, and activities for student involvement.

Bromley, K. D. *Webbing with Literature: Creating Story Maps with Children's Books.* Allyn and Bacon, 1991. The author explains the use of semantic webbing in enhancing children's understanding of literature. She provides examples of webs for 50 books and brief annotations of 145 other books.

Brown, H., and Cambourne, B. *Read and Retell.* Heinemann, 1987. Discusses a strategy, "read and retell," that can be used in teaching literature. Offers specific suggestions for how to use this procedure. The book contains full texts from different genres, with suggestions for how to make use of them.

Brown, H., and Mathie, V. *Inside Whole Language: A Classroom View.* Heinemann, 1991. Offers both a theoretical basis and an account of the practice of teaching whole language in the classroom.

413

Burchby, M. "Literature and Whole Language." *The New Advocate* 1 (Spring 1988): 114–123. The author critiques basal instruction and describes the use of whole language instruction. Includes specific suggestions using children's literature in helping children learn a variety of topics.

Butzow, C. M., and Butzow, J. W. *Science through Children's Literature: An Integrated Approach.* Teacher Ideas Press. Libraries Unlimited, 1989. Provides a rationale for integrating literature and science instruction and offers suggestions for teachers. Includes examples of science units for grades K–3.

Cairney, T. H. *Other Worlds: The Endless Possibilities of Literature.* Heinemann, 1991. A practical guide for teachers to create an environment where literature is valued and enjoyed. The author draws upon both research and his own experience to provide background and suggestions for lessons.

Calkins, L. M. *Lessons from a Child: On the Teaching and Learning of Writing.* Heinemann, 1983. Focusing on one child's development as a writer, the author discusses an approach to teaching writing. Issues such as classroom management, the connection of reading and writing, and getting children to help one another are included.

Carbo, M.; Dunn, R.; and Dunn, K. *Teaching Students to Read through Their Individual Learning Styles.* Prentice-Hall, 1986. Written for teachers, parents, and special educators, this book emphasizes the importance of the individual child's learning style in teaching children to read. Includes discussion of some strategies.

Carroll, J. A. *Picture Books: Integrated Teaching, Writing, Listening, Speaking, Viewing, and Thinking.* Teacher Ideas Press, 1991. The author offers specific suggestions for activities to integrate literature throughout the curriculum, using 28 books as examples.

Clayton, L. R. *Explorations: Educational Activities for Young Children.* Teacher Ideas Press, 1991. Organized around eleven different themes such as the zoo, home, the forest, and the old west. The author provides ideas about how to teach math, reading, motor skills, art, and other areas within each theme. Written for teachers, parents, and others who work with young children.

Cordier, M. H., and Perez-Stable, M. A. *Peoples of the American West: Historical Perspectives through Children's Literature.* Scarecrow, 1989. An annotated bibliography of 100 historical fiction and nonfiction books for children.

Crafton, L. K. *Whole Language: Getting started . . . Moving Forward.* Owen, 1991. A resource book for teachers interested in or already involved in using whole language in the classroom. Discusses a variety of problems teachers have faced in their work with whole language.

Cullinan, B. E., editor. *Children's Literature in the Reading Program.* International Reading Association, 1987. Many well-known authors advocate the inclusion of children's literature in the reading program and offer suggestions for implementation.

Cullinan, B. E., editor. *Invitation to Read: More Children's Literature in the Reading Program.* International Reading Association, 1992. Offers teaching strategies, suggestions of books for a range of students, and ideas about implementing a literature-based reading program.

Cunningham, P. M.; Moore, S. A.; Cunningham, J. W.; and Moore, D. W. *Reading in Elementary Classrooms: Strategies and Observations.* 2nd ed. Longman, 1989. In the first part of this book, the authors discuss effective methods for teaching children to read. They provide background on different stages of language development, discuss the integration of reading throughout the curriculum, and outline diagnostic and assessment techniques. Part Two follows an imaginary group of children from kindergarten to fifth grade, giving examples of the various topics discussed in Part One.

Doll, C. A. *Nonfiction Books for Children.* Teacher Ideas Press, 1990. Provides suggestions for integrating nonfiction books into the curriculum. Looks at specific titles from different types of nonfiction and outlines activities for using them.

Draper, M. K., and Schwietert, L. H. *A Practical Guide to Individualized Reading*, revised and edited by May Lazar. New York City Board of Education, Bureau of Educational Research, 1960.

Dunn, S., with Pamenter, L. *Butterscotch Dreams: Chants for Fun and Learning.* Heinemann, 1987. A collection of chants, with suggestions for activities to be done with each one.

Dwyer, J. *A Sea of Talk*. Heinemann, 1989. This book focuses on the talk that goes on in a classroom. The writers emphasize the importance of talking as a tool for learning and its use throughout the curriculum.

Edelsky, C.; Altwerger, B.; and Flores, B. *Whole Language: What's the Difference?* Heinemann, 1991. The authors provide theoretical and historical background for the concept of whole language. A series of vignettes show examples of whole language classrooms.

Eldredge, J. L., and Butterfield, D. "Alternatives to Traditional Reading Instruction." *The Reading Teacher* 40 (Oct. 1986): 32-37. Report of research that found more gains in achievement and interest in reading in second grade classrooms where children's literature was used than in classrooms where basal instruction was used.

Feeley, J. T.; Strickland, D. S.; and Wepner, S. B., editors. *Process Reading and Writing: A Literature-Based Approach*. Teachers College Press, 1991. This book is designed to help teachers move from a textbook-centered way of teaching literacy to a process-driven method. The writers offer their experiences and suggestions for making the transition at different age levels and for a variety of settings.

Glazer, S. M., and Brown, C. S. *Portfolios and Beyond: Collaborative Assessment in Reading and Writing*. Christopher-Gordon, 1993. Discusses a rationale for alternative assessment procedures in the classroom and provides detailed suggestions for implementation.

Goodman, K. "Basal Readers: A Call for Action." *Language Arts* 63 (April 1986): 358-363. The author points out the widening gap between the basal reading program and the latest theory and research in reading instruction.

Goodman, K. "Look What They've Done to Judy Blume!: The 'Basalization' of Children's Literature." *The New Advocate* 1 (Winter, 1988): 29-41. The author argues for giving children authentic children's literature rather than adaptations that have been rewritten.

Goodman, K. *What's Whole in Whole Language?* Heinemann, 1986. This short book provides an overview of whole language, discussing its theoretical basis as well as examples of whole language programs and suggestions for how they can be implemented.

Goodman, K. S.; Bird, L. B.; and Goodman, Y. M. *The Whole Language Catalog: Supplement on Authentic Assessment*. McGraw-Hill, 1992. Explains how to use authentic assessment for teachers, parents, and school administrators. Looks at the history of standardized testing, critiquing how it has been used and the industry that has been set up.

Goodman, K. S.; Shannon, P.; Freeman, Y. S.; and Murphy, S. *Report Card on Basal Readers*. Owen, 1988. The authors take a critical look at basals and their use. The history and philosophy of basals are provided as background to a discussion of their economics and creation. Suggestions are given for alternative ways of teaching children to read and enjoy reading.

Goodman, Y. M.; Hood, W. J.; and Goodman, K. S. *Organizing for Whole Language.* Heinemann, 1991. Teachers, parents, administrators, and teacher educators provide examples of how whole language can become a part of the curriculum.

Graves, D. *Build a Literate Classroom*. Heinemann, 1991. The author offers specific suggestions for working with children on a reading and writing program. He gives ideas for organizing the classrooms, keeping records, and evaluating progress.

Griffiths, R. and Clyne, M. *Books You Can Count On: Linking Mathematics and Literature*. Heinemann, 1991. A resource for elementary school teachers suggesting ways of teaching mathematics through literature.

Hancock, J., and Hill, S., editors. *Literature-Based Reading Programs at Work.* Heinemann, 1987. Discusses problems teachers encounter when implementing a literature-based reading program and offers possible solutions. Also includes discussion of how teachers' beliefs affect their work with children.

Hansen, J. *When Writers Read.* Heinemann, 1987. The author relates a story about changes that occurred in a school when the process approach to teaching writing was used to teach reading. Discusses how her own thinking has changed.

Harp, B., editor. *Assessment and Evaluation in Whole Language Programs.* Christopher Gordon, 1993. The contributors to this book cover a variety of topics related to assessment and whole language. The first few chapters discuss the theoretical background of whole language and assessment of students. The rest of the chapters look at issues such as multiculturalism, special needs, different age levels, and record keeping in whole language classrooms.

Harp, B., editor. *Bringing Children to Literacy: Classrooms at Work.* Christopher-Gordon, 1993. The contributors are nine teachers who are using whole language as the basis of instruction within their classrooms. Each discusses a different strategy that they implement within the classroom. Some of the topics are the writing process, technology, drama, guided reading, and basic skills instruction.

Harste, J. C. *New Policy Guidelines for Reading: Connecting Research and Practice.* National Council of Teachers of English, 1989. Recommendations about effective policy for reading instruction and research. Based on a program of research designed to evaluate current policies and practices. In general, the policies support a whole language base for reading instruction.

Harste, J. C.; Woodward, V. A.; and Burke, C. L. *Language Stories and Literacy Lessons.* Heinemann, 1984. The authors describe their study of literacy and young children, suggesting implications for teachers and the curriculum. They look at the ways children develop literacy before coming to school and discuss the possible impact of what they find on current school instruction and curriculum.

Hart-Hewins, L., and Wells, J. *Real Books for Reading.* Heinemann, 1990. A guide to using books to encourage a love of reading in children. Includes suggestions for a variety of activities with children and a bibliography of children's books.

Heller, M. F. *Reading-Writing Connections: From Theory to Practice.* Longman, 1991. Provides both theoretical background and practical suggestions for integrating reading and writing in K–middle school. Includes bibliographies of children's books and a list of computer software.

Heltshe, M. A., and Kirchner, A. B. *Joyous Journeys with Books: Multicultural Explorations.* Teacher Ideas Press, 1991. Consists of integrated units of study of six different areas of the world: Hawaii, Japan, Australia, Italy, Kenya, and Brazil. The units emphasize whole language and experiential learning. Useful for elementary teachers or librarians.

Hopkins, L. B. *Let Them Be Themselves,* 3rd ed. Harper, 1992. A resource for teaching the language arts, this book includes activities to introduce children to literature, suggestions for expanding school libraries, and other ideas to assist teachers.

Hornsby, D., and Sukarna, D. *Read On: A Conference Approach to Reading.* Heinemann, 1988. A practical guide to implementing a reading program in the classroom. Including suggestions for planning and organizing, developing reading skills, and evaluation.

Hudson-Ross, S.; Cleary, L. M.; and Casey, M., editors. *Children's Voices: Children Talk about Literacy.* Heinemann, 1993. Fifty children ranging from kindergarten to eighth grade share their ideas about reading and literacy. Using interviews, the authors have gathered profiles of children and their thoughts regarding reading, writing, and school. Contains an appendix on conducting interviews with children.

Jenkins, C., and Freeman, S. *Novel Experiences: Literature Units.* Teacher Ideas Press, 1991. Provides leader guides for 35 books ranging from grade two through grade six. For each book the authors give a summary, suggestions for activities, questions for discussion, and a list of related books.

Johnson, T. D., and Louis, D. R. *Bringing It All Together: A Program for Literacy.* Heinemann, 1990. The authors discuss the theory behind their ideas and offer more suggestions for implementing a literature program in the classroom.

Johnson, T. D., and Louis, D. R. *Literacy through Literature.* Heinemann, 1987. Offers ideas on how to introduce children to literature. Discusses how these activities are related to how children learn to read.

Justice, J. *The Ghost and I: Scary Stories for Participatory Telling.* Yellow Moon, 1992. Using the medium of ghost stories, the contributors to this book provide the story and suggestions for telling the story. Also included are suggestions for follow up activities to be used with children.

Kelly, J. *The Battle of Books.* Teacher Ideas Press, 1990. For anyone who works with children, this book describes a game that can be used to show children the fun and excitement of books and reading. The basic format is to ask children to name titles and authors based on questions about the plot, characters, and setting.

Kruise, C. S. *Those Blooming Books: A Handbook for Extending Thinking Skills.* Libraries Unlimited, 1987. This book presents literature-based activities to be used primarily with children in grades one through three. Sixteen books are discussed with suggestions for activities given for each.

Kulleseid, E. R., and Strickland, D. S. *Literature, Literacy, and Learning.* American Library Association, 1989. Gives theoretical background and findings from research in support of a literature-based literacy program. Suggestions are given for implementing these ideas in a school with emphasis on collaborative work among students, teachers, administrators, and librarians.

Lamme, L. L., and Ledbetter, L. "Libraries: The Heart of Whole Language." *Language Arts* 67 (Nov. 1990): 735-741. The authors describe ways teachers and librarians can work together to maximize the use of a school's library media resources.

Laughlin, M. K., and Street, T. P. *Literature-Based Art and Music.* Oryx, 1992. Provides outlines for units in art and music that make use of books to enhance the topic. Units are for ages kindergarten through fifth grade. Topics include color, shape, space, pitch, tempo, and folk songs.

Laughlin, M. K., and Swisher, C. L. *Literature-Based Reading: Children's Books and Activities to Enrich the K-5 Curriculum.* Oryx Press, 1990. Written for educators responsible for conducting a reading program for children, whether the method used is whole language or basal series. Offers specific activities and suggestions for K-5 classrooms.

Lee, B., and Rudman, M. K. *Leading to Reading.* Berkeley, 1983. A compendium of practical suggestions and activities for helping children enjoy and learn from reading. Everyday materials and experiences as well as TV, books, and travel are used to motivate and instruct young readers and writers.

McGlathery, G., and Livo, N. J. *Who's Endangered on Noah's Art: Literary and Scientific Activities for Teachers and Parents.* Teacher Ideas Press, 1992. Provides an approach to teaching children K-12 about endangered animals by integrating literature and science activities. Uses folklore, news articles, scientific information, and classroom activities.

Meek, M. *On Being Literate.* Heinemann, 1991. Looks at the questions of what it means to be literate and how to evaluate how literate children should be in today's society. The author argues that a society changes dramatically in many different arenas and we can no longer take for granted how literacy manifests itself. Careful thought is needed to determine what children need to be literate in a changing world.

Moffett, J., and Wagner, B. J. *Student-Centered Language Arts, K-12,* 4th ed. Heinemann, 1992. A comprehensive resource book on the teaching of language arts utilizing whole language, collaborative learning, the process approach, student empowerment, and other related activities.

Mohr, C.; Nixon, D.; and Vickers, S. *Books That Heal: A Whole Language Approach.* Teacher Ideas Press, 1991. Focuses on the use of fiction to help children deal with issues such as death, divorce, relationships, and differences. Looks at specific books on these and other topics and provides questions and activities.

Moore, T. J., and Hampton, A. B. *Book Bridges: Story-Inspired Activities for Children Three through Eight.* Teacher Ideas Press, 1991. Designed for use by teachers, parents, and others interested in introducing young children to the world of books. Includes a wide variety of activities to be used in connection with picture books.

Moss, J. F. *Focus Units in Literature: A Handbook for Elementary School Teachers.* National Council of Teachers of English, 1984. Outlines thirteen units on a variety of topics. A bibliography, sample questions for discussion, and other activities are given for each unit.

Neamen, M., and Strong, M. *Literature Circles: Cooperative Learning for Grades 3-8.* Teacher Ideas Press, 1992. Written for teachers of the intermediate grades, this book offers suggestions for activities and projects involving reading and cooperative learning.

Neuman, S. B., and Roskos, K. A. *Language and Literacy Learning in the Early Years: An Integrated Approach.* HBJ, 1993. This book provides a framework for understanding how children develop language and literacy. Guidelines are given for helping teachers, parents, and others who work with young children build upon the skills and understanding the children have already developed.

Newman, J. D., editor. *Whole Language: Theory in Use.* Heinemann, 1985. Essays by teachers about how their teaching has been affected by their understanding of whole language.

Olsen, M. L. *Creative Connections: Literature and the Reading Program.* Libraries Unlimited, 1987. A curriculum resource guide for teachers of grades 1-3. Includes summaries of books and details activities to use in connecting literature with the rest of the curriculum. Also gives suggestions of related books.

Pappas, C. C.; Kiefer, B. Z.; and Levstik, L. S. *An Integrated Language Perspective in the Elementary School.* Longman, 1990. Discusses integrated language theory and provides specific examples of how it can be implemented in the classroom. Includes eight detailed units for use in grades K-6.

Pilger, M. A. *Multicultural Projects Index.* Libraries Unlimited, 1992. An extensive index to handicrafts, food, games, and activities from around the world. Each entry contains a subject, a description, and a book relevant to that particular topic. Over 1000 books are listed. A valuable resources for parents and teachers.

Polkingharn, A. T., and Toohey, C. Illus. by L. Welker. *Creative Encounters: Activities to Expand Children's Responses to Literature.* Libraries Unlimited, 1983. Suggests a variety of activities to stimulate children's interest in books. Uses specific books as examples.

Polkingharn, A. T., and Toohey, C. Illus. by L. Welker. *More Creative Encounters: Activities to Expand Children's Responses to Literature.* Libraries Unlimited, 1988. More activities to enhance children's interest in books.

Routman, R. *Invitations: Changing as Teachers and Learners K-12.* Heinemann, 1991. Provides assistance for teachers attempting to change how they practice. A comprehensive annotated bibliography is included.

Routman, R. *Transitions: From Literature to Literacy.* Heinemann, 1988. The author discusses reading and writing as processes. An extensive section on resources for teachers is included.

Rudman, M. K. "Children's Literature in the Reading Program." In *Children's Literature: Resource for the Classroom.* Christopher-Gordon, 1993. Chapter 8 substantively outlines how to apply children's literature to the classroom, using it as the reading program as well as an integrating element across the curriculum. Other chapters in the book include Jennifer Ladd's "Global Education and Children's Literature" and Leigh Bennett Hopkins's "Poetry-Practically," both of which make specific recommendations for incorporating literature into the classroom.

Sadler, G. E., editor. *Teaching Children's Literature: Issues, Pedagogy, Resources.* Modern Language Association of America, 1992. Provides a comprehensive overview of the state of teaching children's literature at the undergraduate and graduate levels. Includes essays on critical issues and approaches in children's literature, as well as course descriptions sent in response to a nationwide survey.

Saul, W., and Jagusch, S. A., editors. *Vital Connections: Children, Science, and Books.* Heinemann, 1991. A collection of essays focused on the inclusion of children's books in teaching science. Children's books can be used to stimulate interest, illuminate scientific concepts, and make connections between the world of science and other aspects of a child's life.

Shanahan, T. *Reading and Writing Together: New Perspectives for the Classroom.* Christopher-Gordon, 1990. The focus of this book is the connection between reading and writing. It discusses the latest theories of reading and writing, looks at research, and offers ideas about classroom practice.

Simons, E. R. *Student Worlds, Student Words: Teaching Writing through Folklore.* Heinemann, 1990. Looks at the use of the students' folklore—their own traditions and history—in teaching writing. It is designed as a series of units to be used in the classroom. These units include background information, activities, and suggested readings.

Smith, F. *Reading without Nonsense,* 2nd ed. Teachers College Press, 1985. The main theme of this book is that "reading must make sense to the learner, and so must reading instruction." The author includes research regarding children's understanding of literacy before formal schooling. This new edition also includes a section on the use of computers in literacy education.

Smith, F. *Understanding Reading.* Erlbaum, 1986. Looks at the skill of reading and learning to read from a variety of perspectives: linguistic, psychological, social, and physiological. The focus is on what teachers and others need to be aware of as they work with children.

Stephens, D. *Research on Whole Language.* Owen, 1991. Including historical, philosophical, and practical perspectives, the book reports on many research projects in the field of whole language. Focuses on scholarly reflection rather than anecdotal comments. The studies include a focus on teachers as well as students.

Stevenson, C., and Carr, J. F. *Integrated Studies in the Middle Grades: Dancing through Walls.* Teachers College Press, 1993. The authors brought together a group of middle school teachers to discuss and design a new curriculum that responded to the interests and concerns of middle school students. This book represents the teachers' insights and activities, along with detailed curriculum units.

Strickland, D. S., and Morrow, L. M., editors. *Emerging Literacy: Young Children Learn to Read and Write.* International Reading Association, 1989. The contributors to this book offer practical suggestions based on theory and research.

Thomas, J. R. "Books in the Classroom: Unweaving the Rainbow." *The Horn Book,* November/December, 1987, pp. 782–787. The author presents an eloquent argument why children need to be given the opportunity to read children's literature rather than rely on textbook versions of the stories.

Tierney, R. J.; Carter, M. A.; and Desai, L. E. *Portfolio Assessment in the Reading-Writing Classroom.* Christopher-Gordon, 1991. Discusses the use of portfolios as a tool for assessment. Provides information based on research, as well as clear suggestions for getting started on using portfolios in the classroom.

Tunnell, M. O., and Ammon, R., editors. *The Story of Ourselves: Teaching History through Children's Literature.* Heinemann, 1993. The contributors to this book focus on the possibility of using children's literature in teaching history. They offer suggestions for teachers who want to use children's books in the history and social studies curriculum.

Tunnell, M. O., and Jacobs, J. S. "Using 'Real' Books: Research Findings on Literature Based Reading Instruction." *The Reading Teacher* 42 (March 1989): 470–477. The authors review studies that compared literature-based reading programs and basal instruction. They also look at research that studied the reading growth of children in whole language classrooms.

Veatch, J. *Reading in the Elementary School.* 2nd ed., Owen, 1976. An introductory text on teaching reading. Includes chapters on classroom management, various stages of learning to read, and evaluation.

Walker, P. P. *Bring in the Arts.* Heinemann, 1993. Written for teachers in elementary and middle schools, this book contains 20 lesson plans concerning drama, art, and writing stories. Practical suggestions are given for adapting and implementing these lessons.

Watson, D. J. *Ideas and Insights: Language Arts in the Elementary School.* National Council of Teachers of English, 1987. Suggestions for activities for using whole language in the classroom. Includes bibliography of children's books.

Watts, I. N. *Making Stories.* Heinemann, 1992. Practical suggestions for encouraging students to "create, build and dramatize their own stories." Offers ideas for how to get students started and how to make use of readily available materials such as newspapers, letters, and folktales.

Weaver, C. *Understanding Whole Language: From Principles to Practice.* Heinemann, 1990. Written for school administrators, teachers, and teacher educators, this book discusses topics such as the theoretical underpinnings of whole language, the development of literacy, implementing whole language in the classroom, and assessment.

Whiten, D. J., and Wilde, S. *Read Any Good Math Lately?* Heinemann, 1992. The authors make the connection between children's literature and mathematics by discussing specific books that have a mathematical theme or component. Contains bibliographies.

Yeager, D. C. *The Whole Language Companion.* Scott, Foresman, 1992. A resource for teachers interested in implementing whole language in their classroom. Offers rationale, suggestions for planning, and teaching strategies and activities for use with students.

APPENDIX B: ADDITIONAL REFERENCES FOR THE STUDY OF CHILDREN'S LITERATURE

Anderson, W., and Groff, P. *A New Look at Children's Literature.* Wadsworth, 1972. Provides a methodology for literary analysis of children's stories. Also examines and discusses different types of children's literature. Presents a stimulating and intelligent set of recommendations for teaching literature to children. Contains an annotated bibliography of children's books corresponding to the different types of books examined in the text.

Bacon, B., editor. *How Much Do We Tell the Children?: The Politics of Children's Literature.* Marxist Educational Press, 1988. A collection of chapters by various writers, almost all of whom criticize capitalist values and espouse a social, political, and economic thematic approach to children's books. They also support helping children develop a critical stance in reading. Several chapters deal with racism in children's literature.

Bader, B. *American Picture Books from Noah's Ark to the Beast Within.* Macmillan, 1976. In this comprehensive history of art in children's books, the author discusses how advancing reproduction techniques have changed the way artists have worked. Although the book is out of print, it is worth searching for in libraries.

Barton, B., and Booth, D. *Stories in the Classroom.* Heinemann, 1990. The authors are interested in helping classroom teachers make stories and storytelling an important part of the curriculum. These stories include both the children's own work and published books. They are also concerned with creating a community within the classroom as children learn to work with each other as well as with the teacher.

Benedict, S., and Carlisle, L., editors. *Beyond Words: Picture Books for Older Readers and Writers.* Heinemann, 1992. Drawing on classroom teachers, students, college professors, and authors and illustrators of picture books, this book provides a wide variety of ways to think about and make use of picture books for older readers.

Bracken, J., and Wigutoff, S. *Books for Today's Children: An Annotated Bibliography of Non-Stereotyped Picture Books.* Feminist Press, 1979. Discusses and recommends over 100 books for young children containing positive values. The titles are arranged in lists of highly recommended, recommended, and recommended with some reservation.

Bracken, N., and Wigutoff, S., with Baker, I. *Books for Today's Young Readers: An Annotated Bibliography of Recommended Fiction for Ages 10–14.* Feminist Press, 1981. Descriptions and analyses of books for older readers. Gender, peer friendship, special needs, families in transition, foster care and adoption, and views of old people are some of the categories specified. Very helpful discussion and format.

Brooks, P., editor. *The Child's Part.* Beacon Press, 1969. Provides a scholarly and historical approach to children's literature. Focuses on French critics and sources but concerns itself with children's literature in general.

Buncombe, F., and Peetoom, A. *Literature-Based Learning: One School's Journey.* Scholastic, 1988. In this short chronicle of a visit to one school, the authors observe how the teachers are making use of literature-based curriculum. Both the authors' comments and the teachers' comments are included.

Burke, E. M. *Early Childhood Literature: For Love of Child and Book.* 2nd ed. Allyn and Bacon, 1986. For teachers, parents, and others who work with young children, this book looks at how literature can be used to be a creative and productive element in children's development. The author discusses various types of literature and offers suggestions for specific activities.

Cameron, E. *The Green and Burning Tree.* Little, Brown, 1969. A collection of essays about children's books. Sensitive analyses of the feelings and intentions of authors. The book includes discussions of fantasy as well as how to write for children.

Carlsen, G. *Books and the Teenage Reader,* 2nd ed. Harper, 1980. Useful discussion of literary genres for readers age twelve and up, but extremely out of date. Does not acknowledge any of the social issues handled by contemporary books. Bibliographies are briefly annotated.

Carlson, R. K. *Emerging Humanity, Multi-Ethnic Literature for Children and Adolescents.* Brown, 1972. Descriptions and suggestions for using children's books containing characters of different ethnic and cultural backgrounds. Very practical and classroom oriented.

Carlson, R. K. *Enrichment Ideas.* Brown, 1976. Each chapter contains a brief discussion of the topic, the history of language, vocabulary expansion, poetry, and books using loneliness as a theme. Selected references are listed but not annotated. Hundreds of activities are described for children to do as an extension of their reading about and studying the above topics.

Caterson, J. H., editor. *Children and Literature.* International Reading Association, 1970. Articles representing an overview of children's literature. Includes theory as well as practice for classroom teachers.

Cianciolo, P. J., editor. *Picture Books for Children.* 2nd ed. American Library Association, 1981. An excellent resource and guide. The annotations of the books are useful and informational. The categories overlap somewhat, but the book is generally easy to use.

Coles, R. *The Call of Stories: Teaching and the Moral Imagination.* Houghton Mifflin, 1989. A passionate and persuasive argument for the value of literature and discussions about literature to help people face their own situations and work through their problems.

Cullinan, B. E. *Literature and the Child.* 2nd ed. HBJ, 1989. Advocates that critical reading of literature be taught to elementary school children. Presents literary analyses of children's narrative fiction. Suggests activities for teachers and students to extend their critical abilities further.

Davis, J. E., and Davis, H. K. *Your Reading: A Booklist for Junior High and Middle School Students.* National Council of Teachers of English, 1988. Annotated bibliography on a wide variety of topics of interest to adolescents.

Egoff, S.; Stubbs, G. T.; and Ashley, L. F., editors. *Only Connect: Readings on Children's Literature.* Oxford University Press, 1980. A highly literate and stimulating collection of essays critically analyzing and discussing different aspects of children's literature.

Farrel, E. J., and Squire, J. R. *Transactions with Literature: A Fifty-Year Perspective.* National Council of Teachers of English, 1990. A collection of articles written to commemorate the fiftieth anniversary of the publication of Louise M. Rosenblatt's *Literature As Exploration.* The authors of the articles discuss the changes that have taken place in the teaching and use of literature over the past fifty years.

Gallo, D. R., editor. *Authors' Insights: Turning Teenagers into Readers and Writers.* Boynton/Cook, 1992. This collection of essays by authors who write books for teenagers focuses on both literature for young people and encouraging young people to become authors themselves. Suggestions are included regarding the teaching of literature and writing, activities for use in classrooms, and arranging authors' visits to schools.

Gallo, D. R., editor. *Speaking for Ourselves.* National Council of Teachers of English, 1990. A collection of short autobiographical sketches of some authors of books for young people.

Georgiou, C. *Children and Their Literature.* Prentice-Hall, 1969. Presents a genre approach to the study of children's literature. Its uniqueness lies in the lushness of its illustrations and its focus on the aesthetic quality of books. The extrawide blocks of text are difficult to read, but the text itself is interesting.

Gillespie, M. C. *History and Trends.* Brown, 1970. A fascinating and thorough account of the history of children's literature, including several little-known names and interesting bits of information. Little attention is paid to contemporary times, but the book as a whole is entertaining and informative.

Glazer, J. I. *Literature for Young Children,* 3rd ed. Merrill, 1991. Discusses how literature can be an important part of a child's development on many different levels. Offers suggestions for those working with young children.

Hall, S. *Using Picture Storybooks to Teach Literary Devices: Recommended Books for Children and Young Adults.* Oryx Press, 1990. This book is in two parts. The first discusses the use of picture books in teaching literary concepts such as metaphor or irony. The second is a compilation of books organized under the literary concept they can be used to teach.

Harris, V. J., editor. *Teaching Multicultural Literature in Grades K–8.* Christopher-Gordon, 1993. Drawing on the expertise and insights from a wide variety of people, the editor of this book has pulled together an important work on the representation of people of color in children's literature. The authors discuss stereotyping, politics, and the need for accurate portrayals of people of color in children's literature. They provide lists of available books and make suggestions for their use.

Harrison, B., and Maguire, G., editors. *Innocence and Experience: Essays and Conversations on Children's Literature.* Lothrop Lee and Shepard, 1987. All the material in this book was gathered from programs presented at the Simmons College Center for the Study of Children's Literature. The section on realism includes perspectives on censorship, war, writing from the heart, and the importance of truth in literature for children.

Haviland, V. *Children's Literature: A Guide to Reference Sources.* Library of Congress, 1966. *Third Supplement,* 1982. Two books containing an enormous number of annotated references covering the entire field of children's literature. The format is somewhat difficult to use. There are some important references omitted, but the two volumes are extensive resources.

Hearne, B. *Choosing Books for Children: A Commonsense Guide*. Delacorte, 1990. The author discusses her favorite books as a starting point for those interested in children's literature and in helping children learn to enjoy reading.

Hearne, B., editor. *The Zena Sutherland Lectures, 1983–1992*. Clarion Books, 1993. A collection of lectures given by illustrators and authors of children's books.

Hickman, J., and Cullinan, B. E., editors. *Children's Literature in the Classroom: Weaving Charlotte's Web*. Christopher-Gordon, 1989. Teachers, librarians, professors, and children's authors contributed to this book, which is written in honor of Charlotte Huck. They discuss various aspects of children's literature, look at specific genres, and make suggestions for integrating literature into the classroom.

Hopkins, L. B. *Books Are by People*. Citation Press, 1969. Interesting accounts of authors and illustrators of children's books. Hopkins interviewed 104 people for this book. The information is presented in a personal, informal style. *More Books by More People* (1974), adds 65 authors and illustrators to the list.

Huck, C. S.; Hepler, S.; and Hickman, J. *Children's Literature in the Elementary School*, 5th ed. HBJ, 1993. This text is valuable, extensive, and informative. Although the book emphasizes a genre and historical approach to children's literature, it also includes a substantial section on practical and creative methods for the classroom. Descriptions of children's books are sensitively and interestingly written. An awareness is expressed of the issues in children's books.

Issues in Children's Book Selection: A School Library Journal/Library Journal Anthology. Bowker, 1973. A collection of articles presenting perspectives on selecting children's books. Such topics as censorship, moral values, sex, self-image, and feminism are briefly but usefully presented. All the articles are reprinted from *School Library Journal*.

Karolides, N. J., editor. *Reader Response in the Classroom: Evoking and Interpreting Meaning in Literature*. Longman, 1992. Focuses on how teachers can use a reader response approach in teaching literature. Provides suggestions for implementing this approach in the classroom.

Kohn, R., editor. *Once upon . . . a Time for Young People and Their Books: An Annotated Resource Guide*. Scarecrow Press, 1986. An annotated resource guide for materials concerning children's literature.

Krashen, S. *The Power of Reading: Insights from Research*. Libraries Unlimited, 1993. The author looks at research on the effectiveness of voluntary reading on literacy. His argument is that "free voluntary reading" is an important component of increasing literacy.

Lamme, L. L.; Krogh, S. L.; and Yachmetz, K. A. *Literature-Based Moral Education*. Oryx Press, 1992. After presenting a brief overview of what is known about children's moral development, the authors turn to a discussion of ways to use literature to assist that development. Includes practical suggestions for classroom or home activities.

Language Arts. Published monthly September–April. National Council of Teachers of English. Publishes issues on topics related to the content and teaching of language arts. Authors are often classroom teachers.

Larrick, N. *A Parent's Guide to Children's Reading*, 5th ed. Bantam, 1982. Extensive practical information and advice for parents and other concerned adults on how to encourage children to read. Many books are annotated in useful, contemporary categories.

Lehr, S. S. *The Child's Developing Sense of Theme: Responses to Literature*. Teachers College Press, 1991. Focusing on the child's "perspective of meaning," the author discusses work she has done getting children to talk about their responses to stories. She argues that children do think critically about what they hear and, given time and encouragement, can communicate those ideas.

Lickteig, M. J. *An Introduction to Children's Literature.* Merrill, 1975. An overview of all of children's literature. Every topic is lightly touched on with indications for further study. The bibliographies, unfortunately, are not annotated. The author maintains an objectivity about all the topics and all the books. The appendixes and suggested references are useful. The author also contributes some practical suggestions for working with children.

Lipson, E. R. *Parent's Guide to the Best Books for Children.* Times Books, 1988. An extensive, annotated reference guide. Organized by type and cross-referenced.

Little, J. "A Writer's Social Responsibility," *The New Advocate* 3 (Spring 1990): 79–88. The author reflects her feelings about the importance of presenting her perspective without didacticism. She decries the practice of bombarding children with "the message of the story" rather than leaving young readers to think for themselves.

Livo, N. J., and Rietz, S. A. *Storytelling: Folklore Sourcebook.* Libraries Unlimited, 1991. A resource for those concerned about telling stories, whether oral or written, as an important part of education. Offers suggestions, background, and information on many aspects of folklore.

Lonsdale, B. J., and Mackintosh, H. *Children Experience Literature.* Random House, 1973. Combines a genre approach with a practical classroom approach. Includes a chapter on literature and personal growth. Somewhat uncritical but useful reference.

Luecke, F. J., editor. *Children's Books, Views and Values.* Xerox Education Publications, 1973. Eight excellent articles reprinted from several scholarly journals concerning issues in children's literature. Issues included are death, violence, feminism, and multiethnic books.

Lukens, R. J. *A Critical Handbook of Children's Literature,* 4th ed. Harper, 1990. Provides guidelines for critiquing children's literature, looking at different aspects such as plot, theme, characters, and style.

Lurie, A. *Don't Tell the Grownups: Subversive Children's Literature.* Little, Brown, 1990. The author demonstrates how many writers of children's literature "popularized new and controversial, political, social, or psychological ideas." She devotes the book to an examination of children's literature from Mother Goose to *The Secret Garden,* including historical information, as well as critical analyses dealing with values and mores.

Lynch-Brown, C., and Tomlinson, C. M. *Essentials of Children's Literature.* Allyn and Bacon, 1993. Tailored for a beginning survey course in children's literature. The authors start with an overview of the field and then discuss a variety of categories of children's literature. The appendixes are a valuable resource.

Marantz, S. S. *Picture Books for Looking and Learning.* Oryx, 1992. Written by librarians and teachers, this book provides suggestions on how to make use of picture books in raising children's awareness of the visual arts.

Martin, D. *The Telling Line: Essays on Fifteen Contemporary Book Illustrators.* Delacorte, 1989. A look at the backgrounds, techniques, and influences of fifteen illustrators of children's books.

Meeker, A. M. *Enjoying Literature with Children.* Odyssey, 1969. Practical but somewhat traditional ideas for incorporating children's books into the elementary school curriculum.

Meltzer, M. "The Social Responsibility of the Writer," *The New Advocate* 2 (Summer 1989): 155–157. One of Meltzer's goals as a writer is to help his readers understand that "we need not accept the world as it is given to us." He writes to "combat the cynical and defeatist view of human nature that dismisses any attempt to make society more just, more fair, more decent."

Moir, H., editor. *Collected Perspectives: Choosing and Using Books for the Classroom,* 2nd ed. Christopher-Gordon, 1992. An annotated bibliography that includes short reviews of each book. Organized by reading level and type.

Moran, C., and Penfield, E. F., editors. *Conversations: Contemporary Critical Theory and the Teaching of Literature.* National Council of Teachers of English, 1990. This collection of essays offers theoretical and critical views of the teaching of literature.

Moss, J. F. *Focus on Literature: A Context for Literacy Learning.* Owen, 1990. A guide to help teachers integrate literature into the curriculum in their classrooms. The author starts with a theoretical basis and offers suggestions on how to move from theory to practice.

Nelms, B. F., editor. *Literature in the Classroom: Readers, Texts, and Contexts.* National Council of Teachers of English, 1988. The focus of this volume is to assert the central place of literature in the English curriculum. The chapters, written by teachers, professors, and administrators, are organized into three sections that focus on readers, text, and context.

The New Advocate: For Those Involved with Young People and Their Literature. Published quarterly. Christopher-Gordon Publishers. Publishes articles on using children's literature in the classroom, reviews children's books and literature resources, and often includes author and illustrator profiles.

Newell, G. E., and Durst, R. K. *Exploring Texts: The Role of Discussion and Writing in the Teaching and Learning of Literature.* Christopher-Gordon, 1993. Written for educators at many levels, this book presents challenging ideas regarding the teaching of literature. It offers both theoretical background and practical suggestions.

Nodelman, P. *The Pleasures of Children's Literature.* Longman, 1992. Drawing on the fields of developmental psychology, history of childhood, theories of perception, and others, the author presents a way of understanding and thinking about children's literature. Shows how other social forces affect how children respond to literature and suggests techniques for teaching literature to children.

Norton, D. E. *Through the Eyes of a Child: An Introduction to Children's Literature,* 3rd ed. Merrill, 1991. Designed as a textbook for classes in children's literature, this work is also intended for anyone who is interested in selecting and evaluating children's literature.

Pearl, P. *Helping Children through Books: A Selected Booklist,* 3rd rev. ed. Church and Synagogue Library Association, 1990. A comprehensive annotated bibliography on bibliotherapy including books intended for children from a preschool to a sixth-grade reading level.

Purves, A. C., and Monson, D. L. *Experiencing Children's Literature.* Harper, 1984. The authors provide a theoretical basis by discussing transactional theory and its connection to children's literature. They then look at various forms of literature in light of the decisions teachers must make in the classroom.

Purves, A. C.; Rogers, T.; and Soter, A. O. *How Porcupines Make Love II: Teaching a Response-Centered Literature Curriculum.* Longman, 1990. Written for teachers, this book discusses reader-response theory and its implications for teaching literature. The authors offer insights and suggestions for making literature enjoyable and accessible.

Pytowska, E. I. *Theme Centered Bibliography of Children's Literature: Books with Themes of Personal, Cultural and Social Empowerment.* Savanna, 1987. A comprehensive annotated bibliography, with thoughtful commentary.

Rasinski, T. V., and Gillespie, C. S. *Sensitive Issues: An Annotated Guide to Children's Literature K-6.* Oryx Press, 1992. Annotated bibliography organized by topic. Also includes suggestions for activities for each book.

The Reading Teacher. Published monthly during school year. International Reading Association. Publishes articles on research, theory, and practice concerning the teaching of reading. Topics such as instruction, ideas for classroom use, and evaluation of resources are regularly included.

Reasoner, C. F. *Releasing Children to Literature.* Dell, 1968. Interesting and open-ended ideas for encouraging critical reading. This book specifically pertains to the Dell Yearling books, but the activities are imaginative and pertinent to any books. Thirty specific books are included, many of which are concerned with topics such as death, siblings, females, and war.

Reasoner, C. F. *Where the Readers Are.* Dell, 1972. Another invaluable teachers' guide to imaginative and stimulating activities to accompany reading. Reasoner specifically discusses 34 Dell Yearling books, but the ideas extend far beyond the particular books.

Robinson, E. R., editor. *Reading about Children's Literature.* McKay, 1966. A book of readings relating to a genre and pedagogic approach to children's literature. The articles are interesting and provide different perspectives on books for children.

Rosenberg, B., and Herald, D. T. *Genreflecting: A Guide to Reading Interests in Genre Fiction,* 3rd ed. Libraries Unlimited, 1991. A guide to identifying authors or books of a specific genre.

Rudman, M. K., editor. *Children's Literature: Resource for the Classroom.* Christopher-Gordon, 1989. Various authors discuss such topics as evaluation, selection, censorship, bibliotherapy, and literature in the reading program.

Rudman, M. K., and Pearce, A. M. *For Love of Reading: A Parent's Guide to Encouraging Young Readers from Infancy Through Age 5.* Consumers Union, 1988. Authors discuss various aspects of rearing children and some books appropriate for different developmental stages. Includes a list of over 800 books for children and an annotated bibliography.

Russell, D. L. *Literature for Children: A Short Introduction.* Longman, 1991. A survey of books written for children from infancy to adolescence. Includes a short discussion of child development and offers suggestions for teaching literature.

Schniedewind, N., and Davidson, E. *Open Minds to Equality: A Sourcebook of Learning Activities to Promote Race, Sex, Class, and Age Equity.* Allyn and Bacon, 1983. Discussion of the prevalence of stereotypes in literature and the importance of critical reading and thinking, as well as a treasure trove of activities, many involving children's books, form the contents of this helpful book.

Shannon, P. "Overt and Covert Censorship of Children's Books," *The New Advocate* 2 (Spring 1989): 97-104. A discussion of censorship that points out that covert means are as influential as overt ones in deciding to what children will or will not be exposed.

Smith, D. V. *Fifty Years of Children's Books.* National Council of Teachers of English, 1963. A beautifully written, extremely informative, though traditional book on the history of children's literature. No mention is made of any present-day issues.

Smith, J. A. *Creative Teaching of Reading and Literature in the Elementary School.* Allyn and Bacon, 1970. Lesson plans, suggestions, and a discussion of the philosophy of creative teaching make this book useful for teachers.

Smith, J. S. *A Critical Approach to Children's Literature.* McGraw-Hill, 1967. A scholarly literary approach to children's books. The author presents a methodology for critical analysis of children's literature.

Smith, L. H. *The Unreluctant Years.* Viking, 1971. A highly literate series of discussions of the different genres of children's literature. Smith presents her critical approach.

Snodgrass, M. E. *Characters from Young Adult Literature.* Libraries Unlimited, 1991. Provides a brief synopsis and a discussion of the major and minor characters of some "favorite works of young people."

Somers, A. B., and Worthington, J. E. *Response Guides for Teaching Children's Books.* National Council of Teachers of English, 1979. Guides to 27 children's books are provided. Each guide includes a summary, a short appraisal, and suggestions for activities or questions for discussion.

Stewig, J. W. *Children and Literature,* 2nd ed. Houghton Mifflin, 1988. Written as a textbook for an introduction to children's literature, this book looks at different types of literature and provides suggestions for teaching literature.

Stewig, J. W., and Sebasta, S. L. *Using Literature in the Classroom.* National Council of Teachers of English, 1989. Addresses different aspects of reading and literature including the nature of language, illustration, and integrating literature throughout the curriculum.

Sutheland, Z. et al. *Children and Books,* 8th ed. Scott, Foresman, 1991. Revised considerably from the 1964 edition, this valuable reference provides discussions of books based on a genre approach. The appendixes provide the reader with book-selection aids, references, publishers' addresses, children's book awards, and a pronunciation guide. One of the most comprehensive references published in the field of children's literature.

Taxel, J. "Notes from the Editor," *The New Advocate* 3 (Spring 1990): vii–xii. A well constructed, eloquent argument for the social responsibility of a writer, bearing in mind the warnings that Jean Little conveys in her article in this same issue.

Taylor, D., and Dorsey-Gaines, C. *Growing up Literate: Learning from Inner-City Families.* Heinemann, 1988. Based on an ethnographic study, this book looks at the many factors affecting poor, urban African-American children as they become literate. The book raises questions about the connection between literacy and socioeconomic status and suggests new ways of looking at the role of the family in developing literacy.

Temple, C., and Collins, P., editors. *Stories and Readers: New Perspectives on Literature in the Elementary Classroom.* Christopher-Gordon, 1992. Elementary teachers and professors discuss the use of story and literature in the classroom and in children's development.

Townsend, J. R. *Written for Children.* 4th ed. Harper, 1990. A survey of children's literature from pre-1840 to the present, covering many different types of literature such as fantasy, history, and poetry.

Trelease, J. *The New Read-Aloud Handbook.* Penguin, 1989. Discusses reasons for reading aloud to children, as well as suggestions for when and how to do so. Includes an annotated bibliography.

Viguers, R. H. *Margin for Surprise.* Little, Brown, 1964. Essays reflecting on the author's love of books and her respect for their impact on children.

West, M. I. *Children, Culture, and Controversy.* Archon, 1988. Examines the concept of the innocence of childhood and its implications for censorship of television, and such reading material for children as dime novels, comics, and textbooks, among others.

White, M. L. *Adventuring with Books: A Booklist for Pre-K–Grade 6,* rev. ed. National Council of Teachers of English, 1981. Approximately 2,500 children's books, published from 1977 to 1989. Brief but informative annotations.

Whitehead, R. *Children's Literature: Strategies of Teaching.* Prentice-Hall, 1968. Hundreds of practical ideas for using books in the classroom. No mention is made of the impact of issues involved in books, but the intent is to provide a cookbook of ideas for activities.

Wood, K. D., and Moss, A., editors. *Exploring Literature in the Classroom: Contents and Methods.* Christopher-Gordon, 1992. Draws upon two different fields, English literature and reading education, to discuss the integration of literature throughout the curriculum. Includes topics such as technology, multiculturalism, and writing as they relate to the teaching of literature.

Yolen, J. *Writing Books for Children.* The Writer, 1976. Yolen advocates that books for children be written so that the writer and reader can "take joy." The book includes an awareness of the social issues involved in books but also advises authors to refrain from heavy didacticism. A well-written, interesting book.

Zaccaria, J. S., and Moses, H. A. *Facilitating Human Development through Reading: The Use of Bibliotherapy in Teaching and Counseling.* Stipes, 1968. An extensive annotated bibliography follows a theoretical section on how to use books in a therapeutic manner with young readers.

APPENDIX C: ACTIVITIES FOR EXTENDING LITERATURE

The activities suitable for an individualized reading program are varied. The children read independently after selecting books that interest them. They maintain records, participate in diagnosis, engage in small-group instruction, help to teach some small groups, and share their reading with their classmates in as many interesting ways as they can think of. The following ideas are only a few of the hundreds available to teachers and children.

Appropriate Music for Story Theme. Many famous pieces of music have been inspired by children's stories, especially fairy tales. Children can select music they feel reflects the mood of whatever they are reading. By creating a multiarts experience themselves, they are in effect enhancing their own appreciation of both reading and music.

Arrangement on Bookshelf of Similar Books. This can be done by an individual or by a group that has read the same book. Posters and pictures can be added, forming a thematic exhibit.

Autobiography. The student rewrites or tells the story from the viewpoint of one of the characters.

Blurbs. These should be interest-arousers that do not reveal too much of the plot. A collection of blurbs can form a bulletin board display to serve as motivation for the class.

Book for the Day. The entire class or a group of children may wish to dress as characters in a book. They can portray the characters not only in dress but in actions and typical speech habits as well.

Book Jackets. A child can design a jacket to reflect the message of the book.

Book Seller. A child tries to "sell" a book to another child or group of child. This is a good exercise in being persuasive and in analyzing people's interests.

Bulletin Boards. Reviews, three-dimensional titles, and eye-catching titles can attract students' attention, leading them to read.

Cartoons. Use ideas from the story to make a set of cartoon drawings to retell the story. Be sure to put the events in order.

Crossword Puzzle. A crossword puzzle can be constructed using new words learned in a story.

Character Analysis. Which characters would the student like to have as a friend? Who has behaved most admirably? Many such questions can be asked.

Dear Author. Letters to the author in care of the publisher (see Appendix E) telling what aspects of the book impressed them, the book's value to them, a comparison with other books by the same author, or other comments inviting a response.

Dear Diary. Students take on the identity of one of the characters and write three entries of 100 words each in the diary of that person.

Diorama. A three-dimensional representation of a scene, it usually is made in a box, such as a shoe box. Figures and scenery are placed inside.

Dolls Dressed as Characters. A child can make costumes for small dolls to represent characters.

Dramatization. Informal or rehearsed—this can be done by an individual or a group. It can be combined with murals, puppets, and shadow plays.

Exhibits or Collections. May be used with books that are of informational nature. Books that are concerned with a particular issue may be placed on display, with comments written by students.

Happy Holidays. Books describing different holidays are selected, and displays are made of each holiday.

Headlines or Caption for a Newspaper Account. They should be short and to the point. The chapter titles can be changed to headlines or used to transform the story into a newspaper account.

History Mystery. If a book describes a historical incident, other descriptions of that same event can be found, either in fact or in other works of fiction. When students compare the different versions, they can try to unravel the mystery of which is the most accurate.

Interview (Simulated) with an Author. If two students have read the same books, one can answer questions as the author while the other poses as an interviewer. Or real authors can be invited to answer the questions (in person or on the phone).

Library Acquisitions. Students who have read a book give advice on whether it should be purchased for the classroom or school library.

Making Slides. Incidents of stories may be shown on student-made slides. As the slides are shown, accompanying parts can be read or explanations given. The oral parts may be taped for greater effectiveness.

Map or Diagram. Books about treasure hunts and mysteries lend themselves especially to this type of sharing.

Mobiles. A mobile can be made with a coat-hanger and pictures of scenes in a book. They could be the child's own work or from magazines.

Movie Roll. The child can take a roll of paper and draw a series of events from a book. These pictures can be shown individually through an opening in a box. It should look like a TV screen but it can be of any size.

Mural. This can be a group or class activity. The scene can be drawn or pasted on mural paper or on a board with colored chalk.

Opaque Projector. Illustrations or original drawings may be flashed on the wall and used as a background while parts of the story are narrated.

Oral Reading. The student reads an interesting portion of the book aloud. This helps develop oral reading proficiency, as well as interest in the book.

Outline of the Story. Choices in the area are a five-sentence outline, a series of ideas, an arrangement of questions or pictures in sequence, or movie scenes. These activities can be aided by murals, movie rolls, slides, or posters.

Out of Whose Mouth? Find some comments or flavorful quotes. Write them on index cards, and see if other people who read the same book can identify the speaker.

Panel Discussions or Debates. Useful for evaluating plot, characters, and solutions and for accepting and evaluating differences of opinion.

Pantomime. The character is shown in action. The audience is urged to take part by telling what action is being performed and by whom.

Photographs. Student photographs of situations or scenes to illustrate the story can be used to arouse interest and to personalize the book.

Poems. The student writes a comment, summary, or impression of the book in the form of a limerick or poem. Poems can also be written to laud or describe a character in the book.

Point of View. Rewrite the story from one of the other characters' perspectives.

Portraits. A portrait of a favorite character can be drawn and framed. The author's description may be used as a guide. A gallery of portraits can be set up.

Posters. Can be used to advertise the book, the characters, or the theme. Students promote reading the book by combining a 25-to-50-word review with illustrations, lettering, and other eye-catching details in an effective visual arrangement.

Predictions. Students read a part of a book, then try to predict what will happen, how a problem will be solved, or how the story will end. They then complete their reading and compare endings with the author's. (You may like the students' solutions better than the author's.)

Puppets. Incidents can be portrayed, characters impersonated, or the story reported through a variety of puppets: finger, hand, sock, stick, and the like.

Quotable Quotes. Particularly colorful or descriptive quotations are located, put into an appropriate order, and displayed.

Radio Scripts. Transformation of a story into a script for television or radio. Friends can be invited to perform the script, complete with sound effects and commercial breaks.

Reading Log. Notes, pictures, and impressions related to the books a child has read may be maintained regularly in a notebook or log.

Souvenirs. Any items connected with the topic or period dealt with in the book are an aid to reporting.

Story Changes. Students may add a chapter to the story or rewrite the first or last chapter. They may also add new characters, present and solve new problems, or change key incidents.

Tableau. Effective in presenting a story in which action is important. A series of "frozen" actions can convey many messages.

Talk Shows. Students take the role of Oprah, Donahue, or other TV talk-show hosts and interview characters from stories.

Tests. Students write a brief test on the book. Five to ten questions are sufficient. Duplicate the tests, and let each child who reads the book take the test "for fun."

This is Your Life. Personal events from the life of a character in the book can be interestingly reviewed in this manner. The author can also be the subject of this sort of presentation.

Title Changes. Students write other titles for the book, make new dust jackets for each title, and display them with the original on a bulletin board.

T.V. Games. Games based upon Wheel of Fortune, Jeopardy, Family Feud and other TV game shows. Groups of students enjoy this and can write very entertaining commercials to amuse the audience.

Twenty Questions. The sharer answers yes or no to questions from the group. The children can try, in twenty questions, to guess the character's identity, the title of the book or the topic it deals with.

Vocabulary Lists. This technique can be employed for books that present entertaining dialogue, unusual terminology, or simply colorful words.

Where in the World? If the book takes place in an interesting real or imagined location, a travel brochure can be designed to entice others to visit it.

A child who enjoys and is interested in reading books becomes a better reader. Children can usually influence and motivate each other more effectively than adults can; they will probably add other ideas to the list given above. Inventive teachers can adapt these ideas to their own class interests and abilities and invariably add many more.

APPENDIX D: SELECTED CHILDREN'S BOOK AWARDS

Randolph J. Caldecott Medal

Determined each year by a special committee of the American Library Association Children's Services Division, this award is given to the illustrator of the picture book judged to be the most distinguished of the previous year. The book must be published in the United States, and the illustrator must be a citizen or resident of the United States.

1938 *Animals of the Bible,* by Helen Dean Fish, illus. Dorothy P. Lathrop
     Honor Books: *Seven Simeons,* by Boris Artzybasheff
                    Four and Twenty Blackbirds, by Helen Dean Fish, illus. Robert Lawson

1939 *Mei Li,* by Thomas Handforth
     Honor Books: *The Forest Pool,* Laura Adams Armer
                    Wee Gillis, by Munro Leaf, illus. Robert Lawson
                    Snow White and the Seven Dwarfs, illus. Wanda Gág
                    Barkis, by Clare Newberry
                    Andy and the Lion, by James Daugherty

1940 *Abraham Lincoln,* by Ingri and Edgar d'Aulaire
     Honor Books: *Cock-a-Doodle Doo,* by Berta and Elmer Hader
                    Madeline, by Ludwig Bemelmans
                    The Ageless Story, by Lauren Ford

1941 *They Were Strong and Good,* by Robert Lawson
     Honor Book: *April's Kittens,* by Clare Newberry

1942 *Make Way for Ducklings,* by Robert McCloskey
     Honor Books: *An American ABC,* by Maud and Miska Petersham
                    In My Mother's House, by Ann Nolan Clark, illus. Velinô Herrera
                    Paddle-to-the-Sea, by Holling C. Holling
                    Nothing at All, by Wanda Gág

1943 *The Little House,* by Virginia Lee Burton
     Honor Books: *Dash and Dart,* by Mary and Conrad Buff
                    Marshmallow, by Clare Newberry

1944 *Many Moons,* by James Thurber, illus. Louis Slobodkin
     Honor Books: *Small Rain: Verses from the Bible,* selected by Jessie Orton Jones, illus. Elizabeth Orton Jones
                    Pierre Pigeon, by Lee Kingman, illus. Arnold E. Bare
                    The Mighty Hunter, by Berta and Elmer Hader
                    A Child's Good Night Book, by Margaret Wise Brown, illus. Jean Charlot
                    Good Luck Horse, by Chin-Yi Chan, illus. Plao Chan

1945 *Prayer for a Child,* by Rachel Field, illus. Elizabeth Orton Jones
     Honor Books: *Mother Goose,* illus. Tasha Tudor
                    In the Forest, by Marie Hall Ets
                    Yonie Wondernose, by Marguerite de Angeli
                    The Christmas Anna Angel, by Ruth Sawyer, illus. Kate Seredy

1946 *The Rooster Crows,* by Maud and Miska Petersham
     Honor Books: *Little Lost Lamb,* by Golden MacDonald, illus. Leonard Weisgard
                    Sing Mother Goose, by Opal Wheeler, illus. Margorie Torrey
                    My Mother Is the Most Beautiful Woman in the World, by Becky Reyher, illus. Ruth Gannett
                    You Can Write Chinese, by Kurt Wiese

1947   *The Little Island,* by Golden MacDonald, illus. Leonard Weisgard
       Honor Books: *Rain Drop Splash,* by Alvin Tresselt, illus. Leonard Weisgard
                       Boats on the River, by Margorie Flack, illus. Jay Hyde Barnum
                       Timothy Turtle, by Al Graham, illus. Tony Palazzo
                       Pedro, the Angel of Alvera Street, by Leo Politi
                       Sing in Praise: A Collection of the Best Loved Hymns, by Opal
                          Wheeler, illus. Margorie Torrey
1948   *White Snow, Bright Snow,* by Alvin Tresselt, illus. Roger Duvoisin
       Honor Books: *Stone Soup,* by Marcia Brown
                       McElligot's Pool, by Dr. Seuss
                       Bambino the Clown, by George Schreiber
                       Roger and the Fox, by Lavinia Davis, illus. Hildegard Woodward
                       Song of Robin Hood, ed. Anne Malcolmson, illus. Virginia Lee
                          Burton
1949   *The Big Snow,* by Bert and Elmer Hader
       Honor Books: *Blueberries for Sal,* by Robert McCloskey
                       All Around the Town, by Phyllis McGinley, illus. Helen Stone
                       Juanita, by Leo Politi
                       Fish in the Air, by Kurt Wiese
1950   *Song of the Swallows,* by Leo Politi
       Honor Books: *America's Ethan Allen,* by Stewart Holbrook, illus. Lynd Ward
                       The Wild Birthday Cake, by Lavinia Davis, illus. Hildegard
                          Woodward
                       The Happy Day, by Ruth Krauss, illus. Marc Simont
                       Bartholomew and the Oobleck, by Dr. Seuss
                       Henry Fisherman, by Marcia Brown
1951   *The Egg Tree,* by Katherine Milhous
       Honor Books: *Dick Whittington and His Cat,* by Marcia Brown
                       The Two Reds, by Will, illus. Nicolas
                       If I Ran the Zoo, by Dr. Seuss
                       The Most Wonderful Doll in the World, by Phyllis McGinley,
                          illus. Helen Stone
                       T-Bone and Baby Sitter, by Clare Newberry
1952   *Finders Keepers,* by Will, illus. Nicolas
       Honor Books: *Mr. T. W. Anthony Woo,* by Marie Hall Ets
                       Skipper John's Cook, by Marcia Brown
                       All Falling Down, by Gene Zion, illus. Margaret Bloy Graham
                       Bear Party, by William Pene duBois
                       Feather Mountain, by Elizabeth Olds
1953   *The Biggest Bear,* by Lynd Ward
       Honor Books: *Puss in Boots,* by Charles Perrault, illus. and trans. Marcia Brown
                       One Morning in Maine, by Robert McCloskey
                       Ape in a Cape, by Fritz Eichenberg
                       The Storm Book, by Charlotte Zolotow, illus. Margaret Bloy
                          Graham
                       Five Little Monkeys, by Juliet Kepes
1954   *Madeline's Rescue,* by Ludwig Bemelmans
       Honor Books: *Journey Cake, Ho!,* by Ruth Sawyer, illus. Robert McCloskey
                       When Will the World Be Mine?, by Mariam Schlein, illus. Jean
                          Charlot
                       The Steadfast Tin Solider, by Hans Christian Andersen, illus.
                          Marcia Brown
                       A Very Special House, by Ruth Krauss, illus. Maurice Sendak
                       Green Eyes, by A. Birnbaum

1955 *Cinderella, or the Little Glass Slipper,* by Charles Perrault, illus. and trans.
Marcia Brown
Honor Books: *Book of Nursery and Mother Goose Rhymes,* illus. Marguerite
de Angeli
Wheel on the Chimney, by Margaret Wise Brown, illus. Tibor
Gergley
The Thanksgiving Story, by Alice Dalgliesh, illus. James
Daugherty

1956 *Frog Went A-Courtin',* ed. John Langstaff, illus. Feodor Rojankovsky
Honor Books: *Play with Me,* by Marie Hall Ets
Crow Boy, by Taro Yashima

1957 *A Tree Is Nice,* by Janice May Udry, illus. Marc Simont
Honor Books: *Mr. Penny's Race Horse,* by Marie Hall Ets
1 is One, by Tasha Tudor
Anatole, by Eve Titus, illus. Paul Galdone
Gillespie and the Guards, by Benjamin Elkin, illus. James
Daugherty
Lion, by William Pène duBois

1958 *Time of Wonder,* by Robert McCloskey
Honor Books: *Fly High, Fly Low,* by Don Freeman
Anatole and the Cat, by Eve Titus, illus. Paul Galdone

1959 *Chanticleer and the Fox,* adapted from Chaucer, illus. Barbara Cooney
Honor Books: *The House That Jack Built,* by Antonio Frasconi
What Do You Say, Dear?, by Sesyle Joslin, illus. Maurice Sendak
Umbrella, by Taro Yashima

1960 *Nine Days to Christmas,* by Marie Hall Ets and Aurora Labastida, illus. Marie
Hall Ets
Honor Books: *Houses From the Sea,* by Alice E. Goudey, illus. Adrienne Adams
The Moon Jumpers, by Janice May Udry, illus. Maurice Sendak

1961 *Baboushka and the Three Kings,* by Ruth Robbins, illus. Nicholas Sidjakov
Honor Book: *Inch By Inch,* by Leo Lionni

1962 *Once a Mouse,* by Marcia Brown
Honor Books: *The Fox Went Out on a Chilly Night,* illus. Peter Spier
Little Bear's Visit, by Else Holmelund Minarik, illus. Maurice
Sendak
The Day We Saw the Sun Come Up, by Alice E. Goudey, illus.
Adrienne Adams

1963 *The Snowy Day,* by Ezra Jack Keats
Honor Books: *The Sun Is a Golden Earring,* by Natalia M. Belting, illus.
Bernarda Bryson
Mr. Rabbit and the Lovely Present, by Charlotte Zolotow, illus.
Maurice Sendak

1964 *Where the Wild Things Are,* by Maurice Sendak
Honor Books: *Swimmy,* by Leo Lionni
All in the Morning Early, by Sorche Nic Leodhas, illus. Evaline
Ness
Mother Goose and Nursery Rhymes, illus. Philip Reed

1965 *May I Bring a Friend?,* by Beatrice Schenk de Regniers, illus. Beni Montresor
Honor Books: *Rain Makes Applesauce,* by Julian Scheer, illus. Marvin Bileck
The Wave, by Margaret Hodges, illus. Blair Lent
A Pocketful of Cricket, by Rebecca Caudill, illus. Evaline Ness

1966 *Always Room for One More,* by Sorche Nic Leodhas, illus. Nonny Hogrogian
Honor Books: *Hide and Seek Fog,* by Alvin Tresselt, illus. Roger Duvoisin

Just Me, by Marie Hall Ets

Tom Tit Tot, by Evaline Ness

1967 *Sam, Bangs and Moonshine,* by Evaline Ness

Honor Books: *One Wide River to Cross,* by Barbara Emberley, illus. Ed Emberley

1968 *Drummer Hoff,* by Barbara Emberley, illus. Ed. Emberley

Honor Books: *Frederick,* by Leo Lionni

Seashore Story, by Taro Yashima

The Emperor and the Kite, by Jane Yolen, illus. Ed Young

1969 *The Fool of the World and the Flying Ship,* by Arthur Ransome, illus. Uri Shulevitz

Honor Book: *Why the Sun and the Moon Live in the Sky,* by Elphinstone Dayrell, illus. Blair Lent

1970 *Sylvester and the Magic Pebble,* by William Steig

Honor Books: *Goggles,* by Ezra Jack Keats

Alexander and the Wind-up Mouse, by Leo Lionni

Pop Corn and Ma Goodness, by Edna Mitchell Preston, illus. Robert Andrew Parker

Thy Friend, Obadiah, by Brinton Turkle

The Judge, by Harve Zemach, illus. Margot Zemach

1971 *A Story—A Story,* by Gail E. Haley

Honor Books: *The Angry Moon,* by William Sleator, illus. Blair Lent

Frog and Toad Are Friends, by Arnold Lobel

In the Night Kitchen, by Maurice Sendak

1972 *One Fine Day,* by Nonny Hogrogian

Honor Books: *Hildilid's Night,* by Cheli Duran Ryan, illus. Arnold Lobel

If All the Seas Were One Sea, by Janina Domanska

Moja Means One, by Muriel Feelings, illus. Tom Feelings

1973 *The Funny Little Women,* retold by Arlene Mosel, illus. Blair Lent

Honor Books: *Anansi the Spider,* adapted and illus. Gerald McDermott

Hosie's Alphabet, by Hosea, Tobias, and Lisa Baskin, illus. Leonard Baskin

Snow White and the Seven Dwarfs, trans. Randall Jarrell, illus. Nancy Ekholm Burkert

When Clay Sings, by Byrd Baylor, illus. Tom Bahti

1974 *Duffy and the Devil,* retold by Harve Zemach, illus. Margot Zemach

Honor Books: *Three Jovial Huntsmen: A Mother Goose Rhyme,* adapted and illus. Susan Jeffers

Cathedral: The Story of Its Construction, written and illus. David Macaulay

1975 *Arrow to the Sun, A Pueblo Indian Tale,* by Gerald McDermott

Honor Book: *Jambo Means Hello, Swahili Alphabet Book,* by Muriel Feelings, illus. Tom Feelings

1976 *Why Mosquitoes Buzz in People's Ears,* retold by Verna Aardema, illus. Leo and Diane Dillon

Honor Books: *The Desert Is Theirs,* by Byrd Baylor, illus. Peter Parnall

Strega Nona, retold and illus. Tomie de Paola

1977 *Ashanti to Zulu: African Traditions,* by Margaret Musgrove, illus. Leo and Diane Dillon

Honor Books: *Fish for Supper,* by M. B. Goffstein

The Contest, retold and illus. by Nonny Hogrogian

The Golem: A Jewish Legend, by Beverly Brodsky McDermott

Hawk, I'm Your Brother, by Byrd Baylor, illus. Peter Parnall

The Amazing Bone, by William Steig

1978 *Noah's Ark,* by Peter Spier
Honor Books: *Castle,* by David Macaulay
It Could Always Be Worse, retold and illus. by Margot Zemach

1979 *The Girl Who Loved Wild Horses,* by Paul Goble
Honor Books: *Freight Train,* by Donald Crew
The Way To Start a Day, by Byrd Baylor, illus. Peter Parnall

1980 *Ox-Cart Man,* Donald Hall, illus. Barbara Cooney
Honor Books: *Ben's Trumpet,* by Rachel Isadora
The Treasure, by Uri Shulevitz
The Garden of Abdul Gasazi, by Chris Van Allsburg

1981 *Fables,* by Arnold Lobel
Honor Books: *The Grey Lady and the Strawberry Snatcher,* by Molly Bang
Truck, by Donald Crews
Mice Twice, by Joseph Low
The Bremen-Town Musicians, retold and illus. by Ilse Plume

1982 *Jumanji,* by Chris Van Allsburg
Honor Books: *A Visit to William Blake's Inn: Poems for Innocent and Experienced Travelers,* by Nancy Willard
Where the Buffaloes Begin, by Olaf Baker
On Market Street, by Arnold Lobel
Outside, Over There, by Maurice Sendak

1983 *Shadow,* trans. and illus. Marcia Brown
Honor Books: *A Chair for My Mother,* by Vera B. Williams
When I Was Young in the Mountains, by Cynthia Ryland, illus. Diane Goode

1984 *The Glorious Flight across the Channel with Louis Bleriot,* by Alice and Martin Provenson
Honor Books: *Ten, Nine, Eight,* by Molly Bang
Little Red Riding Hood, retold and illus. Trina Schart Hyman

1985 *Saint George and the Dragon,* by Margaret Hodges, illus. Trina Schart Human
Honor Books: *Hansel and Gretel,* by Rika Lesser, illus. Paul O. Zelinksy
The Story of Jumping Mouse, retold and illus. John Steptoe
Have You Seen My Duckling? by Nancy Tafuri

1986 *The Polar Express,* by Chris Van Allsburg
Honor Books: *The Relatives Came,* by Cynthia Rylant, illus. Stephen Gammell
King Bidgood's in the Bathtub, by Audrey Wood, illus. Don Wood

1987 *Hey, Al,* by Arthur Yorinks, illus. Richard Egielski
Honor Books: *The Village of Round and Square Houses,* by Ann Grifalconi
Alphabatics, by Suse MacDonald
Rumpelstiltskin, retold and illus. Paul O. Zelinsky

1988 *Owl Moon,* by Jane Yolen, illus. John Schoenherr
Honor Books: *Mufaro's Beautiful Daughters,* retold John Steptoe

1989 *Song and Dance Man,* by Karen Ackerman, illus. Stephen Gammell
Honor Books: *Free Fall,* by David Wiesner
Goldilocks and the Three Bears, retold and illus. James Marshall
Mirandy and Brother Wind, by Patricia McKissack, illus. Jerry Pinkney
The Boy of the Three-Year Nap, by Diane Snyder, illus. Allen Say

1990 *Lon Po Po: A Red-Riding Hood Story from China,* trans. and illus. Ed Young

Honor Books: *Hershel and the Hanukkah Goblins,* by Eric Kimmel, illus.
Trina Schart Hyman
The Talking Eggs, retold Robert D. San Souci, illus. Jerry
Pinkney
Bill Peet: An Autobiography, by Bill Peet
Color Zoo, by Lois Ehlert

1991   *Black and White,* by David Macaulay
Honor Books: *Puss 'n' Boots,* by Charles Perrault, illus. Fred Marcellino
"More, More, More," Said the Baby: Three Love Stories, by Vera
Williams

1992   *Tuesday,* by David Wiesner
Honor Book: *Tar Beach,* by Faith Ringgold

1993   *Mirette on the High Wire,* by Emily A. McCully
Honor Books: *Seven Blind Mice,* by Ed Young
The Stinky Cheese Man and Other Fairly Stupid Tales, by John
Scieszka, illus. Lane Smith
Working Cotton, by Sherley Anne Williams, illus. Carole Byard

1994   *Grandfather's Journey,* by Allen Say
Honor Books: *Peppe, the Lamplighter,* by Elisa Bartone, illus. Ted Lewin
In the Small, Small Pond, by Denise Fleming
Owen, by Kevin Henkes
Raven, a Trickster Tale, by Gerald McDermott
Yo! Yes?, by Chris Raschka

Council on Interracial Books for Children Award

Awarded each year by the council to minority authors whose unpublished manuscripts
are judged to be outstanding.

1968   *Where Does the Day Go?,* by Walter N. Myers
The Soul Brothers and Sister Lou, by Kristin Hunter

1969   *ABC: The Story of the Alphabet,* by Virginia Cox
Sidewalk Story, by Sharon Bell Mathis
Letters from Uncle David: Underground Hero, by Margot S. Webb

1970   *Jimmy Yellow Hawk,* by Virginia Driving Hawk Sneve
Sneakers, by Ray Anthony Shepard
I Am Magic, by Juan Valenzuela

1971–1972   *Morning Song,* by Minfong Ho
The Rock Cried Out, by Florenz Webbe Maxwell
The Unusual Puerto Rican, by Theodore Laquer-Franceschi

1973   *Morning Arrow,* by Nanabah Chee Dodge
Grandfather's Bridge, by Michele O. Robinson
Eyak, by Dorothy Tomiye Okamoto
Song of the Trees, by Mildred D. Taylor
El Pito De Plata De Pito, by Jack Agueros

1974   *Simba, Midnight (The Stallion of the Night) and Mweusi,* by Aishah S.
Abdullah
My Father Hijacked a Plane, by Abelardo B. Delgado
Yari, by Antonia A. Hernandez

1975   *Letters to a Friend on a Brown Paper Bag,* by Emily R. Moore

1976   *El Mundo Maravilloso de Macu,* by Lydia Milagros Gonzalez

(Award discontinued after 1976)

John Newbery Medal

The most coveted children's book award, this prize is given annually to the book judged by a special committee selected by the American Library Association Children's Services Division to be the most outstanding work of children's literature published during the preceding year. The award is given only to authors who are American citizens, and the book must be published in the United States.

1922   *The Story of Mankind,* by Hendrik Willem van Loon
       Honor Books: *The Great Quest,* by Charles Hawes
                     Cedric the Forester, by Bernard Marshall
                     The Old Tobacco Shop, by William Bowen
                     The Golden Fleece and the Heroes Who Lived before Achilles,
                         by Padraic Colum
                     Windy Hill, by Cornelia Meigs

1923   *The Voyages of Doctor Doolittle,* by Hugh Lofting

1924   *The Dark Frigate,* by Charles Hawes

1925   *Tales from Silver Lands,* By Charles Finger
       Honor Books: *Nicholas,* by Anne Carroll Moore
                     Dream Coach, by Anne Parrish

1926   *Shen of the Sea,* by Arthur Bowie Chrisman
       Honor Book: *Voyagers,* by Padraic Colum

1927   *Smoky, The Cowhorse,* by Will James

1928   *Gayneck, the Story of a Pigeon,* by Dhan Gopal Mukerji
       Honor Books: *The Wonder Smith and His Son,* by Ella Young
                     Downright Dencey, by Caroline Snedeker

1929   *The Trumpeter of Krakow,* by Eric P. Kelly
       Honor Books: *Pigtail of Au Lee Ben Loo,* by John Bennett
                     Millions of Cats, by Wanda Gag
                     The Boy Who Was, by Grace Hallock
                     Clearing Weather, by Cornelia Meigs
                     Runaway Papoose, by Grace Moon
                     Tod of the Fens, by Elinor Whitney

1930   *Hitty, Her First Hundred Years,* by Rachel Field
       Honor Books: *Daughter of the Seine,* by Jeanette Eaton
                     Pran of Albania, by Elizabeth Miller
                     Jumping-Off Place, by Marian Hurd McNeely
                     Tangle-Coated Horse and Other Tales, by Ella Young
                     Vaino, by Julia Davis Adams
                     Little Blacknose, by Hildegard Swift

1931   *The Cat Who Went to Heaven,* by Elizabeth Coatsworth
       Honor Books: *Floating Island,* by Anne Parrish
                     The Dark Star of Itza, by Alida Malkus
                     Queer Person, by Ralph Hubbard
                     Mountains Are Free, by Julia Davis Adams
                     Spice and the Devil's Cave, by Agnes Hewes
                     Meggy Macintosh, by Elizabeth Janet Gray
                     Garram the Hunter, by Herbert Best
                     Ood-le-uk the Wanderer, by Alice Lide and Margaret Johansen

1932   *Waterless Mountain,* by Laura Adams Armer
       Honor Books: *The Fairy Circus,* Dorothy P. Lathrop
                     Calico Bush, by Rachel Field
                     Boy of the South Seas, by Eunice Tietjens

Out of the Flame, by Eloise Lownsbery
Jane's Island, by Marjorie Allee
Truce of the Wolf and Other Tales of Old Italy, by Mary Gould Davis

1933   *Young Fu of the Upper Yangtze,* by Elizabeth Lewis
      Honor Books: *Swift Rivers,* by Cornelia Meigs
                  The Railroad to Freedom, by Hildegarde Swift
                  Children of the Soil, by Nora Burglon

1934   *Invincible Louisa,* by Cornelia Meigs
      Honor Books: *The Forgotten Daughter,* by Caroline Snedeker
                  Swords of Steel, by Elsie Singmaster
                  ABC Bunny, by Wanda Gág
                  Winged Girl of Knossos, by Erik Berry
                  New Land, by Sarah Schmidt
                  Big Tree of Bunlahy, by Padraic Colum
                  Glory of the Seas, by Agnes Hewes
                  Apprentice of Florence, by Anne Kyle

1935   *Dobry,* by Monica Shannon
      Honor Books: *Pageant of Chinese History,* by Elizabeth Seeger
                  Davy Crockett, by Constance Rourke
                  Day on Skates, by Hilda Van Stockum

1936   *Caddie Woodlawn,* by Carol Ryrie Brink
      Honor Books: *Honk, the Moose,* by Phil Stong
                  The Good Master, by Kate Seredy
                  Young Walter Scott, by Elizabeth Janet Gray
                  All Sail Set, by Armstrong Sperry

1937   *Roller Skates,* by Ruth Sawyer
      Honor Books: *Phoebe Fairchild: Her Book,* by Lois Lenski
                  Whistler's Van, by Idwal Jones
                  Golden Basket, by Ludwig Bemelmans
                  Winterbound, by Margery Bianco
                  Audubon, by Constance Rourke
                  The Codfish Musket, by Agnes Hewes

1938   *The White Stag,* by Kat Seredy
      Honor Books: *Pecos Bill,* by James Cloyd Bowman
                  Bright Island, by Mabel Robinson
                  On the Banks of Plum Creek, by Laura Ingalls Wilder

1939   *Thimble Summer,* by Elizabeth Enright
      Honor Books: *Nino,* by Valenti Angelo
                  Mr. Popper's Penguins, by Richard and Florence Atwater
                  Hello the Boat!, by Phyllis Crawford
                  Leader by Destiny: George Washington, Man and Patriot, by Jeanette Eaton
                  Penn, by Elizabeth Janet Gray

1940   *Daniel Boone,* by James Daugherty
      Honor Books: *The Singing Tree,* by Kate Seredy
                  Runner of the Mountain Tops, by Mabel Robinson
                  By the Shores of Silver Lake, by Laura Ingalls Wilder
                  Boy with a Pack, by Stephen W. Meader

1941   *Call It Courage,* by Armstrong Sperry
      Honor Books: *Blue Willow,* by Doris Gates
                  Young Mac of Fort Vancouver, by Mary Jane Carr
                  The Long Winter, by Laura Ingalls Wilder

Nansen, by Anna Gertrude Hall

1942   *The Matchlock Gun,* by Walter D. Edmonds
      Honor Books: *Little Town on the Prairie,* by Laura Ingalls Wilder
                    George Washington's World, by Genevieve Foster
                    Indian Captive: The Story of Mary Jemison, by Lois Lenski
                    Down Ryton Water, by Eva Roe Gaggin

1943   *Adam of the Road,* by Elizabeth Janet Gray
      Honor Books: *The Middle Moffat,* by Eleanor Estes
                    Have You Seen Tom Thumb?, by Mabel Leigh Hunt

1944   *Johnny Tremain,* by Esther Forbes
      Honor Books: *These Happy Golden Years,* by Laura Ingalls Wilder
                    Fog Magic, by Julia Sauer
                    Rufus M., by Eleanor Estes
                    Mountain Born, by Elizabeth Yates

1945   *Rabbit Hill,* by Robert Lawson
      Honor Books: *The Hundred Dresses,* by Eleanor Estes
                    The Silver Pencil, by Alice Dalgliesh
                    Abraham Lincoln's World, by Genevieve Foster
                    Lone Journey: The Life of Roger Williams, by Jeanette Eaton

1946   *Strawberry Girl,* by Lois Lenski
      Honor Books: *Justin Morgan Had a Horse,* by Marguerite Henry
                    The Moved-Outers, by Florence Crannell Means
                    Bhimsa, The Dancing Bear, by Christine Weston
                    New Found World, by Katherine Shippen

1947   *Miss Hickory,* by Carolyn Sherwin Bailey
      Honor Books: *Wonderful Year,* by Nancy Barnes
                    Big Tree, by Mary and Conrad Buff
                    The Heavenly Tenants, by William Maxwell
                    The Avion My Uncle Flew, by Cyrus Fisher
                    The Hidden Treasure of Claston, by Eleanore Jewett

1948   *The Twenty-One Balloons,* by William Pène duBois
      Honor Books: *Pancakes-Paris,* by Claire Huchet Bishop
                    Li Lun, Lad of Courage, by Carolyn Treffinger
                    The Quaint and Curious Quest of Johnny Longfoot, by
                          Catherine Besterman
                    The Cow-Tail Switch and Other West African Stories, by Harold
                          Courlander
                    Misty of Chincoteaque, by Marguerite Henry

1949   *King of the Wind,* by Marguerite Henry
      Honor Books: *Seabirds,* by Holling C. Holling
                    Daughter of the Mountains, by Louise Rankin
                    My Father's Dragon, by Ruth S. Gannett
                    Story of the Negro, by Arna Bontemps

1950   *The Door in the Wall,* by Marguerite de Angeli
      Honor Books: *Tree of Freedom,* by Rebecca Caudill
                    Kildee House, by Rutherford Montgomery
                    George Washington, by Genevieve Foster
                    Song of the Pines, by Walter and Marion Havighurst

1951   *Amos Fortune,* Free Man, by Elizabeth Yates
      Honor Books: *Better Known as Johnny Appleseed,* by Mabel Leigh Hunt
                    Gandhi, Fighter without a Sword, by Jeanette Eaton
                    Abraham Lincoln, Friend of the People, by Clara Ingram Judson
                    The Story of Appleby Capple, by Anne Parrish

1952 *Ginger Pye,* by Eleanor Estes
  Honor Books: *Americans before Columbus,* by Elizabeth Baity
        Minn of the Mississippi, by Holling C. Holling
        The Defender, by Nicholas Kalashnikoff
        The Light at Tern Rocks, by Julia Sauer
        The Apple and the Arrow, by Mary and Conrad Buff

1953 *Secret of the Andes,* by Ann Nolan Clark
  Honor Books: *Charlotte's Web,* by E. B. White
        Moccasin Trail, by Eloise McGraw
        Red Sails to Capri, by Ann Weil
        The Bears on Hemlock Mountain, by Alice Dalgliesh
        Birthdays of Freedom, Vol. 1, by Genevieve Foster

1954 *. . . And Now Miguel,* by Joseph Krumgold
  Honor Books: *All Alone,* by Claire Huchet Bishop
        Shadrach, by Meindert DeJong
        Hurry Home Candy, by Meindert DeJong
        Theodore Roosevelt, Fighting Patriot, by Clara Ingram Judson
        Magic Maize, by Mary and Conrad Buff

1955 *The Wheel on the School,* by Meindert DeJong
  Honor Books: *Courage of Sarah Noble,* by Alice Dalgliesh
        Banner in the Sky, by James Ullman

1956 *Carry On, Mr. Bowditch,* by Jean Lee Latham
  Honor Books: *The Secret River,* by Marjorie Kinnan Rawlings
        The Golden Name Day, by Jennie Lindquist
        Men, Microscopes, and Living Things, by Katherine Shippen

1957 *Miracles on Maple Hill,* by Virginia Sorensen
  Honor Books: *Old Yeller,* by Fred Gipson
        The House of Sixty Fathers, by Meindert DeJong
        Mr. Justice Holmes, by Clara Ingram Judson
        The Corn Grows Ripe, by Dorothy Rhoads
        Black Fox of Lorne, by Marguerite de Angeli

1958 *Rifles for Watie,* by Harold Keith
  Honor Books: *The Horsecatcher,* by Mari Sandoz
        Gone-away Lake, by Elizabeth Enright
        The Great Wheel, by Robert Lawson
        Tom Paine, Freedom's Apostle, by Leo Gurko

1959 *The Witch of Blackbird Pond,* by Elizabeth George Speare
  Honor Books: *The Family under the Bridge,* by Natalie S. Carlson
        Along Came a Dog, by Meindert DeJong
        Chucaro: Wild Pony of the Pampa, by Francis Kalnay
        The Perilous Road, by William O. Steele

1960 *Onion John,* by Joseph Krumgold
  Honor Books: *My Side of the Mountain,* by Jean George
        America Is Born, by Gerald W. Johnson
        The Gammage Cup, by Carol Kendall

1961 *Island of the Blue Dolphins,* by Scott O'Dell
  Honor Books: *America Moves Forward,* by Gerald W. Johnson
        Old Ramon, by Jack Schaefer
        The Cricket in Times Square, by George Selden

1962 *The Bronze Bow,* by Elizabeth George Speare
  Honor Books: *Frontier Living,* by Edwin Tunis
        The Golden Goblet, by Eloise McGraw
        Belling the Tiger, by Mary Stolz

1963 *A Wrinkle in Time*, by Madeleine L'Engle
   Honor Books: *Thistle and Thyme*, by Sorche Nic Leodhas
         Men of Athens, by Olivia Coolidge

1964 *It's Like This, Cat*, by Emily Cheney Neville
   Honor Books: *Rascal*, by Sterling North
         The Loner, by Ester Wier

1965 *Shadow of a Bull*, by Maia Wojciechowska
   Honor Book: *Across Five Aprils*, by Irene Hunt

1966 *I, Juan De Pareja*, by Elizabeth Borten de Treviño
   Honor Books: *The Black Cauldron*, by Lloyd Alexander
         The Animal Family, by Randall Jarrell
         The Noonday Friends, by May Stolz

1967 *Up a Road Slowly*, by Irene Hunt
   Honor Books: *The King's Fifth*, by Scott O'Dell
         Zlateh the Goat and Other Stories, by Isaac Bashevis Singer
         The Jazz Man, by Mary H. Weik

1968 *From the Mixed-up Files of Mrs. Basil E. Frankweiler*, by E. L. Konigsburg
   Honor Books: *Jennifer, Hecate, Macbeth, William McKinley, and Me,*
         Elizabeth, by E. L. Konigsburg
         The Black Pearl, by Scott O'Dell
         The Fearsome Inn, by Isaac Bashevis Singer
         The Egypt Game, by Zilpha Keatley Snyder

1969 *The High King*, by Lloyd Alexander
   Honor Books: *To Be a Slave*, by Julius Lester
         When Shlemiel Went to Warsaw and Other Stories, by Isaac
         Bashevis Singer

1970 *Sounder*, by William H. Armstrong
   Honor Books: *Our Eddie*, by Sulamith Ish-Kishor
         The Many Ways of Seeing: An Introduction to the Pleasures of
         Art, by Janet Gaylord Moore
         Journey Outside, by Mary Q. Steele

1971 *Summer of the Swans*, by Betsy Byars
   Honor Books: *Knee-Knock Rise*, by Natalie Babbitt
         Enchantress from the Stars, by Sylvia Louise Engdahl
         Sing Down the Moon, by Scott O'Dell

1972 *Mrs. Frisby and the Rats of NIMH*, by Robert C. O'Brien
   Honor Books: *Annie and the Old One*, by Miska Miles
         The Headless Cupid, by Zilpha Keatley Snyder
         Incident at Hawk's Hill, by Allan W. Eckert
         The Planet of Junior Brown, by Virginia Hamilton
         The Tombs of Atuan, by Ursula K. LeGuin

1973 *Julie of the Wolves*, by Jean Craighead George
   Honor Books: *Frog and Toad Together*, by Arnold Lobel
         The Upstairs Room, by Johanna Reiss
         The Witches of Work, by Zilpha Keatley Snyder

1974 *The Slave Dancer*, by Paula Fox
   Honor Book: *The Dark is Rising*, by Susan Cooper

1975 *M. C. Higgins, the Great*, by Virginia Hamilton
   Honor Books: *My Brother Sam Is Dead*, by James Lincoln Collier and
         Christopher Collier
         The Perilous Gard, by Elizabeth Marie Pope
         Phillip Hall Likes Me, I Reckon Maybe, Bette Greene
         Figgs and Phantoms, by Ellen Raskin

1976   *The Grey King*, by Susan Cooper
      Honor Books: *Dragonwings*, by Lawrence Yep
                              The Hundred Penny Box, by Sharon Bell Mathis

1977   *Roll of Thunder, Hear My Cry*, by Mildred D. Taylor
      Honor Books: *Abel's Island*, by William Steig
                              A String in the Harp, by Nancy Bond

1978   *Bridge to Terabithia*, by Katherine Paterson
      Honor Books: *Anpao: An American Indian Odyssey*, by Jamake Highwater
                              Ramona and Her Father, by Beverly Cleary

1979   *The Westing Game*, by Ellen Raskin
      Honor Book: *The Great Gilly Hopkins*, by Katherine Paterson

1980   *A Gathering of Days*, by Joan W. Blos
      Honor Book: *The Road from Home: The Story of an Armenian Girl*, by
                              David Kherdian

1981   *Jacob Have I Loved*, by Katherine Paterson
      Honor Books: *The Fledgling*, by Jane Langton
                              A Ring of Endless Light, by Madeleine L'Engle

1982   *A Visit to William Blake's Inn: Poems for Innocent and Experienced Travelers*,
      by Nancy Willard
      Honor Books: *Ramona Quinby, Age 8*, by Beverly Cleary
                              Upon the Head of the Goat, by Aranka Siegal

1983   *Dicey's Song*, by Cynthia Voigt
      Honor Books: *The Blue Sword*, by Robin McKinley
                              Dr. DeSoto, by William Steig
                              Graven Images, by Paul Fleischman, illus. Andrew Class
                              Homesick: My Own Story, by Jean Fritz, illus. Margot Tomes
                              Sweet Whispers, Brother Rush, by Virginia Hamilton

1984   *Dear Mr. Henshaw*, by Beverly Cleary
      Honor Books: *The Wish Game*, by Bill Brittain
                                Sugaring Time, by Kathryn Lasky
                              A Solitary Blue, by Cynthia Voigt
                              Sign of the Beaver, by Elizabeth George Speare

1985   *The Hero and the Crown*, by Robin McKinley
      Honor Books: *Like Jake and Me*, by Mavis Jukes
                              The Moves Make the Man, by Bruce Brooks
                              One-Eyed Cat, by Paula Fox

1986   *Sarah, Plain and Tall*, by Patricia MacLachlan
      Honor Books: *Commodore Perry in the Land of the Shogun*, by Rhoda
                              Blumberg
                              Dogsong, by Gary Paulsen

1987   *The Whipping Boy*, by Sid Fleischman
      Honor Books: *On My Honor*, by Marion Dane Bauer
                                Volcano: The Eruption and Healing of Mount St. Helens, by
                              Patricia Lauber
                              A Fine White Dust, by Cynthia Ryland

1988   *Lincoln: A Photobiography*, by Russell Freedman
      Honor Books: *After the Rain*, by Norma Fox Mazer
                                Hatchet, by Gary Paulsen

1989   *Joyful Noise: Poems for Two Voices*, by Paul Fleischman
      Honor Books: *In the Beginning: Creation Stories from around the World*,
                              by Virginia Hamilton
                              Scorpions, by Walter Dean Myers

1990   *Number the Stars,* by Lois Lowry
      Honor Books: *Afternoon of the Elves,* by Janet Taylor Lisle
                Shabanu, Daughter of the Wind, by Suzanne Fisher Staples
                The Winter Room, by Gary Paulsen

1991   *Maniac Magee,* by Jerry Spinelli
      Honor Book: *True Confessions of Charlotte Doyle,* by Avi

1992   *Shiloh,* by Phyllis Reynolds Naylor
      Honor Books: *Nothing but the Truth,* by Avi
                The Wright Brothers: How They Invented the Airplane, by Russell Freedom

1993   *Missing May,* by Cynthia Rylant
      Honor Books: *The Dark Thirty: Southern Tales of the Supernatural,* by Patricia McKissack
                Somewhere in the Darkness, by Walter Dean Myers
                What Hearts, by Bruce Brooks

1994   *The Giver,* Lois Lowry
      Honor Books: *Crazy Lady,* Jane Leslie Conly
                Dragon's Gate, Laurence Yep
                Eleanor Roosevelt: A Life of Discovery, by Russell Freedman

Coretta Scott King Awards

These awards, founded to commemorate Dr. Martin Luther King, Jr., and his wife, Coretta Scott King, for their work in promoting peace and world brotherhood, are given to an African-American author and, since 1974, an African-American illustrator whose children's books published during the preceding year made outstanding inspirational and educational contributions to literature for children and young people. The awards are sponsored by the Social Responsibilities Round Table of the American Library Association.

1970   *Martin Luther King, Jr.,: Man of Peace,* by Lillie Patterson

1971   *Black Troubadour: Langston Hughes,* by Charlemae Rollins

1972   *17 Black Artists,* by Elton C. Fax

1973   *I Never Had It Made,* by Jackie Robinson, as told to Alfred Duckett

1974   Author: *Ray Charles,* by Sharon Bell Mathis
      Illus.: *Ray Charles,* illus. George Ford

1975   Author: *The Legend of Africana,* by Dorothy Robinson
      Illus.: *The Legend of Africana,* illus. Herbert Temple

1976   Author: *Duey's Tale,* by Pearl Bailey
      Illus.: no award

1977   Author: *The Story of Stevie Wonder,* James Haskins
      Illus.: no award

1978   Author: *Africa Dream,* by Eloise Greenfield
      Illus.: *Africa Dream,* illus. Carole Bayard

1979   Author: *Escape to Freedom,* by Ossie Davis
      Illus.: *Something on My Mind,* illus. Tom Feelings, by Nikki Grimes

1980   Author: *The Young Landlords,* by Walter Dean Myers
      Illus.: *Cornrows,* illus. Carole Bayard, by Camille Yarbrough

1981   Author: *This Life,* by Sidney Poitier
      Illus.: *Beat the Story-Drum, Pum-Pum,* by and illus. Ashley Bryan

1982   Author: *Let the Circle Be Unbroken,* by Mildred Taylor

Illus.:   *Mother Crocodile: An Uncle Amadou Tale from Senegal,* illus. John
Steptoe, adapted by Rosa Guy
1983   Author: *Sweet Whispers, Brother Rush,* by Virginia Hamilton
Illus.:   *Black Child,* by and illus. Peter Magubane
1984   Author: *Everett Anderson's Good-bye,* by Lucille Clifton
Illus.:   *My Mama Needs Me,* illus. Pat Cummings, by Mildred Pitts Walter
1985   Author: *Motown and Didi,* by Walter Dean Myers
Illus.:   no award
1986   Author: *The People Could Fly: American Black Folktales,* by Virginia Hamilton
Illus.:   *Patchwork Quilt,* illus. Jerry Pinkney, by Valerie Flournoy
1987   Author: *Justin and the Best Biscuits in the World,* by Mildred Pitts Walter
Illus.:   *Half Moon and One Whole Star,* illus. Jerry Pinkney, by Crescent
Dragonwagon
1988   Author: *The Friendship,* by Mildred D. Taylor, illus. Max Ginsburg
Illus.:   *Mufaro's Beautiful Daughters: An African Tale,* retold and illus.
John Steptoe
1989   Author: *Fallen Angels,* by Walter Dean Myers
Illus.:   *Mirandy and Brother Wind,* illus. Jerry Pinkney, by Patricia McKissack
1990   Author: *A Long Hard Journey,* by Patricia and Frederick McKissack
Illus.:   *Nathaniel Talking,* illus. Jan Spivey Gilchrist, by Eloise Greenfield
1991   Author: *Road to Memphis,* by Mildred D. Taylor
Illus.:   *Aida,* Illus. Leo and Diane Dillon, retold by Leotyne Price
1992   Author: *Now Is Your Time! The African-American Struggle for Freedom,* by
Walter Dean Myers
Illus.:   *Tar Beach,* by and illus. Faith Ringgold
1993   Author: *The Dark Thirty: Southern Tales of the Supernatural,* by Patricia
McKissack
Illus.:   *The Origin of Life on Earth: An African Creation Myth,* illus.
Kathleen Atkins Wilson, by David A. Anderson (Sankofa)
1994   Author: *Toning the Sweep,* by Angela Johnson
Illus.:   *Soul Looks Back in Wonder,* by Tom Feelings
Author Honor Books: *Brown Honey in Broomwheat Tea,* by Joyce
Carol Thomas
Malcolm X: By Any Means Necessary, by Walter Dean
Myers
Illus. Honor Books: *Brown Honey in Broomwheat Tea,* illus. Floyd Cooper,
by Joyce Carol Thomas
Uncle Jed's Barbershop, illus. James Ransome, by
Margaree King Mitchell

Scott O'Dell Award for Historical Fiction

This award, donated by the author Scott O'Dell and administered by the Bulletin of the
Center of Children's Books, is given to the author of a distinguished work of historical
fiction for children or young adults set in the New World and published in English by a
U.S. publisher.

1984   *The Sign of the Beaver,* by Elizabeth George Speare
1985   *The Fighting Ground,* by Avi
1986   *Sarah, Plain and Tall,* by Patricia MacLachlan
1987   *Streams to the River, River to the Sea: A Novel of Sacagewea,* by Scott O'Dell

1988 *Charlie Skedaddle*, by Patricia Beatty
1989 *The Honorable Prison*, by Lyll Becerra de Jenkins
1990 *Shades of Gray*, by Carolyn Reeder
1991 *A Time of Troubles*, by Pieter van Raven
1992 *Stepping on the Cracks*, by Mary Downing Hahn
1993 *Morning Girl*, by Michael Dorris

Jane Addams Book Award

Given annually in the fall since 1953 by the Women's International League for Peace and Freedom and the Jane Addams Peace Association (777 United Nations Plaza, New York, NY 10017) to the children's book of the year that "most effectively promotes peace, social justice, world community and the equality of the sexes and all races."

1953 *People Are Important*, by Eva Knox Evans
1954 *Stick-in-the-Mud*, by Jean Ketchum
1955 *Rainbow round the World*, by Elizabeth Yates
1956 *Story of the Negro*, by Arna Bontemps
1957 *Blue Mystery*, by Margot Benary-Isbert
1958 *The Perilous Road*, by William O. Steele
1959 No award
1960 *Champions of Peace*, by Edith Patterson Meyer
1961 *What Then, Raman?*, by Shirley L. Arora
1962 *The Road to Agra*, by Aimee Sommerfelt
1963 *The Monkey and the Wild, Wild Wind*, by Ryerson Johnson
1964 *Profiles in Courage*, by John F. Kennedy
1965 *Meeting with a Stranger*, by Duane Bradley
1966 *Berries Goodman*, by Emily Cheney Neville
1967 *Queenie Peavy*, by Robert Burch
1968 *The Little Fishes*, by Erik Christian Haugaard
1969 *The Endless Steppe*, by Esther Hautzig
1970 *The Cay*, by Theodore Taylor
1971 *Jane Addams: Pioneer of Social Justice*, by Cornelia Meigs
1972 *The Tamarack Tree*, by Betty Underwood
1973 *The Riddle of Racism*, by S. Carl Hirsch
1974 *Nilda*, by Nicholasa Mohr
1975 *The Princess and the Admiral*, by Charlotte Pomerantz
1976 *Paul Robeson*, by Eloise Greenfield
1977 *Never to Forget: The Jews of the Holocaust*, by Milton Meltzer
1978 *Child of the Owl*, by Laurence Yep
1979 *Many Smokes, Many Moons*, by Jamake Highwater
1980 *The Road from Home: The Story of an Armenian Girl*, by David Kherdian
1981 *First Woman in Congress: Jeannette Rankin*, by Florence White
1982 *A Spirit to Ride the Whirlwind*, by Athena Lord
1983 *Hiroshima No Pika*, by Toshi Maruki
1984 *Rain of Fire*, by Marion Dane Bauer
1985 *The Short Life of Sophie Scholl*, by Hermann Vinke

1986 *Ain't Gonna Study War No More: The Story of America's Peace Seekers*, by Milton Meltzer

1987 *Nobody Wants a Nuclear War*, by Kathleen Tucker, illus. Judith Vigna

1988 *Waiting for the Rain: A Novel of South Africa*, by Sheila Gordon

1989 *Anthony Burns: The Defeat and Triumph of a Fugitive Slave*, by Virginia Hamilton
      Looking Out, by Victoria Boutis

1990 *Long Hard Journey: The Story of the Pullman Porter*, by Patricia McKissack

1991 *Big Book for Peace*, by Ann Durell and Marilyn Sachs

1992 *Journey of the Sparrows*, by Fran L. Buss

1993 *Taste of Salt*, by Frances Temple
      Aunt Harriet's Underground Railroad in the Sky, written and illus. Faith Ringgold

Association of Jewish Libraries Awards

The award honors the book deemed by a committee of professional Judaica librarians to have made the most outstanding contribution to the field of Jewish literature for children and young people.

1969 *The Endless Steppe*, Esther Hautzig

1970 *Our Eddie*, by Sulamith Ish-Kishor

1971 *The Year*, by Suzanne Lange

1972 *Isaac Bashevis Singer* for general contribution

1973 *Molly Cone* for general contribution

1974 *Uncle Misha's Partisans*, by Yuri Suhl

1975 No award

1976 *Waiting for Mama*, by Marietta Moskin

1977 *Never to Forget: The Jews of the Holocaust*, by Milton Meltzer

1978 *Exit from Home*, by Anita Heyman

1979 *The Devil in Vienna*, by Doris Orgel

1980 *Ike and Mama and the Block Wedding*, by Carol Snyder

1981 *A Russian Farewell*, by Leonard Everett Fisher

1982 Older Readers: *The Night Journey*, by Kathryn Lasky
      Younger Readers: *Yussel's Prayer: A Yom Kippur Story*, by Barbara Cohen

1983 Older Readers: *Call Me Ruth*, by Marilyn Sachs
      Younger Readers: *Castle on Hester Street*, by Linda Heller

1984 Older Readers: *In the Mouth of the Wolf*, by Rose Zar
      Younger Readers: *Bubbie, Me and Memories*, by Barbara Pomerantz

1985 Older Readers: *The Island on Bird Street*, by Uri Orlev
      Younger Readers: *Mrs. Moskowitz and the Sabbath Candlesticks*, by Amy Schwartz

1986 Older Readers: *Brothers: A Hebrew Legend*, by Florence B. Freedman, illus. by Robert A. Parker
      Younger Readers: *Ike and Mama and the Seven Surprises*, by Carol Snyder, illus. by Charles Robinson

1987 Older Readers: *Beyond the High White Wall*, by Nancy Pitt
      Younger Readers: *Poems for Jewish Holidays*, ed. Myra C. Livingston, illus. Lloyd Bloom

1988   Older Readers: *Return*, by Sonia Levitin
        Younger Readers: *Number on My Grandfather's Arm*, by David A. Adler
1989   Older Readers: *Devil's Arithmetic*, by Jane Yolen
        Younger Readers: *Keeping Quilt*, by and illus. Patricia Polacco
1990   Older Readers: *Number the Stars*, by Lois Lowry
        Younger Readers: *Berchick, My Mother's Horse*, by Esther S. Blanc, illus. Tennessee Dixon
1991   Older Readers: *My Grandmother's Stories: A Collection of Jewish Folktales*, by Adele Geras, illus. Jael Jordon
        Younger Readers: *Chanukkah Guest*, by Eric A. Kimmel, illus. Carmi Giora
1992   Older Readers: *The Diamond Tree: Jewish Tales from around the World*, by Howard Schwartz and Barbara Rush, illus. Uri Shulevitz
        Younger Readers: *Daddy's Chair*, by Sandy Lanton, illus. Shelly O. Haas
        Cakes and Miracles: A Purim Tale, by Barbara Diamond Goldin, illus. Erika Weihs
1993   Older Readers: *Letters from Rifka*, by Karen Hesse
        Younger Readers: *Something from Nothing*, by Phoebe Gilman

Child Study Children's Book Committee at Bank Street College Award

Given annually to a distinguished book of the previous year for children or young people that deals honestly and courageously with problems in the world.

1944   *Keystone Kids*, by John R. Tunis
1945   *The House*, by Margorie Allee
1946   *The Moved-Outers*, by Florence Crannell Means
1947   *Heart of Danger*, by Howard Pease
1948   *Judy's Journey*, by Lois Lenski
1949   *The Big Wave*, by Pearl Buck
1950   *Paul Tiber: Forester*, by Maria Gleit
1951   *The United Nations and Youth*, by Eleanor Roosevelt and Helen Ferris
1952   No award
1953   *Jareb*, by Miriam Powell
        Twenty and Ten, by Claire Huchet Bishop
1954   *In a Mirror*, by Mary Stolz
1955   *High Road Home*, by William Corbin
        The Ordeal of the Young Hunter, by Jonreed Lauritzen
1956   *Crow Boy*, by Taro Yashima
        Plain Girl, by Virginia Sorenson
1957   *The House of Sixty Fathers*, by Meindert DeJong
1958   *Shadow across the Campus*, by Helen R. Sattley
1959   *South Town*, by Lorenz Graham
1960   *Jennifer*, by Zoa Sherburne
1961   *Janine*, by Robin McKown
1962   *The Girl from Puerto Rico*, by Hila Colman
        The Road to Agra, by Aimee Sommerfelt
1963   *The Trouble with Terry*, by Joan M. Lexau

1964   *The Peaceable Kingdom*, by Betty Schechter
        The Rock and the Willow, by Mildred Lee
1965   *The High Pasture*, by Ruth Harnden
1966   *The Empty Schoolhouse*, by Natalie Savage Carlson
1967   *Queenie Peavy*, by Robert Burch
        (Special citation) *Curious George Goes to the Hospital*, by Margaret and
        H. A. Rey
1968   *The Contender*, by Robert Lipsyte
1969   *What's It All About*, by Vadim Frolov
        (Special citation) *Where Is Daddy? The Story of a Divorce*, by Beth Goff
1970   *The Empty Moat*, by Margaretha Shemin
1971   *Migrant Girl*, by Carli Laklan
        Rock Star, by James Lincoln Collier
1972   *John Henry McCoy*, by Lillie D. Chaffin
        (Special citation) *The Pair of Shoes*, by Aline Glasgow
1973   *A Sound of Chariots*, by Mollie Hunter
1974   *A Taste of Blackberries*, by Doris Buchanan Smith
1975   *Luke Was There*, by Eleanor Clymer
1976   *The Garden Is Doing Fine*, by Carol Farley
1977   *Somebody Else's Child*, by Roberta Silman
1978   *The Pinballs*, by Betsy Byars
1979   *The Devil in Vienna*, by Doris Orgel
1980   *The Whipman Is Watching*, by T. A. Dyer
1981   *A Boat to Nowhere*, by Maureen Crane Wartski
1982   *A Spirit to Ride the Whirlwind*, by Athena Lord
1983   *Homesick: My Own Story*, by Jean Fritz
1984   *The Sign of the Beaver*, by Elizabeth George Speare
        The Solomon System, by Phyllis Reynolds Naylor
1985   *One-Eyed Cat*, by Paula Fox
        With Westie and the Tin Man, by C. S. Adler
1986   *Ain't Gonna Study War No More: The Story of America's Peace Seekers*, by
        Milton Meltzer
1987   *Journey to Jo'burg: A South African Story*, by Beverly Naidoo
1988   *Rabble Starkey*, by Lois Lowry
1989   *December Stillness*, by Mary D. Hahn
        Most Beautiful Place in the World, by Ann Cameron, trans. Thomas B. Allen
1990   *Shades of Gray*, by Carolyn Reeder
1991   *Secret City, U.S.A.*, by Felice Holman
1992   *Blue Skin of the Sea*, by Graham Salisbury
1993   *Make Lemonade*, by Virginia Ewer Wolff

Christopher Awards

The award is given to works that "have achieved artistic excellence . . . affirming the
highest values of the human spirit."

1970   *Alexander and the Wind-up Mouse*, by Leo Lionni
        Tucker's Countryside, by George Selden

Brother, Can You Spare a Dime, by Milton Meltzer
Escape From Nowhere, by Jeannette Eyerly

1971 *The Erie Canal*, by Peter Spier
A Moment of Silence, by Pierre Janssen
The Changeling, by Zilpha Keatley Snyder
The Guardians, by John Christopher
Sea and Earth: The Life of Rachel Carson, by Philip Sterling
UNICEF Book of Children's Legends, *UNICEF Book of Children's Poems*,
  UNICEF Book of Children's Prayers, and *UNICEF Book of Children's Songs*,
  by William I. Kaufman

1972 *Emmet Otter's Jug-Band Christmas*, by Russell Hoban
On the Day Peter Stuyvesant Sailed into Town, by Arnold Lobel
Annie and the Old One, by Miska Miles
Pocahontas and the Strangers, by Clyde Robert Bulla
The Headless Cupid, by Zilpha Keatley Snyder
The Rights of the People—The Major Decisions of the Warren Court, by Elaine
  and Walter Goodman

1973 *The Adventures of Obadiah*, by Brinton Turkle
The Book of Giant Stories, by David L. Harrison
Tracking the Unearthly Creature of Marsh and Pond, by Howard G. Smith
Freaky Friday, by Mary Rodgers
Vanishing Wings, by Griffling Bancroft
This Star Shall Abide, by Sylvia Louise Engdahl
Dominic, by William Steig

1974 *It's Raining Said John Twaining*, by N. M. Bodecker
I'll Protect You from the Beasts, by Martha Alexander
Gorilla, Gorilla, by Carol Fenner
The Wolf, by Michael Fox
Guests in the Promised Land, by Kristin Hunter
The Right to Know—Censorship in America, by Robert A. Liston

1975 *Dawn*, by Uri Shulevitz
My Grandson Lew, by Charlotte Zolotow
First Snow, by Helen Coutant
Save the Mustang, by Ann E. Weiss
A Billion for Boris, by Mary Rodgers

1976 *Anno's Alphabet*, by Mitsumasa Anno
How the Witch Got Alf, by Cora Annett
Bert Breen's Barn, by Walter D. Edmonds
Pyramid, by David Macaulay

1977 *Willy Bear*, by Mildred Kantrowitz
Frog and Toad All Year, by Arnold Lobel
The Champion of Merrimack County, by Roger W. Drury
Hurry, Hurry, Mary Dear! and Other Nonsense Poems, by N. M. Bodecker
Dear Bill, Remember Me? and Other Stories, by Norma Fox Mazer

1978 *Noah's Ark*, by Peter Spier
The Seeing Stick, by Jane Yolen
Come to the Edge, by Julia Cunningham
Where's Your Head? Psychology for Teenagers, by Dale Carlson
The Wheel of King Asoka, by Ashok Davar

1979 *Panda Cake*, by Rosalie Seidler
Chester Chipmunk's Thanksgiving, by Barbara Williams
The Great Gilly Hopkins, by Katherine Paterson
Gentlehands, by M. E. Kerr

1980 *Frederick's Alligator*, by Esther Allen Peterson

What Happened in Hamelin, by Gloria Skurzynski
All Together Now, by Sue Ellen Bridgers
The New York Kid's Book, by Catherine Edmonds et al., ed.

1981 *People,* by Peter Spier
All Times, All People: A World History of Slavery, by Milton Meltzer
Son for a Day, by Corrine Gerson
Encounter by Easton, by Avi
The Hardest Lesson: Personal Accounts of a School Desegregation Crisis, by Pamela Bullard and Judith Stoia

1982 *My Mom Travels a Lot,* by Caroline Feller Bauer, illus. Nancy Winslow Parker
Even If I Did Something Awful, by Barbara Shook Hazen
A Gift of Mirrorvax, by Malcolm Macloud
The Islanders, by John Rowe Townsend

1983 *We Can't Sleep,* by James Stevenson
Homesick: My Own Story, by Jean Fritz
A Formal Feeling, by Zibby Oneal
Drawing From Nature, by Jim Arnosky

1984 *Posy,* by Charlotte Pomerantz
Dear Mr. Henshaw, by Beverly Cleary
The Sign of the Beaver, by Elizabeth George Speare
The Nuclear Arms Race—Can We Survive It?, by Ann E. Weiss

1985 *Picnic,* by Emily Arnold McCully
How My Parents Learned to Eat, by Ina R. Friedman
Secrets of a Small Brother, by Richard J. Margolis
One-Eyed Cat, by Paula Fox
Imagine That!!! Exploring Make Believe, by Joyce Strauss

1986 *Mount Rushmore Story,* by Judith Saint-George
Patchwork Quilt, by Valerie Flournoy
Promise Not to Tell, by Carolyn Polese, illus. by Jennifer Barrett
Sarah, Plain and Tall, by Patricia MacLachlan

1987 *Borrowed Summer,* by Marion W. Doren
Class Dismissed: More High School Poems, by Mel Glenn, illus. Michael J. Bernstein
Duncan and Dolores, by and illus. Barbara Samuels
Purple Coat, by Amy Hest, illus. Amy Schwartz

1988 *Gold Cadillac,* by Mildred D. Taylor, illus. Michael Hays
Heckedy Peg, by Audrey Wood, illus. Don Wood
Humphrey's Bear, by Jan Wahl, illus. William Joyce
Into a Strange Land: Unaccompanied Refugee Youth in America, by Brent Ashabranner and Melissa Ashabranner

1989 *Family Farm,* by and illus. Thomas Locker
Good-bye Book, by Judith Viorst, illus. Kay Chorao
Lies, Deception and Truth, by Ann E. Weiss
Looking the Tiger in the Eye: Confronting the Nuclear Threat, by Carl B. Feldbaum and Ronald J. Bee

1990 *Can the Whales Be Saved?* by Philip Whitfield
Keeping a Christmas Secret, by Phyllis R. Naylor, illus. Lena Shiffman
So Much to Tell You . . . , by John Marsden
William and Grandpa, by Alice Schertle, illus. Lydia Dabcovich

1991 *Anton the Dove Fancier and Other Tales of the Holocaust,* by Bernard Gotfryd
Mississippi Bridge, by Mildred D. Taylor, illus. Max Ginsburg
Paul Revere's Ride, by Henry Wadsworth Longfellow, illus. Ted Rand

1992   *Gold Coin,* by Alma F. Ada, illus. Neil Waldman
      Somebody Loves You, Mr. Hatch, by Eileen Spinelli, illus. Paul Yalowitz
      Star Fisher, by Laurence Yep
      Stephen's Feast, by Jean Richardson, illus. Alice Englander
      Where Does God Live? Questions and Answers for Parents and Children, by
          Rabbi Marc Gellman and Monsignor Thomas Hartman, illus. William Zdinak
1993   *The Rainbow Fish,* by Marcus Pfister
      Rosie and the Yellow Ribbon, by Paula de Paolo
      Letters from Rifka, Karen Hesse
      Mississippi Challenge, by Mildred P. Walter

National Jewish Book Awards

This awards program is designed to promote American Jewish literary creativity and an appreciation of Jewish literature. Beginning in 1983 an award was also given for illustration (indicated by I).

1952   *All-of-a-kind Family,* by Sydney Taylor
1953   *Star Light Stories* and *Stories of King David,* by Lillian S. Freehof
1954   *The Jewish People: Book Three,* by Deborah Pessin
1955   *King Solomon's Navy,* by Nora Benjamin Kubie
1956   Sadie Rose Weilerstein
1957   Elma E. Levinger
1958   *Jewish Junior Encyclopedia,* by Naomi Ben Asher and Hayim Leaf
1959   *Border Hawk: August Bondi,* by Lloyd Alexander
1960   *Keys to a Magic Door: Issac Leib Peretz,* by Sylvia Rothchild
1961   *Discovering Israel,* by Regina Tor
1962   *Ten and a Kid,* by Sadie Rose Weilerstein
1963   *Return to Freedom,* by Josephine Kamm
1964   *A Boy of Old Prague,* by Sulamith Ish-Kishor
1965   *Worlds Lost and Found,* by Dov Peretz Elkins and Azriel Eisenberg
1966   *The Dreyfus Affair,* by Betty Schechter
1967   *The Story of Israel,* by Meyer Levin
1968–1969   No awards
1970   *Martin Buber: Wisdom in Our Time,* by Charlie May
      The Story of Masada, retold by Gerald Gottlieb
1971   *Journey to America,* by Sonia Levitin
1972   *The Master of Miracle: A New Novel of the Golem,* by Sulamith Ish-Kishor
1973   *The Upstairs Room,* by Johanna Reiss
1974   *Uncle Misha's Partisans,* by Yuri Suhl
1975   *The Holocaust: A History of Courage and Resistance,* by Bea Stadtler
1976   *Haym Salomon: Liberty's Son,* by Shirley Milgrim
1977   *Rifka Grows Up,* by Chaya Burstein
1978   *Never to Forget: The Jews of the Holocaust,* by Milton Meltzer
1979   *Joshua: Fighter for Bar Kochba,* by Irene Narell
1980   *Dita Saxova,* by Arnost Lustig
1981   *A Russian Farewell,* by Leonard Everett Fisher
1982   *The Night Journey,* by Kathryn Lasky

1983   *King of the Seventh Grade,* by Barbara Cohen
      Yussel's Prayer: A Yom Kippur Story, by Barbara Cohen, illus. Michael Deraney (I)
1984   *The Jewish Kids Catalog,* by Chaya M. Burstein
1985   *Good If It Goes,* by Gary Provost and Gail Levine-Freidus
      Mrs. Moskowitz and the Sabbath Candlesticks, by Amy Schwartz (I)
1986   *In Kindling Flame: The Story of Hannah Senesh, 1921–1944,* by Linda Atkinson
      Brothers, by Florence B. Freedman, illus. Robert A. Parker (I)
1987   *Monday in Odessa,* by Eileen B. Sherman
      Poems for Jewish Holidays, by Myra C. Livingston, illus. by Lloyd Bloom (I)
1988   *Return,* by Sonia Levitin
      Exodus, adapted by Miriam Chaikin, illus. Charles Mikolaycak (I)
1989   *Devil's Arithmetic,* by Jane Yolen
      Just Enough is Plenty: A Hanukkah Tale, by Barbara D. Goldin, illus. Seymour Chwast (I)
1990   *Number the Stars,* by Lois Lowry
      Berchick, My Mother's Horse, by Esther S. Blanc, illus. Tennessee Dixon (I)
1991   *Becoming Gershona,* by Nava Semel
      Hannukkah, by Roni Schotter, illus. Marylin Hafner (I)
1992   *Chicken Man,* by Michelle Edwards
      The Man from the Other Side, by Uri Orlev
1993   *Letters from Rifka,* by Karen Hesse
      Elijah's Angel, by Michael Rosen, illus. A. Robinson (I)

Carter G. Woodson Book Award

Established in 1973 in honor of black historian and educator Carter G. Woodson, this award for thematically appropriate nonfiction is intended to "encourage the writing, publishing and dissemination of outstanding social science books for young readers which treat topics related to ethnic minorities and race relations sensitively and accurately." It is sponsored by the National Council for Social Studies.

1974   *Rosa Parks,* by Eloise Greenfield
1975   *Make a Joyful Noise unto the Lord: The Life of Mahalia Jackson, Queen of the Gospel Singers,* by Jesse Jackson
1976   *Dragonwinds,* by Laurence Yep
1977   *The Trouble They Seen,* by Dorothy Sterling
1978   *The Biography of Danial Inouye,* by Jane Goodsell
1979   *Native American Testimony: An Anthology of Indian and White Relations,* edited by Peter Nabokov
1980   *War Cry on a Prayer Feather: Prose and Poetry of the Ute Indians,* by Nancy Wood
1981   *The Chinese Americans,* by Milton Meltzer
1982   *Coming to North American from Mexico, Cuba and Puerto Rico,* by Susan Garver and Paula McGuire
1983   *Morning Star, Black Sun: The Cheyenne Indians and American's Energy Crisis,* by Brent Ashabranner
1984   *Mexico and the United States,* by E. B. Fincher
1985   *To Live in Two Worlds: American Indian Youth Today,* by Brent Ashabranner
1986   *Dark Harvest: Migrant Farmworkers in America,* by Brent Ashabranner
1987   *Happily May I Walk,* by Arlene Hirschfelder

1988   *Black Music in America: A History through Its People*, by James Haskins

1989   *Walking the Road to Freedom: A Story about Sojourner Truth,* by Jeri Ferris, illus. Peter E. Hanson

1990   *In Two Worlds: A Yup'ik Eskimo Family,* by Aylette Jenness and Alice Rivers

1991   *Shirley Chisolm: Teacher and Congresswoman,* by Catherine Scheader
       Sorrow's Kitchen: Zora Hurston, by Mary Lyon

1992   *Last Princess: The Story of Ka'iolani of Hawai'i,* by Fay Stanley, illus. Diane Stanley
       Native American Doctor: The Story of Susas LaFlesche Picotte, by Jeri Ferris

1993   *Madam C. J. Walker,* by Patricia and Frederick McKissack

APPENDIX E

Publishers' Addresses

ABC (Americans before Columbus). National Indian Youth Council, 201 Hermosa, Albuquerque, N.E., NM 87108

Abingdon Press. 201 Eighth Avenue, South Nashville, TN 37202

Ace Books (Berkley Publishing). 200 Madison Ave., New York, NY 10016

Addison-Wesley. Rte. 128, Reading, MA 01867

African-American Images. 9204 Commercial, Suite 308, Chicago, IL 60617-9998

Afro-Am Publishing Company. 407 E. 25th St., No. 600, Chicago, IL 60616-2433

Allyn and Bacon, Inc. 160 Gould St., Needham Heights, MA 02194-2310

American Association of Sex Educators and Counselors. 600 Maryland Ave., S.W., Washington, DC 20024

American Federation of Teachers. 11 Dupont Circle, N.W., Washington, DC 20036

American Jewish Committee. Inst. of Human Relations, 165 E. 56th Street, New York, NY 10022-2746

American Guidance Service. Circle Pines, MN 55014-1796

Archon Books. P.O. Box 4327, 925 Sherman St., Hamden, CT 06514

Astor Honor, Inc. 530 Fifth Ave., New York, NY 10036-5101

Atheneum Publishers (Macmillan). 866 Third Ave., New York, NY 10022

Avon Books. 1350 Ave. of the Americas, New York, NY 10019

Ballard & Tighe, Inc. 480 Atlas St., Brea, CA 92621

Bantam Books. 666 Fifth Ave., New York, NY 10103

Barron's Educational Series, Inc. 250 Wireless Blvd., P.O. Box 8040, Hauppauge, NY 11788

The Beacon Press. 25 Beacon St., Boston, MA 02108

Beaufort Books. 9 East 40th St., New York, NY 10016

Behavioral Publications, Inc. 233 Spring St., New York, NY 10013-1578

Berkley Publishing. 200 Madison Ave., New York, NY 10016

Bethany Press. 2320 Pine Blvd., P.O. Box 179, St. Louis, MO 63166

Bookstore Press. Box 191, R.F.D. 1, Freeport, ME 04032

R.R. Bowker. 245 West 17th St., New York, NY 10011

Boyd's Mills Press. 815 Church St., Honesdale, PA 18431

Broadside Press. P.O. Box 04257, Northwestern St., Detroit, MI 48204

Brookline Books. P.O. Box 1046, Cambridge, MA 02238

Butterfield Associates. 1339 61st St., Emeryville, CA 94608

Campbell and Hall. Box 350, Boston, MA 02117

Candlewick Press. 2067 Massachusetts Ave., Cambridge, MA 02140

Carolrhoda Books. 241 First Ave., North Minneapolis, MN 55401

Charlesbridge Publishing. 85 Main St., Watertown, MA 02172

The Children's Small Press Collection. 719 N. Fourth Ave., Ann Arbor, MI 48104

The Children's Literature Foundation, Inc. West-Marshall School, Waverley St., Watertown, MA 02172

Children's Press. 5440 N. Cumberland Ave., Chicago, IL 60656

Chilton Book Company. Chilton Way, Radnor, PA 19089

Christopher-Gordon Publishers Inc. 480 Washington St., Norwood, MA 02060

Clarion Books/Ticknor & Fields (Houghton Mifflin). 215 Park Ave. S., New York, NY 10003

Cobblestone Publishing. 30 Grove St., Peterborough, NH 03458

Council on Interracial Books for Children. 1841 Broadway, Rm. 500, New York, NY 10023

Coward, McCann & Geohegan, Inc. 200 Madison Ave., New York, NY 10016

Crane Publishing Company. 1301 Hamilton Ave., Box 3713, Trenton, NJ 08629

Creative Arts. 833 Bancroft Way, Berkeley, CA 94710

Creative Education, Inc. 123 S. Broad St., P.O. Box 227, Mankato, MN 56001

Crestwood House. P.O. Box 3427, Mankato, MN 56002

Cricket. 315 Fifth St., Peru, IL 61354

Day Star Publishing. P.O. Box 2026, Pahrump, NV 89041

DDL Books Inc. 6521 N.W. 87 Ave., Miami, Fl 33166

Delacorte Press. 666 Fifth Ave., New York, NY 10103

Dell Publishing Co. 666 Fifth Ave., New York, NY 10103

Dial Books for Young Readers (Penguin USA). 375 Hudson St., New York, NY 10014

Dillon Press. 242 Portland Ave., S. Minneapolis, MN 55415

Dinosaur Publishers/Parkwest Publishers. 238 W. 72nd St., New York, NY 10023

Dodd, Mead & Company, Inc. 71 Fifth Ave., New York, NY 10013

Doubleday and Co., Inc. 666 Fifth Ave., New York, NY 10103

E. P. Dutton (New American Library). 2 Park Ave., New York, NY 10016

Educators for Social Responsibility. 23 Garden St., Cambridge, MA 02138

Enslow Publishers. Bloy St. & Ramsey Ave., Box 777, Hillside, NJ 07205-0777

Evans and Company. 216 E. 49th St., New York, NY 10017

Farrar, Straus & Giroux, Inc. 19 Union Square, West, New York, NY 10003

Feminist Press. City University of New York, 311 E. 94th St., New York, NY 10128

Follett Publishing Company. 1000 W. Washington Blvd., Chicago, IL 60607

The Foundation for Children's Books. 30 Common St., Watertown, MA 02172

Franklin Publishers. Box 1338, Bryn Mawr, PA 19010

Fun Publishing Company. P.O. Box 2049, Scottsdale, AZ 85252

Garrard Publishing Company. 1607 N. Market St., Champaign, IL 61820

Ginn and Company. 191 Spring St., Lexington, MA 02173

David R. Godine Publisher, Inc. Horticulture Hall, 300 Massachusetts Ave., Boston, MA 02115

Golden Books. 850 Third Ave., New York, NY 10022

Good Apple. 1204 Buchanan St., P.O. Box 299, Carthage, IL 62321-0299

Gorsuch Scarisbrick Publishers. 8233 Via Paseo del Norte, Suite F-400, Scottsdale, AZ 85258

Green Tiger Press. 1061 India St., San Diego, CA 92101

Greenwillow Books. 1305 Ave. of the Americas, New York, NY 10019

Grosset & Dunlap, Inc. 51 Madison Ave., New York, NY 10010

Grove Press, Inc. 841 Broadway, New York, NY 10003-4793

Gulliver Books. 1250 Sixth Ave., San Diego, CA 92101

Harcourt Brace Jovanovich, Inc. 1250 Sixth Ave., San Diego, CA 92101

Harper Collins Junior Books Group. 10 E. 53rd St., New York, NY 10022

Harper Collins College Books. 10 E. 53rd St., New York, NY 10022

Harvey House (E. M. Hale & Co.). 20 Waterside Plaza, New York, NY 10010

Hastings House Publishers, Inc. 141 Halstead Ave., Mamaroneck, New York, NY 10543

Hayfen Books. 4300 W. 62nd St., Indianapolis, IN 46268

Heineman Educational Books. 361 Hanover St., Portsmouth, NH 03801-3959

Highlights for Children. P. O. Box 269, Columbus, OH 43216-0269

Hill and Wang, Inc. 19 Union Square, W., New York, NY 10003

Holiday House. 425 Madison Ave., New York, NY 10017

Henry Holt and Company, Inc. 115 W. 18th St., New York, NY 10175

Holt, Rinehart & Winston General Books. 301 Commerce St., Suite 3700, Fort Worth, TX 76102

Horn Book. 14 Beacon St., Boston, MA 02108

Houghton Mifflin. 2 Park St., Boston, MA 02108

Human Science Press (Plenum Pub. Co.). 233 Spring St., New York, NY 10013-1578

Human Policy Press. P.O. Box 127 University Station, Syracuse, New York, NY 13210

Incentive Publications, Inc. 3835 Cleghorn Ave., Nashville, TN 37215

Independent Publishers Group. 814 N. Franklin, Chicago, IL 60610

Indian Historian Press. 1493 Masonic Ave., San Francisco, CA 94117

Instructor Books. P.O. Box 6177, Duluth, MN 55806

International Reading Association. 800 Barksdale Road, Newark, DE 19714-8139

Jewish Publication Society. 1930 Chestnut St., Philadelphia, PA 19103

Kane/Miller Book Publishers. P.O. Box 529, Brooklyn, NY 11231-0005

Michael Kesend Publishing Ltd. 1025 5th Ave., New York, NY 10028

Alfred A. Knopf, Inc. 201 E. 50th St., New York, NY 10022

Ladybird Books, Inc. 49 Omni Cir., Auburn, ME 04210

Learning Publications. 5351 Gulf Drive, Holmes Beach, FL 34218

Lectorum Publications, Inc. 137 W. 14th St., New York, NY 10011

Lerner Publications Company. 241 First Ave., N. Minneapolis, MN 55401

Libraries Unlimited. P.O. Box 6633, Englewood, CO 80155-6633

Lion Books/Sayre Publishing Co., Inc. 210 Nelson Road, Suite B, Scarsdale, NY 10583

J. B. Lippincott Company. 227 E. Washington Sq., Philadelphia, PA 19106-3780

Little, Brown, & Co. 34 Beacon St., Boston, MA 02108

Lollipop Power, Inc. 120 Morris St., Durham, NC 27701

Longman Inc. The Longman Building, 10 Bank St., White Plains, NY 10606-1951

Macmillan Publishing Co. 866 Third Ave., New York, NY 10022

Macmillan/McGraw-Hill School Division. 866 Third Ave., New York, NY 10022

Macrae Smith. Rtes. 547 and Old 147, Turbotville, PA 17772

Madrona Publishers. 113 Madrona Place, E. Seattle, WA 98112

Magic Circle Press. 10 Hyde Ridge, Weston, CT 06880

Manzanita Press. 4777 Hillsborough Dr., Petaluma, CA 94954

McClelland & Stewart/The Canadian Publishers. 481 University Ave., Ste 900, Toronto, Ont., Canada M5G 2E9

David McKay Company, Inc. 201 E. 50th St., New York, NY 10022

Melius & Peterson Publishing Inc. 118 River Road, Pierre, SD 57501

Charles E. Merrill Publishing Company. 1300 Alum Creek Drive, Columbus, OH 43216

Merry Thoughts, Inc. 380 Adams St., Bedford Hills, NY 10507

Julian Messner, Inc. (Division of Simon & Schuster), Rte 9W, Englewood Cliffs, NJ 07632.

Mina Press. P.O. Box 854, Sebastopol, CA 95473

Misty Hill Press. 5024 Turner Road, Sebastopol, CA 95472

Modern Curriculum Press, Inc. 13900 Prospect Road, Cleveland, OH 44136

Morning Glory Press. 6595 San Haroldo Way, Buena Park, CA 90620-3748

William Morrow & Company. 1350 Avenue of the Americas, New York, NY 10019

Mother Courage Press. 1667 Douglas Ave., Racine, WI 53404

National Women's History Project. 7738 Bell Road, Windsor, CA 95492-8515

National Council of Teachers of English. 1111 Kenyon Road, Urbana, IL 61801

National Education Association/Prof. Library. P.O. Box 509, West Haven, CT 06516

National Puerto Rican Coalition. 1700 K Street, Suite 500, Washington, DC 20026

NC Press Limited. 401-260 Richmond St., West Toronto, Ont., Canada M5V 1W5

New American Library (Dutton). 1633 Broadway, New York, NY 10019

New Day Press. c/o Karamu, 2355 E. 89th St., Cleveland, OH 44106

New Seed Press. P.O. Box 9488, Berkeley, CA 94709

New Society Publishers. 4527 Springfield Ave., Philadelphia, PA 19143

Northland Publishing. P.O. Box 1389, Flagstaff, AZ 86002

Odyssey Press. 866 Third Ave., New York, NY 10002

Office of Education. U.S. Dept. of Health and Human Services, Washington, DC 20202

Open Hand Publishing Inc. P.O. Box 22048, Seattle, WA 98122

Orchard Books. 95 Madison Ave., New York, NY 10016

Oryx. 4041 North Central Ave., Suite 700, Phoenix, AZ 85102-3397

Over the Rainbow Press. P.O. Box 7072, Berkeley, CA 94707

Richard C. Owen Publishers, Inc. 135 Katonah Ave., Katonah, NY 10536

Oxford University Press. 200 Madison Ave., New York, NY 10016

Oyate. 2702 Matthews St., Berkeley, CA 94702

Panjandrum Books. 11321 Iowa Ave., Suite 7, Los Angeles, CA 90025

Pantheon Books, Inc. 201 East 50th St., New York, NY 10022

Parent's Choice. Box 185, Waban, MA 02168

Parenting Press. P.O. Box 75267, Seattle, WA 98125

Parents Magazine Press. 685 Third Ave., New York, NY 10017

Peaceable Kingdom Press. 4664 N. Rob's Lane, Bloomington, IN 47408

Pelican Publishing Company. 1101 Monroe St., PO Box 189, Gretna, LA 70053

Pemmican Publications, Inc. 411-504 Main St., Winnipeg, Man., Canada R3C 1B8

Perspectives Press. 629 Deming Place, Chicago, IL 60614

Philomel Books. 200 Madison Ave., New York, NY 10016

Philosophical Library, Inc. 31 W. 21st St., 11th Fl., New York, NY 10010

Picture Book Studio. 10 Central St., Saxonville, MA 01701

Platt and Munk Publications. 200 Madison Ave., New York, NY 10010

Pocket Books, Inc. 1230 Avenue of the Americas, New York, NY 10020

Prentice Hall. 15 Columbus Circle, New York, NY 10023

Putnam & Grosset. 200 Madison Ave., New York, NY 10016

Raintree Publications, Inc. 310 W. Wisconsin Ave., Mezzanine Level, Milwaukee, WI 53203

Rand McNally and Company. P.O. Box 7600, Chicago, IL 60680

Random House, Inc. 225 Park Ave. South, New York, NY 10003

Resources for Teachers, Inc. 27128 B Pasedo Espada #622, San Juan Capistrano, CA 92675

Rigby. P.O. Box 797, Crystal Lake, IL 60014

Roberts Rinehart. P.O. Box 666, Niwot, CO 80544

The Ronald Press. 605 Third Ave., New York, NY 10158

St. Martin's Press, Inc. 175 Fifth Ave., New York, NY 10010

Savanna Books. 858 Massachusetts Ave., Cambridge, MA 02139

Scarecrow Press, Inc. 52 Liberty St., POB 4167, Metuchen, NJ 08840

Schocken Books, Inc., 201 E. 50th St., New York, NY 10022

Scholastic. 730 Broadway, New York, NY 10003

Scott, Foresman, & Co. 1900 E. Lake Ave., Glenview, IL 60025

Charles Scribner's Sons. 866 Third Ave., New York, NY 10016

Silver Burdett Co. 250 James St., Morristown, NJ 07960

Simon & Schuster. 15 Columbus Circle, 21st Floor, New York, NY 10023

Stemmer House. 2627 Caves Road, Owings Mills, MD 21117

Stiles Publishing Co. P.O. Box 526, Champaign, IL 61820

Stone Soup. Box 83, Santa Cruz, CA 94063

Teachers College Press. 1234 Amsterdam Ave., New York, NY 10027

Third World Press. POB 19730, 7822 South Dobson, Chicago, IL 60619

Time-Life Books. 777 Duke St., Alexandria, VA 22314

Tor Books, Tom Doherty Associates, Inc. 175 Fifth Ave., New York, NY 10010

Troubador Press. 11150 Olympic Blvd. Suite 650, Los Angeles, CA 90064

The Trumpet Club. 666 Fifth Ave., New York, NY 10103

Van Nostrand Reinhold Co., Inc. 115 Fifth Ave., New York, NY 10003

Vanguard Press, Inc. 424 Madison Ave., New York, NY 10017

Vantage Press. 516 West 34th St., New York, NY 10001

Viking Penguin, Inc. 375 Hudson St., New York, NY 10014-3657

Wadsworth Pub. Co., Inc. 10 Davis Dr., Belmont, CA 94002

Walker and Company. 720 Fifth Ave., New York, NY 10019

Frederick Warne and Co., Inc. 375 Hudson St., New York, NY 10014-3657

W. Warner, Inc. 198-16 Linden, Albany, NY 11412

Waterfront Books. 98 Brookes Ave., Burlington, VT 05401

Franklin Watts, Inc. 95 Madison Ave., New York, NY 10016

Western Publishing Company. 1220 Mound Ave., Racine, WI 53404

The Westminster Press. 100 Witherspoon St., Louisville, KY 40202-1396

Weston Woods. 389 Newtown Turnpike, Weston, CT 06883

Albert Whitman Company. 5747 Howard St., Niles, IL 60648

John Wiley & Sons, Inc. 605 Third Ave., New York, NY 10158-0012

The H. W. Wilson Company. 950 University Ave., Bronx, NY 10452

Windmill Books. 200 Old Tappan Rd., Old Tappan, NJ 07675

The Wright Group. 10949 Technology Place, San Diego, CA 92127

The Writer, Inc. 120 Boylston St., Boston, MA 02116

Xerox Learning Systems/Learning International. P.O. Box 10211, 1600 Summer St., Stamford, CT 06904

Yellow Moon Press. P.O. Box 1316, Cambridge, MA 02238

Indexes

459

TITLE INDEX

SUBJECT INDEX